CONTENT

LEGEND FOR CLUB STADIUM PLANS

Covered seating
Covered standing
Uncovered seating
Uncovered standing

Disabled Facilities, wheelchairs access and viewing areas
Main entrances
Main exits

LEGEND FOR CLUBS' TEN YEAR LEAGUE RECORD

Premier Division
First Division
Second Division
Third Division

Hatched area indicates where the number of teams in the division have been fewer than 12 or 14. (See below)

FOOTNOTE FOR EACH CLUB'S TEN YEAR PLAYING RECORD

The number of teams playing in each division of The Scottish Football League has altered on several occasions during the past ten seasons and in order to assist the reader, the following information explains the various formats in operation during the following period:-

SEASON	PREMIER DIVISION	FIRST DIVISION	SECOND DIVISION	THIRD DIVISION
1986/87	12	12	14	N/A
1987/88	12	12	14	N/A
1988/89	10	14	14	N/A
1989/90	10	14	14	N/A
1990/91	10	14	14	N/A
1991/92	12	12	14	N/A
1992/93	12	12	14	N/A
1993/94	12	12	14	N/A
1994/95	10	10	10	10
1995/96	10	10	10	10

A VERY WARM WELCOME

On behalf of The Scottish Football League Management Committee, I would like to take this opportunity in extending to all fans, a very warm welcome to the 17th edition of The Scottish Football League Review.

As I have mentioned before in a previous edition of this publication, I believe that the Review acts as a very important vehicle of communication for Scotland's national sport between the League, its member clubs, the media and supporters and as you will have already noticed, I am delighted to announce that we have just secured a new long term sponsorship with Tennent Caledonian Breweries for Tennent's Lager to sponsor the title of this book for the next four years at least. As you will be aware, Tennent Caledonian Breweries have been actively involved in sponsoring a number of aspects of our national game in recent years, and during the past few seasons have enjoyed an excellent working relationship with our colleagues at The Scottish Football Association via their sponsorship of The Scottish Cup Competition. I am confident that they will further strengthen their links with Scottish football and continue to enjoy the resultant benefits following their decision to sponsor this very prestigious publication.

With the publication of this season's Review being delayed slightly in view of our negotiations with Tennent Caledonian Breweries during the past few weeks, the first month or so of action not only on the domestic scene but also on the European and International playing fields has provided me with the opportunity to look ahead with eager anticipation to the remainder of the 1996/97 season. However, before so doing, I think it would be prudent to look back and reflect at the events that shaped and ultimately decided the 1995/96 season. Once again, all four divisions generated tremendous excitement and drama, not to mention uncertainty, right up until the final two or three weeks of the season, with several issues not being decided until referees had blown their whistles for the last time on the final Saturday of the season and this resulted in a further encouraging increase in the total number of spectators attending Bell's League Championship matches.

In the Bell's Premier Division, congratulations are due to Rangers for clinching their eighth successive Championship, however, special mention must also be made of Celtic's remarkable challenge. In most other seasons, to lose only one match throughout an entire League campaign would have normally resulted in a club not only winning a Championship but winning it comfortably, but such was the resilience, determination and character shown by the Ibrox club that they now enter this season endeavouring to emulate the nine-in-a-row achievement of their Old Firm rivals. In the Bell's First Division, the outcome was no less dramatic, with three clubs entering the final Saturday with the opportunity of either winning the Championship or at the very least, reaching the Play-Off stage, and after a tension filled afternoon, Dunfermline Athletic gained the coveted automatic promotion place after having narrowly missed out during the previous two seasons. Dundee United overcame the burden of everyone's expectations of a quick return to the top division by securing the Play-Off spot, although not before enduring much anxiety at Cappielow on the final Saturday of the season where Greenock Morton pushed them all the way, with goal difference being required to separate the two clubs. The Tannadice club and support then had to endure further anxiety against Partick Thistle before clinching their Premier Division place after two dramatic Play-Off matches that required extra-time to settle the outcome. In the Bell's Second Division, Stirling Albion won the Championship in exciting and entertaining fashion with East Fife securing the second promotion spot whilst in the Bell's Third Division, Livingston gained inspiration from playing at their new custom built stadium at Almondvale to impressively capture the title with Brechin City, solid in defence, gaining the second promotion place.

The Coca-Cola Cup once again proved no less exciting and popular a competition and after their trials and tribulations of the previous season, Aberdeen defeated First Division Dundee to win their first major domestic honour since 1990. In the Tennents Scottish Cup, Rangers completed the "Double" with victory over Heart of Midlothian providing one of the most impressive performances seen for a long time by a club in a Final at Hampden Park. In The League Challenge Cup, Stenhousemuir confounded most experts by not only reaching the Final but also winning their first major trophy in their 112 year history, defeating Dundee United in a penalty shoot-out at McDiarmid Park, Perth.

On the International front, Scotland qualified for the Finals of Euro '96 in England and whilst we were ultimately unsuccessful in our attempts to qualify from the group stages of a major competition for the first time in our history, Craig Brown and all of the players performed with great credit, distinction as well as skill and only just missed out on qualifying for the Quarter Final stage on goal difference. Hopefully, the wonderful team spirit built up between Craig Brown and the players during the past couple of years will continue as we enter into the crucial World Cup qualifying matches. With the Under-21 squad having performed with great distinction during the past two years and finishing fourth in Europe last season, I am confident that we have a number of exciting young talented players now capable of breaking into and improving our Full International squad even further.

Friday, 15th December, 1995 was a day which altered the fabric of football in not only Scotland but every other country within the European Economic Area. That was of course, the day when the European Court of Justice ruled on the Bosman case whereby a club from one member state in membership of the E.E.A. could no longer claim a compensation fee from a club in another member state of the E.E.A. when a player's Contract expired. Whilst this decision does not for the time being, affect the compensation system in place between clubs within the United Kingdom, the implications of this decision are now being

Scottish Football League Management Committee – Season 1996/97

J. Y. Craig, J.P., C.A. (President), D.B. Smith (Vice-President), G. S. Brown (Treasurer), D. W. M. Cromb, E.J. Riley, I.R. Donald, R.C. Ogilvie, A.A. Penman, G.W. Peat, C.A., W.P. Hunter, A.T. Bulloch, W.C. Whyte, J.P.

assessed as several of our best players have recently decided to move to clubs on the continent without their former club receiving any compensation.

At the time of writing, there is much debate within football about the repercussions that this decision will have for the game in this country and obviously, the outcome of all the discussions, both domestically and between UEFA and its member associations during the next few months, will determine how football in general and indeed, clubs in particular, will stand-up to the challenges faced by not receiving any compensation when a player decides to sign for another club at the expiry of his contract. I know that there have been a number of different views expressed by numerous officials within football and the popular belief is that this decision will have serious consequences for many clubs, particularly smaller clubs, and that as a result, there will be massive cut backs in youth policies, which in turn, will affect the flow of young talent into our game. Whilst it is still too early to gauge the outcome of the Bosman judgement and its possible effects on the game in this country, I would point out that football has proved to be extremely resilient down through the years and we will all have to adapt and adjust to this ruling in the future. It is important, indeed imperative, that we face this challenge in a positive manner and I remain optimistic that football will continue its long held position as our country's national sport as well as playing an important role within our society as we prepare to enter into the millennium.

Despite increasing costs, we have tried once again to improve the content of this book whilst retaining the same cover price as last season's publication and I am sure you will agree with me when I say that the Review represents the best buy of the season! The preparation of the book involves a tremendous amount of time and effort and I would like to take this opportunity in sincerely thanking the following:-

David C. Thomson (Editor); all other staff at The Scottish Football League; our 40 member clubs; Alan Elliott and Jim Jeffrey, our contributors, the various sectors of the media for their co-operation and assistance; our sponsors, Tennent Caledonian Breweries; Creative Services and in particular Nick and Dave Kelly and Emma Robinson; Programme Publications, especially Bill Cotton and Linda Austin.

Finally, I do hope that you continue to enjoy watching and supporting Scotland's national game and that the 1996/97 season will provide all football fans with excitement, drama and many memorable moments in the months ahead.

HAVE AN ENJOYABLE SEASON.

YULE CRAIG
President,
The Scottish Football League.

A WORD FROM OUR SPONSORS

Generation after generation have been influenced by the magic of Scottish football. Like the game, Tennent's Lager has been recognised for its quality, and enjoyed by millions of Scots for over 110 years.

Our support of Scottish football, as well as our heritage, goes back a long way; from the fun of the Tennents Sixes through to the romance of the Tennents Scottish Cup.

As we embark on a new season we can look forward to League thrills and spills with the Premier Division clubs aiming to stop Rangers from making it nine in a row while non-League clubs have the opportunity to make their mark by qualifying for the Tennents Scottish Cup.

Although the road to the Cup Final will take a different route this year, with Hampden undergoing a major re-development, whatever the outcome of the Cups and the League we are sure to enjoy exciting football.

Tennent's Lager, as the official beer of Scottish football, is delighted to support the 17th edition of The Scottish Football League Review Book – the essential guide for all football fans.

Mark R. Hunter
Director of Brands Marketing
Tennent Caledonian Breweries

COVER PHOTOGRAPHS

Jackie McNamara, Celtic (left) – Scotland's Young Player of the Year 1995/96
Paul Gascoigne, Rangers (right) – Scotland's Player of the Year 1995/96

Rangers' manager Walter Smith celebrates with Paul Gascoigne and Trevor Steven

Straight Eight for Rangers

There is obvious merit in the fearful view expressed by so many of us that Old Firm domination of Scottish football is detrimental to the overall health of the game in this country.

Yet who could deny that the titanic head-to-head battle between Rangers and Celtic for the Bell's Premier Division title last season provided us with the most thrilling championship race for years?

The rejuvenation of the Parkhead club under the astute leadership of Manager, Tommy Burns, pushed Rangers to the limit and made the Ibrox men's success in claiming their eighth successive crown all the more admirable.

Celtic's consistency was astounding and who would believe it possible to lose just one match out of 36 and still finish runners-up?

Yet that was exactly what happened in the final analysis, testimony to the resolve and experience of Walter Smith's team who crucially completed the season unbeaten against their greatest rivals in all competitions.

It undoubtedly overshadowed everything else in the Premier Division, but even non Old Firm fans found themselves absorbed and captivated by the Glasgow giants' title tussle.

Both had been busy at the top level of the summer transfer circus. Rangers stunned everyone with the £4.3 million capture of England midfielder, Paul Gascoigne, from Lazio and added Gordan Petric and Oleg Salenko for good measure.

Celtic responded in a manner their fans would have thought impossible until very recently, splashing out £4 million for German striker, Andreas Thom, and shrewdly snapping up stopper John Hughes from Falkirk.

Both teams started off solidly and unspectacularly on day one, back on 26th August, with 1-0 wins, Stuart McCall's goal marking the unfurling of the previous season's Championship flag at Ibrox with victory over Kilmarnock and Pierre Van Hooijdonk kicking off a superb personal campaign with the only goal against Raith Rovers at Kirkcaldy.

It soon became apparent this was a very different Celtic side from the one which finished 18 points behind Rangers in fourth place in 1995-96, a point illustrated by their remarkable 3-2 win over Aberdeen at Pittodrie after trailing to the Dons in an epic match televised live throughout the United Kingdom.

When Rangers lost 1-0 at home to Hibernian on 23rd September, Celtic's 4-0 demolition of Heart of Midlothian at Tynecastle the same afternoon saw the Parkhead men in a role which had been unfamiliar to them for a long time - Premier Division leaders.

However, as they did whenever it was most needed throughout the campaign, Rangers responded to the threat in emphatic style. Goals from Gascoigne and Alex Cleland earned them a vital 2-0 win at Parkhead in the first Old Firm clash of the season to reclaim their accustomed pole position.

Gascoigne's influence was to increase steadily and spectacularly as the games and months went on.

His fitness and temperament were cast into doubt by many who forecast he could not possibly last the full season without serious injury or major disciplinary problems.

True, the irascible Geordie forged a relationship with Scottish match officials which could most charitably be classed as strained.

However, even his harshest critic could not deny his genius, with a football at his feet enthralling fans at grounds all over Scotland and he will always be remembered as the man who made it eight in a row for Rangers.

The reigning champions and the pretenders to their throne both shrugged off the disappointment of being outclassed in Europe by the ultimate winners of their respective tournaments, Juventus and Paris

St. Germain, to sweep all before them on the domestic front.

A fabulous 3-3 draw between the ancient foes at Ibrox in November - unquestionably the game of the season - told everyone this two-horse race may well require a photo finish.

Rangers, though, suddenly appeared out of sight with a sizzling run over the festive period which included a stunning 7-0 hiding of Hibernian at Ibrox.

Celtic were not helped by a series of postponed games at the same time which left them playing catch-up.

Yet Burns' men displayed their new found mettle and style by reaping maximum points from four games in 12 days against Motherwell, Raith Rovers, Aberdeen and Heart of Midlothian in January, the last three away from home.

It cut the gap at the top to just two points but Celtic were left to ponder a critical afternoon's action on 20th January.

Rangers suffered a shock 3-0 home defeat against Heart of Midlothian, opening the door for Celtic to leapfrog them at the summit with victory over Kilmarnock at Rugby Park.

Crucially, Celtic could only draw 0-0 and although the deficit was now a single point, their failure to beat Killie that day would come back to haunt them.

Rangers recovered superbly from their setback against the Tynecastle club, reeling off four wins on the trot in a period which saw Celtic drop two more points in a goalless draw at doomed Falkirk.

A late header from John Hughes rescued a point for Celtic in the final Old Firm League showdown at Ibrox on 17th March, but Rangers remained firmly in control of their own destiny.

A final window of opportunity was opened to Celtic when Rangers again floundered against Heart of Midlothian, this time 2-0 at Tynecastle, but again the Parkhead men failed to grasp their chance and needed a late goal from the prolific Van Hooijdonk to claim just one point at home to Kilmarnock.

Defiant Tommy Burns refused to concede anything and on the penultimate weekend of the campaign, still believed his team could wrest the crown from Rangers.

A 4-2 win over Partick Thistle at Firhill on Saturday, 27th April, cut the gap to one point ahead of Rangers' live TV clash with Aberdeen at Ibrox 24 hours later.

Suddenly, there was real pressure on the champions who badly wanted to avoid the title race running to the final day.

That appeared a genuine prospect when Brian Irvine gave the Dons the lead in front of an anxious capacity Ibrox crowd.

It was merely the cue, however, for Player of the Year Gascoigne to turn in a command performance worthy of clinching any championship.

He scored a remarkable hat-trick to steer Rangers to a 3-1 win which sparked off wild celebrations on and off the pitch.

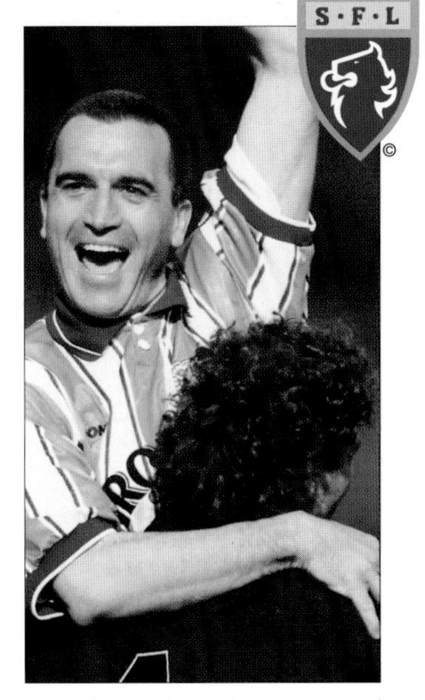
Pasquale Bruno (Hearts)

The Ibrox men were worthy champions once more, while Celtic were left to contemplate what might have been as they received a remarkable ovation from their own grateful support at Parkhead on the final day of the campaign.

By that stage, Falkirk had already lost the fight against relegation which cost John Lambie his job under the kind of acrimonious pressure no manager should face.

Kilmarnock and Motherwell recovered from dreadful starts to finally pull comfortably clear of the drop zone, leaving Partick Thistle to a Play-Off battle they lost in dramatic circumstances against Dundee United.

Aberdeen, already guaranteed European football courtesy of their Coca-Cola Cup triumph, edged out revived Heart of Midlothian for third spot on goal difference with Hibernian, a disappointing and distant fifth.

Huge credit went to Raith Rovers who survived the departure to Millwall of their hugely influential Manager, Jimmy Nicholl, to claim sixth place.

So, Rangers took the prize, Celtic picked up plaudits aplenty and the rest were left to ponder the enormous task of closing the gap on the big two during 1996-97.

STEPHEN HALLIDAY
(Scottish Daily Express)

Andreas Thom (Celtic)

ABERDEEN

Pittodrie Stadium, Pittodrie Street, Aberdeen, AB24 5QH

CHAIRMAN
Ian R. Donald

VICE-CHAIRMAN
Denis J. Miller

DIRECTORS
Gordon A. Buchan & Stewart Milne

GENERAL MANAGER
David Johnston

SECRETARY
Ian J. Taggart

MANAGER
Roy Aitken

RESERVE TEAM COACH
Neil Cooper

COACH/YOUTH DEVELOPMENT
Drew Jarvie

FITNESS COACH
Stuart Hogg

KIT MANAGER
Teddy Scott

CLUB DOCTOR
Dr. Derek Gray

PHYSIOTHERAPISTS
David Wylie & John Sharp

S.F.A. COMMUNITY COACH
Chic McLelland

CHIEF SCOUT
John Kelman

GROUNDSMAN
Jim Warrender

TELEPHONES
Ground/Ticket Office
(01224) 632328
Fax (01224) 644173

CLUB SHOP
c/o Crombie Sports, 23 Bridge Street, Aberdeen, Tel (01224) 593866 and Ticket Office, c/o Aberdeen F.C., Pittodrie Stadium, Aberdeen

OFFICIAL SUPPORTERS CLUB
Association Secretary:
Mrs. Susan Scott, 32 Earns Heugh Crescent, Cove, Aberdeen AB1 4RU

TEAM CAPTAIN
Stewart McKimmie

SHIRT SPONSOR
Living Design

LIST OF PLAYERS 1996-97

SURNAME	FIRST NAME	MIDDLE NAME	DATE OF BIRTH	PLACE OF BIRTH	DATE OF SIGNING	HEIGHT FT INS	WEIGHT ST LBS	PREVIOUS CLUB
Aitken	Robert	Sime	24/11/58	Irvine	27/06/92	6 0.0	13 0	St. Mirren
Anderson	Russell		25/10/78	Aberdeen	19/07/96	5 11.0	10 9	Dyce Juniors
Bernard	Paul		30/12/72	Edinburgh	29/09/95	6 0.0	12 10	Oldham Athletic
Booth	Scott		16/12/71	Aberdeen	28/07/88	5 9.5	11 10	Deeside B.C.
Brown	Robert		04/08/79	Aberdeen	24/08/95	5 10.0	10 13	Hall Russells
Buchan	Martin	James	03/04/77	Manchester	26/08/95	5 10.0	10 10	Stonehaven
Christie	Kevin		01/04/76	Aberdeen	05/10/94	6 1.0	12 3	Lewis United
Cooper	Neil		12/08/58	Aberdeen	23/09/91	5 11.0	12 7	Hibernian
Craig	David	Charles	23/06/77	Dundee	05/10/94	5 8.0	10 9	Banks O'Dee
Craig	Michael		20/09/77	Glasgow	13/09/95	5 9.0	9 12	East End
Dodds	William		05/02/69	New Cumnock	25/07/94	5 8.0	10 10	St. Johnstone
Duncan	Russell		15/09/80	Aberdeen	28/08/96	5 9.5	10 9	Hall Russells
Glass	Stephen		23/05/76	Dundee	06/10/94	5 9.5	10 11	Crombie Sports
Good	Iain	David	09/08/77	Glasgow	14/03/96	6 0.5	11 3	Queen's Park
Grant	Brian		19/06/64	Bannockburn	15/08/84	5 9.0	11 6	Stirling Albion
Inglis	John		16/10/66	Edinburgh	28/10/94	6 0.5	13 0	St. Johnstone
Irvine	Brian	Alexander	24/05/65	Bellshill	19/07/85	6 2.5	13 7	Falkirk
Kiriakov	Ilian		04/08/67	Pavlikeni	14/06/96	5 5.0	11 9	Anorthosis
Kombouare	Antoine		16/11/63	Noumba	03/09/96	6 1.0	12 6	F.C. Sion
Kpedekpo	Malcolm		27/08/76	Aberdeen	08/10/94	6 0.0	12 13	Hermes
McKimmie	Stewart		27/10/62	Aberdeen	12/12/83	5 8.0	11 4	Dundee
Miller	Joseph		08/12/67	Glasgow	30/07/93	5 8.0	10 7	Celtic
Morgan	Kevin	Drummond	31/01/77	Aberdeen	05/10/94	5 8.5	11 4	Hermes
Newlands	Michael		11/08/77	Dufftown	02/03/96	6 2.5	12 0	Huntly
Robertson	Hugh	Scott	19/03/75	Aberdeen	24/08/93	5 9.0	13 11	Lewis United
Robertson	Thomas		25/03/80	Paisley	27/08/96	5 7.5	10 4	Ellon United
Rowson	David	A.	14/09/76	Aberdeen	05/10/94	5 10.5	11 10	F. C. Stoneywood
Shearer	Duncan		28/08/62	Fort William	09/07/92	6 0.0	13 8	Blackburn Rovers
Stillie	Derek		03/12/73	Irvine	03/05/91	6 0.0	12 0	Notts County
Tzvetanov	Tzanko		06/01/70	Svichtov	09/08/96	5 9.0	12 7	S.V. Waldorf-Mannheim
Walker	Joseph	Nicol	29/09/62	Aberdeen	12/08/96	6 2.0	12 7	Partick Thistle
Watt	Michael		27/11/70	Aberdeen	02/07/87	6 1.0	12 9	Cove Rangers "A"
Williamson	Karl		09/11/79	Aberdeen	27/08/96	5 7.0	10 1	Ellon United
Windass	Dean		01/04/69	Hull	01/12/95	5 9.5	13 0	Hull City
Woodthorpe	Colin		13/01/69	Liverpool	19/07/94	6 1.0	12 4	Norwich City
Wyness	Dennis	Middleton	22/03/77	Aberdeen	05/10/94	5 10.5	11 4	F. C. Stoneywood
Young	Darren		13/10/78	Glasgow	16/09/95	5 8.0	10 3	Crombie Sports

MILESTONES

YEAR OF FORMATION: 1903
MOST CAPPED PLAYER: Alex McLeish
NO. OF CAPS: 77
MOST LEAGUE POINTS IN A SEASON: 64 (Premier Division - Season 1992/93) (44 games)(2 Points for a Win)
MOST LEAGUE GOALS SCORED BY A PLAYER IN A SEASON: Benny Yorston (Season 1929/30)
NO. OF GOALS SCORED: 38
RECORD ATTENDANCE: 45,061 (-v- Heart of Midlothian – 13.3.1954)
RECORD VICTORY: 13-0 (-v- Peterhead – Scottish Cup, 9.2.1923)
RECORD DEFEAT: 0-8 (-v- Celtic - Division 1, 30.1.65)

THE DONS' TEN YEAR LEAGUE RECORD

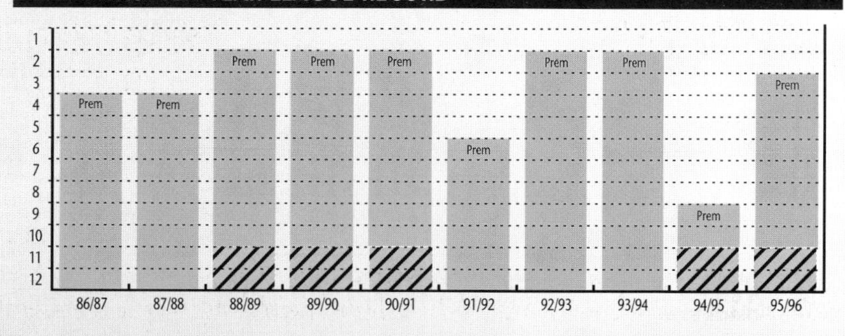

CLUB FACTFILE 1995/96
RESULTS... APPEARANCES... SCORERS

The DONS

Date	Venue	Opponents	Att.	Res	Snelders T.	McKimmie S.	Woodthorpe C.	Hetherston P.	Inglis J.	Smith G.	Miller J.	Jess E.	Booth S.	Dodds W.	Glass S.	Thomson S.	Shearer D.	McKinnon R.	Watt M.	Christie K.	Bernard P.	Grant B.	Robertson H.	Windass D.	Irvine B.	Rowson D.	Buchan J.	Kpedekpo M.	Craig M.
Aug 26	A	Falkirk	6,647	3-2	1	2	3	4	5[1]	6	7	8	9[1]	10[1]	11	12													
Sep 10	H	Celtic	16,489	†2-3	1	2	3	4	5	6	7	8[1]	9	10	11		12	14											
16	A	Hibernian	11,161	1-1	1	2	3	4	5	6	7	8	9	10	11		12[1]												
23	A	Kilmarnock	7,198	2-1		2	3[1]	4	5	6	7[1]	8	9	10	11		12		1	14									
30	H	Raith Rovers	13,983	3-0		2	3	4	5	6	7[1]	8	9[2]	10	11		12		1		14								
Oct 4	A	Heart of Midlothian	10,927	2-1		2	3	4	5	6	7	8	9[1]	10[1]	11		12		1		14								
7	H	Rangers	20,351	0-1		2	3	4	5	6	7	8	9	10	11		12		1		14								
14	A	Motherwell	6,842	1-2		2	3	4	5	6	7	8	9[1]	10	11		12		1		14								
21	H	Partick Thistle	12,719	†3-0		2			5	6	7	11[1]		10	3	14	8		1		9[1]	4							
28	A	Celtic	32,275	0-2	13	2		14	5	6	7	11	9	10	3		12		1		8	4							
Nov 4	H	Hibernian	14,774	1-2	1	2			5	6	7	11	9	10	3[1]		12				8	4							
8	H	Falkirk	11,214	†3-1	1	2		12	5	6	7[1]	11		10[1]	3	14	8				9	4							
11	A	Rangers	45,427	1-1	1	2			5	6	7	11[1]	9	10	3		12				8	4							
18	A	Raith Rovers	5,786	0-1		2		11	5	6	7		9	10	3		12		1		8	4	14						
Dec 2	A	Partick Thistle	4,286	0-1		2			5	6	7	11		10		14	8		1		9	4	3	12					
9	H	Motherwell	11,299	1-0						6	7	11		10	3		8[1]		1		4	2		9	5				
13	H	Kilmarnock	14,060	4-1		2				6	7[3]	11		10	3		8		1		4	12	14	9[1]	5				
16	H	Heart of Midlothian	12,308	1-2						6	7	11		10	3		8		1		4	2	14	9[1]	5				
Jan 8	A	Hibernian	8,191	2-1		2			5	6	7[1]	11		10[1]	3				1		9	4		8					
14	H	Celtic	16,760	1-2		2			5	6	7	11		10[1]	3		12		1		9	4		8					
16	A	Falkirk	4,003	1-1		2			5	6	7	11		10	3		12		1		9	4	15	8[1]					
20	H	Partick Thistle	9,149	1-0		2			5	6	7	11		10[1]	3		12		1		9	4		8	14				
23	A	Kilmarnock	6,703	1-1		2				6	7	11			3		10		1	14	9	4		8	5[1]				
Feb 7	H	Raith Rovers	6,628	1-0		2				6	7	11	12		3		8		1		9	4		10[1]	5				
10	A	Heart of Midlothian	14,314	3-1		2				6	7	11	12		3[1]		8[1]		1		9	4		10[1]	5				
13	A	Motherwell	5,090	0-1		2				6	7	11		14	3		8		1		9	4		10	5				
25	H	Rangers	19,842	0-1		2				6	7		12	10	3		8		1		11	4		9	5				
Mar 2	H	Kilmarnock	7,177	3-0			3			6	7[1]		9[2]	10	11				1		4	2	8		5	14	15		
16	A	Raith Rovers	4,932	2-2			3			6	7[1]		9	12			8		1			2	11	10	5	4	15[1]		
23	H	Hibernian	10,924	2-1			3			6	7		9[1]	12[1]			8		1		10	2	11		5	4	15		
Apr 1	A	Celtic	35,284	0-5			3			6	7		9	10	11				1		4	2	14	8	5	12			
13	H	Motherwell	8,943	†2-1		2	3		6				14	10	11		8		1		7	12		9	5[1]	4		15	
16	A	Partick Thistle	4,568	1-1		2	3		6				9[1]	10			12		1		7		11	8	5	4		15	
20	H	Heart of Midlothian	11,303	1-1		2	3		6				9		11		8		1		7		14	10[1]	5	4		15	
28	A	Rangers	47,247	1-3		2			6	3			9	10	11				1		7			8	5[1]	4		14	
May 4	H	Falkirk	11,831	†2-1					6	4			9		11[1]				1		7	12		8	5	3	2	10	14
TOTAL FULL APPEARANCES					6	29	15	9	24	33	31	25	20	28	32		15		30		27	22	5	19	17	7	1	1	
TOTAL SUB APPEARANCES					(1)			(2)					(4)	(3)		(4)	(15)	(1)		(2)	(4)	(3)	(6)	(1)	(1)	(2)	(3)	(4)	(1)
TOTAL GOALS SCORED							1		1		9	3	9	7	3		3				1			6	3		1		

Small bold figures denote goalscorers. † denotes opponent's own goal.

PITTODRIE STADIUM

CAPACITY: 21,634 (All seated)

PITCH DIMENSIONS: 109 yds x 72 yds

FACILITIES FOR DISABLED SUPPORTERS: Wheelchair section in front of Merkland Stand and in front row of Richard Donald Stand and also front row of Main Stand Section F. (Please telephone Ticket Office and reserve place(s) in advance).

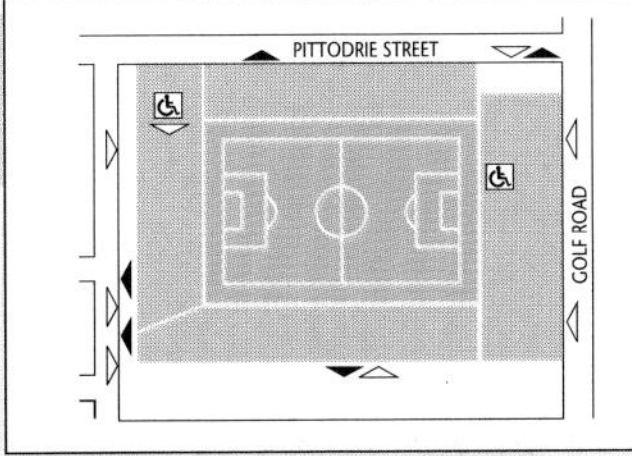

HOW TO GET THERE

You can reach Pittodrie Stadium by these routes:

BUSES: The following buses all depart from the city centre to within a hundred yards of the ground:Nos. 1, 2, 3 and 11.

TRAINS: The main Aberdeen station is in the centre of the city and the above buses will then take fans to the ground.

CARS: Motor vehicles coming from the city centre should travel along Union Street, then turn into King Street and the park will be on your right, about half a mile further on.

Parking on Beach Boulevard, King Street and Golf Road.

CELTIC

Celtic Park, 95 Kerrydale Street,
Glasgow, G40 3RE

CHAIRMAN
Fergus McCann

DIRECTOR
Eric J. Riley

SECRETARY
Dominic W. Keane

MANAGER
Thomas Burns

ASSISTANT MANAGER
William Stark

CHIEF SCOUT
David Hay

RESERVE TEAM MANAGER
Frank Connor

RESERVE TEAM COACH
Tom McAdam

YOUTH TEAM COACH
William McStay

CLUB DOCTOR
Jack Mulhearn

PHYSIOTHERAPIST
Brian Scott

RESERVE TEAM PHYSIOTHERAPIST
Gerry McElhill

GROUNDSMAN
John Hayes

COMMERCIAL MANAGER
David W. Kells
Tel 0141-556 2611

PUBLIC RELATIONS MANAGER
Peter McLean

MANAGING DIRECTOR CELTIC POOLS
John McGuire
Tel 0141-551 9922

TELEPHONES
Ground 0141-556 2611
Fax 0141-551 8106
Ticket Office 0141-551 8654
Credit Card Hotline 0141-551 8653
Celtic Hotline 0891-121888
Celtic View 0141-551 8103
Walfrid Restaurant 0141-551 9955

CLUB SHOPS
18/20 Kerrydale Street, Glasgow G40 3RE Tel 0141-554 4231 (9.00 a.m. to 5.00 p.m. Mon-Sat), 40 Dundas Street, Glasgow G1 2AQ Tel 0141-332 2727 (9.00 a.m. to 5.00 p.m. Mon-Sat) and 21 High Street, Glasgow, G1 1LX Tel 0141-552 7630 (9.30 a.m. to 5.30 p.m. Mon-Sat)

OFFICIAL SUPPORTERS CLUB
Celtic Supporters Association, 1524 London Road, Glasgow G40 3RJ
Tel 0141-556 1882

TEAM CAPTAIN
Paul McStay

SHIRT SPONSOR
C.R. Smith

LIST OF PLAYERS 1996-97

SURNAME	FIRST NAME	MIDDLE NAME	DATE OF BIRTH	PLACE OF BIRTH	DATE OF SIGNING	HEIGHT FT INS	WEIGHT ST LBS	PREVIOUS CLUB
Anthony	Marc		28/03/78	Edinburgh	25/07/95	5 6.0	10 3	Celtic B.C.
Bonner	Patrick	Joseph	24/05/60	Donegal	06/08/94	6 2.0	13 1	Keadue Rovers
Borland	Paul		28/06/79	Rutherglen	12/07/95	5 9.0	9 4	Celtic B.C.
Boyd	Thomas		24/11/65	Glasgow	06/02/92	5 11.0	11 4	Chelsea
Boyle	Charles	Declan	12/02/74	Donegal	21/02/95	5 11.0	12 9	Sligo Rovers
Burns	Thomas		16/12/56	Glasgow	24/11/95	5 10.0	11 3	Kilmarnock
Cadete (Reis)	Jorge	Paulo C.S.	27/08/68	Mozambique	30/03/96	5 11.0	11 10	Sporting Lisbon
Coughlin	Martin		12/04/77	Paisley	09/06/95	5 7.0	10 5	"X" Form
Crossley	Gerard		05/02/80	Belfast	18/07/96	5 7.0	11 0	Celtic B.C.
Culkin	Craig		31/01/79	Jersey	25/07/95	5 9.0	11 2	Jersey Scottish B.C.
Davis	Peter		13/02/79	Dublin	26/10/95	5 11.0	10 8	Shelbourne
Di Canio	Paolo		09/07/68	Rome	03/07/96	5 9.0	11 9	Milan A.C. SpA.
Donnelly	Simon		01/12/74	Glasgow	27/05/93	5 5.0	10 12	Celtic B.C.
Dow	John	Paul	24/09/79	Greenock	18/07/96	5 7.0	11 0	Celtic B.C.
Duggan	Eamon		13/08/79	Rutherglen	18/07/96	6 0.0	10 12	Celtic B.C.
Elliot	Barry	Robert	24/10/78	Carlisle	11/08/95	5 10.0	9 5	Celtic B.C.
Fitzpatrick	Patrick		09/01/80	Wexford	07/02/96	5 6.0	9 12	Taghmon United
Gallagher	James		13/02/80	Letterkenny	30/07/96	5 8.0	10 7	Glenea United
Gilligan	Kevin	Paul	04/01/79	Guernsey	25/07/95	5 8.0	10 4	Guernsey Rovers
Grant	Peter		30/08/65	Bellshill	27/07/82	5 9.0	11 7	Celtic B.C.
Gray	Stuart	Edward	18/12/73	Harrogate	07/07/92	6 1.0	13 1	Giffnock North A.F.C.
Hay	Christopher	Drummond	28/08/74	Glasgow	27/05/93	5 11.0	12 6	Giffnock North A.F.C.
Hughes	John		09/09/64	Edinburgh	07/08/95	6 0.0	13 7	Falkirk
Joyce	Kevin		19/12/79	Alexandria	18/07/96	5 8.0	8 9	Celtic B.C.
Kelly	Patrick		26/04/78	Kirkcaldy	03/08/95	6 2.0	12 0	Celtic B.C.
Kerr	James	Stewart R.	13/11/74	Bellshill	27/05/93	6 2.0	13 0	Celtic B.C.
Lyttle	Gerard		27/11/77	Belfast	09/12/94	5 9.0	10 7	Star of the Sea
MacDonald	Peter		14/08/77	Glasgow	11/08/95	6 1.0	12 0	Celtic B.C.
Mackay	Malcolm	George	19/02/72	Bellshill	06/08/93	6 2.0	13 7	Queen's Park
Marshall	Gordon	George B.	19/04/64	Edinburgh	12/08/91	6 2.0	13 5	Falkirk
McBride	John	Paul	28/11/78	Hamilton	11/08/95	5 10.0	10 2	Celtic B.C.
McCondichie	Andrew		21/08/77	Glasgow	09/06/95	5 10.5	11 9	Celtic B.C.
McGrath	Timothy		16/08/79	Dublin	30/08/95	6 1.0	12 5	Town Celtic
McGuinness	Charles		09/10/78	Bellshill	22/05/96	5 10.0	10 5	Celtic B.C.
McKeown	Philip		04/12/79	Belfast	18/07/96	6 0.0	11 0	Celtic B.C.
McKinlay	Thomas	Valley	03/12/64	Glasgow	04/11/94	5 10.0	11 9	Heart of Midlothian
McLaughlin	Brian		14/05/74	Bellshill	07/07/92	5 4.0	9 3	Giffnock North A.F.C.
McNamara	Jackie		24/10/73	Glasgow	04/10/95	5 8.5	9 7	Dunfermline Athletic
McStay	Paul	Michael L.	22/10/64	Hamilton	20/02/81	5 10.0	11 8	Celtic B.C.
Morrison	Graeme	George	29/10/76	Falkirk	24/12/94	6 0.0	12 9	Celtic B.C.
Morrison	Ryan		14/08/79	Aberdeen	18/07/96	5 10.0	11 0	Celtic B.C.
O'Brien	Andrew		30/04/78	Bellshill	15/08/95	5 4.0	10 0	Celtic B.C.
O'Donnell	Philip		25/03/72	Bellshill	09/09/94	5 10.0	11 5	Motherwell
O'Neil	Brian		06/09/72	Paisley	10/07/91	6 1.0	13 3	Porirua Viard United
Potter	John		15/12/79	Dunfermline	18/07/96	6 0.0	12 8	Celtic B.C.
Queen	Kevin		16/08/78	Bellshill	22/08/96	5 8.0	10 6	Heart of Midlothian
Stark	William		01/12/56	Glasgow	24/11/95	6 1.0	11 11	Kilmarnock
Stubbs	Alan		06/10/71	Kirkby	17/07/96	6 1.0	13 7	Bolton Wanderers
Thom	Andreas		07/09/65	Rudersdorf	04/08/95	5 8.5	11 10	TSV Bayer 04 Leverkusen
Van Hooijdonk	Pierre		29/11/69	Steenbergen	11/01/95	6 4.0	13 5	NAC Breda
Vaugh	Brian		22/08/78	Belfast	11/08/95	6 0.0	11 4	Celtic B.C.
Wieghorst	Morten		25/02/71	Glostrup	08/12/95	6 3.5	12 12	Dundee

MILESTONES

YEAR OF FORMATION: 1888
MOST CAPPED PLAYER: Paul McStay
NO. OF CAPS: 73
MOST LEAGUE POINTS IN A SEASON: 72 (Premier Division – Season 1987/88) (2 points for a Win)
83 (Premier Division – Season 1995/96) (3 points for a Win)
MOST LEAGUE GOALS SCORED BY A PLAYER IN A SEASON: Jimmy McGrory (Season 1935/36)
NO. OF GOALS SCORED: 50
RECORD ATTENDANCE: 92,000 (-v- Rangers – 1.1.1938)
RECORD VICTORY: 11-0 (-v- Dundee – Division 1, 26.10.1895)
RECORD DEFEAT: 0-8 (-v- Motherwell - Division 1, 30.4.1937)

THE BHOYS' TEN YEAR LEAGUE RECORD

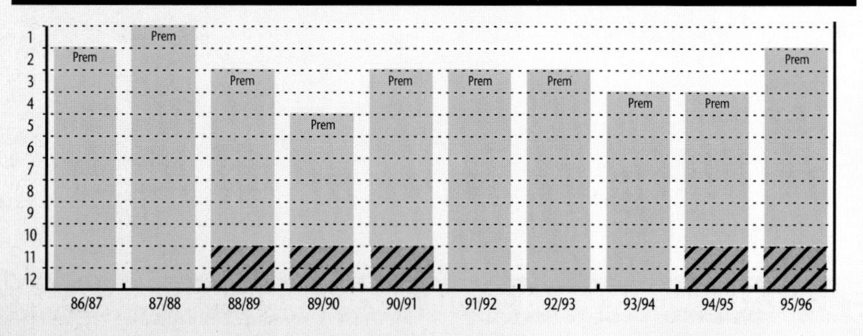

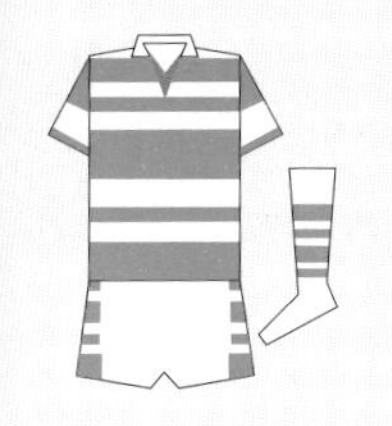

CLUB FACTFILE 1995/96
RESULTS... APPEARANCES... SCORERS

The BHOYS

Date	Venue	Opponents	Att.	Res	Marshall G.	Boyd T.	McKinlay T.	Vata R.	Hughes J.	Grant P.	O'Donnell P.	Donnelly S.	Van Hooijdonk P.	Thom A.	Collins J.	McLaughlin B.	Walker A.	Mackay M.	McStay P.	Falconer W.	Hay C.	Gray S.	McQuilken J.	McNamara J.	Wieghorst M.	O'Neil B.	Cadete (Reis) J.
Aug 26	A	Raith Rovers	9,300	1-0	1	2	3	4	5	6	7	8	9^1	10	11	14											
Sep 10	A	Aberdeen	16,489	3-2	1	2	3	4	5	6	7	8	9	10^1	11^2	15	12	14									
16	H	Motherwell	31,365	1-1	1	2	3	4		6	7^1	10			11	14	9	5	8	12							
23	A	Heart of Midlothian	13,696	4-0	1	2	3	4	5	6		7				11^2	9^2		8	12	10	14					
30	H	Rangers	33,296	0-2	1	2	3	4	5		6	7	9	10	11	14	12		8								
Oct 4	A	Falkirk	9,053	1-0	1	2			5^1	6		7	9	10	11	8							3	4			
7	H	Partick Thistle	29,950	2-1	1	2			5	6		7	9^1	10	11^1	8	12				14		3	4			
14	H	Hibernian	31,738	2-2	1	2			5	6		7	9^1	10	11^1	8							3	4			
21	A	Kilmarnock	14,001	0-0	1	2	3		5	6		8	9	10	11	7	14		12					4			
28	H	Aberdeen	32,275	2-0	1	2	3	12	5	6		7	9^1			11^1	10		8				14	4			
Nov 4	A	Motherwell	12,077	2-0	1	2	3		5	6		7^1	9	10	12^1	11			8					4			
8	H	Raith Rovers	28,832	0-0	1	2	3		5			7	9	10	6	11	12		8					4			
11	A	Partick Thistle	12,223	2-1	1	2	3		5	6		7	9^2	10	11				8					4			
19	A	Rangers	46,640	3-3	1	2	3		5	6		7	9^1	10^1	11^1	14	12		8					4			
25	H	Heart of Midlothian	34,032	3-1	1	2	3		5	6		7	9	10	11^3				8					4			
Dec 2	H	Kilmarnock	33,660	4-2	1	2	3		5	6^1		7	9^2	10^1	11	14			8		15			4			
9	A	Hibernian	13,626	4-0	1	2	3				6^1	7^1	9^1	10	11	14	12	5	8					4^1	15		
16	H	Falkirk	36,466	1-0	1	2	3				6	7	9^1	10	11			5	8		15			4			
Jan 3	H	Rangers	36,719	0-0	1	2	3				6	7	9	10	11	15	12	5	8					4			
6	H	Motherwell	34,629	1-0	1	2	3			12	6	7	9^1	10	11	15		5	8					4			
9	A	Raith Rovers	9,300	3-1	1	2	3		5	4	6^1	7	9^1	10	11^1		14		8						15		
14	A	Aberdeen	16,760	2-1	1	2	3		5	4	6	7	9^1	10	11^1		12		8								
17	A	Heart of Midlothian	15,871	2-1	1	2	3		5	4	6	7	9^1	10	11	15	12^1		8								
20	A	Kilmarnock	16,024	0-0	1	2	3		5	4	6	7	9		11	15	10		8						14		
Feb 3	H	Hibernian	36,976	2-1	1	2	3		5	6		7	9^1	10	11		12		8^1					4			
10	A	Falkirk	10,366	0-0	1	2	3		5	6		7	9	10	11				8					4	14		
24	H	Partick Thistle	36,421	4-0	1		3		5	6^1		7	9^2	10	11	15		12	8					4	14^1	2	
Mar 2	H	Heart of Midlothian	37,034	4-0	1		3		5	6	12	7^1	9^1	10		11^1			8^1					4	14	2	
17	A	Rangers	47,312	1-1	1	2	3		5^1	6	7		9	10	11	15			8					4	14		
23	A	Motherwell	12,394	0-0	1	2	3		5	6	4	7	9	10		11			8			15			14		
Apr 1	H	Aberdeen	35,284	5-0	1	2	3		5	6		7^2	9^2	10					8			11		4		12	15^1
10	H	Kilmarnock	36,476	1-1	1	2	3			6		7	9^1	10		11			8					4	14	5	15
14	A	Hibernian	10,742	2-1	1	2	3			6		7	9^2	12	11			5	8					4	10		15
20	H	Falkirk	35,692	4-0	1	2	3			6		7^1	9	10^2	12			5	8					4	11		15^1
27	A	Partick Thistle	14,693	4-2	1	2				6		7	9^2	10	12	15		5^1	8			3		4			11^1
May 4	H	Raith Rovers	37,318	4-1	1	2	3			6^1		7	9	10		14		5				8^1		4		12	11^2
TOTAL FULL APPEARANCES					36	34	32	5	26	30	14	35	34	31	26	11	4	9	29		1	3	3	26	2	3	2
TOTAL SUB APPEARANCES								(1)		(1)	(1)			(1)	(3)	(15)	(12)	(2)	(1)	(2)	(3)	(2)	(1)		(9)	(2)	(4)
TOTAL GOALS SCORED									2	3	3	6	26	5	11	4	3	1	2			1		1	1		5

Small bold figures denote goalscorers. † denotes opponent's own goal.

CELTIC PARK

CAPACITY: 50,600(Approx) (All Seated)
PITCH DIMENSIONS: 120 yds x 74 yds
FACILITIES FOR DISABLED SUPPORTERS:
77 Wheelchair spaces for Celtic Supporters-front of lower tier. 9 Wheelchair spaces for visiting supporters-max number could be reduced for different segregation conditions. 18 Chair spaces for ambulant disabled supporters allocated at Celtic's discretion in the stand. 54 Chair spaces for helpers. 43 Chair seats at front row adjacent to wheelchair spaces. 11 Chairs allocated at Celtic's discretion in the stand. 22 Chair spaces for blind party-located at the South Stand behind dugouts; induction loop facilities being provided for this area only. Toilet facilities also available.

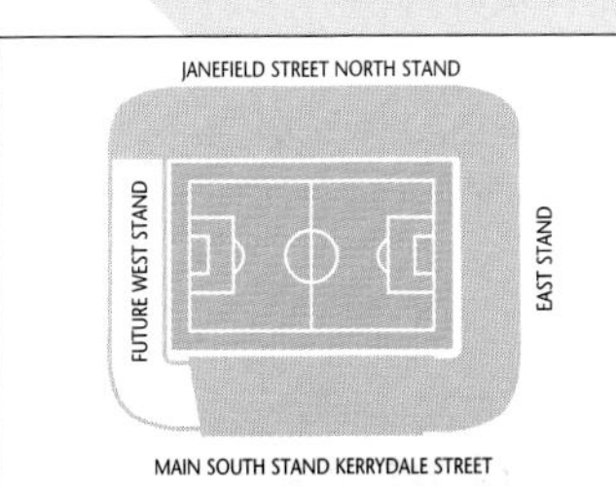

HOW TO GET THERE

The following routes may be used to reach Celtic Park:

BUSES: The following buses all leave from the city centre and pass within 50 yards of the ground. Nos. 61, 62, and 64.

TRAINS: There is a frequent train service from Glasgow Central Low Level station to Bridgeton Cross Station and this is only a ten minute walk from the ground. Belgrove Rail Station is approximately 1 1/2 miles from the ground.

CARS: From the city centre, motor vehicles should travel along London Road and this will take you to the ground. Parking space is available in front of the Main Stand and also on the vacant ground adjacent to the park.

DUNDEE UNITED

Tannadice Park, Tannadice Street, Dundee, DD3 7JW

CHAIRMAN/MANAGING DIRECTOR
James Y. McLean

VICE-CHAIRMAN
Douglas B. Smith

DIRECTORS
Alistair B. Robertson
William M. Littlejohn
John H. McConnachie

COMPANY/CLUB SECRETARY
Miss Priti Trivedi

MANAGER
Thomas McLean

PLAYER/ASSISTANT MANAGER
Maurice Malpas

COACHING STAFF
Gordon Wallace, Ian Campbell, Graeme Liveston

CLUB DOCTOR
Dr. Derek J. McCormack

PHYSIOTHERAPIST
David Rankine

CHIEF SCOUT
Graeme Liveston

S.F.A. COMMUNITY OFFICER
John Holt

COMMERCIAL MANAGER
Bill Campbell

TELEPHONES
Ground/Commercial
(01382) 833166
Fax (01382) 889398

CLUB SHOP
The United Shop, Unit 2, 5/15 Victoria Road, Dundee
Tel (01382) 204066 - Open 9.00 a.m. to 5.30 p.m. Mon-Sat.
Souvenir shops are also situated within the ground and are open on match days

TEAM CAPTAIN
David Bowman

SHIRT SPONSOR
Telewest Communications

LIST OF PLAYERS 1996-97

SURNAME	FIRST NAME	MIDDLE NAME	DATE OF BIRTH	PLACE OF BIRTH	DATE OF SIGNING	HEIGHT FT INS	WEIGHT ST LBS	PREVIOUS CLUB
Benneker	Armand		25/06/69	Tongeren	09/08/96	6 2.0	12 9	M.V.V. Maastricht
Black	Paul	Alexander	30/10/77	Aberdeen	27/07/94	5 9.5	11 6	Dundee United B.C.
Bowman	David		10/03/64	Tunbridge Wells	21/05/86	5 10.0	11 6	Coventry City
Brown	Craig		01/04/80	Dumbarton	03/07/96	5 9.0	10 10	Dundee United B.C.
Bryers	Joseph		07/09/79	Glasgow	03/07/96	5 6.5	9 6	Dundee United B.C.
Coyle	Owen	Columba	14/07/66	Paisley	13/10/95	5 11.0	10 5	Bolton Wanderers
Crabbe	Scott		12/08/68	Edinburgh	03/10/92	5 8.0	11 5	Heart of Midlothian
Devine	Christopher		21/02/79	Bellshill	31/08/95	5 6.0	9 3	Dundee United B.C.
Donachie	Barry		21/12/79	Dundee	03/07/96	5 7.5	10 7	Dundee United B.C.
Duffy	Cornelius		05/06/67	Glasgow	06/08/96	6 1.0	11 13	Dundee
Easton	Craig		26/02/79	Bellshill	31/08/95	5 9.0	9 8	Dundee United B.C.
Fallon	Steven		08/05/79	Paisley	31/08/95	5 8.5	10 7	Dundee United B.C.
Ferreri	Juan	Francisco	13/07/70	Florida, Uruguay	06/01/95	5 10.0	12 4	Defensor Sporting Club
Gallacher	Paul		16/08/79	Glasgow	03/07/96	6 0.0	10 12	Dundee United B.C.
Gray	Dale	Ronald J.	15/02/78	Edinburgh	27/07/94	6 0.5	10 8	Dundee United B.C.
Hannah	David		04/08/73	Airdrie	04/09/91	5 11.5	11 8	Hamilton Thistle
Johnson	Ian	Grant	24/03/72	Dundee	07/09/90	5 11.0	11 2	Broughty Ferry
Keith	Marino		16/12/74	Peterhead	11/10/95	5 10.0	12 12	Fraserburgh
Kennedy	Grahame	David	07/07/77	Dundee	27/07/94	6 0.0	10 6	Dundee United B.C.
Key	Lance		13/05/68	Kettering	26/07/96	6 3.0	15 1	Sheffield United
Malpas	Maurice	Daniel R.	03/08/62	Dunfermline	14/08/79	5 8.0	11 6	"S" Form
Maxwell	Alastair	Espie	16/02/65	Hamilton	27/06/95	5 10.0	10 12	Rangers
McKinnon	Raymond		05/08/70	Dundee	03/11/95	5 10.0	11 10	Aberdeen
McLaren	Andrew		05/06/73	Glasgow	20/06/89	5 10.5	11 7	Rangers B.C.
McQuilken	James	Charles	03/10/74	Glasgow	04/11/95	5 9.0	10 7	Celtic
McSwegan	Gary		24/09/70	Glasgow	06/10/95	5 7.5	10 9	Notts County
Mitchell	David		24/09/76	Irvine	29/03/96	5 11.5	11 11	Dundee St. Josephs
Paterson	James		25/09/79	Bellshill	03/07/96	5 11.0	12 7	Dundee United B.C.
Perry	Mark	George	07/02/71	Aberdeen	09/08/88	6 1.0	12 7	Cove Rangers
Pressley	Steven	John	11/10/73	Elgin	28/07/95	6 0.0	11 0	Coventry City
Robertson	Alexander		26/04/71	Edinburgh	28/07/95	5 9.0	10 7	Coventry City
Shannon	Robert		20/04/66	Bellshill	04/07/95	5 11.0	11 8	Motherwell
Stewart	Andrew	Thomas	02/01/78	Dumfries	31/08/95	6 1.0	12 4	Dundee United B.C.
Stirling	Anthony		07/09/76	Glasgow	27/07/94	6 0.0	11 5	Dundee United B.C.
Thompson	Steven		14/10/78	Paisley	01/07/96	6 2.0	12 5	Dundee United B.C.
Thomson	Richard	James	11/08/77	Perth	31/08/95	6 0.0	11 4	Elwood Juniors
Walker	Paul		20/08/77	Kilwinning	27/07/94	5 5.5	9 7	Dundee United B.C.
Winters	Robert		04/11/74	East Kilbride	11/01/92	5 10.0	11 10	Muirend Amateurs

MILESTONES

YEAR OF FORMATION: 1923 (1909 as Dundee Hibs)
MOST CAPPED PLAYER: Maurice Malpas
NO. OF CAPS: 55
MOST LEAGUE POINTS IN A SEASON: 60 (Premier Division - Season 1986/87) (2 Points for a Win)
67 (First Division - Season 1995/96) (3 Points for a Win)
MOST LEAGUE GOALS SCORED BY A PLAYER IN A SEASON: John Coyle (Season 1955/56)
NO. OF GOALS SCORED: 41
RECORD ATTENDANCE: 28,000 (-v- Barcelona – 16.11.1966)
RECORD VICTORY: 14-0 (-v- Nithsdale Wanderers – Scottish Cup, 17.1.1931)
RECORD DEFEAT: 1-12 (-v- Motherwell – Division 2, 23.1.1954)

THE TERRORS' TEN YEAR LEAGUE RECORD

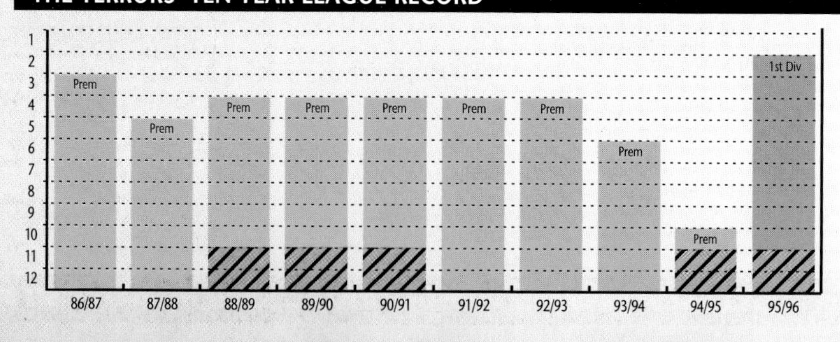

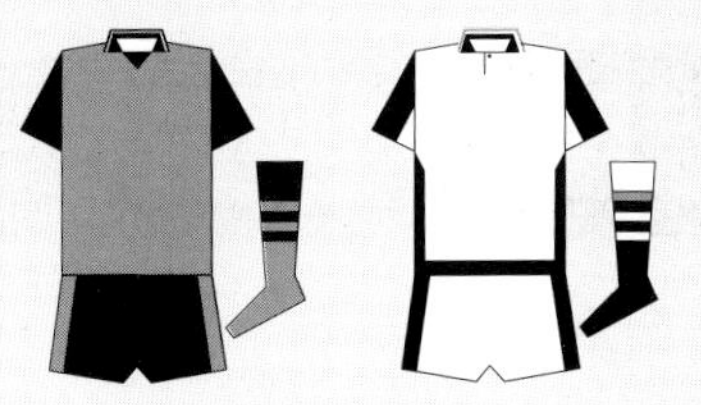

CLUB FACTFILE 1995/96
RESULTS... APPEARANCES... SCORERS

The TERRORS

Date	Venue	Opponents	Att.	Res	Maxwell A.	Perry M.	Shannon R.	Malpas M.	Pressley S.	Hannah D.	McLaren A.	Robertson A.	Winters R.	Brewster C.	Caldwell N.	Connolly P.	Walker P.	Welsh B.	Bowman D.	McKinlay W.	Dailly C.	Bett J.	Crabbe S.	Johnson I. G.	McSwegan G.	Honeyman B.	Coyle O.	McKinnon R.	McQuilken J.	O'Hanlon K.	Keith M.
Aug 12	H	Greenock Morton	6,927	1-1	1	2	3	4	5	6	7	8	9	10^{1}	11	12	14														
26	A	Dunfermline Athletic	7,933	0-3	1	2	3		4		7		9	12	11	10		5	6	8	14										
Sep 2	H	Hamilton Academical	5,194	2-1	1		2	3	4^{1}		7		9			12^{1}			8		5	6	10	11							
9	H	St. Mirren	6,159	†1-0	1		2	3	5		7		9			14		6	11	8	4	10	12								
16	A	Clydebank	1,949	2-1		2	3	6	4		7		9			11		12		8^{1}	5	10^{1}		14						1	
23	H	Airdrieonians	6,005	1-2	1	2^{1}	3	6	4		7		9			11	14			8	5	10									
30	A	Dundee	10,395	3-2	1	2	3	6	4		7		11							8^{3}	5	10		9							
Oct 7	A	Dumbarton	2,013	0-1	1	2	3	6	4		7	12						11			5	10		8	9	14					
14	H	St. Johnstone	7,572	2-1	1		2	3	4		7		11	12				14			5	6^{1}		8	9		10^{1}				
21	A	Hamilton Academical	1,719	1-0	1		2	3	4		7		11	12							5	6		8	9^{1}		10				
28	H	Dunfermline Athletic	9,703	3-1	1		2	3	4		7^{1}		11	12							5	6		8	9^{1}		10^{1}				
31	H	Clydebank	5,428	3-0	1	14	2	3	4		7^{1}		11^{1}	12							5	6		8^{1}	9		10				
Nov 11	A	St. Mirren	3,556	1-1	1		2	3	4		7		11^{1}	12							5	6		8	9		10	14			
18	H	Dundee	10,752	2-3	1		2	3^{1}	4		7		11	12^{1}							5	6		8	14		10	9			
25	A	Airdrieonians	2,504	1-1	1		2	3^{1}	4		7		11	9				5			15	6		8	14		12	10			
Dec 2	H	Dumbarton	5,285	†8-0	1		2	3	4				7	9^{4}				5				6		8^{1}	12^{1}		10^{1}		11		14
9	A	St. Johnstone	5,966	0-0	1		2	3	4		14		7	9				5			15	6		8	12		10		11		
16	A	Greenock Morton	4,660	2-1	1		2	3	4	15	14		7	10				5				6		8^{1}	9^{1}		12		11		
26	H	Hamilton Academical	6,109	1-1	1		2	3	4	14	11		7	10^{1}				5			15	6		8	9		12				
30	H	Airdrieonians	5,855	2-2	1			3	4	7^{1}			11	10^{1}				5	15		2	6		8	9		12		14		
Jan 6	A	Clydebank	1,383	1-1	1		3		4	11			7^{1}	10				5	8		2	6					9				14
9	A	Dundee	9,199	2-0	1		3		4	12	9		7^{2}	10				5	8		2	6			15		14		11		
13	H	St. Mirren	6,523	2-1	1	4	3				11		7	10				5	8		2	6		15	9^{2}		12		14		
20	A	Dumbarton	1,354	3-1	1	14	3^{1}		4		7		11	10^{1}				5	8		2	6			9^{1}		12				15
Feb 3	H	St. Johnstone	7,478	1-3	1		3		4^{1}	9	7		11	10				5			2	6		8	12		14		15		
24	A	Dunfermline Athletic	8,400	2-2	1	2	3	6	4			14	12	10^{1}							5			8	9^{1}		11	7			
27	H	Greenock Morton	6,768	4-0	1	2		3	4		14	15	7	10^{2}					5					12	9^{1}		8^{1}	6	11		
Mar 2	A	Airdrieonians	1,810	1-1	1	2		3	4		12		7	10							14			5	9^{1}		8	6	11		
16	H	Dundee	9,831	2-0		2		3	4		14		11	10^{1}				5	8					6	9^{1}		7	12		1	
23	H	Clydebank	5,973	6-0	1	2		3	4		14		11	10^{3}				5	8					6	9^{2}		7^{1}	12			
30	A	St. Mirren	4,347	†3-1	1	2		3	4		9^{1}		11^{1}	10				5	8		14			6			7				
Apr 6	H	Dumbarton	7,142	6-1	1	2^{1}		3	4		12		11	10^{1}				5	8		14			6	9^{4}		7				
13	A	St. Johnstone	9,973	0-1	1	2	5	3	4		9		11	10					8		12			6			7				14
22	A	Hamilton Academical	3,291	2-0	1	2		3	4				11	10				5	8		14^{1}			6^{1}	9		7				
27	H	Dunfermline Athletic	12,384	0-1	1	2		3	4		12		11	10				5	8		14			6	9		7				
May 4	A	Greenock Morton	12,523	2-2	1	2		3	4		9		11^{1}	10				5^{1}	8		6						7	12			
TOTAL FULL APPEARANCES					34	18	26	30	35	4	23	1	34	23	2	3		21	16	5	20	23	1	25	19		20	5	6	2	
TOTAL SUB APPEARANCES						(2)				(3)	(8)	(3)	(1)	(7)		(3)	(2)	(2)	(1)		(10)		(1)	(3)	(6)	(1)	(8)	(4)	(3)		(4)
TOTAL GOALS SCORED						2	1	2	2	1	3		7	17		1		1		4	1	2		4	17		5				

Small bold figures denote goalscorers. † denotes opponent's own goal.

TANNADICE PARK

CAPACITY: 12,608 (All seated)

PITCH DIMENSIONS: 110 yds x 72 yds

FACILITIES FOR DISABLED SUPPORTERS: Lower Tier – George Fox Stand – Cover for home supporters only on request.

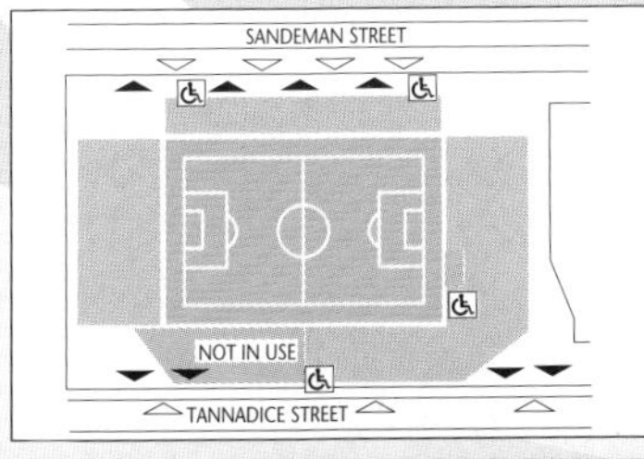

HOW TO GET THERE

Tannadice Park can be reached by the following routes:

BUSES: The following buses leave from the city centre at frequent intervals. Nos. 18, 19 and 21 from Commercial Street and No. 20 from Reform Street.

TRAINS: Trains from all over the country pass through the main Dundee station and fans can then proceed to the ground by the above bus services from stops situated within walking distance of the station.

CARS: There is parking in the streets adjacent to the ground.

DUNFERMLINE ATHLETIC

East End Park, Halbeath Road,
Dunfermline, Fife, KY12 7RB

CHAIRMAN
C. Roy Woodrow

DIRECTORS
William M. Rennie
Gavin G. Masterton, F.I.B. (Scot)
Joseph B. Malcolm, B.Sc., C.Eng.
Andrew T. Gillies
David A.G. Grant, C.A., F.T.I.I.
John Meiklem

SECRETARY/GENERAL MANAGER
Paul A. M. D'Mello

MANAGER
Robert Paton

ASSISTANT MANAGER
Richard Campbell

COACHING STAFF
Ian Campbell & Joe Nelson

CLUB DOCTOR
Dr. Gerry D. Gillespie

PHYSIOTHERAPIST
Philip Yeates, M.C.S.P.

S.F.A. COMMUNITY COACH
Graeme Robertson

YOUTH DEVELOPMENT MANAGER
David McParland

SAFETY/SECURITY ADVISOR
William Nellies

COMMERCIAL MANAGER
Miss Audrey M. Bastianelli

TELEPHONES
Ground/Commercial/Ticket Office
(01383) 724295/721749
Fax (01383) 723468

CLUB SHOP
Intersport, Kingsgate, Dunfermline.
Open 9.00 a.m. – 5.00 p.m.
Mon to Sat

OFFICIAL SUPPORTERS CLUB
c/o Mrs. J. Malcolm, Secretary,
Dunfermline Athletic
Supporters Club,
13 South Knowe,
Crossgates, KY4 8AW

TEAM CAPTAIN
Craig Robertson

SHIRT SPONSOR
Landmark Home Furnishing

LIST OF PLAYERS 1996-97

SURNAME	FIRST NAME	MIDDLE NAME	DATE OF BIRTH	PLACE OF BIRTH	DATE OF SIGNING	HEIGHT FT INS	WEIGHT ST LBS	PREVIOUS CLUB
Alexander	Damien	David	02/03/79	Bellshill	23/10/95	5 10.0	11 3	Bonnybridge
Bingham	David	Thomas	03/09/70	Dunfermline	22/09/95	5 10.0	10 7	Forfar Athletic
Britton	Gerard	Joseph	20/10/70	Glasgow	27/07/96	6 0.0	11 0	Dundee
Clark	John		25/09/64	Edinburgh	03/02/96	6 0.0	14 1	Falkirk
Curran	Henry		09/10/66	Glasgow	14/03/96	5 8.0	11 8	Partick Thistle
Den Bieman	Ivo	Johannes	04/02/67	Wamel	05/08/93	6 2.0	12 10	Dundee
Dickson	John	Alexander	27/04/77	Paisley	19/10/95	5 11.0	11 8	Thornton Hibs
Farrell	Gerard	James	14/06/75	Glasgow	05/10/95	5 8.0	10 10	Possil YM
Ferguson	Steven		18/05/77	Edinburgh	15/08/95	5 8.0	11 6	Rosyth Recreation
Fleming	Derek		05/12/73	Falkirk	07/10/94	5 7.0	10 2	Meadowbank Thistle
Fraser	John		17/01/78	Dunfermline	18/10/95	5 10.0	11 1	Oakley United
French	Hamish	Mackie	07/02/64	Aberdeen	23/10/91	5 10.5	11 7	Dundee United
Hegarty	Ryan	Michael	08/03/76	Edinburgh	21/11/95	5 11.0	10 0	Dundee United
Ireland	Craig		29/11/75	Dundee	12/02/96	6 3.0	13 9	Aberdeen
Lemajic	Zoran		08/11/60	Niksic	30/08/96	6 5.0	13 7	C.S. Maritimo
McCulloch	Mark	Ross	19/05/75	Inverness	02/08/94	5 11.0	12 0	Inverness Clachnacuddin
Millar	Marc		10/04/69	Dundee	14/10/94	5 9.0	10 12	Brechin City
Miller	Colin	Fyfe	04/10/64	Lanark	04/11/95	5 7.0	12 2	Heart of Midlothian
Moore	Allan		25/12/64	Glasgow	26/03/94	5 7.0	10 0	St. Johnstone
Petrie	Stewart	James John	27/02/70	Dundee	27/08/93	5 10.0	11 11	Forfar Athletic
Reynolds	Craig	Robert John	03/10/77	Dunfermline	01/07/96	5 8.0	9 9	St. Johnstone
Rice	Brian		11/10/63	Bellshill	27/10/95	6 1.0	11 7	Falkirk
Robertson	Craig	Peter	22/04/63	Dunfermline	30/08/91	5 10.0	12 0	Aberdeen
Ryan	Robert	James	10/01/78	Dunfermline	18/10/95	5 10.0	11 8	Oakley United
Shaw	Gregory		15/02/70	Dumfries	31/03/95	6 0.0	10 12	Falkirk
Smith	Andrew	Mark	22/11/68	Aberdeen	21/07/95	6 1.0	12 7	Airdrieonians
Tod	Andrew		04/11/71	Dunfermline	04/11/93	6 3.0	12 0	Kelty Hearts
Van De Kamp	Guido		08/02/64	's-Hertogenbosch	21/01/95	6 2.5	12 12	Dundee United
Ward	Kenneth		16/06/63	Blairhall	05/08/94	5 7.0	11 4	Hamilton Academical
Westwater	Ian		08/11/63	Loughborough	30/03/94	6 2.0	14 8	Dundee
Young	Scott	Robertson	05/04/77	Glasgow	05/07/96	5 8.0	9 0	St. Johnstone

MILESTONES

YEAR OF FORMATION: 1885
MOST CAPPED PLAYER: Istvan Kozma
NO. OF CAPS: (13 for Hungary whilst with Dunfermline Athletic)
MOST LEAGUE POINTS IN A SEASON: 65 (First Division – Season 1993/94) (2 Points for a Win)
71 (First Division – Season 1995/96) (3 Points for a Win)
MOST LEAGUE GOALS SCORED BY A PLAYER IN A SEASON: Bobby Skinner (Season 1925/26)
NO. OF GOALS SCORED: 53
RECORD ATTENDANCE: 27,816 (-v- Celtic – 30.4.1968)
RECORD VICTORY: 11-2 (-v- Stenhousemuir – Division 2, 27.9.1930)
RECORD DEFEAT: 0-10 (-v- Dundee – Division 2, 22.3.1947)

THE PARS' TEN YEAR LEAGUE RECORD

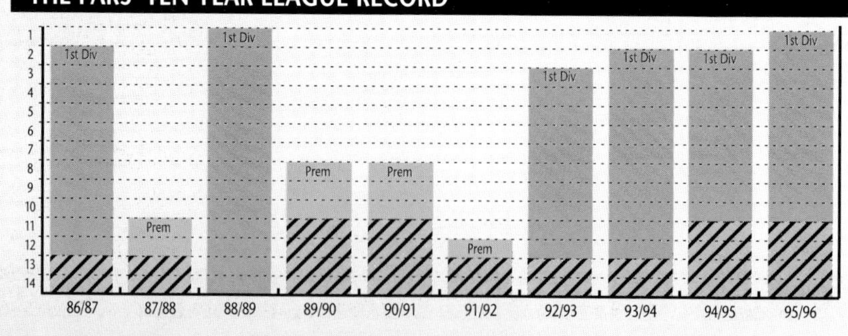

CLUB FACTFILE 1995/96
RESULTS... APPEARANCES... SCORERS

The PARS

Date	Venue	Opponents	Att.	Res	Van De Kamp G.	Den Bieman I.	Millar M.	McCathie N.	Tod A.	Smith P.	Moore A.	McNamara J.	Shaw G.	Petrie S.	Kinnaird P.	McCulloch M.	Fleming D.	Cooper N.	Robertson C.	Fenwick P.	Bingham D.	Farrell G.	French H.	Rice B.	Miller C.	Rissannen K.	Hegarty R.	Ferguson S.	Smith A.	Callaghan T.	Clark J.	Westwater I.	Ireland C.
Aug 12	A	Airdrieonians	2,719	1-0	1	2	3	4	5	6	7	8	9^{1}	10	11	12																	
26	H	Dundee United	7,933	3-0	1	2	3	4	5	6	7^{1}	8	9	10^{1}	11	14	12																
Sep 2	A	Dumbarton	1,952	†4-0	1	2	3	4	5	6	7	8^{1}	9^{1}	10^{1}	11		12	14															
9	H	Clydebank	4,410	2-1	1	2	3	4	5^{1}	6	7^{1}	8	9	10	11		12		14	16													
16	A	St. Mirren	3,479	2-0	1	2	3	4^{1}	5	6	7	8	9	10^{1}	11	14	12																
23	A	Greenock Morton	3,794	0-2	1	2	3	4	5	6	7	8	9	10	11		12				14												
30	H	St. Johnstone	5,737	2-1	1	7		4	5	12		2	9^{1}	10^{1}	14	6	3		8		11												
Oct 7	A	Hamilton Academical	1,473	3-1	1	16		4	5	6	7^{1}		9	10^{1}	12	14	3		8^{1}		11	2											
14	H	Dundee	6,700	0-1	1	14		4	5	6	7		9	10	16	12	3		8		11	2											
21	H	Dumbarton	3,842	3-1	1	7		4	5	6			9^{2}	10^{1}			3		8		11	2	14										
28	A	Dundee United	9,703	1-3	1	2		4	5	6			9^{1}	10		7	3	12			11			8									
Nov 4	H	St. Mirren	4,578	†1-1	1		8	4	5		7		9	10		12	3				11			6	2	14							
11	A	Clydebank	1,304	4-0	1		7	4^{1}	5				9	10			3^{1}		8		12^{2}			6	2	11							
18	A	St. Johnstone	4,559	0-1	1		11		5					10		6	3		8		9	2			4		7	12					
25	H	Greenock Morton	4,857	0-2	1	14	10	4	5		7					6	3		8		11		9		2		12						
Dec 2	H	Hamilton Academical	3,284	4-0	1	12	6	4	5^{1}		7		9^{1}	10^{1}			3^{1}		8				11		2		14						
9	A	Dundee	4,642	4-2	1	14	6	4^{1}	5^{1}		7			10^{1}			3^{1}		8		11		9		2		16						
16	H	Airdrieonians	4,687	2-0	1	14	6	4	5		7^{1}			10^{1}			3		8		11		9		2				16				
Jan 6	A	St. Mirren	3,380	1-2	1	12	6	4	5		7			10			3		8^{1}		11		9		2				14				
13	H	Clydebank	6,642	4-3	1	7	2		5^{1}					10			3	*12	8^{1}		11		6				16		9^{2}				
20	A	Hamilton Academical	1,556	0-0	1	2			5		7			10			11	*12	8				6		3		14		9	16			
Feb 10	A	Airdrieonians	2,453	2-1	1	16	3		5		7			10^{1}			11		8		14^{1}		6		2				9		*12	17	
24	H	Dundee United	8,400	2-2	1	11^{1}			5		7		14	16			3		8				10^{1}		2				9		*12		6
28	H	St. Johnstone	6,348	3-2	1	11			5^{1}		7		14	16			3		8				10		2				9^{1}		$*12^{1}$		6
Mar 2	H	Greenock Morton	4,547	4-1	1				5				14	11			3		8^{1}				10^{1}		2		7^{1}		9^{1}		*12		6
6	H	Dundee	5,580	1-1	1				5				14	11^{1}			3		8				10		2		7		9		*12		6
9	A	Dumbarton	1,477	3-0		14			5		7		8^{2}	11			3					16	10		2				9^{1}		*12	1	6
16	A	St. Johnstone	5,239	2-2			3		5		7		11^{1}	14			16		8				10		2				9^{1}		*12	1	6
19	A	Greenock Morton	3,170	1-1			3^{1}		5		7		11	10			16		8				14		2				9		*12	1	6
23	H	St. Mirren	4,936	2-2			3^{1}		5		7		14	11					8^{1}				10		2				9		*12	1	6
30	A	Clydebank	1,298	3-2			3^{2}		5		7		14	11^{1}					8			16	10		2				9		*12	1	6
Apr 6	H	Hamilton Academical	4,542	1-3			3		5		7		14	11			16		8				10^{1}		2				9		*12	1	6
13	A	Dundee	3,218	1-1		*12	3		5		7		14	11			6		8				10		2				9^{1}	16		1	
20	H	Dumbarton	5,971	4-1		16	3		5		7^{1}		14^{1}	11			6		8				10^{1}	*12	2				9^{1}	17		1	
27	A	Dundee United	12,384	1-0		*12	3		5		7		16	11^{1}			6		8				10	14	2				9			1	
May 4	H	Airdrieonians	13,183	2-1		*12	3^{1}		5		11		14				6		8				7	10	2		16		9^{1}			1	
TOTAL FULL APPEARANCES					26	16	25	18	36	10	28	7	17	31	6	4	25	2	27		12	4	21	5	24	1	3		17		11	10	10
TOTAL SUB APPEARANCES						(10)				(1)			(11)	(3)	(3)	(6)	(8)	(2)	(1)	(1)	(3)	(2)	(2)	(1)		(1)	(6)	(1)	(2)	(3)		(1)	
TOTAL GOALS SCORED						1	5	3	5		5	1	11	13			3		5		3		4				1		9		1		

*Small bold figures denote goalscorers. † denotes opponent's own goal. *denotes full appearance as a result of the tragic death of captain Norrie McCathie. No.4 was not used for the remainder of the season.*

EAST END PARK

CAPACITY: 18,394; Seated 4,074, Standing 14,320

PITCH DIMENSIONS: 115 yds x 68 yds

FACILITIES FOR DISABLED SUPPORTERS: Special ramped area in West Enclosure.

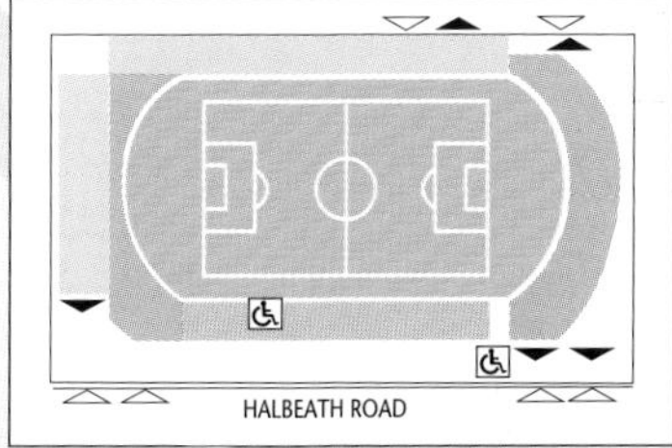

HOW TO GET THERE

East End Park may be reached by the following routes:

TRAINS: Dunfermline Station is served by trains from both Glasgow and Edinburgh and the ground is a 15 minute walk from here.

BUSES: Buses destined for Kelty, Perth, St. Andrews and Kirkcaldy all pass close to East End Park.

CARS: Car Parking is available in a large car park adjoining the East End of the ground and there are also facilities in various side streets. Multi-storey car parking approximately 10 minutes walk from ground.

HEART OF MIDLOTHIAN

Tynecastle Park, Gorgie Road, Edinburgh, EH11 2NL

CHAIRMAN
Christopher P. Robinson

VICE-CHAIRMAN
Leslie G. Deans

DIRECTORS
Fraser S. Jackson, Colin G. Wilson
John G. Frame, Ian D. MacCallum

SECRETARY
Leslie W. Porteous

GENERAL MANAGER
Sally Robinson

MANAGER
James Jefferies

ASSISTANT MANAGER
Billy Brown

COACHES
Paul Hegarty & Peter Houston

CLUB DOCTOR
Dr. Dewar Melvin

PHYSIOTHERAPIST
Alan Rae

S.F.A. COMMUNITY OFFICER
Bobby Jenks

CHIEF SCOUT
John Murray

GROUNDSMAN
Ronnie Blair

COMMERCIAL MANAGER
Tommy Dickson
Tel 0131-337 9011

TICKET MANAGER
Neil Hunter

TELEPHONES
Ground 0131-337 6132
Fax 0131-346 0699
Telex 72694
Ticket Office 0131-337 9011
Information Service 0131-346 8556

CLUB SHOP
Heart of Midlothian Sport & Leisure, Tynecastle Park, McLeod Street, Edinburgh. Tel 0131-346 8511. Open 9.30 a.m. – 5.30 p.m. Mon. to Sat. and match days.

OFFICIAL SUPPORTERS CLUB
Heart of Midlothian Federation, John N. Borthwick, 80 Slateford Road, Edinburgh, EH11 1QU

TEAM CAPTAIN
Gary Locke

SHIRT SPONSOR
Strongbow

LIST OF PLAYERS 1996-97

SURNAME	FIRST NAME	MIDDLE NAME	DATE OF BIRTH	PLACE OF BIRTH	DATE OF SIGNING	HEIGHT FT INS	WEIGHT ST LBS	PREVIOUS CLUB
Barr	Anthony		11/09/77	Bellshill	19/11/94	5 9.0	10 1	Royal Albert
Beckford	Darren	Richard	12/05/67	Manchester	14/08/96	5 8.0	13 0	Oldham Athletic
Bradley	Mark		10/08/76	Glasgow	02/03/95	5 6.0	9 7	Ashfield
Bruno	Pasquale		19/06/62	Lecce	17/11/95	6 0.0	11 7	Fiorentina
Burns	John	Paul	11/03/78	Kirkcaldy	21/11/94	5 6.0	10 9	Newtongrange Star
Callaghan	Stuart		20/07/76	Calderbank	03/08/92	5 8.0	10 3	Blantyre B.C.
Cameron	Colin		23/10/72	Kirkcaldy	31/03/96	5 5.5	9 6	Raith Rovers
Colquhoun	John	Mark	14/07/63	Stirling	27/07/93	5 8.0	11 2	Sunderland
Frail	Stephen	Charles	10/08/69	Glasgow	31/03/94	6 0.0	11 13	Dundee
Fulton	Stephen		10/08/70	Greenock	12/10/95	5 10.0	11 0	Falkirk
Goss	Jeremy		11/05/65	Cyprus	29/07/96	5 8.0	11 7	Norwich City
Hogarth	Myles		30/03/75	Falkirk	16/02/96	6 1.0	11 11	Newtongrange Star
Holmes	Derek		18/10/78	Lanark	05/01/95	6 0.0	12 2	Royal Albert
Horn	Robert	David	03/08/77	Edinburgh	13/05/95	5 9.0	11 0	Edinburgh United
Levein	Craig	William	22/10/64	Dunfermline	25/11/83	6 2.0	13 0	Cowdenbeath
Locke	Gary		16/06/75	Edinburgh	31/07/92	5 10.0	11 8	Whitehill Welfare
Mackay	Gary		23/01/64	Edinburgh	16/06/80	5 9.0	11 8	Salvesen B.C.
McCann	Neil	Docherty	11/08/74	Greenock	30/07/96	5 10.0	10 0	Dundee
McKenzie	Roderick		08/08/75	Bellshill	30/07/96	6 0.0	12 0	Stenhousemuir
McManus	Allan	William	17/11/74	Paisley	03/08/92	6 0.0	12 0	Links United
McNicoll	Grant		07/09/77	Edinburgh	20/07/94	5 9.0	10 1	Yett Farm B.C.
McPherson	David		28/01/64	Paisley	25/10/94	6 3.0	11 11	Rangers
Murie	David		02/08/76	Edinburgh	31/07/92	5 8.0	10 4	Tynecastle B.C.
Murray	Grant	Robert	29/08/75	Edinburgh	02/03/95	5 10.0	12 0	Bonnyrigg Rose
Naysmith	Gary	Andrew	16/11/78	Edinburgh	17/06/96	5 7.0	11 8	Whitehill Welfare Colts
Pointon	Neil	Geoffrey	28/11/67	Church Warsop	10/10/95	5 11.0	12 8	Oldham Athletic
Rafferty	Kenneth		02/04/78	Edinburgh	09/08/96	5 10.0	11 10	Hutchison Vale B.C.
Ritchie	Paul	Simon	21/08/75	Kirkcaldy	31/07/92	5 11.0	12 0	Links United
Robertson	John	Grant	02/10/64	Edinburgh	09/12/88	5 6.0	11 4	Newcastle United
Rousset	Gilles		22/08/63	Hyeres	03/11/95	6 5.0	14 7	Rennes
Salvatori	Stefano		29/12/67	Rome	04/09/96	5 10.0	12 3	Atalanta
Storrar	Andrew	David	06/10/77	Stirling	21/11/94	5 5.0	10 6	Dunipace Juniors
Thomas	Kevin	Roderick	25/04/75	Edinburgh	31/07/92	5 11.0	12 5	Links United
Weir	David	Gillespie	10/05/70	Falkirk	30/07/96	6 2.0	13 7	Falkirk

MILESTONES

YEAR OF FORMATION: 1874
MOST CAPPED PLAYER: Bobby Walker
NO. OF CAPS: 29
MOST LEAGUE POINTS IN A SEASON: 63 (Premier Division - Season 1991/92)
MOST LEAGUE GOALS SCORED BY A PLAYER IN A SEASON: Barney Battles (Season 1930/31)
NO. OF GOALS SCORED: 44
RECORD ATTENDANCE: 53,396 (-v- Rangers – 13.2.1932)
RECORD VICTORY: 21-0 (-v- Anchor – EFA Cup, 1880)
RECORD DEFEAT: 1-8 (-v- Vale of Leven – Scottish Cup, 1883)

THE JAM TARTS' TEN YEAR LEAGUE RECORD

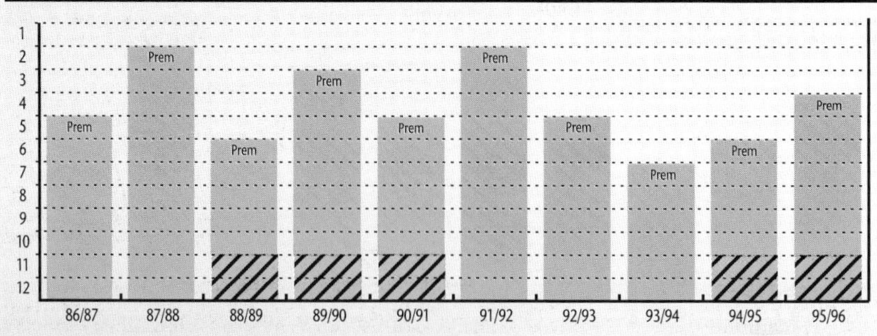

CLUB FACTFILE 1995/96
RESULTS... APPEARANCES... SCORERS

The JAM TARTS

Date	Venue	Opponents	Att.	Res	Smith H.	Locke G.	Wishart F.	Levein C.	McPherson D.	Hamilton B.	Colquhoun J.	Mackay G.	Hagen D.	Johnston A.	Lawrence A.	Leitch S.	Berry N.	Winnie D.	Robertson J.	Jamieson W.	Nelson C.	Ritchie P.	Miller C.	Wright G.	Millar J.	O'Connor G.	Pointon N.	Fulton S.	Rousset G.	Smith P.	Bruno P.	Eskilsson H.	McManus A.	Callaghan S.	Thomas K.	Cameron C.	Hogarth M.	Naysmith G.
Aug 26	H	Motherwell	10,971	1-1	1	2	3	4	5	6	7	8	9^1	10	11	12	14																					
Sep 9	H	Falkirk	11,531	4-1	1	2			5	6	7^1		11	10	8^2	12	4	3	9^1	14																		
16	A	Partick Thistle	5,396	0-2	1	2			5	6	7	12	14	10	8	11	4	3	9																			
23	H	Celtic	13,696	0-4		2			5	6	7		11	10	12	8			9	4	1	3																
Oct 1	A	Hibernian	12,374	2-2		2			5^1	6	12	7	11		8			3	9^1		1		4	10	14													
4	H	Aberdeen	10,927	1-2					5	6	12		11		8	7		3	9^1		1		4	2	10													
7	A	Kilmarnock	6,721	1-3					5	12	7	4	14		8^1	11	2	6	9			3			10	1												
14	H	Raith Rovers	10,133	4-2		2			5	6	7			12	8^2		4		9^1	14					11^1	1	3	10										
21	A	Rangers	45,155	1-4		2			5	6				7	8		4		9				14		11^1	1	3	10										
28	A	Falkirk	6,858	0-2		2			5		7			12	8		14	6	9	4					11		3	10	1									
Nov 4	H	Partick Thistle	10,094	†3-0		2								7	8		5		9	14		3			11^1			10	1	4	6	12^1						
7	A	Motherwell	5,595	0-0		2								7			5		9			3			11			10	1	4	6	8						
11	H	Kilmarnock	10,442	2-1		2^1								7	12		5		9^1			3			11			10	1	4	6	8						
19	H	Hibernian	12,074	2-1		2					14	4		7^1			5		9			3			11^1			10	1		6	8						
25	A	Celtic	34,032	1-3		2					12	4		7	9		5					3			11			10	1	14	6^1	8						
Dec 2	H	Rangers	15,105	0-2		2				15	12	4		7			5		9			3			11			10	1		6	8						
9	A	Raith Rovers	6,349	1-1		2				15	12	4		7			5		9^1			3			11		14	10	1		6	8						
16	A	Aberdeen	12,308	2-1						15	12^1	4		7^1					9			3			11		5	10	1		6	8	2					
Jan 1	A	Hibernian	14,872	1-2							12	4		7	15				9			3			11		5^1	10	1	14	6	8	2					
6	A	Partick Thistle	4,618	1-0		2					9	4		7	8				12			3			10		11		1		6		5^1					
10	H	Motherwell	9,288	4-0		2			15		8^1	4		7^2	12				9			3					11	10^1	1	14	6		5					
13	H	Falkirk	11,560	2-1		2			15		8	4		7	12				9^1			3					11	10^1	1		6		5					
17	H	Celtic	15,871	1-2		2			15		8	4		7	12				9^1			3					11	10	1		6		5					
20	A	Rangers	45,096	3-0		2			4		8	14		7^3	9				12			3					11	10	1		6		5					
Feb 3	H	Raith Rovers	10,183	2-0		2^1			4		8	10		7	12				9^1			3					11		1	14	6		5					
10	H	Aberdeen	14,314	1-3		2			4		8	10		7					9^1			3			15		11		1		6		5					
24	A	Kilmarnock	8,022	2-0		2			4		7^1	6		12	8				9^1			3					11	10	1	14			5	15				
Mar 2	A	Celtic	37,034	0-4		2			4		9	6		7	8				12		1	3			15		11	10			5							
16	H	Hibernian	14,923	1-1		2			4		8	14^1		7	12				9			3			15		11	10	1		6		5					
23	H	Partick Thistle	9,610	2-5					4		8	5		7^1	9				12			3			11			10	1	2	6	15^1	14					
30	A	Falkirk	5,164	2-0		2^1			12		9	8		7			4					3^1					11	10	1		6		5		15			
Apr 10	H	Rangers	15,350	2-0					5		12	4		7^1			15		9			3					11^1	10	1		6		2		14	8		
13	A	Raith Rovers	4,956	3-1					5			4^1		7					9			3					11^1	10	1		6		2			8^1		
20	A	Aberdeen	11,303	1-1		2^1			5		12	14		7			6		9			3					11	10	1				4			8		
27	H	Kilmarnock	11,329	1-0		2			5		8	12		7	15		6		9			3					11	10	1				4^1		14			
May 4	A	Motherwell	8,301	1-1		2			5		14			7	9		6		15			3					11	10					4			8^1	1	12
TOTAL FULL APPEARANCES					3	29	1	1	22	8	20	21	5	30	17	4	16	6	28	2	4	28	2	2	16	3	21	26	25	4	22	8	17			4	1	
TOTAL SUB APPEARANCES									(4)	(4)	(11)	(5)	(2)	(3)	(9)	(2)	(3)		(5)	(3)			(1)		(4)		(1)			(5)		(2)	(1)	(1)	(3)			(1)
TOTAL GOALS SCORED						4			1		4	2	1	9	5				11			1			4		3	2			1	2	2			2		

Small bold figures denote goalscorers. † denotes opponent's own goal.

TYNECASTLE PARK

CAPACITY: 16,613 (All seated)

PITCH DIMENSIONS: 108 yds x 72 yds

FACILITIES FOR DISABLED SUPPORTERS: There are 10 spaces for visiting fans at South end of the Enclosure (must be pre-booked). Regarding facilities for home supporters, contact the club regarding Season Ticket and League Admission Price information.

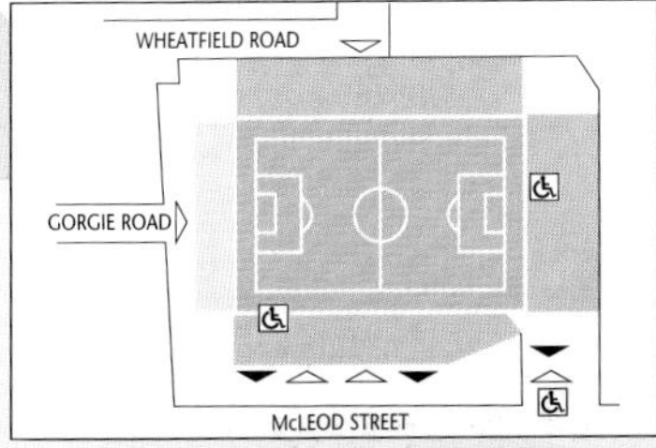

HOW TO GET THERE

Tynecastle Park can be reached by the following routes:

BUSES: A frequent service of buses leaves from the city centre, Nos. 1, 2, 3, 4, 33, 34, 35 and 44 all pass the ground

TRAINS: Haymarket Station is about half a mile from the ground.

CARS: Car Parking facilities exist in the adjacent side streets in Robertson Avenue and also the Westfield area.

HIBERNIAN

Easter Road Stadium,
64 Albion Road,
Edinburgh, EH7 5QG

CHAIRMAN
Douglas W. M. Cromb

DIRECTORS
Robert Huthersall
Thomas J. O'Malley
Ian Brennan

SECRETARY
Robert Huthersall

MANAGER

FIRST TEAM COACH
Jocky Scott

RESERVE TEAM COACH
Donald Park

CLUB DOCTOR
James Ledingham

PHYSIOTHERAPIST
Stuart Collie

S.F.A. COMMUNITY COACH
John Ritchie

COMMERCIAL DEPARTMENT
0131-661 2159

CATERING MANAGER
Keith J. C. Donaldson

BUSINESS DEVELOPMENT MANAGER
Alex Arnott

STADIUM MANAGER
Gordon B. McCabe

GROUNDSMAN
Craig Hildersley

TELEPHONES
Ground 0131-661 2159
Fax 0131-659 6488
Ticket Office 0131-661 1875
Information Service 0891 707070

CLUB SHOP
26 Albion Place, Edinburgh
Open Mon.-Fri.: 9.00 a.m. - 5.00 p.m.,
Home Match Days: 9.30 a.m. - 3.30 p.m. & 4.30 p.m. - 5.30 p.m.
Away First Team Match Days: 9.30 a.m. - 5.30 p.m.
Sunday: 11.00 a.m. - 3.00 p.m.
Tel 0131-661 1875

OFFICIAL SUPPORTERS CLUB
11 Sunnyside Lane, Off Easter Road,
Edinburgh, EH7

TEAM CAPTAIN
Jim Leighton

SHIRT SPONSOR
Carlsberg

LIST OF PLAYERS 1996-97

SURNAME	FIRST NAME	MIDDLE NAME	DATE OF BIRTH	PLACE OF BIRTH	DATE OF SIGNING	HEIGHT FT INS	WEIGHT ST LBS	PREVIOUS CLUB
Anderson	Steven	Ronald	18/09/78	Bangour	18/07/95	5 8.0	9 7	Hutchison Vale B.C.
Bannerman	Scott		21/03/79	Edinburgh	18/07/95	5 6.0	9 12	Hutchison Vale B.C.
Bryson	Graeme		08/01/80	Perth	04/06/96	5 8.0	9 9	Hibernian B.C.
Cameron	Ian		24/08/66	Glasgow	09/08/96	5 9.0	10 4	Partick Thistle
Cook	Paul	Taylor	05/08/78	Broxburn	18/07/95	5 10.0	10 0	Hutchison Vale B.C.
Dods	Darren		07/06/75	Edinburgh	03/08/92	6 1.0	13 2	Hutchison Vale B.C.
Donald	Graeme	Still	14/04/74	Stirling	12/06/91	6 0.0	12 4	Gairdoch United
Dow	Andrew	James	07/02/73	Dundee	05/03/96	5 9.0	10 7	Chelsea
Frame	Andrew		17/10/78	Lanark	19/07/96	5 8.0	9 11	Bellshill B.C.
Gardiner	Jason	Stanley	30/10/73	Edinburgh	14/05/91	6 0.0	13 5	Salvesen B.C.
Harper	Kevin	Patrick	15/01/76	Oldham	03/08/92	5 6.0	11 1	Hutchison Vale B.C.
Hunter	Gordon		03/05/67	Wallyford	10/08/83	5 10.0	12 7	Musselburgh Windsor
Jackson	Christopher		29/10/73	Edinburgh	14/05/91	5 7.0	10 11	Salvesen B.C.
Jackson	Darren		25/07/66	Edinburgh	14/07/92	5 10.0	11 0	Dundee United
Lavety	Barry		21/08/74	Johnstone	13/08/96	6 0.0	12 12	St. Mirren
Leighton	James		24/07/58	Johnstone	14/07/93	6 0.0	13 6	Dundee
Love	Graeme		07/12/73	Bathgate	14/05/91	5 10.0	12 7	Salvesen B.C.
Martin	John		29/01/79	Edinburgh	18/07/95	5 10. 0	11 2	Hutchison Vale B.C.
McAllister	Kevin		08/11/62	Falkirk	29/07/93	5 5.0	11 0	Falkirk
McCaffrey	Stuart		30/05/79	Glasgow	04/06/96	5 10.0	10 4	Duntocher B.C.
McDonald	Ian		07/03/78	Newcastle	19/07/94	6 0.0	12 13	Salvesen B.C.
McGinlay	Patrick	David	30/05/67	Glasgow	01/11/94	5 10.0	11 10	Celtic
McLaughlin	Joseph		02/06/60	Greenock	01/02/96	6 1.0	12 0	Falkirk
McLean	Timothy		21/12/79	Glasgow	22/07/96	5 5.0	9 7	Wolves B.C.
McNab	Ross		12/12/78	Glasgow	18/07/95	5 6.5	10 7	Duntocher B.C.
Millen	Andrew	Frank	10/06/65	Glasgow	21/03/95	5 11.0	11 2	Kilmarnock
Miller	Greg		01/04/76	Glasgow	29/07/94	5 7.5	10 0	Hutchison Vale B.C.
Miller	Kenneth		23/12/79	Edinburgh	22/05/96	5 8.0	9 11	Hutchison Vale B.C.
Miller	William	Nesbit	01/11/69	Edinburgh	14/03/87	5 8.0	11 2	Edina Hibs B.C.
Newman	Andrew		03/10/78	Paisley	18/07/95	5 6.5	11 6	Duntocher B.C.
Paton	Eric	John	01/08/78	Glasgow	19/07/94	5 8.5	11 11	Hutchison Vale B.C.
Reid	Christopher	Thomas	04/11/71	Edinburgh	20/06/88	5 11.0	13 10	Hutchison Vale B.C.
Renwick	Michael		29/02/76	Edinburgh	03/08/92	5 9.0	11 6	Hutchison Vale B.C.
Riley	Paul		07/08/75	Edinburgh	03/08/92	5 7.0	10 6	Hutchison Vale B.C.
Tortolano	Joseph		06/04/66	Stirling	29/08/85	5 8.0	11 6	West Bromwich Albion
Weir	Michael	Graham	16/01/66	Edinburgh	14/01/88	5 4.0	10 3	Luton Town
Welsh	Brian		23/02/69	Edinburgh	07/08/96	6 2.0	13 8	Dundee United
Wight	Craig	MacDonald	24/07/78	Glasgow	15/09/95	5 11.0	11 10	Haddington Athletic
Wilkins	Raymond	Colin	14/09/56	Hillingdon	13/09/96	5 10.0	11 9	Wycombe Wanderers
Wright	Keith		17/05/65	Edinburgh	01/08/91	5 11.0	12 6	Dundee

MILESTONES

YEAR OF FORMATION: 1875
MOST CAPPED PLAYER: Lawrie Reilly
NO. OF CAPS: 38
MOST LEAGUE POINTS IN A SEASON: 57 (First Division – Season 1980/81)
MOST LEAGUE GOALS SCORED BY A PLAYER IN A SEASON: Joe Baker (Season 1959/60)
NO. OF GOALS SCORED: 42
RECORD ATTENDANCE: 65,860 (-v- Heart of Midlothian – 2.1.1950)
RECORD VICTORY: 22-1 (-v- 42nd Highlanders 3.9.1881)
RECORD DEFEAT: 0-10 (-v- Rangers – 24.12.1898)

THE HIBEES' TEN YEAR LEAGUE RECORD

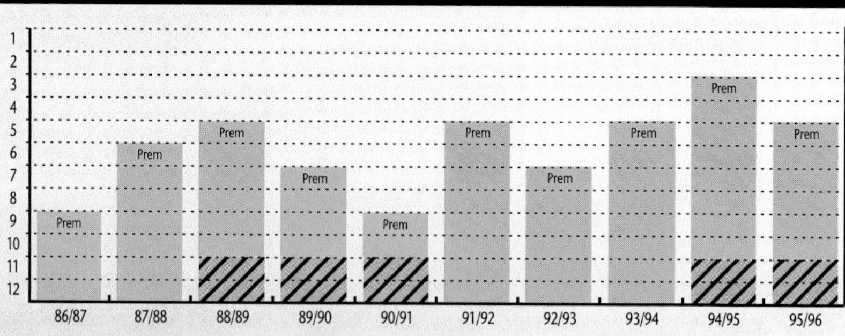

CLUB FACTFILE 1995/96
RESULTS... APPEARANCES... SCORERS

The HIBEES

Date	Venue	Opponents	Att.	Res	Leighton J.	Jackson C.	Dods D.	McGinlay P.	Tweed S.	Millen A.	McAllister K.	Donald G.	Harper K.	Jackson D.	O'Neill M.	Miller W.	Hunter G.	Evans G.	Wright K.	Weir M.	Love G.	Tortolano J.	Miller Greg	Miller Graeme	Renwick M.	Farrell D.	McLaughlin J.	Mitchell G.	Dow A.
Aug 26	A	Partick Thistle	5,327	1-1	1	2	3	4	5	6	7	8	9	10	11^{1}														
Sep 9	A	Kilmarnock	7,014	3-0	1	8	15	4	5	3	12			10	11	2	6	7^{1}	9^{2}	14									
16	H	Aberdeen	11,161	1-1	1	8		4	5	2			12	10^{1}	11		6	7	9		3								
23	A	Rangers	44,221	1-0	1	2		4	5	6	7	15	8	10^{1}	11				9		3								
Oct 1	H	Heart of Midlothian	12,374	2-2	1	2		4^{1}	5	8		12^{1}		10	11		6	7	9		3								
4	A	Raith Rovers	6,051	0-3	1	8		4	5			2	7	10	11		6	12	9		3								
7	H	Falkirk	8,356	2-1	1	3	2	4	5		7^{1}		8	10^{1}	11		6	9			14								
14	A	Celtic	31,738	2-2	1	8	2	4	5		7	15	9^{1}	10^{1}	11		6	14	12		3								
21	H	Motherwell	9,803	4-2	1	14	2	4	5		7	15	8	10^{2}	11^{1}		6	12	9^{1}			3							
28	H	Kilmarnock	9,888	2-0	1		2	4	5		7		8	10	11^{1}		6		9^{1}			3							
Nov 4	A	Aberdeen	14,774	2-1	1	7	2	4	5		12		8	10	11^{1}		6		9^{1}			3							
11	A	Falkirk	6,046	0-2	1	11	2	4	5		7	14	8	10			6	12	9			3	15						
19	A	Heart of Midlothian	12,074	1-2	1	8^{1}		4	5	2	7			10	11		6	9		12		3							
22	H	Partick Thistle	6,783	3-0	1	11	2	4	5	8	7^{1}	14		10^{1}			6	12		9^{1}		3	15						
25	H	Rangers	13,558	1-4	1	8^{1}	2		5	4	7	12		10	11		6	9			14	3		15					
Dec 2	A	Motherwell	5,362	2-0	1	3	2	4	5	8	7			10	11		6		9^{2}										
9	H	Celtic	13,626	0-4	1	3	2	4	5	8	7			10			6		9	11		12							
16	H	Raith Rovers	8,507	1-2	1	8		4^{1}	5	2	7			10			6	14	9	12		3	11						
30	A	Rangers	44,692	0-7	1	8		4	5	2	7		12	10			6		9	11		3							
Jan 1	H	Heart of Midlothian	14,872	2-1	1			4	5	2	7		8^{1}	10	11^{1}		6	14	9			3							
8	H	Aberdeen	8,191	1-2	1			4	5	2	7		8^{1}	10	11		6		9			3							
13	A	Kilmarnock	6,686	2-3	1	6	4		5	2	7		8	10	11^{1}				9^{1}			3			12				
16	A	Partick Thistle	2,811	0-0	1	8		4	5	2	7			10	11				9		15	3			6				
20	H	Motherwell	7,658	0-0	1		5	4		2	7		8	10	11				9		6	3							
Feb 3	A	Celtic	36,976	1-2	1	14				8	7		9	10^{1}	11	2			12		3					4	5	6	
10	A	Raith Rovers	4,832	0-1	1	12				8	7			10	11	2			9	14	3					4	5	6	
24	H	Falkirk	7,609	2-1	1			4	6		7			10	11	2		8^{1}	9^{1}	15						12	5	3	
Mar 3	H	Rangers	11,923	0-2	1			4	6					10	11	2		12	9	7						8	5	3	
16	A	Heart of Midlothian	14,923	1-1	1			4	6					10	12	2		7	9							8	5	3	11^{1}
23	A	Aberdeen	10,924	1-2	1			12	6	4	7^{1}			10	14	2		9								8	5	3	11
30	H	Kilmarnock	8,001	1-1	1				4		7^{1}			10	11	2	6	9								8	5		3
Apr 6	A	Motherwell	5,964	0-3	1	14		4	5	7	9			10	11	2		12			6					8			3
14	H	Celtic	10,742	1-2	1			4^{1}	5	8	7	14		10	11	2		9	15		6								3
20	H	Raith Rovers	7,214	1-1	1		6	4^{1}	5	8	7	15		10	11	2		12	9										3
27	A	Falkirk	2,813	1-1	1			4^{1}		8	7	15		10		2	6	11	9								5		3
May 4	H	Partick Thistle	6,885	1-0	1			4		8	7	12		10^{1}		2	6	14	9		11						5		3
TOTAL FULL APPEARANCES					36	19	14	30	31	25	29	2	14	36	27	13	22	12	25	4	11	14	1		1	7	9	6	8
TOTAL SUB APPEARANCES						(4)	(1)	(1)			(2)	(11)	(2)		(2)			(11)	(3)	(5)	(3)	(1)	(2)	(1)	(1)	(1)			
TOTAL GOALS SCORED						2		5			4	1	3	9	6			2	9	1									1

Small bold figures denote goalscorers. † denotes opponent's own goal.

EASTER ROAD STADIUM

CAPACITY: 15,745 (All seated)

PITCH DIMENSIONS: 112 yds x 74 yds

FACILITIES FOR DISABLED SUPPORTERS: Area in South Seated Enclosure, new North Stand, new South Stand.

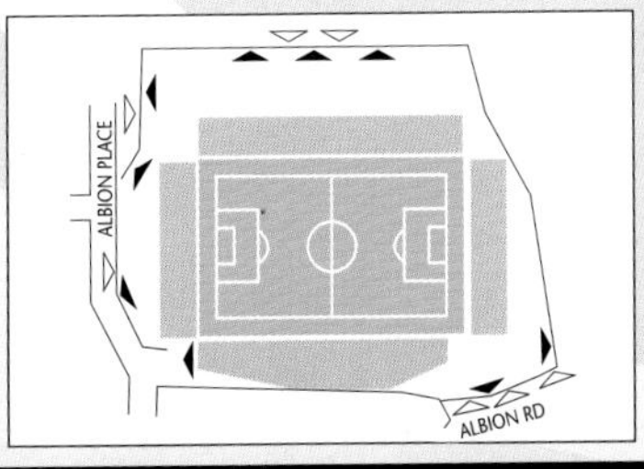

HOW TO GET THERE

Easter Road Stadium can be reached by the following routes:

BUSES: The main bus station in the city is served by buses from all over the country and the following local buses departing from Princes Street all stop near the ground. Nos. 4, 15, 42 and 44.

TRAINS: Edinburgh Waverley Station is served by trains from all parts of the country and the above buses all stop near the ground.

KILMARNOCK

Rugby Park, Rugby Road,
Kilmarnock, KA1 2DP

CHAIRMAN
James H. Moffat

VICE-CHAIRMAN
John Paton

DIRECTORS
Ronald D. Hamilton
William Costley
James H. Clark
Robert Wyper

SECRETARY
Kevin D. Collins

MANAGER
Alexander Totten

FIRST TEAM COACH
Kenneth Thomson

RESERVE COACH
Bobby Williamson

GOALKEEPING COACH
Jim Stewart

YOUTH COACHES
Alan Robertson & Paul Clarke

HON. MEDICAL OFFICER
Dr. Robin Magee

CROWD DOCTOR
Dr. Zaidi

PHYSIOTHERAPISTS
Hugh Allan M.B.E. &
Andrew McLeod, B.Sc.,M.C.S.P.

S.F.A. COMMUNITY OFFICER
Jim Clark

CHIEF SCOUT
Alex Wright

COMMERCIAL MANAGER
Denny Martin

STADIUM MANAGER
Angus Hollas

TELEPHONES
Ground/Commercial
(01563) 525184
Fax (01563) 522181
Matchday/Ticket Information
(01563) 542999

CLUB SHOP
Killie Sports, 36 Bank Street,
Kilmarnock. Tel (01563) 534210.
Open Mon to Sat
9.00 a.m. – 5.00 p.m.
Also shop at ground.

OFFICIAL SUPPORTERS CLUB
c/o Rugby Park, Kilmarnock, KA1 2DP

TEAM CAPTAIN
Ray Montgomerie

SHIRT SPONSOR
A.T. Mays, Travel Agents

LIST OF PLAYERS 1996-97

SURNAME	FIRST NAME	MIDDLE NAME	DATE OF BIRTH	PLACE OF BIRTH	DATE OF SIGNING	HEIGHT FT INS	WEIGHT ST LBS	PREVIOUS CLUB
Agostini	Damiano		22/11/78	Irvine	15/05/96	5 11.0	12 9	Kilmarnock Youth
Anderson	Derek	Christopher	15/05/72	Paisley	15/11/94	6 0.0	11 0	Kilwinning Rangers
Bagen	David		26/04/77	Irvine	16/11/95	5 6.0	9 7	Troon Juniors
Brown	Thomas		01/04/68	Glasgow	27/08/93	5 7.0	10 7	Glenafton Athletic
Burke	Alexander		11/11/77	Glasgow	18/08/95	5 7.5	9 11	Kilmarnock B.C.
Davidson	Stuart		03/08/79	Glasgow	18/08/95	5 7.0	9 2	Glasgow City B.C.
Dillon	John		16/12/78	Vale of Leven	15/05/96	5 7.0	10 0	Kilmarnock Youth
Doig	Kevin		06/11/75	Glasgow	15/05/95	6 0.0	12 5	Troon Juniors
Findlay	William	McCall	29/08/70	Kilmarnock	21/03/95	5 10.0	12 13	Hibernian
Graham	Martin		21/02/79	Irvine	15/05/96	5 9.0	10 5	Kilmarnock Youth Team
Hamilton	Steven	James	19/03/75	Baillieston	26/08/94	5 9.0	12 10	Troon Juniors
Hay	Gary		07/09/77	Irvine	18/08/95	5 7.5	10 0	Kilmarnock B.C.
Henry	John		31/12/71	Vale of Leven	15/08/94	5 10.0	10 5	Clydebank
Holt	Gary		09/03/73	Irvine	18/08/95	5 11.5	11 3	Stoke City
Kerr	Alan		07/05/76	Irvine	11/05/95	5 8.0	10 9	Troon Juniors
Lauchlan	James	Harley	02/02/77	Glasgow	20/07/94	6 1.0	10 13	Kilmarnock B.C.
Lekovic	Dragoje		21/11/67	Sivac, Montenegro	26/11/94	6 2.5	12 9	Buducnost Podgorica
Lennox	Rodney		02/09/78	Irvine	12/06/96	5 6.5	10 0	Kilmarnock Youth Team
MacPherson	Angus	Ian	11/10/68	Glasgow	10/06/86	5 11.0	11 8	Rangers
McClelland	John		20/05/80	Glasgow	20/07/96	5 10.5	10 0	Hearts U'16s
McCutcheon	Gary		08/10/78	Dumfries	18/08/95	5 4.5	9 11	Kilmarnock B.C.
McGowne	Kevin		16/12/69	Kilmarnock	02/09/96	6 0.0	12 3	St. Johnstone
McIntyre	James		24/05/72	Alexandria	22/03/96	5 11.0	11 5	Airdrieonians
McKee	Colin		22/08/73	Glasgow	06/09/94	5 10.0	11 3	Manchester United
Meldrum	Colin	George	26/11/75	Kilmarnock	03/09/93	5 10.5	13 4	Kilwinning Rangers
Mitchell	Alistair	Robert	03/12/68	Kirkcaldy	05/07/91	5 7.0	11 8	East Fife
Montgomerie	Samuel	Raymond	17/04/61	Irvine	12/08/88	5 8.0	11 12	Dumbarton
Morrison	Steven		09/02/80	Stirling	29/07/96	5 10.0	11 1	Tillicoultry B.C.
Reilly	Mark		30/03/69	Bellshill	05/07/91	5 8.0	10 10	Motherwell
Roberts	Mark	Kingsley	29/10/75	Irvine	07/02/92	5 10.5	11 2	Bellfield B.C.
Ryan	Alexander		07/09/79	Glasgow	18/08/95	5 5.0	9 9	Highbury B.C.
Skilling	Mark	James	06/10/72	Irvine	01/10/91	5 9.5	11 2	Saltcoats Victoria
Tallon	Gerrit	Thomas	05/09/73	Drogheda	20/06/96	5 8.5	12 7	Blackburn Rovers
Vincent	Robert		13/11/77	Glasgow	12/06/96	5 6.5	10 1	Kilmarnock Youth Team
Walker	Scott		05/03/75	Glasgow	02/11/95	6 1.0	13 9	Dalry Thistle
Whitworth	Neil		12/04/72	Wigan	02/09/94	6 0.5	12 9	Manchester United
Wright	Paul	Hamilton	17/08/67	East Kilbride	31/03/95	5 8.0	11 7	St. Johnstone

MILESTONES

YEAR OF FORMATION: 1869
MOST CAPPED PLAYER: Joe Nibloe; **NO. OF CAPS:** 11
MOST LEAGUE POINTS IN A SEASON: 58 (Division 2 - Season 1973/74)
MOST LEAGUE GOALS SCORED BY A PLAYER IN A SEASON: Harry "Peerie" Cunningham (Season 1927/28) and Andy Kerr (Season 1960/61)
NO. OF GOALS SCORED: 34
RECORD ATTENDANCE: 34,246 (-v- Rangers – August 1963)
RECORD VICTORY: 13-2 (-v- Saltcoats – Scottish Cup, 12.9.1896)
RECORD DEFEAT: 0-8 (-v- Rangers and Hibernian - Division 1)

KILLIE'S TEN YEAR LEAGUE RECORD

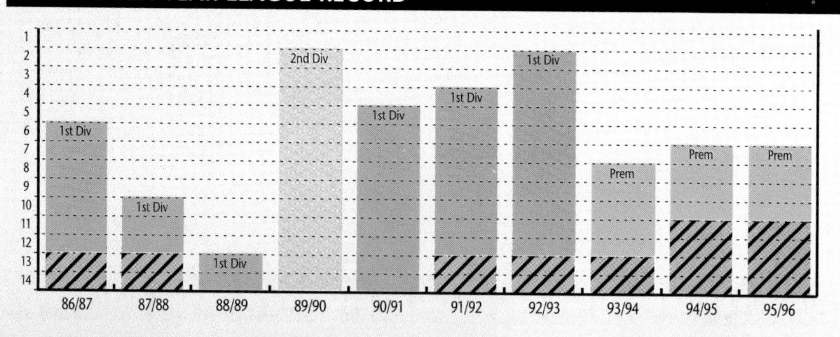

CLUB FACTFILE 1995/96
RESULTS... APPEARANCES... SCORERS

KILLIE

Date	Venue	Opponents	Att.	Res	Lekovic D.	Skilling M.	Black T.	Montgomerie R.	Whitworth N.	Connor R.	Mitchell A.	Henry J.	Wright P.	Brown T.	Reilly M.	Roberts M.	Geddes R.	MacPherson A.	McKee C.	Findlay W.	Anderson D.	Holt G.	Maskrey S.	Meldrum C.	Lauchlan J.	McIntyre J.
Aug 26	A	Rangers	44,430	0-1	1	2	3	4	5	6	7	8	9	10	11	14										
Sep 9	H	Hibernian	7,014	0-3		11	3	4	5	6	7	8	9	14	13	10	1	2								
16	A	Raith Rovers	4,441	0-2		8		4	5	6	7	10	14		3	9	1	2	11	12						
23	H	Aberdeen	7,198	1-2	1	8			5	4	7	13	10	11^{1}	3	14		2	9		6					
30	A	Motherwell	6,356	0-3	1	8	3		5	4	7		10	11				2	9		6	13	14			
Oct 4	A	Partick Thistle	3,419	†1-1	1	4	3		5	8	7		9	10				2	11		6		14			
7	H	Heart of Midlothian	6,721	3-1	1	4	3		5	8	7		9	10^{1}				2	11^{2}		6	12	14			
14	A	Falkirk	4,878	2-0	1	4	3		5	8	7^{1}		9^{1}	10	13			2	11		6	12	14			
21	H	Celtic	14,001	0-0	1	4	3		5	8		13	9	10				2	11	7	6	12	14			
28	A	Hibernian	9,888	0-2	1		3		5	8	10	13	9					2	11	7	6	4	14			
Nov 4	H	Raith Rovers	6,440	5-1	1		3		5	8	7	4^{2}	9^{2}	10^{1}	13			2			6	14	11			
8	H	Rangers	14,613	0-2			3		5	8	7	4	9	10	12			2	11		6	14		1		
11	A	Heart of Midlothian	10,442	1-2	1		3		5	8	7	4	9			14		2	11^{1}		6	10				
18	H	Motherwell	6,608	1-1	1		3		5	8	7^{1}	4	9	10				2	11		6	13	14			
Dec 2	A	Celtic	33,660	2-4	1		3		5	8	7^{1}	12	9	10^{1}	4			2	14		6	11				
9	H	Falkirk	6,017	4-0	1		3^{1}		5	8	7	4	9	10^{2}	12			2^{1}			6	11	13			
13	A	Aberdeen	14,060	1-4	1				5	8	7	4	9^{1}	10	3			2			6	11				
16	H	Partick Thistle	6,581	2-1	1				5	8	7	4	9^{2}	10	3			2				11			6	
26	A	Rangers	45,143	0-3	1				5	8	7	4	9	10	3			2				11			6	
Jan 6	A	Raith Rovers	4,781	1-1	1		3^{1}		5	8	7	13	9		4	14		2				11	10		6	
13	H	Hibernian	6,686	3-2	1		3		5		7	8^{1}	9^{1}		4			2	14		6	11	10^{1}			
16	A	Motherwell	5,781	1-0	1		3	13	5		7	8	9^{1}		4			2	14		6	11	10			
20	H	Celtic	16,024	0-0	1		3		5		7	8	9		4			2	14		6	11	10			
23	H	Aberdeen	6,703	1-1	1		3		5		7	8	9^{1}	13	4			2	14		6	11	10			
Feb 3	A	Falkirk	4,143	2-4	1		3		5			8	9^{2}	10	4	14		2	7		6	11				
10	A	Partick Thistle	4,857	1-0	1		3^{1}	5				8	9	10	4			2	7		6	11				
24	H	Heart of Midlothian	8,022	0-2	1		3	5			7	8	9	10	4	14		2	11		6					
Mar 2	A	Aberdeen	7,177	0-3	1		3	12	5	10	7	14	9	8	4			2	11		6					
16	H	Motherwell	7,035	0-1	1	12	3		5		7	8	9		4	13		2	14		6	11	10			
23	H	Raith Rovers	6,143	2-0	1	8		4	5				9^{1}	13	12			2	7^{1}		3	6	11			10
30	A	Hibernian	8,001	1-1	1		3	4				8	9^{1}	14	6			2	7		5		11			10
Apr 10	A	Celtic	36,476	1-1	1	12	3	4				8	9	13	6			2	7		5	11	14			10^{1}
13	H	Falkirk	6,505	1-0	1		3	4			14	8	9		6			2	7		5	12	11			10^{1}
20	H	Partick Thistle	7,276	2-1	1	8^{1}	3^{1}	4			7		9	13	6			2	14		5	12	11			10
27	A	Heart of Midlothian	11,329	0-1	1	8	3	4		6	7		9			13		2	14				11		5	10
May 4	H	Rangers	17,102	0-3	1	8	3	4		12	7		9		6	13		2	14				11		5	10
TOTAL FULL APPEARANCES					33	13	30	12	28	22	29	22	35	19	22	2	2	35	19	2	28	17	13	1	5	7
TOTAL SUB APPEARANCES						(2)		(2)		(1)	(1)	(6)	(1)	(6)	(6)	(9)			(9)	(1)		(9)	(9)			
TOTAL GOALS SCORED						1	4				3	3	13	6				1	4				1			2

Small bold figures denote goalscorers. † denotes opponent's own goal.

RUGBY PARK

CAPACITY: 18,128 (All Seated)

PITCH DIMENSIONS: 112 yds x 74 yds

FACILITIES FOR DISABLED SUPPORTERS:
Contact: John Tual, Secretary, Persons with a Disability Association, 72 Morris Crescent, Hurlford, Kilmarnock, KA1 5BH. Tel: 01563 530117

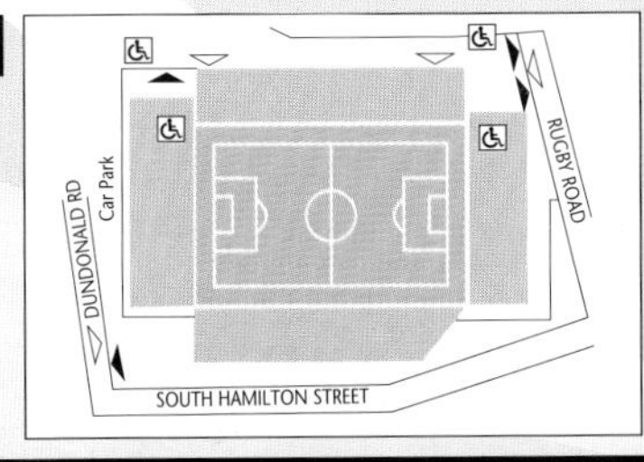

HOW TO GET THERE

Rugby Park can be reached by the following routes:

BUSES: The main bus station, which is served by buses from all over the country, is ten minutes walk from the ground, but there are three local services which run from here to within a two minute walk of the park. These are the Kilmarnock-Saltcoats, Kilmarnock-Ardrossan and Kilmarnock-Largs.

TRAINS: Kilmarnock station is well served by trains from Glasgow and the West Coast, and the station is only 15 minutes walk from the ground.

CARS: Car parking is available in the club car park by permit only Entry ONLY from Dundonald Road. Visiting supporters enter ONLY from Rugby Road Entrance.

MOTHERWELL

Fir Park, Firpark Street,
Motherwell, ML1 2QN

CHAIRMAN
John C. Chapman, O.B.E., A.R.A.gS

VICE-CHAIRMAN
William H. Dickie, R.I.B.A., A.R.I.A.S

GENERAL MANAGER/SECRETARY
Alan C. Dick

PLAYER/MANAGER
Alexander McLeish

ASSISTANT MANAGER
Andrew Watson

COACH
Jim Griffin

HON. MEDICAL OFFICERS
Mr. Ian Kerr & Dr. Robert Liddle

PHYSIOTHERAPIST
John Porteous

S.F.A. COMMUNITY OFFICER
William McLean

YOUTH DEVELOPMENT OFFICER/ CHIEF SCOUT
John Park

GROUNDSMAN
Christopher Westwood

COMMERCIAL MANAGER
John Swinburne

TELEPHONES
Ground/Commercial
(01698) 333333
Fax (01698) 276333
Ticket Office (01698) 333030
Information Service 0891 121553

CLUB SHOP
Motherwell Football & Athletic Club, Firpark Street, Motherwell, ML1 2QN
Tel (01698) 333333.
Open 9.00 a.m. – 4.30 p.m. Mon. to Fri. (Open Saturdays from 10.00 a.m. to 5.00 p.m. on first team home match days and 10.00 a.m. to 1.00 p.m. when the team is playing away from home.)

OFFICIAL SUPPORTERS CLUB
c/o Fir Park, Firpark Street,
Motherwell, ML1 2QN.

TEAM CAPTAIN
Chris McCart

SHIRT SPONSOR
Motorola

LIST OF PLAYERS 1996-97

SURNAME	FIRST NAME	MIDDLE NAME	DATE OF BIRTH	PLACE OF BIRTH	DATE OF SIGNING	HEIGHT FT INS	WEIGHT ST LBS	PREVIOUS CLUB
Arnott	Douglas		05/08/61	Lanark	29/10/86	5 7.0	10 7	Pollok Juniors
Burns	Alexander		04/08/73	Bellshill	06/08/91	5 8.0	10 0	Shotts Bon-Accord
Coyne	Thomas		14/11/62	Glasgow	30/11/93	6 0.0	10 7	Tranmere Rovers
Craigan	Stephen		21/10/76	Newtownards	07/09/95	5 10.0	10 9	Blantyre Vics
Davies	William	McIntosh	31/05/64	Glasgow	12/03/94	5 6.0	10 9	Dunfermline Athletic
Denham	Greig	Paterson	05/10/76	Glasgow	19/08/93	6 0.0	12 2	Cumbernauld United
Dolan	James		22/02/69	Salsburgh	13/06/87	5 9.0	10 7	Motherwell B.C.
Essandoh	Roy		17/02/76	Belfast	09/12/94	6 0.0	12 3	Cumbernauld Juniors
Ewing	Christopher		12/10/78	Glasgow	20/08/96	6 4.0	12 2	Cumbernauld United
Falconer	William	Henry	05/04/66	Aberdeen	16/01/96	6 1.0	13 0	Celtic
Gow	Garry		24/06/77	Glasgow	31/08/96	5 11.0	11 12	Irvine Vics
Hamilton	Brian		13/08/78	Lanark	31/08/96	5 10.0	9 12	Vale of Clyde
Hendry	John		06/01/70	Glasgow	12/07/95	5 11.0	10 0	Tottenham Hotspur
Howie	Scott		04/01/72	Glasgow	13/10/94	6 3.0	13 5	Norwich City
Jamieson	Ross		31/10/77	Bellshill	31/08/96	5 11.0	11 1	Irvine Vics
Martin	Brian		24/02/63	Bellshill	14/11/91	6 0.0	13 0	St. Mirren
May	Edward		30/08/67	Edinburgh	24/02/95	5 7.5	10 3	Falkirk
McCallum	David	John	07/09/77	Bellshill	20/08/96	5 11.0	10 12	Bearsden B.C.
McCart	Christopher		17/04/67	Motherwell	19/12/84	6 1.0	12 10	Motherwell B.C.
McCulloch	Lee		14/05/78	Bellshill	17/08/95	5 11.0	12 5	Cumbernauld United
McLeish	Alexander		21/01/59	Glasgow	15/07/94	6 1.5	13 4	Aberdeen
McMillan	Stephen		19/01/76	Edinburgh	19/08/93	5 10.0	11 0	Troon Juniors
McSkimming	Shaun	Peter	29/05/70	Stranraer	03/11/94	5 11.0	10 8	Kilmarnock
Philliben	John		14/03/64	Stirling	05/09/86	5 11.5	12 7	Doncaster Rovers
Ritchie	Innes		24/08/73	Edinburgh	14/08/93	6 0.0	12 7	Bathgate Thistle
Roddie	Andrew	Robert	04/11/71	Glasgow	20/08/94	5 10.5	11 6	Aberdeen
Ross	Ian		27/08/74	Broxburn	14/08/93	5 10.0	10 7	Bathgate Thistle
Van Der Gaag	Mitchell		27/10/71	Zutphen	22/03/95	6 2.0	12 4	PSV Eindhoven
Wishart	Fraser		01/03/65	Johnstone	13/08/96	5 8.0	10 0	Heart of Midlothian
Woods	Stephen	Gerard	23/02/70	Glasgow	22/07/94	6 2.0	12 0	Preston North End

MILESTONES

YEAR OF FORMATION: 1886
MOST CAPPED PLAYER: George Stevenson (Scotland) and Tommy Coyne (Republic of Ireland)
NO. OF CAPS: 12
MOST LEAGUE POINTS IN A SEASON: 66 (Division 1 - Season 1931/32)
MOST LEAGUE GOALS SCORED BY A PLAYER IN A SEASON: William McFadyen (Season 1931/32)
NO. OF GOALS SCORED: 52
RECORD ATTENDANCE: 35,632 (-v- Rangers – Scottish Cup, 12.3.1952)
RECORD VICTORY: 12-1 (-v- Dundee United – Division 2, 23.1.1954)
RECORD DEFEAT: 0-8 (-v- Aberdeen - Premier Division, 26.3.1979)

THE WELL'S TEN YEAR LEAGUE RECORD

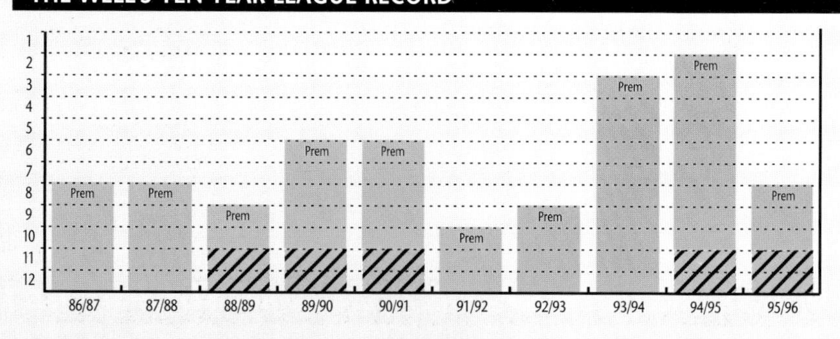

CLUB FACTFILE 1995/96
RESULTS... APPEARANCES... SCORERS

The WELL

Date	Venue	Opponents	Att.	Res	Howie S.	May E.	McKinnon R.	Roddie A.	Martin B.	McCart C.	Lambert P.	Dolan J.	Burns A.	Arnott D.	Davies W.	Philliben J.	McSkimming S.	Ritchie I.	Coyne T.	Krivokapic M.	Hendry J.	Denham G.	McMillan S.	Essandoh R.	Ferguson P.	McLeish A.	Falconer W.	Van der Gaag M.	Ross I.	McCulloch L.
Aug 26	A	Heart of Midlothian	10,971	1-1	1	2	3	4	5	6	7	8	9	10[1]	11	12	14													
Sep 9	H	Partick Thistle	6,155	†1-1	1	2		4	5		7	8	9	10	12	6	11	3												
16	A	Celtic	31,365	1-1	1	2	3	14	5	6	7	8		10[1]		4	11		9											
23	A	Falkirk	4,246	0-0	1	2		11	5	6	7	8		10	14	4	3		9											
30	H	Kilmarnock	6,356	3-0	1	2[1]	3	14	5	6	7		15	10	8	4	11		9[2]											
Oct 3	A	Rangers	39,891	1-2	1	2	3	14	5	6	7	8	15	10	12	4	11[1]		9											
7	H	Raith Rovers	5,727	0-2	1	2	3	11	5	6	7		14	10	8	4			9											
14	H	Aberdeen	6,842	2-1	1	2	3	14	5		7[1]	8		10	11	4			9[1]	6	12	15								
21	A	Hibernian	9,803	2-4	1	2		3	5		7	8	12	10	11	6			9	4	14[2]									
28	A	Partick Thistle	4,029	0-1	1			15	5	6	7	8	14		11	2			9	4	10		3							
Nov 4	H	Celtic	12,077	0-2	1	2		14	5	6	7	8	12	10	11	4		15			9		3							
7	H	Heart of Midlothian	5,595	0-0	1			10	5	6	7	8	9		11	2				4			3	12						
11	A	Raith Rovers	4,293	0-0	1			10	5	6	7	8	9	12	11	2				4		14	3							
18	A	Kilmarnock	6,608	1-1	1		3	12	5		7		9[1]	10	11			15			14	4	8		2	6				
25	H	Falkirk	5,201	1-1	1		3	12	5		7	8	9[1]	10	11			2		4	14	6	15							
Dec 2	H	Hibernian	5,362	0-2	1		3	11			7	8	9	10	12		2	5		4	14	6								
9	A	Aberdeen	11,299	0-1	1	2	3	12	5		7	8	9	10	11					4	14	6								
19	H	Rangers	10,197	0-0	1	2	3	10	5		7	12	9		11		8	14		4		6		15						
Jan 6	A	Celtic	34,629	0-1	1	2	3	14	5		7	12	9	10	11		8			4		6								
10	A	Heart of Midlothian	9,288	0-4	1	7	3	12	5			8	9	10	11			2		4		6	14	15						
13	H	Partick Thistle	5,226	0-2	1	2	3	14			7	8	10	9	12			5		4		6	11	15						
16	H	Kilmarnock	5,781	0-1	1	2	3	11			7	8	14	9		5		15		4	12	6					10			
20	A	Hibernian	7,658	0-0	1	2	3		5		7			12	11	4					9	6	8				10			
23	A	Falkirk	3,845	†1-0	1	2	3		5		7		14	9	11	4						6	8				10			
Feb 10	A	Rangers	44,871	2-3	1	2	3		5[1]	6	7	14		9			11				12		8				10[1]	4		
13	H	Aberdeen	5,090	1-0	1	2	3		5	6	7		14[1]		15	12	11				9		8				10	4		
24	H	Raith Rovers	5,569	1-0	1	2	3		5	6	7	8	14		12		11		15		9						10[1]	4		
Mar 2	H	Falkirk	5,037	1-0	1	2	3		5	6	7	8	12		11				14		9						10[1]	4		
16	A	Kilmarnock	7,035	1-0	1	2	3		5	6	7[1]	8	9		11				12								10	4		
23	H	Celtic	12,394	0-0	1	2	3		5		7	8	9	14	11	6			12								10	4		
30	A	Partick Thistle	4,846	2-0	1	2	3		5	6	7		12	9	11[1]	8			14								10	4[1]		
Apr 6	H	Hibernian	5,964	3-0	1	2	3		5[1]	6	7	8		14	11	12			9[1]								10[1]	4		
13	A	Aberdeen	8,943	1-2	1	2	3		5	6	7	8	14	9	11	12											10[1]	4		
20	H	Rangers	13,128	1-3	1	2	3		5	6	7	8	12	9[1]	11	14	15										10	4		
27	A	Raith Rovers	3,653	0-2	1			8	5	6	7				11	2	3	14			9						10	4		
May 4	H	Heart of Midlothian	8,301	1-1	1			2	5		7				11[1]	6	3				9						10	4	8	14
TOTAL FULL APPEARANCES					36	28	27	12	33	20	35	24	14	23	26	19	13	5	9	13	8	11	10		1	1	15	12	1	
TOTAL SUB APPEARANCES								(12)				(3)	(14)	(4)	(7)	(5)	(2)	(5)	(5)		(8)	(2)	(2)	(4)						(1)
TOTAL GOALS SCORED						1			2		2		3	3	2		1		4		2						5	1		

Small bold figures denote goalscorers. † denotes opponent's own goal.

FIR PARK

CAPACITY: 13,742 (All seated)

PITCH DIMENSIONS: 110 yds x 75 yds

FACILITIES FOR DISABLED SUPPORTERS: Area between Main Stand and South Stand. Prior arrangement must be made with the Secretary and a ticket obtained.

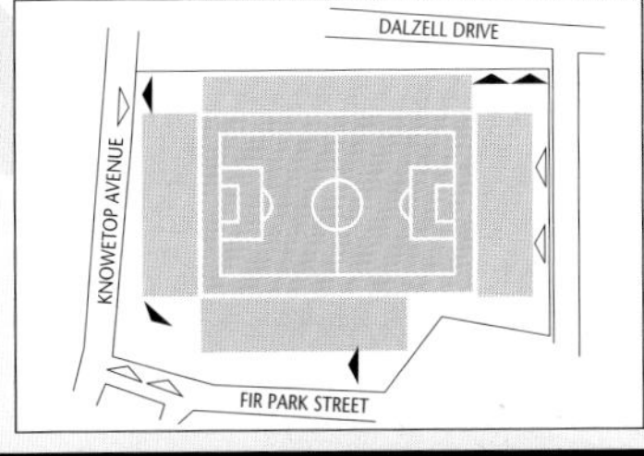

HOW TO GET THERE

The following routes can be used to reach Fir Park:

BUSES: Fir Park is less than a quarter of a mile from the main thoroughfare through the town and numerous buses serving Lanarkshire and Glasgow all pass along this road. De-bus at the Civic Centre.

TRAINS: Motherwell Station is a main-line station on the Glasgow–London (Euston) route, and the station is particularly well served by trains running from numerous points throughout the Strathclyde Region. Motherwell station is a twenty minute walk from Fir Park, while the new station at Airbles is only fifteen minutes away.

CARS: Car Parking is only available in the many side streets around the ground. There is no major parking area close to Fir Park.

RAITH ROVERS

Stark's Park, Pratt Street,
Kirkcaldy, Fife, KY1 1SA

CHAIRMAN
Alexander A. Penman

VICE-CHAIRMAN
William Shedden

DIRECTORS
Charles A. Cant
William H. Gray

GENERAL MANAGER
William McPhee

MANAGER
Iain Munro

OFFICE MANAGER
Deborah Muir

YOUTH COACHES
Stevie Kirk & Miodrag Krivokapic

CLUB DOCTOR
Dr. G. K. N. Hall

PHYSIOTHERAPIST
Gerry Docherty

CHIEF SCOUT
Andy Harrow

GROUNDSMAN
John Murray

COMMERCIAL ADMINISTRATOR
Lynn Penman
Home (01592) 201993
Mobile (0374) 685808

TELEPHONES
Ground/Commercial
(01592) 263514
Fax (01592) 642833
Ticket Office (01592) 263514
Club Call (0891) 884479

CLUB SHOP
16 Links Street, Kirkcaldy
Tel (01592) 201993.
Open Mon-Fri 9.00 am – 5.00 pm
(Early Closing Wed at 1.00 pm).
Sat 9.00 am – 3.00 pm on Home
Match Days and 9.00 am – 5.00 pm
on Away Match Days.

OFFICIAL SUPPORTERS CLUB
c/o Fraser Hamilton,
22 Tower Terrace, Kirkcaldy, Fife

TEAM CAPTAIN
Shaun Dennis

SHIRT SPONSOR
Kelly's Copiers

LIST OF PLAYERS 1996-97

SURNAME	FIRST NAME	MIDDLE NAME	DATE OF BIRTH	PLACE OF BIRTH	DATE OF SIGNING	HEIGHT FT INS	WEIGHT ST LBS	PREVIOUS CLUB
Bogie	Graeme		07/08/79	Kirkcaldy	11/10/95	5 9.0	11 3	Glenrothes Strollers
Bonar	Paul		28/12/76	Robroyston	31/03/96	5 11.0	10 7	Airdrieonians
Browne	Paul		17/02/75	Glasgow	03/07/96	6 2.0	12 6	Aston Villa
Byers	Kevin		23/08/79	Kirkcaldy	09/07/96	5 10.0	9 2	Glenrothes Strollers
Craig	David	William	11/06/69	Glasgow	10/05/96	6 2.0	13 0	Hamilton Academical
Dargo	Craig	Peter	03/01/78	Edinburgh	11/10/95	5 6.0	10 1	Links United
Dennis	Shaun		20/12/69	Kirkcaldy	03/08/88	6 1.0	13 7	Lochgelly Albert
Duffield	Peter		04/02/69	Middlesbrough	29/02/96	5 6.0	10 4	Airdrieonians
Francis	Christopher	Douglas	20/02/79	Dunfermline	11/10/95	5 10.0	11 3	Valleyfield
Geddes	Alexander	Robert	12/08/60	Inverness	26/01/96	6 0.0	12 8	Kilmarnock
Harvey	Paul	Edward	28/08/68	Glasgow	03/07/96	5 8.0	10 7	Airdrieonians
Humphries	Mark		23/12/71	Glasgow	01/12/95	5 11.0	13 0	Bristol City
Hynd	Alistair		31/10/79	Kirkcaldy	26/06/96	6 0.0	9 10	Glenrothes Strollers
Johnston	Leslie		28/02/80	Kirkcaldy	09/07/96	5 9.0	9 10	Glenrothes Strollers
Kirk	Stephen	David	03/01/63	Kirkcaldy	01/03/96	5 11.0	11 4	Falkirk
Kirkwood	David	Stewart	27/08/67	St. Andrews	10/08/94	5 10.0	11 7	Airdrieonians
Krivokapic	Miodrag		06/09/59	Niksic Crna Gora	29/03/96	6 1.0	12 6	Motherwell
Landels	Graeme	John	27/03/78	Broxburn	11/10/95	5 11.0	12 5	I.C.I. Juveniles
Lennon	Daniel	Joseph	06/04/69	Whitburn	31/03/94	5 5.0	10 8	Hibernian
Mauchlen	Iain		11/06/79	Irvine	11/10/95	5 7.0	10 0	Leicester City
McCulloch	Greig		18/04/76	Girvan	24/02/96	5 8.0	10 7	Aberdeen
McInally	James	Edward	19/02/64	Glasgow	07/07/95	5 8.5	11 4	Dundee United
McPherson	Dean		07/06/78	Aberdeen	06/08/94	5 10.0	9 9	Hutchison Vale B.C.
Millar	John		08/12/66	Bellshill	31/03/96	5 10.0	11 10	Heart of Midlothian
Rougier	Anthony	Leo	17/07/71	Trinidad & Tobago	13/03/95	6 0.0	14 1	Trinity Pros
Sellars	Neil	Andrew	09/05/77	Kirkcaldy	03/08/94	5 8.0	9 11	Kirkcaldy Y.M.
Smart	Craig		26/11/78	Kirkcaldy	11/10/95	5 7.5	10 4	Valleyfield
Stein	Jay		13/01/79	Dunfermline	11/10/95	5 6.5	10 4	Inverkeithing United
Taylor	Alexander		13/06/62	Baillieston	05/07/95	5 9.5	11 7	Partick Thistle
Taylor	Russell	Thomas	30/07/80	Dunfermline	16/07/96	5 10.0	10 6	Glenrothes Strollers
Thomson	Scott	Munro	29/01/72	Aberdeen	01/03/96	5 10.0	11 10	Aberdeen
Thomson	Scott	Yuill	08/11/66	Edinburgh	08/09/93	6 0.0	11 9	Forfar Athletic
Twaddle	Kevin		31/10/71	Edinburgh	03/07/96	6 3.0	12 2	St. Johnstone
Wilson	David	William	19/09/79	Dunfermline	09/07/96	5 11.0	9 2	Rosyth Recreation

MILESTONES

YEAR OF FORMATION: 1883
MOST CAPPED PLAYER: David Morris
NO. OF CAPS: 6
MOST LEAGUE POINTS IN A SEASON: 65 (First Division - Season 1992/93) – 2 points for a win
69 (First Division - Season 1994/95) – 3 points for a win
MOST LEAGUE GOALS SCORED BY A PLAYER IN A SEASON: Norman Heywood (Season 1937/38)
NO. OF GOALS SCORED: 42
RECORD ATTENDANCE: 31,306 (-v- Heart of Midlothian – Scottish Cup, 7.2.1953)
RECORD VICTORY: 10-1 (-v- Coldstream – Scottish Cup, 13.2.1954)
RECORD DEFEAT: 2-11 (-v- Morton – Division 2, 18.3.1936)

THE ROVERS' TEN YEAR LEAGUE RECORD

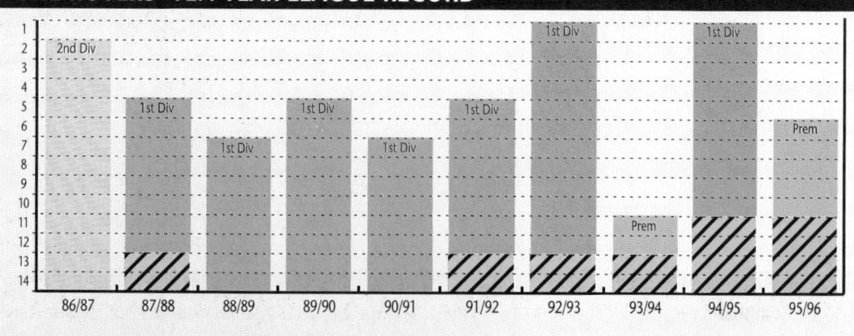

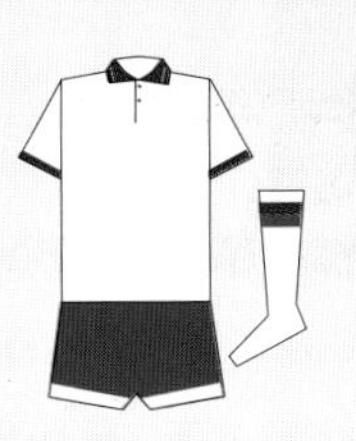

CLUB FACTFILE 1995/96
RESULTS... APPEARANCES... SCORERS

The ROVERS

Date	Venue	Opponents	Att.	Res	Thomson S. Y.	Kirkwood D.	Broddle J.	McInally J.	Dennis S.	Sinclair D.	Wilson B.	Cameron C.	Graham A.	Crawford S.	Rougier A.	Lennon D.	Raeside R.	Coyle R.	McAnespie S.	Dair J.	Nicholl J.	Taylor A.	McMillan I.	Buist M.	Humphries M.	McKilligan N.	Forrest G.	Fridge L.	Geddes R.	McCulloch G.	Thomson S. M.	Duffield P.	Kirk S.	Krivokapic M.	Millar J.	Bonar P.	Dargo C.	Landels G.	Sellars N.
Aug 26	H	Celtic	9,300	0-1	1	2	3	4	5	6	7	8	9	10	11	12	14																						
Sep 9	A	Rangers	43,284	0-4	1	2	3	4	5	6	7	8	12	9	11	10		14	16																				
16	H	Kilmarnock	4,441	2-0	1	6	3	12		5	7	8	9^{1}	14	16	10		4	2	11^{1}																			
23	H	Partick Thistle	4,342	3-1	1	6	3	12		5	16	8^{2}	9	14	7	10		4	2	11^{1}																			
30	A	Aberdeen	13,983	0-3	1	2	3	4	5	6	7	8		9		10	14	12		11	16																		
Oct 4	H	Hibernian	6,051	3-0	1	2	3	7	5	6^{1}		8^{2}	9			10		4		11																			
7	A	Motherwell	5,727	2-0	1	2	3	7	5	6^{1}		8	9	12		10		4		11^{1}																			
14	A	Heart of Midlothian	10,133	2-4	1	2	3	7	5	6		8	9^{1}	12^{1}		10		4		11		14	16																
21	H	Falkirk	4,715	0-1	1	2	3	7	5	6		8	9	12	14	10		4		11																			
28	H	Rangers	9,300	2-2	1		3			6		8^{1}	12	9	11	10^{1}		4		7		14	5	2															
Nov 4	A	Kilmarnock	6,440	1-5	1	2	3	7	5	6		8^{1}	12	9		10		4		11		14	16																
8	A	Celtic	28,832	0-0	1	2	3	7	5	6		8	12	9		10		4		11																			
11	H	Motherwell	4,293	0-0	1	2	3	7	5	6		8	12	9	16	10		4		11																			
18	H	Aberdeen	5,786	1-0	1		3	2	5	6	16	8	9	7		10^{1}		4		11																			
25	A	Partick Thistle	3,503	2-0	1	12	3	2	5	6		8	9^{1}	7^{1}		10		4		11		14																	
Dec 2	A	Falkirk	4,442	1-2	1		3	2	5	6	11	8	9^{1}	7	16	10		4				14																	
9	H	Heart of Midlothian	6,349	1-1	1		3	2		5	11	8	9	7	16	10^{1}		4							6														
16	A	Hibernian	8,507	2-1	1	16	3		5	12	14	8	9^{1}	7^{1}	11	10		4							6	2													
Jan 6	H	Kilmarnock	4,781	1-1	1	11	3		5	2	14	8	9	7		10^{1}		4							6														
9	H	Celtic	9,300	1-3	1		3		5	6	7	8^{1}	9	11		10		4				12			2	14	16												
13	A	Rangers	42,498	0-4	1		12	2	5	6	7	8	9	11		10		4					16		3														
20	H	Falkirk	4,123	1-0	1		14		5	6^{1}		8	9	10	7	4				11			2		3														
23	H	Partick Thistle	3,651	0-2	1	16	14		5	6		8	9	10	11	4				7			2		3														
Feb 3	A	Heart of Midlothian	10,183	0-2		2	3		5			8	9	7	10			4		11			12		6	14		1											
7	A	Aberdeen	6,628	0-1		2	14		5	6		8	12	9	11	10		4		7					3				1										
10	H	Hibernian	4,832	1-0		2^{1}	3		5	6		8	14	9	7	10		4		11									1										
24	A	Motherwell	5,569	0-1		10	3	11		6	16	8			7		5	4		9		14							1	2									
Mar 2	A	Partick Thistle	2,336	3-0		3		4		6		8^{1}		9			5												1	2^{1}	7	10^{1}	11						
16	H	Aberdeen	4,932	2-2		3		4		6		8^{1}		12	16	10	5												1	2	7	9	11^{1}						
23	A	Kilmarnock	6,143	0-2		3		4		6		8		12		10	5												1	2	7	9	11						
30	H	Rangers	9,300	2-4		3^{1}		4							11	10	6			12		14							1	2	7	9^{1}	8	5					
Apr 6	A	Falkirk	3,766	3-2		3		4							11^{1}	10	6^{1}												1	2	7	9^{1}		5	8	12			
13	H	Heart of Midlothian	4,956	1-3											11	10^{1}							5	6					1	2	7	9	12	4	8	3			
20	A	Hibernian	7,214	1-1	1	2			5	6					11	12															7	9	8	4	10^{1}	3			
27	H	Motherwell	3,653	2-0	1	2		10	5	6					11	12															7^{1}	9^{1}	8	4		3			
May 4	A	Celtic	37,318	1-4	1	2		4	5	6					11	7						8									10	9^{1}				3	12	14	16
TOTAL FULL APPEARANCES					26	25	23	23	25	31	8	30	18	21	17	30	6	22	2	19		1	4	2	9	1		1	9	7	9	9	6	5	3	4			
TOTAL SUB APPEARANCES						(3)	(4)	(2)		(1)	(5)		(7)	(7)	(6)	(3)	(2)	(2)	(1)	(1)	(1)	(8)	(4)			(2)	(1)						(1)			(1)	(1)	(1)	(1)
TOTAL GOALS SCORED						2				3		9	5	3	1	5	1			3										1	1	5	1		1				

Small bold figures denote goalscorers. † denotes opponent's own goal.

STARK'S PARK

CAPACITY: 11,877; Seated 10,277, Standing 1,600

PITCH DIMENSIONS: 113 yds x 70 yds

FACILITIES FOR DISABLED SUPPORTERS: By prior arrangement with the Secretary.

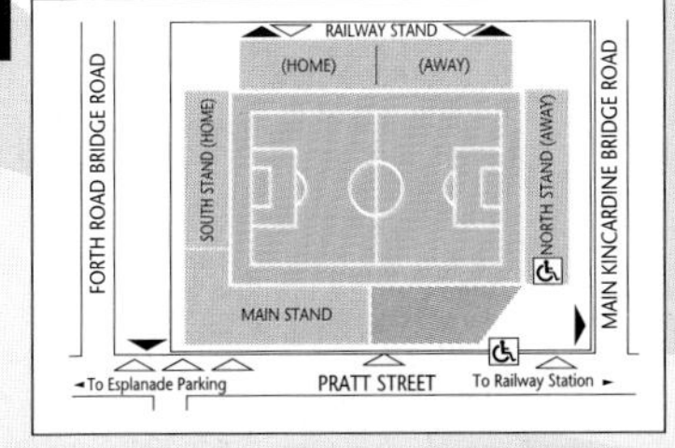

HOW TO GET THERE

The following routes may be used to reach Stark's Park:

TRAINS: Kirkcaldy railway station is served by trains from Dundee, Edinburgh and Glasgow (via Edinburgh) and the ground is within walking distance of the station.

BUSES: The main bus station in Kirkcaldy is also within 15 minutes walking distance of the ground, but the Edinburgh, Dunfermline and Leven services pass close by the park.

CARS: Car parking is available in the Esplanade, which is on the south side of the ground, in Beveridge Park, which is on the north side of Stark's Road, and in ground adjacent to the railway station.

RANGERS

Ibrox Stadium,150 Edmiston Drive,
Glasgow, G51 2XD

CHAIRMAN
David E. Murray

VICE-CHAIRMAN
Donald R. Findlay, Q.C., LL.B.

DIRECTORS
Hugh R. W. Adam, John Gillespie,
R. Campbell Ogilvie,
Ian Skelly, Walter Smith

SECRETARY
R. Campbell Ogilvie

MANAGER
Walter Smith

ASSISTANT MANAGER
Archie Knox

FIRST TEAM COACH
Davie Dodds

RESERVE COACH
John McGregor

YOUTH COACH
John Chalmers

S.F.A. COMMUNITY OFFICER
Ewan Chester

CLUB DOCTOR
Dr. Donald Cruickshank

PHYSIOTHERAPIST
Grant Downie

PUBLIC RELATIONS EXECUTIVE
John Greig, M.B.E.

FINANCIAL CONTROLLER
Douglas Odam

OPERATIONS EXECUTIVE
Alistair Hood, Q.P.M.

RANGERS CATERING MANAGER
Peter Kingstone

MANAGER, MARKETING & PUBLICATIONS DEPARTMENT
Brian Main

COMMERCIAL SALES EXECUTIVE
Scott Gardiner

STADIUM ACCESS ADMINISTRATOR
Ian Hosie

PITCH SUPERINTENDENT
Alan Ferguson

COMMERCIAL MANAGER
Bob Reilly 0141-427 8822

STADIUM PROPERTY MANAGER
Tom Onions

TELEPHONES
Ground/Public Relations Department
Tel 0141-427 8500 Fax 0141-427 2676
Stadium Access Administration (Tickets)
Tel 0141-427 8800 Fax 0141-427 8504

CLUB SHOPS
The Rangers Shop, 150 Copland Road, Glasgow, G51. Open 11.00 a.m.–3.00 p.m. Matchdays Only.
The Rangers Shop, 103 St. Vincent Street, Glasgow, G2. Open 9.30 a.m.–5.30 p.m.
The Rangers Shop, 100 Edmiston Drive, Glasgow, G51. Open 9.30 a.m.–5.30 p.m. Mon to Sat & 10.30 a.m.– 4.30 p.m. on Sunday.
The Rangers Shop, 21 Trongate, Glasgow. Open 9.30 a.m.– 5.30 p.m. Mon to Sat & 12.00 Noon to 5.00 p.m. on Sunday

OFFICIAL SUPPORTERS CLUB
Rangers F.C. Supporters' Association, 250 Edmiston Drive, Glasgow, G51 1YU

TEAM CAPTAIN
Richard Gough

SHIRT SPONSOR
McEwan's Lager

LIST OF PLAYERS 1996-97

SURNAME	FIRST NAME	MIDDLE NAME	DATE OF BIRTH	PLACE OF BIRTH	DATE OF SIGNING	HEIGHT FT INS	WEIGHT ST LBS	PREVIOUS CLUB
Albertz	Jorg		29/01/71	Monchengladbach	16/07/96	6 2.0	13 5	Hamburger S.V.
Andersen	Erik Bo		14/11/70	Randers	01/03/96	6 4.0	12 4	Aalborg Boldspilklub A/S
Bjorklund	Joachim		15/03/71	Vaxjo	15/07/96	5 11.0	12 8	Vicenza Calcio
Bollan	Gary		24/03/73	Dundee	27/01/95	5 11.0	12 12	Dundee United
Boyack	Steven		04/09/76	Edinburgh	01/07/93	5 10.0	10 7	Rangers B.C.
Brown	John		26/01/62	Stirling	15/01/88	5 11.0	11 2	Dundee
Cleland	Alexander		10/12/70	Glasgow	27/01/95	5 8.5	11 7	Dundee United
Dair	Lee		28/05/77	Dunfermline	01/07/93	5 10.0	11 10	Rangers B.C.
Durie	Gordon	Scott	06/12/65	Paisley	24/11/93	5 10.0	12 13	Tottenham Hotspur
Durrant	Ian		29/10/66	Glasgow	27/07/84	5 8.0	9 7	Glasgow United
Ferguson	Barry		02/02/78	Glasgow	06/07/94	5 7.0	9 10	Rangers S.A.B.C.
Ferguson	Ian		15/03/67	Glasgow	15/02/88	5 10.0	10 11	St. Mirren
Fitzgerald	Darren		13/10/78	Belfast	06/07/94	5 8.0	10 0	St. Andrews B.C.
Gascoigne	Paul		27/05/67	Gateshead	10/07/95	5 9.0	11 10	Lazio Societa Sportiva
Gibson	James		19/02/80	Bellshill	01/07/96	5 7.0	10 5	"S" Form
Goram	Andrew	Lewis	13/04/64	Bury	27/06/91	5 11.0	12 13	Hibernian
Gough	Charles	Richard	05/04/62	Stockholm	02/10/87	6 0.0	11 12	Tottenham Hotspur
Graham	David		06/10/78	Edinburgh	03/07/95	5 10.0	10 10	Rangers S.A.B.C.
Haggarty	Francis		16/11/78	Glasgow	03/07/95	5 7.0	9 3	Rangers S.A.B.C.
Jardine	Christopher		26/11/78	Dumfries	03/07/95	5 6.0	8 10	Rangers S.A.B.C.
Juttla	Jaswinder	Singh	02/08/77	Glasgow	06/07/94	5 6.0	9 13	Rangers S.A.B.C.
Laudrup	Brian		22/02/69	Vienna	21/07/94	6 0.0	13 0	Fiorentina AC
McCall	Stuart		10/06/64	Leeds	15/08/91	5 8.0	11 12	Everton
McCoist	Alistair		24/09/62	Bellshill	09/06/83	5 10.0	12 0	Sunderland
McGinty	Brian		10/12/76	East Kilbride	01/07/93	6 1.0	11 4	Rangers B.C.
McInnes	Derek	John	05/07/71	Paisley	14/11/95	5 7.0	11 4	Greenock Morton
McKnight	Paul		08/02/77	Belfast	05/08/93	5 7.0	11 4	St. Andrews B.C.
McLaren	Alan	James	04/01/71	Edinburgh	26/10/94	6 0.0	13 0	Heart of Midlothian
McShane	Paul		13/04/78	Alexandria	06/07/94	5 8.0	10 7	Rangers S.A.B.C.
Miller	Charles		18/03/76	Glasgow	02/07/92	5 9.0	10 8	Rangers B.C.
Milligan	Ross		02/06/78	Dumfries	03/07/95	6 0.0	12 6	Maxwellton Thistle
Moore	Craig	Andrew	12/12/75	Canterbury, Aus.	16/09/93	6 1.0	12 0	Australian Institute
Murray	Neil		21/02/73	Bellshill	23/08/89	5 9.0	10 10	Rangers Amateurs F.C.
Nicholson	Barry		24/08/78	Dumfries	03/07/95	5 7.0	9 1	Rangers S.A.B.C.
Nicolson	Iain		13/10/76	Glasgow	04/06/93	5 10.0	10 4	Rangers B.C.
Petric	Gordan		30/07/69	Belgrade	29/07/95	6 2.5	13 9	Dundee United
Rae	Michael		24/11/76	Inverness	06/07/94	5 10.0	12 4	Mayburgh A.F.C.
Robertson	David		17/10/68	Aberdeen	02/07/91	5 11.0	11 0	Aberdeen
Robson	Barry		07/11/78	Aberdeen	10/07/95	5 11.0	12 0	Rangers S.A.B.C.
Shields	Greg		21/08/76	Falkirk	01/07/93	5 9.0	10 10	Rangers B.C.
Snelders	Theodorus	G.A.	07/12/63	Westervoort	29/03/96	6 2.0	14 12	Aberdeen
Steven	Trevor		21/09/63	Berwick upon Tweed	29/07/92	5 9.0	10 12	Olympique de Marseille
Stone	Michael		15/01/79	Stirling	03/07/95	6 0.0	13 3	Rangers S.A.B.C.
Van Vossen	Peter	Jacobus	21/04/68	Zierikzee	16/01/96	6 0.0	12 2	Istanbulspor Kulubu
Watt	James		09/02/79	Dunfermline	03/07/95	5 11.0	11 7	Rangers S.A.B.C.
Wilson	Scott		19/03/77	Edinburgh	01/07/93	6 1.0	11 4	Rangers B.C.
Wright	Stephen		27/08/71	Bellshill	05/07/95	5 10.5	11 2	Aberdeen
Young	David		01/03/79	Glasgow	03/07/95	5 8.0	10 0	Rangers S.A.B.C.

MILESTONES

YEAR OF FORMATION: 1873
MOST CAPPED PLAYER: Alistair McCoist
NO. OF CAPS: 55
MOST LEAGUE POINTS IN A SEASON: 76 (Division 1 - Season 1920/21) (2 points for a win)
87 (Premier Division - Season 1995/96) (3 points for a win)
MOST LEAGUE GOALS SCORED BY A PLAYER IN A SEASON: Sam English (Season 1931/32)
NO. OF GOALS SCORED: 44
RECORD ATTENDANCE: 118,567 (-v- Celtic – 2.1.1939)
RECORD VICTORY: 14-2 (-v- Blairgowrie – Scottish Cup, 20.1.1934)
RECORD DEFEAT: 2-10 (-v- Airdrieonians – 1886)

THE GERS' TEN YEAR LEAGUE RECORD

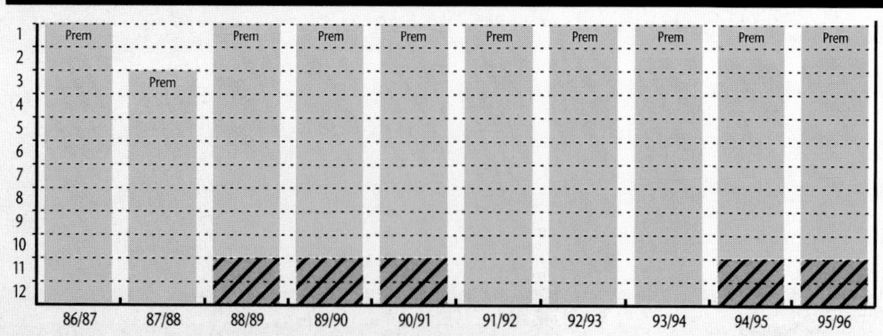

CLUB FACTFILE 1995/96
RESULTS... APPEARANCES... SCORERS

The GERS

Date	Venue	Opponents	Att.	Res	Goram A.	Wright S.	Robertson D.	Gough R.	McLaren A.	Petric G.	Steven T.	Miller C.	McCoist A.	McCall S.	Durie G.	Durrant I.	Salenko O.	Gascoigne P.	Laudrup B.	Moore C.	Murray N.	Mikhailitchenko A.	Cleland A.	Ferguson I.	Brown J.	Scott C.	Bollan G.	Thomson W.	McGinty B.	McInnes D.	Van Vossen P.	Andersen E.B.	Snelders T.	Shields G.
Aug 26	H	Kilmarnock	44,430	1-0	1	2	3	4	5	6	7	8	9	10^{1}	11	12	14																	
Sep 9	H	Raith Rovers	43,284	4-0	1	2	3^{1}	4	5	6		7^{1}	9^{2}			12	10	8	11															
16	A	Falkirk	11,480	2-0	1		3^{1}	4	5	6		10	14		8		9^{1}	12		2	7	11	15											
23	H	Hibernian	44,221	0-1	1	2		4	5	6		7	9		14		10	8	11		16		3											
30	A	Celtic	33,296	2-0	1	2		4	5	6		12	9	7			10	8^{1}					3^{1}	11										
Oct 3	H	Motherwell	39,891	2-1	1			4	5	6			9^{1}	14	7	12		8^{1}		2	16	11	3	10										
7	A	Aberdeen	20,351	1-0	1	2	3	4	5	6				10	11	8	9			14^{1}	16		7											
14	A	Partick Thistle	16,066	4-0	1	2	3	4^{1}	5	6			14	10	9^{3}	8				16		11	7		12									
21	H	Heart of Midlothian	45,155	4-1	1		3	4	5	6					10^{1}	12	9^{2}	8^{1}		2		11	7		16									
28	A	Raith Rovers	9,300	2-2	1			4^{1}	5	6^{1}		16	9		11		10	8		2	7	14	3											
Nov 4	H	Falkirk	42,059	2-0				4	5	6		12	9^{2}	10	11	7							2	8		1	3							
8	A	Kilmarnock	14,613	2-0				4	5^{1}	6			9			7	10^{1}	8				12	2	11	16	1	3							
11	H	Aberdeen	45,427	1-1				4	5	6			14	10		12	9^{1}	8				11	2	7	16		3	1						
19	H	Celtic	46,640	†3-3	1		3	4	5	6		12	14^{1}	10			9	8	11^{1}				2	7										
25	A	Hibernian	13,558	†4-1	1			4	5	6		7^{1}	9^{1}		14^{1}	12	10	8					2				3		11					
Dec 2	A	Heart of Midlothian	15,105	2-0	1		3	4	5	6		10	9^{1}	12	14			8^{1}	11				2						7					
9	H	Partick Thistle	43,137	1-0	1		3	4	5	6		7	9		10^{1}	12			11	2										8				
19	A	Motherwell	10,197	0-0	1		3	4	5	6		9			10				11			7		8						2				
26	H	Kilmarnock	45,143	3-0	1		3	4	5	6		7			10^{1}	12	9^{1}	8^{1}	11					2						14				
30	H	Hibernian	44,692	7-0	1		3	4	5	6		7^{1}			10^{4}		9^{1}	8^{1}	11					2										
Jan 3	A	Celtic	36,719	0-0	1		3	4	5	6		7			10		9	8	11				16	2										
6	A	Falkirk	10,348	4-0	1		3^{1}	4	5	6			9^{2}		10^{1}		16	8					7	2						11				
13	H	Raith Rovers	42,498	4-0	1		3	4	5	6			9^{1}		10^{2}			8	11				12	2^{1}						7				
20	H	Heart of Midlothian	45,096	0-3	1		3	4	5	6		7			10	9			11			12	8	2							14			
Feb 3	A	Partick Thistle	16,488	2-1	1		3		5	6		9		10				8^{2}	11			16	2		4						7			
10	H	Motherwell	44,871	3-2	1		3		5^{1}	6		7	14^{1}	10				8	11	4				2^{1}							9			
25	A	Aberdeen	19,842	1-0	1		3		5	4		7		10				8^{1}	11	2			14	9	6						12			
Mar 3	A	Hibernian	11,923	†2-0	1		3	4	5	6		12	16	10				8	11^{1}	2					14						7	9		
17	H	Celtic	47,312	1-1	1				5^{1}	4		7	9	10	14			8	11	2			3		6									
23	H	Falkirk	46,361	3-2					5	4		2	9	10	12			8^{1}	11			16	3		6	1						7^{2}		
30	A	Raith Rovers	9,300	4-2					5	2			9^{3}	10	4^{1}			8	11				3	12	6						14	7	1	
Apr 10	A	Heart of Midlothian	15,350	0-2	1		3	4	5	6	7		9	10	12			8	11				2	16	14									
13	H	Partick Thistle	46,438	5-0	1		3	4^{1}	5		16			10^{1}	7			8	11				2		6							9^{3}		
20	A	Motherwell	13,128	3-1	1		3	4	5		2			10^{1}	7			8^{1}	11						6							9^{1}		
28	H	Aberdeen	47,247	3-1	1		3	4	5	16	2		14	10	7	12		8^{3}	11						6							9		
May 4	A	Kilmarnock	17,102	3-0			3		5		7	16	9^{1}	4	10^{2}	6								8						11	14		1	2
TOTAL FULL APPEARANCES					30	6	25	29	36	32	5	17	18	19	21	6	14	27	22	9	2	6	21	16	8	3	4	1	2	5	3	6	2	1
TOTAL SUB APPEARANCES										(1)	(1)	(6)	(7)	(2)	(6)	(9)	(2)	(1)		(2)	(3)	(5)	(4)	(2)	(6)					(1)	(4)			
TOTAL GOALS SCORED							3	3	3	1		3	16	3	17		7	14	2	1			1	2								6		

Small bold figures denote goalscorers. † denotes opponent's own goal.

IBROX STADIUM

CAPACITY: 50,411 (All seated)

PITCH DIMENSIONS: 115 yds x 78 yds

FACILITIES FOR DISABLED SUPPORTERS: Special area within stadium and also special toilet facilities provided. The club also have a Rangers Disabled Supporters' Club. Contact: David Milne, Secretary, Disabled Supporters' Club, c/o Ibrox Stadium, Glasgow, G51 2XD.

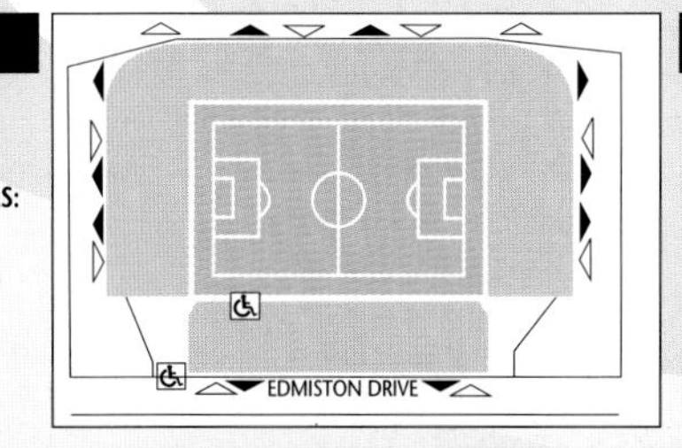

HOW TO GET THERE

You can reach Ibrox Stadium by these routes:

BUSES: The following buses all pass within 300 yards of the Stadium and can be boarded from Glasgow city centre. Nos. 4, 9A, 23, 23A, 52, 53, 53A, 54A, 54B, 65, 89 and 91.

UNDERGROUND: GGPTE Underground station is Ibrox, which is two minutes walk from the Stadium.

CARS: Motor Vehicles can head for the Stadium from the city centre by joining the M8 Motorway from Waterloo Street. Take the B768 turn-off for Govan. This will then take you to the ground. There are parking facilities available at the Albion car park.

Dunfermline Athletic – 1995/96 Bells First Division Champions

Triumph over Tragedy

Tragedy hung over Scottish football and, in particular, Dunfermline Athletic, overpowering the excitement generated by the tension laden promotion scene in the First Division.

The tragic death of the Dunfermline captain and inspirational leader Norrie McCathie in January, 1996, affected everyone connected to the club emotionally – players, officials and supporters alike. However, the memory of the East End Park skipper acted as a spur to the players over the final months of the season and it was fitting that, somehow, everyone at the club rose above the personal grief felt as the Pars dramatically won the championship on the final day of the League season to gain a coveted place in the Premier Division.

Each and every player voiced the same thought at the end of a tempestuous and grief stricken campaign by declaring that "we won the championship for Norrie". All football supporters, of course, have their favourite team, but following the Pars' Championship success, everyone across the country publicly and privately agreed that it was fitting that Dunfermline should attain their ambition of Premier Division football.

A season which had begun with a one goal win away to Airdrieonians at Broadwood eventually ended in triumphant fashion for the Pars in front of vastly increased crowds. However, they suffered several disappointments along the way and it was not until the second last Saturday of the season, when they collected three points against fellow promotion challengers, Dundee United, with a one goal win at Tannadice thanks to a goal from Stewart Petrie, that their destiny was in their own hands. Then, on the final day of the season, over 13,000 fans packed into East End Park anticipating a Championship victory and the automatic promotion spot that rewards the champion club of that division.

However, what a tension filled and dramatic afternoon's action arose on that final day at both East End Park and Cappielow, as the other two clubs involved in the promotion race, Dundee United and Greenock Morton, were involved in their own drama filled epic in front of a crowd in excess of 12,000, with hundreds locked outside.

Walkmans and mobile phones were on green alert as the action unfolded and with the match at East End Park being delayed to allow the huge crowd in, it wasn't until Marc Millar coolly slotted home a penalty in the final quarter of the game that all Pars' players and fans alike could start to celebrate, in the knowledge that Greenock Morton and Dundee United had already finished all square at two goals apiece.

Dunfermline were celebrating as champions with 71 points from their 36 games – four points ahead of joint second Dundee United and Greenock Morton. But what a climax to the season at Greenock as twice, United had gone into the lead, only for Morton to hit back on both occasions and that result left the Tannadice side second on goal difference! What a finish on that last day of the season and it was still not over for the Tannadice side!

They were seemingly now only 180 minutes away from clinching a place in the Premier Division, but that meant that they now endured a two leg Play-Off against Partick Thistle, who had finished second bottom of the top division.

The first game was played on Sunday, 12th May, at Firhill and a Christian Dailly goal four minutes from time saw United return to Tannadice still on level terms after a pulsating afternoon's entertainment had ended 1–1, with Andy Lyons having earlier been on target for the Jags, scoring with a spectacular 25 yard free kick.

Over 12,000 fans turned out at Tannadice the following Thursday and the outcome could not be settled during the regulation 90 minutes, with both sides locked at one goal each and 2–2 on aggregate. It was another dramatic filled match and after Ian Cameron had netted for the Firhill club from the penalty spot with 15 minutes remaining, it looked likely that they had secured their place among the elite for another season. However, as the match moved into injury time, United snatched a dramatic equaliser with Brian Welsh scoring to take the Play-Off into extra-time. Despite United dominating the extra-time period, it looked as though further drama would ensue via a penalty shoot-out. However, with five minutes remaining, Owen Coyle struck the matchwinner to take the Tangerine Terrors back into the Premier Division at the first time of asking. It was that tight and whilst the United players, officials and supporters celebrated a last gasp victory, everyone connected to the Firhill club left Tannadice disappointed and utterly dejected.

However, as always, there has to be a winner and a loser in such circumstances and once again, there was a fantastic finish to yet another outstanding season of thrills and spills in the Bell's First Division.

Greenock Morton, who had won the Second Division Championship the previous season, came so close to gaining promotion for the second successive season despite the loss of the midfield skills of Derek McInnes, who moved to Rangers during the early part of the season. Their Finnish pair, Janne Lindberg and Marko Rajamaki, along with the strong running striker Derek Lilley, were outstanding, as manager Allan McGraw continued his stated policy, "I want to play good football and attack."

St. Johnstone, after a disappointing spell prior to Christmas, enjoyed the fruits of their twice a day training methods and came so close to at least making the Play-Off stage before running out of games, whilst Dundee were unable to find any consistency after their Coca-Cola Cup exploits earlier in the season. St. Mirren, with a squad full of talented youngsters, struggled badly in the early part of the season, however, the young players showed tremendous character and the Paisley club eventually secured a comfortable mid table position.

However, it was a season in which two clubs without their own grounds, Airdrieonians and Hamilton Academical, struggled. The Diamonds, who had several talented players in their ranks including Kenny Black and Paul Harvey, now transferred to Raith Rovers, could not mount a serious challenge from their ground sharing base at Broadwood in Cumbernauld. Their players even took home their strips to be washed and trained daily in Strathclyde Park and it was no surprise that in the circumstances, they laboured rather than flourished on a Saturday. However, the good news from the club's point of view is that it has now received permission to build a new stadium and they will be hoping that this will act as a catalyst in the future.

Their Lanarkshire neighbours,

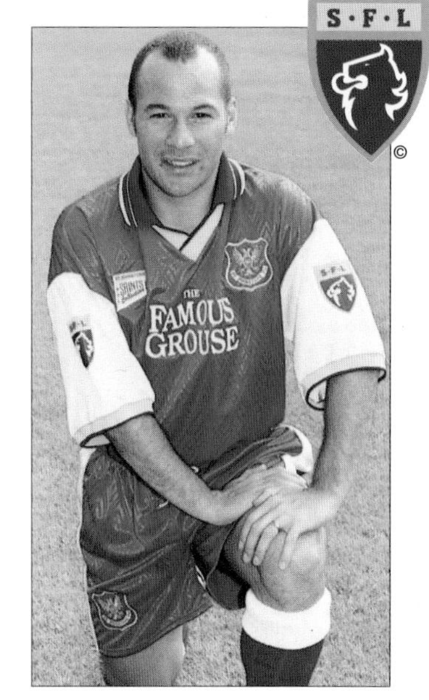

George O'Boyle (St. Johnstone)

Hamilton Academical, were also forced into ground sharing policy once again, and they played at Firhill, the home of Partick Thistle. Their struggles finally ended in misery for the Accies, who despite a dreadful start, rallied superbly, but unfortunately for them, were unable to close that gap significantly, although they made Clydebank sweat as they eroded their points difference before running out of games.

Dumbarton, after being top of the table after winning their first two matches, suffered what can only be described as an absolutely disastrous season, gaining only 11 points and indeed, lost their final 19 matches. They will be hoping for better things this time around and indeed, will be supplementing their income by taking in as lodgers , their near neighbours Clydebank, who, at the end of the season, announced that they were selling their Kilbowie Park and hoped to build a new stadium. Meantime, the Bankies will be playing their home games at Boghead this season.

With uncertainty right up until the final few minutes of the season, fans responded in tremendous numbers, with crowds on the increase once again. There is only one certainty and it is that we are in for another season of uncertainty in the Bell's First Division in the season ahead.

Dundee United's Play-Off goal heroes – Owen Coyle and Brian Welsh

BILL MARWICK
(Freelance)

AIRDRIEONIANS

Broadwood Stadium,
Cumbernauld, G68 9NE
ALL CORRESPONDENCE SHOULD BE ADDRESSED TO:
G. W. PEAT, C.A., Esq.,
32 Stirling Street, Airdrie, ML6 0AH

CHAIRMAN
George W. Peat, C.A.

VICE-CHAIRMAN
David W. Smith, C.Eng., M.I.C.E.

DIRECTORS
Joseph M. Rowan
Alexander MacDonald
A. McI. Campbell Craig

SECRETARY
George W. Peat, C.A.

MANAGER
Alexander MacDonald

ASSISTANT MANAGER
John McVeigh

COACH
John Binnie

CLUB DOCTOR
Brian Dunn, M.B.,C.L.B.,M.R.C.P.(UK)

PHYSIOTHERAPIST
Ian Constable, M.C.S.P., S.R.P.

YOUTH DEVELOPMENT OFFICER
Roy Tomnay

COMMERCIAL CONSULTANTS
The Sports Business
Tel 0141-332 9003

TELEPHONES
Ground
(01236) 451511 (Match Days Only)
Office (01236) 762067
Fax (01236) 760698
Ticket Office (01236) 747255
Information Service (01236) 762067

CLUB SHOP
93 Graham Street, Airdrie, ML6 6DE.
Tel (01236) 747255. Open Mon-Fri.
10.00 a.m. till 1.00 p.m. and 2.00 p.m. till 4.00 p.m. (Closed Wednesday)
Sat 9.00 a.m. – 3.00 p.m.

OFFICIAL SUPPORTERS CLUB
c/o David Johnstone,
16 Deveron Street, Coatbridge
Tel (01236) 423812

TEAM CAPTAIN
James Sandison

SHIRT SPONSOR
Gillespie Mining

LIST OF PLAYERS 1996-97

SURNAME	FIRST NAME	MIDDLE NAME	DATE OF BIRTH	PLACE OF BIRTH	DATE OF SIGNING	HEIGHT FT INS	WEIGHT ST LBS	PREVIOUS CLUB
Black	Kenneth	George	29/11/63	Stenhousemuir	12/09/91	5 9.0	11 10	Portsmouth
Boyle	James		19/02/67	Glasgow	11/08/89	5 6.0	11 2	Queen's Park
Connelly	Gordon		01/11/76	Glasgow	11/08/95	6 0.0	12 0	Milngavie Wanderers
Connolly	Patrick		25/06/70	Glasgow	29/03/96	5 9.5	11 0	Dundee United
Cooper	Stephen		22/06/64	Birmingham	30/09/94	5 11.0	12 2	York City
Davies	John		25/09/66	Glasgow	09/09/94	5 7.0	10 0	St. Johnstone
Eadie	Kenneth	William	26/02/61	Paisley	22/07/96	5 10.0	11 8	Clydebank
Hay	Graham	Stuart	27/11/65	Falkirk	25/01/94	6 0.0	12 7	Clydebank
Hetherston	Peter		06/11/64	Bellshill	01/03/96	5 9.0	10 7	Aberdeen
Jack	Paul	Dunn	15/05/65	Malaya	05/08/89	5 10.0	11 7	Arbroath
Johnston	Forbes	Duthie S.	03/08/71	Aberdeen	13/08/96	5 10.0	10 12	Falkirk
Lamb	John		12/08/77	Bellshill	11/04/96	5 10.5	11 4	Dundee United
Lawrence	Alan		19/08/62	Edinburgh	13/08/96	5 7.0	10 0	Heart of Midlothian
Martin	John	Galloway K.	27/10/58	Edinburgh	30/04/80	6 1.0	12 0	Tranent Juniors
McClelland	John	Stephen	26/04/77	Glasgow	11/08/95	5 9.0	10 4	Milngavie Wanderers
McIntyre	Thomas		26/12/63	Bellshill	29/07/94	6 0.0	12 5	Hibernian
McKenna	Gerard		02/02/77	Bellshill	11/08/95	5 8.0	10 9	Milngavie Wanderers
McPeak	Anthony		22/05/74	Glasgow	10/08/95	6 0.0	12 0	Knightswood Juveniles
McPhee	Brian		23/10/70	Glasgow	03/08/96	5 10.0	11 4	Queen's Park
Rhodes	Andrew	Charles	23/08/64	Doncaster	12/12/95	6 1.0	14 2	St. Johnstone
Sandison	James	William	22/06/65	Edinburgh	27/07/91	5 10.5	10 10	Heart of Midlothian
Smith	Anthony		28/10/73	Bellshill	02/06/93	5 8.0	9 7	Heart of Midlothian
Stewart	Alexander		14/10/65	Bellshill	14/10/89	5 8.0	11 0	Kilmarnock
Sweeney	Sean	Brian	17/08/69	Glasgow	10/08/95	6 0.0	11 0	Clydebank
Tait	Stephen	James	15/10/76	Glasgow	11/08/95	6 0.0	11 8	Milngavie Wanderers
Wilson	Marvyn		01/12/73	Bellshill	22/07/92	5 7.5	10 0	Heart of Midlothian

MILESTONES

YEAR OF FORMATION: 1878
MOST CAPPED PLAYER: Jimmy Crapnell
NO. OF CAPS: 9
MOST LEAGUE POINTS IN A SEASON: 60 (Division 2 - Season 1973/74) (2 Points for a Win)
61 (First Division - Season 1994/95) (3 Points for a Win)
MOST LEAGUE GOALS SCORED BY A PLAYER IN A SEASON: Bert Yarnell (Season 1916/17)
NO. OF GOALS SCORED: 39
RECORD ATTENDANCE: 24,000 (-v- Heart of Midlothian – 8.3.1952)
RECORD VICTORY: 15-1 (-v- Dundee Wanderers – Division 2, 1.12.1894)
RECORD DEFEAT: 1-11 (-v- Hibernian - Division 1, 24.10.1959)

THE DIAMONDS' TEN YEAR LEAGUE RECORD

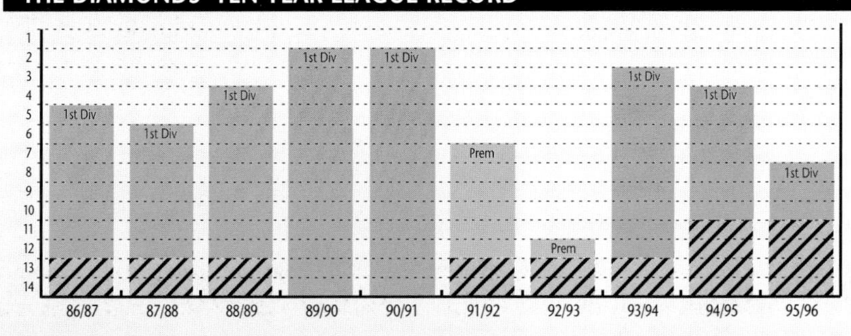

CLUB FACTFILE 1995/96
RESULTS... APPEARANCES... SCORERS

The DIAMONDS

Date	Venue	Opponents	Att.	Res	Martin J.	Boyle J.	Jack P.	Sandison J.	McIntyre T.	Black K.	Davies J.	Harvey P.	Cooper S.	Duffield P.	Stewart A.
Aug 12	H	Dunfermline Athletic	2,719	0-1	1	2	3	4	5	6	7	8	9	10	11
26	A	Dundee	3,536	1-1	1	2		4	12	6	8	14	9	10[1]	3
Sep 2	H	St. Mirren	2,142	1-2	1	7	12	4	5		6	10	9[1]		2
9	A	Dumbarton	1,320	2-1	1	7[1]	3	4	5[1]	6	8	10	9		2
16	H	Greenock Morton	1,927	†3-2	1	7	3	4		6	8	10	9	14	2
23	A	Dundee United	6,005	2-1	1	7		4	2	6	8	10	9[1]	12[1]	
30	H	Hamilton Academical	1,586	0-0	1	7	3	4		6	8	10	9	12	2
Oct 7	A	St. Johnstone	2,839	0-1	1	7	3	4	12	6	8	11		10	2
14	H	Clydebank	1,306	1-1	1	7	4		5	6	8[1]	12	9	10	3
21	A	St. Mirren	2,459	2-1	1	7		4		6	8	12[1]	9	10	2
28	H	Dundee	1,925	2-3	1	7		4		6	8	10		11[2]	2
Nov 4	A	Greenock Morton	3,856	1-2	1	7			4	6[1]	8	10		9	2
11	H	Dumbarton	1,205	2-1	1	7			4	6[1]	8[1]	10	9	12	2
18	A	Hamilton Academical	1,169	2-1	1	7		4[1]		6	8	11	9	10	2
25	H	Dundee United	2,504	1-1	1	7		4	14	6	8	11	9	10	2
Dec 2	H	St. Johnstone	1,660	1-1	1	7		4	3	6	8	11		10	2
16	A	Dunfermline Athletic	4,687	0-2		7		4	5	6	8	11		10	2
30	A	Dundee United	5,855	†2-2		7		4		6	8	11		10	2
Jan 9	A	Clydebank	865	1-1		7	15	4		6	8	11		10	2
13	A	Dumbarton	1,045	2-1		7	5	4		6	8	12	9	10[1]	2
16	H	St. Mirren	1,554	1-3		7		4		6	8	12	9	10[1]	
20	A	St. Johnstone	2,761	0-0		7		4		6	12	11	9	10	
23	H	Greenock Morton	1,605	0-2		7		4		6	12	10	9	14	
Feb 10	H	Dunfermline Athletic	2,453	1-2		7		4		6	11[1]	14	9	10	2
13	H	Clydebank	851	1-1		7[1]		4		6	11	14	9	10	2
24	A	Dundee	2,116	0-2	1	7		4		6	11		9	10	2
Mar 2	H	Dundee United	1,810	1-1	1	7		4			6	10	9[1]		2
6	H	Hamilton Academical	1,021	3-0	1	7		4		6	8	10[1]	9[1]		2
16	A	Hamilton Academical	909	1-4	1	7		4		6	8	10	9		2
23	A	Greenock Morton	2,889	0-3		7	12			6	8	11	9		2
30	H	Dumbarton	1,062	5-1		7	2		14[1]	6	8	10			
Apr 6	H	St. Johnstone	2,018	1-3		7	2		4	6	8	10			
13	A	Clydebank	831	1-2		7	15	4	14	6	8		10		2
20	A	St. Mirren	2,117	1-2		7	12	4		6	8	10			2
27	H	Dundee	1,454	0-0		7		4	5			11			2
May 4	A	Dunfermline Athletic	13,183	1-2		7		4	5	6	8	10			2
TOTAL FULL APPEARANCES					20	36	9	30	12	33	33	27	24	19	30
TOTAL SUB APPEARANCES							(5)		(5)		(2)	(7)		(5)	
TOTAL GOALS SCORED						2		1	2	2	3	2	4	6	

Date	Opponents	McIntyre J.	Sweeney S.	Smith A.	Wilson M.	Connelly G.	Rhodes A.	Bonar P.	Tait S.	Hetherston P.	Connolly P.	McClelland J.	McPeak A.
Aug 12	Dunfermline Athletic	15											
26	Dundee	7	5	11									
Sep 2	St. Mirren	11		3	8								
9	Dumbarton	11		12		15							
16	Greenock Morton	11[2]	5	12	15								
23	Dundee United	11	5	3									
30	Hamilton Academical	11	5										
Oct 7	St. Johnstone	9	5	14									
14	Clydebank	7		11									
21	St. Mirren	11[1]	5	3									
28	Dundee	9	5	3									
Nov 4	Greenock Morton	11	5	3									
11	Dumbarton	11	5	3		15							
18	Hamilton Academical	12	5	3[1]									
25	Dundee United	12[1]	5	3									
Dec 2	St. Johnstone	9[1]	5			12							
16	Dunfermline Athletic	9		3			1	14					
30	Dundee United	9[1]		3	12	14	1	5					
Jan 9	Clydebank	9[1]		3			1	5					
13	Dumbarton	11[1]		3			1						
16	St. Mirren	11		3		15	1	5	2				
20	St. Johnstone	14		3	8		1	5	2				
23	Greenock Morton	11	2	3	8		1	5	15				
Feb 10	Dunfermline Athletic	12	5	3	8		1						
13	Clydebank	12	5	3	8		1						
24	Dundee	14	5	3	8			15					
Mar 2	Dundee United	11	5					3		8			
6	Hamilton Academical	11	5	3[1]	12	15		14					
16	Hamilton Academical	11[1]	5					3		12			
23	Greenock Morton		5	4	10	15	1	3		14			
30	Dumbarton		5	3[1]	12	15	1	4		11[1]	9[2]		
Apr 6	St. Johnstone		5	3			1			11[1]	9	14	
13	Clydebank		5	3			1			11[1]	9		
20	St. Mirren		5	3			1			11	9[1]		
27	Dundee			3	8		1			10	9	6	14
May 4	Dunfermline Athletic			3	12		1		14	11[1]	9	15	
TOTAL FULL APPEARANCES		22	24	28	8		16	9	2	7	6	1	
TOTAL SUB APPEARANCES		(7)		(3)	(5)	(8)		(3)	(2)	(2)		(2)	(1)
TOTAL GOALS SCORED		9		3						4	3		

Small bold figures denote goalscorers. † denotes opponent's own goal.

BROADWOOD STADIUM

CAPACITY: 8,003 (All seated)

PITCH DIMENSIONS: 112 yds x 76 yds

FACILITIES FOR DISABLED SUPPORTERS: Facilities available in both Home, Away and New Stands.

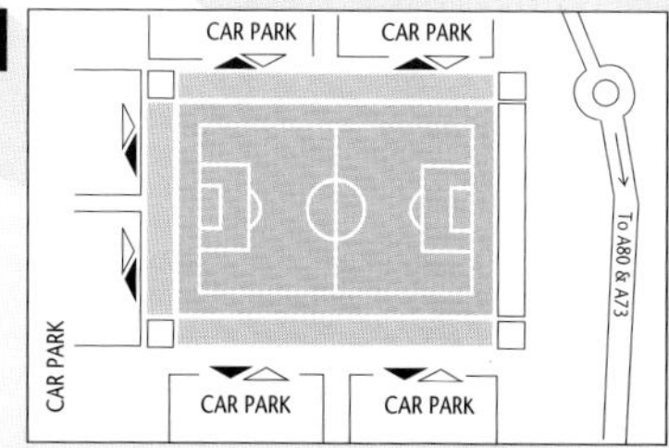

HOW TO GET THERE

Broadwood Stadium can be reached by the following routes:

BUSES: From Buchanan Street Bus Station, Glasgow. Bus No. 36A (Glasgow to Westfield).

TRAINS: From Queen Street Station, Glasgow to Croy Station. The Stadium is a 15 minute walk from here.

CARS: From Glasgow City Centre via Stepps By Pass joining A80 towards Stirling. Take Broadwood turn-off to Stadium.

CLYDEBANK

Boghead Park,
Dumbarton, G82 2JA

ALL CORRESPONDENCE SHOULD BE ADDRESSED TO:
c/o West of Scotland R.F.C.,
Burnbrae, Milngavie, G62 6HX

CHAIRMAN
C. Graham Steedman

DIRECTORS
John S. Steedman, C.B.E.
Charles A. Steedman
William Howat
Colin L. Steedman, B.Acc, C.A.
James H. Heggie

MANAGING DIRECTOR
Ian C. Steedman, C.A.

SECRETARY
Andrew Steedman

COACH
Brian Wright

ASSISTANT COACH
David Irons

CLUB DOCTORS
Stuart Hillis & Andrew Renwick

PHYSIOTHERAPIST
Peter Salila

S.F.A. COMMUNITY COACH
Tony Gervaise

CHIEF SCOUT
Robert Gallie

GROUNDSMAN
George Furze

COMMERCIAL MANAGER
David Curwood

TELEPHONES
Ground 01389-762569/767864
(Match Days Only)
Office/Commercial 0141-955 9048
Fax 0141-955 9049

OFFICIAL SUPPORTERS CLUB
c/o West of Scotland R.F.C.,
Burnbrae, Milngavie, G62 6HX

TEAM CAPTAIN
David Irons

SHIRT SPONSOR
Wet Wet Wet

LIST OF PLAYERS 1996-97

SURNAME	FIRST NAME	MIDDLE NAME	DATE OF BIRTH	PLACE OF BIRTH	DATE OF SIGNING	HEIGHT FT INS	WEIGHT ST LBS	PREVIOUS CLUB
Agnew	Paul		28/06/72	Coatbridge	14/06/94	5 7.0	10 10	Arthurlie Juniors
Barnes	Derek		20/09/77	Glasgow	14/08/96	6 0.0	11 3	Heart of Midlothian
Bowman	Gary		12/08/74	Glasgow	30/03/94	5 11.0	11 4	Knightswood Juveniles
Brannigan	Kenneth		08/06/65	Glasgow	29/03/96	6 0.0	12 4	Stenhousemuir
Connell	Graham		31/10/74	Glasgow	03/07/95	5 11.0	11 10	Ipswich Town
Currie	Thomas		06/11/70	Vale of Leven	29/08/92	6 1.0	12 7	Shettleston Juniors
Davidson	William		09/07/78	Glasgow	14/08/96	5 8.0	10 0	Rangers
Grady	James		14/03/71	Paisley	14/06/94	5 7.0	10 0	Arthurlie Juniors
Irons	David	John	18/07/61	Glasgow	16/03/96	6 0.0	11 4	St. Johnstone
Lovering	Paul	James	25/11/75	Glasgow	31/03/95	5 10.0	10 0	Neilston Juniors
Matthews	Gary		15/03/70	Paisley	21/03/94	6 3.5	16 2	Kilmarnock
McMahon	Steven		22/04/70	Glasgow	14/08/96	6 5.0	11 12	Darlington
Miller	Scott	Kerr	04/05/75	Balornock	25/10/95	5 9.0	10 5	Shettleston Juniors
Murdoch	Scott	McKenzie	27/02/69	Glasgow	22/10/92	5 7.0	10 7	St. Rochs
Nicholls	David	Clarkson	05/04/72	Bellshill	11/08/95	5 8.0	12 6	Cork City
Robertson	Joseph		12/04/77	Glasgow	15/05/95	5 8.0	11 5	Clydebank B.C.
Sutherland	Colin		15/03/75	Glasgow	24/02/95	5 11.0	11 10	Kilpatrick Juveniles
Teale	Gary		21/07/78	Glasgow	19/06/96	6 0.0	11 4	Clydebank B.C.
Wright	Brian	Vincent	05/10/58	Glasgow	19/06/96	5 11.0	11 3	Queen of the South

MILESTONES

YEAR OF FORMATION: 1965
MOST LEAGUE POINTS IN A SEASON: 58 (Division 1 – Season 1976/77)
MOST LEAGUE GOALS SCORED BY A PLAYER IN A SEASON: Ken Eadie (Season 1990/91)
NO. OF GOALS SCORED: 29
RECORD ATTENDANCE: 14,900 (-v- Hibernian – 10.2.1965)
RECORD VICTORY: 8-1 (-v- Arbroath – Division 1, 3.1.1977)
RECORD DEFEAT: 1-9 (-v- Gala Fairydean – Scottish Cup, 15.9.1965)

THE BANKIES' TEN YEAR LEAGUE RECORD

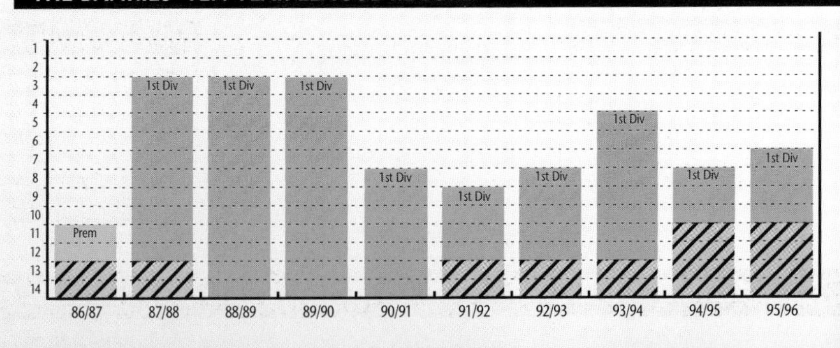

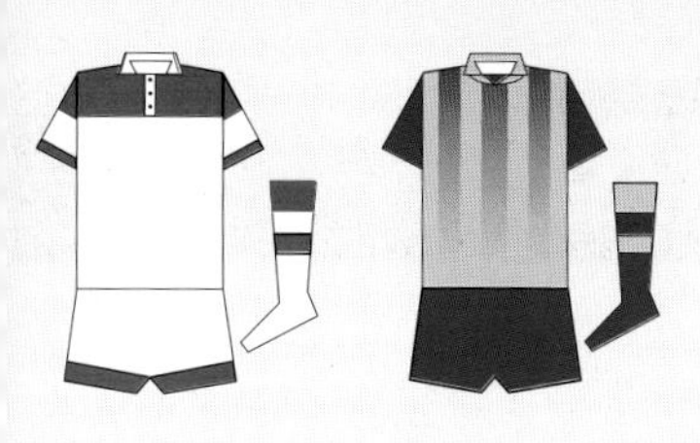

CLUB FACTFILE 1995/96
RESULTS... APPEARANCES... SCORERS

The BANKIES

Date	Venue	Opponents	Att.	Res	Matthews G.	Tomlinson C.	Sutherland C.	Murdoch S.	Currie T.	Nicholls D.	Robertson J.	Connell G.	Eadie K.	Grady J.	Bowman G.	Miller S.	Kerrigan S.	Teale G.	Lovering P.	Flannigan C.	Agnew P.	Lansdowne A.	Dunn R.	Connelly D.	Jack S.	Melvin W.	Crawford D.	McLaughlin I.	Keane G.	Irons D.	Brannigan K.	Hardie D.
Aug 12	H	St. Mirren	1,886	1-1	1	2	3	4	5	6	7	8	9^1	10	11	14																
26	A	Hamilton Academical	845	2-0	1	2	3	4	5	6	7^1	8	9^1	10	11		12	14	15													
Sep 2	H	Dundee	1,467	1-1	1	2	3	4	5	6	7	8^1	9	10	11																	
9	A	Dunfermline Athletic	4,410	1-2	1	2	3	4	5	6	7^1	8	9	10	11				14	12												
16	H	Dundee United	1,949	1-2	1	2	3	4	5	6	7	8	9	10^1	11				15	12	14											
23	A	St. Johnstone	2,482	2-2	1	2	3		5	6^1	7	8	12^1	9	11			14	15	10	4											
30	H	Dumbarton	913	2-1	1	2	3^1		5	6	7	8	9	10^1	11			14	12		4	15										
Oct 7	H	Greenock Morton	2,343	1-0	1	2	3	4	5	6	7	8	9^1	10	11					15		14										
14	A	Airdrieonians	1,306	1-1	1	2	3	4	5	6		8	9	10^1	11			7	12	14	15											
21	A	Dundee	2,708	1-1	1	2		4	5	6	7	8	9	10	11^1				3	12												
28	H	Hamilton Academical	814	2-0	1	2		4	5	6	7^1	8	9^1	10	11				3	12		15										
31	A	Dundee United	5,428	0-3	1	2			5	6	12	8	9	10	11				3	7			4	14								
Nov 11	H	Dunfermline Athletic	1,304	0-4	1	2	3	4	5	6	7	8	9	10	11					14				15								
18	A	Dumbarton	1,043	2-1	1		3	4	5	6	7	8	9^1	10^1	11				14	12				2								
25	H	St. Johnstone	923	2-0	1		3^1	4	5	6	7	8	9^1	10	11			14	2													
Dec 2	A	Greenock Morton	3,002	0-3	1		3	4	5	6	7	8	9	10	11			15	2					12	14							
16	A	St. Mirren	1,828	1-2	1			4	5	6	7^1	8		10	11	14				9				2	3	15						
Jan 6	H	Dundee United	1,383	1-1	1	2		4	5	6	9	8		10	11				3^1						7		15					
9	H	Airdrieonians	865	1-1	1		14	4	5	6	9^1	8		10	11	7			3						2							
13	A	Dunfermline Athletic	6,642	3-4	1		3	4	5	6	7	8^1	9	10^2	11			15	2						14							
16	H	Dundee	644	0-1	1		3	4	5	6	7	8	12	9	11			10	2	14					15							
20	H	Greenock Morton	1,685	0-1	1		3	4	5	6	12			10	11			7		9		8		15	2							
23	A	St. Johnstone	2,167	1-3	1		3	4	5	6		8	9	10^1				12	15	7		14		11	2							
Feb 10	H	St. Mirren	1,515	1-2	1			4		5	7	8		10	11^1	9			3	12			6		2							
13	A	Airdrieonians	851	1-1	1			4		6^1	14	8	9	10	11	15			3			5			2			7	12			
17	H	Dumbarton	612	1-0	1		3	4		6	7	8	9^1	10	11					14		2	15		5							
24	A	Hamilton Academical	835	1-1	1		3	4		6^1	7	8	9	10	11					12		2	15		5							
Mar 2	H	St. Johnstone	705	1-2	1		3		5	6	7	8	9^1	10						12		4	11		2							
16	A	Dumbarton	654	1-0	1				5	6	7	8	9	10	11					14^1		2			3					4		
23	A	Dundee United	5,973	0-6	1				5	6	11	8	9	7		15				12	10	2			3					4		
30	H	Dunfermline Athletic	1,298	2-3	1				6	3		8	9	10^2	11			7		12	15				2					4	5	
Apr 6	A	Greenock Morton	3,001	0-0	1		3			6		8	9	10	11			7		14		2								4	5	
13	H	Airdrieonians	831	2-1	1		3	12		6	15	8		10	11			7		9^1		2			14					4^1	5	
20	A	Dundee	1,403	0-3	1		3	2		6	12	8		10	11			7	15	9					5					4		
27	H	Hamilton Academical	3,665	1-3	1		3	6			14	8	9^1	12	11			7		10		2								4	5	
May 4	A	St. Mirren	1,657	2-1	1		3	4	12	6				10^1	11	9		7^1	14		2									8	5	15
TOTAL FULL APPEARANCES					36	14	25	27	27	35	25	34	26	35	33	3		9	11	8	4	10	3	3	14			1		8	5	
TOTAL SUB APPEARANCES							(1)	(1)	(1)		(6)		(2)	(1)		(4)	(1)	(7)	(10)	(17)	(3)	(4)	(2)	(4)	(4)	(1)	(1)		(1)			(1)
TOTAL GOALS SCORED							2			3	5	2	10	10	2			1	1	2										1		

Small bold figures denote goalscorers. † denotes opponent's own goal.

BOGHEAD PARK

CAPACITY: 5,007; Seated 303, Standing 4,704

PITCH DIMENSIONS: 110 yds x 72 yds

FACILITIES FOR DISABLED SUPPORTERS: Wheelchairs are accommodated on the track.

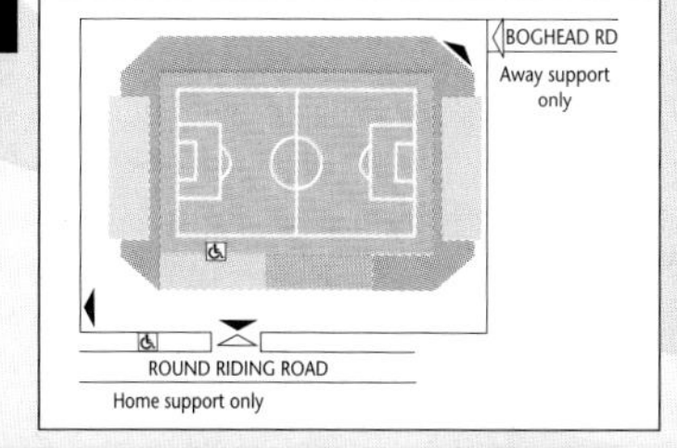

HOW TO GET THERE

Boghead Park can be reached by the following routes:

TRAINS: The train service from Glasgow Queen Street and Glasgow Central Low Level both pass through Dumbarton East Station (away fans best choice) and Dumbarton Central Station, both of which are situated just under a ten minute walk from the ground.

BUSES: There are two main services which pass close to the ground. These are bound for Helensburgh and Balloch from Glasgow.

CARS: Car parking is available in certain side streets around the ground. Supporters buses should follow Police signposts to designated parking area.

DUNDEE

Dens Park Stadium,
Sandeman Street,
Dundee, DD3 7JY

CHAIRMAN
Ronald N. Dixon

VICE-CHAIRMAN
Malcolm Reid

MANAGING DIRECTOR
Nigel R. Squire

DIRECTORS
Robert W. Hynd
John F. Black
Henry J. Leadingham

SECRETARIES
Blackadder, Reid, Johnston
(30-34 Reform Street, Dundee)

PLAYER/MANAGER
James Duffy

ASSISTANT MANAGER
John McCormack

CLUB DOCTOR
Dr. Phyllis Windsor

PHYSIOTHERAPIST
James Crosby, B.Sc., MCSP, SRP

GROUNDSMAN
Brian Robertson

COMMERCIAL MANAGER
Stuart Rafferty
01382 889966

TELEPHONES
Football (01382) 826104
Administration (01382) 889966
Fax (01382) 832284

CLUB SHOP
Dundee F.C. Shop,
David Low Sports,
21 Commercial Street, Dundee.
Tel (01382) 224501

TEAM CAPTAIN
Thomas McQueen

SHIRT SPONSOR
The Firkin Brewery

LIST OF PLAYERS 1996-97

SURNAME	FIRST NAME	MIDDLE NAME	DATE OF BIRTH	PLACE OF BIRTH	DATE OF SIGNING	HEIGHT FT INS	WEIGHT ST LBS	PREVIOUS CLUB
Adamczuk	Dariusz		20/10/69	Stettin	18/01/96	5 10.0	12 0	Pogon Stettin
Anderson	Iain		23/07/77	Glasgow	10/08/94	5 8.0	9 7	"X" Form
Bain	Kevin		19/09/72	Kirkcaldy	28/06/89	6 0.0	11 9	Abbey Star
Cargill	Andrew		02/09/75	Dundee	23/09/94	5 6.5	10 8	Dundee United
Charnley	James	Callaghan	11/06/63	Glasgow	06/01/96	5 10.0	11 12	Dumbarton
Duffy	James		27/04/59	Glasgow	03/07/96	5 10.0	11 11	Partick Thistle
Farningham	Raymond	Paul	10/04/61	Dundee	06/06/94	5 8.0	11 5	Partick Thistle
Ferguson	Iain	John H.	04/08/62	Newharthill	23/08/96	5 9.0	10 7	Portadown
Fisher	David	John	23/08/73	Dundee	30/10/95	5 7.0	10 4	Lochee United
Grieg	Martin		28/08/78	Aberdeen	11/09/96	5 11.0	11 0	Dyce Juniors
Hamilton	James		09/02/76	Aberdeen	31/01/94	6 0.0	10 10	Keith
Harris	Brian		15/07/79	Dundee	11/09/96	5 6.0	9 7	Maryfield United
Magee	Kevin		10/04/71	Bangour	08/08/96	5 10.0	11 1	Scarborough
McBain	Roy	Adam	07/11/74	Aberdeen	11/09/95	5 11.0	11 5	Dundee United
McGlynn	Gary	D.	24/11/77	Falkirk	04/06/96	5 11.0	12 5	Bellshill B.C.
McKeown	Gary		19/10/70	Oxford	31/07/92	5 10.5	11 8	Arsenal
McQueen	Thomas	Feeney	01/04/63	Glasgow	10/08/95	5 9.0	11 7	Falkirk
Miller	Gary		04/05/78	Lanark	18/06/96	5 10.0	10 11	Lesmahagow B.C.
O'Driscoll	Jerry		04/04/78	Aberdeen	01/09/95	6 0.0	11 9	Crombie Juniors
Rae	Gavin		28/11/77	Aberdeen	01/09/95	5 11.0	10 4	Hermes Juniors
Raeside	Robert		07/07/72	South Africa	10/07/96	6 0.0	11 10	Raith Rovers
Shaw	George		10/02/69	Glasgow	11/01/94	5 7.0	10 9	Partick Thistle
Slater	Mark	Andrew	02/04/79	Buckie	11/09/96	5 11.0	11 5	Buckie Thistle
Smith	Barry	Martin	19/02/74	Paisley	08/12/95	5 10.0	12 0	Celtic
Thomson	William	Marshall	10/02/58	Linwood	08/08/96	6 2.0	12 3	Rangers
Tosh	Paul	James	18/10/73	Arbroath	04/08/93	6 0.0	11 10	Arbroath
Tully	Craig		07/01/76	Stirling	18/04/94	5 11.0	11 0	Victoria Juveniles
Wilkie	Lee		20/04/80	Dundee	04/06/96	6 4.0	13 0	Dundee West B.C.
Winnie	David		26/10/66	Glasgow	27/08/96	6 1.5	12 7	Heart of Midlothian

MILESTONES

YEAR OF FORMATION: 1893
MOST CAPPED PLAYER: Alex Hamilton
NO. OF CAPS: 24
MOST LEAGUE POINTS IN A SEASON: 58 (First Division – Season 1991/92) (2 points for a Win)
68 (First Division – Season 1994/95) (3 points for a Win)
MOST LEAGUE GOALS SCORED BY A PLAYER IN A SEASON: Alan Gilzean (Season 1963/64)
NO. OF GOALS SCORED: 52
RECORD ATTENDANCE: 43,024 (-v- Rangers – 1953)
RECORD VICTORY: 10-0 (-v- Fraserburgh, 1931; -v- Alloa, 1947; -v- Dunfermline Athletic, 1947; -v- Queen of the South, 1962)
RECORD DEFEAT: 0-11 (-v- Celtic – Division 1, 26.10.1895)

THE DARK BLUES' TEN YEAR LEAGUE RECORD

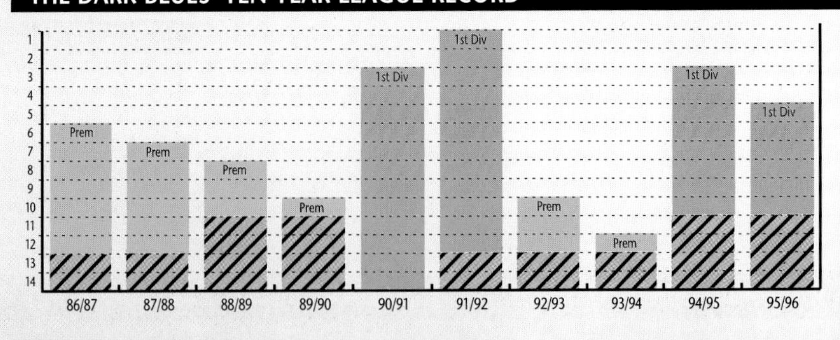

CLUB FACTFILE 1995/96
RESULTS... APPEARANCES... SCORERS

The DARK BLUES

Date	Venue	Opponents	Att.	Res	Pageaud M.	Bain K.	Cargill A.	Manley R.	Wieghorst M.	Duffy C.	Tosh P.	Vrto D.	Britton G.	Hamilton J.	McCann N.	Shaw G.	Anderson I.	McQueen T.	Farningham R.	Mathers P.	McBain R.	Teasdale M.	Duffy J.	McKeown G.	Smith B.	Charnley J.	Adamczuk D.	Magee D.	O'Driscoll J.	Rae G.	Tully C.	Hutchison M.
Aug 12	A	St. Johnstone	5,236	†2-0	1	2	3	4	5	6	7	8	9^1	10	11	12	14															
26	H	Airdrieonians	3,536	1-1	1	2	6^1	4	5		7	8	9	10	11	12		3														
Sep 2	A	Clydebank	1,467	1-1	1	2	5	4		6	9	8		10^1	11	7	14	3	12													
9	A	Greenock Morton	3,384	2-2	1	2	4		5	6	9^1	8		10	11	7	14	3	12^1	15												
16	H	Hamilton Academical	2,395	1-1	1		5	4		6	9	8		10	11	7^1	12	3	2		14											
23	A	Dumbarton	1,207	†5-1	1	8^1	14		5	6	9			12^1	11	7^2	10	3				2	4									
30	H	Dundee United	10,395	2-3	1		5	4	8	6	9		12	10^2	11	7		3	2													
Oct 7	H	St. Mirren	3,555	3-1	1	8			5^1	6	9^1		12	10^1	11	7	15	3	2				4									
14	A	Dunfermline Athletic	6,700	1-0	1			4	8	6	9^1		12	10	11	7		3	2				5									
21	H	Clydebank	2,708	1-1	1			4	8	6^1	9	12	7	10	11	14		3	2				5									
28	A	Airdrieonians	1,925	3-2	1			4	5^2			8	10	14^1	11	7	9	3	2				6									
Nov 4	A	Hamilton Academical	1,131	2-1	1				5	6^1	9^1	8	10		11	7		3	2				4									
11	H	Greenock Morton	4,060	0-0	1			4	5	6	9	8	10	12	11	7		3					2									
18	A	Dundee United	10,752	3-2	1			4	5^1	6	9	8	12	10	11	7^2		3					2									
Dec 2	A	St. Mirren	2,278	2-1	1				5	6	9^1	8	12	10		7^1	11	3	2		15		4	14								
5	H	Dumbarton	2,804	1-1	1		8	4	5	6	9^1		10			7	11	3	2		15											
9	H	Dunfermline Athletic	4,642	2-4	1	14	5	4		6	9		11	10^1		7^1	12	3	8					15	2							
16	H	St. Johnstone	3,034	0-1	1	5	12			6		8	10			7	11	3			9		4		2							
Jan 6	H	Hamilton Academical	2,020	2-1	1		15			4		8	11	10		7	9		3^1				5		2	6^1						
9	H	Dundee United	9,199	0-2	1	14	12			4	9	8		10		7					3		5	11	2	6						
13	A	Greenock Morton	3,163	0-1	1		12				9	8	14	10		7		3	6		11		5	4	2							
16	A	Clydebank	644	1-0	1		12				9	8	11^1	10		7		3	14				5	4	2	6						
20	H	St. Mirren	2,698	1-2	1					4	9	8	11	10		7		3	12					5	2	6^1	14					
23	A	Dumbarton	761	2-1	1		11			4	9	8		10^2		7		3	6					5	2		12	14				
Feb 13	A	St. Johnstone	3,960	2-3				3		4	9	8	11	10		7			12^1	1				14^1	2	6	5					
24	H	Airdrieonians	2,116	2-0	1	15				6	9	8	12	10^1	11^1	7							3	4	2	5						
Mar 2	H	Dumbarton	1,712	3-0	1		15			6	9^1	8	12	10^2	11	7							3	4	2	5	14					
6	A	Dunfermline Athletic	5,580	1-1	1					6^1	9	8		10		7							3	4	2	5	11					
16	A	Dundee United	9,831	0-2	1					4	9		12	10		7	11						5	8	2	6	3					
23	A	Hamilton Academical	828	1-0	1		4	5		6	9^1		8	10		7	11								2		3		12	14		
30	H	Greenock Morton	2,734	1-1	1			4			9^1		12	10	11	7	14						5	8	2		6			3		
Apr 6	A	St. Mirren	2,175	1-2	1			6		4		12	9	10^1	11	7								5	2		8		14	3		
13	H	Dunfermline Athletic	3,218	1-1	1			4		6	12	8		10	11	7								5	2		9		14^1	3		
20	H	Clydebank	1,403	3-0	1					4		8		10^1	11^1	7	9							6	2	5^1	12		14	3		
27	A	Airdrieonians	1,454	0-0	1					4	9	8		10	11	7								12	2	5	6				3	14
May 4	H	St. Johnstone	2,710	0-0	1		4			6		8		10	11	7	12								2	5	15		9	14	3	
TOTAL FULL APPEARANCES					35	7	11	17	14	31	29	25	15	30	22	33	9	21	13	1	3	1	19	13	20	12	8		1	4	2	
TOTAL SUB APPEARANCES						(3)	(7)				(1)	(2)	(10)	(3)		(3)	(8)		(5)	(1)	(3)			(4)			(5)	(1)	(4)	(2)		(1)
TOTAL GOALS SCORED						1	1		4	3	9		2	14	2	7			3					1		3			1			

Small bold figures denote goalscorers. † denotes opponent's own goal.

DENS PARK STADIUM

CAPACITY: 14,481; Seated 11,181, Standing 3,300

PITCH DIMENSIONS: 110 yds x 72 yds

FACILITIES FOR DISABLED SUPPORTERS: East End of Stand Enclosure.

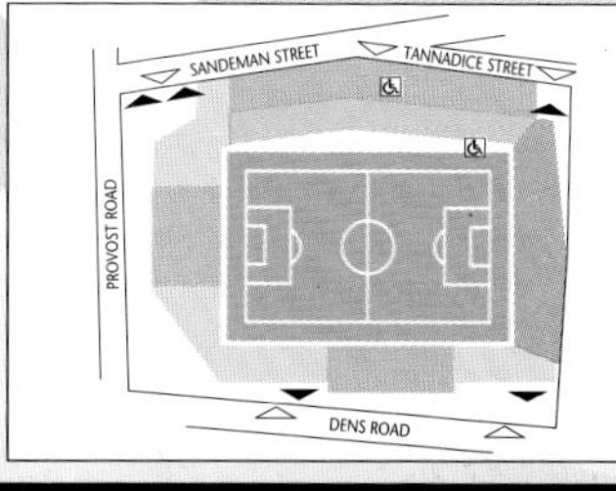

HOW TO GET THERE

You can reach Dens Park by the following routes:

BUSES: There is a frequent service of buses from the city centre. Nos. 1A and 1B leave from Albert Square and Nos. 18, 19 and 21 leave from Commercial Street.

TRAINS: Trains from all over the country pass through the mainline Dundee station and fans can then proceed to the ground by the above buses from stops situated close to the station.

CARS: Cars may be parked in the car park and local streets adjacent to the ground.

EAST FIFE

Bayview Park, Wellesley Road,
Methil, Fife, KY8 3AG

MANAGING DIRECTOR
Julian S. Danskin

DIRECTORS
James W. Baxter
Stephen Baxter
John Fleming
James Taylor

ADMINISTRATION
J. Derrick Brown
(01333) 423441

SECRETARIAL ASSISTANT
Mrs. Leona R. G. Walker

PLAYER/MANAGER

PLAYER/ASSISTANT MANAGER
Alan Sneddon

PLAYER/COACH
Gordon Rae

CLUB DOCTOR
Dr. William McCrossan

PHYSIOTHERAPIST
Alex MacQueen, L.V.M.C.

YOUTH DEVELOPMENT MANAGER
Donald Mackay

ASSISTANT YOUTH DEVELOPMENT OFFICERS
Tom Auld
Ken Halley
Dominic Schiavone

GROUNDSMAN
James Hay

KIT MAN
Alexander Doig

COMMERCIAL MANAGER
Jake Young

STADIUM MANAGER
David Gorman

TELEPHONES
Ground/Commercial
(01333) 426323
Fax (01333) 426376

CLUB SHOP
A Supporters' Club Shop
is situated within the Ground

OFFICIAL SUPPORTERS CLUB
Levenmouth: Mr. Michael McCoull,
60 Rothes Road, Glenrothes, Fife.
(01592) 757249
East Neuk O'Fife: Mr. Ian Anderson,
1 East Shore, Pittenweem, Fife.
(01334) 310080

TEAM CAPTAIN
John McStay

SHIRT SPONSOR
Jones & McComb (Hyundai Dealers)

LIST OF PLAYERS 1996-97

SURNAME	FIRST NAME	MIDDLE NAME	DATE OF BIRTH	PLACE OF BIRTH	DATE OF SIGNING	HEIGHT FT INS	WEIGHT ST LBS	PREVIOUS CLUB
Allan	Gilbert	Chapman	21/02/73	St. Andrews	16/11/93	6 0.0	9 7	Anstruther Colts
Andrew	Benjamin		05/02/73	Perth	20/08/90	5 8.0	9 6	Lochore Welfare
Archibald	Steven		27/09/56	Glasgow	22/08/94	5 10.5	11 7	Clyde
Beaton	David	Robert	08/08/67	Bridge of Allan	24/11/90	5 11.0	11 4	Falkirk
Bell	Graham		29/03/71	St. Andrews	12/08/87	5 10.0	11 0	St. Andrews
Burns	William		10/12/69	Motherwell	07/08/91	5 10.0	11 7	Rochdale
Cusick	John	James	16/01/75	Kirkcaldy	18/03/94	5 8.0	10 0	Dundonald Bluebell
Demmin	Craig		21/05/71	Trinidad & Tobago	19/12/95	6 3.0	13 4	Trinity Pros
Dixon	Alan		14/01/73	Musselburgh	07/11/95	5 9.0	10 13	Gala Fairydean
Donaghy	Mark		29/08/72	Glasgow	22/10/94	5 8.0	9 13	Shettleston Juniors
Dunnett	Mark		31/12/77	Dunfermline	01/11/95	5 8.0	10 3	Inverkeithing United
Dwarika	Arnold		23/08/73	Trinidad & Tobago	31/03/95	5 8.0	10 4	Superstar Rangers
Gartshore	Philip		02/04/76	Kirkcaldy	29/10/94	5 10.0	9 7	Methilhill Strollers
Gibb	Richard		22/04/65	Bangour	17/09/93	5 7.0	11 0	Armadale Thistle
Hamill	Alexander		30/10/61	Coatbridge	13/01/95	5 8.0	11 4	Cowdenbeath
Hamilton	Lindsay		11/08/62	Bellshill	04/08/95	6 2.0	13 4	Portadown
Henderson	David		03/07/66	Edinburgh	22/12/95	5 10.0	11 0	Hutchison Vale U'21s
Hildersley	Ronald		06/04/65	Kirkcaldy	17/09/93	5 5.0	10 7	Halifax Town
Hope	Douglas		14/06/71	Edinburgh	15/08/88	5 8.0	11 0	Hutchison Vale B.C.
Hutcheon	Stephen		20/05/70	St. Andrews	07/10/94	6 0.0	12 7	Cupar Hearts A.F.C.
Kinnell	Andrew		24/07/78	Dunfermline	28/08/96	5 10.0	12 0	Inverkeithing United U'18
Lewis	Gavin		01/06/76	Nottingham	05/07/96	5 6.0	10 7	Barnsley
Long	Derek		20/08/74	Broxburn	31/03/93	5 10.0	12 0	Newburgh Juniors
Mair	Ian		01/08/76	Kirkcaldy	16/10/95	5 6.0	10 4	Thornton Hibs
McLeod	Darren		28/06/78	Kirkcaldy	24/02/95	5 6.0	9 10	Northern Colts U'16
McStay	John		24/12/65	Larkhall	11/07/95	5 9.5	10 12	Clydebank
Rae	Gordon		03/05/58	Edinburgh	20/02/95	6 0.0	15 0	Gala Fairydean
Robertson	Dean		06/07/74	Johannesburg	20/05/95	5 11.0	12 0	Norton House
Scott	Robert		13/01/64	Bathgate	19/07/90	5 9.0	11 2	Colchester United
Sneddon	Alan		12/03/58	Baillieston	27/07/93	5 11.0	12 3	Motherwell
Winiarski	Stefan	Antoni	08/09/77	Dunfermline	10/03/96	5 8.0	10 7	Inverkeithing United

MILESTONES

YEAR OF FORMATION: 1903
MOST CAPPED PLAYER: George Aitken
NO. OF CAPS: 5
MOST LEAGUE POINTS IN A SEASON: 57 (Division 2 – Season 1929/30)(2 Points for a Win)
67 (Second Division – Season 1995/96)(3 Points for a Win)
MOST LEAGUE GOALS SCORED BY A PLAYER IN A SEASON: Henry Morris (Season 1947/48)
NO. OF GOALS SCORED: 41
RECORD ATTENDANCE: 22,515 (-v- Raith Rovers – 2.1.1950)
RECORD VICTORY: 13-2 (-v- Edinburgh City – Division 2, 11.12.1937)
RECORD DEFEAT: 0-9 (-v- Heart of Midlothian – Division 1, 5.10.1957)

THE FIFERS' TEN YEAR LEAGUE RECORD

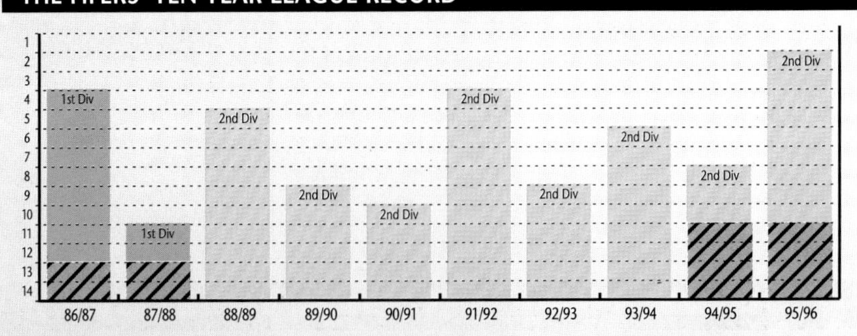

CLUB FACTFILE 1995/96
RESULTS... APPEARANCES... SCORERS

The FIFERS

Date	Venue	Opponents	Att.	Res	Hamilton L.	McStay J.	Hamill A.	Cusick J.	Beaton D.	Balmain K.	Hildersley R.	Andrew B.	Scott R.	Allan G.	Hope D.	Hutcheson S.	Gartshore P.	Donaghy M.	Archibald S.	Hunter P.	Struthers D.	Gibb R.	Dwarika A.	Robertson D.	Dixon A.	Sneddon A.	Demmin C.	Chalmers P.	Broddle J.	Ferguson P.	Winiarkski S.
Aug 12	A	Forfar Athletic	711	2-0	1	2	3	4	5^{1}	6	7	8	9	10	11	15^{1}															
26	H	Ayr United	684	1-0	1	2		5			7	10	9^{1}	4	11	15	3	6	8	12	14										
Sep 2	A	Stirling Albion	942	2-0	1	2		4^{1}	5^{1}		7	12	9	10	11	15	3	6	8		14										
9	H	Montrose	702	3-0	1	2		4^{1}	5		7	12	9^{2}	10	11	15	3	6	8	14											
16	A	Stranraer	634	0-2	1	2		4	5		7		9	10	11		3	6	8	15											
23	H	Queen of the South	700	2-1	1	2		4	5				9	10^{1}	11	15	7	6^{1}	8			3	14								
30	A	Stenhousemuir	789	1-0	1	2		4	5			7	9	10	11	15	3	6	8				12^{1}								
Oct 7	A	Berwick Rangers	655	1-0	1	2		4	5			7	9	10	11	15		6	8^{1}			3	14								
14	H	Clyde	1,128	0-0	1	2		4	5			7	9	10	11	15		6	8			3	14								
21	H	Forfar Athletic	794	1-1		2		4	5				9^{1}	10	11	15		6	8			3	7	1							
28	A	Ayr United	1,278	1-0	1	2		4	5			7	9^{1}	10	11	15		6	8			3									
Nov 4	H	Stranraer	850	3-3	1	2		4	5^{1}			7	9	10	11	15^{1}		6	8^{1}			3	12								
11	A	Montrose	802	2-1	1	2		4	5			7		10	11	9^{2}	12	6	8			3	15								
18	H	Stenhousemuir	815	0-2	1	2		4	5			7		10	11	9		6	8			3	14		15						
25	A	Queen of the South	1,081	2-0	1	2	11	4	5				9^{1}	10		7		6	8			3	12^{1}			14					
Dec 2	H	Berwick Rangers	903	1-0	1	2	4		5			7	9	10		11		6^{1}	8			3	14			12					
16	A	Clyde	982	1-0	1	2	7		5				9	10^{1}	12	8		6	15			3	11		4	14					
Jan 9	A	Forfar Athletic	621	2-0	1	2	11	7	5				9	10			12^{1}	6	8^{1}			3			4						
17	H	Stirling Albion	1,529	0-3	1	2	7	4	5				9	10	11	15		6	8			3									
20	A	Berwick Rangers	382	2-1	1	2	11	4	5^{1}			15	9	10^{1}		14		6				3	8		12		7				
23	A	Stenhousemuir	594	2-2	1	2	11	4	5				9	10	15			6				3^{1}	8^{1}		14		7				
31	H	Queen of the South	732	1-2	1	2	11	7	5				9	10	14	12	15	6				3	8^{1}		4						
Feb 3	H	Clyde	774	1-1	1	2		7	5				9	10		14		6	8^{1}			3	11		4						
10	A	Stranraer	531	0-0	1	2		4				15	9	10	14	11		7	8			3			6		5				
21	H	Montrose	425	7-0	1	2	12	5					9^{3}	10^{1}	7	14	15^{1}	6^{1}	8			3			4			11^{1}			
24	H	Ayr United	834	1-1	1		12	2	5				9	10	7			6	8^{1}			3			4			11			
Mar 2	A	Stirling Albion	1,166	2-2	1	2^{1}		7	5				9	10	15	14		6	8^{1}			3			4			11			
9	A	Queen of the South	1,476	0-1	1		6	2	5			15	9	10	11	7			8			3			4						
16	H	Stenhousemuir	621	3-1	1	2	11	6	5				9^{1}	10					8				7^{2}		4				3		
23	H	Stranraer	738	2-1	1	6	11	4	5			15	9	10	14				8				7^{2}		2				3		
30	A	Montrose	696	1-0	1	4		3	5				9^{1}	10				6					11		2				8	7	
Apr 6	H	Berwick Rangers	1,603	0-0	1	2		3	5				9	10				6	8				7		4			14	11	12	
13	A	Clyde	1,145	2-2	1	2		3	5				9	10				6	15				7		4			14^{2}	11	8	
20	H	Forfar Athletic	1,462	1-0	1	2		3	5				12	10				6	8				15		4			9^{1}	11	7	
27	A	Ayr United	1,304	0-1	1	11	14	4	15				9	5	12			6	8			3			2			10		7	
May 4	H	Stirling Albion	1,185	0-1	1	4			5				12	3		14		6	8			11	10		2			9		7	15
TOTAL FULL APPEARANCES					35	34	12	33	32	1	5	10	32	36	18	7	6	32	29			24	12	1	17		3	6	6	5	
TOTAL SUB APPEARANCES							(3)		(1)			(6)	(2)		(7)	(18)	(4)		(2)	(3)	(2)		(10)		(3)	(3)		(2)		(1)	(1)
TOTAL GOALS SCORED						1		2	4				11	4		4	2	3	6			1	8					4			

Small bold figures denote goalscorers. † denotes opponent's own goal.

BAYVIEW PARK

CAPACITY: 5,433; Seated 648, Standing 4,785

PITCH DIMENSIONS: 110 yds x 71 yds

FACILITIES FOR DISABLED SUPPORTERS: Area available at East End of Stand.

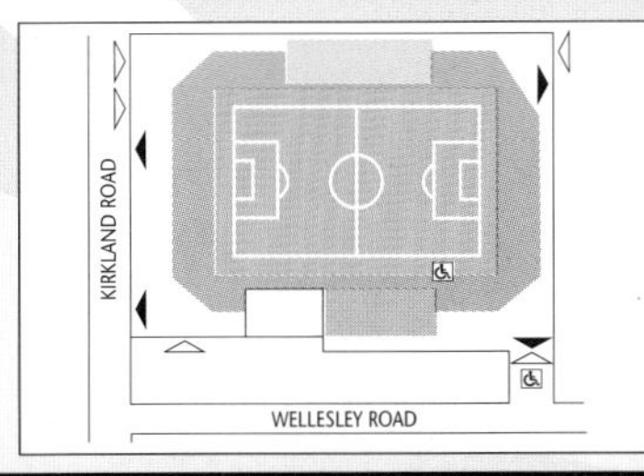

HOW TO GET THERE

Bayview Park can be reached by the following routes:

TRAINS: The nearest railway station is Kirkcaldy (8 miles away), and fans will have to catch an inter-linking service from here to the ground.

BUSES: A regular service from Kirkcaldy to Leven passes outside the ground, as does the Leven to Dunfermline service.

CARS: There is a car park behind the ground, with entry through Kirkland Road.

FALKIRK

Brockville Park, Hope Street,
Falkirk, FK1 5AX

CHAIRMAN
George J. Fulston

DIRECTORS
Alexander D. Moffat
David L. Bayne
James S. Turnbull, M.A., LL.B., NP
Brian J. Paterson
A. Neil Binnie

SECRETARY
Alexander D. Moffat

GENERAL MANAGER
Jim Hendry

PLAYER/MANAGER
Eamonn J. Bannon

ASSISTANT MANAGER/ COACH
Walter Kidd

CLUB DOCTOR
Dr. Alan Mitchell, M.B., Ch.B., M.R.C.G.P., D.R.C.O.G., D.F.F.P.

PHYSIOTHERAPIST
Bob McCallum

COMMUNITY DEVELOPMENT OFFICER
Tommy O'Neill

COMMERCIAL/YOUTH DEVELOPMENT OFFICER
Sarah Scott

GROUNDSMAN
James Dawson

TELEPHONES
Ground/Commercial/
Ticket Office/Information
Service (01324) 624121
Fax (01324) 612418

CLUB SHOP
47 Glebe Street, Falkirk, FK1 1HX
Open Mon. – Sat. 9.30 a.m. –
12 Noon and 1.00 p.m. – 5.00 p.m.
(Closed Wed)

OFFICIAL SUPPORTERS CLUB
Association of Falkirk F.C. Supporters
Clubs–Chairman : Alex Hastings
Tel (01324) 627793

TEAM CAPTAIN
Albert Craig

SHIRT SPONSOR
Square Deal Motors

LIST OF PLAYERS 1996-97

SURNAME	FIRST NAME	MIDDLE NAME	DATE OF BIRTH	PLACE OF BIRTH	DATE OF SIGNING	HEIGHT FT INS	WEIGHT ST LBS	PREVIOUS CLUB
Abbott	Gordon	Thomas K.	24/02/79	Edinburgh	16/07/96	5 10.0	11 9	Falkirk U'16s
Bannon	Eamonn	John	18/04/58	Edinburgh	29/08/96	5 9.0	11 11	Stenhousemuir
Berry	Neil		06/04/63	Edinburgh	02/08/96	6 0.0	12 7	Heart of Midlothian
Corrigan	Martyn		14/08/77	Glasgow	02/08/95	5 9.0	10 9	Gairdoch United
Craig	Albert	Hughes	03/01/62	Glasgow	21/12/95	5 8.0	11 5	Partick Thistle
De Massis	Sabatino		25/03/70	Pescara	30/07/96	5 7.0	10 12	L'Aquila
Elliot	David		13/11/69	Glasgow	18/08/95	5 9.0	11 0	St. Mirren
Ferguson	Derek		31/07/67	Glasgow	07/09/95	5 8.5	11 6	Sunderland
Foster	Wayne	Paul	11/09/63	Tyldesley	30/08/96	5 10.0	12 3	Partick Thistle
Graham	Alastair		11/08/66	Glasgow	01/03/96	6 3.0	12 7	Raith Rovers
Graham	Bruce	Aston	13/10/77	Melbourne	17/04/96	5 8.0	11 0	Kilsyth Rangers U'18
Gray	Andrew	Arthur	22/02/64	London	22/12/95	5 11.0	13 9	Athletico Marbella
Hagen	David		05/05/73	Edinburgh	13/10/95	5 11.0	13 0	Heart of Midlothian
Hamilton	Brian		05/08/67	Paisley	01/08/96	6 0.0	12 6	Heart of Midlothian
James	Kevin	Francis	03/12/75	Edinburgh	17/11/93	6 0.0	12 0	Musselburgh Athletic
Kidd	Walter	Joseph	10/03/58	Edinburgh	29/08/96	5 11.0	12 3	Heart of Midlothian
Lawrie	Andrew		24/11/78	Galashiels	18/06/96	6 0.0	12 1	Falkirk U'16s
Mathers	Paul		17/01/70	Aberdeen	26/07/96	5 11.0	11 6	Dundee
McGowan	Jamie		05/12/70	Morecambe	02/03/94	6 0.0	11 1	Dundee
McGraw	Mark	Robertson	05/01/71	Rutherglen	18/08/95	5 11.5	11 2	Hibernian
McGrillen	Paul	Alexander	19/08/71	Glasgow	24/02/95	5 8.0	10 5	Motherwell
McKenzie	Scott		07/07/70	Glasgow	08/09/90	5 9.0	10 5	Musselburgh Athletic
Mitchell	Graham		02/11/62	Glasgow	09/08/96	5 10.0	11 12	Hibernian
Nelson	Craig	Robert	28/05/71	Coatbridge	01/08/96	6 1.0	12 3	Heart of Midlothian
Oliver	Neil		11/04/67	Berwick-upon-Tweed	07/08/91	5 11.0	11 10	Blackburn Rovers
Seaton	Andrew	Murray	16/09/77	Edinburgh	18/04/96	5 9.0	11 9	Stoneyburn Juniors
Waddle	Christopher		14/12/60	Gateshead	13/09/96	6 1.0	13 3	Sheffield Wednesday
Whiteside	Garry	Andrew	06/09/73	Glasgow	31/03/96	5 7.0	10 8	St. Rochs

MILESTONES

YEAR OF FORMATION: 1876
MOST CAPPED PLAYER: Alex H. Parker
NO. OF CAPS: 14
MOST LEAGUE POINTS IN A SEASON: 59 (Division 2 – Season 1935/36)
MOST LEAGUE GOALS SCORED BY A PLAYER IN A SEASON: E. Morrison (Season 1928/29)
NO. OF GOALS SCORED: 43
RECORD ATTENDANCE: 23,100 (-v- Celtic – 21.2.1953)
RECORD VICTORY: 12-1 (-v- Laurieston – Scottish Cup, 23.3.1893)
RECORD DEFEAT: 1-11 (-v- Airdrieonians – Division 1, 28.4.1951)

THE BAIRNS' TEN YEAR LEAGUE RECORD

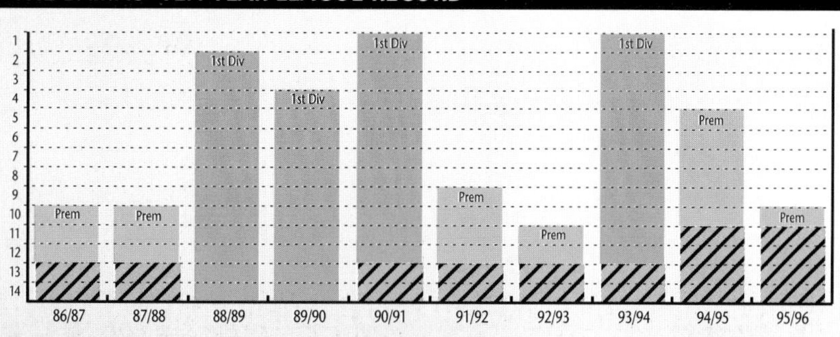

CLUB FACTFILE 1995/96
RESULTS... APPEARANCES... SCORERS

The BAIRNS

Date	Venue	Opponents	Att.	Res	Parks A.	Clark J.	Napier C.	Oliver N.	McLaughlin J.	Rice B.	McGowan J.	Kirk S.	McDonald C.	Johnston M.	Elliot D.	McGraw M.	Inglis N.	Weir D.	McKenzie S.	Ferguson D.	Henderson N.	Fulton S.	McGrillen P.	Lamont W.	Hagen D.	Munro S.	Johnston F.	Wright G.	James K.	Gray A.	Craig A.	Finnigan A.	Iorfa D.	Graham A.	Seaton A.	Whiteside G.	Lawrie A.	Hamilton G.	Abbott G.
Aug 26	H	Aberdeen	6,647	2-3	1	2	3	4	5^1	6	7	8^1	9	10	11	12																							
Sep 9	A	Heart of Midlothian	11,531	1-4		16		3	5		2	7	9^1	10	11		1	4	6	8	14																		
16	H	Rangers	11,480	0-2	1	2		3			5	7	9	10	11			4	6	8	14	12																	
23	H	Motherwell	4,246	0-0	1	2	14			12	3	7		10	11	16		5	4	8		6	9																
30	A	Partick Thistle	4,078	1-1	1	2				12	3	7	14	10^1	11			5	4	8		6	9																
Oct 4	H	Celtic	9,053	0-1		2			16	12	3	7	9	10	11			5	4	8		6	14	1															
7	A	Hibernian	8,356	1-2			3		5			7	12	10	11			2	4^1	8	14	6	9	1															
14	H	Kilmarnock	4,878	0-2			3		5	16	4	7		10	11			2	6	8	12		14	1	9														
21	A	Raith Rovers	4,715	1-0					5		4	7	16	10	11			2	6				9^1	1	8	3	12												
28	H	Heart of Midlothian	6,858	2-0					5		4			10^1	11			2^1	6	8	16		9	1	7	3													
Nov 4	A	Rangers	42,059	0-2		12			5		4			10	11			2	6	8	14		9	1	7	3													
8	A	Aberdeen	11,214	1-3	1	4			5		8		12	10				2	6				9^1		11	3	7												
11	H	Hibernian	6,046	2-0	1				5		4			10^2	11			2	6				9		7	3	8												
18	H	Partick Thistle	4,127	0-1	1	16			5		4	12		10	11			2	6		14		9		7	3	8												
25	A	Motherwell	5,201	1-1	1	4^1			5			8		10	11			2	6		16		9		7	3													
Dec 2	H	Raith Rovers	4,442	2-1	1	4			5		14			10	11			2	6	8			9^2		7	3													
9	A	Kilmarnock	6,017	0-4	1	4			5			6		10	11			2	3	8	16		9		7														
16	A	Celtic	36,466	0-1	1	4					5			10	11	14		2		8			9		7	3		6	16										
Jan 6	H	Rangers	10,348	0-4	1	4					5			10		16		2		8			9		11	3				6	7								
9	A	Partick Thistle	2,708	3-0	1	4					3^1	12		10	11			2^1	6	8			16		7				14	5	9^1								
13	A	Heart of Midlothian	11,560	1-2	1	4					5	14^1			3	10		2	6	8					7				16	11	9								
16	H	Aberdeen	4,003	1-1	1	4^1						10			11			2		8			9		12	3		16	5	6	7								
20	A	Raith Rovers	4,123	0-1	1				5			10			11			2		8			9		14	3			6	4	7								
23	H	Motherwell	3,845	0-1	1				5			12		10	11			2		8			9		14	3			6	4	7								
Feb 3	H	Kilmarnock	4,143	4-2	1						3	7^1		10	14			2	12	8					11					5	6^1	4^1	9^1						
10	H	Celtic	10,366	0-0	1						3	7		10				2	16	8			12		11					5	6	4	9						
24	A	Hibernian	7,609	1-2	1						3	7^1	12		11			4	6	8			10							5		2	9						
Mar 2	A	Motherwell	5,037	0-1	1						3			10				4	6	8			11		7					5		2	16	9					
16	H	Partick Thistle	3,711	1-2	1						3			10	6			2^1	4	8			11		7				16	5				9					
23	A	Rangers	46,361	2-3	1						14			10^1	3	16		2	12	8					11				5^1	4	6	7		9					
30	H	Heart of Midlothian	5,164	0-2							6			10	3			2	7	8			16	1	11				5	4				9					
Apr 6	H	Raith Rovers	3,766	2-3	1						4			10	3	14		2	7	8			11		12				5^1		6^1	16		9					
13	A	Kilmarnock	6,505	0-1	1									10	3	16		4	7				8		11		14		5		6	2		9	12				
20	A	Celtic	35,692	0-4	1						3			10	11	7		2	6				16				14		5	4	8			9					
27	H	Hibernian	2,813	1-1	1						3			10	11			4	7				9^1						5	6	8	2				14			
May 4	A	Aberdeen	11,831	1-2	1						3				11				7				10^1						5	6	8	2		9		16	4	12	14
TOTAL FULL APPEARANCES					28	14	3	3	15	1	27	16	4	31	31	2	1	34	27	26		4	24	7	21	13	3	1	10	16	14	8	3	8			1		
TOTAL SUB APPEARANCES						(3)	(1)		(1)	(4)	(2)	(4)	(5)		(1)	(7)			(3)		(9)	(1)	(6)		(4)		(3)	(1)	(4)			(1)	(1)		(1)	(2)		(1)	(1)
TOTAL GOALS SCORED						2			1		1	4	1	5				3	1				6						2		3	1	1						

Small bold figures denote goalscorers. † denotes opponent's own goal.

BROCKVILLE PARK

CAPACITY: 11,953; Seated 2,661, Standing 9,292

PITCH DIMENSIONS: 110 yds x 71 yds

FACILITIES FOR DISABLED SUPPORTERS: Disabled Enclosure Opposite Main Stand - Takes 7 Disabled Fans in Wheelchairs plus 1 Helper Each.

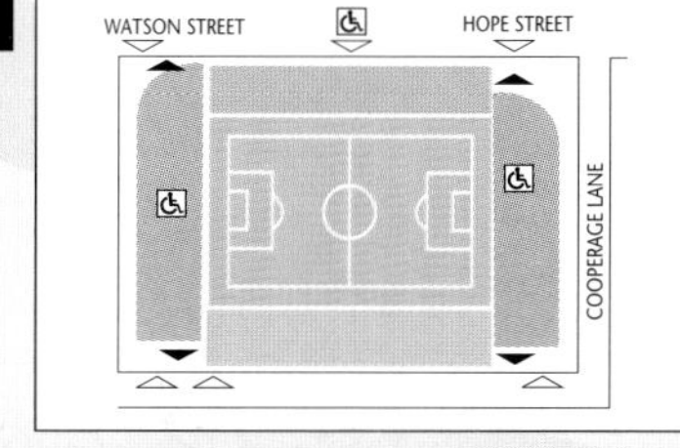

HOW TO GET THERE

Brockville Park can be reached by the following routes:

TRAINS: The main Edinburgh-Glasgow railway line passes by the ground and passengers can alight at Grahamston Station. They will then have a walk of 100 yards to the ground.

BUSES: All buses departing from the city centre pass by Brockville.

CARS: Car parking facilities are available in the Meeks Road car park for coaches and cars and also in a local shopping car park which can hold 500 cars. Supporters coaches and cars will be directed to the appropriate parking area by the police on duty.

GREENOCK MORTON

Cappielow Park, Sinclair Street,
Greenock, PA15 2TY

CHAIRMAN
John Wilson

DIRECTORS
Duncan D. F. Rae
Kenneth Woods
Andrew Gemmell
W. Arthur Montford

SECRETARY
Mrs Jane W. Rankin

MANAGER
Allan McGraw

ASSISTANT MANAGER
Peter Cormack

SENIOR COACH
John McMaster

CLUB DOCTOR
Dr. R. Craig Speirs

CROWD DOCTOR
Dr. Fraser Gray

PHYSIOTHERAPIST
John Tierney

GROUNDSMAN
Ian Lyle

KIT MANAGER
William Gray

COMMERCIAL DIRECTOR
Duncan D.F. Rae
(01475) 728771

SALES & MARKETING
Ms. Sandra Fisher

LOTTERY MANAGER
Chris Norris

STADIUM MANAGER
Alex Renfrew

SAFETY OFFICER
Michael Scott

TELEPHONES
Ground/Ticket Office
(01475) 723571
Fax (01475) 781084

CLUB SHOP
Greenock Morton F.C. Enterprises,
85 Cathcart Street, Greenock.
Open 9.00 a.m. - 5.30 p.m. Mon - Sat.

OFFICIAL SUPPORTERS CLUB
Greenock Morton Supporters Club,
Regent Street, Greenock

TEAM CAPTAIN
Janne Lindberg

SHIRT SPONSOR
James Watt College

LIST OF PLAYERS 1996-97

SURNAME	FIRST NAME	MIDDLE NAME	DATE OF BIRTH	PLACE OF BIRTH	DATE OF SIGNING	HEIGHT FT INS	WEIGHT ST LBS	PREVIOUS CLUB
Aitken	Stephen	Smith	25/09/76	Glasgow	05/12/95	5 6.0	9 7	Beith Juniors
Anderson	John	Patton	02/10/72	Greenock	25/01/94	6 2.0	12 2	Gourock Y.A.C.
Blaikie	Alan		25/08/72	Greenock	30/12/94	6 1.0	12 0	Greenock Juniors
Blair	Paul		05/07/76	Greenock	21/06/94	5 7.0	10 8	Ferguslie United
Collins	Derek	J.	15/04/69	Glasgow	23/07/87	5 8.0	10 7	Renfrew Waverley
Cormack	Peter	Robert	08/06/74	Liverpool	11/08/94	6 0.0	11 5	Newcastle United
Fanning	Ross	Stewart	04/09/76	Vale of Leven	22/12/95	5 9.5	10 11	Vale of Leven
Flannery	Patrick		23/07/76	Glasgow	29/03/96	5 11.0	10 12	Beith Juniors
Hawke	Warren	Robert	20/09/70	Durham	28/07/95	5 10.5	11 4	Berwick Rangers
Hunter	James	Addison	20/12/64	Johnstone	16/09/96	5 9.0	10 10	Glentyan Thistle
Inglis	Neil	David	10/09/74	Glasgow	16/08/96	6 1.0	12 2	Falkirk
Johnstone	Douglas	Iain	12/03/69	Irvine	31/08/91	6 2.0	12 8	Glasgow University
Lilley	Derek	Symon	09/02/74	Paisley	13/08/91	5 10.5	12 7	Everton B.C.
Lindberg	Janne		24/05/66	Finland	11/11/94	5 7.0	11 0	MyPa–47
Mahood	Alan	Scott	26/03/73	Kilwinning	23/03/92	5 8.0	10 10	Nottingham Forest
Matheson	Ross		15/11/77	Greenock	02/07/96	5 6.0	9 10	Rangers
McArthur	Scott		28/02/68	Johnstone	26/12/92	5 11.0	11 10	Heart of Midlothian
McCahill	Stephen	Joseph	03/09/66	Greenock	02/10/92	6 2.0	12 0	Celtic
McPherson	Craig		27/03/71	Greenock	07/10/94	5 9.0	11 3	Gourock Amateurs
Powers	Marc		13/12/74	Glasgow	18/09/96	6 0.0	11 6	Greenock Juniors
Rajamaki	Marko		03/10/68	Finland	11/11/94	5 7.0	11 3	MyPa–47
Reeley	Derek		26/12/74	Glasgow	19/02/96	5 8.0	11 0	Aberdeen
Reid	Brian	Robertson	15/06/70	Paisley	12/03/96	6 2.0	11 12	Rangers
Slavin	Bryan		23/09/77	Irvine	29/11/95	5 9.0	11 1	Dalry Thistle
Wylie	David		04/04/66	Johnstone	01/08/85	6 0.0	13 0	Ferguslie United

MILESTONES

YEAR OF FORMATION: 1874
MOST CAPPED PLAYER: Jimmy Cowan
NO. OF CAPS: 25
MOST LEAGUE POINTS IN A SEASON: 69 (Division 2 – Season 1966/67)
MOST LEAGUE GOALS SCORED BY A PLAYER IN A SEASON: Allan McGraw (Season 1963/64)
NO. OF GOALS SCORED: 58
RECORD ATTENDANCE: 23,500 (-v- Celtic – 1922)
RECORD VICTORY: 11-0 (-v- Carfin Shamrock – Scottish Cup, 13.11.1886)
RECORD DEFEAT: 1-10 (-v- Port Glasgow Athletic – Division 2, 5.5.1884)

THE TON'S TEN YEAR LEAGUE RECORD

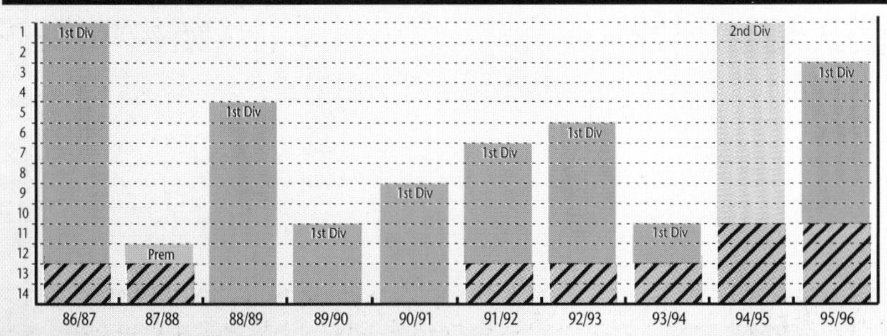

CLUB FACTFILE 1995/96
RESULTS... APPEARANCES... SCORERS

The TON

Date	Venue	Opponents	Att.	Res	Wylie D.	Johnstone D.	Collins D.	Anderson J.	McCahill S.	Lindberg J.	Lilley D.	Mahood A.	Hawke W.	McInnes D.	Rajamaki M.	Laing D.	Blair P.	McArthur S.	McPherson C.	Cormack P.	Hunter J.	Blaikie A.	Boe A.	Reid B.
Aug 12	A	Dundee United	6,927	1-1	1	2	3	4	5	6	7	8^1	9	10	11	12	15							
26	H	Dumbarton	2,612	1-2	1	3	2	4	5	6	7^1	8	9	10	11									
Sep 2	A	St. Johnstone	3,134	2-0	1	4	2		5	6	7^2	8	9	10	11	12	15	3	14					
9	H	Dundee	3,384	2-2	1	4	2	14	5	6	7^2	8	9	10	11	12	15	3						
16	A	Airdrieonians	1,927	2-3	1		2	4	5	6	7	8	9^2	10	11	12	15	3						
23	H	Dunfermline Athletic	3,794	2-0	1		2	4	5	6	7	8	9^1	10^1	11	12	14	3						
30	A	St. Mirren	5,436	4-1	1		2	4	5	6	7^1	8	9^2	10	11^1			3						
Oct 7	A	Clydebank	2,343	0-1	1	15	2	4	5	6	7	8	9	10	11	12	14	3						
14	H	Hamilton Academical	2,875	2-0	1	5	2	4		6	7	8^1	9^1	10	11			3	15	14				
21	H	St. Johnstone	3,313	4-0	1	5	2	4^1		6	7	8	9^3	10	11		14			3				
28	A	Dumbarton	2,378	2-0	1	5	2	4		6	7	8	9^2		11	12	10			3				
Nov 4	H	Airdrieonians	3,856	2-1	1	5	2	4		6	7	8^1	9	10	11^1					3				
11	A	Dundee	4,060	0-0	1	5	2	4		6	7	8	9	10	11		15			3				
18	H	St. Mirren	6,217	0-3	1	5	2	4	10	6	7	8	9		11	12				3				
25	A	Dunfermline Athletic	4,857	2-0	1	5	2	4		6	7^1	8	9^1		11	12		3	10					
Dec 2	H	Clydebank	3,002	3-0	1	5	2	4		6	7^1	8	9		11^2	12		3	10		14	15		
9	A	Hamilton Academical	1,813	3-2	1	5	2^1	4^1		6	7^1	8	9		11	12		3	10			15		
16	H	Dundee United	4,660	1-2	1	5	2	4		6	7^1	8			11	9		3	10	12				
Jan 9	A	St. Johnstone	3,253	1-6	1	5	2	4		6^1	7	8	9		11	12	14	15	10	3				
13	H	Dundee	3,163	1-0	1		2	4^1	5	6	7	8	9		11	12		3	14	10				
20	A	Clydebank	1,685	1-0	1		2	4	5	6	7	8	9^1		11	12		3	14	10				
23	A	Airdrieonians	1,605	2-0	1		2	4	5	6^1	7^1	8	9		11	12		3	14	10		15		
31	A	St. Mirren	5,312	1-0	1	15	2	4	5	6	7		9		11	12	8	3	14	10^1				
Feb 24	H	Dumbarton	2,833	2-0		5	2	4		6	7^1	8^1	9		12	14	11	3	15	10			1	
27	A	Dundee United	6,768	0-4		5	2	4		6	7	8	9		12	14		3	11	10			1	
Mar 2	A	Dunfermline Athletic	4,547	1-4			2	4	5	6	7	8	9		11^1	12		14	3	10			1	
9	H	Hamilton Academical	2,560	4-1	1	3^1	2	4	5			8	9		11^1	7^1			6	10^1				
16	H	St. Mirren	4,204	1-2	1	3	2		5		7	8	12		11^1	9			6	10				4
19	H	Dunfermline Athletic	3,170	1-1	1	3	2		5		7	8	9		11^1		14		6	10				4
23	H	Airdrieonians	2,889	3-0	1	3	2		5^1		7^1	8	9		11^1	14	15	12	6	10				4
30	A	Dundee	2,734	1-1	1	3	2		5		7^1	8	9		11		14	12	6	10				4
Apr 6	H	Clydebank	3,001	0-0	1	3	2		5		7	8	9		11	14	15		6	10				4
13	A	Hamilton Academical	1,519	1-0	1	3	2	6	5		7		9		11^1	14	15		8	10				4
20	H	St. Johnstone	5,808	1-0	1	3^1	2	6	5		7		9		11	14		12	8	10				4
27	A	Dumbarton	2,733	1-0	1	3	2	6^1	5		7		9		11				8	10				4
May 4	H	Dundee United	12,523	2-2	1	3^1	2	6	5		7		9		11^1		15	12	8	10				4
TOTAL FULL APPEARANCES					33	27	36	29	24	26	35	31	34	12	34	3	3	17	17	23			3	9
TOTAL SUB APPEARANCES						(2)		(1)					(1)		(2)	(23)	(15)	(6)	(7)	(2)	(1)	(3)		
TOTAL GOALS SCORED						3	1	4	1	2	14	4	13	1	11	1				2				

Small bold figures denote goalscorers. † denotes opponent's own goal.

CAPPIELOW PARK

CAPACITY: 14,267; Seating 5,257, Standing 9,010

PITCH DIMENSIONS: 110 yds x 71 yds

FACILITIES FOR DISABLED SUPPORTERS: Seating facilities below Grandstand.

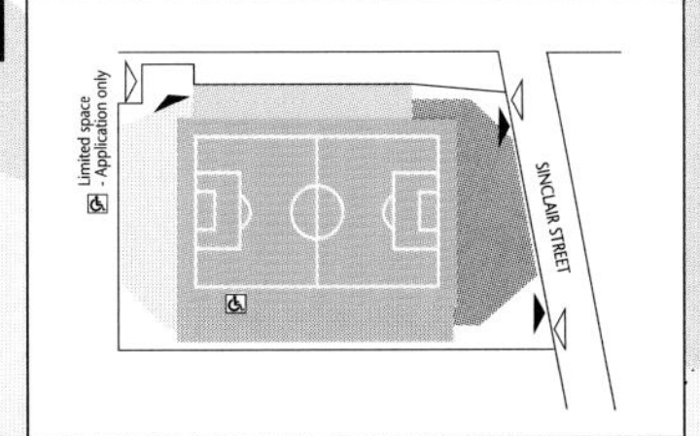

HOW TO GET THERE

Cappielow Park may be reached by the following routes:

BUSES: Services from Glasgow stop just outside the park. There are also services from Port Glasgow and Gourock.

TRAINS: The nearest local station is Cartsdyke and it is a five minute walk from here to the ground. There are two to three trains every hour from Glasgow and from Gourock.

CARS: Temporary Car Park adjacent to Stadium.

PARTICK THISTLE

Firhill Stadium, 80 Firhill Road, Glasgow, G20 7BA

CHAIRMAN
James Oliver

VICE-CHAIRMAN
T. Brown McMaster

DIRECTORS
Angus MacSween
Harry F. Scott
Robert G.S. McCamley

PRESIDENT
James R. Aitken

SECRETARY
Ms. Lorna Bryce

PLAYER/MANAGER
Murdo MacLeod

ASSISTANT MANAGER
Gordon Chisholm

CLUB DOCTOR
Alan W. Robertson

PHYSIOTHERAPISTS
Graham Hebenton
& Iain McFadyen

S.F.A. COMMUNITY COACH
Graham Diamond

CHIEF SCOUT
Robert Dinnie

CHIEF OF SECURITY
Bill McPhie

GROUND MAINTENANCE
Souters of Stirling

COMMERCIAL MANAGER
John Lawson

LOTTERY MANAGER
Bobby Briggs

TELEPHONES
Ground/Ticket Office/Commercial
0141- 945 4811
Fax 0141-945 1525

CLUB SHOP
c/o 90 Firhill Road, Glasgow, G20 7AL
Tel 0141-945 4811.
Open Matchdays/evenings only

OFFICIAL SUPPORTERS CLUB
Ms. Morag McHaffie
99 Somerville Drive, Glasgow,
G42 9BH. Tel 0141-632 3604

TEAM CAPTAIN
Alan Dinnie

SHIRT SPONSOR
D. C. S.

PARTICK THISTLE 18 76

LIST OF PLAYERS 1996-97

SURNAME	FIRST NAME	MIDDLE NAME	DATE OF BIRTH	PLACE OF BIRTH	DATE OF SIGNING	HEIGHT FT INS	WEIGHT ST LBS	PREVIOUS CLUB
Adams	Charles	Stuart S.	21/03/76	Irvine	13/09/96	5 10.0	11 5	Kilwinning Rangers
Ayton	Stuart		19/10/75	Glasgow	01/07/94	5 8.0	10 12	Rangers
Budinauckas	Kevin		16/09/74	Bellshill	10/08/92	5 10.0	11 0	Armadale Thistle
Cairns	Mark	Henry	25/09/69	Edinburgh	28/10/94	6 0.0	13 2	Gala Fairydean
Dinnie	Alan		14/05/63	Glasgow	27/08/94	5 10.0	11 5	Dundee
Docherty	Stephen		18/02/76	Glasgow	25/08/93	5 8.0	10 10	Pollok Juniors
Evans	Gareth	John	14/01/67	Coventry	09/08/96	5 7.5	11 6	Hibernian
Farrell	David		29/10/69	Glasgow	09/08/96	5 9.0	11 4	Hibernian
Henderson	Nicholas	Sinclair	08/02/69	Edinburgh	22/12/95	5 10.0	11 1	Falkirk
Lyons	Andrew		19/10/66	Blackpool	01/03/96	5 9.0	12 7	Wigan Athletic
Macdonald	William	James	17/09/76	Irvine	21/11/95	5 7.5	11 0	West Bromwich Albion
MacLeod	Murdo	Davidson	24/09/58	Glasgow	16/08/95	5 9.0	12 4	Dumbarton
Maskrey	Stephen	William	16/08/62	Edinburgh	02/08/96	5 7.5	9 10	Kilmarnock
McWilliams	Derek		16/01/66	Broxburn	02/08/94	5 10 .0	12 0	Dunfermline Athletic
Milne	Callum		27/08/65	Edinburgh	04/09/93	5 8.5	10 7	Hibernian
Moss	David		15/11/68	Doncaster	13/09/96	6 2.0	13 3	Scunthorpe United
Slavin	James		18/01/75	Lanark	15/03/96	6 2.0	14 0	Celtic
Smith	Thomas	William	12/10/73	Glasgow	12/01/95	5 8.5	11 7	Portadown
Stirling	Jered		13/10/76	Stirling	16/10/95	6 0.0	11 6	Shettleston Juniors
Turner	Thomas	Gibson	11/10/63	Johnstone	31/12/94	5 10.0	10 7	St. Johnstone
Watson	Gregg		21/09/70	Glasgow	14/08/93	5 9.5	10 9	Aberdeen

MILESTONES

YEAR OF FORMATION: 1876
MOST CAPPED PLAYER: Alan Rough
NO. OF CAPS: 53
MOST LEAGUE POINTS IN A SEASON: 57 (First Division - Season 1991/92)
MOST LEAGUE GOALS SCORED BY A PLAYER IN A SEASON: Alec Hair (Season 1926/27)
NO. OF GOALS SCORED: 41
RECORD ATTENDANCE: 49,838 (-v- Rangers – 18.2.1922)
RECORD VICTORY: 16-0 (-v- Royal Albert – Scottish Cup, 17.1.1931)
RECORD DEFEAT: 0-10 (-v- Queen's Park - Scottish Cup, 3.12.1881)

THE JAGS' TEN YEAR LEAGUE RECORD

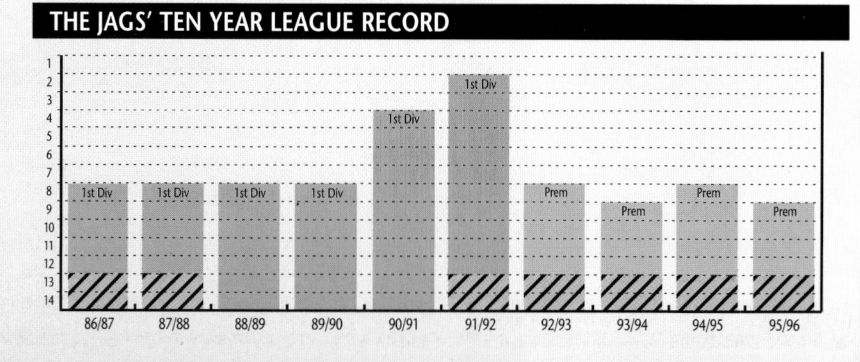

CLUB FACTFILE 1995/96
RESULTS... APPEARANCES... SCORERS

The JAGS

Date	Venue	Opponents	Att.	Res	Walker J. N.	Dinnie A.	Pittman S.	McWilliams D.	Watson G.	Welsh S.	Gibson A.	Craig A.	Foster W.	Curran H.	Cameron I.	McDonald R.	Milne C.	McKee K.	Docherty S.	Tierney P. G.	Smith T.	Shepherd A.	Turner T.	Ayton S.	MacLeod M.	Macdonald W.	Cairns M.	Adams C.	Henderson N.	McMahon S.	Lyons A.	McCue J.	Slavin J.	Stirling J.
Aug 26	H	Hibernian	5,327	1-1	1	2	3	4	5	6	7^1	8	9	10	11																			
Sep 9	A	Motherwell	6,155	1-1	1	2	3	4	6	5	15	8	9	14	11	7^1	10	12																
16	H	Heart of Midlothian	5,396	2-0	1	2	3	7^1	6	5		8	9	12	11		10	4	15^1															
23	A	Raith Rovers	4,342	1-3	1	2		4		5	15		9		11	7^1	3		10	6	8	14												
30	H	Falkirk	4,078	1-1	1	2			6	5	9	8^1			12	7	3	4	11				10											
Oct 4	H	Kilmarnock	3,419	1-1	1	2		11	6	5	9	8^1		15	14	7	3	4	12				10											
7	A	Celtic	29,950	1-2	1	2		9	6	5		8			11	7	3		12		4^1		10											
14	H	Rangers	16,066	0-4	1	2		11	6	5	15	8		7			3		9		4		10	14										
21	A	Aberdeen	12,719	0-3	1	2		14	6	5	12	8			15	7	3	4	9		11				10									
28	H	Motherwell	4,029	1-0	1	2	3	7	6	5	9				11				8^1		4		10	15										
Nov 4	A	Heart of Midlothian	10,094	0-3	1	2	3	7	6	5	9	8	11		10				12		4													
11	H	Celtic	12,223	1-2	1	2	3	7	6	5	12		9	15	10				11^1		4		8											
18	A	Falkirk	4,127	1-0	1	2	3	7	6	5	14		9^1		10				11		4		8											
22	A	Hibernian	6,783	0-3	1	2	3	7	6	5	14		9	15	10		12		11		4		8											
25	H	Raith Rovers	3,503	0-2	1	2	3	7	6	5	12				10	9	4		11				8			14								
Dec 2	H	Aberdeen	4,286	1-0		2	3	7		5	9				10		6		11		4^1		8			12	1							
9	A	Rangers	43,137	0-1		2		7	6	5	12		9		10			3	11		4		8				1							
16	A	Kilmarnock	6,581	1-2		2		7^1	6	5	9				10			3	11		4		8	14		12	1	15						
Jan 6	H	Heart of Midlothian	4,618	0-1	1	2		7	6	5	12				10		3		11		4		8			15			9					
9	H	Falkirk	2,708	0-3	1	2			6	5	11			7	10		3						8			14		4	9	15				
13	A	Motherwell	5,226	2-0	1	2			6^1	5					10	15	3		11		4		8^1	12		7		14	9					
16	H	Hibernian	2,811	0-0	1	2			6	5			8		10	15	3		11		4					7			9					
20	A	Aberdeen	9,149	0-1	1	2			6	5			8		10	15	3		11		4					7			9					
23	A	Raith Rovers	3,651	2-0	1	2	4		6	5			8		10	11^2	3									7			9					
Feb 3	H	Rangers	16,488	1-2	1	2		11	6	5			9		10	7^1		3	14		4					8								
10	H	Kilmarnock	4,857	0-1	1	2		11	6	5			9		10	7	3		8		4		15						12					
24	A	Celtic	36,421	0-4	1	2	11	14	6	5			9		10	7		3	8		4								12					
Mar 2	H	Raith Rovers	2,336	0-3	1	2	3		6	5			9		10	7			8							14			4		11	15		
16	A	Falkirk	3,711	2-1	1	2	3			6			9		10						4		8			7			14		11^2		5	
23	A	Heart of Midlothian	9,610	5-2	1	2		9	3	6					10^1		14				4		8^1			7^1					11^2		5	
30	H	Motherwell	4,846	0-2	1	2		9	3	6					10						4		8			7		15	12		11		5	
Apr 13	A	Rangers	46,438	0-5	1				3	6	14				10			2			4		8			7			9		11		5	
16	H	Aberdeen	4,568	1-1	1			4^1	3	6	15		8		10		12	2								7			9		11		5	
20	A	Kilmarnock	7,276	1-2	1			4	3	6	14		8		10		2				15		12^1			7			9		11		5	
27	H	Celtic	14,693	2-4	1			4		6	12				10						2			7				15	8^1		11^1	9	5	3
May 4	A	Hibernian	6,885	0-1	1			4	6						10	14	2						8						7		11	9	5	3
TOTAL FULL APPEARANCES					33	31	14	25	32	35	8	9	19	3	32	12	19	10	19	1	24		20	1	1	11	3	1	12		9	2	8	2
TOTAL SUB APPEARANCES								(2)			(14)			(5)	(3)	(4)	(3)	(1)	(5)		(1)	(1)	(2)	(4)		(6)		(4)	(4)	(1)		(1)		
TOTAL GOALS SCORED								3	1		1	2	1		1	5			3		2		3			1			1		5			

Small bold figures denote goalscorers. † denotes opponent's own goal.

FIRHILL STADIUM

CAPACITY: 20,876; Seated 9,076 Standing 11,800

PITCH DIMENSIONS: 110 yds x 75 yds

FACILITIES FOR DISABLED SUPPORTERS: Covered places available in North Enclosure. 10 Wheelchair spectators, 10 attendants, 10 ambulant disabled. Telephone call in advance to Office Secretary for arrangements.

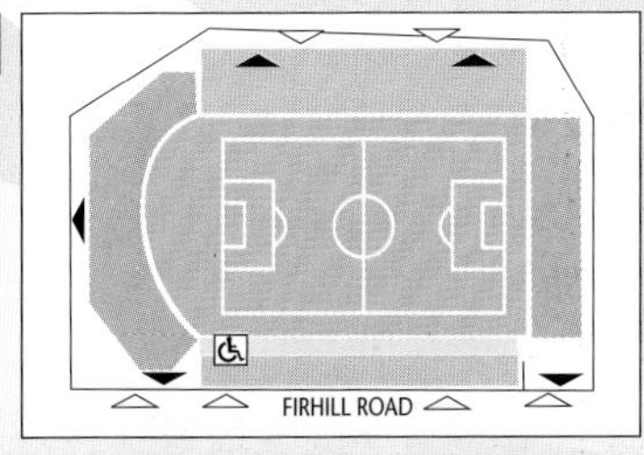

HOW TO GET THERE

The following routes may be used to reach Firhill Stadium:

TRAINS: The nearest railway stations are Glasgow Queen Street and Glasgow Central and buses from the centre of the city pass within 100 yards of the ground.

BUSES: The following buses from the city centre all pass by the park. Nos. 1, 18, 21, 21A, 57, 60, 61 and 61B and the frequency of the buses is just over 12 minutes.

UNDERGROUND: The nearest GGPTE Underground station is St.George's Cross and supporters walking from here should pass through Cromwell Street into Maryhill Road and then walk up this road as far as Firhill Street. The ground is then on the right. The Kelvinbridge Underground Station is also not far from the park and supporters from here should walk along Great Western Road as far as Napiershill Street and then follow this into Maryhill Road.

CARS: Car Parking is available at the north end of the ground.

ST. JOHNSTONE

McDiarmid Park, Crieff Road,
Perth, PH1 2SJ

CHAIRMAN
Geoffrey S. Brown

DIRECTORS
Douglas B. McIntyre
Henry S. Ritchie
David F. Sidey
Henry G. Stewart

HONORARY PRESIDENT
Bruce McDiarmid

MANAGING DIRECTOR/ SECRETARY
A. Stewart M. Duff

MANAGER
Paul W. Sturrock

FIRST TEAM COACH
John Blackley

YOUTH COACH
Alastair Stevenson

CLUB DOCTOR
Alistair McCracken

PHYSIOTHERAPIST
David Henderson

S.F.A. COMMUNITY OFFICER
Atholl Henderson

STADIUM MANAGER
Jimmy Hogg

COMMERCIAL MANAGER
Helen Harcus

LOTTERY MANAGER
Anne Connolly

CATERING MANAGER
Scott Ritchie

TELEPHONES
Ground/Commercial/Ticket Office
(01738) 626961
Fax (01738) 625771
Information Service 0891 121559

CLUB SHOP
Open Mon-Fri at Ticket Office
at Ground and Sat. Matchdays.
Situated at South Stand

OFFICIAL SUPPORTERS CLUB
c/o McDiarmid Park,
Crieff Road, Perth

TEAM CAPTAIN
Jim Weir

SHIRT SPONSOR
The Famous Grouse

LIST OF PLAYERS 1996-97

SURNAME	FIRST NAME	MIDDLE NAME	DATE OF BIRTH	PLACE OF BIRTH	DATE OF SIGNING	HEIGHT FT INS	WEIGHT ST LBS	PREVIOUS CLUB
Brown	Gordon		21/10/79	Broxburn	12/01/96	5 10.5	11 1	Celtic B.C.
Davidson	Callum	Ian	25/06/76	Stirling	08/06/94	5 10.0	11 0	"S" Form
Donaldson	Euan	Gordon	20/08/75	Falkirk	16/05/95	5 10.0	10 7	Stenhousemuir
Farquhar	Gary	Robert	23/02/71	Wick	14/10/94	5 7.0	11 4	Brora Rangers
Ferguson	Ian		05/08/68	Dunfermline	30/11/93	6 1.0	13 12	Heart of Midlothian
Freedman	Gordon	James	27/11/78	Glasgow	22/07/95	5 10.0	10 4	Celtic B.C.
Grant	Roderick	John	16/09/66	Gloucester	29/07/95	5 11.0	11 0	Partick Thistle
Greenock	Robert		04/01/80	Coatbridge	12/01/96	5 8.0	10 0	St. Johnstone U'15s
Griffin	Daniel	Joseph	10/08/77	Belfast	18/02/94	5 10.0	10 5	St. Andrews Belfast
Jenkinson	Leigh		09/07/69	Doncaster	08/12/95	6 2.0	13 0	Coventry City
King	Charles		15/11/79	Edinburgh	12/01/96	5 7.0	10 2	Celtic B.C.
Main	Alan	David	05/12/67	Elgin	05/01/95	5 11.5	12 13	Dundee United
Malcolm	Stuart		20/08/79	Edinburgh	12/07/96	6 1.0	11 0	Hutchison Vale B.C.
McAnespie	Kieran	Liam	11/09/79	Gosport	14/09/95	5 8.0	10 13	St. Johnstone B.C.
McCluskey	Stuart	Campbell	29/10/77	Bellshill	07/07/94	5 11.0	10 3	"S" Form
McCulloch	Marc	Raymond	14/03/80	Edinburgh	12/07/96	5 8.0	10 10	Musselburgh Union
McQuillan	John		20/07/70	Stranraer	04/07/95	5 10.0	11 7	Dundee
O'Boyle	George		14/12/67	Belfast	24/07/94	5 8.0	11 9	Dunfermline Athletic
O'Neil	John		06/07/71	Bellshill	04/08/94	5 7.0	11 7	Dundee United
Preston	Allan		16/08/69	Edinburgh	26/03/94	5 10.0	11 4	Dunfermline Athletic
Robertson	Stephen		16/03/77	Glasgow	16/09/94	5 10.0	11 13	Ashfield Juniors
Scott	Philip	Campbell	14/11/74	Perth	30/07/91	5 9.0	11 1	Scone Thistle
Sekerlioglu	Attila		27/01/65	Linz	06/12/95	6 1.0	12 7	F.C. Tirol Milch Innsbruck
Sturrock	Paul	Whitehead	10/10/56	Ellon	26/11/93	5 8.5	12 2	Dundee United
Tosh	Steven	William	27/04/73	Kirkcaldy	22/07/95	5 9.0	10 2	Arbroath
Weir	James	McIntosh	15/06/69	Motherwell	18/11/94	6 1.0	12 5	Heart of Midlothian
Whiteford	Andrew		22/08/77	Bellshill	09/06/94	5 10.0	11 4	Possil Y.M.C.A.

MILESTONES

YEAR OF FORMATION: 1884
MOST CAPPED PLAYER: Sandy McLaren
NO. OF CAPS: 5
MOST LEAGUE POINTS IN A SEASON: 59 (Second Division – Season 1987/88)(2 Points for a Win)
65 (First Division – Season 1995/96)(3 Points for a Win)
MOST LEAGUE GOALS SCORED BY A PLAYER IN A SEASON: Jimmy Benson (Season 1931/32)
NO. OF GOALS SCORED: 38
RECORD ATTENDANCE: 29,972 (-v- Dundee 10.2.1951 at Muirton Park)
10,504 (-v- Rangers – Premier Division, 20.10.1990 at McDiarmid Park)
RECORD VICTORY: 8-1 (-v- Partick Thistle – League Cup, 16.8.1969)
RECORD DEFEAT: 0-12 (-v- Cowdenbeath – Scottish Cup, 21.1.1928)

THE SAINTS' TEN YEAR LEAGUE RECORD

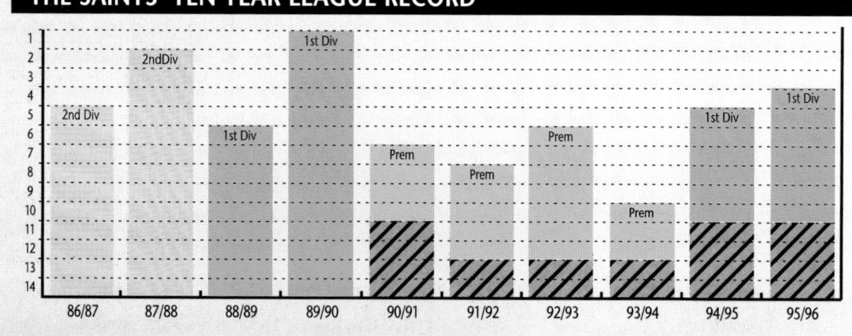

CLUB FACTFILE 1995/96

RESULTS... APPEARANCES... SCORERS

The SAINTS

Date	Venue	Opponents	Att.	Res	Main A.	McQuillan J.	Donaldson E.	Cherry P.	Irons D.	McGowne K.	Scott P.	Griffin D.	Twaddle K.	Grant R.	Preston A.	Farquhar G.	Ferguson I.	Proctor M.	McCluskey S.	O'Neil J.	O'Boyle G.	Tosh S.	McLean S.	Weir J.	English I.	Whiteford A.	Sekerlioglu A.	Jenkinson L.	Young S.	Robertson S.	Davidson C.
Aug 12	H	Dundee	5,236	0-2	1	2	3	4	5	6	7	8	9	10	11	12	14														
26	A	St. Mirren	2,430	0-0	1	2			12		7	5	16	8	3			4	6	9	10	11									
Sep 2	H	Greenock Morton	3,134	0-2	1	2			12	6	7	5	16	8	3	11		4		9	10	14									
9	A	Hamilton Academical	803	3-0	1	2		6	4		7	5	9	14	3	11		12		8^2	10^1		16								
16	H	Dumbarton	2,273	4-1	1	2			4		7	5	9^1	14	3	11^1		12		8^1	10^1		16	6							
23	H	Clydebank	2,482	2-2	1	2		12	4		7	5	9	14^1	3	11				8	10^1			6	16						
30	A	Dunfermline Athletic	5,737	1-2	1	2		12	4		7	5	9		3	11	16			8	10^1			6							
Oct 7	H	Airdrieonians	2,839	1-0	1	2	3	6	4		7^1	5	9	16		11		12		8	10										
14	A	Dundee United	7,572	1-2	1	2^1		6	4			5	9	16	3	11		14		8	10			7							
21	A	Greenock Morton	3,313	0-4	1	2		4	6		8	12	9	14	3					11	10	7		5							
28	H	St. Mirren	3,028	0-0	1	2	3		12		7	6	11	9	8		16		5	4	10										
Nov 4	A	Dumbarton	1,050	3-1	1	2	3			6	7	4	9^2		14	8				11	10^1			5							
11	H	Hamilton Academical	2,348	2-0	1		3			6	7	4	9		11^1					8^1	10		16	5		2					
18	H	Dunfermline Athletic	4,559	1-0	1		3			6	7	4	9^1		11					8	10		16	5		2					
25	A	Clydebank	923	0-2	1		3		12	6	7	4	9		11		14			8	10		16	5		2					
Dec 2	A	Airdrieonians	1,660	1-1	1		3	2	12	6	7^1	4	9		16		11			8	10			5							
9	H	Dundee United	5,966	0-0	1			2		6	7		9		3					8	10			5			4	11			
16	A	Dundee	3,034	1-0	1			2			7^1	6	9		3		16			8	10			5			4	11			
Jan 6	H	Dumbarton	2,448	†3-0	1			2	12		7	6		16	3		9			8	10^2			5			4	11	14		
9	H	Greenock Morton	3,253	6-1	1			2			7^1	6		9	3		16^1			8	10^3			5			4^1	11	14		
13	A	Hamilton Academical	1,197	1-2	1			2	14		7	6		9	3^1	12	16			8	10			5			4	11			
20	H	Airdrieonians	2,761	0-0				2		4	7	6	11	16	3	14	9			8	10			5						1	
23	H	Clydebank	2,167	3-1	1	2				6	7^2		16	9	3	14				8	10^1			5			4	11			
Feb 3	A	Dundee United	7,478	3-1	1	2				6	7			9	3					8^1	10^2			5			4	11			
13	H	Dundee	3,960	3-2	1	2			4	6^1	7	12		9^1	3					8	10^1			5				11			
24	A	St. Mirren	2,568	3-1	1	2				6	7^2		16	9	3					8	10^1			5			4	11			
28	A	Dunfermline Athletic	6,348	2-3	1	2			14	6	7	12	16	9^1	3					8	10^1			5			4	11			
Mar 2	A	Clydebank	705	2-1	1	2				6		12		9	3					8^1	10	7^1		5			4	11			
16	H	Dunfermline Athletic	5,239	2-2	1	2	3			6		5^1	16	9		7				8	10						4	11^1			
23	A	Dumbarton	903	3-0	1	2	3			6		12	16	9^1		14				8	10^1	7		5			4	11^1			
30	H	Hamilton Academical	2,614	4-1	1	2	3			6^1		12	16	9^1						8	10^1	7		5			4^1	11	14		
Apr 6	A	Airdrieonians	2,018	3-1	1	2^1	3			6				9						8	10^2	7		5			4	11			
13	H	Dundee United	9,973	†1-0	1	2	3			6	7	12		9						8	10			5			4	11			
20	A	Greenock Morton	5,808	0-1	1	2	3			6	7	12	16	9						8	10			5			4	11			
27	H	St. Mirren	3,687	1-0	1	2				6		12		9						8	10^1	7		5			4	11			3
May 4	A	Dundee	2,710	0-0				2		6		4				8					10	7	9	5		16			11	1	3
TOTAL FULL APPEARANCES					34	25	14	13	9	23	28	22	17	19	25	10	3	2	2	34	35	8	1	29		3	17	18	1	2	2
TOTAL SUB APPEARANCES								(2)	(8)			(9)	(9)	(8)	(2)	(5)	(7)	(4)				(1)	(5)		(1)	(1)			(3)		
TOTAL GOALS SCORED						2				2	8	1	4	5	2	1	1			6	21	1					2	2			

Small bold figures denote goalscorers. † denotes opponent's own goal.

McDIARMID PARK

CAPACITY: 10,673 (All Seated)

PITCH DIMENSIONS: 115 yds x 75 yds

FACILITIES FOR DISABLED SUPPORTERS: Entrance via south end of West Stand and south end of East Stand. Visiting disabled fans should contact the club in advance. Headphones available in West and North Stands for blind and partially sighted supporters.

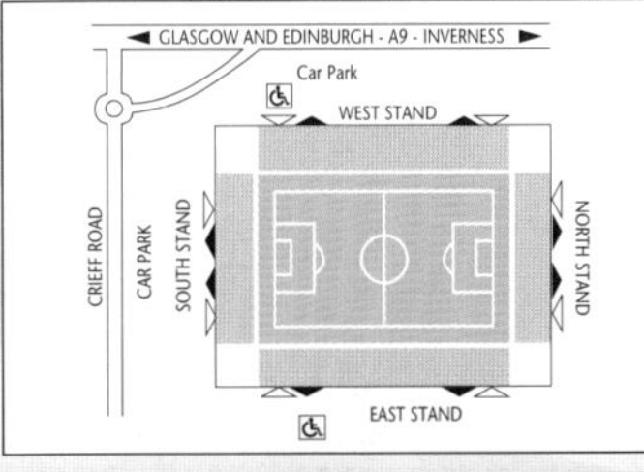

HOW TO GET THERE

The following routes can be used to reach McDiarmid Park:

TRAINS: Perth Station is well served by trains from all parts of the country. The station is about 40 minutes walk from the park.

BUSES: Local services nos. 1 and 2 pass near the ground. Both leave from Mill Street in the town centre.

CARS: The car park at the park holds 1,500 cars and 100 coaches. Vehicles should follow signs A9 to Inverness on Perth City by-pass, then follow "Football Stadium" signs at Inveralmond Roundabout South onto slip road adjacent to McDiarmid Park. Vehicle charges are £1.00 for cars and £5.00 for coaches.

St. Mirren Park, Love Street,
Paisley, PA3 2EJ

CHAIRMAN
Robert Earlie

VICE-CHAIRMAN
William W. Waters, F.R.I.C.S.

HON. PRESIDENT
William Todd, M.B.E., J.P.

DIRECTORS
Allan W. Marshall, LL.B.
J. Yule Craig, J.P., C.A.
Charles G. Palmer
George P. Campbell
John F. Paton
Stewart G. Gilmour

SECRETARY
Jack Copland

MANAGER
Tony Fitzpatrick

CLUB DOCTOR
Stuart McCormick, M.B., Ch.B.

PHYSIOTHERAPIST
Andrew Binning, B.Sc., M.C.S.P.

CHIEF SCOUT
Joe Hughes

GROUNDSMAN
Tom Docherty

COMMERCIAL MANAGER
Peter Dallas
0141-840 1337

CATERING MANAGER
Mrs. Sally A. MacDonald

TELEPHONES
Ground 0141-889 2558/840 1337
Enquiries 0141-849 0661
Sports/Leisure Complex
0141-849 0609
Fax 0141-848 6444

CLUB SHOP
Situated at Ground
Open 10.30 a.m. – 2.30 p.m.
Mon to Fri
and 10.00 a.m. – 3.00 p.m.
on Saturdays

OFFICIAL SUPPORTERS CLUB
St. Mirren Supporters Club,
11 Knox Street, Paisley

TEAM CAPTAIN
Norman McWhirter

SHIRT SPONSOR
Phoenix Honda

ST. MIRREN

LIST OF PLAYERS 1996-97

SURNAME	FIRST NAME	MIDDLE NAME	DATE OF BIRTH	PLACE OF BIRTH	DATE OF SIGNING	HEIGHT FT INS	WEIGHT ST LBS	PREVIOUS CLUB
Archdeacon	Paul		11/10/76	Greenock	22/04/94	5 9.0	11 5	St. Mirren B.C.
Baker	Martin		08/06/74	Govan	16/09/92	6 0.0	10 12	St. Mirren B.C.
Combe	Alan		03/04/74	Edinburgh	07/08/93	6 1.0	12 2	Cowdenbeath
Dick	James		21/06/72	Bellshill	06/07/93	5 11.0	10 8	Airdrieonians
Fenwick	Paul	Joseph	25/08/69	London	13/10/95	6 2.0	12 7	Dunfermline Athletic
Fullarton	James		20/07/74	Bellshill	13/06/91	5 11.0	11 12	Motherwell B.C.
Gillies	Richard	Charles	24/08/76	Glasgow	12/12/92	5 10.0	11 0	St. Mirren B.C.
Hetherston	Brian		23/11/76	Bellshill	26/03/94	6 0.0	10 6	St. Mirren B.C.
Iwelumo	Christopher	Robert	01/08/78	Coatbridge	05/08/96	6 3.0	13 7	"S" Form
Love	Fraser		16/05/78	Motherwell	21/02/96	5 9.0	10 4	Giffnock North
McGuire	James		10/02/79	Paisley	13/08/96	5 10.0	10 2	St. Peters B.C.
McLaughlin	Barry	John	19/04/73	Paisley	01/08/91	6 1.0	12 7	St. Mirren B.C.
McWhirter	Norman		04/09/69	Johnstone	16/09/85	5 10.0	11 4	Linwood Rangers B.C.
Mendes	Junior	Albert	15/09/76	London	30/04/96	5 10.0	11 0	Chelsea
Pollock	Christopher	Jon	06/11/77	Kilwinning	04/08/95	5 8.0	10 12	Rangers
Prentice	Alan	Gilmour	18/11/77	Glasgow	21/02/96	6 0.0	10 4	Giffnock North
Scrimgour	Derek		29/03/78	Glasgow	06/09/95	6 3.0	12 7	Largs Thistle
Smith	Brian		26/10/76	Paisley	10/08/95	5 11.0	10 2	"S" Form
Taylor	Stuart		26/11/74	Glasgow	16/09/92	6 1.0	11 4	St. Mirren B.C.
Watson	Stephen		04/04/73	Liverpool	28/07/94	6 1.0	13 0	Rangers
Yardley	Mark		14/09/69	Livingston	22/09/95	6 2.0	13 1	Cowdenbeath

MILESTONES

YEAR OF FORMATION: 1877
MOST CAPPED PLAYERS: Iain Munro & Billy Thomson
NO. OF CAPS: 7
MOST LEAGUE POINTS IN A SEASON: 62 (Division 2 – Season 1967/68)
MOST LEAGUE GOALS SCORED BY A PLAYER IN A SEASON: Dunky Walker (Season 1921/22)
NO. OF GOALS SCORED: 45
RECORD ATTENDANCE: 47,438 (-v- Celtic 7.3.1925)
RECORD VICTORY: 15-0 (-v- Glasgow University – Scottish Cup, 30.1.1960)
RECORD DEFEAT: 0-9 (-v- Rangers – Division 1, 4.12.1897)

THE BUDDIES' TEN YEAR LEAGUE RECORD

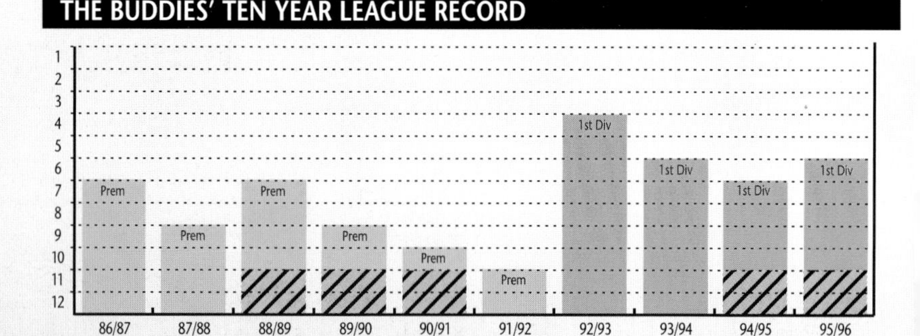

CLUB FACTFILE 1995/96
RESULTS... APPEARANCES... SCORERS

The BUDDIES

Date	Venue	Opponents	Att.	Res	Money C.	Dawson R.	Baker M.	McWhirter N.	Watson S.	McLaughlin B.	Law R.	Fullarton J.	Lavety B.	Bone A.	Boyd J.	Taylor S.	Gillies R.	Combe A.	Dick J.	McGrotty G.	Hetherston B.	McIntyre P.	Smith B.	Archdeacon P.	Inglis G.	Yardley M.	Fenwick P.	Makela J.	Prentice A.	Scrimgour D.	McMillan J.	Iwelumo C.	Hringsson H.	Milne D.	Galloway G.	Love F.
Aug 12	A	Clydebank	1,886	1-1	1	2	3	4	5	6	7	8^{1}	9	10	11	12	14																			
26	H	St. Johnstone	2,430	0-0		2	3		5	6	7	8	9	10	11	4	15	1	12	14																
Sep 2	A	Airdrieonians	2,142	2-1		2	3		5	6	7	8	15^{1}	10^{1}	11	4	9	1	12		14															
9	A	Dundee United	6,159	0-1		2	3		5	6	7	8	10	15	12	4	9	1	11		14															
16	H	Dunfermline Athletic	3,479	0-2		2	3		5		4	10	9		11	8	7	1				6	12	14	15											
23	A	Hamilton Academical	1,451	2-2		2	3		5		7				11^{1}	4	10	1	8	16		6				9^{1}										
30	H	Greenock Morton	5,436	1-4		2	3		5	6	4	8			11^{1}	12	10	1	7	15						9										
Oct 7	A	Dundee	3,555	1-3		2			5	6	3				11^{1}		10	1			7	8	4	14		9										
14	H	Dumbarton	2,377	3-2					5	6				15	11		14	1	10^{1}	7	8	2	12	3^{1}		9^{1}	4									
21	H	Airdrieonians	2,459	1-2					5	6	12					11^{1}	7	1	10		8	14		3		9	4	2								
28	A	St. Johnstone	3,028	0-0					5	6	7					11	10	1	8		14	2	12	3		9	4									
Nov 4	A	Dunfermline Athletic	4,578	†1-1					5	6	7		15				10	1	8		11	2	12	3		9	4		14							
11	H	Dundee United	3,556	1-1			3		5	6	7		10				8^{1}	1		15	14	2	12	11		9	4									
18	A	Greenock Morton	6,217	3-0			3			6	7		10^{1}		14	5	8			15	12	2		11		9^{2}	4			1						
25	H	Hamilton Academical	2,546	0-3			3		12	6	5		10		11	14	8			7		2		15		9	4			1						
Dec 2	H	Dundee	2,278	1-2	1		3			6			10^{1}			5	8		7	15	11	2		14		9	4									
9	A	Dumbarton	1,461	0-0	1		3			6		14	10			12	8		5	7	11	2				9	4				15					
16	H	Clydebank	1,828	2-1	1		3	4	14			6	10			12	8		7^{1}		11	2				9^{1}	5				15					
Jan 6	H	Dunfermline Athletic	3,380	2-1	1		3	4	12		14	6	10				8^{1}		7		11^{1}	2				9	5									
13	A	Dundee United	6,523	1-2			3	4	11	5	8	6	10^{1}				14	1	7		12	2				9					15					
16	A	Airdrieonians	1,554	3-1	1		3	4	14	5	12	6	10				8		7		11^{1}	2				9^{2}					15					
20	A	Dundee	2,698	2-1	1		3	4	14	8	12	6^{1}	10						7		11	2				9	5				15^{1}					
24	A	Hamilton Academical	1,531	0-3			3	4	14	8		6	10				12	1	7		11	2				9	5				15					
31	H	Greenock Morton	5,312	0-1	1		3	4	14	12	2		10				8		7				6	11		9	5				15					
Feb 3	H	Dumbarton	1,838	5-0	1		3	4	12^{1}				10^{2}				8		7	14	11		2	6		9	5^{1}					15^{1}				
10	A	Clydebank	1,515	2-1	1		3	4	11		12		10				8^{1}		7				2	6		9	5^{1}					15				
24	H	St. Johnstone	2,568	1-3	1			4	3	7		6	10			14	8				11	12	2			9^{1}	5				15					
Mar 2	H	Hamilton Academical	1,243	0-1	1			4	3	7		6	10			11	8					12	2			9	5						14			
16	A	Greenock Morton	4,204	2-1				4		2^{1}		6	10^{1}		3	14	8	1			11	15		7		9	5									
23	A	Dunfermline Athletic	4,936	2-2				4		2		6	10^{2}		3	14	8	1			11	15		7		9	5									
30	H	Dundee United	4,347	1-3						2^{1}		6	10		3	14	8	1	9		11	4	12	7			5					15				
Apr 6	H	Dundee	2,175	2-1			3	4	14	2			10			6^{1}	8	1	7			12		11			5^{1}					9		15		
13	A	Dumbarton	1,139	1-0			3	4	14	2		12				6	8	1	7					11^{1}		9	5					10		15		
20	H	Airdrieonians	2,117	2-1			3	4	14	2		12	10^{1}			6^{1}	8	1	7					11		9	5							15		
27	A	St. Johnstone	3,687	0-1			3		12	2		8	10			6		1	7		15	4		11		9	5							14		
May 4	H	Clydebank	1,657	1-2			3		11	2		6	10^{1}			14			7							9	5		15	1				8	4	12
TOTAL FULL APPEARANCES					12	8	26	17	18	29	15	19	27	3	12	14	28	21	24	3	16	19	6	16		29	26	1		3		2		1	1	
TOTAL SUB APPEARANCES									(12)	(1)	(5)	(3)	(2)	(2)	(2)	(10)	(5)		(2)	(7)	(7)	(6)	(6)	(4)	(1)				(2)		(8)	(3)	(1)	(4)		(1)
TOTAL GOALS SCORED									1	2		2	11	1	3	3	3		2		2			2		8	3				1	1				

Small bold figures denote goalscorers. † denotes opponent's own goal.

ST. MIRREN PARK

CAPACITY: 15,410; Seated 9,395, Standing 6,015

PITCH DIMENSIONS: 112 yds x 73 yds

FACILITIES FOR DISABLED SUPPORTERS: Full wheelchair facilities available for visiting supporters in the West Stand.

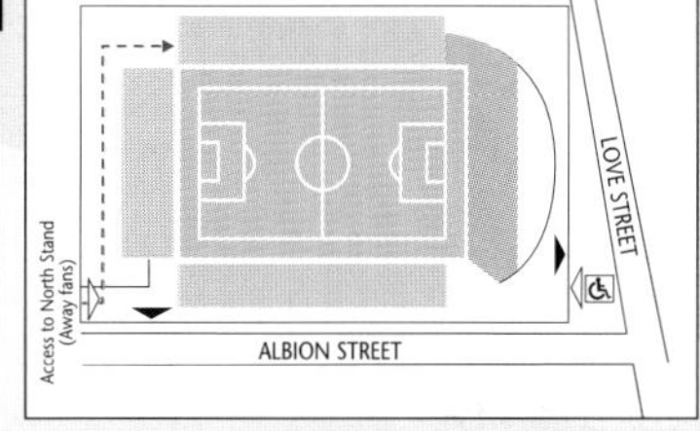

HOW TO GET THERE

St. Mirren Park can be reached by the following routes:

TRAINS: There is a frequent train service from Glasgow Central Station and all coastal routes pass through Gilmour Street. The ground is about 400 yards from the station.

BUSES: All SMT coastal services, plus buses to Johnstone and Kilbarchan, pass within 300 yards of the ground.

CARS: The only facilities for car parking are in the streets surrounding the ground.

STIRLING ALBION

Forthbank Stadium, Springkerse,
Stirling, FK7 7UJ

CHAIRMAN
Peter McKenzie

VICE-CHAIRMAN
Peter Gardiner, C.A.

DIRECTORS
Duncan B. MacGregor
John L. Smith

SECRETARY
Mrs. Marlyn Hallam

MANAGER
Kevin Drinkell

ASSISTANT MANAGER/YOUTH DEVELOPMENT OFFICER
Ray Stewart

CLUB DOCTOR
Dr. Duncan B. MacGregor

PHYSIOTHERAPIST
George Cameron

ASSISTANT PHYSIOTHERAPIST
Danny Cunning

GROUND MAINTENANCE
Souters of Stirling

COMMERCIAL MANAGER
Mrs. Marlyn Hallam

KIT MAN
Alan Grieve

TELEPHONES
Ground/Commercial/Ticket Office
(01786) 450399
Sec. Home (01786) 816274
Fax (01786) 448592

CLUB SHOP
Situated at Forthbank Stadium
Open Mon. – Fri. and
Home Match Days.

OFFICIAL SUPPORTERS CLUB
Stephen Torrance, Secretary,
Forthbank Stadium, Springkerse,
Stirling, FK7 7UJ

TEAM CAPTAIN
Thomas Tait

SHIRT SPONSOR
McKenzie Trailers

LIST OF PLAYERS 1996-97

SURNAME	FIRST	MIDDLE	DATE OF	PLACE OF	DATE OF	HEIGHT	WEIGHT	PREVIOUS CLUB
Armstrong	Paul		27/10/65	Glasgow	25/07/91	5 11.0	11 6	Cork City
Bennett	John	Neil	22/08/71	Falkirk	26/02/96	5 7.0	10 0	Alloa
Bone	Alexander	Syme Frew	26/02/71	Stirling	19/10/95	5 9.0	10 7	St. Mirren
Buist	Mark		13/09/75	Kirkcaldy	16/08/96	6 0.0	11 12	Raith Rovers
Deas	Paul	Andrew	22/02/72	Perth	10/03/95	5 11.0	11 7	St. Johnstone
Forrest	Edward	Alexander	17/12/78	Edinburgh	20/07/96	6 0.0	10 10	Stirling Albion Youth
Gibson	John		20/04/67	Blantyre	26/11/93	5 10.0	10 5	Alloa
Jack	Stephen	J.	27/03/71	Bellshill	08/08/96	5 11.0	10 0	Clydebank
Kirkham	David	Gordon	20/10/73	Falkirk	07/10/95	6 1.0	11 0	Alloa
McCormick	Stephen		14/08/69	Dumbarton	07/07/95	6 4.0	11 4	Queen's Park
McGeown	Mark		10/05/70	Paisley	13/10/88	5 10.5	11 6	Blantyre Victoria
McGrotty	Gary		26/09/76	Glasgow	29/03/96	5 6.0	8 10	St. Mirren
McInnes	Ian		22/03/67	Hamilton	09/08/90	5 8.0	10 5	Stranraer
McLeod	Joseph		30/12/67	Edinburgh	09/12/93	5 7.0	11 3	Portadown
McQuilter	Ronald		24/12/70	Glasgow	24/12/93	6 1.0	12 2	Ayr United
Mitchell	Colin		25/05/65	Bellshill	28/07/88	5 10.0	12 8	Airdrieonians
Monaghan	Michael	Joseph	28/06/63	Glasgow	22/02/94	6 1.0	15 2	Dumbarton
Mortimer	Paul		14/02/80	Falkirk	20/07/96	5 11.0	10 9	Denny F.C. U'16s
Mullen	Martynn		23/05/78	Glasgow	09/08/96	5 10.0	11 0	St. Johnstone
Paterson	Andrew		05/05/72	Glasgow	26/08/94	5 9.0	11 3	St. Mirren
Paterson	Garry		10/11/69	Dunfermline	07/03/95	6 5.0	15 1	Dunfermline Athletic
Stewart	Raymond	Straun McD.	07/09/59	Stanley	26/08/94	5 11.0	12 2	St. Johnstone
Taggart	Craig		17/01/73	Glasgow	12/08/94	5 9.0	11 6	Falkirk
Tait	Thomas		08/09/67	Ayr	12/09/92	5 10.5	12 7	Kilmarnock
Watson	Paul		16/07/68	Bellshill	08/12/90	6 0.0	12 6	Thorniewood United
Wood	David	Wilson	30/12/75	Broxburn	20/10/95	5 9.5	11 2	Partick Thistle

MILESTONES

YEAR OF FORMATION: 1945
MOST LEAGUE POINTS IN A SEASON: 59 (Division 2 – Season 1964/65)(2 Points for a Win)
81 (Second Division – Season 1995/96)(3 Points for a Win)
MOST LEAGUE GOALS SCORED BY A PLAYER IN A SEASON: Joe Hughes (Season 1969/70)
NO. OF GOALS SCORED: 26
RECORD ATTENDANCE: 26,400 (-v- Celtic – Scottish Cup, 11.3.1959)
RECORD VICTORY: 20-0 (-v- Selkirk – Scottish Cup, 8.12.1984)
RECORD DEFEAT: 0-9 (-v- Dundee United – League, 30.12.1967)

THE ALBION'S TEN YEAR LEAGUE RECORD

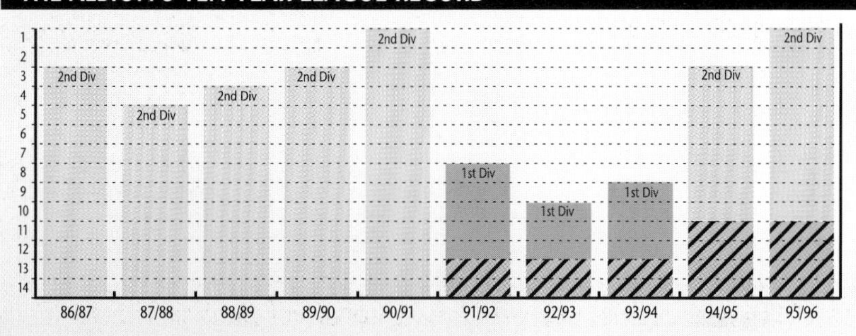

CLUB FACTFILE 1995/96
RESULTS... APPEARANCES... SCORERS

The ALBION

Date	Venue	Opponents	Att.	Res	McGeown M.	McKechnie M.	Watson P.	Mitchell C.	McQuilter R.	Tait T.	McInnes I.	Deas P.	McCormick S.	Taggart C.	McLeod J.	Farquhar A.	Gibson J.	Paterson A.	Roberts P.	Watters W.	Monaghan M.	Kirkham D.	Bone A.	Wood D.	Paterson G.	Bennett N.	McGrotty G.
Aug 12	H	Montrose	752	3-0	1	2	3	4^{1}	5	6^{1}	7	8	9^{1}	10	11	14											
26	A	Berwick Rangers	434	0-3	1	2	3	4	5	6	7	8	9	10	11	14											
Sep 2	H	East Fife	942	0-2	1	2	3	4	5	6	7	8	9	10	11	14	12										
9	A	Stenhousemuir	674	1-1	1		3^{1}	4	5	6	7	8	9	10	11			2	14								
16	H	Ayr United	760	2-0	1		3	4	5	6	7	8	9	10^{1}			11^{1}	2									
23	A	Stranraer	658	0-0	1			4	5	6	7	8	9	10	11		3	2		14							
30	H	Clyde	1,011	1-1				4	5	6	7	8	9	10^{1}	11		3	2		14	1						
Oct 7	A	Forfar Athletic	624	6-0			12	4	5	6	7^{2}	8	9^{3}	10^{1}	11		3	2	15		1	14					
14	H	Queen of the South	748	2-2			12	4	5	6^{1}	7	8	9	10	11^{1}		3	2	14		1						
21	A	Montrose	629	2-2			12	4	5^{1}	6		3	9	10			8	2			1		7^{1}	11			
28	H	Berwick Rangers	811	1-0				4	5			3	9^{1}	10			8	2			1	14	7	11	6		
Nov 4	A	Ayr United	1,233	2-1				4	5		14	3	9	10			8^{1}	2			1		7	11^{1}	6		
11	H	Stenhousemuir	903	2-1				4	5		10^{1}	3	9				8	2			1		7^{1}	11	6		
18	A	Clyde	1,200	2-1				4	5		10	3	9^{1}	14^{1}			8	2			1		7	11	6		
25	H	Stranraer	811	1-1				4	5		10	3	9	14			8	2			1		7^{1}	11	6		
Dec 2	H	Forfar Athletic	734	4-1	1			4	5^{1}		8^{1}	3	9^{2}	10	14		12	2					7	11	6		
16	A	Queen of the South	1,004	5-1	1			4	5		8	3	9^{3}	10	14			2					7^{1}	11	6^{1}		
23	H	Montrose	1,056	2-0	1			4	5		8	3	9^{2}	10	14			2					7	11	6		
Jan 13	A	Stranraer	587	2-2	1			4	5	8		3	9	10			11	2					7^{1}		6^{1}		
17	A	East Fife	1,529	3-0	1			4	5	8		3	9	10^{1}	11			2					7^{1}		6^{1}		
20	A	Forfar Athletic	611	4-1	1			4	5	8		3	9^{1}	10^{1}	11^{1}			2					7^{1}		6		
24	H	Clyde	1,068	3-0	1			4	5	8^{1}		3	9	10	11		12	2					7^{2}		6		
Feb 3	H	Queen of the South	1,042	4-1	1			4	5	8		3	9^{3}	10^{1}	11		12	2					7		6		
14	H	Ayr United	834	2-0	1			4	5	8		3	9^{1}	10	11		12	2					7^{1}		6		
24	A	Berwick Rangers	483	3-0	1			4	5	8		3	9^{2}	10	11		12	2					7^{1}		6		
27	A	Stenhousemuir	864	1-0	1			4	5	8		3	9	10			12^{1}	2					7	11	6	14	
Mar 2	H	East Fife	1,166	2-2	1			4	5^{1}	8		3	9^{1}	10	11		12	2					7	14	6		
9	H	Stranraer	1,023	2-0	1			4	5	8^{1}		3	9^{1}	10	11		12	2					7		6	14	
16	A	Clyde	1,183	3-1	1			4^{1}	5	8		3	9^{1}	10	11		12	2					7^{1}		6		
23	A	Ayr United	1,732	2-2	1			4	5	8^{1}		3	9^{1}	10	11		12	2					7		6		
30	H	Stenhousemuir	1,132	0-1	1			4	5	8		3		10	11		9	2					7		6	14	12
Apr 6	H	Forfar Athletic	788	1-0	1			12	5	8		3		10	11		4	2					7	15^{1}	6	14	9
13	A	Queen of the South	1,394	7-0	1			12	5	8^{1}		3		10	11		4^{2}	2					7^{3}	15	6^{1}	14	9
20	A	Montrose	824	†3-0	1			14	5	8		3	9	10^{1}	11		4	2					7^{1}		6	12	15
27	H	Berwick Rangers	1,238	4-3	1			14	5	8^{1}		3	9^{1}	10	11		4^{1}	2					7^{1}		6	12	15
May 4	A	East Fife	1,185	1-0				5		8			9	10			4	2			1		7^{1}	11	6	3	15
TOTAL FULL APPEARANCES					26	3	5	32	35	28	15	35	33	33	23		18	33			10		27	11	26	1	2
TOTAL SUB APPEARANCES							(3)	(4)			(1)			(2)	(3)	(3)	(11)		(3)	(2)		(2)		(3)		(7)	(4)
TOTAL GOALS SCORED							1	2	3	7	4		25	8	2		6						18	2	4		

Small bold figures denote goalscorers. † denotes opponent's own goal.

FORTHBANK STADIUM

CAPACITY: 3,808, Seated 2,508, Standing 1,300

PITCH DIMENSIONS: 110 yds x 74 yds

FACILITIES FOR DISABLED SUPPORTERS: Disabled access, toilets and spaces for 36.

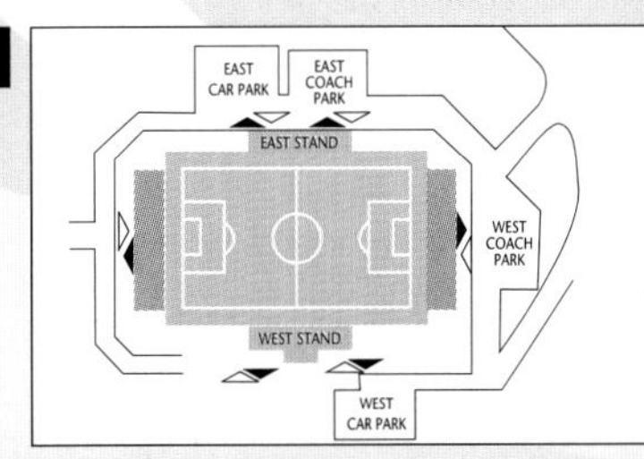

HOW TO GET THERE

Forthbank Stadium can be reached by the following routes.

TRAINS: The nearest station is Stirling Railway Station, which is approximately 2 miles from the ground. A bus service from Goosecroft Road travels to the stadium (buses run every 25 minutes from 1.50 p.m. – 2.40 p.m. and returns to town at 4.50 p.m.).

BUSES: To Goosecroft Bus Station, Stirling, and bus to stadium from Goosecroft Road (outside Bus Station) every 25 minutes from 1.50 p.m. – 2.40 p.m. and return to town at 4.50 p.m.

CARS: Follow signs for A91 St Andrews/Alloa. Car Parking is available in the club car park. Home support in West Car Park and visiting support in East Car Park.

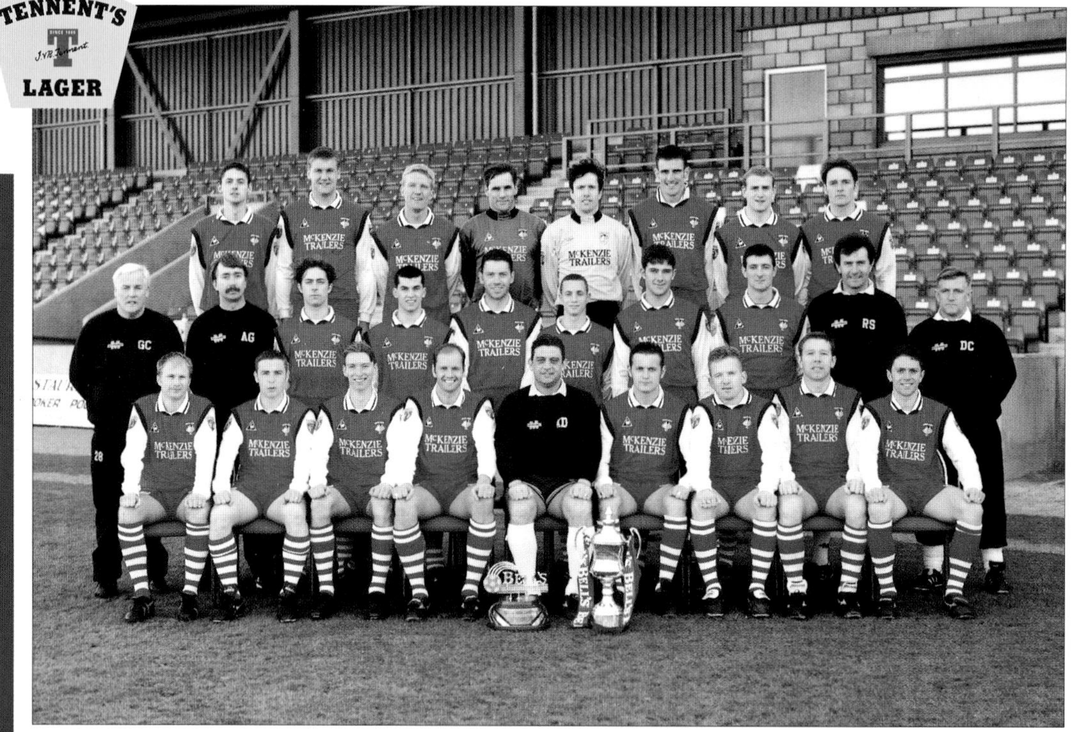

Stirling Albion – Bell's Second Division Champions 1995/96

BELL'S LEAGUE DIVISION 2

A Stirling Performance

Stirling Albion manager, Kevin Drinkell, knew as the 1995/96 season beckoned that he had a prolific scoring side. The Forthbank manager had seen Stirling come desperately close to gaining promotion the previous season and the pressure was on him and his players to go one better this time around.

That led him to laying down a target to be aimed at in the ensuing months and he told his players, "Continue the prolific rate of goalscoring and match it with the number of points gained, and that will get us promotion out of the Second Division."

But even Drinkell could not have expected the positive reaction he was to receive with Stirling Albion scoring 83 League goals and gaining 81 points which saw them earn not only promotion but the Bell's Second Division Championship by a clear 14 point margin from second placed East Fife, who also stepped up with them to the First Division.

Admitted Drinkell, "It was a stuttering start. We were busily engaged in pre-season games, then cup-ties and League matches and felt we had done well. Yet when we sat down to look at the results, we realised after those first few weeks that we had lost two out of the first three of our opening League games. But we restored that early damage by losing only one of our next 33 matches.

"The year before when we narrowly missed promotion, we had been caught out late in games by losing last minute goals. But I had put that down to a lack of belief in ourselves. This time around, we did have that belief and killer instinct and we worked hard as a group.

"If we had the ball we attacked, people went into wide positions and we looked to score at every opportunity.

"If we lost the ball, everyone was expected to defend and that was underlined by the sight of our leading goalscorer, Steve McCormick, battling for possession."

Shrewdly, during the season, Drinkell entered into the transfer market to sign striker Alex Bone, a local lad, from St. Mirren and his combative style of non-stop action combined with the goalscoring ability of McCormick proved a lethal combination.

At one stage, Bone remarked, "I know if I can get the ball into the penalty area, Steve will hit the target."

In the end, McCormick collected 25 League goals to provide the proof that this statement was correct.

However, the Second Division scene did not wholly revolve around Stirling Albion. Former Scotland international, Steve Archibald, who had been successful in a playing career which stretched from Scotland into England and then Spain, earned the plaudits as he guided the Fifers to the First Division.

Archibald moulded a team full of experience, with Jock McStay providing a steadying influence in defence. Indeed, Archibald also revealed his own "superstar" in Arnold Dwarika from the quaintly named Superstar Rangers of Trinidad.

While Stirling Albion and East Fife eventually emerged as promotion winners, neither was able to relax, for the chasing Berwick Rangers and Stenhousemuir kept the pressure on them until the last quarter of the season.

Indeed, Drinkell paid tribute to Berwick when he remarked, "At one time, I thought they were out of it, but then they came back strongly and we realised we could not relax!"

That was all the more surprising as the Shielfield club had lost manager, Tom Hendrie, and his assistant, John Coughlin, who decided that a better future lay elsewhere and dropped a division to take over at Alloa.

Hendrie had devised the style of play associated with Berwick by giving his players specific instructions of their duties in each match and it was to both his credit and that of his successor, Ian Ross, that the Shielfield club continued to operate successfully and keep alive their hopes of promotion virtually until the end of the season.

Stenhousemuir, too, kept the pressure on in the League race until the last few weeks, when their manager, Terry Christie, had to admit, "Tiredness took over. Some of our players are getting on in years and, being part-time, they may have just had too many games."

That was not a surprise, for the Larbert club had exceeded all expectations by winning the League Challenge Cup, defeating the full-time Dundee and even more sensationally, Dundee United in a penalty shoot-out in the Final at McDiarmid Park, and had also come out triumphant in their Tennents Scottish Cup tie against Premier Division neighbours Falkirk.

Ironically, Eamonn Bannon, in the

Steve McCormick (Stirling Albion)

twilight of a distinguished playing career, was part of their defence and he has since taken over as manager of Falkirk. But Bannon and Archibald were not the only big name personalities in the Second Division who had seen life at the top. Former Scotland, Celtic, Arsenal and Aberdeen star, Charlie Nicholas, was continuing to show his undoubted skills at Clyde, but probably, in hindsight, had mixed feelings about the season. The midfielder was the focus of attention in a live televised Tennents Scottish Cup tie that was shown throughout the United Kingdom, as Clyde, for 60 minutes, threatened a major upset against the mighty Rangers. But in the League, Clyde never got going and it was a disappointment for manager Alex Smith that his side did not mount a serious challenge for promotion.

That disappointment was more seriously mirrored by Forfar manager, Tommy Campbell, as his players fought valiantly but failed to halt a slide back into the Third Division.

Elsewhere, the managerial heads were falling as an indication of the pressure for success at every level of the senior game increasingly became apparent. The ebullient Simon Stainrod gave way to former Rangers, Manchester City and Raith Rovers striker, Gordon Dalziel, who took over at Ayr and faced a lengthy period of worry before leading the Somerset Park side out of the relegation area.

Stranraer's long-serving manager, Alex McAnespie, was shattered when he learned that he was being discarded and was subsequently replaced by the former Scotland and St. Mirren goalkeeper, Campbell Money. He immediately experienced the intense pressure in the hot seat for he was sent to the stand by the referee for comments he made during his first game in charge!

"I'll be more careful in the future. It was my first game in charge and I reacted too intensely," pleaded the repentant Money.

Queen of the South decided on co-managers after parting company with Billy McLaren, with the experienced striker, Rowan Alexander, and Mark Shanks, an SFA community coach in the Dumfries area, sharing the dual role. The ambitious Doonhamers intend to build the nucleus of their squad from youth and they offered full-time contracts to a number of teenage players linking their football training with their education.

Relegated Montrose parted company with manager Andy Dornan as their fate became clear and replaced him with Dave Smith, who had enjoyed much success in charge at Whitehill Welfare, including a spirited showing against Celtic in the Tennents Scottish Cup during the course of last season and they will look to him to restore confidence in the Gable Endies in their quest to a quick return to the Second Division.

BILL MARWICK
(Freelance)

Charlie Nicholas (Clyde)

AYR UNITED

Somerset Park, Tryfield Place,
Ayr, KA8 9NB

CHAIRMAN
William J. Barr, OBE,
C. Eng., F.I.C.E., F.I.Mgt

VICE-CHAIRMAN
Donald R. Cameron

DIRECTORS
Donald McK. MacIntyre
George H. Smith
John E. Eyley, B.A., A.C.M.A.
Kenneth W. MacLeod, A.R.I.C.S
Roy G. Kennedy

SECRETARY
John E. Eyley, B.A., A.C.M.A.

ADMINISTRATOR
Brian Caldwell

PLAYER/MANAGER
Gordon Dalziel

ASSISTANT MANAGER
Alistair Dawson

COACH
Michael Oliver

CLUB DOCTOR
Dr. John A.M. Hannah, B.Sc (Hons)
M.B.Ch.B., M.R.C.G.P., D.R.C.O.G.

CROWD DOCTOR
Dr. Robert Paterson, M.B., CH.B.

PHYSIOTHERAPIST
John Kerr, L.V.M.C. Inst. of H.T.

GROUNDSMAN
David Harkness

SALES & MARKETING EXECUTIVE
Mrs Angela Smith

LOTTERY MANAGER
Andrew Downie

TELEPHONES
Ground/Ticket Office/
Sales & Marketing
(01292) 263435
Fax (01292) 281314

CLUB SHOP
Ayr United Enterprises, Tryfield Place,
Ayr, KA8 9NB. (01292) 263435.
Open 8.30 a.m.-5.30 p.m. Mon-Fri
and 10.00 a.m.-3.00 p.m. on all first
team matchdays.

OFFICIAL SUPPORTERS CLUB
c/o Ayr United F.C., Somerset Park,
Ayr, KA8 9NB

TEAM CAPTAIN
Ronald Coyle

SHIRT SPONSOR
Ayrshire Post

LIST OF PLAYERS 1996-97

SURNAME	FIRST NAME	MIDDLE NAME	DATE OF BIRTH	PLACE OF BIRTH	DATE OF SIGNING	HEIGHT FT INS	WEIGHT ST LBS	PREVIOUS CLUB
Bell	Robert		11/03/76	Springburn	29/03/96	5 9.5	10 12	Aberdeen
Biggart	Kevin		10/11/73	Kilmarnock	13/01/94	5 8.5	11 1	Dundee United
Burns	Gordon		02/12/78	Glasgow	22/05/96	6 1.0	11 6	"S" Form
Cameron	Justin		07/11/77	Edinburgh	05/07/96	6 1.0	13 0	Wimbledon
Connor	Robert		04/08/60	Kilmarnock	02/07/96	5 11.0	11 4	Kilmarnock
Coyle	Ronald		04/08/64	Glasgow	22/03/96	5 11.0	12 9	Raith Rovers
Dalziel	Gordon		16/03/62	Motherwell	09/08/95	5 10.5	10 13	Raith Rovers
English	Isaac		12/11/71	Paisley	16/03/96	5 9.0	10 11	St. Johnstone
George	Duncan	Henry	04/12/67	Paisley	29/03/91	5 10.0	10 7	Stranraer
Henderson	Darren		12/10/66	Kilmarnock	23/02/96	5 11.0	11 0	Stranraer
Hewitt	Scott		13/03/78	Oldham	20/06/96	5 9.0	11 1	Blackburn Rovers
Hood	Gregg		29/05/74	Bellshill	01/07/91	6 0.0	12 7	Ayr United B.C.
Jamieson	William	George	27/04/63	Barnsley	21/11/95	5 11.0	12 0	Heart of Midlothian
Kerrigan	Steven	John	09/10/72	Bellshill	25/06/96	6 0.0	11 8	Stranraer
Kinnaird	Paul		11/11/66	Glasgow	20/12/95	5 8.0	11 11	Scarborough
Law	Robert	Shearer	24/12/65	Bellshill	29/03/96	5 9.5	11 12	St. Mirren
McCulloch	William		02/04/73	Baillieston	02/08/96	6 6.0	12 6	Airdrieonians
Mercer	James		30/07/74	Glasgow	23/07/96	6 5.0	13 7	Campsie Black Watch
Smith	Colin		17/11/74	Glasgow	22/07/96	5 11.0	11 0	Campsie Black Watch
Smith	Henry	George	10/03/56	Lanark	26/01/96	6 2.0	13 2	Heart of Midlothian
Smith	Paul	McKinnon	02/11/62	Edinburgh	17/07/96	5 11.0	12 0	Heart of Midlothian
Stewart	David		14/08/78	Irvine	22/05/96	6 1.0	12 2	"S" Form
Taylor	Philip	Matthew	09/11/77	Salford	20/06/96	5 8.0	10 2	Blackburn Rovers
Traynor	John	Francis C.	10/12/66	Glasgow	07/11/91	5 10.0	11 0	Clydebank
Wilson	William	Stewart	19/08/72	Glasgow	17/10/95	5 3.0	10 0	Kirkintilloch Rob Roy

MILESTONES

YEAR OF FORMATION: 1910
MOST CAPPED PLAYER: Jim Nisbett
NO. OF CAPS: 3
MOST LEAGUE POINTS IN A SEASON: 61 (Second Division – Season 1987/88)
MOST LEAGUE GOALS SCORED BY A PLAYER IN A SEASON: Jimmy Smith (Season 1927/28)
NO. OF GOALS SCORED: 66
RECORD ATTENDANCE: 25,225 (-v- Rangers – 13.9.1969)
RECORD VICTORY: 11-1 (-v- Dumbarton – League Cup, 13.8.1952)
RECORD DEFEAT: 0-9 (-v- Rangers, Heart of Midlothian, Third Lanark – Division 1)

THE HONEST MEN'S TEN YEAR LEAGUE RECORD

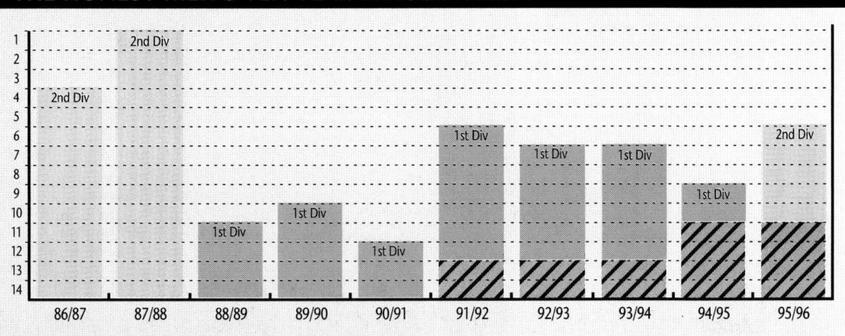

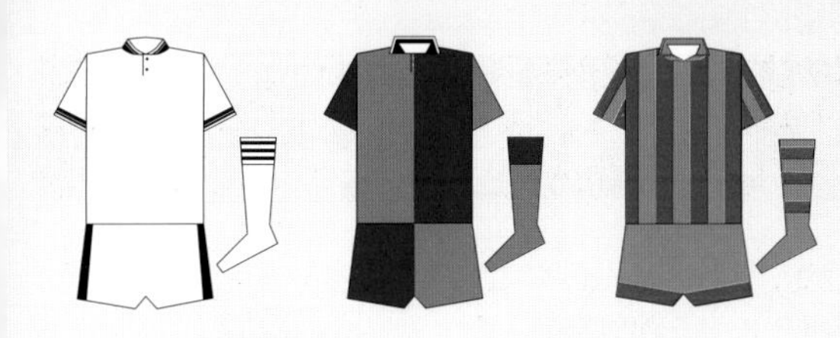

CLUB FACTFILE 1995/96

RESULTS... APPEARANCES... SCORERS

The HONEST MEN

Date	Venue	Opponents	Att.	Res	Lamont W.	Biggart K.	Boyce D.	George D.	Rolling F.	Sharples J.	Shepherd A.	Dalziel G.	Wilson S.	Stainrod S.	Moore V.	MacFarlane C.	Bilsland B.	Tannock R.	Byrne D.	Traynor J.	McKilligan N.	Chalmers P.	Connie C.	Agnew S.	Connolly S.	Duncan C.	Yule R.	Wilson W.	Smith M.	Hood G.	Clarke J.	Mooney S.	Steel T.	Balfour E.	Jamieson W.	Barnstaple K.	Napier C.	Scott M.	Kinnaird P.	Smith H.	Paavoli T.	Henderson D.	Diver D.	English I.	Coyle R.	Law R.	Bell R.	Nolan J.	Burns G.
Aug 12	H	Clyde	1,963	1-1	1	2	3	4	5	6	7	8	9	10	11[1]	12	14																																
26	A	East Fife	684	0-1	1	12	3		5	6	7	8	10			4	9	2	11																														
Sep 2	H	Berwick Rangers	1,221	1-4	1		3			6[1]	4	10	9	8	7	14	12	11	2	5	16																												
9	H	Forfar Athletic	1,152	1-3	1	16	3				7	8[1]	9					6	2	4	14	5	10	11	12																								
16	A	Stirling Albion	760	0-2		3						8			4		7	6	2	5	12	9	10	11		1																							
23	A	Montrose	409	1-0		3						8	11		6		14	4	7	5	2	9[1]	10			1																							
30	H	Stranraer	1,455	0-0		3		12				8	7					6	4	5	2	11	10	14		1	9																						
Oct 7	A	Queen of the South	1,147	0-0		12		11		5	7	8			10		14	6	2	4	3	9				1																							
14	H	Stenhousemuir	1,106	1-2		14				5	7	8	16		10		9	6	2	4	3					1	12	11[1]																					
21	A	Clyde	1,125	2-1				7		5	8				10[1]		9[1]	6		4	3		14			1		2	11	16																			
28	H	East Fife	1,278	0-1		12		7		5	8				10		9	6		4	3		14			1		2	11																				
Nov 4	H	Stirling Albion	1,233	1-2		3		7		6	14	12			8	5	9[1]			4	2		10			1			11																				
11	A	Forfar Athletic	534	1-2				7[1]		6	4	12			8	5	9			2						1		14	11		3	10																	
18	A	Stranraer	891	0-2				8		5	4				11		14	6		2						1			9		3		7	10															
25	H	Montrose	1,166	2-0				10		6		9[2]					7	14	12	3						1			11		2		4	8	5														
Dec 2	H	Queen of the South	1,434	2-0				10		6		9					7	14	12	3						1			11[1]		2		4[1]	8	5	15													
16	A	Stenhousemuir	525	1-1		14		10		6		9[1]					7	2		3			12			1			11				4	8	5														
Jan 13	A	Montrose	587	1-0		12		7		6		10					8[1]													4	2		14		5	1	3	9	11										
16	A	Berwick Rangers	355	2-2				7		6		12					8[1]													4	2		14	10[1]	5	1	3	9	11										
20	A	Queen of the South	1,264	2-2				7		6[1]		12					8			14						1				4[1]			2	10	5		3	9	11										
27	H	Stranraer	1,919	0-0		14		7		6		9					12													4			2	10	5		3	8	11	1									
Feb 3	H	Stenhousemuir	1,181	1-1				7		6		8					9[1]			12										4			2		5		3	10	11	1									
14	A	Stirling Albion	834	0-2		14		7		6		8					9			10										4	3		2		5	15		11	12	1									
24	A	East Fife	834	1-1				7		6													8			1				4			2		5		3		11		9	10[1]							
27	H	Clyde	1,378	2-1		14		7		6[1]													8			1				4[1]	12		2		5		3		11		9	10							
Mar 2	H	Berwick Rangers	907	5-0		14				6		12											3			1				4				7	5	15	2		11		9[2]	10	8[3]						
5	H	Forfar Athletic	1,322	1-1		2				6		12											10			1				4				7	5		3		11[1]			9	8						
9	H	Montrose	1,326	2-0		12		7		6													3			1				4				14	5		2	9	11[1]			10	8[1]						
16	A	Stranraer	806	1-1		2		7		6																1				4	14		12	10	5				11			3[1]	8	9					
23	H	Stirling Albion	1,732	2-2		3		7		6[1]																1				2			14	10	5				11				8	9[1]	4				
30	A	Forfar Athletic	442	0-1		12		7												14								2		6			15	10	5					1			8	9	4	3	11		
Apr 6	H	Queen of the South	1,764	3-0				7				14								6								2		4					5[1]				11	1		10	8	9[2]		3	12		
13	A	Stenhousemuir	559	1-0		3		7												5								2	14	4				12					11	1		10[1]	8	9		6			
20	A	Clyde	1,075	0-2		12														5								2	14	6									11	1		10	8	9	4	3	7		
27	H	East Fife	1,304	1-0		14														12					8			2		6					5				11	1		10		9[1]	4	3	7		
May 4	A	Berwick Rangers	681	1-2		15							7							6								2		4					5				14	1		10		9[1]		3	11	8	12
TOTAL FULL APPEARANCES					4	9	4	24	2	26	10	16	7	2	11	3	15	12	8	20	7	5	10	2	1	21	1	9	8	19	7	1	10	12	20	2	10	7	16	9	3	11	9	8	4	6	4	1	
TOTAL SUB APPEARANCES						(16)		(1)			(1)	(7)	(1)			(2)	(6)	(2)	(2)	(4)	(3)		(3)	(1)	(1)		(1)	(1)	(2)	(1)	(2)		(5)	(2)		(3)			(2)								(1)		(1)
TOTAL GOALS SCORED								1		4		4			2		5					1						1	1	2			1	1	1				2		2	3	4	5					

Small bold figures denote goalscorers. † denotes opponent's own goal.

SOMERSET PARK

CAPACITY: 12,128; Seated 1,450, Standing 10,678

PITCH DIMENSIONS: 110 yds x 72 yds

FACILITIES FOR DISABLED SUPPORTERS: Enclosure and toilet facilities for wheelchairs. Match commentary available for blind persons at all first team matches.

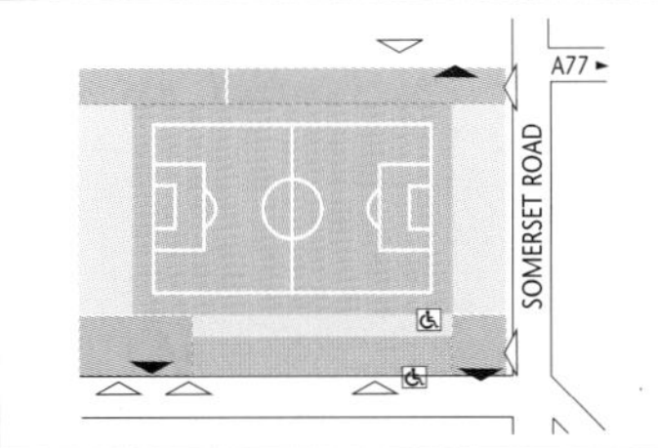

HOW TO GET THERE

Somerset Park can be reached by the following routes.

TRAINS: There is a half hourly train service from Glasgow to either Ayr or Newton-on-Ayr. The ground is a ten minute walk from both stations.

BUSES: There are several buses from the town centre with a frequency approximately every five minutes. Fans should board buses bound for Dalmilling, Whitletts or any bus passing Ayr Racecourse. The ground is only a ten minute walk from the town centre.

CARS: Car parking facilities are available at Craigie Park and at Ayr Racecourse and also at Somerset Road car park.

BERWICK RANGERS

Shielfield Park,
Shielfield Terrace, Tweedmouth,
Berwick Upon Tweed, TD15 2EF

CHAIRMAN

VICE-CHAIRMAN
Thomas Davidson

DIRECTORS
John H. Hush
Peter McAskill
William M. McLaren
James M.S. Rose

HONORARY PRESIDENT
James F. Reed

CLUB SECRETARY
Dennis J. McCleary

MANAGER
Ian Ross

COACHING STAFF
Ian Smith, Ian Oliver

KIT MAN
Ian Oliver

PHYSIO STAFF
Ian Oliver &
Rev. Glynn Jones

GROUNDSMEN
Jim Sim & Ian Oliver

COMMERCIAL MANAGER
Conrad I. Turner
(01289) 307969

TELEPHONES
Ground/Ticket Office/Fax
(01289) 307424
Club Sec. Home/Fax
(01289) 307623
Information Service
0891 800697

CLUB SHOP
Supporters Shop situated within the ground. Open during first team matchdays.

OFFICIAL SUPPORTERS CLUB
c/o Shielfield Park, Tweedmouth,
Berwick Upon Tweed, TD15 2EF

TEAM CAPTAIN
Graeme Fraser

SHIRT SPONSOR
Federation Brewery (L.C.L. Pils)

LIST OF PLAYERS 1996-97

SURNAME	FIRST NAME	MIDDLE NAME	DATE OF BIRTH	PLACE OF BIRTH	DATE OF SIGNING	HEIGHT FT INS	WEIGHT ST LBS	PREVIOUS CLUB
Burgess	Michael	Andrew	06/09/77	Edinburgh	04/08/96	6 0.0	11 2	Hutchison Vale B.C.
Coates	Scott	Lee	07/09/76	Consett	27/07/96	5 11.0	13 4	Sunderland A.F.C.
Craig	Kevin		02/06/74	Edinburgh	27/07/96	5 9.0	11 4	Easthouses B.C.
Forrester	Paul		03/11/72	Edinburgh	30/03/94	5 9.0	12 0	Middlesbrough
Fraser	Graeme	William	07/08/73	Edinburgh	31/03/94	5 11.0	11 8	Dunfermline Athletic
Graham	Thomas	Newlands	25/08/65	Edinburgh	03/07/87	5 8.0	11 7	Edina Hibs
Grant	Derek		19/05/66	Edinburgh	06/09/96	6 2.0	12 8	Montrose
King	Thomas	Richard	07/03/76	St. Albans	18/09/96	5 11.0	11 7	Dundee North End
McGlynn	David	John	26/06/75	Edinburgh	23/12/95	6 0.0	11 3	Musselburgh Athletic
Miller	Graeme		21/02/73	Glasgow	09/08/96	5 7.0	10 3	Livingston
Neil	Martin		16/04/70	Ashington	17/11/94	5 8.0	11 7	Bolton Wanderers
Reid	Alastair		16/12/68	Edinburgh	15/02/95	6 1.0	11 6	Ormiston Primrose
Rutherford	Paul		23/02/67	Sunderland	30/12/94	5 11.0	11 0	Scarborough
Smith	Stephen		16/02/68	Sunderland	27/07/96	6 0.0	12 0	Chester-Le-Street Town
Stewart	Grant		24/10/74	Edinburgh	27/07/96	5 11.0	11 6	Easthouses B.C.
Walton	Kevin		02/05/75	Durham City	05/07/95	5 10.0	11 2	Edinburgh University
Ward	Barry		11/07/78	Perth	21/11/95	5 7.0	10 0	Bankfoot Juniors
Watkins	Darren		17/03/77	Middlesbrough	22/08/96	6 0.0	11 0	Nottingham Forest
Wilson	Mark		31/07/74	Dechmont	17/02/93	5 11.0	10 8	Fauldhouse United B.C.
Young	Neil	Andrew	14/10/67	Beverley	31/03/94	5 10.0	11 8	Goole Town

MILESTONES

YEAR OF FORMATION: 1881
MOST LEAGUE POINTS IN A SEASON: 54 (Second Division – Season 1978/79) (2 Points for a Win)
60 (Second Division – Season 1995/96) (3 Points for a Win)
MOST LEAGUE GOALS SCORED BY A PLAYER IN A SEASON: Ken Bowron (Season 1963/64)
NO. OF GOALS SCORED: 38
RECORD ATTENDANCE: 13,365 (-v- Rangers – 28.1.1967)
RECORD VICTORY: 8-1 (-v- Forfar Athletic (H) – Division 2, 25.12.1965)
8-1 (-v- Vale of Leithen – Scottish Cup at Innerleithen 17.12.1966)
RECORD DEFEAT: 1-9 (-v- Hamilton Academical – First Division, 9.8.1980)

THE BORDERERS' TEN YEAR LEAGUE RECORD

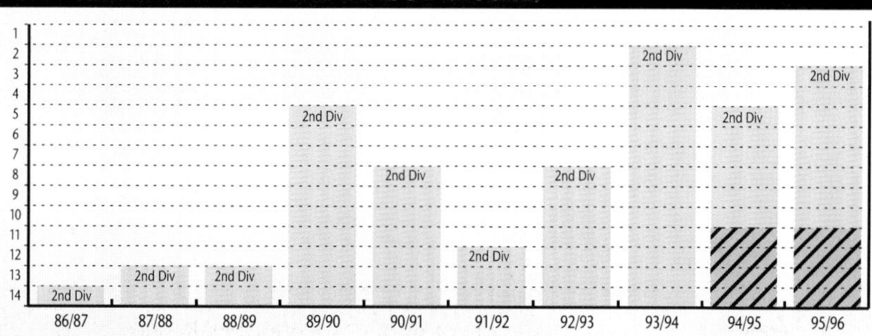

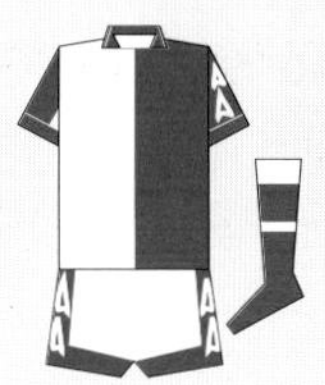
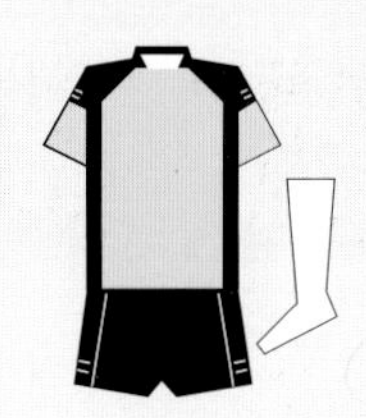

CLUB FACTFILE 1995/96
RESULTS... APPEARANCES... SCORERS

The BORDERERS

Date	Venue	Opponents	Att.	Res	Young N.	Valentine C.	Banks A.	Reid A.	Cowan M.	Fraser G.	Forrester P.	Neil M.	Rutherford P.	Irvine W.	Graham T.	Kane K.	Walton K.	Clegg N.	Cole A.	Wilson M.	Clarke J.	Thomson M.	Govan M.	Coughlin J.	McQueen J.	McGlynn D.	Chivers D.	Gallacher J.
Aug 12	A	Stranraer	507	0-0	1	2	3	4	5	6	7	8	9	10	11	12												
26	H	Stirling Albion	434	3-0	1	2	3	4	5	6[1]	7	8	9	10[2]	11	14												
Sep 2	A	Ayr United	1,221	4-1	1	2	3[1]	4	5	6	7	8	9[1]	10[2]	11	12												
9	A	Clyde	1,103	1-3	1	2	3	4	5	6	7	8	9	10[1]	11		12	14										
16	H	Stenhousemuir	362	3-1	1	2		4	5	6	7	8	9[1]	10[2]	11	14			3	15								
23	H	Forfar Athletic	450	1-0	1	2		4	5	6		8	9	10	11[1]	7			3									
30	A	Queen of the South	1,056	4-1	1	2		4	5[1]	6[2]	9	8		10	11	7	14	15	3[1]	12								
Oct 7	H	East Fife	655	0-1	1	2		4	5	6	9	8		10	11	7	14		3	12	15							
14	A	Montrose	503	3-1	1	2		4	5	6[1]	9	8		10[2]	11	7	14		3	12	15							
21	H	Stranraer	433	4-0	1	5	14	4		6[1]	9[1]	8[1]		10[1]	11	7			3	12	2							
28	A	Stirling Albion	811	0-1	1		14	4	5	6	9	8		10	11	7	15		3	12	2							
31	A	Stenhousemuir	402	1-4	1		15	5		6[1]	9	8		10	11	7			3		2	4	14					
Nov 11	H	Clyde	468	0-0	1		3	5		4	10	8			11	9	6	15		7				2				
21	H	Queen of the South	324	0-0	1		3	4	5	6	12	8	15	10	11	9				7				2				
25	A	Forfar Athletic	523	4-1	1	2	3	4	5	6[1]	7	8[1]	14	10[1]	11	9[1]	15											
Dec 2	A	East Fife	903	0-1		4	3	5		6	15	8	12	10		9	11			7				2	1			
16	H	Montrose	314	2-2	1	2	3[1]	4[1]	5	6	12	8		10	11	9				7								
Jan 10	A	Stranraer	433	3-0	1	4	3		5	6	14	8		10	11	7	12			2						9[3]		
16	H	Ayr United	355	2-2	1	3		4	5[1]	6	14	8		10[1]	11	7	12			2						9		
20	H	East Fife	382	1-2	1	4	3		5	6	14	8[1]		10	11	7				2						9		
23	A	Queen of the South	840	0-3	1	5	14	4		6	8	12		10	11	7	3			2						9		
30	H	Forfar Athletic	309	1-0	1	4	3		5	6	14	8[1]		10	11	7				2						9		
Feb 3	A	Montrose	520	2-1		4	3	5		6	12	8[1]		10	11[1]	7				2					1	9		
10	H	Stenhousemuir	333	2-1	1	2	3[1]	4		6	14	8		10[1]	11	9				7		5			15	12		
18	A	Clyde	667	1-2		2	3	4	5	6	12	8		10	11	9	15[1]			7					1	14		
24	H	Stirling Albion	483	0-3		4	3		5	6	9	8		10	11	7	14	15		2					1			
Mar 2	A	Ayr United	907	0-5		2	3	4	5	6	9	8		10		7	11	14							1		15	
9	A	Forfar Athletic	440	3-1	1	2	3			5	9[1]	4		10	11	12	6[1]									8[1]		7
16	H	Queen of the South	363	4-1	1	2	3			5	8[3]	4		10	11		6			14						9[1]		7
23	A	Stenhousemuir	419	3-0	1	2	3		14	5	8[1]	4		10	11	15	6[2]			7						9		
30	H	Clyde	433	2-3	1	2	3[1]			5	8[1]	4		10	11		6									9		7
Apr 6	A	East Fife	1,603	0-0	1	2	3		5	6	9	4		10	11		8									7		
13	H	Montrose	367	4-1	1	2	3	14[1]	5	4	8[3]			10	11		6			12						9		7
20	H	Stranraer	373	1-0	1	2	3[1]		5	4	8	12		10	11		6			7						9		
27	A	Stirling Albion	1,238	3-4	1		3		5[1]	4	8	7		10	11[1]		6	14		2						9[1]		
May 4	H	Ayr United	681	2-1	1	2	3		5	4	8	7		10			6[1]			11[1]						9		
TOTAL FULL APPEARANCES					31	31	26	23	25	36	25	33	6	35	33	22	13		8	17	3	2		3	5	15		4
TOTAL SUB APPEARANCES							(4)	(1)	(1)		(10)	(2)	(3)			(6)	(10)	(6)		(8)	(2)		(1)		(1)	(2)	(1)	
TOTAL GOALS SCORED							5	2	3	7	10	5	2	13	3	1	5		1	1						6		

Small bold figures denote goalscorers. † denotes opponent's own goal.

SHIELFIELD PARK

CAPACITY: 4,131; Seated 1,366, Standing 2,765

PITCH DIMENSIONS: 110 yds x 70 yds

FACILITIES FOR DISABLED SUPPORTERS: Supporters should enter via gate adjacent to ground turnstiles (see ground plan) or via official entrance

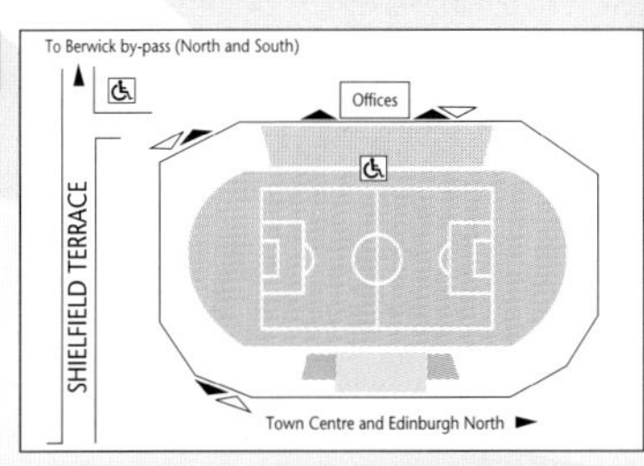

HOW TO GET THERE

Shielfield Park can be reached by the following routes.

The ground is approximately 1½ miles south of Berwick town centre and is situated in Shielfield Terrace, Tweedmouth.

BUSES: The local bus route from the town centre is the Prior Park service and the nearest stop to the ground is in Shielfield Terrace. The bus stop is only yards away from the ground.

TRAINS: The only railway station is Berwick, which is situated on the East Coast line and a frequent service operates at various stages during the day. The ground is approximately 1½ miles from the station and a taxi service operates from there or alternatively, fans can take the local bus service as detailed above.

CARS: There is a large car park at the rear of the ground. (Nominal charge).

BRECHIN CITY

Glebe Park, Trinity Road,
Brechin, Angus, DD9 6BJ

CHAIRMAN
Hugh A. Campbell Adamson

VICE-CHAIRMAN
David H. Birse

HONORARY PRESIDENT
Ricardo Gallaccio

DIRECTORS
Martin Smith (Treasurer)
I. Michael Holland
(Assistant Treasurer)
David H. Will
Kenneth W. Ferguson
Calum I. McK. Brown
James G. Black

SECRETARY
Kenneth W. Ferguson

MANAGER
John Young

ASSISTANT MANAGERS
Jimmy Cant & Cammy Evans

CLUB DOCTOR
Dr. Archibald McInnes

SPORTS THERAPIST
Tom Gilmartin

CHIEF SCOUT
Jake Ferrier

GROUNDSMAN
Alex Laing

COMMERCIAL CONTACT
Kenneth W. Ferguson

TELEPHONES
Ground (01356) 622856
Sec. Home (01356) 625691
Sec. Bus. (01356) 625285/
(01674) 678910
Sec. Bus. Fax (01356) 625524

CLUB SHOP
Glebe Park, Brechin, Angus, DD9 6BJ
Open during home match days.

OFFICIAL SUPPORTERS CLUB
c/o Glebe Park, Brechin,
Angus, DD9 6BJ

TEAM CAPTAIN
Harry Cairney

SHIRT SPONSOR
ROWCO International

LIST OF PLAYERS 1996-97

SURNAME	FIRST NAME	MIDDLE NAME	DATE OF BIRTH	PLACE OF BIRTH	DATE OF SIGNING	HEIGHT FT INS	WEIGHT ST LBS	PREVIOUS CLUB
Allan	Raymond	George K.	05/03/55	Cowdenbeath	24/07/95	6 0.0	11 7	Raith Rovers
Baillie	Richard	Ketchen	06/06/68	Dunfermline	24/11/89	5 5.5	10 0	Cowdenbeath
Black	Roddy		22/02/78	Dundee	10/09/95	5 9.0	11 0	Carnoustie Panmure
Brand	Ralph		17/07/70	Dundee	10/08/91	5 9.0	10 3	Lochee United
Brown	Robert		11/11/59	Lincoln	10/01/85	5 10.0	11 4	Dundee North End
Buick	Garry	Robert	12/01/75	Arbroath	25/11/94	5 5.5	10 4	Keith
Cairney	Henry		01/09/61	Holytown	12/02/92	5 7.0	10 8	Stenhousemuir
Cargill	Harry		17/01/77	Arbroath	31/08/95	5 10.0	11 0	Arbroath Sporting Club
Christie	Graeme		01/01/71	Dundee	04/08/93	6 1.0	11 0	Carnoustie Panmure
Conway	Francis	Joseph	29/12/69	Dundee	25/11/89	5 11.0	11 4	Lochee Harp
Davidson	Graham		30/12/77	Dundee	04/10/95	5 10.0	9 7	Elmwood JFC
Ewan	Neil	David	11/03/79	Aberdeen	15/09/95	5 9.0	11 0	Banchory St.Ternan
Farnan	Craig		07/04/71	Dundee	07/06/95	5 10.0	13 3	Arbroath
Ferguson	Scott		04/11/77	Broxburn	08/08/95	5 8.0	10 7	"X" Form
Feroz	Craig		24/10/77	Aberdeen	12/03/96	5 8.0	10 7	Lewis United
Garden	Stuart	Robertson	10/02/72	Dundee	01/09/95	5 11.5	12 3	Dundee United
Heddle	Ian	Alexander	21/03/63	Dunfermline	16/03/96	5 10.0	11 0	Forfar Athletic
Kerrigan	Steven	Paul	29/09/70	Wolverhampton	01/02/96	5 9.0	10 0	Kirriemuir Thistle
McKellar	James	Robert	29/12/76	Bellshill	26/07/94	5 6.0	10 4	Arbroath Lads Club
McNeill	William	John	12/03/67	Toronto	05/03/93	5 9.0	11 0	Meadowbank Thistle
Mitchell	Brian	Charles	29/02/68	Arbroath	06/10/94	5 8.0	13 0	Arbroath
Reid	Scott	Lawrence	06/05/78	Dundee	10/09/95	5 8.5	9 8	Forfar Albion
Scott	Walter	Douglas	01/01/64	Dundee	25/05/94	5 9.0	10 7	Dundee
Smith	Greig	Robert	26/03/76	Aberdeen	21/12/94	5 9.0	10 12	Culter Juniors
Smollet	Ronnie	David	28/11/75	Kirkcaldy	15/09/94	5 8.0	10 8	Hall Russell United
Sorbie	Stuart	Graham	07/09/63	Glasgow	16/02/96	5 9.5	10 5	Livingston

MILESTONES

YEAR OF FORMATION: 1906
MOST LEAGUE POINTS IN A SEASON: 55 (Second Division – Season 1982/83)(2 Points for a Win)
63 (Third Division – Season 1995/96)(3 Points for a Win)
MOST LEAGUE GOALS SCORED BY A PLAYER IN A SEASON: W. McIntosh (Season 1959/60)
NO. OF GOALS SCORED: 26
RECORD ATTENDANCE: 8,122 (-v- Aberdeen – 3.2.1973)
RECORD VICTORY: 12-1 (-v- Thornhill – Scottish Cup, 28.1.1926)
RECORD DEFEAT: 0-10 (-v- Airdrieonians, Albion Rovers and Cowdenbeath – Division 2, 1937/38)

THE CITY'S TEN YEAR LEAGUE RECORD

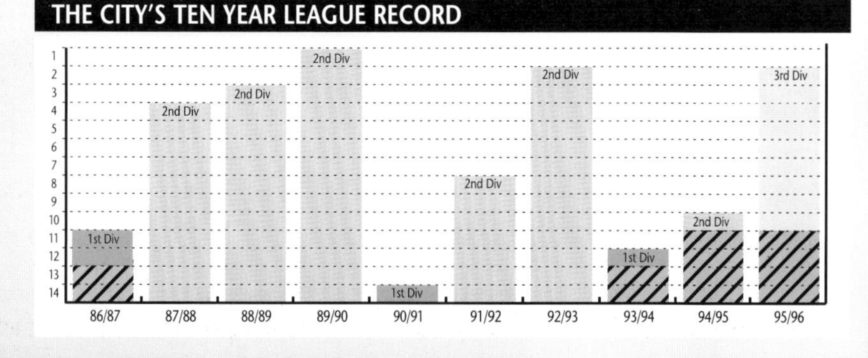

CLUB FACTFILE 1995/96
RESULTS... APPEARANCES... SCORERS

The CITY

Date	Venue	Opponents	Att.	Res	Allan R.	Mitchell B.	Christie G.	Brown R.	Conway F.	Mearns G.	Smith R.	Farnan C.	Price G.	Brand R.	Marr S.	Cairney H.	Scott W.D.	Ferguson S.	Ross A.	McNeill W.	McKellar J.	Reid S.	Garden S.	Brown B.	Balfour D.	Graham R.	Buick G.	Baillie R.	Kerrigan S.	Sorbie S.	Heddle I.
Aug 12	H	East Stirlingshire	326	3-1	1	2	3	4	5	6	7	8	9^{2}	10^{1}	11																
26	A	Caledonian Thistle	1,029	2-1	1	2	6	3	5		9^{1}	8		7		4	10	11	16^{1}												
Sep 2	H	Alloa	355	0-1	1	2	6	3	5	8	7			12		4	10	11	9												
9	H	Ross County	479	2-1	1	2	6	3^{1}	5		7	8		14		4	10	11	9^{1}												
16	A	Cowdenbeath	251	1-0	1	2		3	5	10	7	8		11^{1}		4		6	9	12											
23	A	Queen's Park	422	2-0	1	2		3	5	10		8		11^{2}		4		6	9	12	7										
30	H	Arbroath	632	1-1	1	2		3	5	10		8		11		4		6	9	12	7^{1}										
Oct 7	H	Albion Rovers	341	0-1	1	2		3	5	10		8				4		6	9	11	7	12	15								
14	A	Livingston	273	0-0		2		3	5			8				4	10	6	9	11	7		1								
21	A	Alloa	371	2-3		2	15	3	5			8				4	10	6	9^{1}	11^{1}	7			1							
28	H	Caledonian Thistle	374	0-0		2	5	3			14	8				4	10	6		11	7				1	9					
Nov 4	H	Cowdenbeath	338	2-0	1	2	5	3		10	11	8^{1}				4		6		9	7^{1}					12					
11	A	Ross County	1,653	0-0	1	2	5	3		10	9	8				4		6	12	11	7										
18	A	Arbroath	572	1-1	1	2	5	3			9	8				4		6^{1}	12	11	7						10				
25	H	Queen's Park	306	1-0	1	2^{1}	5	3			12	8				4		6	9	11	7						10				
Dec 2	A	Albion Rovers	289	0-1	1	2	5	3			14	8				4		6	9	11	7						10				
9	H	East Stirlingshire	253	4-1	1	2	5^{1}	3^{1}	6			8^{1}				4^{1}			9	11	7						10	12			
16	H	Livingston	419	2-0	1	2	5	3	6			8				4^{1}			9	11	7^{1}						10				
Jan 13	A	Queen's Park	505	0-0	1	2	6	3	5		14	8				4	10	12	9	11	7										
20	H	Albion Rovers	296	1-0	1	2	5	3	4			8					10	6	9^{1}	11	7							14			
23	H	Alloa	349	3-0	1	2	5	3	4		12	8					6		9^{2}	11^{1}	7						10				
31	H	Arbroath	777	0-1	1	2	6	3	5			8				4	10		9	11							7		12		
Feb 3	A	Livingston	2,386	1-0	1	2	6	3	5			8				4	10		9	11							7^{1}		14		
14	A	Cowdenbeath	160	0-0	1	2	6	3	5		7	8		14		4	10			11									9		
17	H	Ross County	506	0-0	1	2	6	3	5			8		12		4	10		9	11										7	
24	A	Caledonian Thistle	2,514	1-0	1	2	6	3	5			8				4	10			11							7			9^{1}	
Mar 2	A	East Stirlingshire	268	0-2	1	2	6	3	5			8		12		4	10			11							7	14		9	
9	H	Queen's Park	363	4-0	1	2^{1}	6^{1}	3	5			8		9		4	10			11^{2}	7							12	14		
16	A	Arbroath	605	1-0	1	2	6	3	5			8				4	10		9^{1}	7											11
23	H	Cowdenbeath	368	2-0	1	2	6	3	5			8				4	10		9^{1}	7^{1}	14							12			11
30	A	Ross County	2,362	2-1	1	2	6	3	5			8				4	10		9	7^{2}	14										11
Apr 6	A	Albion Rovers	329	0-0	1	2		3	5			8				4	10		9	7								6			11
13	H	Livingston	768	0-1	1	2		3	5			8				4	10	6	9	7	14										11
20	A	Alloa	369	3-0	1	2		3	5			8		9^{2}		4		6		7							10^{1}	12			11
27	H	Caledonian Thistle	656	0-1	1	2		3	5			8		9		4		6		7	11						10		14		16
May 4	A	East Stirlingshire	305	0-3	1	2	14	3	5			10		9		4		6			12							8	7		11
TOTAL FULL APPEARANCES					33	36	25	36	30	8	9	35	1	9	1	33	21	20	23	28	18		1	1	1	1	12	2	2	3	7
TOTAL SUB APPEARANCES							(2)				(5)			(5)				(1)	(3)	(3)	(4)	(1)	(1)			(1)		(6)	(4)		(1)
TOTAL GOALS SCORED						2	2	2			1	2	2	6		2		1	8	7	3						2			1	

Small bold figures denote goalscorers. † denotes opponent's own goal.

GLEBE PARK

CAPACITY: 3,960; Seated 1,519, Standing 2,441

PITCH DIMENSIONS: 110 yds x 67 yds

FACILITIES FOR DISABLED SUPPORTERS: Section of Terracing designated for disabled supporters.

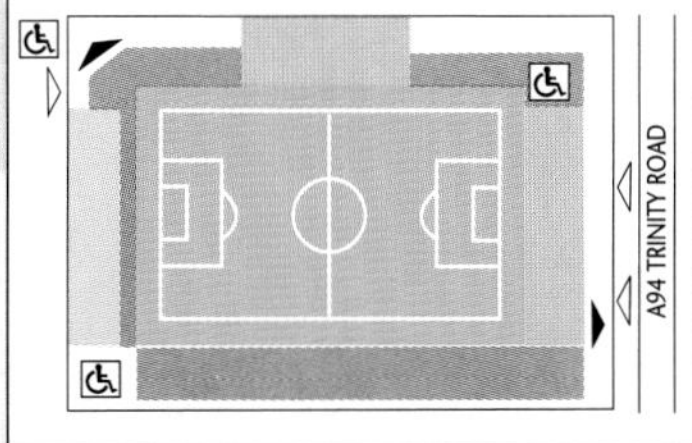

HOW TO GET THERE

The following routes may be used to reach Glebe Park:

TRAINS: The nearest railway station is Montrose, which is eight miles away. There is a regular Inter-City service from all parts of the country and fans alighting at Montrose can then catch a connecting bus service to Brechin.

BUSES: Brechin bus station is only a few hundred yards from the ground and buses on the Aberdeen-Dundee and Montrose-Edzell routes stop here.

CARS: Car parking is available in the Brechin City car park, which is capable of holding 50 vehicles. There are also a number of side streets which may be used for this purpose.

CLYDE

Broadwood Stadium,
Cumbernauld, G68 9NE

CHAIRMAN
William B. Carmichael

DIRECTORS
J. Sean Fallon
Robert B. Jack, C.B.E., M.A., LL.B.
Harry McCall, B.A., C.Eng., M.I.C.E.
John F. McBeth, F.R.I.C.S.
John D. Taylor, A.I.B.
Gerard W. Dunn

SECRETARY
John D. Taylor, A.I.B.
0141-248 6808

MANAGER

ASSISTANT MANAGER

RESERVE COACH
Gardner Speirs

CLUB DOCTOR
John A. MacLean

PHYSIOTHERAPIST
John Watson

S.F.A. COMMUNITY COACH
Bill Munro

CHIEF SCOUTS
George Peebles & George Rankin

COMMERCIAL MANAGER
John Donnelly

GROUNDSMAN
Douglas Fraser

TELEPHONES
Ground/Commercial
(01236) 451511
Fax (01236) 733490

CLUB SHOP
Situated at Ground

OFFICIAL SUPPORTERS CLUB
180 Main Street, Rutherglen

TEAM CAPTAIN
Keith Knox

SHIRT SPONSOR
OKI

LIST OF PLAYERS 1996-97

SURNAME	FIRST NAME	MIDDLE NAME	DATE OF BIRTH	PLACE OF BIRTH	DATE OF SIGNING	HEIGHT FT INS	WEIGHT ST LBS	PREVIOUS CLUB
Annand	Edward		24/03/73	Glasgow	28/07/95	5 11.0	11 1	Sligo Rovers
Brown	James		21/10/74	Bellshill	09/07/93	6 0.0	10 0	Rangers
Brownlie	Paul		30/08/77	Falkirk	25/08/95	5 9.0	10 4	Dunipace Juniors
Campbell	Paul	John	26/11/77	Bellshill	10/09/95	5 9.0	10 7	Bellshill Athletic
Ferguson	Graeme	William	03/03/71	Stirling	22/07/95	5 10.0	11 10	Clydebank
Gibson	Andrew		02/02/69	Dechmont	08/08/96	5 9.5	11 10	Partick Thistle
Gillies	Kenneth		20/07/74	Glasgow	25/07/95	5 10.0	11 10	St. Mirren
Harrison	Thomas	Edward	22/01/74	Edinburgh	04/08/95	5 9.0	11 8	Dunfermline Athletic
Knox	Keith		06/08/64	Stranraer	16/03/88	5 10.0	12 2	Stranraer
Mathieson	Miller	Stewart	19/12/64	Surrey	24/07/96	5 11.0	11 12	Stenhousemuir
McCheyne	Graeme		21/12/73	Bellshill	29/07/92	6 1.0	11 3	Dundee United
McConnell	Ian	Paul	06/01/75	Glasgow	04/10/93	6 1.0	12 8	Derry City
McEwan	Craig		03/10/77	Glasgow	04/07/96	5 8.0	10 0	Possil Y.M.
McInulty	Stephen	James	22/09/71	Bellshill	07/07/96	5 11.0	11 0	Hamilton Academical
McLay	John		12/10/76	Glasgow	11/07/95	6 3.0	11 8	Gleniffer Thistle B.C.
McLean	Mark	Andrew	30/03/72	Paisley	02/08/96	6 1.0	13 0	Sligo Rovers
O'Neill	Martin		17/06/75	Glasgow	08/06/93	5 7.5	10 10	Clyde B.C.
O'Neill	Michael		27/07/78	Glasgow	23/07/96	6 1.0	10 8	Kilsyth Rangers Youth Club
Parks	Gordon	John	19/11/72	Glasgow	18/08/92	5 9.5	10 7	Shettleston Juniors
Prunty	James		21/09/74	Bellshill	08/06/93	5 8.5	10 8	Clyde B.C.

MILESTONES

YEAR OF FORMATION: 1878
MOST CAPPED PLAYER: Tommy Ring
NO. OF CAPS: 12
MOST LEAGUE POINTS IN A SEASON: 64 (Division 2 – Season 1956/57)
MOST LEAGUE GOALS SCORED BY A PLAYER IN A SEASON: Bill Boyd (Season 1932/33)
NO. OF GOALS SCORED: 32
RECORD ATTENDANCE: 52,000 (-v- Rangers – 21.11.1908 – at Shawfield Stadium)
7,382 (-v- Celtic – 14.8.1996 (Coca-Cola Cup) – at Broadwood Stadium)
RECORD VICTORY: 11-1 (-v- Cowdenbeath – Division 2, 6.10.1951)
RECORD DEFEAT: 0-11 (-v- Dumbarton and Rangers, Scottish Cup)

THE BULLY WEE'S TEN YEAR LEAGUE RECORD

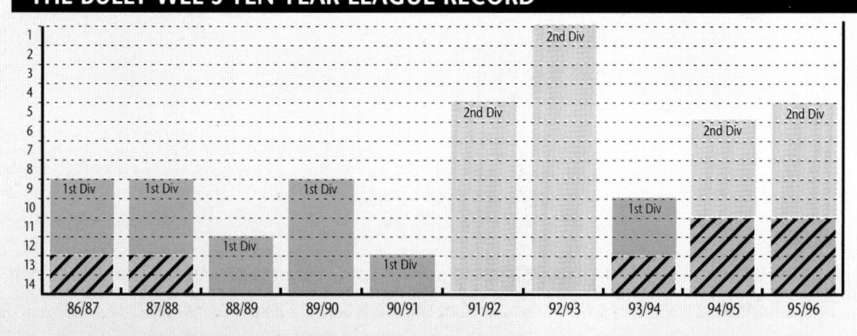

CLUB FACTFILE 1995/96
RESULTS... APPEARANCES... SCORERS

The BULLY WEE

Date	Venue	Opponents	Att.	Res	Hillcoat J.	Ferguson G.	Angus I.	Gillies K.	Knox K.	Brown J.	O'Neill M.	Nicholas C.	Annand E.	Harrison T.	Parks G.	McCluskey G.	McCarron J.	Watson G.	McLay J.	McCheyne G.	Patterson P.	Nisbet I.	McQueen J.	Thomson J.	McConnell I.	Dickson J.	Prunty J.	Falconer M.	Brownlie P.	Dawson R.	Muir J.	Campbell P.	McEwan C.	Coleman S.
Aug 12	A	Ayr United	1,963	1-1	1	2	3	4	5	6	7	8[1]	9	10	11	12	14																	
26	H	Forfar Athletic	1,163	1-2	1		3		5	6	7	8	9[1]	10				2	4	11	12	14												
Sep 2	A	Queen of the South	1,897	3-0			3	4	2	6	7	8[1]	9[1]	10[1]		12			11	14			1	5										
9	H	Berwick Rangers	1,103	3-1			3	4	2	6	7	8[1]	9[1]	10[1]		12			11	14			1	5										
16	A	Montrose	763	0-0			3	4	2	6	7	8	9	10		12			11	14			1	5										
23	H	Stenhousemuir	1,088	0-1			3	4	2	6	7	8	9	10		12			11	14			1	5										
30	A	Stirling Albion	1,011	1-1		11	3	4	2			8	9	10				7		14	12		1	5	6[1]									
Oct 7	H	Stranraer	1,048	1-1	1	11	3	4	2	6		8	9	14				7		15	10[1]			5	12									
14	A	East Fife	1,128	0-0		11	3	4	2	6	14	8	9	10							7		1	5		15								
21	H	Ayr United	1,125	1-2		11	3		2		4	8	9[1]	10		12			6		7		1	5	14	15								
28	A	Forfar Athletic	645	0-1		11	3		2	6		8	9					10		4	15	14	1	5	12	7								
Nov 4	H	Montrose	849	3-0		11	3	4	2				9[2]	10				8				14	1	5	12	7	6	15[1]						
11	A	Berwick Rangers	468	0-0		11	3	4	2				9	10				8				14	1	5	12	15	6	7						
18	H	Stirling Albion	1,200	1-2			3	4	2				9[1]					7	15	12		10	1	5	8	11	6	14						
25	A	Stenhousemuir	714	1-0	1		3	4	2			8	9			15	11[1]	10		6		14			5	7		12						
Dec 2	A	Stranraer	683	0-0	1	11		4	2			8	9			15		10		6		7			5		3	12						
16	H	East Fife	982	0-1	1	11	3	4	2			8	9					10		6					5	7		15	12					
Jan 13	H	Stenhousemuir	958	3-0	1	11	3[1]		2			8	9[2]	12		15		10		6				4	5	14	7							
20	H	Stranraer	942	2-2	1	11	3	10	2			8	9[1]	14		15				6		12[1]		4	5		7							
24	A	Stirling Albion	1,068	0-3	1	11		4	2		14	8	9	10								7		6	5	12	3							
Feb 3	A	East Fife	774	1-1	1	11		4	2		7	8	9[1]	10					3		12	14		5			6							
18	H	Berwick Rangers	667	2-1	1	11	3	4	2		7	8	9[2]	6				10			15	14		5										
24	H	Forfar Athletic	878	3-1	1	11	3	4	2[1]		7[1]	8	9[1]	6				10			15	14		5			12							
27	A	Ayr United	1,378	1-2	1	11	3	4	2		7	8	9[1]	6				10				14		5			12							
Mar 2	A	Queen of the South	877	1-2	1	11	3	4	2		7	8	9	14				6			10			5[1]		15	12							
5	H	Queen of the South	776	2-1	1	11	3	4			12	8	9	7[1]				6	14		15			5[1]				10		2				
9	A	Stenhousemuir	674	0-1	1	11	3				7	8	9	14				10	6	4	15			5			12			2				
12	A	Montrose	226	3-2	1	11	3					8[1]	9	7[1]				10		6[1]	12	14		5			4			2				
16	H	Stirling Albion	1,183	1-3	1	11	3	4			7[1]	8		10				6		9				5		14	12			2	15			
23	H	Montrose	791	1-3	1		3[1]	4			7	8	9					6		10		15			5	12	11	14		2				
30	A	Berwick Rangers	433	3-2	1	11	3	4				8	9[2]	7		10[1]		6		15					5		12	14		2				
Apr 6	A	Stranraer	655	2-2	1	11	3	4			14	8	9	7		10[1]		6		15					5[1]		12			2				
13	H	East Fife	1,145	2-2	1	11	3	4	14		7	8[1]	9	12		10[1]		6							5					2				
20	H	Ayr United	1,075	2-0	1		3	4	2		7	8	9[2]			10		6				11			5		12		14					
27	A	Forfar Athletic	472	2-4	1	14	3	4	2		7		9[2]			8		6	10	15					5				11			12		
May 4	H	Queen of the South	1,095	0-0	1	11	3	4	2		7		9			15									5		6		10			12	8	14
TOTAL FULL APPEARANCES					25	26	33	30	28	9	19	31	35	21	1	5	1	25	9	11	4	4	11	24	15	5	11	2	2	8			1	
TOTAL SUB APPEARANCES						(1)			(1)		(4)			(6)		(11)	(1)		(2)	(10)	(9)	(12)			(5)	(8)	(8)	(7)	(2)		(1)	(2)		(1)
TOTAL GOALS SCORED							2		1		2	5	21	4		3	1			1	1	1		2	2			1						

Small bold figures denote goalscorers. † denotes opponent's own goal.

BROADWOOD STADIUM

CAPACITY: 8,003 (All Seated)

PITCH DIMENSIONS: 112 yds x 76 yds

FACILITIES FOR DISABLED SUPPORTERS: Facilities available in both Home, Away and New Stands.

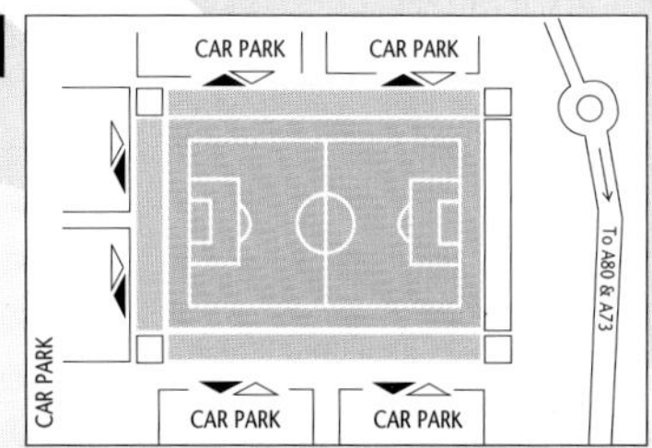

HOW TO GET THERE

The following routes may be used to reach Broadwood Stadium:

BUSES: From Buchanan Street Bus Station, Glasgow. Bus No. 36A (Glasgow to Westfield).

TRAINS: From Queen Street Station, Glasgow to Croy Station. The Stadium is a 15 minute walk from here.

CARS: From Glasgow City Centre via Stepps By-Pass joining A80 towards Stirling. Take Broadwood turn-off to Stadium.

DUMBARTON

Boghead Park, Miller Street,
Dumbarton, G82 2JA

CHAIRMAN
Douglas S. Dalgleish

MANAGING DIRECTOR
Neil Rankine

DIRECTORS
David Wright
G. James Innes
David O. Stark

HON. PRESIDENTS
Ian A. Bell
R. Campbell Ward, C.A.

CLUB SECRETARY
Colin J. Hosie

ASSISTANT SECRETARY
J. David Prophet

MANAGER
Jim Fallon

ASSISTANT MANAGER
Alastair MacLeod

CLUB DOCTORS
James Goldie & Paul Jackson

PHYSIOTHERAPIST
David Stobie

GROUNDSMAN
George Furze

KIT MAN
Richard Jackson

COMMERCIAL MANAGER
Alec Couper

TELEPHONES
Ground/Commercial
(01389) 762569/767864
Sec. Bus. (01236) 769377
Fax (01389) 762629

CLUB SHOP
Situated in ground – open on matchdays and 10.00 a.m. – 4.00 p.m. Mon-Fri

OFFICIAL SUPPORTERS CLUB
c/o Boghead Park, Miller Street, Dumbarton

TEAM CAPTAIN
James Meechan

SHIRT SPONSOR
Methode

LIST OF PLAYERS 1996-97

SURNAME	FIRST NAME	MIDDLE NAME	DATE OF BIRTH	PLACE OF BIRTH	DATE OF SIGNING	HEIGHT FT INS	WEIGHT ST LBS	PREVIOUS CLUB
Dallas	Stephen		02/11/74	Glasgow	31/03/95	5 7.0	10 4	Hibernian
Glancy	Martin	Paul	24/03/76	Glasgow	16/01/96	5 8.0	10 0	Petershill Juniors
Goldie	Joseph		17/08/77	Vale of Leven	21/05/96	5 11.0	10 6	Leven Valley Juveniles
Gow	Stephen		06/12/68	Dumbarton	23/07/87	6 0.0	11 1	Dumbarton United
Granger	Alan	William	16/09/71	Glasgow	09/08/95	5 9.0	11 0	Pollok Juniors
King	Thomas	David	23/01/70	Dumbarton	30/09/94	5 9.0	11 0	Arbroath
MacFarlane	Ian		05/12/68	Bellshill	12/07/91	6 1.0	12 7	Hamilton Academical
Marsland	James		28/08/68	Dumbarton	15/06/90	5 8.0	10 12	Kilpatrick Juveniles
McGall	James		02/10/78	Glasgow	30/08/96	5 7.0	9 0	Arsenal B.C.
McGarvey	Martin		16/01/72	Glasgow	20/02/91	5 8.0	11 0	Irvine Meadow
McGivern	Samuel	Walker	09/10/63	Kilwinning	11/08/95	5 8.0	10 10	Ayr United
McKinnon	Colin		29/08/69	Glasgow	30/09/94	6 0.0	11 7	Arbroath
Meechan	James		14/10/63	Alexandria	05/10/90	5 9.0	11 7	Irvine Meadow
Meechan	Kenneth		16/02/72	Greenock	04/12/95	6 0.0	12 8	Greenock Juniors
Melvin	Martin		07/08/69	Glasgow	22/12/ 90	5 11.0	11 6	Falkirk
Mooney	Martin	James	25/09/70	Alexandria	24/09/92	5 7.5	9 11	Falkirk
Sharp	Lee		22/05/75	Glasgow	11/12/95	5 8.0	11 7	Ashfield Juniors
Ward	Hugh		09/03/70	Dumbarton	05/11/93	5 8.0	9 12	Greenock Juniors

MILESTONES

YEAR OF FORMATION: 1872
MOST CAPPED PLAYERS: J. Lindsay and J. McAulay
NO. OF CAPS: 8 each
MOST LEAGUE POINTS IN A SEASON: 53 (First Division – Season 1986/87) (2 Points for a Win)
60 (Second Division – Season 1994/95) (3 Points for a Win)
MOST LEAGUE GOALS SCORED BY A PLAYER IN A SEASON: Kenneth Wilson (Season 1971/72)
NO. OF GOALS SCORED: 38
RECORD ATTENDANCE: 18,001 (-v- Raith Rovers – 2.3.1957)
RECORD VICTORY: 13-2 (-v- Kirkintilloch – Scottish Cup)
RECORD DEFEAT: 1-11 (-v- Ayr United and Albion Rovers)

THE SONS' TEN YEAR LEAGUE RECORD

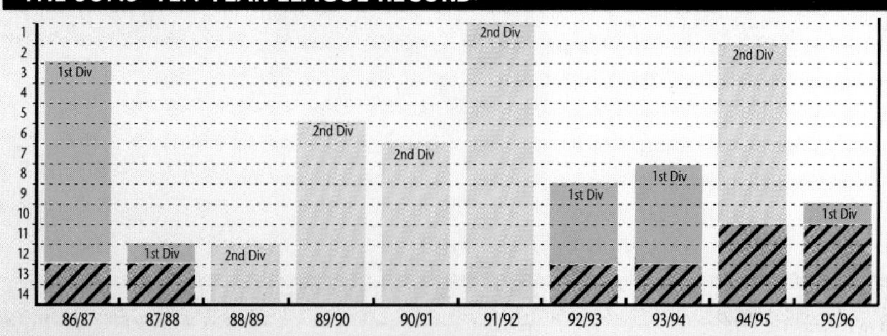

CLUB FACTFILE 1995/96
RESULTS... APPEARANCES... SCORERS

The SONS

Date	Venue	Opponents	Att.	Res	MacFarlane I.	Burns H.	Fabiani R.	Meechan J.	Martin P.	Marsland J.	Mooney M.	King T.	McGivern S.	Charnley J.	Granger A.	Gibson C.	McGarvey M.	Gow S.	McKinnon C.	Melvin M.	Hamilton J.	Foster A.	Dallas S.	Dennison P.	Meechan K.	Ward H.	Sharp L.	Glancy M.	Goldie J.
Aug 12	H	Hamilton Academical	1,191	1-0	1	2[1]	3	4	5	6	7	8	9	10	11	12	14												
26	A	Greenock Morton	2,612	2-1	1	2	3		5	6	7[1]	8	9	11[1]	15		14	4	10										
Sep 2	H	Dunfermline Athletic	1,952	0-4	1	2	3	10	5	6	7	8	9	15	14			4	11	12									
9	H	Airdrieonians	1,320	1-2	1		3		5[1]	6	7	8	9	11	14	12			10	4	2								
16	A	St. Johnstone	2,273	1-4	1		3		5	6	7	8	9	11	12	14			10[1]	4	2								
23	H	Dundee	1,207	1-5	1			14	5	6	7			11	10	9	12[1]		8	4	2	3							
30	A	Clydebank	913	1-2	1				5	6	14	8		11	10	9[1]	2		7	4		3							
Oct 7	H	Dundee United	2,013	1-0	1		14	4	5	6	15[1]	8		11	7	9	12		10	2		3							
14	A	St. Mirren	2,377	2-3	1	15	3	5		6	7[1]	8	12	11		9	14[1]		4	2		10							
21	A	Dunfermline Athletic	3,842	1-3	1		3	4		6	7			11	10	9[1]	12	5	8	2									
28	H	Greenock Morton	2,378	0-2	1		3	4		6	7			11	10	9	15	5	8	2									
Nov 4	H	St. Johnstone	1,050	1-3	1		3	2	5	6	7[1]	4		11	10	9			8										
11	A	Airdrieonians	1,205	†1-2	1		3	4	5	6	7	10	12	11	9				8	2			14						
18	H	Clydebank	1,043	1-2			3	4	5	6	7[1]	14	10	11		9			8	2			12	1					
Dec 2	A	Dundee United	5,285	0-8			3	4	5	6	14	8		12	15	9			7	2		11	10	1					
5	A	Dundee	2,804	1-1			3	5		6	7	4		11	15				8	2		10	9[1]		1				
9	H	St. Mirren	1,461	0-0			3	5		6	7	2		11	15	14	10		8	4			9		1				
16	A	Hamilton Academical	762	0-3	1		3	5		6	7	2		11	14	12	10		8	4		15	9						
Jan 6	A	St. Johnstone	2,448	0-3	1	2	3	6			7					9	10	5	8	4			11			14			
13	H	Airdrieonians	1,045	1-2	1	2	3	6			7				14[1]	9	10	5	8	4						11			
20	H	Dundee United	1,354	1-3	1	2	3	6			7	10			12	9	14	5	8	4			15			11[1]			
23	H	Dundee	761	1-2		2	3	6			7	10				9	12	5	8	4			15		1	11[1]	14		
Feb 3	A	St. Mirren	1,838	0-5		2		5			7	6			8	12	15	14		4		10	9		1	11	3		
13	H	Hamilton Academical	654	1-2				5			7	10			12[1]	9	6	2	8	4					1	11	3		
17	A	Clydebank	612	0-1				5			7	6			8	9		2	10	4			14		1	11	3		
24	A	Greenock Morton	2,833	0-2				5			7	6			10	9		2	8	4			15		1	11	3		
Mar 2	A	Dundee	1,712	0-3				5			7	6			10	9	11	2	8	4			14		1	12	3		
9	H	Dunfermline Athletic	1,477	0-3		6		5			7				10	9	8	2		4			12		1	11	3		
16	H	Clydebank	654	0-1		2		5			7		9				8	6	12	4			14		1	11	3	10	
23	H	St. Johnstone	903	0-3				5			7				8	9	6	2	12	4		10	14		1	11	3		
30	A	Airdrieonians	1,062	1-5				5			7	6			11	9		2	8	4		10[1]	14		1		3		12
Apr 6	A	Dundee United	7,142	1-6	1			5			7	6			11	9	10	2	8	4		14	12				3[1]		
13	H	St. Mirren	1,139	0-1	1			5			7	6	9		11		10	2	8	4			12				3		
20	A	Dunfermline Athletic	5,971	1-4	1			5			12	6	9		7		10		8	4		2	11[1]		15	14	3		
27	H	Greenock Morton	2,733	0-1	1			5			7	6			8	9		2	10	4			11			12	3		
May 4	A	Hamilton Academical	657	1-2	1			5			12	6			11[1]	9	10	2	7	4			14				3		8
TOTAL FULL APPEARANCES					22	10	19	31	12	18	31	27	9	16	20	23	14	20	31	32	3	10	8	2	12	10	14	1	1
TOTAL SUB APPEARANCES						(1)	(1)	(1)			(5)	(1)	(2)	(2)	(11)	(6)	(10)	(1)	(2)	(1)		(2)	(14)		(1)	(4)	(1)		(1)
TOTAL GOALS SCORED						1			1		5			1	3	2	2		1			1	2			2	1		

Small bold figures denote goalscorers. † denotes opponent's own goal.

BOGHEAD PARK

CAPACITY: 5,007; Seated 303, Standing 4,704

PITCH DIMENSIONS: 110 yds x 72 yds

FACILITIES FOR DISABLED SUPPORTERS: Wheelchairs are accommodated on the track.

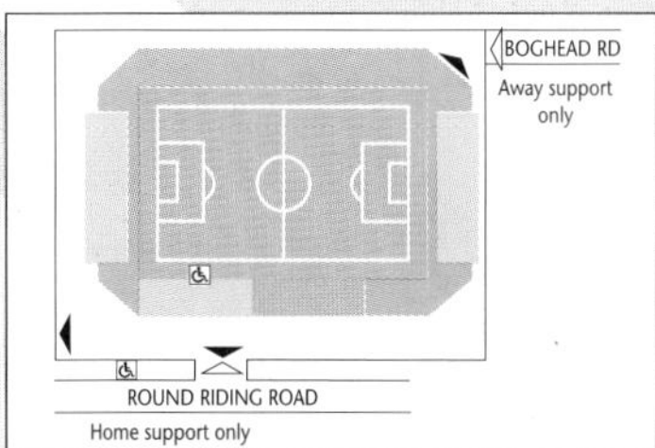

HOW TO GET THERE

Boghead Park can be reached by the following routes:

TRAINS: The train service from Glasgow Queen Street and Glasgow Central Low Level both pass through Dumbarton East Station (away fans best choice) and Dumbarton Central Station, both of which are situated just under a ten minute walk from the ground.

BUSES: There are two main services which pass close to the ground. These are bound for Helensburgh and Balloch from Glasgow.

CARS: Car parking is available in certain side streets around the ground. Supporters buses should follow Police signposts to designated parking area.

HAMILTON ACADEMICAL

Cliftonhill Stadium, Main Street, Coatbridge, ML5 9XX

OFFICE ADDRESS
Tudor Lodge, 51 Burnbank Road, Hamilton, ML3 9AQ

CHAIRMAN
David Campbell

CHIEF EXECUTIVE
Alistair R. Duguid

DIRECTORS
David Campbell Jnr.
William Whitelaw

SECRETARY
Scott A. Struthers, B.A. (Hons)

HON. LIFE PRESIDENT
Dr. Alexander A. Wilson

MANAGER
Alexander Clark

HON. MEDICAL OFFICER
Dr. Brian Lynas

PHYSIOTHERAPISTS
Michael McBride
Alan Mackay

S.F.A. COMMUNITY COACH
Jim Chapman

TELEPHONES
Office/Commercial (01698) 286103
Ground (01236) 606334
(Matchdays Only)
Fax (01698) 285422
Information Service
(0891) 666492

CLUB SHOP
"The Acciesshop",
c/o Accies Stand Club,
51 Burnbank Road,
Hamilton, ML3 9AQ

OFFICIAL SUPPORTERS CLUB
The Stand Club,
c/o 51 Burnbank Road,
Hamilton, ML3 9AQ

TEAM CAPTAIN
Crawford Baptie

SHIRT SPONSOR
Wilson Homebuilders

LIST OF PLAYERS 1996-97

SURNAME	FIRST NAME	MIDDLE NAME	DATE OF BIRTH	PLACE OF BIRTH	DATE OF SIGNING	HEIGHT FT INS	WEIGHT ST LBS	PREVIOUS CLUB
Baptie	Crawford	Bowie	24/02/59	Glasgow	11/08/95	6 1.0	11 7	Falkirk
Bruce	Jamie	Ross	29/08/76	East Kilbride	06/10/95	6 0.0	11 4	East Kilbride Thistle
Clark	Gary		13/09/64	Glasgow	25/06/91	5 10.0	11 10	Clyde
Davidson	William	Andrew	01/12/77	Bellshill	08/08/96	5 10.0	10 0	"X" Form
Ferguson	Allan	Thomas	21/03/69	Lanark	31/12/87	5 10.5	12 6	Netherdale Com A.F.C
Geraghty	Michael	John	30/10/70	Glasgow	03/11/95	5 10.0	10 6	East Stirlingshire
Hillcoat	Christopher	Patrick	03/10/69	Glasgow	19/05/87	5 10.0	11 3	St. Bridget's B.G.
Laird	David	James	18/08/77	Bellshill	13/12/95	5 11.0	11 0	Lesmahagow Juniors
Lorimer	David	James	26/01/74	Bellshill	04/08/93	5 9.5	11 0	Hamilton Accies B.C.
McBride	Joseph		17/08/60	Glasgow	07/08/96	5 8.5	11 2	Livingston
McCormick	Steven	Walter	10/11/75	Bellshill	02/06/94	5 6.0	9 10	Mill United
McCulloch	Scott	Anderson J.	29/11/75	Cumnock	24/03/95	6 0.0	12 4	Rangers
McEntegart	Sean	David	01/03/70	Dublin	24/07/92	6 0.0	12 7	Queen's Park
McFarlane	David		10/04/79	Glasgow	06/08/96	5 11.0	11 7	"S" Form
McGill	Derek		14/10/75	Lanark	17/09/96	5 11.5	11 4	Falkirk
McIntosh	Martin	Wylie	19/03/71	East Kilbride	01/02/94	6 2.0	12 4	Clydebank
McKenzie	Paul	Vincent	22/09/64	Glasgow	30/01/91	5 11.0	12 4	Dumbarton
McQuade	John		08/07/70	Glasgow	31/08/93	5 9.0	10 4	Dumbarton
Paris	Steven	Robert	01/08/78	Uphall	12/07/96	6 2.5	13 12	Newcastle United
Quitongo	Jose	Manuel	18/11/74	Luanda	15/11/95	5 7.5	10 7	Darlington
Renicks	Steven	John	28/11/75	Bellshill	01/06/94	5 8.5	10 7	Hamilton Accies B.C.
Ritchie	Paul	Michael	25/01/69	St. Andrews	06/08/96	5 11.0	12 0	Derry City
Scott	Colin		19/05/70	Glasgow	24/08/96	6 1.0	12 4	Rangers
Sherry	James	Cunningham	09/09/73	Glasgow	19/05/92	5 8.0	11 9	Hamilton Accies B.C.
Thomson	Steven	William	19/04/73	Glasgow	06/01/95	6 0.0	10 12	Kirkintilloch Rob Roy

MILESTONES

YEAR OF FORMATION: 1874
MOST CAPPED PLAYER: Colin Miller (Canada)
NO. OF CAPS: 29
MOST LEAGUE POINTS IN A SEASON: 57 (First Division – Season 1991/92)
MOST LEAGUE GOALS SCORED BY A PLAYER IN A SEASON: David Wilson (Season 1936/37)
NO. OF GOALS SCORED: 34
RECORD ATTENDANCE: 28,690 (-v- Heart of Midlothian – Scottish Cup 3.3.1937)
RECORD VICTORY: 10-2 (-v- Cowdenbeath – Division 1, 15.10.1932)
RECORD DEFEAT: 1-11 (-v- Hibernian – Division 1, 6.11.1965)

THE ACCIES' TEN YEAR LEAGUE RECORD

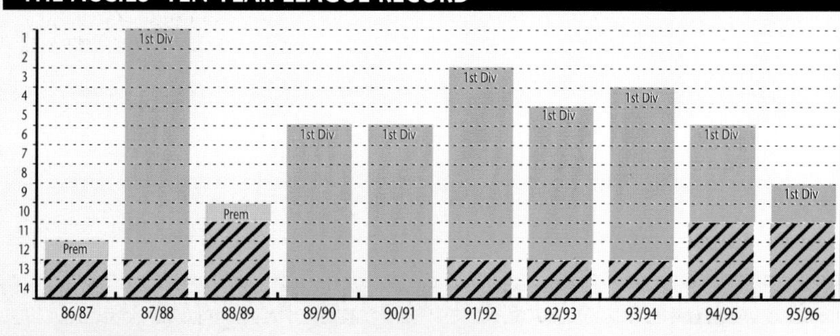

CLUB FACTFILE 1995/96
RESULTS... APPEARANCES... SCORERS

The ACCIES

Date	Venue	Opponents	Att.	Res	Cormack D.	Renicks S.	McInulty S.	Thomson S.	Paterson C.	McIntosh M.	Hartley P.	McEntegart S.	Chalmers P.	McQuade J.	McCulloch S.	Clark G.	Lorimer D.	McKenzie P.	Sherry J.	Baptie C.	McCormick S.	McParland J. I.	McCarrison D.	Ferguson A.	Hillcoat C.	McStay R.	McCloy S.	Geraghty M.	Quitongo J.	Craig D.	Diver D.	Tighe M.	McFarlane D.
Aug 12	A	Dumbarton	1,191	0-1	1	2	3	4	5	6	7	8	9	10	11	12	14																
27	H	Clydebank	845	0-2	1		3		5	6		4		10	15	7	14	2	8	9	11	12											
Sep 2	A	Dundee United	5,194	1-2	1	12		5		6	14	4		10^{1}	11	7	8	3	2	9			15										
9	H	St. Johnstone	803	0-3			3	9	5	6	12	4		10		7	11	2	8				15	1									
16	A	Dundee	2,395	1-1		3		8	5	6	7^{1}	4				10			11	9			15	1	2	12							
23	H	St. Mirren	1,451	2-2		3		8	5	6	7^{1}	4^{1}		15		10			11	9				1	2		14						
30	A	Airdrieonians	1,586	0-0			3	8	5	6	7	4				10		15	11	9				1	2		12						
Oct 7	H	Dunfermline Athletic	1,473	1-3			3	8	5	6	7	4		12		10^{1}		15	11	9				1	2		14						
14	A	Greenock Morton	2,875	0-2			3	8		6	7					10	12	4	11	5				1	2	14	9						
21	H	Dundee United	1,719	0-1		3	11	8		6		14				10		4	7	5	9			1	2		15						
28	A	Clydebank	814	0-2		3		8		6	11				15	10		4	7	5	9			1	2	14							
Nov 4	H	Dundee	1,131	1-2		3		8	5	6^{1}	7				14			12	11	9	15			1	2	4		10					
11	A	St. Johnstone	2,348	0-2		3	11	8		6	7				14		15	12	10	5				1	2	4		9					
18	H	Airdrieonians	1,169	1-2		3				6	7	8			12	10	11	14		5				1	2	4^{1}		9	15				
25	A	St. Mirren	2,546	3-0		3				6	11^{1}	8			15	10		12		5				1	2	4		9^{1}	7^{1}				
Dec 2	A	Dunfermline Athletic	3,284	0-4		3	14			6	11	8				10		12		5	9			1	2	4			7				
9	H	Greenock Morton	1,813	2-3		3	11			6	9	10				12^{1}		4		5	14			1	2	8^{1}			7				
16	H	Dumbarton	762	3-0		3	6				11^{1}	8				10^{1}		5		9				1	2	4^{1}			7				
26	A	Dundee United	6,109	1-1	17	3^{1}		14	6			8					10		7	5	12			1	2	4		9	11				
Jan 6	A	Dundee	2,020	1-2	1	3					11	8					10		7	5					2	4^{1}		9	15	6			
13	H	St. Johnstone	1,197	2-1	1	3	14				10^{1}	8^{1}				12	15		7	5					2	4		9	11	6			
20	H	Dunfermline Athletic	1,556	0-0	1	3	11	4			10	8					15			5					2			9	7	6	14		
24	H	St. Mirren	1,531	3-0	1	3	11	4			10	8^{1}					15	12		5					2			9^{2}	7	6	14		
Feb 13	A	Dumbarton	654	2-1		2	3	4		5	7^{2}	8			11				15		14			1				10		6	9		
24	H	Clydebank	835	1-1		3	10				7	8			11^{1}				4	5	9			1	2				14	6	12		
Mar 2	A	St. Mirren	1,243	1-0		3	11				10			12					8	5				1	2	4		9	7	6^{1}			
6	A	Airdrieonians	1,021	0-3		3	11	15						10			12	14	8	5				1	2	4		9	7	6			
9	A	Greenock Morton	2,560	1-4		3						8		10				15	7	5				1	2	4		9	11^{1}	6			
16	H	Airdrieonians	909	†4-1		3					11^{2}	4		10					8	5				1	2	14		9	7^{1}	6			
23	H	Dundee	828	0-1			3	9			11	4		10					8	5				1	2			12	7	6			
30	A	St. Johnstone	2,614	1-4	1	3		10			11	4						14	8^{1}	5					2			9	7	6			
Apr 6	A	Dunfermline Athletic	4,542	3-1	1	3		9		5	11^{1}	10^{1}							8						2	4			7^{1}	6			
13	H	Greenock Morton	1,519	0-1	1	3		9		5	11	10		14				15	8						2	4		12	7	6			
22	H	Dundee United	3,291	0-2		3				5	11	8		10				4		9				1	2			14	12	6		7	
27	A	Clydebank	3,665	3-1		3				5	11	8					12	4		9^{1}				1	2			10^{2}	7	6			
May 4	H	Dumbarton	657	2-1		3				5	11^{1}						12	4		9				1	2	8		10^{1}	7	6			15
TOTAL FULL APPEARANCES					10	29	17	19	9	23	29	28	1	9	4	14	5	11	24	31	5			26	31	16	1	17	18	17	1	1	
TOTAL SUB APPEARANCES					(1)	(1)	(2)	(2)			(2)	(1)		(4)	(6)	(3)	(10)	(12)	(1)		(4)	(1)	(3)			(4)	(4)	(3)	(4)		(3)		(1)
TOTAL GOALS SCORED						1				1	11	4		1	1	3			1	1						4		6	4	1			

Small bold figures denote goalscorers. † denotes opponent's own goal.

CLIFTONHILL STADIUM

CAPACITY: 1,238; Seated 538, Standing 700

PITCH DIMENSIONS: 100 yds x 70 yds

FACILITIES FOR DISABLED SUPPORTERS: Access from East Stewart Street with toilet facilities and space for wheelchairs, cars etc. Advanced contact with club advised – this area is uncovered.

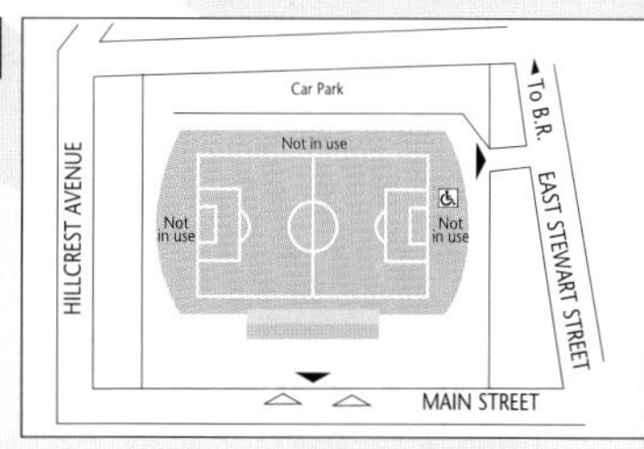

HOW TO GET THERE

The following routes can be used to reach Cliftonhill Stadium:

BUSES: The ground is conveniently situated on the main Glasgow-Airdrie bus route and there is a stop near the ground. Local buses serving most areas of Coatbridge and Airdrie pass by the stadium every few minutes

TRAINS: The nearest railway station is Coatdyke on the Glasgow-Airdrie line and the ground is a ten minute walk from there. The frequency of service is 15 minutes.

CARS: A large car park is situated behind the ground with access off Albion Street, and vehicles may also be parked in Hillcrest Avenue, Albion Street and East Stewart Street, which are all adjacent to the ground.

LIVINGSTON

Almondvale Stadium,
Alderstone Road, Livingston,
West Lothian, EH54 7DN

CHAIRMAN
William P. Hunter

VICE-CHAIRMAN
Hugh Cowan

DIRECTORS
Robert Clark (Treasurer)
James R. S. Renton
Anthony K. Kinder

HONORARY PRESIDENT
John P. Blacklaw, C.Eng, M.I.E.E.

HONORARY VICE-PRESIDENT
William L. Mill
John L. Bain B.E.M.

SECRETARY
James R. S. Renton

ASSISTANT SECRETARY
Morris Kaplan

MANAGER
James Leishman

ASSISTANT MANAGER
George McNeill

RESERVE TEAM COACH
Michael Korotkich

YOUTH TEAM COACH
James Henderson

CLUB DOCTOR
Dr. Box

PHYSIOTHERAPIST
Arthur Duncan

COMMERCIAL MANAGER
Mrs. Morna Watkins

TELEPHONES
Ground/Commercial
(01506) 417000
Sec. Home (0802) 933263
Sec. Bus. (01738) 476430
Fax (01506) 418888

OFFICIAL SUPPORTERS CLUB
Marilyn McMillan,
41 Deanswood, Deanswood Park,
Deans, Livingston.
(01506) 490666

TEAM CAPTAIN
Gordon McLeod

SHIRT SPONSOR
Mitsubishi Electric

LIST OF PLAYERS 1996-97

SURNAME	FIRST NAME	MIDDLE NAME	DATE OF BIRTH	PLACE OF BIRTH	DATE OF SIGNING	HEIGHT FT INS	WEIGHT ST LBS	PREVIOUS CLUB
Alleyne	David	Richardo	15/02/72	Barbados	13/03/95	5 11.0	12 0	Lambada (Barbados)
Bailey	Lee		10/07/72	Edinburgh	04/08/92	5 6.0	10 0	Hibernian
Black	Derek	John	15/12/77	Uphall	13/08/96	5 11.0	10 4	Livingston Juniors
Bowsher	Colin		11/06/73	Musselburgh	16/11/95	6 2.0	12 0	Ormiston Juniors
Callaghan	Thomas		28/08/69	Glasgow	19/07/96	5 10.0	11 4	Dunfermline Athletic
Callaghan	William	Thomas	23/03/67	Dunfermline	24/03/95	5 10.5	12 7	Cowdenbeath
Campbell	Stephen		20/11/67	Dundee	04/01/96	5 7.0	11 0	Coleraine
Davidson	Graeme		18/01/68	Edinburgh	23/07/93	5 10.0	11 0	Berwick Rangers
Douglas	Robert	James	24/04/72	Lanark	26/10/93	6 3.0	14 12	Forth Wanderers
Duthie	Mark	James	19/08/72	Edinburgh	25/08/90	5 8.0	10 0	Edina Hibs
Forrest	Gordon	Ian	14/01/77	Dunfermline	05/09/96	5 6.0	8 2	Raith Rovers
Graham	Thomas		12/05/68	Edinburgh	18/06/90	6 0.0	13 0	Cavalry Park B.C.
Harvey	Graham		23/04/61	Musselburgh	04/08/95	5 10.5	11 7	Instant Dict (Hong Kong)
Korotkich	Michael	James	26/05/63	Edinburgh	08/06/95	5 9.0	12 0	Dunbar
Laidlaw	Steven	James	17/06/73	Edinburgh	13/06/96	6 0.0	12 0	Ormiston Juniors
Martin	Craig	Richard S.	16/04/71	Haddington	16/08/94	6 0.0	11 10	Arbroath
McLeod	Gordon	Thomas	02/09/67	Edinburgh	25/09/92	5 9.0	11 2	Dundee
McMartin	Grant	Thomas	31/12/70	Linlithgow	01/08/95	5 10.0	10 5	St. Johnstone
O'Hara	Gerard		29/09/77	Broxburn	13/08/96	5 9.0	10 8	Livingston Juniors
Sinclair	Christopher		11/11/70	Sheffield	07/10/94	5 9.0	10 10	Dunfermline Athletic
Smart	Craig	William	23/03/75	Dunfermline	01/08/95	6 0.0	10 3	Dunfermline Athletic
Stoute	Horace	Antonio	29/05/71	Barbados	13/03/95	6 2.0	13 7	Lambada (Barbados)
Tierney	Peter	Grant	11/10/61	Falkirk	16/01/96	6 0.5	13 13	Partick Thistle
Watson	Graham		10/09/70	St. Andrews	01/08/96	5 9.5	11 6	Clyde
Williamson	Stewart		10/12/61	Lasswade	02/08/88	6 0.0	11 7	Cowdenbeath
Wood	Barry	Wilson	19/06/77	Edinburgh	16/11/95	5 7.0	11 0	Bonnyrigg Rose
Young	Jason	Anthony	01/03/72	Edinburgh	14/02/95	5 7.0	10 0	Wissen (Germany)

MILESTONES

YEAR OF FORMATION: 1974 (From Seasons 1974/75 to 1994/95 known as Meadowbank Thistle F.C.)
MOST LEAGUE POINTS IN A SEASON: 55 (Second Division – Season 1986/87)(2 Points for a Win)
72 (Third Division – Season 1995/96)(3 Points for a Win)
MOST LEAGUE GOALS SCORED BY A PLAYER IN A SEASON: John McGachie (Season 1986/87)
NO. OF GOALS SCORED: 21
RECORD ATTENDANCE: 2,818 (-v- Albion Rovers, 10.8.1974 at Meadowbank Stadium)
4,000 (-v- East Stirlingshire, 11.11.1995 at Almondvale Stadium)
RECORD VICTORY: 6-0 (-v- Raith Rovers – Second Division, 9.11.1985)
RECORD DEFEAT: 0-8 (-v- Hamilton Academical – Division 2, 14.12.1974)

LIVVY'S LIONS' TEN YEAR LEAGUE RECORD

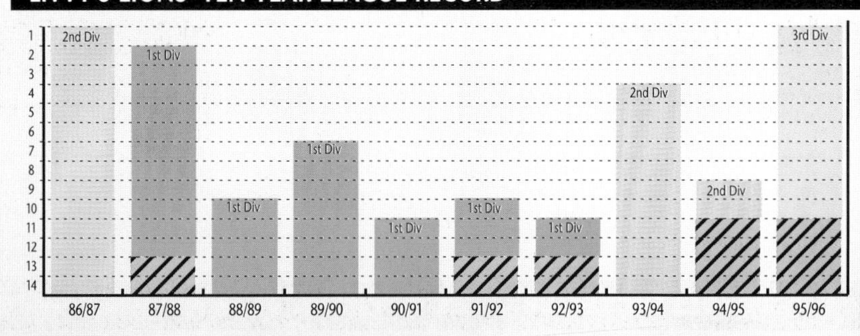

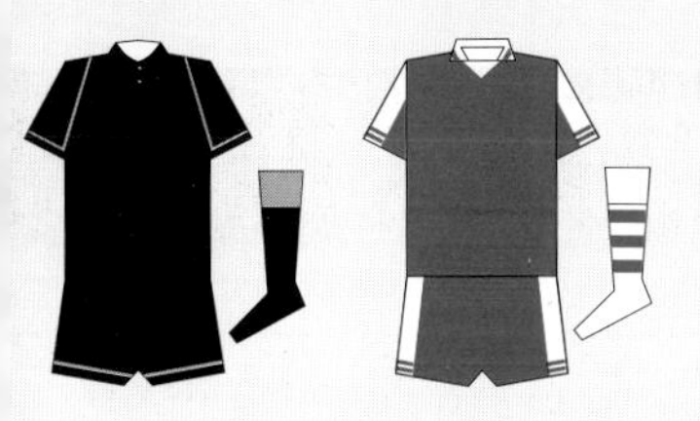

CLUB FACTFILE 1995/96
RESULTS... APPEARANCES... SCORERS

LIVVY'S LIONS

Date	Venue	Opponents	Att.	Res	Stoute H.	Smart C.	McCartney C.	Davidson G.	Williamson S.	Alleyne D.	McMartin G.	Bailey L.	Young J.	McLeod G.	Duthie M.	Harvey G.	Sinclair C.	Sorbie S.	Martin C.	Callaghan W.	Graham T.	Douglas R.	Thorburn S.	Campbell S.	McBride J.	Coulston D.	Tierney P. G.	Wright G.	Hislop T.	Laidlaw S.
Aug 12	A	Caledonian Thistle	1,259	3-0	1	2	3	4	5	6	7	8[2]	9	10[1]	11	12	15													
26	A	Arbroath	721	3-1	1	2		4	5	10	7	8	9[2]	6	3	15[1]	11	12												
Sep 9	A	East Stirlingshire	409	2-1	1	2		4	5	10	7	8	9[2]	6	11	14		12	3	15										
16	H	Alloa	249	2-0	1	10[1]		4	2[1]		7	8	9	6	3		11				5									
20	H	Queen's Park	223	2-0	1	10		4	2		7[1]	8	9	6[1]	3	14	11	12			5									
23	H	Albion Rovers	229	2-1	1	10		4	2[1]		7[1]	8	9	6	3	14	11			15	5									
30	A	Cowdenbeath	340	1-0	1	2		4		6	7		8[1]	10	3		11	15		9	5									
Oct 7	A	Ross County	2,120	1-1	1	6		4	2	8	7		9[1]	10	3	14				11	5									
14	H	Brechin City	273	0-0	1	8	11	4	2		7	10	9	6	3	12	15	14			5									
21	A	Queen's Park	540	1-0	1	8		4	2		7	11	9[1]	6	3	12		10			5									
28	H	Arbroath	236	0-1		8		4	2	15	7	10	9	6	3	14		11		12	5	1								
Nov 4	A	Alloa	548	2-0		11		4	2	8	7	10	9	6	3[2]						5	1								
11	H	East Stirlingshire	4,000	1-1		6		4	5		7	11	9[1]	10	3	12		8		14	2	1	15							
18	H	Cowdenbeath	3,880	0-1		6		4	5		7	11	9	10	3	14		8		12	2	1	15							
25	A	Albion Rovers	433	2-0		8	3	4	2		7		9[2]	6	11					10	5	1								
Dec 2	H	Ross County	3,444	0-0		8		4	2	3	7	12	10	6	11	14		15		9	5	1								
16	A	Brechin City	419	0-2			2	4		3	7	12	9	6	11	10		8		15	5	1	14							
Jan 10	H	Queen's Park	1,822	3-1				4	5	8	7		9	6[1]	11[1]	10[1]				14		1	2	3	15					
13	H	Albion Rovers	2,509	0-1				4	5	8	7		9	6	11	10				14		1	2	3	15	12				
17	H	Caledonian Thistle	2,578	0-2	1	8			4		7	12	9	6	11	10							2	3			5			
Feb 3	H	Brechin City	2,386	0-1	1	6		4	2		7	12	8	10	11					9				3			5			
10	H	Alloa	2,066	1-0		2		4		8	7		9[1]	6	11	10	14					1		3			5			
13	A	Ross County	2,300	2-2		2		4		8	7	12	9[1]	6	11	10[1]	14					1		3			5			
17	A	East Stirlingshire	472	3-0		2		4	15	8	7	10	9[2]	6			11[1]			14		1		3			5			
24	A	Arbroath	772	2-1		2		4		8[1]	7	10	9	6[1]			11					1		3			5			
28	A	Cowdenbeath	272	3-0		2		4		8	7[1]	10[1]	9[1]	6			11			14		1		3			5	15		
Mar 2	H	Caledonian Thistle	2,152	2-2		2		4		8	7	10[1]	9[1]	6			11					1		3			5			
9	A	Albion Rovers	623	1-0		2		4		8[1]	7	10	9	6			11			14		1		3			5	15		
16	H	Cowdenbeath	2,147	2-1		2		4		10	7	8	9	6			11[1]			15		1		3			5[1]	14		
23	A	Alloa	541	1-1		2		4	12		7	8[1]	9	6	14		11			15		1		3			5	10		
30	H	East Stirlingshire	2,084	1-1		2		4	15	10	7	8	9[1]		14		11					1		3			5	6		
Apr 6	H	Ross County	2,333	2-1		2			4		7		9	6	12		11[1]			15		1		3[1]			5	8	10	
13	A	Brechin City	768	1-0		2			4		7		9	6			11			15		1		3			5[1]	8	10	
20	A	Queen's Park	928	0-0		2			4		7		9	6	11					15		1		3			5	8	10	
27	H	Arbroath	2,993	3-0				6	4		7	14	9[1]	10	15		11			12		1		3[1]			5	2	8[1]	
May 4	A	Caledonian Thistle	1,403	2-1				4			7	12	10		2		11			9	5	1		3				6		8[2]
TOTAL FULL APPEARANCES					12	31	4	32	23	19	36	20	36	34	25	6	17	5	1	6	15	24	3	19			16	7	4	1
TOTAL SUB APPEARANCES									(3)	(1)		(7)			(4)	(12)	(4)	(6)		(17)			(3)		(2)	(1)		(3)		
TOTAL GOALS SCORED						1			2	2	3	5	18	4	3	3	3							2			2		1	2

Small bold figures denote goalscorers. † denotes opponent's own goal.

ALMONDVALE STADIUM

CAPACITY: 4,000 (All Seated)
PITCH DIMENSIONS: 110yds x 75yds
FACILITIES FOR DISABLED SUPPORTERS: By prior arrangement with Secretary.

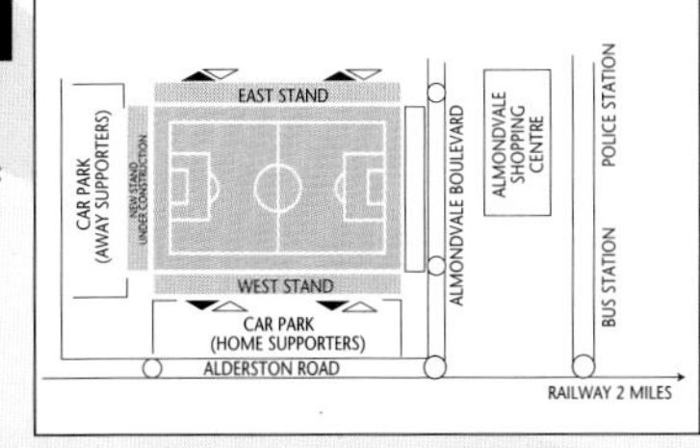

HOW TO GET THERE

Almondvale Stadium can be reached by the following routes:

BUSES: By bus to terminus at Almondvale Shopping Centre. Follow direction signs for St. John's Hospital or Almondvale Stadium and it is a short 5 minute walk.

TRAINS: To either Livingston North or South, and by taxi to stadium. Approximate cost is £2.00.

CARS: Leave M8 at Livingston Junction (East). Follow signs for St. John's Hospital or Almondvale Stadium.

QUEEN OF THE SOUTH

Palmerston Park, Terregles Street, Dumfries, DG2 9BA

CHAIRMAN
Norman G. Blount

VICE-CHAIRMAN
Gordon R. McKerrow

DIRECTORS
Thomas G. Harkness
Keith M. Houliston

COMPANY SECRETARY
Richard Shaw, MBE

CO-MANAGERS
Rowan Alexander & Mark Shanks

CHIEF SCOUT
Scott Stirling

EDUCATION OFFICER
Brian Oakes

CLUB COACHES
Trevor Wilson, Gordon Doig, Jim Grant, Derek McHarg, Tommy Bryce, Walter MacAdam, Gordon Campbell & Whitey Moffat

CAREERS OFFICER
Walter MacAdam

MATCH ANALYST
Iain McChesney

CLUB DOCTORS
Dr. Phil Clayton, Dr. Steven Morris
Dr. Andrew Lyon

ORTHOPAEDIC SURGEONS
Clark Dreghorn, Andrew Ogden
Miss Pat Costigan

PHYSIOTHERAPIST
Marion Hamilton

MASSEUR
Gordon Johnstone

GROUNDSMAN
Kevin McCormick

COMMERCIAL MANAGER
Robert McKinnell (01387) 258565

TELEPHONES
Ground/Ticket Office/Information
(01387) 254853
Fax (01387) 254853
Restaurant (01387) 252241
Football Office Only (01387) 251666

CLUB SHOP
Palmerston Park, Terregles Street, Dumfries (01387) 254853
Open 9.00 a.m. – 4.00 p.m. Mon. to Fri. and 1.30 p.m. – 5.00 p.m. on home match days.

OFFICIAL SUPPORTERS CLUB
c/o Palmerston Park, Terregles Street, Dumfries, DG2 9BA

TEAM CAPTAIN
David Kennedy

SHIRT SPONSOR
The Open University

LIST OF PLAYERS 1996-97

SURNAME	FIRST NAME	MIDDLE NAME	DATE OF BIRTH	PLACE OF BIRTH	DATE OF SIGNING	HEIGHT FT INS	WEIGHT ST LBS	PREVIOUS CLUB
Aitken	Andrew	Robert	02/02/78	Dumfries	10/07/96	6 1.0	12 0	Annan Athletic
Alexander	Rowan	Samuel	28/01/61	Ayr	25/01/96	5 7.0	11 10	Greenock Morton
Allen	Craig		25/10/77	Paisley	10/07/96	5 10.0	11 3	Bellshill B.C.
Brown	James	William	29/01/72	Dumfries	08/08/94	5 10.0	10 0	Cumnock Juniors
Bryce	Thomas	Charles	27/01/60	Johnstone	03/08/93	5 8.0	11 10	Clydebank
Brydson	Euan		13/09/73	Dumfries	16/07/96	5 8.0	9 0	Maybole Juniors
Burnett	Andrew	John	21/10/68	Dumfries	06/09/96	5 10.0	12 0	Annan Athletic
Cleeland	Marc		15/12/75	Whitehaven	10/07/96	5 8.0	10 2	Unattached
Cochrane	Gary		20/02/76	Dumfries	29/06/94	5 10.0	11 0	Ayr Boswell B.C.
Flannigan	Craig		11/02/73	Dumfries	10/07/96	5 6.0	10 2	Clydebank
Irving	Craig		19/04/78	Dumfries	10/07/96	5 8.0	10 7	Annan Athletic
Johnstone	Neil	William	21/06/79	Dumfries	07/07/95	5 6.0	11 7	"S" Form
Kennedy	David	John	07/10/66	Ayr	24/12/93	5 10.0	11 0	Ayr United
Laing	Derek	James	11/11/73	Haddington	15/07/96	5 10.0	11 7	Greenock Morton
Lancaster	Ian	Robert	04/09/77	Ruthin	12/08/96	5 8.0	10 8	Carlisle United
Leslie	Steven		06/02/76	Dumfries	29/01/96	5 5.5	10 0	Annan Athletic
Lilley	David	William	31/10/77	Bellshill	26/10/95	6 1.0	11 4	"X" Form
MacLean	Jeffrey	Duncan C.	18/07/78	Ontario	10/07/96	6 0.0	12 0	Unattached
Mallan	Stephen	Patrick	30/08/67	Glasgow	03/08/93	5 11.0	12 4	Clyde
Mathieson	David	James	18/01/78	Dumfries	02/08/96	5 11.0	10 13	St. Johnstone
McAllister	James	Reynolds	26/04/78	Glasgow	10/07/96	5 10.0	11 0	Bellshill B.C.
McFarlane	Andrew		22/02/70	Glasgow	30/10/90	5 7.0	10 7	Arthurlie
McIntosh	Stuart	Russell	06/02/74	Ayr	27/07/96	6 1.0	12 7	Maybole Juniors
McKeown	Brian		31/10/56	Motherwell	09/11/90	5 7.0	11 7	Airdrieonians
McKeown	Desmond	Michael	18/01/70	Glasgow	09/08/94	5 11.0	11 0	Albion Rovers
Nesovic	Alexander		10/11/72	Bradford	27/08/96	6 1.0	12 7	Eccleshill United
Nicoll	Mark	Charles	20/11/77	Dumfries	02/08/96	5 7.0	10 12	Rangers
Pettit	Steven		13/11/77	Bellshill	10/07/96	5 8.0	12 0	Bellshill B.C.
Proudfoot	Kevin	David	20/01/76	Dumfries	23/03/96	6 2.0	12 7	Glenafton Athletic
Rowe	John	George	23/08/68	Glasgow	26/08/92	6 0.0	11 7	Clydebank
Townsley	Derek		21/03/73	Carlisle	27/08/96	6 5.0	13 0	Gretna
Wilson	Stuart	Joseph	21/09/65	Edinburgh	16/07/96	5 10.0	12 0	Livingston

MILESTONES

YEAR OF FORMATION: 1919
MOST CAPPED PLAYER: William Houliston
NO. OF CAPS: 3
MOST LEAGUE POINTS IN A SEASON: 55 (Division 2 – 1985/86)
MOST LEAGUE GOALS SCORED BY A PLAYER IN A SEASON: J. Gray (Season 1927/28)
NO. OF GOALS SCORED: 37
RECORD ATTENDANCE: 24,500 (-v- Heart of Midlothian – Scottish Cup, 23.2.1952)
RECORD VICTORY: 11-1 (-v- Stranraer – Scottish Cup, 16.1.1932)
RECORD DEFEAT: 2-10 (-v- Dundee – Division 1, 1.12.1962)

THE DOONHAMERS' TEN YEAR LEAGUE RECORD

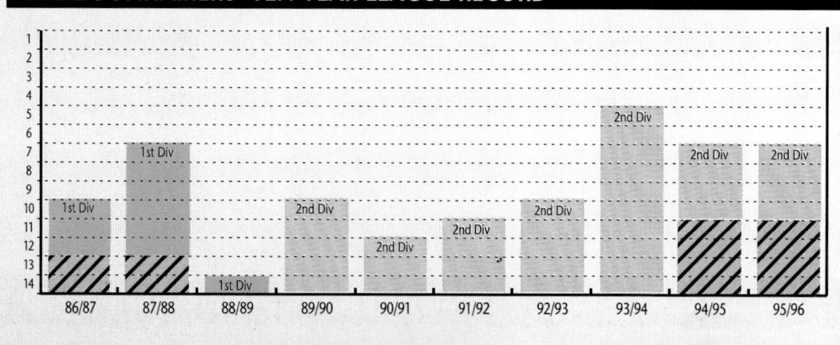

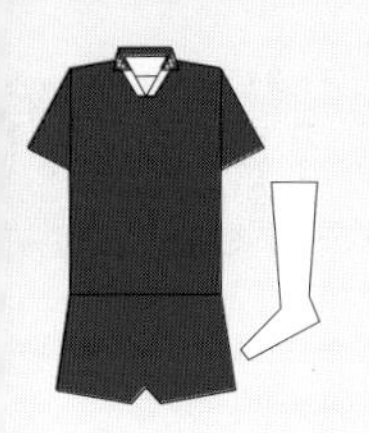

CLUB FACTFILE 1995/96
RESULTS... APPEARANCES... SCORERS

The DOONHAMERS

Date	Venue	Opponents	Att.	Res	Butter J.	McKeown D.	Brown J.	McKeown B.	Hetherington K.	Ramsay S.	Wilson S.	Kennedy D.	Campbell D.	Harris C.	Mallan S.	McFarlane A.	Cody S.	Bryce T.	McLaren J.	Campbell C.	McColm R.	Jackson D.	Lilley D.	Telfer G.	Millar J.	Dobie M.	Graham C.	Leslie S.	Burridge J.	Allen C.	McAllister J.	Pettit S.	Alexander R.
Aug 12	H	Stenhousemuir	1,300	2-2	1	2	3	4	5	6	7	8	9	10^{1}	11^{1}	12	14	15															
26	A	Montrose	557	4-1	1		3	4	2	8	7	5		9^{2}	12	6	14	10	11^{2}														
Sep 2	H	Clyde	1,897	0-3	1		3	4	2	11	7	5	14	9	12	6	8	10	15														
9	H	Stranraer	1,531	0-3	1	2	3	4		14	7	5	9	12	11	6	8	10		16													
16	A	Forfar Athletic	589	1-2	1		3		5	6	7	2	9	12	14	11	8^{1}	10		4													
23	A	East Fife	700	†1-2		15	3	2	5	6	7		12	9		11	8	10	14	4	1												
30	H	Berwick Rangers	1,056	1-4	1	12	3		5	6	7	2	15	10^{1}	11		8	9		4													
Oct 7	H	Ayr United	1,147	0-0	1	3	14			6		2	9	10	11	7	5	8		4		15											
14	A	Stirling Albion	748	2-2	1	3		12		6		2	9^{1}	10	11	7	5	8	15^{1}	4													
21	A	Stenhousemuir	509	1-2	1	3	15			8	7	2	10	9	6		5	11^{1}	14	4													
28	H	Montrose	902	4-2	1	3		2			7	8	9^{1}	12				10^{1}	6^{1}	4		11^{1}	5	15									
Nov 4	H	Forfar Athletic	1,147	1-1	1	3		2			7	10	9^{1}	12				8	11	4		6	5										
11	A	Stranraer	1,006	0-0	1	3	15	2			7	8	9	12				10	11	4		6	5										
21	A	Berwick Rangers	324	0-0	1	3		2			7	8	9	12	6			10	11	4			5										
25	H	East Fife	1,081	0-2	1	3		2			7	8	9	12	14		15	6	10	4		11	5										
Dec 2	A	Ayr United	1,434	0-2	1	3		2				6	12	7	11		8	10	9	4			5		15								
16	H	Stirling Albion	1,004	1-5	1	3		2		6	12	10	14	7	11^{1}		8	9		4			5										
Jan 10	H	Stenhousemuir	743	3-3	1	3		4				7		9	11^{1}		8	6		2			5	15^{1}		10^{1}							
20	H	Ayr United	1,264	2-2	1	3		6				2		7^{1}	9^{1}	11	4	10					5			8	12						
23	H	Berwick Rangers	840	3-0	1	3	15	6		14		2		7	9^{2}	11	4	10^{1}					5			8	12						
31	A	East Fife	732	2-1	1	3		6		14		2		7	8^{1}	11		10^{1}					5			9		4					
Feb 3	A	Stirling Albion	1,042	1-4	1	3	6					2		7^{1}	8	11		10					5			9	12	4					
13	A	Forfar Athletic	427	3-0	1	3		6		4	14	2		7	10^{2}	11		8	12				5			9^{1}							
17	H	Stranraer	1,229	†2-1	1	3		6		4		2		7	10	11^{1}		8	12				5			9		15					
24	A	Montrose	545	6-0	1	3		6		4	14	2		7	10^{2}	11		8	12^{1}				5			9^{3}		15					
Mar 2	H	Clyde	877	2-1	1	3		6		4	12^{1}	2		7	10^{1}	11		8	14				5			9		15					
5	A	Clyde	776	1-2	1	3		6		14	7	2		15	10	11		8^{1}	9				5					4					
9	H	East Fife	1,476	1-0		3		6		14	7	2		5^{1}	10	11		8	9							12		4	1				
16	A	Berwick Rangers	363	1-4		3		6				2		7^{1}	10	11		8					5			9		4	1				
23	H	Forfar Athletic	1,279	4-1		3		6		12	14	2		7	10	11		8^{3}	16^{1}				5			9		4	1				
30	A	Stranraer	722	1-3		3		6		14		2		7^{1}	10	11		8	12				5			9		4	1				
Apr 6	A	Ayr United	1,764	0-3		3		6		16		2	12	7	10	11		8	14	5						9		4	1				
13	H	Stirling Albion	1,394	0-7		3	11	6		16	7	2		5	12	14		8	10							9		4	1				
20	A	Stenhousemuir	471	3-1		3	16	6		12	7^{1}	2			10	11		8^{2}	14		1		5			9		4					
27	H	Montrose	1,227	1-1		14		6		4	7	12			10	11		8	16		1		5			9^{1}				2	3		
May 4	A	Clyde	1,095	0-0		3	12	6		4	7	2			10			8			1		5			9					11	14	15
TOTAL FULL APPEARANCES					26	30	9	30	6	16	19	34	11	25	27	23	13	35	10	15	4	4	23			17		10	6	1	2		
TOTAL SUB APPEARANCES						(3)	(6)	(1)		(10)	(5)	(1)	(6)	(8)	(5)	(2)	(3)	(1)	(13)	(1)		(1)		(2)	(1)	(1)	(3)	(3)				(1)	(1)
TOTAL GOALS SCORED											2		3	9	12	1	1	10	6			1		1		6							

Small bold figures denote goalscorers. † denotes opponent's own goal.

PALMERSTON PARK

CAPACITY: 8,312; Seated 3,509, Standing 4,803

PITCH DIMENSIONS: 112 yds x 73 yds

FACILITIES FOR DISABLED SUPPORTERS: Situated in East Stand.

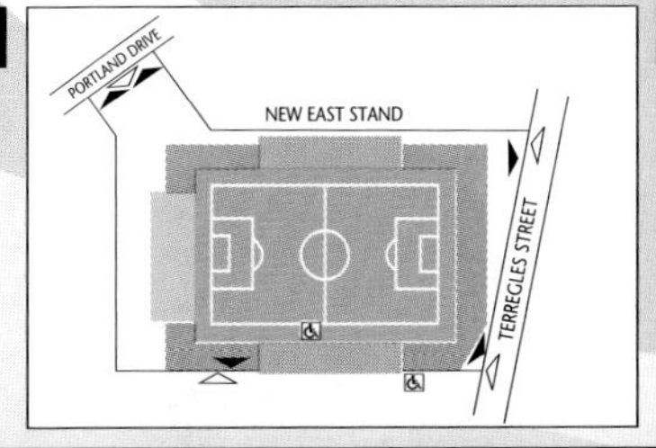

HOW TO GET THERE

Palmerston Park can be reached by the following routes:

TRAINS: There is a reasonable service to Dumfries Station from Glasgow on Saturdays, but the service is more limited in midweek. The station is about 3/4 mile from the ground.

BUSES: Buses from Glasgow, Edinburgh, Ayr and Stranraer all pass within a short distance of the park.

CARS: The car park may be reached from Portland Drive or King Street and has a capacity for approximately 174 cars.

STENHOUSEMUIR

Ochilview Park, Gladstone Road, Stenhousemuir, FK5 4QL

CHAIRMAN
A. Terry Bulloch

VICE-CHAIRMAN
Sidney S. Collumbine

DIRECTORS
David O. Reid
Gordon T. Cook (Treasurer)
James S. B. Gillespie
John G. Sharp
Alan J. McNeill
John Rolland
Martin I. McNairney
Kenneth Baird

SECRETARY
David O. Reid

MANAGER
Terry Christie

PLAYER/ASSISTANT MANAGER
Graeme Armstrong

COACH
Gordon Buchanan

CLUB DOCTOR
Steven Brown

YOUTH INITIATIVE DIRECTOR
Alan J. McNeill

PHYSIOTHERAPIST
Mrs. Lee Campbell

COMMERCIAL MANAGER
John G. Sharp
Bus. (01324) 711189

TELEPHONES
Ground/Fax (01324) 562992
Sec. Home (01324) 631895
Sec. Bus. 0141-204 2511 Ext. 231

CLUB SHOP
Ochilview Park, Gladstone Road, Stenhousemuir, FK5 4QL.
(01324) 562992
Open during first team home match days between 2.00 p.m. until 5.00 p.m. & Mon to Fri 9.00 a.m. till 4 p.m.
Contact Mrs C. Walker.

OFFICIAL SUPPORTERS CLUB
Ochilview Park, Gladstone Road, Stenhousemuir, FK5 4QL

TEAM CAPTAIN
Graeme Armstrong

SHIRT SPONSOR
Four in One

LIST OF PLAYERS 1996-97

SURNAME	FIRST NAME	MIDDLE NAME	DATE OF BIRTH	PLACE OF BIRTH	DATE OF SIGNING	HEIGHT FT INS	WEIGHT ST LBS	PREVIOUS CLUB
Aitken	Neil		27/04/71	Edinburgh	26/01/90	6 1.0	11 7	Penicuik Athletic
Alexander	Neil		10/03/78	Edinburgh	08/08/96	6 0.0	11 7	Edina Hibs
Armstrong	Graeme	John	23/06/56	Edinburgh	31/10/92	5 9.0	10 12	Meadowbank Thistle
Banks	Alan		25/02/70	Edinburgh	29/05/96	5 11.0	11 0	Berwick Rangers
Brown	Scott		05/03/80	Edinburgh	05/09/96	5 5.0	10 0	Salvesen B.C.
Buchanan	Gordon		20/10/61	Glasgow	08/08/95	6 0.0	11 12	Unattached
Christie	Martin	Peter	07/11/71	Edinburgh	04/12/93	5 6.0	10 4	Dundee
Ellison	Steven		03/03/70	Edinburgh	03/06/96	6 1.0	12 3	Livingston
Fisher	James		14/10/67	Bridge of Allan	18/01/92	5 10.0	10 11	Bo'ness United
Haddow	Lloyd	Simon	21/01/71	Lanark	13/02/92	6 1.0	11 6	Fauldhouse United
Henderson	James	Charles	18/10/76	Falkirk	05/03/96	6 1.0	11 0	Sauchie Juniors
Hume	Andrew		30/06/68	Falkirk	05/09/96	6 5.0	14 7	Bonnybridge Juniors
Hunter	Paul		30/08/68	Kirkcaldy	22/09/95	5 9.0	10 7	East Fife
Hutchison	Gareth		04/06/72	Edinburgh	26/07/94	5 10.0	12 0	Tranent Juniors
Little	Ian	James	10/12/73	Edinburgh	06/06/95	5 6.0	8 12	Livingston
Logan	Paul	Michael	13/06/76	Sheffield	06/01/94	5 11.0	11 4	Bonnybridge Juniors
McGeachie	George		05/02/59	Bothkennar	26/07/94	5 11.5	11 12	Raith Rovers
McKee	Kevin	George	10/06/66	Edinburgh	24/07/96	5 8.0	11 11	Partick Thistle
Roseburgh	David		30/06/59	Loanhead	26/08/93	5 10.5	9 9	Meadowbank Thistle
Scott	Colin	Andrew	30/11/66	Edinburgh	22/09/95	5 8.0	13 0	East Stirlingshire
Sprott	Adrian		23/03/62	Edinburgh	05/08/93	5 8.0	10 0	Meadowbank Thistle
Stewart	Iain	Scott	06/01/79	Falkirk	14/06/96	5 10.0	12 0	I.C.I. Juveniles
Thomson	James		15/05/71	Stirling	19/06/96	6 1.0	12 7	Clyde

MILESTONES

YEAR OF FORMATION: 1884
MOST LEAGUE POINTS IN A SEASON: 50 (Division 2 – Season 1960/61) (2 Points for a Win)
56 (Second Division – Season 1994/95) (3 Points for a Win)
MOST LEAGUE GOALS SCORED BY A PLAYER IN A SEASON Evelyn Morrison (Season 1927/28) and Robert Murray (Season 1936/37)
NO. OF GOALS SCORED: 31
RECORD ATTENDANCE: 12,500 (-v- East Fife – 11.3.1950)
RECORD VICTORY: 9-2 (-v- Dundee United – Division 2, 16.4.1937)
RECORD DEFEAT: 2-11 (-v- Dunfermline Athletic – Division 2, 27.9.1930)

THE WARRIORS' TEN YEAR LEAGUE RECORD

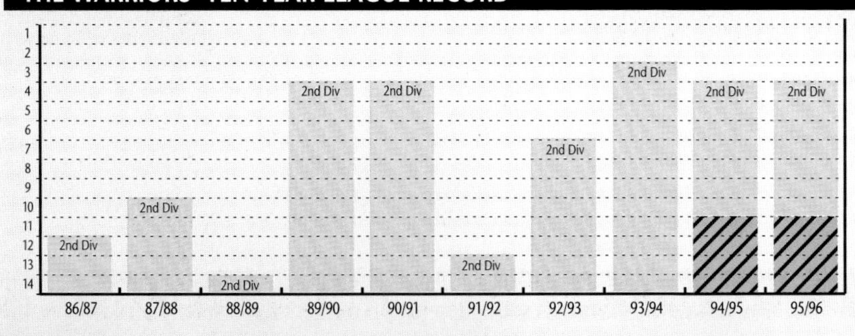

The WARRIORS

Date	Venue	Opponents	Att.	Res	McKenzie R.	Bannon E.	Haddow L.	Armstrong G.	McGeachie G.	Christie M.	Logan P.	Fisher J.	Mathieson M.	Hutchison G.	Little I.	Clarke J.	Henderson J.	Aitken N.	Swanson D.	Sprott A.	Scott C.	Hunter P.	Brannigan K.	Steel T.	Roseburgh D.	Little G.
Aug 12	A	Queen of the South	1,300	2-2	1	2	3	4	5	6	7	8	9	10[1]	11[1]											
26	H	Stranraer	336	3-0	1	2	3	4	5	6	7	8[1]	9[1]	10	11[1]	12	14									
Sep 2	A	Forfar Athletic	542	0-1	1	2	3	4	5		7	8	9	10	11		14	6	12							
9	H	Stirling Albion	674	1-1	1	2	3	4	5		7	8	9	10	11[1]		6	12		14						
16	A	Berwick Rangers	362	1-3	1	2	3	4	5		7	8	9	10	11		14[1]	12		6						
23	A	Clyde	1,088	1-0	1	2		4	5			8	9	10	11[1]			12		6	3	7				
30	H	East Fife	789	0-1	1	2	3	4	5			8	9	10	11		15	12		6		7				
Oct 7	H	Montrose	521	3-1	1		3	4	5		6[1]	8	9[1]	10[1]	11		14	12				7	2			
14	A	Ayr United	1,106	†2-1	1		3	4	5		6	8	9	10[1]	11			12	15			7	2			
21	H	Queen of the South	509	2-1	1	2	3	4	5			8	9	10[1]	11[1]			12		6		7				
28	A	Stranraer	566	1-2	1	2		4			14	8	9[1]	10	11			12		3		7	5	6		
31	H	Berwick Rangers	402	4-1	1	2	3	4			14	8	9	10	11			5		6[4]		7		12		
Nov 11	A	Stirling Albion	903	1-2	1	2	3	4	5			8	9	10	11			12		6[1]		7		15	14	
18	A	East Fife	815	2-0	1		3	4	5	6		8	9[1]	10	11[1]				7	2						
25	H	Clyde	714	0-1	1	7	3	4	5	6		8	9	10	11					2		14				15
Dec 2	A	Montrose	504	4-1	1	7	3	4	5	6		8	9[2]	10[1]	11[1]					2					12	15
16	H	Ayr United	525	1-1	1	7	3	4				8	9[1]	10	11			5	14	2		6				12
Jan 10	A	Queen of the South	743	3-3	1	7	3	4	5	6	15	8	9[1]	10[2]				11		2		12				
13	A	Clyde	958	0-3	1	7	3	4		6	15	8	9	10						2	14	12	5			11
16	H	Forfar Athletic	381	3-1	1	3[1]		4		6		8	9	10	11[1]					2	15	7[1]	5			
20	H	Montrose	378	3-1	1	7	3	4	12	6		8[1]	9[2]	10	11					2			5			14
23	H	East Fife	594	2-2	1			4		6	12	8		10[1]	11			7		2	5	9[1]	3		14	
Feb 3	A	Ayr United	1,181	1-1	1			4	5	6		8		10	11			14		2		9[1]	3		7	
10	A	Berwick Rangers	333	1-2	1	3	12	4		6				10	11			14		2[1]	8	9	5		7	15
24	H	Stranraer	406	2-0	1	3		4				8	9	10	11			12[1]		2[1]		7	5		6	
27	H	Stirling Albion	864	0-1	1	3		4				8	9	10	11			6		2		7	5		12	
Mar 2	A	Forfar Athletic	371	1-3	1		3	4	5	6		8	14	12[1]				7		2	11	9				10
9	H	Clyde	674	1-0	1	3		4	5			8		10	11			12		2[1]	7	9			6	
16	A	East Fife	621	1-3	1		15	4	5	6	8		9	10	11			12		2		7[1]			3	
23	H	Berwick Rangers	419	0-3	1	5	8	4		6	12		9	10	11					2		7			3	
30	A	Stirling Albion	1,132	1-0	1	5	3	4				8	9	10	11		6			2		7[1]				
Apr 6	A	Montrose	507	3-1	1	5	3	4				8	9	10	11[1]		6			2		7[2]				
13	H	Ayr United	559	0-1	1	5	3			14		8	9	10	11		6			2	4	7				
20	H	Queen of the South	471	1-3	1	5	3	4		6		8	9	10	11					2		7[1]				
27	A	Stranraer	503	0-0	1	3			5	6		8	9	10	11		4			2		7				
May 4	H	Forfar Athletic	431	0-2	1	3		4	5	6		8		10	11		9	15		2		7				
TOTAL FULL APPEARANCES					36	29	24	34	21	18	8	33	30	35	33		6	7	1	30	6	25	11	1	6	2
TOTAL SUB APPEARANCES							(2)		(1)	(1)	(6)		(1)	(1)		(1)	(5)	(15)	(3)	(1)	(2)	(3)		(2)	(4)	(5)
TOTAL GOALS SCORED						1					1	2	10	9	9		1	1		8		8				

Small bold figures denote goalscorers. † denotes opponent's own goal.

OCHILVIEW PARK

CAPACITY: 2,770; Seated 1000, Standing 1,770

PITCH DIMENSIONS: 110 yds x 72 yds

FACILITIES FOR DISABLED SUPPORTERS: Accommodation for disabled in new Stand. Toilet facilities also provided.

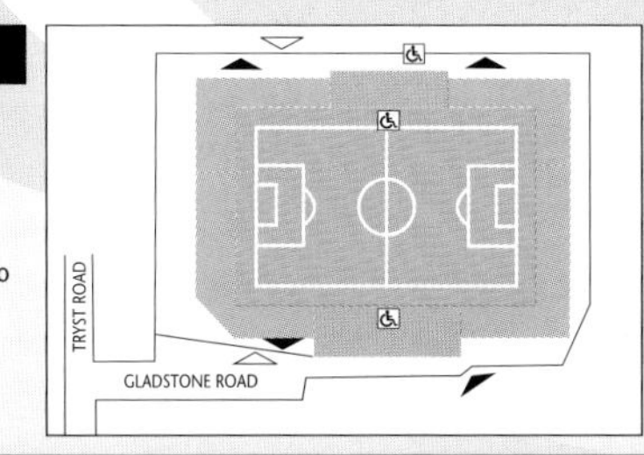

HOW TO GET THERE

Ochilview Park can be reached by the following routes:

TRAINS: The nearest station is Larbert, which is about a mile away from the ground.

BUSES: Buses from Glasgow to Dunfermline, Leven, Dundee and Kirkcaldy pass through Stenhousemuir town centre and this is only a short distance from the park. There is also a regular bus service from Falkirk.

CARS: There is a large car park on the north side of the ground.

STRANRAER

Stair Park, London Road,
Stranraer, DG9 8BS

CHAIRMAN
R. A. Graham Rodgers

VICE-CHAIRMAN
James Hannah

COMMITTEE
Andrew Hannah (Treasurer)
James T. Robertson
George F. Compton
Robert J. Clanachan
Thomas Rice
James Bark
Leo R. Sprott
Alexander McKie
Nigel C. Redhead
Thomas L. Sutherland

SECRETARY
R. A. Graham Rodgers

PLAYER/MANAGER
I. Campbell Money

COACH/PHYSIOTHERAPIST
James Denny

GROUNDSMEN
Patrick Dowey & Wilson Hamilton

KIT MAN
William Milliken, M.B.E.

COMMERCIAL MANAGER
Thomas L. Sutherland
(01776) 707070

TELEPHONES
Ground (01776) 703271
Sec. Home/Ticket Office/
Information Service
(01776) 702194
Fax (01776) 702194

CLUB SHOP
Situated at Ground
2.30 p.m. – 3.00 p.m. and
half-time on matchdays

TEAM CAPTAIN
Graham Millar

SHIRT SPONSOR
Stena Line

LIST OF PLAYERS 1996-97

SURNAME	FIRST NAME	MIDDLE NAME	DATE OF BIRTH	PLACE OF BIRTH	DATE OF SIGNING	HEIGHT FT INS	WEIGHT ST LBS	PREVIOUS CLUB
Bilsland	Brian		06/08/71	Glasgow	24/02/96	5 10.0	10 0	Ayr United
Black	Thomas		11/10/62	Lanark	24/07/96	5 11.5	13 3	Kilmarnock
Crawford	Derek		18/06/74	Glasgow	13/01/96	5 8.0	10 0	Clydebank
Docherty	Robert	John	11/09/65	Glasgow	01/08/96	5 8.0	10 12	East Stirlingshire
Duffy	Bernard	John	28/07/61	Kilmarnock	22/06/88	5 10.5	11 7	Annbank United
Duncan	Graham		02/02/69	Glasgow	30/06/89	5 11.0	11 6	Dumbarton
Gallacher	Iain	Ronald	22/03/74	Irvine	13/07/96	5 9.5	10 9	Maybole Juniors
Gallagher	Anthony		16/03/63	Bellshill	31/03/88	6 1.0	14 3	Albion Rovers
Harvie	Scott	Smith	22/11/68	Glasgow	06/09/96	5 7.5	11 8	St. Mirren
Howard	Nigel		06/10/70	Morecambe	27/06/94	6 0.0	13 8	Ayr United
Hughes	James	Francis	07/05/65	Kilwinning	29/03/91	5 10.0	11 5	Ayr United
Lansdowne	Alan		08/04/70	Glasgow	06/06/96	5 11.0	11 4	Clydebank
McAulay	Ian		06/06/74	Glasgow	21/08/95	5 4.0	10 0	Tower Hearts
McCaffrey	John	Brendan	17/10/72	Glasgow	11/03/94	6 1.0	12 7	Albion Rovers
McCrindle	Scott		30/09/77	Stranraer	05/07/96	5 9.0	10 5	Partick Thistle
McIntyre	Paul		18/01/67	Girvan	11/07/96	6 0.0	12 11	Maybole Juniors
McLaren	John	Stuart	20/04/75	Glasgow	07/08/96	6 0.0	10 8	Queen of the South
McMillan	John	David	09/08/76	Irvine	31/03/96	5 8.0	10 12	St. Mirren
Millar	Graham		12/03/65	Bellshill	25/03/93	5 8.0	11 0	Albion Rovers
Money	Israel	Campbell	31/08/60	Maybole	31/03/96	5 11.0	13 10	St. Mirren
Robertson	John		28/03/76	Irvine	19/09/94	6 0.0	11 0	Unattached
Sloan	Thomas		24/08/64	Irvine	19/07/91	5 9.5	10 10	Kilmarnock
Young	Gordon		01/05/72	Glasgow	06/06/96	6 1.0	12 8	Albion Rovers

MILESTONES

YEAR OF FORMATION: 1870
MOST LEAGUE POINTS IN A SEASON: 56 (Second Division – 1993/94)
MOST LEAGUE GOALS SCORED BY A PLAYER IN A SEASON: D. Frye (Season 1977/78)
NO. OF GOALS SCORED: 27
RECORD ATTENDANCE: 6,500 (-v- Rangers – 24.1.1948)
RECORD VICTORY: 7-0 (-v- Brechin City – Division 2, 6.2.1965)
RECORD DEFEAT: 1-11 (-v- Queen of the South – Scottish Cup, 16.1.1932)

THE BLUES' TEN YEAR LEAGUE RECORD

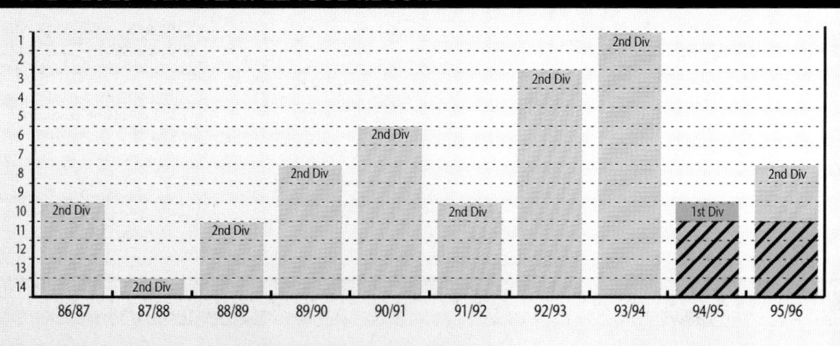

CLUB FACTFILE 1995/96
RESULTS... APPEARANCES... SCORERS

The BLUES

Date	Venue	Opponents	Att.	Res	Ross S.	Hughes J.	McLean P.	Robertson J.	Howard N.	Gallagher A.	Sloan T.	Walker T.	Duncan G.	McGuire D.	Henderson D.	Callaghan T.	McCaffrey J.	Grant A.	McAulay I.	Ferguson W.	Millar G.	McGowan N.	Reilly R.	Pickering M.	Kerrigan S.	Skippen R.	Crawford D.	Shepherd A.	Bilsland B.	Duffy B.	McMillan J.	Connelly D.
Aug 12	H	Berwick Rangers	507	0-0	1	2	3	4	5	6	7	8	9	10	11	12																
26	A	Stenhousemuir	336	0-3	1	2	15	4			7	9	3	14	11	6	5	8	10	12												
Sep 2	H	Montrose	503	4-1	1	2	14	4[1]	5		7	9[1]			11	12	6	8[2]	10		3	15										
9	A	Queen of the South	1,531	3-0	1	3	15	2	5		7[1]	9	12		11[1]	14	6	8[1]	10		4											
16	H	East Fife	634	2-0	1	3		2	5		7	9	12		11[1]		6	8	10	14[1]	4		15									
23	H	Stirling Albion	658	0-0	1	3		2	5		7	9	12		11		6	8	10	14	4		15									
30	A	Ayr United	1,455	0-0	1	3		2	5		7	9	12		11		6	8	10		4		14									
Oct 7	A	Clyde	1,048	1-1	1	3		2	5		7	9	6		11[1]	14		8	10	12	4		15									
14	H	Forfar Athletic	635	1-1	1	3		2	5	4	7	9	6		11	14		8[1]		12			10									
21	A	Berwick Rangers	433	0-4	1	3		2	5		7	9	6		11	14		8		12	4		10	15								
28	H	Stenhousemuir	566	2-1	1	3			5	4	7	9	6[1]		11	2		8	14	12			10[1]									
Nov 4	A	East Fife	850	3-3	1	3		2	5	4	7	10	6		11			8[2]			14		15		9[1]							
11	H	Queen of the South	1,006	0-0	1	3		2	4		7	10	11	14			5	8		12	6		15		9							
18	H	Ayr United	891	2-0	1	3		2	4	5	7	8	10[1]		11					12	6		14		9[1]							
25	A	Stirling Albion	811	1-1	1	3		2	4	5	7	9	10	14	11	15			6	12[1]			8									
Dec 2	H	Clyde	683	0-0	1			2	4	5	7	8	6	12	11			15	3	9			10									
16	A	Forfar Athletic	430	0-0	1	3		2	4	5	7	8	6	12	11				10						9							
Jan 10	H	Berwick Rangers	433	0-3	1	3			4	5	7	8	6	12					10			11	2		9	14						
13	H	Stirling Albion	587	2-2	1	6		2	12	5	7[1]	8[1]	4						11						9		3	10				
16	A	Montrose	334	2-4	1	6		2	5		7	8	4	12[1]					11[1]				15		9		3	10				
20	A	Clyde	942	†2-2	1	6		2	5		7	8	4						11				10		9		3[1]					
27	A	Ayr United	1,919	0-0	1	6		2	4	5	7		8		11			14	10						9		3					
Feb 3	H	Forfar Athletic	476	1-0	1	6		2		5	7	10[1]	4		11			8					3		9							
10	H	East Fife	531	0-0	1	6		2		5	7	10	4		11			8					3		9		12					
17	A	Queen of the South	1,229	1-2	1	6		2		5	7	10[1]	4		11			8			15		12		9		3					
24	A	Stenhousemuir	406	0-2	1	6		2			7	10	4					9	11		5				14		3		8			
Mar 2	H	Montrose	436	1-2	1	6		15	14	5	7	10	4					12	11				2		9[1]		3		8			
9	A	Stirling Albion	1,023	0-2		3		2	5		7	12	4	15				8	11		6		10				14		9	1		
16	H	Ayr United	806	1-1		3[1]		4	5		10	9	6	8							11		2				7		12	1		
23	A	East Fife	738	1-2		2		6	5		11	9	8[1]	7							4		10		15		3		12	1		
30	H	Queen of the South	722	3-1		3		4	5		10		11	7[1]					14		6		2		9[1]		8		12[1]	1	15	
Apr 6	H	Clyde	655	2-2		3		2	5[1]		8[1]		6	7					11		4	12			9				10	1	15	14
13	A	Forfar Athletic	388	2-2		3		2	5	12	7		6					14	11		4				9				15	1	10[2]	8
20	A	Berwick Rangers	373	0-1				2	5	6	7	12	3	14					11		4				9				15	1	10	8
27	H	Stenhousemuir	503	0-0				2		5	7	6		14				10	11		4	15			9		3			1	8	12
May 4	A	Montrose	347	1-0				2	5	6	7	12							11		4				9[1]		3		14	1	10	8
TOTAL FULL APPEARANCES					27	32	1	33	28	18	36	29	29	5	20	2	7	18	23	1	19	1	14		19		12	2	4	9	4	3
TOTAL SUB APPEARANCES							(3)	(1)	(2)	(1)		(3)	(4)	(10)		(7)		(4)	(2)	(10)	(2)	(3)	(9)	(1)	(2)	(1)	(2)		(6)		(2)	(2)
TOTAL GOALS SCORED						1		1	1		3	4	3	2	3			6	1	2			1		5		1		1		2	

Small bold figures denote goalscorers. † denotes opponent's own goal.

STAIR PARK

CAPACITY: 6,100; Seated 1,800, Standing 4,300

PITCH DIMENSIONS: 110 yds x 70 yds

FACILITIES FOR DISABLED SUPPORTERS: By prior arrangement with Club Secretary.

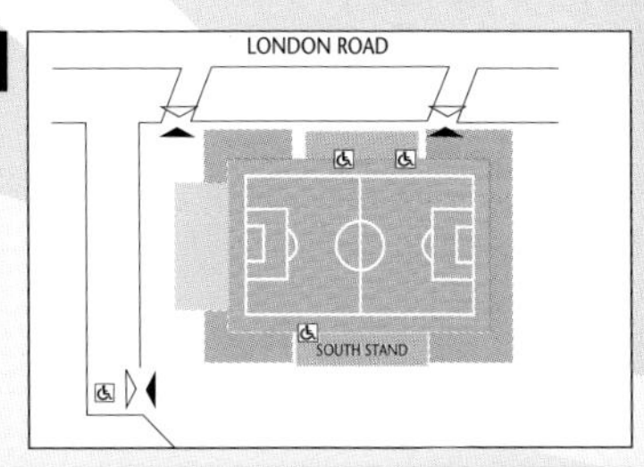

HOW TO GET THERE

Stair Park can be reached by the following routes.

TRAINS: There is a regular service of trains from Ayr and the station is only 1 mile from the ground.

BUSES: Two services pass the park. These are the buses from Glenluce to Portroadie and the Dumfries-Stranraer service.

CARS: Car parking is available in the club car park at the ground, where there is space for approximately 50 vehicles and also in the side streets around the park. Signs for away supporters will be displayed and parking situated at Stranraer Academy, McMasters Road.

Livingston – Third Division Champions, 1995/96

Livingston Discovered

Livingston began the new season with a new name, but in the familiar surroundings of the Meadowbank Stadium in Edinburgh that had been their "home" for 21 years. On 11th November, 1995, they played their first match at their newly built all seated Almondvale Stadium in the New Town against East Stirlingshire and they ended the campaign as champions of the Third Division.

During the 40 weeks which separated the start and the end of the season, the players and officials had overcome the nervous strain of a removal into new palatial surroundings and a promotion campaign which had threatened to come unstuck. However, for chairman, Bill Hunter, and manager, Jim Leishman, the season was a success of huge proportions and an impressive ratification of their ambition. Admitted Leishman, "The upheaval of moving in mid-season into a new stadium added its own pressures, but in the end it was well worth it.

"We now have a superb new venue from which to build with confidence for the future and the people of Livingston have responded and have been magnificent so far."

Certainly, the change from the sparse following that watched the club in its previous guise as Meadowbank Thistle, with average crowds now in excess of 2,000 now enthusiastically turning out to support Livingston in their new surrounds, has been nothing short of phenomenal. This is now a thriving club and chairman Hunter believes that promotion to the Second Division is the first step in their ambition to lift the club into the top echelons of the game.

Livingston is building from the grass roots of the game, for manager Leishman and his backroom staff are regularly coaching in local schools, colleges and youth clubs while aiming to raise the awareness and profile of the club in the community.

"It was a proud moment for all of us to finally realise that we had gained promotion. This is not just down to me, but the result of a lot of hard work by everyone at the club, both on and off the pitch," said an excited Leishman reflecting thoughtfully a few weeks after the Championship was clinched.

However, it had been a difficult campaign to win, for the race to gain promotion had been extremely tight throughout a nail-biting season.

Brechin, re-shaped by the deep-thinking manager, John Young, also had cause to celebrate, for their second place finish clinched another opportunity of playing in the Second Division.

A resolute defence which gave little away and proved to be a major cause of disappointment for each and every one of their opponents, proved to be the basis of their outstanding success. Time after time, opposition managers were heard to moan about the inability of their strikers to pierce the well martialled Brechin rearguard.

That led to a number of games won by the odd goal, but nonetheless, an important three points gained on each occasion. Yet again, the main challenge to the eventual promotion winners came from the Highlands, where Caledonian Thistle and Ross County proved that the decision to offer them a place in senior football had been the correct one.

But it was surprising that, at the end of a rigorous season, Ross County should part company with their manager, Bobby Wilson, who had steered them to much success in the Highland League and then had coped admirably with the transition to senior football in the Third Division. Former Aberdeen, Aston Villa, Rangers and Dunfermline Athletic defender, Neale Cooper, was appointed in his place and he will require all the experience gained from a playing career that saw him win countless winners' medals, including a European Cup Winners' Cup Winners medal with Aberdeen, in order to take the Dingwall club into one of the two promotion places.

Steve Paterson remains at the helm of Caledonian Thistle, who have now added "Inverness" to their title.

Arbroath, under manager John Brogan, spent much of the season rebuilding, but by the spring and the final weeks of the season, had shown that the groundwork had been laid for a club which will be actively seeking a place in the promotion scene in the years to come.

However, life in the Third Division is never easy with the line between success and failure extremely delicate. That was brought home to East Stirlingshire and their hard working manager, Billy Little, in no uncertain manner. The previous season, the 'Shire had narrowly missed promotion and Little had expected to be very much involved again in that issue during the course of the 1995/96 campaign.

But a series of severe injuries to a number of his players took their toll as they were left on the sidelines for lengthy periods and the high hopes expected could not be realised.

Indeed, Little commented wryly before one of the final games of the season, "I have had to wait all through the autumn, the winter and now the spring until there are only a few games remaining, to be able to say that I have almost got my first choice selection available for Saturday."

Lack of finance is also a major problem among all of the clubs at this level and the Cowdenbeath chairman, Gordon McDougall, and manager, Tom Steven, spent much of the year planning their youth campaign which, they hope, will provide a much needed injection of life for their club.

Said Steven, "By the end of the season, my team was full of lads under the age of 21. We do not have money to spend, and finding and developing our own talent is the only answer."

Development of youth was also a season-long quest for the Queen's Park coach, Hugh McCann, who knows that he may not benefit from much of his outstanding work as the "Amateurs" tend to lose their better players to the paid ranks. But McCann kept Queen's away from the bottom rung while laying a foundation which he anticipates will see his side participate in the promotion campaign in the future.

Jason Young

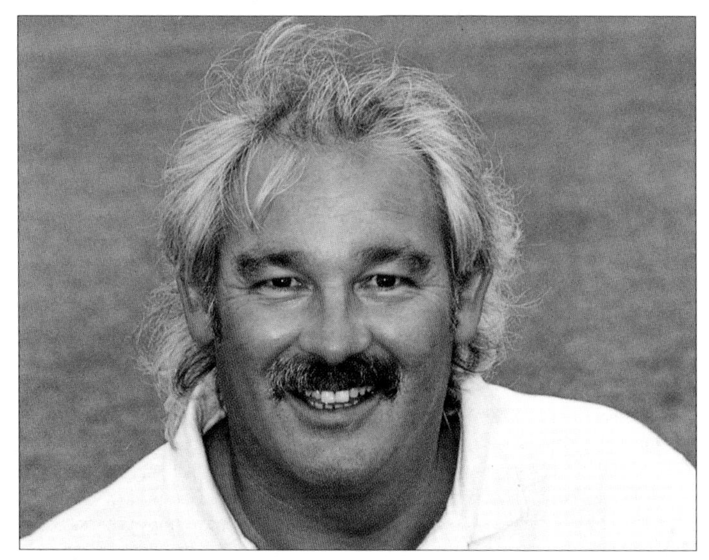
Jim Leishman

Ambition runs through every club despite the lack of finance and Alloa, although finishing second bottom, showed their impatience at the lack of success when, after parting with manager Pat McAulay, they shocked many by tempting manager, Tom Hendrie, and his assistant, John Coughlin, to leave Berwick, who were involved at the time in the Second Division promotion scene. That could have far-reaching effects.

But bottom of the table Albion Rovers went even further for, not only did manager Jimmy Crease leave during the season, but a number of their directors also moved out in a disagreement over the direction to be taken by the club.

The split had been caused by plans for the club to leave its Cliftonhill home in Coatbridge and goundshare with Airdrie sometime in the future when their neighbours had developed a new stadium.

As the new Board of Directors took over, the former Ayr and Stirling Albion midfielder, Vinnie Moore, came in as manager. He brought with him new players and although, in the short term, that was not good enough to lift the club out of the bottom of the League position, there is hope that better days could yet lie ahead.

As always, there is no shortage of optimism within the rank and file of our clubs in the lower divisions.

BILL MARWICK
(Freelance)

ALBION ROVERS

Cliftonhill Stadium, Main Street, Coatbridge, ML5 9XX

CHAIRMAN
David T. Shanks, B.Sc.

VICE-CHAIRMAN
James B. Greenhalgh, C.A.

DIRECTORS
Hugh S. Munro, B.Sc., A.R.I.C.S.
Andrew Dick
Gordon Dishington
Edward P. Hagerty
John Hughes, F.C.C.A.
Alan H. Brown
Robert Watt

SECRETARY
John Hughes, F.C.C.A.

PLAYER/MANAGER
Vincent Moore

ASSISTANT MANAGER
Stuart Robertson

COACHES
Robert Russell, David Byrne

CLUB DOCTOR
Dr. Alisdair Purdie, M.B., Ch.B.

PHYSIOTHERAPIST
Derek Kelly

CHIEF SCOUT
Robert Watt

GROUNDSMAN
Hugh McBride

COMMERCIAL DIRECTOR
Gordon Dishington
(01698) 853108

TELEPHONES
Ground (01236) 606334
Telefax (01236) 427192
Sec. Home (01236) 434759
Sec. Bus. (01236) 422651

CLUB SHOP
Cliftonhill Stadium, Main Street, Coatbridge, ML5 3RB. Open one hour prior to kick-off at first team home matches.

OFFICIAL SUPPORTERS CLUB
Andy Morrison, 98 Dundyvan Road, Coatbridge. (01236) 402336

TEAM CAPTAIN
Paul Martin

SHIRT SPONSOR
Morrison Homes

LIST OF PLAYERS 1996-97

SURNAME	FIRST NAME	MIDDLE NAME	DATE OF BIRTH	PLACE OF BIRTH	DATE OF SIGNING	HEIGHT FT INS	WEIGHT ST LBS	PREVIOUS CLUB
Angus	Ian	Allan	19/11/61	Glasgow	03/09/96	5 10.0	10 3	Clyde
Brown	Martin		26/01/64	Bellshill	31/03/96	6 1.0	12 2	Dalziel H.S.F.P.
Byrne	David	Stuart	05/03/61	London	12/01/96	5 9.0	10 9	Ayr United
Clark	Martin	John	13/10/68	Holytown	16/02/96	5 9.0	11 4	Macclesfield Town
Cody	Stephen		01/06/69	Calderbank	02/08/96	5 9.0	12 3	Queen of the South
Dickson	John		23/12/69	Glasgow	19/06/96	5 5.0	9 7	Clyde
Gallagher	John		02/06/69	Glasgow	29/11/91	5 9.0	10 10	Arbroath
Harty	Ian	McGuinness	08/04/78	Bellshill	09/08/96	5 8.0	10 7	Heart of Midlothian
MacFarlane	Colin		03/07/70	Bellshill	19/01/96	6 3.0	12 3	Ayr United
Martin	Paul	John	08/03/65	Bellshill	02/08/96	5 11.5	11 0	Dumbarton
McGowan	Neil	William	15/04/77	Glasgow	09/08/96	5 10.0	10 12	Stranraer
McGuire	Douglas	John	06/09/67	Bathgate	13/06/96	5 8.0	11 4	Stranraer
McInally	Anthony	Charles	24/02/68	Glasgow	31/03/96	5 8.0	11 0	Dalziel H.S.F.P.
McKenna	Adrian	Paul	31/03/71	Glasgow	02/08/96	6 2.0	10 9	Stirling Albion
McKenzie	David		30/04/75	Glasgow	02/08/96	5 10.5	11 7	Tower Hearts
Mitchell	Anthony		10/01/79	Glasgow	09/08/96	6 0.0	12 2	St. Mirren
Moore	Vincent		21/08/64	Scunthorpe	12/01/96	5 11.0	12 0	Ayr United
Osborne	Marc	Leslie	05/08/72	Broxburn	12/09/95	6 3.0	11 10	Berwick Rangers
Pickering	Mark	Fulton	11/06/65	Glasgow	02/02/96	5 8.0	11 4	Ardeer Thistle
Reid	Alan		19/01/75	Glasgow	02/08/96	5 7.0	10 0	Tower Hearts
Reilly	Robert	Piper	23/09/59	Kilmarnock	31/03/96	5 10.0	11 1	Stranraer
Ross	Stephen		27/01/65	Glasgow	13/06/96	5 9.0	10 10	Stranraer
Russell	Robert		11/02/57	Glasgow	13/01/96	5 8.5	10 3	Cumbernauld United
Strain	Barry		04/08/71	Glasgow	05/08/95	5 11.0	12 7	Clyde
Walker	Thomas		23/12/64	Glasgow	13/06/96	5 7.5	10 10	Stranraer

MILESTONES

YEAR OF FORMATION: 1882
MOST CAPPED PLAYER: John White
NO. OF CAPS: 1
MOST LEAGUE POINTS IN A SEASON: 54 (Division 2 – Season 1929/30)
MOST LEAGUE GOALS SCORED BY A PLAYER IN A SEASON: John Renwick (Season 1932/33)
NO. OF GOALS SCORED: 41
RECORD ATTENDANCE: 27,381 (-v- Rangers 8.2.1936)
RECORD VICTORY: 12-0 (-v- Airdriehill – Scottish Cup, 3.9.1887)
RECORD DEFEAT: 1-11 (-v- Partick Thistle – League Cup, 11.8.1993)

THE WEE ROVERS' TEN YEAR LEAGUE RECORD

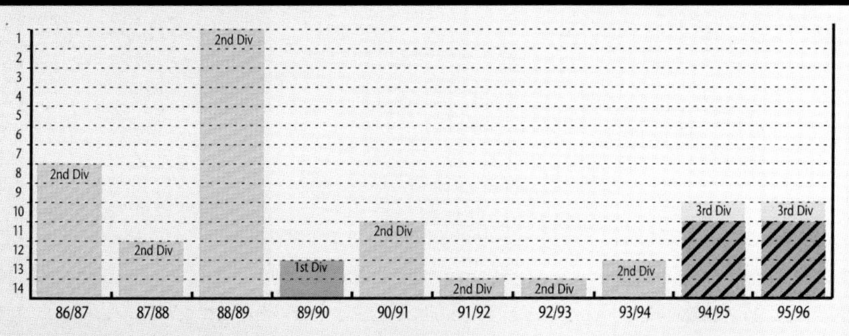

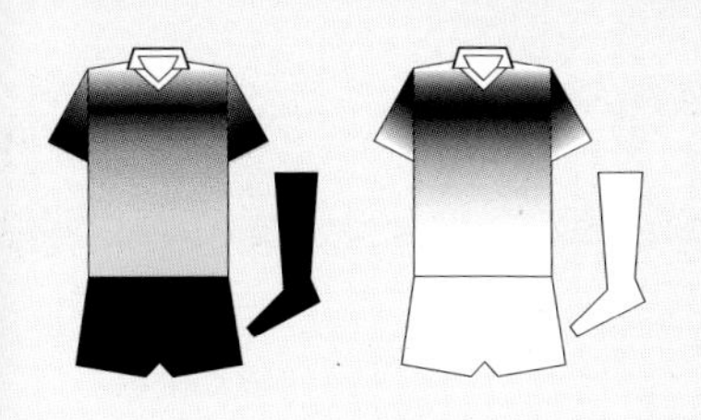

CLUB FACTFILE 1995/96

RESULTS... APPEARANCES... SCORERS

The WEE ROVERS

Date	Venue	Opponents	Att.	Res	Moonie D.	Riley D.	Gallacher J.	Shanks C.	Ryan M.	Strain B.	Deeley B.	Collins L.	Scott M.	McBride J.	Young G.	Crawford P.	Seggie D.	McDonald D.	Wright A.	Bell D.	Duncan M.	Russell R.	Osborne M.	Lavery J.	Quinn K.	Richardson J.	Spiers C.	Willock A.	McEwan A.	Thompson D.	McConville R.	Friar P.	Yule R.	Moffat J.	Smith B.	Miller D.	Byrne D.	Moore V.	Henderson B.	McFarlane C.	Pickering M.	Clark M.	Reilly J.	Percy A.	Robertson S.	Morrison A.	Brown M.	Watson B.	McInally A.	Reilly R.
Aug 12	H	Arbroath	378	0-2	1	2	3	4	5	6	7	8	9	10	11	12	14																																	
26	A	Alloa	427	2-3	1		3	6		4	5	8	9^1		11^1		12	2	7	10	14																													
Sep 2	H	Caledonian Thistle	284	2-2	1		3	6	5	4	7	8	9	10^1	11^1		14	2																																
9	H	Cowdenbeath	680	2-3	1		3	6		4	5	8^1		10^1	11	9	15	2		7		14																												
16	A	Ross County	1,419	1-5			3		5	4	6	8		10	11^1	9						7	1	2	14																									
23	A	Livingston	229	1-2			3	6		4		8		10	9^1	14		2		7		11	1			5																								
30	H	Queen's Park	378	3-1			3	6		4		8		10^1	9^2	14		2		7			1				5	11																						
Oct 7	A	Brechin City	341	1-0			3	6		4		8		10	9^1			2		7	14		1				5	11																						
14	H	East Stirlingshire	334	1-2				6	12	3	4				9^1	14	10	2		7	8		1				5	11	15																					
21	A	Caledonian Thistle	1,222	1-6			3	4	5		6			14	9	12	10	2		7			1					11	8^1	4	6																			
28	H	Alloa	427	2-1										10^1	9^1			2		7		14	1				5	11	12	8		3																		
Nov 4	H	Ross County	399	3-4				6		2	4			10^1	9^1					7		14	1				5^1	11		8		3	15																	
11	A	Cowdenbeath	166	1-4			3			6	4			10	9			15^1		7		8	1				5			2			11																	
18	A	Queen's Park	467	1-4			3	6	12	4^1	5			10	9	15		2		7		14						11	1	8																				
25	H	Livingston	433	0-2			3	8		6				10	9	14		2		7		12					5		11	4				1																
Dec 2	H	Brechin City	289	1-0			10	6		4	14				9	15		2									5	11^1		7		3		1	8															
19	A	East Stirlingshire	245	1-5			10	6	4		14				9	12		2									5	11^1	8			3		1	7															
Jan 1	A	Queen's Park	617	1-5			8	4			3				9	12^1		2		7								11	10			5		1	14	6														
6	A	Arbroath	306	0-2			3	6	5		11				9	10		2		8				4										1		7														
13	A	Livingston	2,509	1-0			7	12	5		3				9	15^1		2		8				6										1			4	10	11											
20	A	Brechin City	296	0-1			7		6		12				9	11		2		8				3										1			4	10	15	5										
Feb 17	H	Cowdenbeath	348	2-0			7		6	12					9^1	15		2																1			4	10^1		5	3	8	11							
24	A	Alloa	342	1-3			7		6	9	14					12		2										15						1			4	10		5	3	8	11^1							
28	H	Caledonian Thistle	364	0-2			7	14		6	15					12		2				8						9						1			4	10		5	3		11							
Mar 2	H	Arbroath	237	1-1			7		6	15								2		14								12						1			8	10^1	9	5	3	4		11						
6	A	Ross County	1,031	1-1			7		6	12								2		14								11									8^1	10	9	5	3	4			1					
9	H	Livingston	623	0-1			7		6	12					9			2		15								14						1			8	10		5	3	4	11							
16	H	Queen's Park	387	0-2			7		12	6					9					8		15												1	3		10			5	2	4	14			11				
20	H	East Stirlingshire	199	2-2			7			6^1					9					12		8						15						1			10			5	3	4	14				2	11^1		
23	H	Ross County	364	0-3			7	8	6	12	3				9	11		2										15						1			4			5			10							
30	A	Cowdenbeath	173	1-1			7		6	8	3				9	11																		1			4			5^1							2		10	
Apr 6	H	Brechin City	329	0-0			7		4	6					9	11																		1			3			5							2		10	8
13	A	East Stirlingshire	293	1-1			7		4						9^1	11																		1			3		12	5		6					2		8	10
20	A	Caledonian Thistle	769	1-1			7		4						9	11																		1			3		15	5		6	12				2		8	10^1
27	H	Alloa	454	1-0			7		4	14					9	11																		1			3		15	5		6	10				2		8^1	
May 4	A	Arbroath	350	1-2			7		4	12					9	11						15												1			3			5^1	14	6	8				2		10	
TOTAL FULL APPEARANCES					4	1	33	17	20	20	15	8	3	12	32	11	2	24	1	17	1	5	9	4		1	9	12	5	7	1	5	1	21	3	2	17	8	3	16	8	11	7	1	1	1	7	1	6	3
TOTAL SUB APPEARANCES								(2)	(3)	(7)	(5)			(1)		(14)	(4)	(1)		(4)	(2)	(7)			(1)			(5)	(2)				(1)		(1)				(4)		(1)		(3)							
TOTAL GOALS SCORED										2		1	1	5	12	2		1									1	2	1								1	2		2			1					1	1	1

Small bold figures denote goalscorers. † denotes opponent's own goal.

CLIFTONHILL STADIUM

CAPACITY: 1,238; Seated 538, Standing 700

PITCH DIMENSIONS: 100 yds x 70 yds

FACILITIES FOR DISABLED SUPPORTERS: Access from East Stewart Street with toilet facilities and space for wheelchairs, cars etc. Advanced contact with club advised – this area is uncovered.

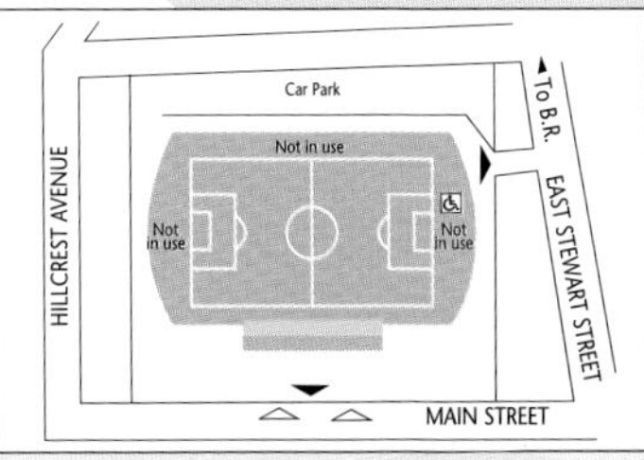

HOW TO GET THERE

The following routes can be used to reach Cliftonhill Stadium:

BUSES: The ground is conveniently situated on the main Glasgow-Airdrie bus route and there is a stop near the ground. Local buses serving most areas of Coatbridge and Airdrie pass by the stadium every few minutes.

TRAINS: The nearest railway station is Coatdyke on the Glasgow-Airdrie line and the ground is a ten minute walk from there. The frequency of service is 15 minutes.

CARS: A large car park is situated behind the ground with access off Albion Street, and vehicles may also be parked in Hillcrest Avenue, Albion Street and East Stewart Street, which are all adjacent to the ground.

ALLOA

Recreation Park,
Clackmannan Road,
Alloa, FK10 1RR

CHAIRMAN
Patrick Lawlor

VICE-CHAIRMAN
Robert F. Hopkins

DIRECTORS
George Ormiston
Ronald J. Todd
Ewen G. Cameron
William J. McKie

SECRETARY
Ewen G. Cameron

MANAGER
Thomas Hendrie

ASSISTANT MANAGER
John Coughlin

RESERVE TEAM/ YOUTH TEAM COACH
Walter Boyd

CLUB DOCTOR
Dr. Clarke Mullen

PHYSIOTHERAPIST
Alan Anderson

CHIEF SCOUT
Bill Barclay

GROUNDSMAN
Lachie McKinnon

KIT MEN
Craig Robertson & Nicol Campbell

COMMERCIAL MANAGER
William McKie
Home (01259) 730572

TELEPHONES
Ground/Commercial/Fax
(01259) 722695
Sec. Bus. (01324) 612472
Sec. Home (01259) 750899

CLUB SHOP
Adjacent to refreshment kiosk

OFFICIAL SUPPORTERS CLUB
c/o Recreation Park,
Clackmannan Road,
Alloa, FK10 1RR

TEAM CAPTAIN
Keith McCulloch

SHIRT SPONSOR
Alloa Advertiser

LIST OF PLAYERS 1996-97

SURNAME	FIRST NAME	MIDDLE NAME	DATE OF BIRTH	PLACE OF BIRTH	DATE OF SIGNING	HEIGHT FT INS	WEIGHT ST LBS	PREVIOUS CLUB
Balfour	Robert		26/12/69	Bellshill	10/08/95	5 11.0	11 0	Bathgate Thistle
Cadden	Stephen	Joseph	26/11/68	Baillieston	04/03/94	6 0.0	11 6	Albion Rovers
Cowan	Mark		16/01/71	Edinburgh	17/06/96	6 0.0	12 7	Berwick Rangers
Dwyer	Peter		18/08/65	Glasgow	13/06/96	6 1.0	12 10	East Stirlingshire
Gilmour	James		17/12/61	Bellshill	08/09/95	5 6.0	9 4	Bo'ness United
Irvine	William		28/12/63	Stirling	31/05/96	5 10.0	11 3	Berwick Rangers
Johnston	Neil	James	31/08/76	Dunfermline	09/09/95	5 10.0	10 2	Steelend Vics U'18s
Kane	Kevin		30/12/69	Edinburgh	31/03/96	5 10.0	12 0	Berwick Rangers
Little	Thomas	Francis	13/02/78	Glasgow	20/07/95	5 4.0	9 8	Kilsyth Rangers U'18s
Lonzi	Giacomo		07/05/71	Livorno	16/09/96	6 0.0	12 7	Armando Picchi Calcio Livorno
Mackay	Stuart	John	03/03/75	Inverness	16/12/95	5 8.0	12 6	Clachnacuddin
McAnenay	Michael	Samuel P.	16/09/66	Glasgow	09/10/93	5 10.0	10 7	Dumbarton
McAneny	Paul	James	11/11/73	Glasgow	07/10/95	5 11.0	12 1	Stirling Albion
McAvoy	Neil		29/07/72	Stirling	24/11/95	6 2.0	11 7	Montrose
McCormack	John	Thomas	22/07/65	Stirling	26/11/93	5 9.0	10 0	Stirling Albion
McCulloch	Keith	George	27/05/67	Edinburgh	28/08/87	5 10.0	12 0	Cowdenbeath
McDonaugh	James		16/11/77	Edinburgh	10/09/96	5 7.0	9 4	Livingston Juniors
McKenzie	Grant		27/09/77	Stirling	28/08/96	5 9.0	11 1	Sauchie Juniors
Moffat	Barrie		27/12/72	Bangour	09/10/90	5 8.0	11 0	Gairdoch Colts U'18
Nelson	Mark		09/08/69	Bellshill	01/03/94	5 11.0	11 0	Dumbarton
Nicholson	Neil	Dennis J.	09/12/77	Edinburgh	10/09/96	5 7.0	10 7	Dalkeith Thistle
Valentine	Craig		16/07/70	Edinburgh	20/07/96	5 8.0	11 0	Berwick Rangers
Wilson	Robert	Alexander	07/07/79	Alexandria	28/08/96	5 7.0	10 7	Sauchie Juniors
Wilson	William	John McK.	30/05/78	Kirkcaldy	28/08/96	6 2.0	12 7	Sauchie Juniors
Wylie	Roderick		31/01/69	Glasgow	03/02/95	5 11.0	13 0	Cumbernauld Juniors

MILESTONES

YEAR OF FORMATION: 1883
MOST CAPPED PLAYER: Jock Hepburn
NO. OF CAPS: 1
MOST LEAGUE POINTS IN A SEASON: 60 (Division 2 – Season 1921/22)
MOST LEAGUE GOALS SCORED BY A PLAYER IN A SEASON: William Crilley (Season 1921/22)
NO. OF GOALS SCORED: 49
RECORD ATTENDANCE: 13,000 (-v- Dunfermline Athletic – 26.2.1939)
RECORD VICTORY: 9-2 (-v- Forfar Athletic – Division 2, 18.3.1933)
RECORD DEFEAT: 0-10 (-v- Dundee – Division 2 and Third Lanark – League Cup)

THE WASPS' TEN YEAR LEAGUE RECORD

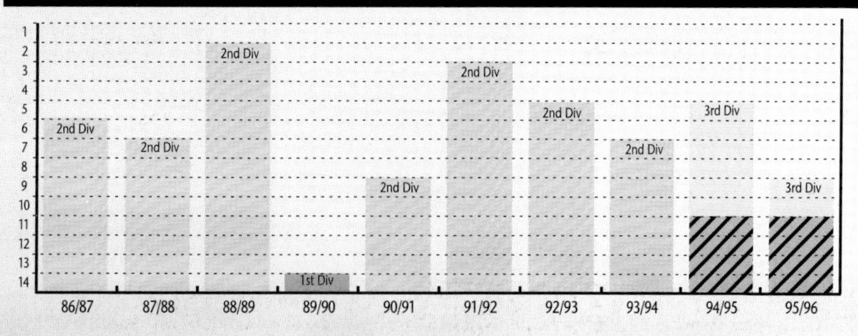

CLUB FACTFILE 1995/96
RESULTS... APPEARANCES... SCORERS

The WASPS

Date	Venue	Opponents	Att.	Res	Graham P.	Newbigging W.	Bennett N.	McCormack J.	Lawrie D.	Conway V.	Cadden S.	Diver D.	Rixon S.	Whyte M.	Morrison S.	Kirkham D.	McKenzie C.	Wylie R.	Cully D.	Moffat B.	Smith G.	Nelson M.	Hannah K.	Gilmour J.	Johnston N.	Lamont W.	Balfour R.	McAneny P.	Watters W.	McAvoy N.	McCulloch K.	Mackay S.	Little T.	Stewart W.	McCardle R.	Cummings P.	Kane K.
Aug 12	A	Cowdenbeath	281	0-1	1	2	3	4	5	6	7	8	9	10	11	12	14	15																			
26	H	Albion Rovers	427	3-2	1	2	3[1]		5		6	8	10[1]	14	7		11		4	9[1]	12																
Sep 2	A	Brechin City	355	1-0	1	2	3		5			8		10	7		11			9[1]	6	4	12	15													
9	H	Arbroath	475	0-2	1	2	3		5		12	8	10	11	7		14			9	6	4		15													
16	A	Livingston	249	0-2	1	2	3	4			11	8	10	14	12	7		5		9		15		6													
23	H	Caledonian Thistle	387	0-5	1		3		5			8		10	11	7	6			9	14	4	2		12												
30	A	East Stirlingshire	305	2-2		4[1]	6	3			11	8		10[1]				5		9	2		7		15	1											
Oct 7	A	Queen's Park	483	0-0		4	6	2			11	12							3	9			7	8			1	5	10								
14	H	Ross County	501	1-0		4	3			6	8		9	15[1]	7			5	14	10		2					1	11	12								
21	H	Brechin City	371	3-2		4	3			6			9[1]	7				5		14[1]		2		11			1	8	10[1]								
28	A	Albion Rovers	427	1-2		4	3			15		8		7				5	14	9		2		6			1	11[1]	10								
Nov 4	H	Livingston	548	0-2			3	4		6			10	7	8				14	9	2	15	12	11			1	5									
11	A	Arbroath	508	1-1		4	3					7			8			6		11	2			10[1]	9		1	5									
18	H	East Stirlingshire	357	1-3		4	3				8	7	14	12				6		11[1]	2			10	9		1	5									
25	A	Caledonian Thistle	1,181	1-1			3				8		11[1]					5		7	2			10	9		1	4		6							
Dec 2	H	Queen's Park	352	0-0			3	12			8		11	14				5		7	2			10	9		1	4		6	15						
16	A	Ross County	1,303	2-2			3	2			8[1]	9	11[1]					5		12		14		10			1	4		6		7					
Jan 13	H	Caledonian Thistle	410	0-2			3	2		6			9	12	15				14	11		4	8	10			1	5				7					
16	H	Cowdenbeath	289	2-3			3	2					10		8					9[1]		4	12[1]	6	11		1	5				7					
20	A	Queen's Park	467	0-0			3				8		12	11	14				4	9	2		7	10			1	5				6	15				
23	A	Brechin City	349	0-3			3				8		11		14			12	4	9	2		7	10			1	5				6	15				
31	A	East Stirlingshire	310	0-1	1		3											5		9	2			6	12			4		8		7	15	10	11		
Feb 3	H	Ross County	373	0-4	1		3			6	8		15	11				5		9	2		12					4		10		7					
10	A	Livingston	2,066	0-1	1		3	12						14	8			6		9	2	7		11				4		10	5						
17	H	Arbroath	360	0-3			3	12					10		8			14		9	2	7		11			1	4		6	5						
24	H	Albion Rovers	342	3-1				7			12		10[1]		8			14		9		3		6[1]	15[1]		1	2		4	5		11				
Mar 2	A	Cowdenbeath	190	0-3				7			12		10		8					9		3		6	14		1	2		4	5	15	11				
12	A	Caledonian Thistle	1,162	0-0		12		2					14		8					9		15			10		1	5		3	4	6	7			11	
16	H	East Stirlingshire	309	2-2		2							14	7	8			12		9		15			10		1	5		3	4	6[2]	11				
23	H	Livingston	541	1-1		4								7	6[1]					9		3					1	2		10	5	8	11				
30	A	Arbroath	397	0-1		6		12					14	7	8			5		9		4			15		1	2		3		10	11				
Apr 6	H	Queen's Park	403	0-1				8					14	7	2					9				15	10		1	5		3	4	6	12				11
13	A	Ross County	1,068	0-0				8					12	7	2					9				14	10		1	5		3	4	6	11				
20	H	Brechin City	369	0-3				8					9	7	2					10				15	14		1	5		3	4	6	12				11
27	A	Albion Rovers	454	0-1				4		6			14	7	12					9		3		10			1	2			5	8	15				11
May 4	H	Cowdenbeath	260	2-1										10	2[1]					9		3					1	5		6	4[1]	8	11				7
TOTAL FULL APPEARANCES					9	15	25	15	5	7	13	11	17	18	21	2	3	14	4	33	14	16	6	20	9	1	26	29	3	17	12	16	8	1	1	1	4
TOTAL SUB APPEARANCES						(1)		(4)		(1)	(3)	(1)	(9)	(7)	(5)	(1)	(2)	(5)	(4)	(2)	(2)	(5)	(4)	(5)	(7)				(1)		(1)	(1)	(6)				
TOTAL GOALS SCORED						1	1				1		5	2	2					5			1	2	1			1	1		1	2					

Small bold figures denote goalscorers. † denotes opponent's own goal.

RECREATION PARK

CAPACITY: 4,111; Seated 424, Standing 3,687

PITCH DIMENSIONS: 110 yds x 75 yds

FACILITIES FOR DISABLED SUPPORTERS: Accommodation for wheelchairs and invalid carriages in front of Stand. Disabled toilets are also available.

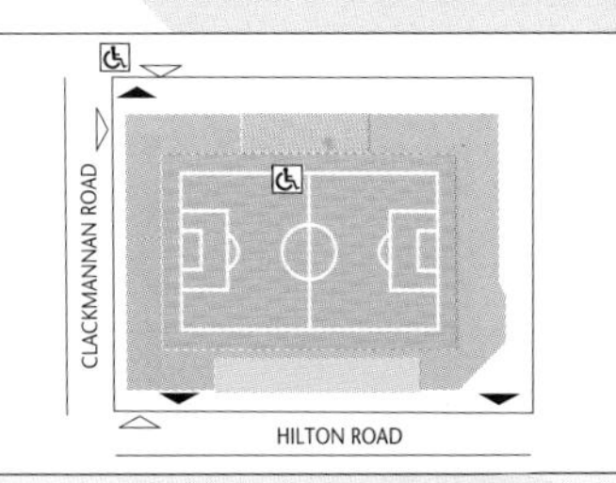

HOW TO GET THERE

Recreation Park can be reached by the following routes.

TRAINS: The nearest railway station is Stirling, which is seven miles away. Fans would have to connect with an inter-linking bus service to reach the ground from here.

BUSES: There are three main services which stop outside the ground. These are the Dunfermline-Stirling, Stirling-Clackmannan and Falkirk-Alloa buses.

CARS: Car Parking is available in the car park adjacent to the ground and this can hold 175 vehicles.

ARBROATH

Gayfield Park,
Arbroath, DD11 1QB

PRESIDENT
John D. Christison

VICE-PRESIDENT
Charles Kinnear

COMMITTEE
R. Alan Ripley (Treasurer)
William J. Thomson
George Johnson
David G. Hodgens
Alexander C. Watt
James A.F. Jack

SECRETARY
Charles Kinnear

MANAGER
John Brogan

ASSISTANT MANAGER
James Kerr

YOUTH COACH
John Martin

CLUB DOCTOR
Dr. Dick Spiers

PHYSIOTHERAPIST
William Shearer

CHIEF SCOUTS
John Martin
Tom Fairweather

GROUNDSMAN
Iain Gunn

COMMERCIAL MANAGER
Alexander C. Watt
(01241) 876116
Mobile 0831 408642

TELEPHONES
Ground/Fax/Ticket Office/Club Shop
(01241) 872157
Sec. Home (01241) 875677
Sec. Bus. (01382) 313452

CLUB SHOP
Gayfield Park, Arbroath, DD11 1QB.
Open on matchdays
Premier Sports, West Port, Arbroath,
DD11 1RF. Open Mon. to Sat.

TEAM CAPTAIN
John Ward

SHIRT SPONSOR
Perimax Diana

LIST OF PLAYERS 1996-97

SURNAME	FIRST NAME	MIDDLE NAME	DATE OF BIRTH	PLACE OF BIRTH	DATE OF SIGNING	HEIGHT FT INS	WEIGHT ST LBS	PREVIOUS CLUB
Balfour	Gary	Shaw	30/09/78	Dundee	31/08/95	5 6.0	11 0	Forfar Albion
Burnett	Ross	Alexander	27/08/79	Plymouth	29/08/96	6 1.0	11 0	Arbroath Victoria
Burns	Steven	Patrick	12/01/80	Dundee	29/08/96	5 6.0	10 7	Arbroath Victoria
Clark	Patrick	John	13/03/74	Hamilton	29/07/95	5 11.0	11 1	Hamilton Academical
Crawford	Jonathan		14/10/69	Johnstone	31/03/95	6 1.0	12 7	Arthurlie Juniors
Dunn	Gordon		21/01/62	Dundee	08/08/96	5 9.0	11 8	Forfar West End
Elliot	David	Euan	23/12/74	Dundee	30/03/94	5 9.5	10 3	Arbroath Sporting Club
Florence	Steven		28/10/71	Dundee	20/05/88	5 6.0	11 5	Arbroath Lads Club
Fowler	John	James	30/01/65	Glasgow	11/07/95	5 7.0	11 12	Greenock Morton
Gardner	Robert	Lee	11/07/70	Ayr	22/10/94	5 5.0	9 5	Meadowbank Thistle
Hinchcliffe	Craig	Peter	05/05/72	Glasgow	04/08/95	5 11.0	13 0	Elgin City
Kerr	James		17/01/59	Hamilton	21/02/95	5 11.0	11 7	Albion Rovers
Mackie	Brian	John	02/11/70	Dundee	19/06/96	5 11.0	11 4	Forfar West End
McAulay	John		28/04/72	Glasgow	04/07/95	5 9.0	11 7	Clyde
McCarron	James		31/10/71	Glasgow	01/08/96	5 6.0	9 12	Clyde
McCormick	Stephen		19/03/65	Seafield	04/08/95	5 11.0	12 10	Forfar Athletic
McMillan	Thomas		08/08/72	Falkirk	21/10/94	5 10.5	11 13	Dundee United
McVicar	Donald	Frederick	06/11/62	Perth	16/03/96	5 9.0	11 12	Forfar Athletic
McWalter	Mark	Nicoll	20/06/68	Arbroath	02/08/96	5 11.0	13 2	Ballymena United
Murray	Iain	Alexander	04/09/79	Dundee	05/09/96	5 11.0	10 7	Forfar West End
Peters	Scott		09/12/72	Dundee	06/06/95	5 11.0	11 7	Forfar West End
Pew	David	John	28/08/71	Glasgow	04/02/95	5 10.0	10 5	Stirling Albion
Phinn	James	Bruce	03/10/76	Dundee	27/10/95	6 2.0	12 12	Forfar West End
Roberts	Paul		24/03/70	Glasgow	09/02/96	6 0.0	13 6	Stirling Albion
Scott	Steve		15/11/78	Arbroath	02/08/96	5 11.0	12 0	"S" Form
Ward	John		25/11/77	Dundee	02/06/95	6 4.0	12 10	Duncraig U'18s
Waters	Michael	Joseph	28/09/72	Stirling	15/12/95	5 8.0	12 10	Zurriqu, Malta
Watters	William	Devlin	05/06/64	Bellshill	08/11/95	5 10.0	12 2	Alloa
Welsh	Brian		22/06/77	Glasgow	12/12/95	5 9.0	11 0	Rutherglen Glencairn

MILESTONES

YEAR OF FORMATION: 1878
MOST CAPPED PLAYER: Ned Doig
NO. OF CAPS: 2
MOST LEAGUE POINTS IN A SEASON: 57 (Division 2 – Season 1966/67)
MOST LEAGUE GOALS SCORED BY A PLAYER IN A SEASON: David Easson (Season 1958/59)
NO. OF GOALS SCORED: 45
RECORD ATTENDANCE: 13,510 (-v- Rangers – Scottish Cup, 23.2.1952)
RECORD VICTORY: 36-0 (-v- Bon Accord – Scottish Cup, 12.9.1885)
RECORD DEFEAT: 1-9 (-v- Celtic – League Cup, 25.8.1993)

THE RED LICHTIES' TEN YEAR LEAGUE RECORD

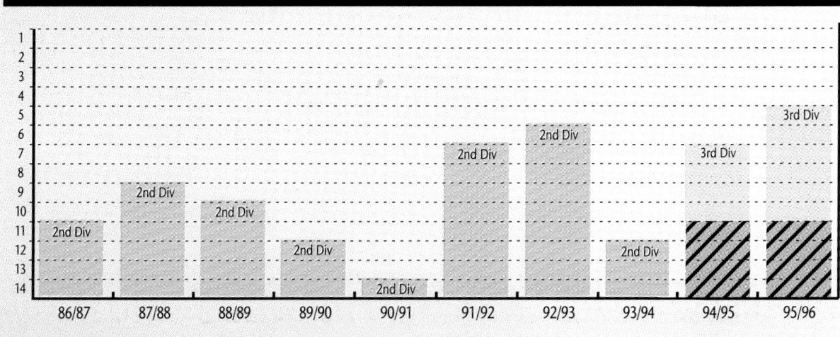

CLUB FACTFILE 1995/96

RESULTS... APPEARANCES... SCORERS

The RED LICHTIES

Date	Venue	Opponents	Att.	Res	Hinchcliffe C.	McMillan T.	Florence S.	Peters S.	Fowler J.	Clark P.	Lindsay J.	Porteous I.	McCormick S.	Kennedy A.	McAulay J.	Pew D.	Sexton B.	Kerr J.	Crawford J.	Elliot D.	Gardner R.L.	McLean C.	Dunn G.	Middleton A.	Elder S.	Welsh B.	McCabe G.	Waters M.	Watters W.	Ward J.	Phinn J.	Roberts P.	McVicar D.	Kerr R.	Scott S.
Aug 12	A	Albion Rovers	378	2-0	1	2	3	4	5	6	7	8^{1}	9^{1}	10	11	12	14																		
26	H	Livingston	721	1-3	1	2	3	11	5	4		8	9^{1}	14	12	7		6	10																
Sep 2	A	Ross County	1,400	2-4	1	2		4		5	8	14	9	10		11^{2}		6	3	7	12	16													
9	A	Alloa	475	2-0				5	16		14	12	9^{1}	10	2	8^{1}			6	7	11		1	3	4										
16	H	Caledonian Thistle	579	2-1				5	16		14	12	9^{1}	8	2	11^{1}			6	7	10		1	3	4										
23	H	East Stirlingshire	570	2-2			3		6		14	8^{1}	9	10^{1}	2	7			5	12	11		1		4										
30	A	Brechin City	632	1-1	1		3	14	12	6		8		10	2	7	9^{1}		5					11	4	16									
Oct 7	A	Cowdenbeath	308	1-1	1		11		12	6		8	9	14	2	7	3		5		10^{1}				4										
17	H	Queen's Park	361	1-1	1		3	14		6		8	9	10^{1}	2	7			5	12	11				4										
21	H	Ross County	603	1-2	1		3	10	2	6		8^{1}	9	16	14	7			5	11	12				4										
28	A	Livingston	236	1-0				3	14	6		8	9^{1}		2	7	12		5		11		1		4		10								
Nov 4	A	Caledonian Thistle	1,525	1-5					10	6		8^{1}	9		2	7	14		5		11		1		4		3	12							
11	H	Alloa	508	1-1				5				8	9		2	7			6		11		1	3	4^{1}				10						
18	H	Brechin City	572	1-1				5		6	7	12	9^{1}		2	14			16		11		1	3	4		8		10						
25	A	East Stirlingshire	335	1-0				6		5	7		9		2	16			12	14	11^{1}		1	3	4		8		10						
Dec 2	H	Cowdenbeath	464	2-1				6		5					2	7	14			12	11		1	3	4		8	9^{1}	10^{1}						
16	A	Queen's Park	464	0-2			6	3				16	9		2	7			5	12	11		1		4		14	8	10						
Jan 6	H	Albion Rovers	306	2-0	1			2			8	14	9		6	7			3		11						12	4	10^{2}	5					
10	A	Ross County	944	0-0	1		16	2			8		9		6	7			3	14				11			12	4	10	5					
13	H	East Stirlingshire	447	2-1				2			8		9		6	7^{1}			3	16	11		1	14			12	4^{1}	10	5					
20	A	Cowdenbeath	223	2-1	1			2					12		6	7			3	9^{2}			15	11	14		8	4	10	5					
31	A	Brechin City	777	1-0			14	2					12		6	7			3	9			1	11	8			4	10	5^{1}					
Feb 3	H	Queen's Park	572	1-1			16	2	12				9		6	7			3	14	8^{1}		1	11	4				10	5					
17	A	Alloa	360	3-0				2	14				9		6	8^{2}		16		7^{1}			1	11	4				10	5	3	12			
21	H	Caledonian Thistle	703	1-2				2	14				9		6	8	16	12		7^{1}			1	11	4				10	5	3				
24	H	Livingston	772	1-2				2	14				9^{1}		6	8				7			1	11	4	12			10	5	3	16			
Mar 2	A	Albion Rovers	237	1-1				2					9^{1}		6	7				11			1		4			8	10	5	3				
9	A	East Stirlingshire	358	0-1				2					9		7	11		6		16			1		4		12	8	10	5	3	14			
16	H	Brechin City	605	0-1				2					9		7	14		6					1		4		16	8	10	5		12	3	11	
23	A	Caledonian Thistle	1,105	1-1				2					10		6	11		12		7			1		4		8		16	5		9^{1}	3		
30	H	Alloa	397	1-0		16		2					10		6	11				7^{1}			1		4		8	12	14	5		9	3		
Apr 6	H	Cowdenbeath	387	0-0		12		2					14		6	11				7			1		4	10	8	16		5		9	3		
13	A	Queen's Park	401	0-0				2		10			9		6	11				12			1		4		8	7	14	5		16	3		
20	H	Ross County	439	1-1		11		2		12					6	7^{1}							1		4	16	8	10	9	5		14	3		
27	A	Livingston	2,993	0-3		11		2							6	7							1		4	12	10	8	9	5		14	3		
May 4	H	Albion Rovers	350	2-1	1			2							6	7				16				11	4^{1}	8	12	5	9			10^{1}	3		14
TOTAL FULL APPEARANCES					11	5	8	31	5	13	7	10	28	7	33	32	2	4	19	13	15		25	15	29	2	12	14	20	18	5	4	8	1	
TOTAL SUB APPEARANCES						(2)	(3)	(2)	(9)	(1)	(3)	(6)	(3)	(3)	(2)	(4)	(5)	(3)	(2)	(11)	(2)	(1)	(1)	(1)	(1)	(4)	(7)	(3)	(3)			(7)			(1)
TOTAL GOALS SCORED												4	8	2		8	1			5	3				2			2	3	1		2			

Small bold figures denote goalscorers. † denotes opponent's own goal.

GAYFIELD PARK

CAPACITY: 6,488; Seated 715, Standing 5,773

PITCH DIMENSIONS: 115 yds x 71 yds

FACILITIES FOR DISABLED SUPPORTERS: Enclosure at West end of Stand with wide steps to take a wheelchair. Toilet facilities are also available.

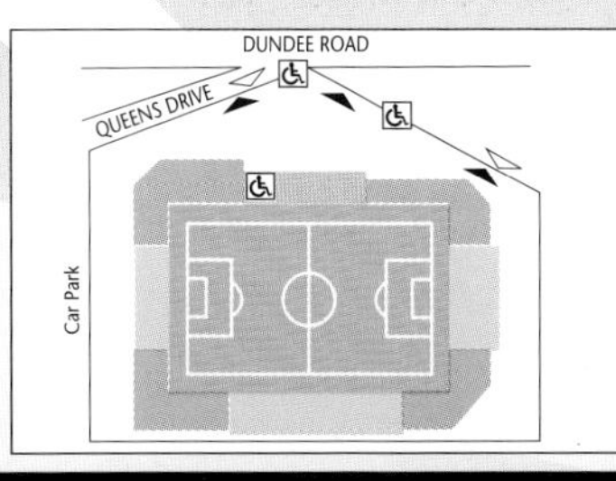

HOW TO GET THERE

The following routes may be used to reach Gayfield Park:

BUSES: Arbroath is on the main route from both Glasgow and Edinburgh to Aberdeen. Buses from these three cities, plus Stirling, Dundee and Perth all stop at Arbroath Bus Station at hourly intervals. There is also a local service between Dundee-Arbroath and Montrose and this service is half hourly until 7.00 p.m. Between 7.00 p.m. and 10.45 p.m. the service is hourly. The bus station is 10 minutes walk from the ground.

TRAINS: Arbroath is on the Inter-City 125 route from London to Aberdeen and there are frequent local services between Arbroath, Dundee and Edinburgh. Trains also travel north from Glasgow, Stirling and Perth. The station is a 15 minute walk from the ground.

CARS: There is free parking for 500 cars just next to the ground in Queen's Drive.

COWDENBEATH

Central Park, High Street,
Cowdenbeath, KY4 9QQ

CHAIRMAN
Gordon McDougall

VICE-CHAIRMAN
Eric Mitchell

DIRECTORS
Ian Fraser
Albert Tait
George T. Mowat
Patrick M. Munro
James Stevenson

SECRETARY
Thomas Ogilvie

MANAGER
Thomas Steven

PLAYER/COACH
Samuel Conn

YOUTH TEAM COACH
William Aitchison

SPRINT COACH
Bert Oliver

CLUB DOCTOR
Dr. Robert Brownlee

PHYSIOTHERAPIST
Kenneth Cotterell

GROUNDSMAN
Gordon McDougall

COMMERCIAL MANAGER
Joe McNamara

TELEPHONES
Ground/Commercial/
Ticket Office/Information Service
(01383) 610166
Sec. Home (01383) 513013
Fax (01383) 512132

CLUB SHOP
Situated at Stadium
Open 10.00 a.m. – 3.00 p.m.
and at Home Match Days

OFFICIAL SUPPORTERS CLUB
Central Park,
Cowdenbeath, KY4 9QQ

TEAM CAPTAIN
Barry McMahon

SHIRT SPONSOR

LIST OF PLAYERS 1996-97

SURNAME	FIRST NAME	MIDDLE NAME	DATE OF BIRTH	PLACE OF BIRTH	DATE OF SIGNING	HEIGHT FT INS	WEIGHT ST LBS	PREVIOUS CLUB
Baillie	Robert		04/04/78	Edinburgh	13/07/96	5 10.0	11 8	Broxburn Athletic
Bowmaker	Kevin		03/04/75	Edinburgh	15/02/95	5 11.0	11 13	Musselburgh Athletic
Brough	Grant		24/09/77	Dunfermline	18/12/95	5 10.0	11 2	Leslie Hearts B.C.
Chapman	Graham		08/08/77	Edinburgh	21/08/96	6 1.0	13 0	Musselburgh Athletic
Conn	Samuel	Craig	26/10/61	Lanark	29/10/94	5 11.0	12 0	Albion Rovers
Hamilton	Alistair	Strathern	12/11/75	Irvine	29/04/95	5 7.0	10 7	Musselburgh Athletic
Humphreys	Martin	Jay	16/03/76	Dunfermline	24/02/95	6 0.0	12 11	Links United
Hutchison	Kevin		28/02/77	Glasgow	17/08/95	5 9.0	10 9	Thorniewood United
Malloy	Brian	John	04/05/67	Paisley	26/05/94	5 11.0	12 0	Bo'ness United
McGregor	James	Scott	05/04/78	Melbourne	28/05/96	6 2.0	13 0	Ferguslie United
McKinnon	Michael		17/07/70	Edinburgh	20/08/96	6 0.0	11 7	Eyemouth United
McMahon	Barry		08/04/71	Edinburgh	23/11/92	6 1.0	12 2	Kelty Hearts
Meldrum	Graham	Ian	27/02/73	Bangour	22/07/95	5 8.0	10 7	Bo'ness United
Moffat	James		27/01/60	Dunfermline	26/07/96	6 0.0	12 0	Albion Rovers
Munro	Kenneth	Neil	08/08/77	Edinburgh	13/07/96	5 10.0	11 0	Salvesen B.C.
O'Neill	Hugh		03/01/75	Dunfermline	27/10/95	6 0.0	11 0	Forfar Athletic
Petrie	Edward		15/06/73	Bathgate	02/09/96	5 10.0	12 7	Bathgate United U'21
Ritchie	Alan		02/07/71	Edinburgh	04/06/96	5 11.0	12 0	Gala Fairydean
Russell	Neil		29/05/71	Kirkcaldy	31/05/94	6 3.0	13 9	Forfar Athletic
Sinclair	Craig		19/07/72	Edinburgh	25/06/96	5 11.0	12 0	Gala Fairydean
Steven	Thomas		05/09/54	Edinburgh	21/08/96	5 9.5	12 0	Edinburgh United
Stewart	William	Paul	16/04/77	Glasgow	28/08/95	5 10.0	10 0	Thorniewood United
Winter	Craig	John	30/06/76	Dunfermline	19/07/94	5 9.0	10 0	Raith Rovers
Wood	Garry	Pringle G.	18/09/76	Edinburgh	23/02/95	5 11.0	12 7	Hutchison Vale B.C.

MILESTONES

YEAR OF FORMATION: 1881
MOST CAPPED PLAYER: Jim Paterson
NO. OF CAPS: 3
MOST LEAGUE POINTS IN A SEASON: 60 (Division 2 – Season 1938/39)
MOST LEAGUE GOALS SCORED BY A PLAYER IN A SEASON: Willie Devlin (Season 1925/26)
NO. OF GOALS SCORED: 40
RECORD ATTENDANCE: 25,586 (-v- Rangers – 21.9.1949)
RECORD VICTORY: 12-0 (-v- Johnstone – Scottish Cup, 21.1.1928)
RECORD DEFEAT: 1-11 (-v- Clyde – Division 2, 6.10.1951)

THE BLUE BRAZIL'S TEN YEAR LEAGUE RECORD

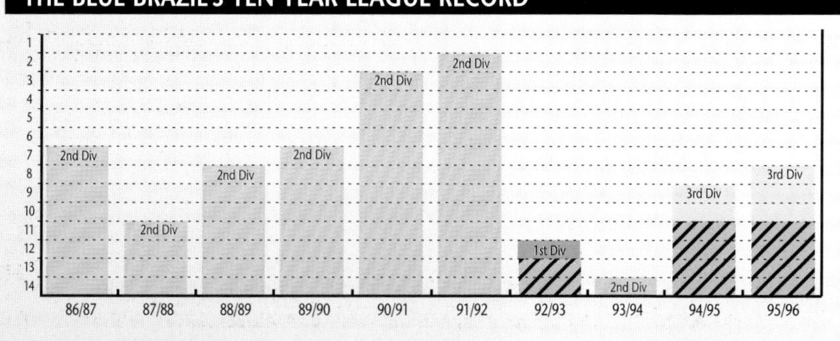

CLUB FACTFILE 1995/96
RESULTS... APPEARANCES... SCORERS

The BLUE BRAZIL

Date	Venue	Opponents	Att.	Res	Russell N.	Steven S.	Meldrum G.	McMahon B.	Malloy B.	Maratea D.	Winter C.	Wood G.	Wardell S.	Smith C.	Hutchison K.	Buckley G.	De Melo A.	Humphreys M.	Scott D.	Yardley M.	Petrie E.	Chapman G.	Soutar G.	Bowmaker K.	Brock J.	MacKenzie A.	O'Neill H.	Conn S.	Hamilton A.	Brough G.	Millar G.	Oliver S.	Stewart W.	Spence J.	McGregor S.
Aug 12	H	Alloa	281	1-0	1	2	3	4	5	6	7	8	9	10	11	12^{1}	14																		
26	A	Queen's Park	444	1-3	1	8	3	5^{1}	6	12	7	4		11		14		2	9	10															
Sep 2	H	East Stirlingshire	203	4-2	1	7	3	6	5	14	4	8		12		11		2	9^{3}	10^{1}	15														
9	A	Albion Rovers	680	3-2	1	2	3	5	6		8	7^{1}		12		11^{1}		4	9	10^{1}	14														
16	H	Brechin City	251	0-1	1	8	3	5	6		4	7				11		2	9	10		14													
23	A	Ross County	1,571	2-2	1	10	3	5	6		2	7^{1}			14	11^{1}	8	4	9				12												
30	H	Livingston	340	0-1	1	8	3	5	6		2	7				11	15	4	9				12	10	14										
Oct 7	H	Arbroath	308	1-1	1	2	3	5	6		8	7		14		12		4	9^{1}					11	10										
14	A	Caledonian Thistle	1,378	2-3	1	2	3	6			5	7		14		12		4	9^{2}					8	10	11									
21	A	East Stirlingshire	284	1-3	1	2	3	6	5			7						4	9				11^{1}		10	8									
28	H	Queen's Park	222	3-2	1	2	3	6	5^{1}		8	7				12	15	4	9^{2}				11		14		10								
Nov 4	A	Brechin City	338	0-2	1	8	3	6	5		4	7						2	9				10		14		11	12							
11	H	Albion Rovers	166	4-1	1	6	11	4	5	15	8	7^{3}				12		2	9						14		10	3^{1}							
18	A	Livingston	3,880	1-0	1	10	3	6	5		11	7				12		2	9					15^{1}	14		8	4							
25	H	Ross County	318	2-0	1	7	3	5			10					12		2	9					11	14		8	4^{2}	6	15					
Dec 2	A	Arbroath	464	1-2	1	7	3	5	6		11					14		4^{1}	9						10		12	8	2						
16	H	Caledonian Thistle	230	0-0	1	6	3			2	8							5	9				14	11		10		4			7				
Jan 9	H	East Stirlingshire	154	1-4	1	7	3			2	10	15				11		5^{1}					14	6		9		4	12		8				
13	A	Ross County	1,369	1-4	1	7	3		6	2	8	9						5					14	11		10^{1}		4			12				
16	A	Alloa	289	3-2		8	3	6	5	2	11	10^{1}						4								9^{2}		7				1			
20	H	Arbroath	223	1-2	1	8	3^{1}	6	5	2	11	10						4						12		9		7			15				
Feb 3	H	Caledonian Thistle	229	2-1	1	11^{2}	3	5		2	8	9						4								10	6				7		14		
14	H	Brechin City	160	0-0	1	9	3	5		2	7	10						6	14					11				4			8		12		
17	A	Albion Rovers	348	0-2	1	8	3	6		2	9	10						4	14					11				5			7		12		
24	A	Queen's Park	468	1-2	1	11^{1}	3	6		2	8	9						4									10	5	14		7		12		
28	H	Livingston	272	0-3	1	6	3	5		9	7	8						4						11			10		2		14		12		
Mar 2	H	Alloa	190	3-0	1	10	3^{1}	5			6^{1}	8						4	9					11			7^{1}		2	14	12				
9	H	Ross County	290	1-1	1	10	3	5			7	6						4	9^{1}								8		2		12		11	14	
16	A	Livingston	2,147	1-2	1	8	3	5				7						4	9^{1}		6			11			10		2		12		14		
23	A	Brechin City	368	0-2	17	8	3	5				7						4	9		6			11				12	2		14	1	10		
30	H	Albion Rovers	173	1-1		8	3	5										4	9		6			11			7^{1}		2			1	12	15	10
Apr 6	A	Arbroath	387	0-0	1	5	3				6	8						4	9					11			10	7	2	14				12	
13	A	Caledonian Thistle	721	0-2	1	5	3				6	8						4	9					14			10	7	2	11		17	12		
20	A	East Stirlingshire	294	1-1	1	2				6	8	7						4	9^{1}					12			11	5	10	3			14		
27	H	Queen's Park	231	2-3		4	3			6	7^{1}	8^{1}						2	9					15			11	5	12	14		1	10		
May 4	A	Alloa	260	1-2	1	5	3		6	15	7							4	9					8^{1}			14		2	11			12		10
TOTAL FULL APPEARANCES					32	36	35	28	18	13	32	30	1	2	1	6	1	35	26	4	3		3	16	4	8	16	16	12	3	6	4	3		2
TOTAL SUB APPEARANCES					(1)					(4)		(1)		(4)	(1)	(9)	(3)		(2)		(2)	(1)	(5)	(5)	(6)		(2)	(2)	(3)	(4)	(7)	(1)	(10)	(3)	
TOTAL GOALS SCORED						**3**	**2**	**1**	**1**		**2**	**7**				**3**		**2**	**11**	**2**			**1**	**2**		**3**	**2**	**3**							

Small bold figures denote goalscorers. † denotes opponent's own goal.

CENTRAL PARK

CAPACITY: 5,258; Seated 1,552, Standing 3,706

PITCH DIMENSIONS: 107 yds x 66 yds

FACILITIES FOR DISABLED SUPPORTERS: Direct access from car park into designated area within ground. Toilet and catering facilities also provided.

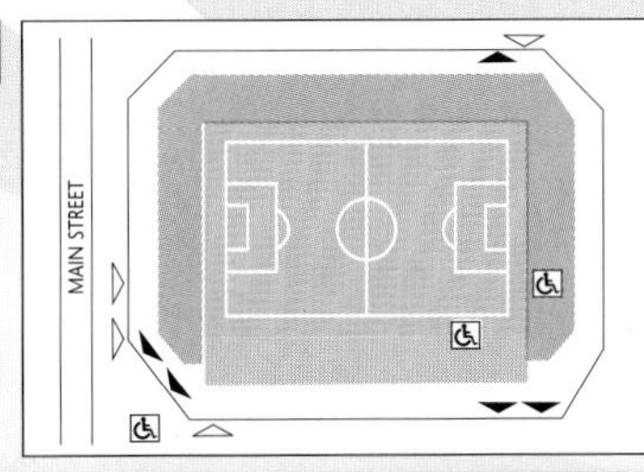

HOW TO GET THERE

You can get to Central Park by the following routes:

TRAINS: There is a regular service of trains from Edinburgh and Glasgow (via Edinburgh) which call at Cowdenbeath and the station is only 400 yards from the ground.

BUSES: A limited Edinburgh-Cowdenbeath service stops just outside the ground on matchdays and a frequent service of Dunfermline-Ballingry buses also stop outside the ground, as does the Edinburgh-Glenrothes service.

CARS: Car parking facilities are available in the public car park adjacent to the ground for 190 cars. There are also another 300 spaces at the Stenhouse Street car park, which is 200 yards from the ground.

EAST STIRLINGSHIRE

Firs Park, Firs Street, Falkirk, FK2 7AY

CHAIRMAN
William C. Whyte

VICE-CHAIRMAN
G. Marshall Paterson

DIRECTORS
William W. H. Lawless
Alexander S. H. Forsyth
Alexander C. Mitchell
Angus Williamson

SECRETARY
Mrs. Margaret Thomson

MANAGER
William Little

ASSISTANT MANAGER/COACH
Lenny Reid

CLUB DOCTOR
Dr. Alan Buchan, M.B., C.B.

PHYSIOTHERAPIST
Angus Williamson

COMMERCIAL COMMITTEE
c/o The Secretary,
Mrs Margaret Thomson

TELEPHONES
Ground/Commercial
(01324) 623583
Sec. Home (01324) 552946
Fax (01324) 637862

CLUB SHOP
Situated at ground. Open Mon-Fri 10 a.m.- 3.30 p.m. (except Thursday) and on all home matchdays

TEAM CAPTAIN
Brian Ross

SHIRT SPONSOR
Angus Williamson Therapy Clinic

EAST STIRLINGSHIRE F.C. EST 1881

LIST OF PLAYERS 1996-97

SURNAME	FIRST NAME	MIDDLE NAME	DATE OF BIRTH	PLACE OF BIRTH	DATE OF SIGNING	HEIGHT FT INS	WEIGHT ST LBS	PREVIOUS CLUB
Abercromby	Mark	Henry	14/07/74	Glasgow	08/11/94	5 10.0	10 7	Kitchee (Hong Kong)
Campbell	Colin	James	05/01/70	Edinburgh	30/07/96	5 11.0	11 0	Queen of the South
Cochrane	Matthew		06/04/77	Bellshill	30/07/96	5 11.0	11 4	Raith Rovers
Conway	Vincent	Matthew	25/02/75	Bellshill	20/08/96	5 11.0	12 6	Alloa
Farquhar	Alastair	John	15/08/76	Aberfeldy	19/01/96	5 8.5	11 5	Stirling Albion
Hamilton	Graeme	John	22/01/74	Stirling	22/08/96	5 10.0	10 10	Falkirk
Hunter	Murray	Russell	08/01/71	Edinburgh	14/03/95	6 1.0	12 0	Whitehill Welfare
Inglis	Grant	Hugh	29/12/66	Corby	23/08/96	5 7.0	11 1	Forfar Athletic
Kerr	Ross	Hutchison	19/04/76	Hamilton	09/08/96	5 11.0	10 6	Stirling Albion
McBride	Martin	Joseph	22/03/71	Glasgow	11/08/95	5 9.0	10 7	Albion Rovers
McDougall	Gordon		17/02/71	Bellshill	16/07/93	6 2.0	12 3	Falkirk
Murray	Neil	Fraser	01/05/72	Paisley	02/08/96	5 8.0	11 0	Partizan Amateurs
Neill	Alan	John	13/12/70	Baillieston	03/08/95	6 1.0	12 7	Clyde
Ramsay	Steven		13/04/67	Germiston, S.A.	30/07/96	5 9.0	11 0	Queen of the South
Ronald	Paul		19/07/71	Glasgow	07/08/96	6 2.0	12 7	Happy Valley (Hong Kong)
Ross	Brian		15/08/67	Stirling	31/03/91	5 11.0	11 7	Ayr United
Russell	Gordon	Alan	03/03/68	Falkirk	23/09/95	5 9.5	10 0	Stenhousemuir
Scott	Martin		27/04/71	Bellshill	09/08/96	5 10.0	10 0	Ayr United
Sneddon	Scott		07/12/71	Dechmont	08/11/94	6 2.0	11 4	Queen's Park
Watt	David		05/03/67	Edinburgh	19/07/94	5 7.0	11 6	Cowdenbeath
Wilson	Ewan	McKinley	01/10/68	Dunfermline	14/12/95	6 2.0	12 0	East Fife

MILESTONES

YEAR OF FORMATION: 1881
MOST CAPPED PLAYER: Humphrey Jones
NO. OF CAPS: 5 (for Wales)
MOST LEAGUE POINTS IN A SEASON: 55 (Division 2 – Season 1931/32) (2 Points for a Win)
59 (Third Division – Season 1994/95) (3 Points for a Win)
MOST LEAGUE GOALS SCORED BY A PLAYER IN A SEASON: Malcolm Morrison (Season 1938/39)
NO. OF GOALS SCORED: 36
RECORD ATTENDANCE: 11,500 (-v- Hibernian – 10.2.1969)
RECORD VICTORY: 10-1 (-v- Stenhousemuir – Scottish Cup, 1.9.1888)
RECORD DEFEAT: 1-12 (-v- Dundee United – Division 2, 13.4.1936)

THE SHIRE'S TEN YEAR LEAGUE RECORD

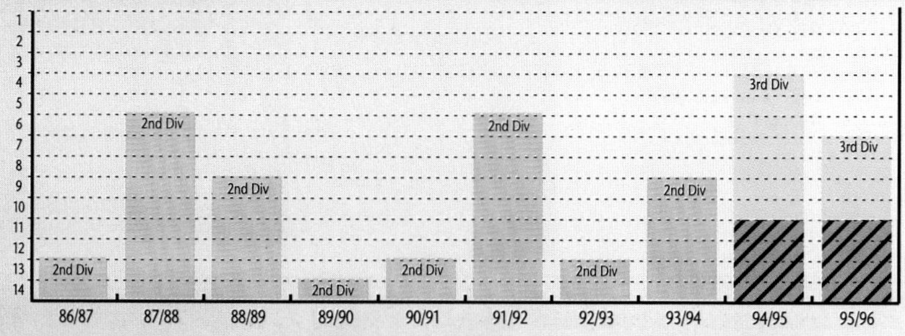

1 2 3 4 5 6 7 8 9 10 11 12 13 14

2nd Div 2nd Div 2nd Div 2nd Div 2nd Div 2nd Div 2nd Div 2nd Div 3rd Div 3rd Div

86/87 87/88 88/89 89/90 90/91 91/92 92/93 93/94 94/95 95/96

CLUB FACTFILE 1995/96
RESULTS... APPEARANCES... SCORERS

The SHIRE

Date	Venue	Opponents	Att.	Res	McDougall G.	Orr J.	Lee R.	MacLean S.	Ross B.	Neill A.	McBride M.	Hunter M.	Geraghty M.	Abercromby M.	Dwyer P.	Watt D.	Millar G.	Sneddon S.	Scott C.	McKenna T.	Moffat J.	Lee I.	Lamont P.	Russell G.	Cameron D.	Stirling D.	Cuthbert L.	Lawrie D.	Farquhar A.	Frater A.	Docherty R.	Dodds J.	Murray N.
Aug 12	A	Brechin City	326	1-3	1	2	3	4^1	5	6	7	8	9	10	11																		
27	H	Ross County	478	†1-2	1		3			6	7		9	8	11	2	4	5	10	15													
Sep 2	A	Cowdenbeath	203	2-4		2	3	8^2		6	7	4	9	15	11		14	5	10		1	12											
9	H	Livingston	409	1-2		6	3	8		12	7		9		11^1	2	4	5	10		1	15											
16	A	Queen's Park	627	0-1		6	3	4		12	7		9	15	10	2		5		11	1	8	14										
23	A	Arbroath	570	2-2		6	3	4		5^1		14	9^1	8		2				11	1	10		7	12	15							
30	H	Alloa	305	2-2		6	3	4		5	7^1	14	9		10					11	1	8^1		2	15	12							
Oct 7	H	Caledonian Thistle	381	0-5			3		6	5	7	8	9	4	11						1	10		2	12								
14	A	Albion Rovers	334	2-1			3	8	6			7	9^2	15	11	2		5			1	10		4		14	12						
21	H	Cowdenbeath	284	3-1			3		6	10		7^2	9		11	2^1	8	5			1			4			12						
28	A	Ross County	1,646	1-1	1		3		6	8		7^1	9	15	11	2		5				10		4		14							
Nov 4	H	Queen's Park	407	1-2	1		3		6	8	14			9^1	11	2		5				10	15	4		7							
11	A	Livingston	4,000	1-1	1		3	8^1		6	7			9	11			5				10	12	2		4							
18	A	Alloa	357	3-1	1		3	8		6		7^1		9	11^2	15		5				10	14	2		4							
25	H	Arbroath	335	0-1	1		3	8		6	14	7		9	11	15		5				10	12	2		4							
Dec 2	A	Caledonian Thistle	1,142	1-1	1		3	15	12	6	7	11				8		5				10	9^1	2	14	4							
9	A	Brechin City	253	1-4	1		3			6	14	7		9	11	10		5				8^1	12	2		4							
19	H	Albion Rovers	245	†5-1	1		3	14	6	4	7	8			11^4	2		5				10	9		15	12							
Jan 9	A	Cowdenbeath	154	4-1	1		3	7	6	5	10^1	4			9^2							8	11^1	2		12							
13	A	Arbroath	447	1-2	1		3	7	6	5	10				9	4^1						8	11	2	15	12							
20	H	Caledonian Thistle	353	1-5	1		3	14	6		7				11	8		5				10^1		2		12		4	9				
31	H	Alloa	310	1-0	1		3	8	6		7				9^1	2						10	11	4		5			12				
Feb 10	A	Queen's Park	522	2-2	1		3	8	6	5	7^1				9^1	4						10		2		14			11	15			
17	H	Livingston	472	0-3	1		3	12		5	11					2						10	7	6		4			9	8	14		
24	H	Ross County	353	2-4	1		3		6	5^1	7				9^1	2						10	12	4		15			11		8		
Mar 2	H	Brechin City	268	2-0	1		3	8	6	5	7				9^2	2						10		4		14					11		
9	H	Arbroath	358	1-0	1		3		6	7	11			12	9	2		5^1				10		4							8		
16	A	Alloa	309	2-2	1		3	14	6	7	11			9		2^1		5^1				10		4		15			12		8		
20	A	Albion Rovers	199	2-2	1			8	6	3	7			9	11^1	2		5				10^1		4					12				
23	H	Queen's Park	364	1-2	1			14	6	5	4			8	11^1	2		9				10		3		15			7				
30	A	Livingston	2,084	1-1	1		3		6	7	8			9	11^1	2		5				10		4		15							
Apr 6	A	Caledonian Thistle	1,071	3-0	1		3	11^1		6	7^1				9^1	2		5				10		4		8						12	15
13	H	Albion Rovers	293	1-1	1		3	11		6	7			9^1		2		5				10		4		8							14
20	H	Cowdenbeath	294	1-1	1		3	12		6	7^1			9	11	2		5				10		4		15							8
27	A	Ross County	914	3-1	1	14	3			5	7^2			9	11^1	2						10		4		6				12			8
May 4	H	Brechin City	305	3-0	1		3	14	6	5	7^1			9	11^2	2						10		4							12		8
TOTAL FULL APPEARANCES					28	6	34	18	20	31	28	12	11	17	31	28	3	23	3	3	8	31	6	30		11		1	5	1	4		3
TOTAL SUB APPEARANCES						(1)		(8)	(1)	(2)	(3)	(2)		(5)		(2)	(1)			(1)		(2)	(7)		(6)	(15)	(2)		(3)	(2)	(2)	(1)	(2)
TOTAL GOALS SCORED								5		2	8	4	3	2	21	3		2				4	2										

Small bold figures denote goalscorers. † denotes opponent's own goal.

FIRS PARK

CAPACITY: 1,880; Seated 297, Standing 1,583

PITCH DIMENSIONS: 106 yds x 73 yds

FACILITIES FOR DISABLED SUPPORTERS: By prior arrangement with Secretary.

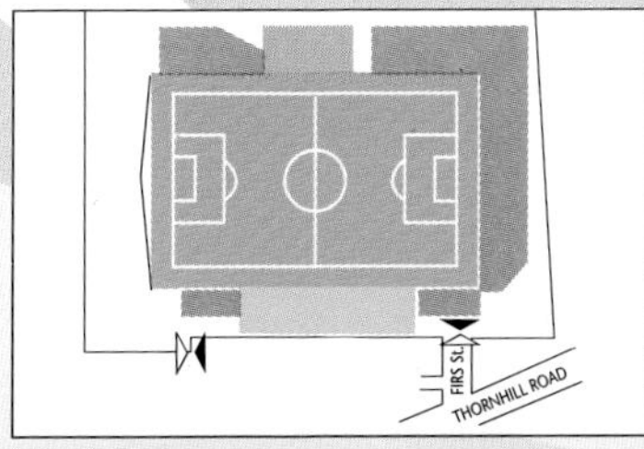

HOW TO GET THERE

The following routes may be used to reach Firs Park:

TRAINS: Passengers should alight at Grahamston station and the ground is then ten minutes walk.

BUSES: All buses running from the city centre pass close by the ground. The Grangemouth via Burnbank Road and Tamfourhill via Kennard Street services both stop almost outside the ground.

CARS: Car parking is available in the adjacent side streets. There are also spaces available in the car park adjacent to the major stores around the ground.

FORFAR ATHLETIC

Station Park, Carseview Road, Forfar, DD8 3BT

CHAIRMAN
George A. Enston

VICE-CHAIRMAN
David McGregor

DIRECTORS
James G. Robertson
Alastair S. Nicoll
Michael S. McEwan
Gordon Menmuir

SECRETARY
David McGregor

MANAGER
Tom Campbell

ASSISTANT MANAGER
Brian McLaughlin

COACHING STAFF
Tom McCallum
Gordon Arthur

PHYSIOTHERAPIST
Jim Peacock

GROUNDSMAN
Martin Gray

COMMERCIAL DIRECTOR
James G. Robertson
(01250) 874588

TELEPHONES
Ground (01307) 463576/462259
Sec. Home (01307) 464924
Sec. Bus. (01307) 462255
Fax (01307) 466956

CLUB SHOP
45 East High Street, Forfar
(01307) 465959.
Open 9.00 a.m.-5.00 p.m.
Mon, Tue, Thur and Fri.

OFFICIAL SUPPORTERS CLUB
c/o Mrs. Yvonne Nicoll,
24 Turfbeg Drive, Forfar

TEAM CAPTAIN
James Hamilton

SHIRT SPONSOR
Webster Contracts Ltd.

LIST OF PLAYERS 1996-97

SURNAME	FIRST NAME	MIDDLE NAME	DATE OF BIRTH	PLACE OF BIRTH	DATE OF SIGNING	HEIGHT FT INS	WEIGHT ST LBS	PREVIOUS CLUB
Allison	John		05/06/70	Dunfermline	22/09/95	5 6.0	10 4	Kelty Hearts
Arthur	Gordon		30/05/58	Kirkcaldy	08/09/93	5 11.0	12 5	Raith Rovers
Bowes	Mark	John	17/02/73	Bangour	28/07/95	5 8.0	10 10	Dunfermline Athletic
Christie	Sean		15/07/80	Dundee	23/07/96	5 9.0	10 7	"S" Form
Craig	Douglas	Ewing	30/01/71	London	05/11/94	5 10.0	12 9	Forfar Albion
Donegan	John	Francis J.	19/05/71	Cork	18/07/95	6 1.0	12 8	St. Johnstone
Farquaharson	Stuart		05/03/79	Dundee	23/07/96	5 6.0	10 7	St. Josephs U'18
Gardiner	Barry		11/06/77	Perth	06/09/95	5 7.0	10 2	Bankfoot Juniors
Glennie	Stuart	Philip	07/10/75	Torphins	14/09/93	6 0.0	13 0	Banchory St. Ternan
Guthrie	Derek		16/08/77	Forfar	15/08/95	5 6.0	10 0	Forfar Albion
Hamilton	James	Michael	09/12/66	Duntocher	22/12/95	5 9.0	11 0	Dumbarton
Hannigan	Paul	William	10/07/70	Perth	19/10/94	5 7.0	10 0	Jeanfield Swifts
Higgins	Gary		15/09/72	Stirling	22/09/95	5 11.0	11 5	Dunfermline Athletic
Honeyman	Ben		14/02/77	Adelaide	23/07/96	5 9.0	10 3	Dundee United
Irvine	Neil	Donald	13/10/65	Edinburgh	22/07/94	5 10.0	12 7	Montrose
Lee	Iain	Caird C.	07/07/67	Hamilton	24/08/96	5 9.0	10 7	East Stirlingshire
Loney	James		29/08/75	Stirling	11/03/95	5 8.0	10 0	East Stirlingshire
Lowe	Ian	Andrew	06/10/78	Dundee	31/03/96	5 11.0	11 0	Dundee United
Mann	Robert	Alexander	11/01/74	Dundee	21/07/92	6 3.0	13 7	St. Johnstone
McPhee	Ian		31/01/61	Perth	27/09/91	5 8.0	11 10	Airdrieonians
Morgan	Andrew	Alan	10/12/74	Glasgow	06/01/95	5 9.0	10 12	St. Johnstone
Sexton	Brian		23/08/75	Glasgow	16/03/96	6 1.0	11 2	Arbroath

MILESTONES

YEAR OF FORMATION: 1885
MOST LEAGUE POINTS IN A SEASON: 63 (Second Division – Season 1983/84) (2 Points for a Win)
80 (Third Division – Season 1994/95) (3 Points for a Win)
MOST LEAGUE GOALS SCORED BY A PLAYER IN A SEASON: Dave Kilgour (Season 1929/30)
NO. OF GOALS SCORED: 45
RECORD ATTENDANCE: 10,800 (-v- Rangers – 7.2.1970)
RECORD VICTORY: 14-1 (-v- Lindertis – Scottish Cup, 1.9.1888)
RECORD DEFEAT: 2-12 (-v- King's Park – Division 2, 2.1.1930)

THE LOONS' TEN YEAR LEAGUE RECORD

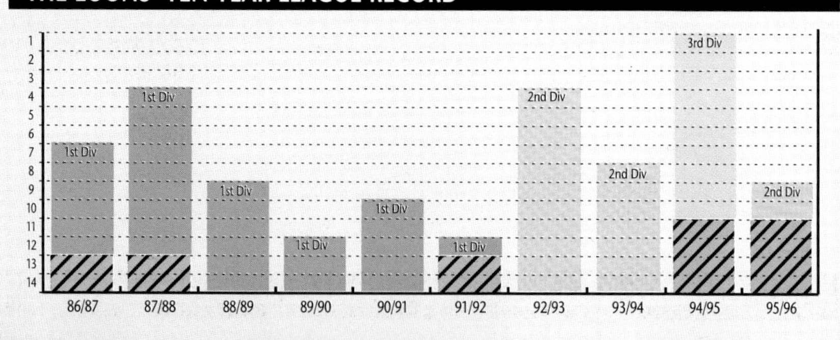

CLUB FACTFILE 1995/96
RESULTS... APPEARANCES... SCORERS

The LOONS

Date	Venue	Opponents	Att.	Res	Arthur G.	Bowes M.	Craig D.	Mann R.	McKillop A.	Glennie S.	Morgan A.	McPhee I.	Paterson A.	McVicar D.	Bingham D.	Hannigan P.	Loney J.	Irvine N.	O'Neill H.	Higgins G.	Allison J.	Inglis G.	Archibald E.	Donegan J.	Christie S.	Henderson D.	Heddle I.	Hamilton J.	Strain J.	Sexton B.
Aug 12	H	East Fife	711	0-2	1	2	3	4	5	6	7	8	9	10	11	12	14													
26	A	Clyde	1,163	2-1	1	8	6^1	4	5	2	7		12	3	10^1	9		11												
Sep 2	H	Stenhousemuir	542	1-0	1	8	6	4	5	2	7^1	11	12	3	10	9			14											
9	A	Ayr United	1,152	3-1	1	8	6	4	5		7	11	12	3	10^1	9^2	14		2											
16	H	Queen of the South	589	2-1	1	8	6	4^1	5		7	11	9	3	10^1		14		2											
23	A	Berwick Rangers	450	0-1	1	8	6	4	5		7	11	12	3		9			2	10	14									
30	H	Montrose	660	0-0	1	8	6	4	5	2	7	3	12			9	11		14	10										
Oct 7	H	Stirling Albion	624	0-6	1	8			5	4	7		14	3		12	11		6	9	2	10								
14	A	Stranraer	635	1-1	1		11	4	5	2	7	3		6		12				9^1		10	8							
21	A	East Fife	794	1-1	1	2	11	4	5		7	3		6						9^1		10	8							
28	H	Clyde	645	1-0	1	2	11	4	5		7	3		6		14				9^1		10	8	15						
Nov 4	A	Queen of the South	1,147	1-1	1	2	11	4	5	3	7^1			6		12				9	14	10	8							
11	H	Ayr United	534	2-1	1	2	11	4	5		7			6		10^1				9^1	3		8							
18	A	Montrose	730	0-1	1	2	11		5	4	7			6		10		12		9	3	14	8							
25	H	Berwick Rangers	523	1-4	1	2	12	4		6	7			3		10^1		8		9	11		5		14					
Dec 2	A	Stirling Albion	734	1-4	1	2^1	3	4	5		7	10				12		8		9	11		6		14					
16	H	Stranraer	430	0-0	1	10	5			4	7	6				14				9	2	8				3	11			
Jan 9	H	East Fife	621	0-2	1	10	5	4		6	7					14		11		9		8				3	12	2		
16	A	Stenhousemuir	381	1-3	1	10	5	4		2	7^1			3		12		11		9	14	8						6		
20	H	Stirling Albion	611	1-4	1	8		4^1			7	6		3		9					10			15		5	11	2		
23	H	Montrose	589	2-1		10^1		5		6	7	4		3		9^1					8			1			11	2		
30	A	Berwick Rangers	309	0-1	1	10	6	5			7	4		3		9				14	8						11	2		
Feb 3	A	Stranraer	476	0-1	1	10	6			5		4		3		9		12		7	8	14					11	2		
13	H	Queen of the South	427	0-3	1		4		5	12		8		3		9		10			7	14	6				11	2		
24	A	Clyde	878	1-3		10		5		6	7	4		3		9^1		12			8	11		1			14	2		
Mar 2	H	Stenhousemuir	371	3-1	1					5	7					9		8		10^3	4	11				6		2	3	
5	A	Ayr United	1,322	1-1	1	6				5	7			3		9		8		10	4^1	11		15				2	14	
9	H	Berwick Rangers	440	1-3	1	11			6	5	7^1			3		9		8		10	4	12						2	14	
16	A	Montrose	585	1-3	1	6	3	4		5	7^1					9		8			10	11						2		14
23	A	Queen of the South	1,279	1-4	1		6		5	2	10					9		8		14	7	12^1				3		4		11
30	H	Ayr United	442	1-0	1	10		6	5	2	7					12		8		9	14	11^1						4		3
Apr 6	A	Stirling Albion	788	0-1	1		2	6	5		7					12		8		9	10	11						4		3
13	H	Stranraer	388	2-2	1		3	6	5		7	10						8		9^2	2	11						4		12
20	A	East Fife	1,462	0-1	1		3	6	5	8	7	10				14				9	2	11						4		
27	H	Clyde	472	4-2	1	14	3^1			5	7^1					11		8		9^2	4	10		15				2		6
May 4	A	Stenhousemuir	431	2-0		14	3	12^1		5	7					11		8		9^1	4	10		1				2		6
TOTAL FULL APPEARANCES					33	27	27	25	22	24	34	19	2	23	5	21	2	16	4	24	22	18	9	3		5	6	19	1	5
TOTAL SUB APPEARANCES						(2)	(1)	(1)		(1)			(6)			(12)	(3)	(3)	(2)	(2)	(4)	(5)		(4)	(2)		(2)		(2)	(2)
TOTAL GOALS SCORED						2	2	3			6				3	6				12	1	2								

Small bold figures denote goalscorers. † denotes opponent's own goal.

STATION PARK

CAPACITY: 8,732; Seated 739, Standing 7,993

PITCH DIMENSIONS: 115 yds x 69 yds

FACILITIES FOR DISABLED SUPPORTERS: Ramp entrance via Main Stand.

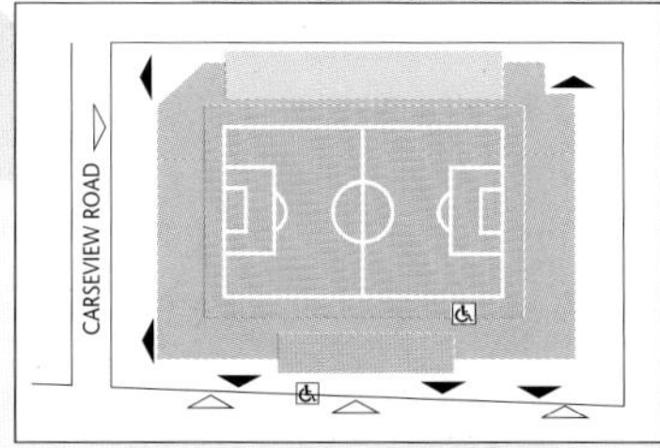

HOW TO GET THERE

Station Park can be reached by the following routes:

BUSES: There is a regular service of buses departing from Dundee City Centre into Forfar. The bus station in the town is about half a mile from the ground. There is also a local service

TRAINS: The nearest railway station is Dundee (14 miles away) and fans who travel to here should then board a bus for Forfar from the city centre. Arbroath station is also about 14 miles away.

CARS: There are car parking facilities in adjacent streets to the ground and also in the Market Muir car park.

INVERNESS CALEDONIAN THISTLE

Telford Street Park,
Telford Street,
Inverness, IV3 5LU

PRESIDENT
Dugald M. McGilvray

VICE-PRESIDENT
Norman H. Miller

HON. LIFE PRESIDENT
John S. McDonald

DIRECTORS
John Price
Alister I. MacKenzie
Craig R. MacLean
Ian Gordon
Kenneth A. Thomson
Roy MacLennan
Douglas Riach
James A. Jarvie

SECRETARY
James Falconer

GENERAL MANAGER
Bruce K. Graham
(01463) 243526

MANAGER
Steven W. Paterson

ASSISTANT MANAGER
Alex Caldwell

RESERVE TEAM MANAGER/ COMMUNITY COACH
Danny MacDonald

RESERVE TEAM COACH
Mike Fridge

YOUTH COACHES
John Beaton
Jackie Sutherland

TRAINER
Alex Young

CLUB DOCTOR
Dr. John N. MacAskill

PHYSIOTHERAPIST
Ian Manning

GROUNDSMAN/KIT MAN
Tommy Cumming

TELEPHONES
Ground (01463) 230274
Fax (01463) 715816
Sec. Home (01463) 792358
Sec. Bus. (01463) 724484

CLUB SHOP
Situated at the Ground and at Club Office, 28 Greig Street, Inverness

TEAM CAPTAIN
Michael Noble

SHIRT SPONSOR
Scottish Citylink Coaches

LIST OF PLAYERS 1996-97

SURNAME	FIRST NAME	MIDDLE NAME	DATE OF BIRTH	PLACE OF BIRTH	DATE OF SIGNING	HEIGHT FT INS	WEIGHT ST LBS	PREVIOUS CLUB
Bennett	Graeme	Peter	07/05/65	Inverness	08/08/94	5 10.0	12 7	Clachnacuddin
Benson	Robert		09/04/68	Inverness	03/08/95	5 9.0	12 5	Clachnacuddin
Calder	James	Evan	29/07/60	Grantown-on-Spey	29/06/94	5 11.0	13 4	Inverness Thistle
Cherry	Paul	Robert	14/10/64	Derby	07/07/96	6 0.0	11 6	St. Johnstone
Christie	Charles		30/03/66	Inverness	05/08/94	5 8.5	11 2	Caledonian
De Barros	Marco		18/08/71	London	12/09/96	5 9.5	10 10	Huntly
Hastings	Richard	Corey	18/05/77	Prince George, B.C.	19/07/95	6 0.0	11 8	"S" Form
Hercher	Alan	Alexander	11/08/65	Dingwall	29/06/94	6 1.0	14 3	Caledonian
MacArthur	Iain		18/10/67	Elgin	10/08/95	5 11.0	12 10	Elgin City
McAllister	Mark		13/02/71	Inverness	20/10/94	6 0.0	12 0	Caledonian
McGinlay	David		09/02/69	Fort William	01/08/95	6 0.0	11 10	Huntly
McLean	Scott	James	17/06/76	East Kilbride	12/07/96	5 11.5	12 5	St. Johnstone
Noble	Michael		18/05/66	Inverness	08/08/94	5 11.0	12 2	Caledonian
Ross	David	William	30/06/70	Inverness	23/06/95	6 2.0	12 7	Brora Rangers
Sinclair	Neal	Andrew	01/03/77	Dingwall	12/07/96	5 10.0	10 7	Nairn County
Stewart	Iain	Angus	23/10/69	Dundee	09/06/95	5 7.0	9 12	Lossiemouth
Teasdale	Michael	Joseph	28/07/69	Elgin	08/12/95	6 0.0	13 0	Dundee
Thomson	Brian	Fraser	19/06/66	Fraserburgh	08/12/95	5 11.0	13 6	Huntly
Tokely	Ross	Norman	08/03/79	Aberdeen	03/06/96	6 3.0	12 0	Huntly
Wilson	Barry	John	16/02/72	Kirkcaldy	20/07/96	5 11.0	12 4	Raith Rovers

MILESTONES

YEAR OF FORMATION: 1994
MOST LEAGUE POINTS IN A SEASON: 57 (Third Division – Season 1995/96) (3 points for a Win)
MOST LEAGUE GOALS SCORED BY A PLAYER IN A SEASON: Iain Stewart (Season 1995/96)
NO. OF GOALS SCORED: 23
RECORD ATTENDANCE: 4,931 (-v- Ross County – 23.1.1996)
RECORD VICTORY: 6-1 (-v- Albion Rovers – Third Division, 21.10.1995)
RECORD DEFEAT: 0-4 (-v- Queen's Park – Third Division, 20.8.1994)
(-v- Montrose – Third Division, 14.2.1995)

CALEY THISTLE'S LEAGUE RECORD

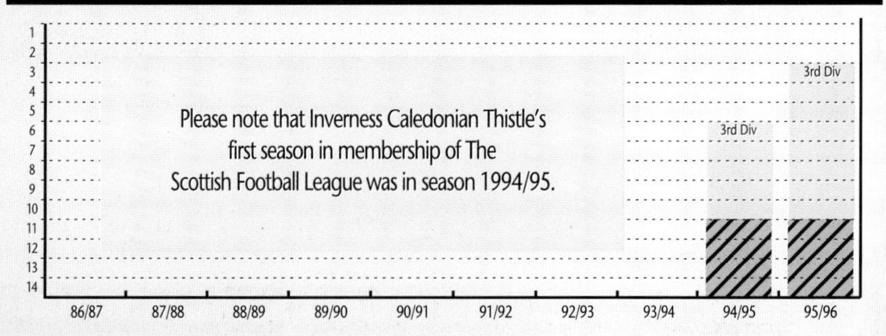

CLUB FACTFILE 1995/96
RESULTS... APPEARANCES... SCORERS

CALEY THISTLE

Date	Venue	Opponents	Att.	Res	McRitchie M.	McGinlay D.	McAllister M.	Noble M.	Benson R.	Ross D.	Mitchell C.	Lisle M.	Stewart I.	Christie C.	Green D.	Bennett G.	MacMillan N.	Brennan D.	Hastings R.	Hercher A.	Calder J.	MacArthur I.	Scott J.	Teasdale M.	Thomson B.	McKenzie P.
Aug 12	H	Livingston	1,259	0-3	1	2	3	4	5	6	7	8	9	10	11	14	15									
26	H	Brechin City	1,029	1-2	1			4	5	6	14		9^{1}	10		8	7	2	3	11						
Sep 2	A	Albion Rovers	284	2-2				4	5	7	12		9	10	14	8	6	2	3	11^{2}	1					
9	H	Queen's Park	1,141	3-1				5		7	12		9^{1}	10	6^{1}	4			3	11^{1}	1	2	8			
16	A	Arbroath	579	1-2				5		7			9^{1}	10	6	4			3	11	1	2	8			
23	A	Alloa	387	5-0				5		7	12	14	9^{2}	10^{3}	6	4	15		3	11	1	2	8			
30	H	Ross County	3,627	1-1			12	5		7		15	9	10		4	6		3	11^{1}	1	2	8			
Oct 7	A	East Stirlingshire	381	5-0				5		6^{1}	10^{1}	7	9^{2}		15		14	2^{1}	3	11	1	4	8			
14	H	Cowdenbeath	1,378	3-2		14		5		6	10	7	9^{1}		15	12		2	3^{1}	11^{1}	1	4	8			
21	H	Albion Rovers	1,222	6-1			6	5		7^{1}	10^{2}	14	9^{3}		12	4	15	2	3	11	1		8			
28	A	Brechin City	374	0-0		14	6	5		7	10		9	12	15	4		2	3	11	1		8			
Nov 4	H	Arbroath	1,525	5-1			6	5		7	10	15	9^{2}	12^{2}		4	14	2	3^{1}	11	1		8			
11	A	Queen's Park	597	3-0		14	6	5			7	12	9^{2}	10	15	4		2	3	11^{1}	1		8			
18	A	Ross County	4,288	0-2		14	6	5			7		9	10	15	4		2	3	11	1		8			
25	H	Alloa	1,181	1-1		14	6	5		15	7		9	10^{1}		4		2	3	11	1		8			
Dec 2	H	East Stirlingshire	1,142	1-1		11	6	5		7^{1}	12		9	10		4			3	14	1	2	8			
16	A	Cowdenbeath	230	0-0		2		5		6			9	10		4			3	14	1		8	7	11	
Jan 13	A	Alloa	410	2-0				5		6			14	10^{1}		4			3	11	1	2	8	7	9^{1}	
17	A	Livingston	2,578	2-0				5		6			14	10^{1}		4			3	11	1	2	8	7^{1}	9	
20	A	East Stirlingshire	353	5-1		2	14	5		12^{1}			9^{3}	10				15	3	11	1	4	8^{1}	7	6	
23	H	Ross County	4,931	1-1				5		6			9^{1}	15		4			3	11	1	2	8	7	10	
Feb 3	A	Cowdenbeath	229	1-2		6	12	5		11			9	10^{1}		4			3		1	2		7	8	
21	A	Arbroath	703	2-1				5		6			9^{1}			4			3	11	1	2	8^{1}	7	10	
24	H	Brechin City	2,514	0-1		14		5		6	15		9			4			3	11	1	2	8	7	10	
28	A	Albion Rovers	364	2-0		12	14	5		6	15		9^{1}			4			3	11^{1}	1	2	8	7	10	
Mar 2	A	Livingston	2,152	†2-2		15		5		6	14		9	12		4			3	11	1	2	8	7^{1}	10	
5	H	Queen's Park	1,245	1-1		2		5		12	10		9			4		14	3	11^{1}	1		8	7	6	15
12	H	Alloa	1,162	0-0		12		5		10	14		9	15		4			3	11	1	2	8	7	6	
16	A	Ross County	3,670	1-2		14	15^{1}	5		6			9	10		4			3	11	1	2	8	7	12	
23	H	Arbroath	1,105	1-1		11	3	5			6	7	9	10		4				12^{1}	1	2	14		8	15
30	A	Queen's Park	526	2-1		6	3	5				8	9^{1}	10^{1}		4		2		11	1		15	7	12	
Apr 6	H	East Stirlingshire	1,071	0-3		6	3	5		15		8	9	10		4		14		11	1	2		7	12	
13	H	Cowdenbeath	721	2-0			3	5		7			9	10^{1}						4	1	6	8	2	11^{1}	15
20	H	Albion Rovers	769	1-1		15	3	5		7	8		9	10^{1}		12				4	1	6		2	11	14
27	A	Brechin City	656	1-0		14	3	5		11			12	10		6				4^{1}	1	2	8	7	9	
May 4	H	Livingston	1,403	1-2		15	3	5		11		8	9^{1}	10		4				12	1	2	6	7	14	
TOTAL FULL APPEARANCES					2	9	15	36	3	28	12	7	33	24	4	30	3	11	28	30	34	24	28	19	16	
TOTAL SUB APPEARANCES						(13)	(5)			(4)	(9)	(5)	(3)	(5)	(7)	(3)	(5)	(3)		(4)			(2)		(4)	(4)
TOTAL GOALS SCORED							1			4	3		23	12	1			1	2	10			2	2	2	

Small bold figures denote goalscorers. † denotes opponent's own goal.

TELFORD STREET PARK

CAPACITY: 5,480;
Seated 480, Standing 5,000

PLEASE NOTE THAT THE CLUB IS SCHEDULED TO MOVE TO A NEW STADIUM IN EARLY NOVEMBER, 1996 WITH AN INITIAL CAPACITY FOR 5,500 SPECTATORS. THE GROUND IS LOCATED ON THE A9 WITH ACCESS OFF THE ROUNDABOUNT TO THE SOUTH SIDE OF THE KESSOCK BRIDGE. THERE WILL BE AMPLE PARKING AT THE GROUND.

PITCH DIMENSIONS: 110 yds x 70 yds

FACILITIES FOR DISABLED SUPPORTERS:
By prior arrangement with the Secretary

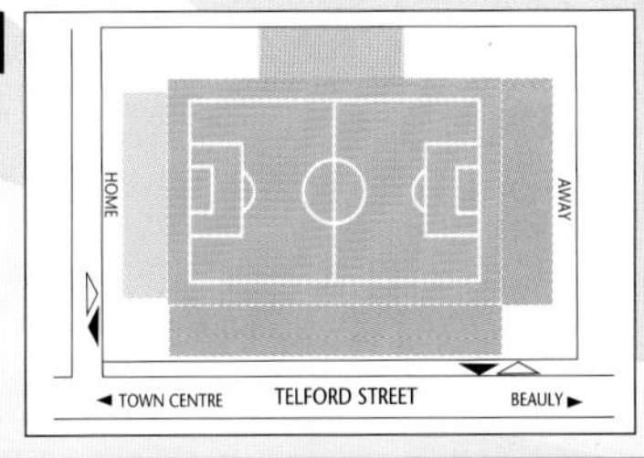

HOW TO GET THERE

The following routes may be used to reach Telford Street Park:

TRAINS: Nearest Railway Station is Inverness which is approximately one mile from ground.

BUSES: Local services available from Bus Station situated close to Inverness town centre.

CARS: The Ground is located to the West of Inverness on the old A9 Road. If approaching from North, South or East follow signs for town centre and Beauly. Car and bus parking is available within the Carsegate Industrial Estate area adjacent to the ground.

MONTROSE

Links Park Stadium,
Wellington Street,
Montrose, DD10 8QD

CHAIRMAN
Michael G. Craig

DIRECTORS
Malcolm J. Watters
John D. Crawford
John Archbold

HONORARY PRESIDENT
William Johnston, M.B.E., J.P.

SECRETARY
Malcolm J. Watters

MATCH DAY SECRETARY
Andrew Stephen

MANAGER
David Smith

ASSISTANT MANAGER
Graeme Woodward

YOUTH TEAM COACH
Charlie Guthrie

CLUB SCOUTS
Bill Moir, Steve Samson,
Jim Chalmers, Derek Hardie

COMMERCIAL REPRESENTATIVES
Merpro Leisure Ltd

CLUB DOCTOR
Dr. A. Walker

PHYSIOTHERAPIST
Allan Borthwick

TELEPHONES
Ground (01674) 673200
Sec. Home (01674) 830354
Sec. Bus. (01674) 674941
Sec. Fax (01674) 677830
Ground Fax (01674) 677311

CLUB SHOP
Situated at Stadium
(01674) 674941.
Open 10.30 a.m. – 5.00 p.m. Fri.
and on matchdays

OFFICIAL SUPPORTERS CLUB
c/o Links Park, Wellington Street,
Montrose, DD10 8QD

TEAM CAPTAIN
Mark Haro

SHIRT SPONSOR
Bon Accord Glass

LIST OF PLAYERS 1996-97

SURNAME	FIRST NAME	MIDDLE NAME	DATE OF BIRTH	PLACE OF BIRTH	DATE OF SIGNING	HEIGHT FT INS	WEIGHT ST LBS	PREVIOUS CLUB
Bird	John		14/03/70	Edinburgh	30/07/96	5 11.0	11 8	Whitehill Welfare
Brady	Scott		06/02/77	Aberdeen	09/09/96	5 11.0	10 12	Culter Juniors
Brown	Justin		12/02/78	Aberdeen	11/09/95	6 0.0	12 0	Bon Accord
Butter	James	Ross	14/12/66	Dundee	09/09/96	6 1.0	12 12	Queen of the South
Constable	Ryan	David	08/07/78	Aberdeen	02/10/95	5 9.0	11 0	Crombie Sports
Cooper	Craig		17/01/73	Arbroath	19/06/93	5 10.0	10 13	Portcullis
Craib	Mark		08/02/70	St. Andrews	17/07/92	5 10.0	11 12	Dundee
Ferrie	Alistair	Alexander	13/03/78	Montrose	02/09/95	5 8.0	11 2	Stonehaven Juniors
Glass	Scott		04/02/72	South Africa	02/08/96	5 8.0	10 4	Downfield
Haro	Mark		21/10/71	Irvine	12/07/93	6 2.0	11 7	Dunfermline Athletic
Ingram	Nicholas	Charles	23/08/73	Edinburgh	02/08/96	5 8.5	10 9	Livingston
Kennedy	Allan		11/03/64	Arbroath	02/11/95	5 9.0	10 0	Arbroath
Kydd	Stephen		13/06/76	Carnoustie	09/09/96	6 1.0	11 4	Forfar West End
Larter	David		18/03/60	Edinburgh	27/07/87	5 10.5	11 4	Dalkeith
Lavelle	Mark		26/04/74	Hitchin	10/05/95	5 11.0	11 5	Bon Accord Juniors
Lawrie	Graham		03/11/76	Aberdeen	12/10/95	5 10.0	11 7	Lewis United
MacDonald	Innes	James	19/10/62	Inverness	01/08/94	5 10.0	11 3	Luxol St. Andrews
Mailer	Craig	James	27/09/67	Perth	20/02/95	5 11.0	11 7	Kinnoull Juniors
Massie	Ronald	Wilson	04/10/75	Montrose	09/09/96	5 11.0	11 5	Carnoustie Panmure
Masson	Paul	Thomas	07/12/74	Aberdeen	27/10/93	5 9.0	10 7	Carnoustie Panmure
McGlashan	Colin	James	17/03/64	Perth	12/07/94	5 7.0	10 12	Ayr United
Purves	Stewart		15/10/62	Edinburgh	30/07/96	6 1.0	12 0	Whitehill Welfare
Robb	Mark	David	02/04/77	Aberdeen	11/09/95	6 0.0	11 10	Bon Accord
Ross	Michael		14/11/77	Montrose	02/10/95	6 1.0	11 6	Montrose Rosslea
Smith	Shaun		13/04/71	Bangour	17/03/95	6 0.0	12 2	Clydebank
Stephen	Levi		19/03/74	Hastings	06/08/93	5 8.0	11 0	Clydebank
Taylor	Scott	Andrew	23/01/77	Forfar	02/08/95	5 9.0	10 0	Dundee United
Tindal	Kevin	Douglas	11/04/71	Arbroath	20/11/93	5 9.0	12 7	Arbroath
Tosh	James	David	12/09/74	Arbroath	19/06/93	6 0.0	10 11	Arbroath Lads Club
Wood	Robert		31/08/77	Aberdeen	11/09/95	5 11.0	11 0	Banks O'Dee

MILESTONES

YEAR OF FORMATION: 1879
MOST CAPPED PLAYER: Sandy Keiller
NO. OF CAPS: 6 (2 whilst with Montrose)
MOST LEAGUE POINTS IN A SEASON: 53 (Division 2 – 1974/75 and Second Division 1984/85) (2 Points for a Win)
67 (Third Division – Season 1994/95) (3 Points for a Win)
RECORD ATTENDANCE: 8,983 (-v- Dundee – 17.3.1973)
RECORD VICTORY: 12-0 (-v- Vale of Leithen – Scottish Cup, 4.1.1975)
RECORD DEFEAT: 0-13 (-v- Aberdeen, 17.3.1951)

THE GABLE ENDIES' TEN YEAR LEAGUE RECORD

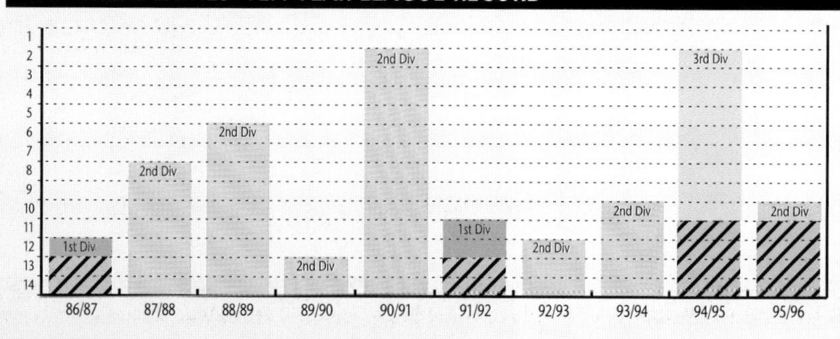

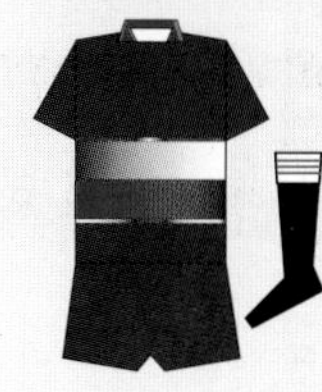

CLUB FACTFILE 1995/96
RESULTS... APPEARANCES... SCORERS

The GABLE ENDIES

Date	Venue	Opponents	Att.	Res	Larter D.	Robertson I.	Mailer C.	Masson P.	Grant D.	Tosh J.	Cooper C.	MacDonald I.	McGlashan C.	Smith S.	MacRonald C.	Stephen L.	Brown M.	Massie R.	McAvoy N.	Taylor S.	Tindal K.	Ferrie A.	Garden M.	Masson C.	Craib M.	Kennedy A.	Kydd S.	Haro M.
Aug 12	A	Stirling Albion	752	0-3	1	2	3	4	5	6	7	8	9	10	11	12	15											
26	H	Queen of the South	557	1-4			2	4	5	6	7	8	9[1]	10	11	3		1	12	15								
Sep 2	A	Stranraer	503	1-4			2	4	5	6	7	8[1]		10	14	3		1	11	9	12	15						
9	A	East Fife	702	0-3	1		2		5	6	7	4	9	10	11	3			8	15		14						
16	H	Clyde	763	0-0	1		6	4	5		7	10	9			3			11		2		8					
23	H	Ayr United	409	0-1	1			4	5	6	7	8	9	10		3			11	12	2	14		15				
30	A	Forfar Athletic	660	0-0	1	2		12	5	6		8	9	10		4			11	7	3							
Oct 7	A	Stenhousemuir	521	1-3	1	2	12	14	5	6		8	9	10[1]		4			11	7	3				15			
14	H	Berwick Rangers	503	1-3	1	2	6	4	5		7	8	9	10		3			11[1]	14		15						
21	H	Stirling Albion	629	2-2	1	2	6	4	5		12	7	9[1]	10[1]		3			11						8			
28	A	Queen of the South	902	2-4	1	2	6	4	5		14	7	9[2]	10		3			11		12				8			
Nov 4	A	Clyde	849	0-3	1	2	6		5		7	8				3			11	9					4	10	15	
11	H	East Fife	802	1-2	1	2	3	4[1]	6			7							11	12		15		5	8	10	9	
18	H	Forfar Athletic	730	1-0	1	2	3	4		6		7	9						11					5	8	10[1]	12	
25	A	Ayr United	1,166	0-2	1	2	3			6		7	9			4						11		5	8	10	15	
Dec 2	H	Stenhousemuir	504	1-4	1	2	3	4		6		7	9[1]							12	15	14		5	8	10	11	
16	A	Berwick Rangers	314	2-2	1		2	4	5[1]	6		7	9	14							3	11			8	10[1]		
23	A	Stirling Albion	1,056	0-2	1		2	4	5			7	9	14						12	3	11			8	10		6
Jan 13	H	Ayr United	587	0-1	1		8	4	5	2		7	9	14						12	3				11	10		6
16	H	Stranraer	334	4-2	1		8	4	5	2		7	9[3]	10		14				12[1]	3				11			6
20	A	Stenhousemuir	378	1-3	1		5	4		2		7	9[1]	10		11				12	3	15			8	14		6
23	A	Forfar Athletic	589	1-2	1		8	4	5	2		7	9[1]							14	3				11	12	10	6
Feb 3	H	Berwick Rangers	520	1-2	1		2		5		7		9[1]	10		4				11	3	14			8			6
21	A	East Fife	425	0-7					5	2		11	9	10		4		1		12	3				8	7	14	6
24	H	Queen of the South	545	0-6	1		2		4	5			9	10		11				12	3	14			8	7		6
Mar 2	A	Stranraer	436	2-1	1		2				7	8	9	10						14		11		3	4	6[2]		5
9	A	Ayr United	1,326	0-2	1		2				7	8	9	10								11		5	3	4		6
12	H	Clyde	226	2-3	1		2				7	8[1]	9[1]	10						12		11		5	3	6		4
16	H	Forfar Athletic	585	3-1	1		2		5		7	8	9[1]	10						6[2]		11			3			4
23	A	Clyde	791	3-1	1		2		5		7	8	9[1]	10		12				6[2]		11			3		15	4
30	H	East Fife	696	0-1	1		2		5		7	8	9	10		11				6		12			3			4
Apr 6	H	Stenhousemuir	507	1-3	1		2				7	8	9[1]	10		11						12		5	3	6		4
13	A	Berwick Rangers	367	1-4	1		2[1]		14	5	7	8	9	10		11				6	3	12					15	4
20	H	Stirling Albion	824	0-3	1		2				7	8	9	10		11				6	3	12			5		14	4
27	A	Queen of the South	1,227	1-1	1		2	6			7	8	9[1]	10		11				15	3	12			5			4
May 4	H	Stranraer	347	0-1	1		2	6		15	14	8	9			11				7	3				5		10	4
TOTAL FULL APPEARANCES					33	11	32	19	24	18	19	34	33	25	3	22		3	12	11	17	8	1	8	26	14	4	19
TOTAL SUB APPEARANCES							(1)	(2)	(1)	(1)	(3)			(3)	(1)	(3)	(1)		(1)	(16)	(3)	(14)		(1)	(1)	(2)	(7)	
TOTAL GOALS SCORED							1	1	1			2	16	2					1	5						4		

Small bold figures denote goalscorers. † denotes opponent's own goal.

LINKS PARK STADIUM

CAPACITY: 4,338; Seated 1,338, Standing 3,000

PITCH DIMENSIONS: 113 yds x 70 yds

FACILITIES FOR DISABLED SUPPORTERS: Area set aside for wheelchairs and designated area in new stand.

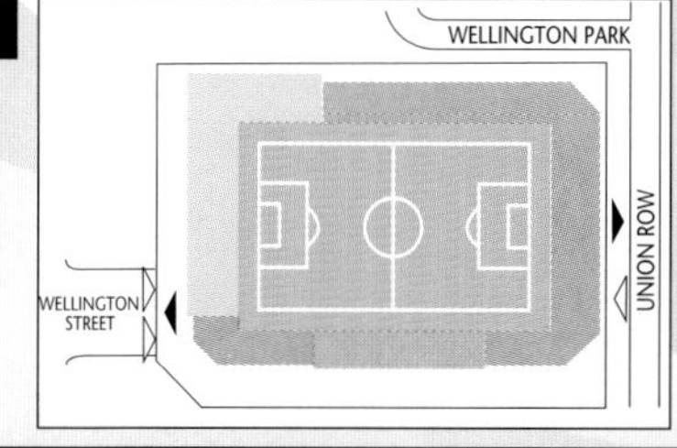

HOW TO GET THERE

Links Park can be reached by the following routes:

TRAINS: Montrose is on the Inter-City 125 route from London to Aberdeen and also on the Glasgow-Aberdeen route. There is a regular service and the station is about 15 minutes walk from the ground.

BUSES: An hourly service of buses from Aberdeen and Dundee stop in the town centre and it is a 15 minute walk from here to the ground.

CARS: Car parking is available in the car park at the ground and there are numerous side streets all round the park which can be used if necessary.

QUEEN'S PARK

Hampden Park, Letherby Drive,
Mount Florida, Glasgow, G42 9BA

PRESIDENT
H. Gordon Wilson

COMMITTEE
James C. Rutherford (Treasurer)
Malcolm Mackay
Martin B. Smith, LL.B., N.P.
Peter G. Buchanan
John C. Campbell
William Omand
Austin Reilly
James Nicholson
A. Kenneth C. Harvey
David Gordon

SECRETARY
Alistair MacKay

COACH
Hugh McCann

ASSISTANT COACH
Andrew McGlennan

CLUB DOCTOR
Alan S. Hutchison

PHYSIOTHERAPIST
Robert C. Findlay

CHIEF SCOUT
William S. Burgess

STADIUM FOREMAN
Norman Henderson

KIT MANAGER
Sam McNaughton

KIT ASSISTANT
Russell Greig

COMMERCIAL MANAGER
Ms. Carol J. Cairns
0141-649 9256

TELEPHONES
Ground 0141-632 1275
Fax 0141-636 1612

CLUB SHOP
Home matches only – Hampden Park (Kiosk within North Stand) 2.15 p.m. – 3.00 p.m. and 4.45 p.m. – 5.00 p.m. on home match days. Mail Orders may be obtained through the Secretary of the Official Supporters Club.

OFFICIAL SUPPORTERS CLUB
c/o Secretary, Keith McAllister,
58 Brunton Street,
Glasgow, G44 3NQ

TEAM CAPTAIN
Graeme Elder

SHIRT SPONSOR
British Engine Insurance

LIST OF PLAYERS 1996-97

SURNAME	FIRST NAME	MIDDLE NAME	DATE OF BIRTH	PLACE OF BIRTH	DATE OF SIGNING	HEIGHT FT INS	WEIGHT ST LBS	PREVIOUS CLUB
Arbuckle	David		12/08/73	Bellshill	23/06/95	5 10.0	11 5	Gartferry Amateur
Bruce	Gordon		10/07/75	Edinburgh	23/06/95	5 11.0	11 12	Stoneyburn Juniors
Callan	Dominic		20/09/66	Glasgow	14/08/90	5 10.0	10 7	Vale of Leven
Cameron	Craig	Douglas	09/05/73	Bellshill	09/07/96	6 1.0	11 4	Blantyre Victoria
Caven	Ross		04/08/65	Glasgow	12/08/82	6 0.0	12 0	Possil Y.M.C.A.
Edgar	Scott		10/06/76	Glasgow	27/07/94	6 4.0	13 0	Milngavie Wanderers
Elder	Graeme		21/11/61	Glasgow	08/07/86	6 1.0	13 0	Drumchapel Y.M.C.A.
Falconer	Marc		04/11/72	Glasgow	02/08/96	5 10.0	11 2	Clyde
Ferguson	Paul		10/09/73	Glasgow	25/03/94	6 0.0	10 7	Wolves B.C.
Ferry	Daniel		31/01/77	Glasgow	23/06/95	5 7.0	11 4	Queen's Park U'18s
Fraser	Robert	Scott	02/10/67	Paisley	31/03/95	6 0.0	12 0	Renfrew Juniors
Graham	David		27/01/71	Bellshill	25/07/91	5 10.0	10 8	Queen's Park Youth
Hardie	Martin		22/04/76	Alexandria	17/09/96	5 11.0	11 0	Yoker Athletic
Kennedy	Kenneth	Leslie	11/03/77	Edinburgh	29/06/95	6 4.0	11 6	Bothkennar Y.M. U'18s
Maxwell	Ian		02/05/75	Glasgow	24/07/93	6 3.0	12 5	Unattached
McGarrigle	John	Joseph	08/10/73	Greenock	02/08/96	6 1.0	11 6	Port Glasgow Juniors
McGoldrick	Kevin		12/05/72	Glasgow	03/09/94	5 10.0	11 7	Campsie Black Watch
McLauchlan	Mark		02/01/70	Bellshill	31/07/96	6 0.0	12 13	Kilsyth Rangers
Orr	Garry		27/11/73	Glasgow	14/02/92	5 4.0	10 10	Dundee United
Smith	Daniel		30/05/77	Falkirk	05/07/96	5 11.0	10 6	Dunipace Juniors
Smith	Mark	Alexander	16/12/64	Bellshill	17/09/96	5 9.0	9 7	Ayr United
Ward	James		25/04/72	Paisley	29/03/96	5 9.0	11 3	Glenafton Athletic
Wilson	Derek	William	30/05/76	Bellshill	03/09/94	5 10.0	11 6	Airdrieonians

MILESTONES

YEAR OF FORMATION: 1867
MOST CAPPED PLAYER: Walter Arnott
NO. OF CAPS: 14
MOST LEAGUE POINTS IN A SEASON: 57 (Division 2 – Season 1922/23)
MOST LEAGUE GOALS SCORED BY A PLAYER IN A SEASON: William Martin (Season 1937/38)
NO. OF GOALS SCORED: 30
RECORD ATTENDANCE: 149,547 (Scotland v England – 17.4.1937)
RECORD VICTORY: 16-0 (-v- St. Peters – Scottish Cup, 29.8.1885)
RECORD DEFEAT: 0-9 (-v- Motherwell – Division 1, 29.4.1930)

THE SPIDERS' TEN YEAR LEAGUE RECORD

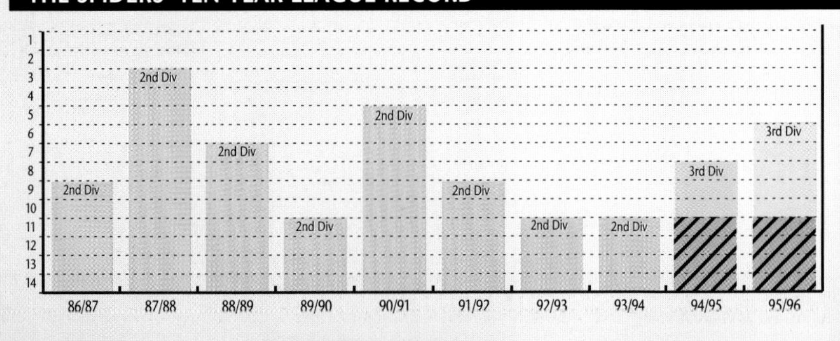

CLUB FACTFILE 1995/96
RESULTS... APPEARANCES... SCORERS

The SPIDERS

Date	Venue	Opponents	Att.	Res	Chalmers J.	Graham D.	McGoldrick K.	McGrath D.	Caven R.	Maxwell I.	McInally A.	Arbuckle D.	McCusker J.	McPhee B.	Matchett J.	Brodie D.	Kerr G.	Porter C.	Ferguson P.	Elder G.	Edgar S.	Callan D.	Wilson D.	Smith M.	Fraser R.	Ferry D.	McGinlay M.	Orr G.	Kennedy K.	Bruce G.	Ward J.
Aug 12	A	Ross County	1,515	0-2	1	2	3	4	5	6	7	8	9	10	11	12	15	16													
26	H	Cowdenbeath	444	3-1	1	2	11	4	8	6	12		9[2]	14	15		7		3	5	10[1]										
Sep 9	A	Caledonian Thistle	1,141	1-3	1	11	10	4	5	6		8		15		7			3		9[1]	2									
16	H	East Stirlingshire	627	1-0	1	2	11		8[1]	6	7	4	9	14		12			3	5	10	15									
20	A	Livingston	223	0-2	1	2	11	4		6	7	8	14	10		15			3	5	9	12									
23	H	Brechin City	422	0-2	1	8	11		7	6	12	4	14	10		15			3	5	9	2									
30	A	Albion Rovers	378	1-3	1	3	11[1]	4	7	6		8	15	10		14				5	9	12	2								
Oct 7	H	Alloa	483	0-0	1	3	11		8	6		4		15			12	10		5	9		2	7	14						
17	A	Arbroath	361	1-1	1	3	11			6	12	4		14				10	5		9[1]	8	2		7						
21	H	Livingston	540	0-1	1		11		5	6	12	4		14			15	10	3		9	8	2		7						
28	A	Cowdenbeath	222	2-3	1		3		6[1]	5	11	4	14	12			8	9			10[1]	7	2								
Nov 4	A	East Stirlingshire	407	2-1	1	3	11		5[1]	6		4		10			8	13			9[1]	2	12		7						
11	H	Caledonian Thistle	597	0-3	1	3	11		8	6		4		10			12	14		5	9	2			7	15					
18	H	Albion Rovers	467	4-1	1	2	11[2]		5	6		8		10			7	14[1]	3	4	9[1]	15			12						
25	A	Brechin City	306	0-1	1	2	11		5	6		8		10					3	4	9	12			7		15				
Dec 2	A	Alloa	352	0-0	1		3		5	6		11		10				9		4		2			8	14		7			
16	H	Arbroath	464	2-0	1	15	11		5	6		3				14		10		4	9	2[1]			8	12[1]		7			
30	H	Ross County	699	1-1	1	6	11		5			3				7		12		4	9	2			8[1]	10					
Jan 1	H	Albion Rovers	617	5-1	1	6	11[1]	14	5[1]			3				10		12		4	9	2			8[1]	7[2]			15		
10	A	Livingston	1,822	1-3	1	6	11		5			3		12		7				4	9		2		8	10[1]		14			
13	H	Brechin City	505	0-0	1	6	11		5			3		12		7		14		4	9	2			8	10			15		
20	H	Alloa	467	0-0	1	3	11		5			8		7		14		12	6	4	9	2				10			15		
Feb 3	A	Arbroath	572	1-1	1	3	11		5			8		9		10			6	4	14	2				15		7[1]	12		
10	H	East Stirlingshire	522	2-2	1	11	3		5			8		15		10			6	4	9	2				12[1]		7[1]	14		
24	H	Cowdenbeath	468	2-1	1	3[1]	11		5	4		8		12[1]	14				6		9	2				10		7			
Mar 2	H	Ross County	238	0-0	1	8	11		5	4		3		10					6		9	2				12		7			
5	A	Caledonian Thistle	1,245	1-1	1	3[1]	11		5	4		8			10				6		9	2				12		7			
9	A	Brechin City	363	0-4	1	3	11		5	4		8		14	10	15			6		9	2	12					7			
16	A	Albion Rovers	387	2-0		7	11[1]		5	6		8[1]		9					3	4	14	2				10				1	
23	A	East Stirlingshire	364	2-1		7	11		5	6[2]		8		9		15			3	4	14	2				10				1	
30	H	Caledonian Thistle	526	1-2		8	11		5	6		7		9[1]				15	3	4	14	2	12			10				1	
Apr 6	A	Alloa	403	1-0		8	11[1]		5	6		7		9		14			3	4	10	2				12				1	15
13	H	Arbroath	401	0-0		8	3		5	6		7		9		14				4	10	12	2					11		1	
20	H	Livingston	928	0-0		8	11			5		7		9				15	6	4			2		14			10		1	3
27	A	Cowdenbeath	231	†3-2		11	3			5		7		9[2]					6	4	14		2		8			10	15	1	
May 4	A	Ross County	916	1-0		11	3			5		7		9[1]					6	4	10	12	2		8				15	1	
TOTAL FULL APPEARANCES					28	32	36	5	31	29	4	35	3	20	3	7	4	6	23	26	28	23	10	1	13	9		11		8	1
TOTAL SUB APPEARANCES						(1)		(1)			(4)		(4)	(12)	(2)	(11)	(4)	(10)			(5)	(7)	(3)		(3)	(8)	(1)	(1)	(7)		(1)
TOTAL GOALS SCORED						2	6		4	2		1	2	5				1			6	1			2	5		2			

Small bold figures denote goalscorers. † denotes opponent's own goal.

HAMPDEN PARK

CAPACITY: 9,222 (All Seated)
PLEASE NOTE: Only North Stand and North Stand Gantry will be used.

PITCH DIMENSIONS: 115 yds x 75 yds

FACILITIES FOR DISABLED SUPPORTERS: Disabled facilities (including toilet) will be available at North Stand trackside.

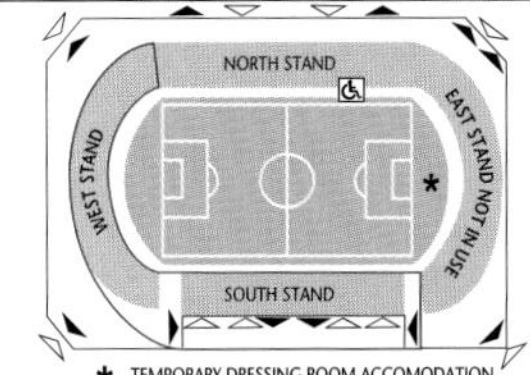

HOW TO GET THERE

The following routes may be used to reach Hampden Park:

TRAINS: There are two stations within five minutes walk of the ground. Mount Florida Station, on the Cathcart Circle and King's Park Station. A 15 minute service runs from Glasgow Central.

BUSES: Services to approach Mount Florida end of Stadium: From City Centre: 5, 5A, 5B, M5, M14, 31, 37, 66, 66A, 66B, 66C; From Govan Cross; 34; From Drumchapel: 96, 97, Circular Service: 89, 90; G.C.T. Service: 1; Services to approach King's Park end of Stadium; From City Centre: 12, 12A, 74; Circular Service: 89, 90; G.C.T. Service: 19.

CARS: Car and Coach parking facilities are available in the car park in Letherby Drive, which is capable of holding 200 vehicles. Side streets can also be used.

ROSS COUNTY

Victoria Park, Jubilee Road,
Dingwall, Ross-shire, IV15 9QW

DIRECTORS
Kenneth D. Cameron
Roy J. MacGregor
Ian Dingwall
Donald R. MacLean
Gordon M. R. Macrae
Alistair Mackintosh
Hector MacLennan
Donald MacBean

SECRETARY
Donald MacBean

OFFICE SECRETARIES
Mrs. Cathy Caird
& Mrs. Helen Walker

PLAYER/MANAGER
Neale J. Cooper

ASSISTANT MANAGER
Jim Kelly

RESERVE COACH
Donald Stuart

YOUTH COACH
Tommy Regan

CLUB DOCTOR
Dr. Gordon Bruce

PHYSIOTHERAPISTS
Chick Ogilvie & Dougie Sim

S.F.A. COMMUNITY COACH
Ross Jack

GROUND CONVENOR AND SAFETY OFFICER
Gordon M. R. Macrae

GROUNDSMAN
Dougie MacDonald

KIT MAN
David Hamilton

COMMERCIAL MANAGER
Brian Campbell
Mobile (01589) 644047

TELEPHONES
Ground/Commercial/Ticket Office
(01349) 862253
Fax (01349) 866277

CLUB SHOP
Situated at Ground

OFFICIAL SUPPORTERS CLUB
George Shiels, 4 Tulloch Place,
Dingwall (01349) 865135

TEAM CAPTAIN
Johnston Bellshaw

SHIRT SPONSOR
John MacLean & Sons

LIST OF PLAYERS 1996-97

SURNAME	FIRST NAME	MIDDLE NAME	DATE OF BIRTH	PLACE OF BIRTH	DATE OF SIGNING	HEIGHT FT INS	WEIGHT ST LBS	PREVIOUS CLUB
Adams	Derek		25/06/75	Glasgow	31/07/96	5 10.0	10 12	Burnley
Bellshaw	Johnston	Cunningham	06/12/63	Dingwall	18/11/94	6 1.0	13 4	Inverness Caledonian
Bradshaw	Paul	Allan	25/09/79	Inverness	02/03/96	6 2.0	10 7	Unattached
Broddle	Julian		01/11/64	Sheffield	28/07/96	5 9.0	12 8	East Fife
Connelly	Gordon	Paul	20/09/67	Stirling	12/08/94	5 7.0	11 2	Dunfermline Athletic
Cooper	Neale	James	24/11/63	Darjeeling	02/08/96	6 0.0	12 7	Dunfermline Athletic
Cormack	David		29/11/70	Lanark	02/08/96	6 2.0	13 7	Hamilton Academical
Ferries	Keith		16/08/65	Inverness	08/08/94	5 8.0	10 10	Elgin City
Fotheringham	Kevin	George	13/08/75	Dunfermline	05/09/96	5 10.0	11 4	Rangers
Furphy	William		07/05/66	London	23/09/94	5 11.0	11 7	Elgin City
Golabek	Stuart		05/11/74	Inverness	16/11/95	5 10.0	11 0	Clachnacuddin
Grant	Brian		13/12/68	Inverness	08/08/94	5 10.0	11 0	Brechin City
Herd	William	David	03/09/65	Buckhaven	08/08/94	5 11.0	12 0	Cowdenbeath
Hutchison	Stephen		18/09/70	Glasgow	08/08/94	5 11.5	12 10	Falkirk
Mackay	David		17/09/75	Dingwall	16/09/94	5 11.0	12 1	Ross County B.C.
MacLeod	Andrew	Donald	14/08/69	Glasgow	08/08/94	5 8.0	10 2	Fortuna Sittard
Matheson	David		27/06/78	Elgin	31/07/96	5 8.0	10 12	Aberdeen
Ross	Alexander	Robert	01/08/63	Bellshill	06/09/96	6 0.0	11 8	Brechin City
Ruickbie	Ross	Murray	12/07/78	Aberdeen	10/08/96	6 1.0	12 7	Unattached
Somerville	Christopher	Ian	08/12/67	Larne	08/08/94	5 5.0	10 0	Brora Rangers
Watt	William	George	08/10/76	Inverness	01/08/95	6 0.0	10 7	Unattached
Williamson	Robert		25/04/69	Inverness	08/08/94	5 10.0	11 4	Inverness Clachnacuddin

MILESTONES

YEAR OF FORMATION: 1929
MOST LEAGUE POINTS IN A SEASON: 60 (Third Division – Season 1994/95) (3 Points for a Win)
MOST LEAGUE GOALS SCORED BY A PLAYER IN A SEASON: Colin Milne (Season 1995/96)
NO. OF GOALS SCORED: 15
RECORD ATTENDANCE: 8,000 (-v- Rangers – Scottish Cup, 28.2.66)
RECORD VICTORY: 11-0 (-v- St. Cuthbert Wanderers – Scottish Cup, 1994)
RECORD DEFEAT: 1-10 (-v- Inverness Thistle – Highland League)

COUNTY'S LEAGUE RECORD

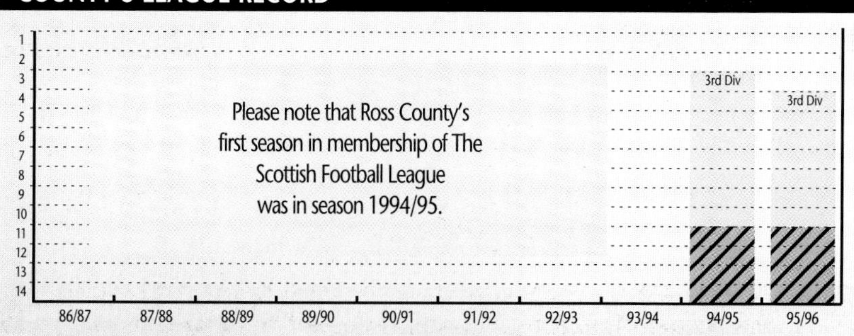

CLUB FACTFILE 1995/96
RESULTS... APPEARANCES... SCORERS

The COUNTY

Date	Venue	Opponents	Att.	Res	Hutchison S.	Herd W.	Mackay D.	Williamson R.	Bellshaw J.	Furphy W.	Ferries K.	Grant B.	Milne C.	Connelly G.	Crainie D.	MacPherson J.	McFee R.	Somerville C.	Watt W.	Robertson C.	MacLeod Andrew	MacMillan D.	Golabek S.	Ruickbie R.	Bradshaw P.	Stewart R.
Aug 12	H	Queen's Park	1,515	2-0	1	2	3	4	5	6	7	8	9^{1}	10	11	15^{1}										
27	A	East Stirlingshire	478	2-1	1	2	3	4	5^{1}	6	7	16	9	10	11	8^{1}	15									
Sep 2	H	Arbroath	1,400	4-2	1	2	3	4	5^{1}	6	7	15	9^{1}	10^{1}	11	8^{1}	14	12								
9	A	Brechin City	479	1-2	1	2	3	4	5	6	7	15	9	10	11	8^{1}	12		14							
16	H	Albion Rovers	1,419	5-1	1	2	3	4	5	6	7	15^{2}	9^{2}	10	11	8^{1}				12	14					
23	H	Cowdenbeath	1,571	2-2	1	2	3	4	5	6	7	15	9^{1}	10		8^{1}	14			11						
30	A	Caledonian Thistle	3,627	1-1	1	2	3	4	5	6	7	15	9	10		8^{1}				11	12					
Oct 7	H	Livingston	2,120	1-1	1	2	3	4	5	6	7	8	9^{1}	10			14			11	15					
14	A	Alloa	501	0-1	1	2	3	4	5	6	7	15	9	10		8				11	12					
21	A	Arbroath	603	2-1	1	2	3	4^{1}	5	6	7	15	9	10^{1}		8	14			11						
28	H	East Stirlingshire	1,646	1-1		2	3	4	5	6^{1}	7	15	9	10		8	14			11		1				
Nov 4	A	Albion Rovers	399	4-3		2	3	4	5	6	7^{1}	8^{1}	9^{2}	10						11	14	1				
11	H	Brechin City	1,653	0-0	1	4	3		5	6	7	8	9	10		15		2		11	14					
18	H	Caledonian Thistle	4,288	2-0		4	3		5	6	7	15	9	10		8^{2}		2		12	14	1	11			
25	A	Cowdenbeath	318	0-2		4	3	12	5	6	7	15	9	10		8		2		14		1	11			
Dec 2	A	Livingston	3,444	0-0	1	7	3	4	5	6	14	8	15	10		9		2			12		11			
16	H	Alloa	1,303	2-2	1	4	3	15	5	6	7	14	9	10		8		2^{1}		12			11^{1}			
30	A	Queen's Park	699	1-1	1	4	3		5	6	7	14	9	10		8^{1}		2		12			11			
Jan 10	H	Arbroath	944	0-0	1	2	3	15	5	6	7	8	14	10		9				4	12		11			
13	H	Cowdenbeath	1,369	4-1	1	4	3		5	6	14	8^{2}	9^{1}	12^{1}				2		7	10		11			
23	A	Caledonian Thistle	4,931	1-1	1	4	3		5	6	14	8	9^{1}	10		15		2			7		11			
Feb 3	A	Alloa	373	4-0	1	7	3	4^{1}	5	6	14		9^{2}	10		8^{1}		2					11	12		
13	H	Livingston	2,300	2-2	1	4	3		5	6	14		9	10		8^{1}		2			7^{1}		11			
17	A	Brechin City	506	0-0	1	4	3		5		7	15	9	10		8		2			6		11			
24	A	East Stirlingshire	353	4-2	1	4	3		5		7^{1}	15	9^{1}	10		8	14	2^{1}	12		6^{1}		11			
Mar 2	A	Queen's Park	238	0-0	1	4	3		5		7	8	9	10				2		15	6		11		12	
6	H	Albion Rovers	1,031	1-1	1	4	3		5	14	7	8	9^{1}	10			15	2		11	6					
9	A	Cowdenbeath	290	1-1	1	4	3		5	6	7	15	9				14	2			8		11^{1}		10	
16	H	Caledonian Thistle	3,670	2-1	1	4	3		5	6	7	15^{1}	9				14	2			8^{1}		11		10	
23	A	Albion Rovers	364	3-0	1	4	3		5	6	7	8^{3}	9	14				2			10		11		12	
30	H	Brechin City	2,362	1-2	1	4	3		5	6	7	8	9	14			15	2			10		11		12^{1}	
Apr 6	A	Livingston	2,333	1-2	1	4	3		5	6	7	8	9^{1}	14			15	2			10		11		12	
13	H	Alloa	1,068	0-0	1	8	3	4	5		7	15		10				2	6		14		11	12	9	
20	A	Arbroath	439	1-1	1	10	3	4		14	7	8^{1}				15		2	6		9		11	5		12
27	H	East Stirlingshire	914	1-3	1	6	3	4	5	14	7	8^{1}	15					2			10		11	12	9	
May 4	H	Queen's Park	916	0-1	1	6	3	4	5		7	8	9			16		2	15		10		11	12		
TOTAL FULL APPEARANCES					32	36	36	18	35	28	31	16	31	27	5	19		23	2	11	15	4	22	1	4	
TOTAL SUB APPEARANCES								(3)		(3)	(5)	(18)	(3)	(4)		(5)	(13)	(1)	(3)	(6)	(10)			(4)	(4)	(1)
TOTAL GOALS SCORED								2	2	1	2	11	15	3		12		2			3		2		1	

Small bold figures denote goalscorers. † denotes opponent's own goal.

VICTORIA PARK

CAPACITY: 5,400, Seated 1,520, Standing 3,880

PITCH DIMENSIONS: 110 yds x 75 yds

FACILITIES FOR DISABLED SUPPORTERS: Areas in Main Stand and Terracing. Toilet facilities are also available.

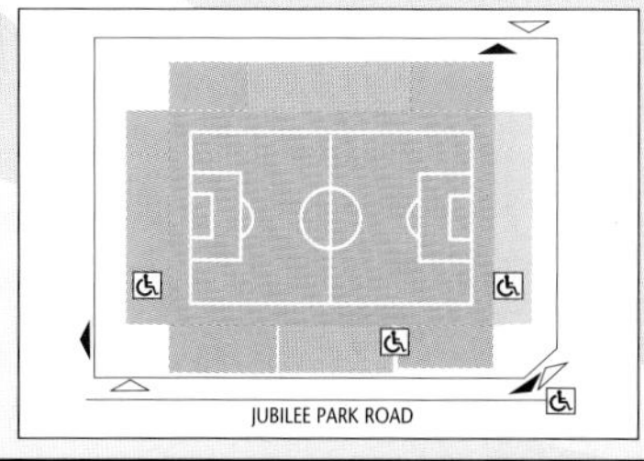

HOW TO GET THERE

The following routes may be used to reach Victoria Park:

TRAINS: The nearest mainline station is Inverness and fans travelling from the south should alight and board a train that takes them direct to Dingwall Station.

BUSES: Regular buses on a daily basis from Glasgow, Edinburgh and Perth.

CARS: The major trunk roads, A9 and A96, connect Dingwall with the North, the South and the East.

S·F·L

PREMIER DIVISION CHAMPIONSHIP

	P	W	L	D	F	A	Pts
Rangers	36	27	3	6	85	25	87
Celtic	36	24	1	11	74	25	83
Aberdeen	36	16	13	7	52	45	55
Heart of Midlothian	36	16	13	7	55	53	55
Hibernian	36	11	15	10	43	57	43
Raith Rovers	36	12	17	7	41	57	43
Kilmarnock	36	11	17	8	39	54	41
Motherwell	36	9	15	12	28	39	39
** Partick Thistle	36	8	22	6	29	62	30
Falkirk	36	6	24	6	31	60	24

FIRST DIVISION CHAMPIONSHIP

	P	W	L	D	F	A	Pts
Dunfermline Athletic	36	21	7	8	73	41	71
** Dundee United	36	19	7	10	73	37	67
Greenock Morton	36	20	9	7	57	39	67
St. Johnstone	36	19	9	8	60	36	65
Dundee	36	15	9	12	53	40	57
St. Mirren	36	13	15	8	46	51	47
Clydebank	36	10	16	10	39	58	40
Airdrieonians	36	9	16	11	43	54	38
Hamilton Academical	36	10	20	6	40	57	36
Dumbarton	36	3	31	2	23	94	11

** In the Premier Division/First Division Play-Off matches, Dundee United F.C. defeated Partick Thistle F.C. by 3 goals to 2 on aggregate. Therefore, Dundee United F.C. have been promoted to the Premier Division and Partick Thistle F.C. have been relegated to the First Division.

SECOND DIVISION CHAMPIONSHIP

	P	W	L	D	F	A	Pts
Stirling Albion	36	24	3	9	83	30	81
East Fife	36	19	7	10	50	29	67
Berwick Rangers	36	18	12	6	64	47	60
Stenhousemuir	36	14	15	7	51	49	49
Clyde	36	11	13	12	47	45	45
Ayr United	36	11	13	12	40	40	45
Queen of the South	36	11	15	10	54	67	43
Stranraer	36	8	10	18	38	43	42
Forfar Athletic	36	11	18	7	37	61	40
Montrose	36	5	26	5	33	86	20

THIRD DIVISION CHAMPIONSHIP

	P	W	L	D	F	A	Pts
Livingston	36	21	6	9	51	24	72
Brechin City	36	18	9	9	41	21	63
Caledonian Thistle	36	15	9	12	64	38	57
Ross County	36	12	7	17	56	39	53
Arbroath	36	13	10	13	41	41	52
Queen's Park	36	12	12	12	40	43	48
East Stirlingshire	36	11	14	11	58	62	44
Cowdenbeath	36	10	18	8	45	59	38
Alloa	36	6	19	11	26	58	29
Albion Rovers	36	7	21	8	37	74	29

PREMIER RESERVE LEAGUE

	P	W	L	D	F	A	Pts
Rangers	36	17	8	11	76	55	62
Heart of Midlothian	36	17	11	8	58	45	59
Aberdeen	36	16	12	8	73	54	56
Falkirk	36	13	9	14	48	44	53
Kilmarnock	36	14	14	8	52	50	50
Partick Thistle	36	10	11	15	48	49	45
Celtic	36	11	14	11	51	45	44
Motherwell	36	10	12	14	24	31	44
Hibernian	36	9	16	11	36	55	38
Raith Rovers	36	11	21	4	32	70	37

RESERVE LEAGUE EAST

	P	W	L	D	F	A	Pts
St. Johnstone	28	24	2	2	102	18	74
Dunfermline Athletic	28	20	4	4	73	28	64
Dundee United	28	20	5	3	85	25	63
Dundee	28	14	6	8	51	34	50
Livingston	28	14	10	4	48	53	46
Hibernian	28	12	9	7	31	34	43
Arbroath	28	12	13	3	49	45	39
Raith Rovers	28	12	14	2	42	49	38
Montrose	28	10	12	6	67	57	36
East Fife	28	11	14	3	43	62	36
Alloa	28	10	13	5	50	55	35
Forfar Athletic	28	7	16	5	31	55	26
Brechin City	28	6	16	6	33	57	24
Berwick Rangers	28	4	22	2	31	102	14
Cowdenbeath	28	2	22	4	25	87	10

RESERVE LEAGUE WEST

	P	W	L	D	F	A	Pts
St. Mirren	22	16	3	3	66	23	51
Airdrieonians	22	14	4	4	39	21	46
Clyde	22	13	4	5	53	31	44
Greenock Morton	22	13	5	4	38	23	43
Clydebank	22	10	9	3	43	37	33
Stirling Albion	22	9	10	3	35	43	30
Stranraer	22	8	12	2	42	61	26
Hamilton Academical	22	7	11	4	38	41	25
Queen of the South	22	7	12	3	32	45	24
Queen's Park	22	6	13	3	37	54	21
Stenhousemuir	22	6	15	1	31	57	19
Dumbarton	22	4	15	3	39	57	15

YOUTH DIVISION

	P	W	L	D	F	A	Pts
Rangers	28	23	1	4	120	16	73
Celtic	28	23	3	2	87	26	71
Dundee United	28	16	3	9	90	19	57
Heart of Midlothian	28	17	8	3	83	26	54
Aberdeen	28	16	9	3	87	38	51
Kilmarnock	28	15	8	5	67	49	50
St. Johnstone	28	14	8	6	63	49	48
Dundee	28	9	10	9	44	47	36
Falkirk	28	10	15	3	48	60	33
Greenock Morton	28	8	19	1	58	90	25
Cowdenbeath	28	7	18	3	34	66	24
Ayr United	28	6	17	5	28	71	23
Queen of the South	28	4	16	8	27	88	20
Livingston	28	3	18	7	34	99	16
Alloa	28	3	21	4	25	151	13

Bell's League Championship Play-off Matches

FIRST LEG

Sunday, 12th May, 1996

PARTICK THISTLE 1 — A. Lyons
DUNDEE UNITED 1 — C. Dailly

Partick Thistle: J.N. Walker, C. Milne, G. Watson, D. McWilliams, (T. Smith), J. Slavin, S. Welsh, R. McDonald, W. Macdonald, (T. Turner), J. McCue, I. Cameron, A. Lyons
Substitute not used: N. Henderson

Dundee United: A. Maxwell, C. Dailly, R. Shannon, S. Pressley, B. Welsh, R. McKinnon, (G. McSwegan), R. Winters, D. Bowman, A. McLaren, (O. Coyle), C. Brewster, J. McQuilken
Substitute not used: K. O'Hanlon (Goalkeeper)

Attendance: 10,414

SECOND LEG

Thursday, 16th May, 1996

DUNDEE UNITED 2 (AET– 1-1 After 90 Minutes) — B. Welsh, O. Coyle
PARTICK THISTLE 1 — I. Cameron

Dundee United: A. Maxwell, R. Shannon, J. McQuilken, S. Pressley, B. Welsh, C. Dailly, R. Winters, (I.G.Johnson), D. Bowman, G. McSwegan, (O. Coyle), C. Brewster, (R. McKinnon), A. McLaren

Partick Thistle: J.N. Walker, C. Milne, G. Watson, T. Smith, J. Slavin, S. Welsh, W. Macdonald, D. McWilliams, (A. Dinnie), J. McCue, (N. Henderson), I. Cameron, A. Lyons
Substitute not used: M. Cairns (Goalkeeper)

Attendance: 12,120

Dundee United won 3-2 on aggregate and were promoted to the Premier Division for Season 1996/97 and Partick Thistle were relegated to the First Division

Bell's Award Winners 1995/96

MONTHLY AWARD WINNERS

AUGUST, 1995

Manager	**Craig Brown** *(Scotland)*
Player	**Ally McCoist** *(Rangers)*
Young Player	**Charlie Miller** *(Rangers)/* **Neil McCann** *(Dundee)*
Premier Division	**Roy Aitken** *(Aberdeen)*
First Division	**Jim Duffy** *(Dundee)*
Second Division	**Steve Archibald** *(East Fife)*
Third Division	**Jim Leishman** *(Livingston)*

SEPTEMBER, 1995

Manager	**Jimmy Nicholl** *(Raith Rovers)*
Player	**Scott Booth** *(Aberdeen)*
Young Player	**Stephen Glass** *(Aberdeen)*
First Division	**Allan McGraw** *(Greenock Morton)*
Second Division	**Tom Hendrie** *(Berwick Rangers)*
Third Division	**Jim Leishman** *(Livingston)*

OCTOBER, 1995

Manager	**Jim Duffy** *(Dundee)*
Player	**Darren Jackson** *(Hibernian)*
Young Player	**Neil McCann** *(Dundee)*
Premier Division	**Alex Miller** *(Hibernian)*
Second Division	**Terry Christie** *(Stenhousemuir)*
Third Division	**Steve Paterson** *(Caledonian Thistle)*

NOVEMBER, 1995

Manager	**Craig Brown** *(Scotland)*
Player	**Andy Goram** *(Rangers)*
Young Player	**Stephen Glass** *(Aberdeen)*
Premier Division	**Jimmy Nicholl** *(Raith Rovers)*
First Division	**Jim Duffy** *(Dundee)*
Second Division	**Kevin Drinkell** *(Stirling Albion)*
Third Division	**Tom Steven** *(Cowdenbeath)*

DECEMBER, 1995

Manager	**Walter Smith** *(Rangers)*
Player	**Gordon Durie** *(Rangers)*
Young Player	**Jackie McNamara** *(Celtic)*
First Division	**Bert Paton** *(Dunfermline Athletic)*
Second Division	**Kevin Drinkell** *(Stirling Albion)*
Third Division	**Hugh McCann** *(Queen's Park)*

JANUARY, 1996

Manager	**Alex Totten** *(Kilmarnock)*
Player	**Pierre Van Hooijdonk** *(Celtic)*
Young Player	**Gary Locke** *(Heart of Midlothian)*
First Division	**Billy Kirkwood** *(Dundee United)*
Second Division	**Kevin Drinkell** *(Stirling Albion)*
Third Division	**Steve Paterson** *(Caledonian Thistle)*

FEBRUARY, 1996

Manager	**Jim Jefferies** *(Heart of Midlothian)*
Player	**Paul Gascoigne** *(Rangers)*
Young Player	**Paul Ritchie** *(Heart of Midlothian)*
First Division	**Paul Sturrock** *(St. Johnstone)*
Second Division	**Kevin Drinkell** *(Stirling Albion)*
Third Division	**Steve Paterson** *(Caledonian Thistle)*

MARCH, 1996

Manager	**Alex McLeish** *(Motherwell)*
Player	**Ally McCoist** *(Rangers)*
Young Player	**Derek Stillie** *(Aberdeen)*
First Division	**Billy Kirkwood** *(Dundee United)*
Second Division	**Steve Archibald** *(East Fife)*
Third Division	**John Young** *(Brechin City)*

APRIL, 1996

Manager	**Jim Jefferies** *(Heart of Midlothian)*
Player	**Paul Gascoigne** *(Rangers)*
Young Player	**Gary Locke** *(Heart of Midlothian)*
First Division	**Allan McGraw** *(Greenock Morton)*
Second Division	**Kevin Drinkell** *(Stirling Albion)*
Third Division	**Vinnie Moore** *(Albion Rovers)*

SEASON AWARD WINNERS

Manager of the Year	**Walter Smith** *(Rangers)*
Player of the Year	**Paul Gascoigne** *(Rangers)*
Young Player of the Year	**Jackie McNamara** *(Celtic)*
First Division Manager of the Year	**Allan McGraw** *(Greenock Morton)*
Second Division Manager of the Year	**Kevin Drinkell** *(Stirling Albion)*
Third Division Manager of the Year	**Jim Leishman** *(Livingston)*

Walter Smith (Rangers) Bell's Manager of the Year

Scottish League Champions since inception

SEASON	DIVISION ONE	POINTS	DIVISION TWO	POINTS
1890/91	Dumbarton/Rangers	29	(No Competition)	
1891/92	Dumbarton	37	(No Competition)	
1892/93	Celtic	29	(No Competition)	
1893/94	Celtic	29	Hibernian	29
1894/95	Heart of Midlothian	31	Hibernian	30
1895/96	Celtic	30	Abercorn	27
1896/97	Heart of Midlothian	28	Partick Thistle	31
1897/98	Celtic	33	Kilmarnock	29
1898/99	Rangers	36	Kilmarnock	32
1899-1900	Rangers	32	Partick Thistle	29
1900/01	Rangers	35	St. Bernards	25
1901/02	Rangers	28	Port Glasgow	32
1902/03	Hibernian	37	Airdrieonians	35
1903/04	Third Lanark	43	Hamilton Academical	37
1904/05	Celtic (after play-off)	41	Clyde	32
1905/06	Celtic	49	Leith Athletic	34
1906/07	Celtic	55	St. Bernards	32
1907/08	Celtic	55	Raith Rovers	30
1908/09	Celtic	51	Abercorn	31
1909/10	Celtic	54	Leith Athletic	33
1910/11	Rangers	52	Dumbarton	31
1911/12	Rangers	51	Ayr United	35
1912/13	Rangers	53	Ayr United	34
1913/14	Celtic	65	Cowdenbeath	31
1914/15	Celtic	65	Cowdenbeath	37
1915/16	Celtic	67	(No Competition)	
1916/17	Celtic	64	(No Competition)	
1917/18	Rangers	56	(No Competition)	
1918/19	Celtic	58	(No Competition)	
1919/20	Rangers	71	(No Competition)	
1920/21	Rangers	76	(No Competition)	
1921/22	Celtic	67	Alloa	60
1922/23	Rangers	55	Queen's Park	57
1923/24	Rangers	59	St. Johnstone	56
1924/25	Rangers	60	Dundee United	50
1925/26	Celtic	58	Dunfermline Athletic	59
1926/27	Rangers	56	Bo'ness	56
1927/28	Rangers	60	Ayr United	54
1928/29	Rangers	67	Dundee United	51
1929/30	Rangers	60	Leith Athletic*	57
1930/31	Rangers	60	Third Lanark	61
1931/32	Motherwell	66	East Stirlingshire*	55
1932/33	Rangers	62	Hibernian	54
1933/34	Rangers	66	Albion Rovers	45
1934/35	Rangers	55	Third Lanark	52
1935/36	Celtic	66	Falkirk	59
1936/37	Rangers	61	Ayr United	54
1937/38	Celtic	61	Raith Rovers	59
1938/39	Rangers	59	Cowdenbeath	60
1939/40	(No Competition)		(No Competition)	
1940/41	(No Competition)		(No Competition)	
1941/42	(No Competition)		(No Competition)	
1942/43	(No Competition)		(No Competition)	
1943/44	(No Competition)		(No Competition)	
1944/45	(No Competition)		(No Competition)	

# of The Scottish Football League in 1890

SEASON	DIVISION ONE	POINTS	DIVISION TWO	POINTS
1945/46	(No Competition)		(No Competition)	
1946/47	Rangers	46	Dundee	45
1947/48	Hibernian	48	East Fife	53
1948/49	Rangers	46	Raith Rovers*	42
1949/50	Rangers	50	Morton	47
1950/51	Hibernian	48	Queen of the South*	45
1951/52	Hibernian	45	Clyde	44
1952/53	Rangers*	43	Stirling Albion	44
1953/54	Celtic	43	Motherwell	45
1954/55	Aberdeen	49	Airdrieonians	46
1955/56	Rangers	52	Queen's Park	54
1956/57	Rangers	55	Clyde	64
1957/58	Heart of Midlothian	62	Stirling Albion	55
1958/59	Rangers	50	Ayr United	60
1959/60	Heart of Midlothian	54	St. Johnstone	53
1960/61	Rangers	51	Stirling Albion	55
1961/62	Dundee	54	Clyde	54
1962/63	Rangers	57	St. Johnstone	55
1963/64	Rangers	55	Morton	67
1964/65	Kilmarnock*	50	Stirling Albion	59
1965/66	Celtic	57	Ayr United	53
1966/67	Celtic	58	Morton	69
1967/68	Celtic	63	St. Mirren	62
1968/69	Celtic	54	Motherwell	64
1969/70	Celtic	57	Falkirk	56
1970/71	Celtic	56	Partick Thistle	56
1971/72	Celtic	60	Dumbarton¥	52
1972/73	Celtic	57	Clyde	56
1973/74	Celtic	53	Airdrieonians	60
1974/75	Rangers	56	Falkirk	54

SEASON	PREMIER DIVISION	POINTS	FIRST DIVISION	POINTS	SECOND DIVISION	POINTS	THIRD DIVISION	POINTS
1975/76	Rangers	54	Partick Thistle	41	Clydebank¥	40		
1976/77	Celtic	55	St. Mirren	62	Stirling Albion	55		
1977/78	Rangers	55	Morton¥	58	Clyde¥	53		
1978/79	Celtic	48	Dundee	55	Berwick Rangers	54		
1979/80	Aberdeen	48	Heart of Midlothian	53	Falkirk	50		
1980/81	Celtic	56	Hibernian	57	Queen's Park	50		
1981/82	Celtic	55	Motherwell	61	Clyde	59		
1982/83	Dundee United	56	St. Johnstone	55	Brechin City	55		
1983/84	Aberdeen	57	Morton	54	Forfar Athletic	63		
1984/85	Aberdeen	59	Motherwell	50	Montrose	53		
1985/86•	Celtic¥	50	Hamilton Academical	56	Dunfermline Athletic	57		
1986/87•	Rangers	69	Morton	57	Meadowbank Thistle	55		
1987/88•	Celtic	72	Hamilton Academical	56	Ayr United	61		
1988/89§	Rangers	56	Dunfermline Athletic	54	Albion Rovers	50		
1989/90§	Rangers	51	St. Johnstone	58	Brechin City	49		
1990/91§	Rangers	55	Falkirk	54	Stirling Albion	54		
1991/92§	Rangers	72	Dundee	58	Dumbarton	52		
1992/93	Rangers	73	Raith Rovers	65	Clyde	54		
1993/94	Rangers	58	Falkirk	66	Stranraer	56		
1994/95†	Rangers	69	Raith Rovers	69	Greenock Morton	64	Forfar Athletic	80
1995/96†	Rangers	87	Dunfermline Athletic	71	Stirling Albion	81	Livingston	72

* *Champions on goal average.* • *Competition known as Fine Fare League.* † *Competition known as Bell's League Championship.*
¥ *Champions on goal difference.* § *Competition known as B & Q League.*

Aberdeen - Winners of The Coca-Cola Cup 1995

Aberdeen Triumphant

Right from day one on 5th August, 1995, when the First Round ties were played, the tone of the 1995-96 Coca-Cola Cup Competition was set. There was a penalty shoot-out between Berwick Rangers and Caledonian Thistle, which the Wee Rangers won 5-3. From then on, it was penalties-a-popping, Motherwell overcoming Clydebank 4-1 in the Second Round, while the lesser fancied Livingston were on the mark to turf out St. Johnstone 4-2.

There were two pot-shot parades in the Quarter Finals where Airdrieonians eased through 3-2 against Partick Thistle and it was even more nerve-wracking for Dundee, who made it to the Semis by virtue of a 5-4 penalty shoot-out success against Heart of Midlothian.

In a competition which would provide three and a half months of exciting and exhilarating action, it took only 24 seconds for the competition to explode into action, when Ralph Brand gave Brechin City the lead over East Fife at Glebe Park. Although his quick fire strike was not enough to ultimately win the match for Brechin, Brand had the consolation of securing £500 for having scored the fastest goal of the First Round. Although he didn't know it at the time, his £500 jackpot was doubled after 25 seconds of goalless action in the Final, when it was confirmed that he would also have the honour of scoring the fastest goal overall in the competition.

After Raith Rovers heroics in winning The Coca-Cola Cup the previous season as a First Division club, it was the turn of both Dundee and Airdrieonians to fly the flag for that division, with both teams claiming the scalps of more fancied Premier Division opposition.

Dundee's Coca-Cola Cup campaign got off to a six-hit start against East Stirlingshire with four of them being scored by Neil McCann (who won himself a £500 incentive hat-trick bonus) and then followed this up with a 3-1 win over Premier Division Kilmarnock.

Their Fourth Round clash with Hearts at Dens Park was sensational to say the least. They were level at 3-3 after 90 minutes and with both clubs each scoring in extra-time to take the tie to penalties, Dundee kept their nerve to win the shoot-out 5-4. Incidentally, Hearts' goalkeeper, Henry Smith, took one of his team's spot kicks - and missed!

With Airdrieonians also accounting for two Premier Division clubs, defeating Hibernian 2-0 in the Third Round and following it up with a penalty shoot-out victory over Partick Thistle, the Semi-Final draw paired the First Division clubs together. The Dens men made it to the Final thanks to a brilliant last minute winner from Neil McCann, scoring with a superb chip over John Martin from a tight angle after the Diamonds' Peter Duffield had earlier cancelled out a Paul Tosh strike in a pulsating tie at McDiarmid Park. It was the kind of goal that was produced so often in a Coca-Cola Cup Competition which fizzed with style and skill.

After defeating St. Mirren 3-1 in their opening Coca-Cola Cup tie at Pittodrie, eventual trophy winners, Aberdeen, thumped Falkirk 4-1 at Brockville and then managed to avoid the penalty plague afflicting other cup ties.

However, they did need extra-time to beat Motherwell in a tough Quarter Final match at Fir Park, where big John Inglis eventually eased the Dons through with a header from a Joe Miller cross in the 115th minute.

The Semi-Final meeting of Rangers and Aberdeen was the seventh time that both clubs had met each other in this competition during the past nine seasons. Although Rangers were the bookmakers' favourites to win the trophy, Aberdeen had other ideas and achieved their success in some style as a perky Pittodrie side caught the Ibrox club cold with a pacy performance at Hampden, with Eoin Jess in particular running the show. £850,000 striker Billy Dodds, who was to finish up joint top Coca-Cola Cup scorer for the season alongside Dundee's Neil McCann, with each claiming £1,000 for this honour, netted twice in the second half to take the Dons through despite a late strike from Russian Oleg Salenko for Rangers.

The Semi exit was a surprise to Rangers, who were nursing ambitions of bringing off the treble. Having comfortably disposed of Greenock Morton 3-0 at Ibrox, they followed this up by building a similar three goal lead against Stirling Albion before slacking off and nearly being embarrassed by two late Albion goals. Then when the Light Blues went to Parkhead for the Quarter Final which they eventually won in a blistering live televised game, thanks to a flying header from Ally McCoist, everyone believed their name was on the trophy. Except Dons that is!

Duncan Shearer (Aberdeen)

That Aberdeen deserved their name on the trophy cannot be understated. The team that only the season before had to face a Play-Off survival game to stay in the Premier Division, powered through The Coca-Cola Cup Competition in impressive form. Any team that wallop four past Falkirk at Brockville, beat Motherwell at Fir Park and knock over Rangers at Hampden in the Semi-Final can be acclaimed true Cup battlers. Dons rounded it all off with their 2-0 Final win over Dundee at the National Stadium on Sunday, 26th November. It was a victory which took them back into Europe in the UEFA Cup and confirmed that big Roy Aitken had indeed succeeded in turning the club round in six short months as manager.

It was Aberdeen's first trophy since 1990 and the Pittodrie fans and players savoured the sweet moment of success. First Division Dundee's hopes of following in Raith Rovers' bootsteps by winning the trophy against Premier opposition foundered against the pace and power of an Aberdeen side which had Under-21 cap Stephen Glass in superb form on the left.

It was a surging run and shot by Glass which set up the killer opening goal in the 33rd minute. French goalkeeper, Michel Pageaud, could only parry the ball, and there was one of the game's most menacing predators, Billy Dodds, waiting to net against his old club.

It was all over just after the interval when "Man of the Match" Glass - he received a mountain bike as a prize for that nomination - broke down the left and fired in a cross which big Duncan Shearer met at the near post to bullet a magnificent header into the net.

It was a trophy well won. Dons scored 13 goals and conceded only four in their five ties. 20,000 Aberdeen fans celebrated as skipper, Stewart McKimmie, received the trophy and the celebrations lasted all the way back up the road to the Granite City.

In a competition that constantly produced excitement, entertainment and drama, a total of 333,442 fans attended the 39 Coca-Cola Cup ties witnessing an extremely healthy average 3.2 goals per game. Here's hoping that this season's tournament provides more of the same!

DIXON BLACKSTOCK
(Scottish Sunday Express)

Stephen Glass (Aberdeen)

Billy Dodds (Aberdeen)

FIRST ROUND

Saturday, 5th August, 1995

ROSS COUNTY 0 — ARBROATH 2
J. Lindsay, S. McCormick

Ross County: S. Hutchison, C. Somerville, (K. Ferries), G. Campbell, R. Williamson, J. Bellshaw, W. Furphy, D. Mackay, J. MacPherson, C. Milne, (B. Grant), G. Connelly, W. Herd
Substitute not used: W. Watt

Arbroath: C. Hinchcliffe, T. McMillan, S. Florence, S. Peters, J. Fowler, P. Clark, J. Lindsay, I. Porteous, S. McCormick, A. Kennedy, (D. Pew), J. McAulay
Substitutes not used: B. Scott, G. Dunn (Goalkeeper)
Attendance: 1,128

BRECHIN CITY 2 — EAST FIFE 3
(A.E.T. - 2-2 After 90 Minutes)
R. Brand (2) — R. Scott (2), S. Hutcheon
Brechin City: R. Allan, B. Mitchell, R. Brown, H. Cairney, F. Conway, W.D. Scott, W. McNeill, (R. Vannett), C. Farnan, G. Price, R. Brand, S. Marr, (R. Smith)
Substitute not used: R. Smollet

East Fife: D. Robertson, J. McStay, A. Hamill, J. Cusick, D. Beaton, A. Sneddon, (G. Allan), R. Hildersley, K. Balmain, (M. Donaghy), R. Scott, B. Andrew, (S. Hutcheon), D. Hope
Attendance: 476

QUEEN OF THE SOUTH 3 — QUEEN'S PARK 1
D. Campbell, C. Harris, S. Mallan — B. McPhee
Queen of the South: J. Butter, D. McKeown, J. Brown, B. McKeown, D. Kennedy, S. Ramsay, D. Campbell, (A. McFarlane), S. Wilson, C. Harris, T. Bryce, (S. Cody), S. Mallan
Substitute not used: K. Hetherington

Queen's Park: G. Bruce, G. Kerr, D. Graham, D. McGrath, R. Caven, I. Maxwell, R. Fraser, D. Arbuckle, (S. Edgar), D. Brodie, B. McPhee, A. McInally, (K. McGoldrick)
Substitute not used: C. Bruce (Goalkeeper)
Attendance: 1,202

CLYDE 1 — EAST STIRLINGSHIRE 2
E. Annand — M. Abercromby (2)

Clyde: J. Hillcoat, J. Prunty, (I. McConnell), G. Ferguson, (P. Patterson), G. Watson, K. Knox, J. Brown, M. O'Neill, I. Nisbet, E. Annand, T. Harrison, J. Dickson
Substitute not used: J. McQueen (Goalkeeper)

East Stirlingshire: G. McDougall, J. Orr, A. Neill, D. Stirling, B. Ross, R. Lee, G. Millar, M. Hunter, M. Geraghty, (T. McKenna), M. Abercromby, (C. Scott), S. MacLean, (L. Cuthbert)
Attendance: 834

BERWICK RANGERS 1 — CALEDONIAN THISTLE 1
(A.E.T. - 1-1 After 90 Minutes)
N. Clegg — C. Valentine (o.g.)
Berwick Rangers won 5-3 on Kicks from the Penalty Mark
Berwick Rangers: N. Young, C. Valentine, A. Banks, A. Reid, M. Cowan, G. Fraser, T. Graham, M. Wilson, P. Forrester, P. Rutherford, (K. Walton), K. Kane, (N. Clegg)
Substitute not used: M. Osborne (Goalkeeper)

Caledonian Thistle: M. McRitchie, D. McGinlay, M. McAllister, M. Noble, R. Benson, D. Ross, C. Mitchell, (R. Hastings), M. Lisle, (G. Bennett), I. Stewart, C. Christie, D. Green
Substitute not used: D. Brennan
Attendance: 482

ALBION ROVERS 0 — COWDENBEATH 1
D. Scott
Albion Rovers: D. Moonie, D. McDonald, (G. Young), J. Gallagher, B. Strain, M. Ryan, C. Shanks, M. Duncan, L. Collins, M. Scott, P. Crawford, D. Seggie, (J. McBride)
Substitute not used: J. Wight (Goalkeeper)

Cowdenbeath: N. Russell, S. Steven, G. Meldrum, G. Wood, B. Malloy, B. McMahon, E. Petrie, K. Bowmaker, (C. Smith), D. Scott, C. Winter, A. De Melo, (S. Wardell)
Substitute not used: S. Chappell (Goalkeeper)
Attendance: 430

MONTROSE 0 — LIVINGSTON 2
G. McMartin, J. Young
Montrose: D. Larter, I. Robertson, C. Mailer, K. Tindal, (M. Garden), D. Grant, J. Tosh, I. MacDonald, L. Stephen, (P. Masson), C. McGlashan, S. Taylor, (S. Smith), C. MacRonald

Livingston: H. Stoute, C. Smart, C. McCartney, G. Davidson, S. Williamson, D. Alleyne, G. McMartin, L. Bailey, (G. Harvey), J. Young, G. McLeod, M. Duthie, (C. Sinclair)
Substitute not used: S. Sorbie
Attendance: 636

ALLOA 2 — FORFAR ATHLETIC 1
S. Rixon, B. Moffat — J. Loney
Alloa: P. Graham, W. Newbigging, N. Bennett, J. McCormack, D. Lawrie, D. Kirkham, S. Cadden, D. Diver, S. Rixon, B. Moffat, (M. Whyte), S. Morrison
Substitutes not used: D. Cully, C. McKenzie (Goalkeeper)

Forfar Athletic: G. Arthur, M. Bowes, I. McPhee, R. Mann, A. McKillop, D. Craig, A. Morgan, D. McVicar, A. Ross, (J. Loney), P. Hannigan, (H. O'Neill), D. Bingham
Substitute not used: J. Donegan (Goalkeeper)
Attendance: 512

SECOND ROUND

Saturday, 19th August, 1995

ABERDEEN 3 — ST. MIRREN 1
S. Booth (2), W. Dodds — B. McLaughlin
Aberdeen: T. Snelders, S. McKimmie, C. Ireland, R. McKinnon, (E. Verveer), J. Inglis, P. Hetherston, J. Miller, E. Jess, S. Booth, W. Dodds, S. Glass
Substitutes not used: S. Thomson, M. Watt (Goalkeeper)

St. Mirren: C. Money, R. Dawson, M. Baker, S. Taylor, B. McLaughlin, S. Watson, R. Law, J. Fullarton, R. Gillies, (B. Lavety), A. Bone, J. Boyd, (J. Dick)
Substitute not used: A. Combe (Goalkeeper)
Attendance: 10,397

CLYDEBANK 1 — MOTHERWELL 1
(A.E.T. - 1-1 After 90 Minutes)
J. Robertson — D. Arnott
Motherwell won 4-1 on Kicks from the Penalty Mark
Clydebank: G. Matthews, C. Tomlinson, C. Sutherland, (D. Crawford), S. Murdoch, T. Currie, D. Nicholls, J. Robertson, G. Connell, K. Eadie, S. Kerrigan, (G. Teale), G. Bowman
Substitute not used: A. Monaghan (Goalkeeper)

Motherwell: S. Howie, E. May, (J. Philliben), R. McKinnon, M. Van Der Gaag, (S. Woods), B. Martin, S. McSkimming, P. Lambert, J. Dolan, (A. Roddie), T. Coyne, D. Arnott, W. Davies
Attendance: 2,192

DUNFERMLINE ATHLETIC 3 — STRANRAER 0
N. McCathie, A. Moore, S. Petrie
Dunfermline Athletic: G. Van De Kamp, I. Den Bieman, M. Millar, N. McCathie, A. Tod, P. Smith, A. Moore, J. McNamara, (M. McCulloch), G. Shaw, S. Petrie, P. Kinnaird, (D. Fleming)
Substitute not used: I. Westwater (Goalkeeper)

Stranraer: S. Ross, P. McLean, J. Hughes, (N. McGowan), J. Robertson, N. Howard, J. McCaffrey, T. Sloan, T. Callaghan, T. Walker, G. Duncan, (A. Grant), D. Henderson, (D. McGuire)
Attendance: 3,089

COWDENBEATH 0 — DUNDEE UNITED 4
W. McKinlay, P. Connolly (2), N. Caldwell
Cowdenbeath: N. Russell, D. Maratea, (S. Wardell), G. Meldrum, G. Wood, B. Malloy, B. McMahon, S. Steven, C. Winter, D. Scott, (G. Buckley), M. Yardley, C. Smith, (A. De Melo)

Dundee United: A. Maxwell, M. Perry, R. Shannon, S. Pressley, B. Welsh, D. Bowman, A. McLaren, W. McKinlay, R. Winters, P. Connolly, N. Caldwell
Substitutes not used: C. Brewster, A. Robertson, K. O'Hanlon (Goalkeeper)
Attendance: 2,077

S·F·L ©

RAITH ROVERS 2 — **ARBROATH 1**
D. Kirkwood (2) — S. McCormick

Raith Rovers: S.Y. Thomson, D. Kirkwood, J. Broddle, J. McInally, (D. Lennon), S. Dennis, D. Sinclair, A. Rougier, C. Cameron, S. Crawford, A. Taylor, J. Dair, (A. Graham)
Substitute not used: L. Fridge (Goalkeeper)

Arbroath: C. Hinchcliffe, T. McMillan, J. Crawford, S. Peters, J. Fowler, P. Clark, D. Pew, (J. McAulay), I. Porteous, S. McCormick, A. Kennedy, (C. McLean), J. Lindsay
Substitute not used: G. Dunn (Goalkeeper)
Attendance: 3,012

QUEEN OF THE SOUTH 0 — **FALKIRK 2**
M. Johnston, N. Henderson

Queen of the South: J. Butter, K. Hetherington, J. Brown, B. McKeown, D. Kennedy, S. Ramsay, (T. Bryce), S. Wilson, S. Mallan, C. Harris, (G. Friels), A. McFarlane, D. Campbell, (S. Cody)

Falkirk: A. Parks, J. Clark, (F. Johnston), C. Napier, N. Oliver, J. McLaughlin, B. Rice, J. McGowan, S. Kirk, M. McGraw, (N. Henderson), M. Johnston, D. Elliot
Substitute not used: N. Inglis (Goalkeeper)
Attendance: 2,507

KILMARNOCK 1 — **DUMBARTON 0 (A.E.T.)**
M. Roberts

Kilmarnock: D. Lekovic, A. MacPherson, (W. Findlay), T. Black, R. Montgomerie, N. Whitworth, M. Skilling, A. Mitchell, J. Henry, (M. Roberts), P. Wright, R. Connor, T. Brown, (M. Reilly)

Dumbarton: I. MacFarlane, H. Burns, R. Fabiani, J. Marsland, P. Martin, T. King, M. Mooney, J. Meechan, S. McGivern, (C. Gibson), M. McGarvey, (A. Granger), J. Charnley
Substitute not used: P. Dennison (Goalkeeper)
Attendance: 5,011

AYR UNITED 0 — **CELTIC 3**
P. Van Hooijdonk, A. Thom, J. Collins

Ayr United: W. Lamont, R. Tannock, D. Boyce, D. George, (S. Wilson), F. Rolling, J. Sharples, A. Shepherd, N. McKilligan, (C. MacFarlane), B. Bilsland, S. Stainrod, V. Moore
Substitute not used: K. McKay

Celtic: G. Marshall, T. Boyd, T. McKinlay, R. Vata, J. Hughes, (M. Mackay), P. Grant, P. O'Donnell, S. Donnelly, P. Van Hooijdonk, A. Thom, (B. McLaughlin), J. Collins
Substitute not used: P. Bonner (Goalkeeper)
Attendance: 9,128

ST. JOHNSTONE 1 — **LIVINGSTON 1**
(A.E.T. -1-1 After 90 Minutes)
G. O'Boyle — L. Bailey
Livingston won 4-2 on Kicks from the Penalty Mark

St. Johnstone: A. Main, J. McQuillan, A. Preston, D. Griffin, D. Irons, (P. Cherry), K. McGowne, P. Scott, (J. O'Neil), R. Grant, (S. McLean), K. Twaddle, G. O'Boyle, G. Farquhar

Livingston: H. Stoute, C. Smart, C. McCartney, (C. Sinclair), G. Davidson, S. Williamson, D. Alleyne, G. McMartin, L. Bailey, (G. Harvey), J. Young, G. McLeod, M. Duthie
Substitute not used: S. Sorbie
Attendance: 2,226

EAST STIRLINGSHIRE 0 — **DUNDEE 6**
M. Wieghorst, J. Hamilton, N. McCann (4)

East Stirlingshire: G. McDougall, J. Orr, (T. McKenna), R. Lee, D. Watt, S. Sneddon, A. Neill, M. Hunter, (S. MacLean), C. Scott, M. Geraghty, M. Abercromby, D. Stirling, (P. Dwyer)

Dundee: M. Pageaud, K. Bain, (I. Anderson), A. Cargill, R. Manley, M. Wieghorst, C. Duffy, P. Tosh, D. Vrto, G. Britton, J. Hamilton, (G. Shaw), N. McCann
Substitute not used: P. Mathers (Goalkeeper)
Attendance: 1,140

RANGERS 3 — **GREENOCK MORTON 0**
P. Gascoigne, A. McCoist, M. Hateley

Rangers: A. Goram, S. Wright, (A. Cleland), D. Robertson, R. Gough, C. Moore, I. Ferguson, C. Miller, (I. Durrant), P. Gascoigne, A. McCoist, M. Hateley, A. Mikhailitchenko
Substitute not used: W. Thomson (Goalkeeper)

Greenock Morton: D. Wylie, D. Johnstone, D. Collins, J. Anderson, S. McCahill, J. Lindberg, D. Lilley, A. Mahood, W. Hawke, (D. Laing), D. McInnes, M. Rajamaki, (P. Blair)
Substitute not used: C. McPherson
Attendance: 43,396

BERWICK RANGERS 0 — **PARTICK THISTLE 7**
S. Pittman, D. McWilliams (2), R. McDonald, A. Craig (2), H. Curran

Berwick Rangers: N. Young, C. Valentine, A. Banks, A. Reid, M. Cowan, G. Fraser, (M. Wilson), P. Forrester, (K. Kane), M. Neil, P. Rutherford, W. Irvine, T. Graham, (K. Walton)

Partick Thistle: J.N. Walker, A. Dinnie, S. Pittman, D. McWilliams, P.G. Tierney, S. Welsh, R. McDonald, A. Craig, W. Foster, H. Curran, I. Cameron
Substitutes not used: A. Gibson, G. Watson, T. Smith
Attendance: 1,120

HIBERNIAN 3 — **STENHOUSEMUIR 1**
P. McGinlay, D. Jackson (2 (1 Pen)) — G. Hutchison

Hibernian: J. Leighton, G. Donald, G. Mitchell, P. McGinlay, S. Tweed, C. Jackson, M. Weir, (K. McAllister), A. Millen, K. Harper, (Graeme Miller), D. Jackson, M. O'Neill
Substitute not used: D. Dods

Stenhousemuir: R. McKenzie, E. Bannon, L. Haddow, G. Armstrong, G. McGeachie, M. Christie, (D. Swanson), P. Logan, (J. Clarke), J. Fisher, M. Mathieson, (J. Henderson), G. Hutchison, I. Little
Attendance: 7,053

EAST FIFE 2 — **AIRDRIEONIANS 3**
R. Scott, G. Allan — J. Boyle, S. Cooper, P. Duffield

East Fife: L. Hamilton, J. McStay, A. Hamill, J. Cusick, D. Beaton, M. Donaghy, K. Balmain, (G. Allan), R. Hildersley, (S. Hutcheon), R. Scott, (S. Archibald), B. Andrew, D. Hope

Airdrieonians: J. Martin, J. Boyle, P. Jack, J. Sandison, T. McIntyre, (J. McIntyre), A. Stewart, J. Davies, P. Harvey, (M. Wilson), S. Cooper, P. Duffield, A. Smith
Substitute not used: G. Connelly
Attendance: 1,187

HEART OF MIDLOTHIAN 3 — **ALLOA 0**
D. McPherson, B. Hamilton, S. Leitch

Heart of Midlothian: H. Smith, G. Locke, F. Wishart, C. Levein, D. McPherson, B. Hamilton, J. Colquhoun, G. Mackay, D. Hagen, A. Johnston, S. Leitch, (S. Callaghan)
Substitutes not used: W. Jamieson, C. Nelson (Goalkeeper)

Alloa: P. Graham, W. Newbigging, N. Bennett, J. McCormack, D. Lawrie, T. Little, (C. McKenzie), R. Wylie, (D. Cully), D. Diver, B. Moffat, S. Rixon, (M. Whyte), S. Morrison
Attendance: 7,732

STIRLING ALBION 2 — **HAMILTON ACADEMICAL 0**
T. Tait, J. McLeod

Stirling Albion: M. McGeown, M. McKechnie, P. Watson, (J. Gibson), C. Mitchell, R. McQuilter, T. Tait, I. McInnes, P. Deas, S. McCormick, (A. Farquhar), C. Taggart, J. McLeod
Substitute not used: M. Monaghan (Goalkeeper)

Hamilton Academical: D. Cormack, S. Renicks, S. McInulty, S. Thomson, C. Paterson, M. McIntosh, P. Hartley, G. Clark, (C. Baptie), S. McCormick, (D. McCarrison), J. McQuade, D. Lorimer, (S. McCulloch)
Attendance: 921

THIRD ROUND

Tuesday, 29th August, 1995

DUNDEE UNITED 1 — **MOTHERWELL 2**
R. Winters — P. Lambert, D. Arnott

Dundee United: A. Maxwell, M. Perry, R. Shannon, C. Dailly, S. Pressley, B. Welsh, A. McLaren, W. McKinlay, A. Robertson,(P. Connolly), J. Bett, (S. Crabbe), R. Winters
Substitute not used: K. O'Hanlon (Goalkeeper)

Motherwell: S. Howie, E. May, R. McKinnon, A. Roddie, (W. Davies), B. Martin, J. Philliben, P. Lambert, J. Dolan, A. Burns, D. Arnott, S. McSkimming
Substitutes not used: I. Ritchie, S. Woods (Goalkeeper)
Attendance: 6,839

AIRDRIEONIANS 2 — **HIBERNIAN 0**
S. Tweed (o.g.), J. Boyle

Airdrieonians: J. Martin, J. Boyle, T. McIntyre, J. Sandison, S. Sweeney, (S. Tait), J. Davies, M. Wilson, P. Harvey, J. McIntyre, (S. Cooper), P. Duffield, A. Smith
Substitute not used: G. Connelly

Hibernian: J. Leighton, C. Jackson, D. Dods, P. McGinlay, S. Tweed, G. Hunter, (M. Weir), K. McAllister, (G. Donald), A. Millen, K. Harper, D. Jackson, M. O'Neill
Substitute not used: G. Love
Attendance: 3,201

Wednesday, 30th August, 1995

RANGERS 3 — **STIRLING ALBION 2**
S. McCall, A. McCoist, M. Hateley — S. McCormick, C. Taggart

Rangers: A. Goram, S. Wright, D. Robertson, R. Gough, A. McLaren, G. Petric, S. McCall, C. Miller, A. McCoist, M. Hateley, A. Mikhailitchenko
Substitutes not used: I. Durrant, G. Durie, W. Thomson (Goalkeeper)

Stirling Albion: M. McGeown, M. McKechnie, (P. Armstrong), P. Watson, C. Mitchell, R. McQuilter, T. Tait, I. McInnes, P. Deas, (J. Gibson), S. McCormick, C. Taggart, J. McLeod
Substitute not used: A. Farquhar
Attendance: 39,540

HEART OF MIDLOTHIAN 2 — **DUNFERMLINE ATHLETIC 1**
D. McPherson, D. Hagen — I. Den Bieman

Heart of Midlothian: H. Smith, G. Locke, D. Winnie, C. Levein, (N. Berry), D. McPherson, B. Hamilton, J. Colquhoun, (A. Lawrence), G. Mackay, D. Hagen, A. Johnston, J. Robertson
Substitute not used: C. Nelson (Goalkeeper)

Dunfermline Athletic: G. Van De Kamp, I. Den Bieman, M. Millar, N. McCathie, A. Tod, P. Smith, A. Moore, J. McNamara, G. Shaw, (N. Cooper), S. Petrie, M. McCulloch, (D. Fleming)
Substitute not used: I. Westwater (Goalkeeper)
Attendance: 12,498

DUNDEE 3 — **KILMARNOCK 1**
M. Wieghorst, G. Shaw, J. Hamilton — P. Wright

Dundee: M. Pageaud, K. Bain, A. Cargill, (T. McQueen), R. Manley, M. Wieghorst, C. Duffy, G. Shaw, D. Vrto, (I. Anderson), G. Britton, (P. Tosh), J. Hamilton, N. McCann

Kilmarnock: D. Lekovic, M. Skilling, T. Black, R. Montgomerie, N. Whitworth, R. Connor, A. Mitchell, J. Henry, (G. Holt), P. Wright, T. Brown, M. Reilly, (M. Roberts)
Substitute not used: D. Anderson
Attendance: 4,324

FALKIRK 1 — **ABERDEEN 4**
M. Johnston — C. Woodthorpe, J. Miller, S. Booth, J. Clark (o.g.)

Falkirk: A. Parks, J. Clark, C. Napier, (N. Inglis), N. Oliver, J. McLaughlin, S. McKenzie, (B. Rice), J. McGowan, S. Kirk, C. McDonald, (N. Henderson), M. Johnston, D. Elliot

Aberdeen: T. Snelders, S. McKimmie, C. Woodthorpe, P. Hetherston, (R. McKinnon), J. Inglis, G. Smith, J. Miller, E. Jess, S. Booth, (S. Thomson), W. Dodds, S. Glass
Substitute not used: M. Watt (Goalkeeper)
Attendance: 6,387

LIVINGSTON 1 — **PARTICK THISTLE 2**
J. Young — A. Craig (2)

Livingston: H. Stoute, C. Smart, C. Martin, (C. Sinclair), G. Davidson, S. Williamson, S. Sorbie, (G. Harvey), G. McMartin, L. Bailey, (W. Callaghan), J. Young, D. Alleyne, M. Duthie

Partick Thistle: J.N. Walker, A. Dinnie, S. Pittman, D. McWilliams, G. Watson, S. Welsh, R. McDonald, A. Craig, W. Foster, T. Turner, I. Cameron, (A. Gibson)
Substitutes not used: P.G. Tierney, H. Curran
Attendance: 1,280

Thursday, 31st August, 1995

CELTIC 2 — **RAITH ROVERS 1**
(A.E.T. - 1-1 After 90 Minutes)
P. Van Hooijdonk, S. Donnelly — A. Rougier

Celtic: G. Marshall, T. Boyd, T. McKinlay, R. Vata, J. Hughes, P. Grant, P. O'Donnell, B. McLaughlin, (S. Donnelly), P. Van Hooijdonk, A. Thom, (A. Walker), J. Collins
Substitute not used: P. Bonner (Goalkeeper)

Raith Rovers: S.Y. Thomson, D. Kirkwood, J. Broddle, J. McInally, (A. Graham), S. Dennis, (R. Coyle), D. Sinclair, A. Rougier, C. Cameron, S. Crawford, D. Lennon, J. Dair, (B. Wilson)
Attendance: 27,546

FOURTH ROUND

Tuesday, 19th September, 1995

CELTIC 0 — **RANGERS 1**
A. McCoist

Celtic: G. Marshall, T. Boyd, T. McKinlay, R. Vata, J. Hughes, P. Grant, S. Donnelly, P. McStay, A. Walker, (P. Van Hooijdonk), A. Thom, (B. McLaughlin), J. Collins
Substitute not used: P. Bonner (Goalkeeper)

Rangers: A. Goram, S. Wright, D. Robertson, (A. Cleland), R. Gough, A. McLaren, G. Petric, C. Miller, P. Gascoigne, A. McCoist, O. Salenko, (G. Durie), B. Laudrup
Substitute not used: W. Thomson (Goalkeeper)
Attendance: 32,803

Wednesday, 20th September, 1995

MOTHERWELL 1 — **ABERDEEN 2**
(A.E.T. - 1-1 After 90 Minutes)
D. Arnott — J. Inglis, W. Dodds

Motherwell: S. Howie, E. May, R. McKinnon, (W. Davies), J. Philliben, B. Martin, C. McCart, P. Lambert, (A. Roddie), J. Dolan, T. Coyne, D. Arnott, (A. Burns), S. McSkimming

Aberdeen: M. Watt, S. McKimmie, C. Woodthorpe, P. Hetherston, (K. Christie), J. Inglis, G. Smith, J. Miller, E. Jess, S. Booth, W. Dodds, S. Glass, (D. Shearer)
Substitute not used: D. Stillie (Goalkeeper)
Attendance: 9,137

AIRDRIEONIANS 1 — **PARTICK THISTLE 1**
(A.E.T. - 1-1 After 90 Minutes)
J. McIntyre — W. Foster
Airdrieonians Won 3-2 on Kicks from the Penalty Mark

Airdrieonians: J. Martin, A. Stewart, P. Jack, (A. Smith), J. Sandison, S. Sweeney, K. Black, J. Boyle, J. Davies, S. Cooper, (P. Duffield), P. Harvey, J. McIntyre
Substitute not used: T. McIntyre

Partick Thistle: J.N. Walker, A. Dinnie, S. Pittman, (H. Curran), K. McKee, (R. McDonald), S. Welsh, G. Watson, D. McWilliams, A. Craig, W. Foster, C. Milne, I. Cameron
Substitute not used: S. Docherty
Attendance: 4,311

DUNDEE 4 — **HEART OF MIDLOTHIAN 4**
(A.E.T. - 3-3 After 90 Minutes)
M. Wieghorst, G. Shaw (2), P. Tosh — D. McPherson, J. Colquhoun, J. Robertson, A. Lawrence
Dundee Won 5-4 on Kicks from the Penalty Mark

Dundee: M. Pageaud, R. Farningham, T. McQueen, A. Cargill, (J. Duffy), M. Wieghorst, C. Duffy, G. Shaw, D. Vrto, (K. Bain), P. Tosh, J. Hamilton, (I. Anderson), N. McCann

Heart of Midlothian: H. Smith, G. Locke, D. Winnie, (W. Jamieson), N. Berry, D. McPherson, B. Hamilton, J. Colquhoun, G. Mackay, (S. Leitch), J. Robertson, D. Hagen, A. Lawrence
Substitute not used: C. Nelson (Goalkeeper)
Attendance: 9,528

SEMI-FINALS

Tuesday, 24th October, 1995
Hampden Park, Glasgow

RANGERS 1	ABERDEEN 2
O. Salenko	W. Dodds (2)

Rangers: A. Goram, S. Wright, J. Brown, C. Moore, (I. Durrant), A. McLaren, G. Petric, A. Cleland, (A. Mikhailitchenko), P. Gascoigne, A. McCoist, O. Salenko, G. Durie
Substitute not used: N. Murray

Aberdeen: M. Watt, S. McKimmie, S. Glass, B. Grant, J. Inglis, G. Smith, J. Miller, (P. Hetherston), P. Bernard, S. Booth, W. Dodds, E. Jess
Substitutes not used: D. Shearer, T. Snelders (Goalkeeper)
Attendance: 26,131

Wednesday, 25th October, 1995
McDiarmid Park, Perth

DUNDEE 2	AIRDRIEONIANS 1
P. Tosh, N. McCann	P. Duffield

Dundee: M. Pageaud, R. Farningham, T. McQueen, R. Manley, M. Wieghorst, J. Duffy, G. Shaw, D. Vrto, P. Tosh, (G. Britton), J. Hamilton, N. McCann
Substitutes not used: I. Anderson, K. Bain

Airdrieonians: J. Martin, A. Stewart, A. Smith, (P. Duffield), J. Sandison, S. Sweeney, K. Black, J. Boyle, J. Davies, S. Cooper, P. Harvey, J. McIntyre
Substitutes not used: T. McIntyre, M. Wilson
Attendance: 8,930

The Final – Paul Tosh (Dundee) and Stephen Glass (Aberdeen)

S·F·L ©

FINAL

Sunday, 26th November, 1995

HAMPDEN PARK, GLASGOW

ABERDEEN 2 — DUNDEE 0

Aberdeen: M. Watt, S. McKimmie, S. Glass, B. Grant, J. Inglis, G. Smith, J. Miller, (H. Robertson), D. Shearer, P. Bernard, W. Dodds, E. Jess, (P. Hetherston)
Substitute not used: D. Stillie (Goalkeeper)

Dundee: M. Pageaud, J. Duffy, T. McQueen, R. Manley, M. Wieghorst, C. Duffy, G. Shaw, D. Vrto, (R. Farningham), P. Tosh, (G. Britton), J. Hamilton, N. McCann, (I. Anderson)

Scorers: Aberdeen: D. Shearer, W. Dodds

Referee: L.W. Mottram (Forth)

Attendance: 33,099

COCA-COLA CUP – SEASON 1995/96

ROUND BY ROUND GOALS ANALYSIS

	No. of Goals Scored	Ties Played	Average Per Game
First Round	22	8	2.8
Second Round	54	16	3.4
Third Round	28	8	3.5
Fourth Round	14	4	3.5
Semi-Final	6	2	3.0
Final	2	1	2.0

Total No. of Goals Scored:	126
Ties Played	39
Average Goals per Game:	3.2

The Coca-Cola Cup

It's Aberdeen's Cup!

Billy Dodds (Aberdeen) – the pleasure of goalscoring!

SEASON 1946/47

5th April, 1947 at Hampden Park; Attendance 82,584; Referee: Mr R. Calder (Rutherglen)

RANGERS 4 — **ABERDEEN 0**
Gillick, Williamson, Duncanson (2)

SEASON 1947/48

25th October, 1947 at Hampden Park; Attendance 52,781; Referee: Mr P. Craigmyle (Aberdeen)

EAST FIFE 0 — **FALKIRK 0**
After Extra Time

REPLAY
1st November, 1947 at Hampden Park; Attendance 30,664; Referee: Mr. P. Craigmyle (Aberdeen)

EAST FIFE 4 — **FALKIRK 1**
Duncan (3), Adams — Aikman

SEASON 1948/49

12th March, 1949 at Hampden Park; Attendance 53,359; Referee: Mr W. G. Livingstone (Glasgow)

RANGERS 2 — **RAITH ROVERS 0**
Gillick, Paton

SEASON 1949/50

29th October, 1949 at Hampden Park; Attendance 38,897; Referee: Mr W. Webb (Glasgow)

EAST FIFE 3 — **DUNFERMLINE ATHLETIC 0**
Fleming, Duncan, Morris

SEASON 1950/51

28th October, 1950 at Hampden Park; Attendance 63,074; Referee: Mr J. A. Mowat (Glasgow)

MOTHERWELL 3 — **HIBERNIAN 0**
Kelly, Forrest, Watters

SEASON 1951/52

27th October, 1951 at Hampden Park; Attendance 91,075; Referee: Mr J. A. Mowat (Glasgow)

DUNDEE 3 — **RANGERS 2**
Flavell, Pattillo, Boyd — Findlay, Thornton

SEASON 1952/53

25th October, 1952 at Hampden Park; Attendance 51,830; Referee: Mr J. A. Mowat (Glasgow)

DUNDEE 2 — **KILMARNOCK 0**
Flavell (2)

SEASON 1953/54

24th October, 1953 at Hampden Park; Attendance 88,529; Referee: Mr J. S. Cox (Rutherglen)

EAST FIFE 3 — **PARTICK THISTLE 2**
Gardiner, Fleming, Christie — Walker, McKenzie

SEASON 1954/55

23rd October, 1954 at Hampden Park; Attendance 55,640; Referee: Mr J. A. Mowat (Glasgow)

HEART OF MIDLOTHIAN 4 — **MOTHERWELL 2**
Bauld (3), Wardhaugh — Redpath (pen), Bain

SEASON 1955/56

22nd October, 1955 at Hampden Park; Attendance 44,103; Referee: Mr H. Phillips (Wishaw)

ABERDEEN 2 — **ST. MIRREN 1**
Mallan (og), Leggat — Holmes

SEASON 1956/57

27th October, 1956 at Hampden Park; Attendance 58,973; Referee: Mr J. A. Mowat (Glasgow)

CELTIC 0 — **PARTICK THISTLE 0**

REPLAY
31st October, 1956 at Hampden Park; Attendance 31,126; Referee: Mr J. A. Mowat (Glasgow)

CELTIC 3 — **PARTICK THISTLE 0**
McPhail (2), Collins

SEASON 1957/58

19th October, 1957 at Hampden Park; Attendance 82,293; Referee: Mr J. A. Mowat (Glasgow)

CELTIC 7 — **RANGERS 1**
Mochan (2), McPhail (3), Wilson, Fernie (pen) — Simpson

SEASON 1958/59

25th October, 1958 at Hampden Park; Attendance 59,960; Referee: Mr R. H. Davidson (Airdrie)

HEART OF MIDLOTHIAN 5 — **PARTICK THISTLE 1**
Murray (2), Bauld (2), Hamilton — Smith

SEASON 1959/60

24th October, 1959 at Hampden Park; Attendance 57,974; Referee: Mr R. H. Davidson (Airdrie)

HEART OF MIDLOTHIAN 2 — **THIRD LANARK 1**
Hamilton, Young — Gray

SEASON 1960/61

29th October, 1960 at Hampden Park; Attendance 82,063; Referee: Mr T. Wharton (Glasgow)

RANGERS 2 — **KILMARNOCK 0**
Brand, Scott

SEASON 1961/62

28th October, 1961 at Hampden Park; Attendance 88,635; Referee: Mr R. H. Davidson (Airdrie)

RANGERS 1 — **HEART OF MIDLOTHIAN 1**
Millar — Cumming (pen)

REPLAY
18th December, 1961 at Hampden Park; Attendance 47,552; Referee: Mr R. H. Davidson (Airdrie)

RANGERS 3 — **HEART OF MIDLOTHIAN 1**
Millar, Brand, McMillan — Davidson

SEASON 1962/63

27th October, 1962 at Hampden Park; Attendance 51,280; Referee: Mr T. Wharton (Glasgow)

HEART OF MIDLOTHIAN 1 — **KILMARNOCK 0**
Davidson

S·F·L ©

SEASON 1963/64

26th October, 1963 at Hampden Park;
Attendance 105,907; Referee: Mr H. Phillips (Wishaw)

RANGERS 5 **MORTON 0**
Forrest (4), Willoughby

SEASON 1964/65

24th October, 1964 at Hampden Park;
Attendance 91,000; Referee: Mr H. Phillips (Wishaw)

RANGERS 2 **CELTIC 1**
Forrest (2) Johnstone

SEASON 1965/66

23rd October, 1965 at Hampden Park;
Attendance 107,609; Referee: Mr H. Phillips (Wishaw)

CELTIC 2 **RANGERS 1**
Hughes (2 (2 pen)) Young (o.g.)

SEASON 1966/67

29th October, 1966 at Hampden Park;
Attendance 94,532; Referee: Mr T. Wharton (Glasgow)

CELTIC 1 **RANGERS 0**
Lennox

SEASON 1967/68

28th October, 1967 at Hampden Park;
Attendance 66,660; Referee: Mr R. H. Davidson (Airdrie)

CELTIC 5 **DUNDEE 3**
Chalmers (2), Hughes, Wallace, Lennox G. McLean (2), J. McLean

SEASON 1968/69

5th April, 1969 at Hampden Park;
Attendance 74,000; Referee: Mr W. M. M. Syme (Airdrie)

CELTIC 6 **HIBERNIAN 2**
Lennox (3), Wallace, Auld, Craig O'Rourke, Stevenson

SEASON 1969/70

25th October, 1969 at Hampden Park;
Attendance 73,067; Referee: Mr J. W. Paterson (Bothwell)

CELTIC 1 **ST. JOHNSTONE 0**
Auld

SEASON 1970/71

24th October, 1970 at Hampden Park;
Attendance 106,263; Referee: Mr T. Wharton (Glasgow)

RANGERS 1 **CELTIC 0**
Johnstone

SEASON 1971/72

23rd October, 1971 at Hampden Park;
Attendance 62,740; Referee: Mr W. J. Mullan (Dalkeith)

PARTICK THISTLE 4 **CELTIC 1**
Rae, Lawrie, McQuade, Bone Dalglish

SEASON 1972/73

9th December, 1972 at Hampden Park;
Attendance 71,696; Referee: Mr A. MacKenzie (Larbert)

HIBERNIAN 2 **CELTIC 1**
Stanton, O'Rourke Dalglish

SEASON 1973/74

15th December, 1973 at Hampden Park;
Attendance 27,974; Referee: Mr R. H. Davidson (Airdrie)

DUNDEE 1 **CELTIC 0**
Wallace

SEASON 1974/75

26th October, 1974 at Hampden Park;
Attendance 53,848; Referee: Mr J. R. P. Gordon (Newport on Tay)

CELTIC 6 **HIBERNIAN 3**
Johnstone, Deans (3), Wilson, Murray Harper (3)

SEASON 1975/76

25th October, 1975 at Hampden Park;
Attendance 58,806; Referee: Mr W. Anderson (East Kilbride)

RANGERS 1 **CELTIC 0**
MacDonald

SEASON 1976/77

6th November, 1976 at Hampden Park;
Attendance 69,268; Referee: Mr J. W. Paterson (Bothwell)

ABERDEEN 2 **CELTIC 1**
Jarvie, Robb Dalglish (pen.)
After extra-time – 1-1 After 90 Minutes

SEASON 1977/78

18th March, 1978 at Hampden Park;
Attendance 60,168; Referee: Mr D. F. T. Syme (Rutherglen)

RANGERS 2 **CELTIC 1**
Cooper, Smith Edvaldsson
After extra-time – 1-1 After 90 Minutes

SEASON 1978/79

31st March, 1979 at Hampden Park;
Attendance 54,000; Referee: Mr I. M. D. Foote (Glasgow)

RANGERS 2 **ABERDEEN 1**
McMaster (o.g.), Jackson Davidson

SEASON 1979/80 – BELL'S LEAGUE CUP

8th December, 1979 at Hampden Park;
Attendance 27,299; Referee: Mr B. R. McGinlay (Balfron)

DUNDEE UNITED 0 **ABERDEEN 0**
After extra-time

REPLAY

12th December, 1979 at Dens Park;
Attendance 28,984; Referee: Mr B. R. McGinlay (Balfron)

DUNDEE UNITED 3 **ABERDEEN 0**
Pettigrew (2), Sturrock

SEASON 1980/81 – BELL'S LEAGUE CUP

6th December, 1980 at Dens Park;
Attendance 24,466; Referee: Mr R. B. Valentine (Dundee)

DUNDEE UNITED 3 **DUNDEE 0**
Dodds, Sturrock (2)

SEASON 1981/82

28th November, 1981 at Hampden Park; Attendance 53,795; Referee: Mr E. H. Pringle (Edinburgh)

RANGERS 2 – **DUNDEE UNITED 1**
Cooper, Redford – Milne

SEASON 1982/83

4th December, 1982 at Hampden Park; Attendance 55,372; Referee: Mr K. J. Hope (Clarkston)

CELTIC 2 – **RANGERS 1**
Nicholas, MacLeod – Bett

SEASON 1983/84

25th March, 1984 at Hampden Park; Attendance 66,369; Referee: Mr R. B. Valentine (Dundee)

RANGERS 3 – **CELTIC 2**
McCoist 3 (1 pen) – McClair, Reid (pen)
After extra-time – 2-2 After 90 Minutes

SEASON 1984/85 – SKOL CUP

28th October, 1984 at Hampden Park; Attendance 44,698; Referee: Mr B. R. McGinlay (Balfron)

RANGERS 1 – **DUNDEE UNITED 0**
Ferguson

SEASON 1985/86 – SKOL CUP

27th October, 1985 at Hampden Park; Attendance 40,065; Referee: Mr R. B. Valentine (Dundee)

ABERDEEN 3 – **HIBERNIAN 0**
Black (2), Stark

SEASON 1986/87 – SKOL CUP

26th October, 1986 at Hampden Park; Attendance 74,219; Referee: Mr D. F. T. Syme (Rutherglen)

RANGERS 2 – **CELTIC 1**
Durrant, Cooper (pen) – McClair

SEASON 1987/88 – SKOL CUP

25th October, 1987 at Hampden Park; Attendance 71,961; Referee: Mr R. B. Valentine (Dundee)

RANGERS 3 – **ABERDEEN 3**
Cooper, Durrant, Fleck – Bett, Falconer, Hewitt
After extra-time – 3-3 After 90 Minutes
Rangers won 5-3 on Kicks from the Penalty Mark

SEASON 1988/89 – SKOL CUP

23rd October, 1988 at Hampden Park; Attendance 72,122; Referee: Mr G. B. Smith (Edinburgh)

RANGERS 3 – **ABERDEEN 2**
McCoist (2), I. Ferguson – Dodds (2)

SEASON 1989/90 – SKOL CUP

22nd October, 1989 at Hampden Park; Attendance 61,190; Referee: Mr G. B. Smith (Edinburgh)

ABERDEEN 2 – **RANGERS 1**
Mason (2) – Walters (pen)
After extra-time – 1-1 after 90 minutes

SEASON 1990/91 – SKOL CUP

28th October, 1990 at Hampden Park; Attendance 62,817; Referee: Mr J. McCluskey (Stewarton)

RANGERS 2 – **CELTIC 1**
Walters, Gough – Elliott

SEASON 1991/92 – SKOL CUP

27th October, 1991 at Hampden Park; Attendance 40,377; Referee: Mr B. R. McGinlay (Balfron)

HIBERNIAN 2 – **DUNFERMLINE ATHLETIC 0**
McIntyre (pen), Wright

SEASON 1992/93 – SKOL CUP

25th October, 1992 at Hampden Park; Attendance 45,298; Referee: Mr D. D. Hope (Erskine)

RANGERS 2 – **ABERDEEN 1**
McCall, Smith (o.g.) – Shearer
After extra-time – 1-1 after 90 minutes

SEASON 1993/94

24th October, 1993 at Celtic Park; Attendance 47,632; Referee: Mr J. McCluskey (Stewarton)

RANGERS 2 – **HIBERNIAN 1**
Durrant, McCoist – McPherson (o.g.)

SEASON 1994/95 – COCA-COLA CUP

27th November, 1994 at Ibrox Stadium; Attendance 45,384; Referee: Mr J. McCluskey (Stewarton)

RAITH ROVERS 2 – **CELTIC 2**
S. Crawford, G. Dalziel – C. Nicholas, A. Walker
After extra-time – 2-2 after 90 minutes

Raith Rovers won 6-5 on Kicks from the Penalty Mark

SEASON 1995/96 – COCA-COLA CUP

26th November, 1995 at Hampden Park; Attendance 33,099; Referee: Mr L.W. Mottram (Forth)

ABERDEEN 2 – **DUNDEE 0**
D. Shearer, W. Dodds

WINNERS AT A GLANCE

RANGERS	19
CELTIC	9
ABERDEEN	5
HEART OF MIDLOTHIAN	4
DUNDEE	3
EAST FIFE	3
DUNDEE UNITED	2
HIBERNIAN	2
MOTHERWELL	1
PARTICK THISTLE	1
RAITH ROVERS	1

APPEARANCES IN FINALS

(Figures do not include replays)

Club	Apps	Club	Apps
RANGERS	25	KILMARNOCK	3
CELTIC	21	DUNFERMLINE ATHLETIC	2
ABERDEEN	11	MOTHERWELL	2
HIBERNIAN	7	RAITH ROVERS	2
DUNDEE	6	FALKIRK	1
HEART OF MIDLOTHIAN	5	GREENOCK MORTON	1
DUNDEE UNITED	4	ST. JOHNSTONE	1
PARTICK THISTLE	4	ST. MIRREN	1
EAST FIFE	3	THIRD LANARK	1

Player of the Year Awards

Scottish Professional Footballers' Association

1977/78

Premier Division	**Derek Johnstone** *(Rangers)*
First Division	**Billy Pirie** *(Dundee)*
Second Division	**Dave Smith** *(Berwick Rangers)*
Young Player of the Year	**Graeme Payne** *(Dundee United)*

1978/79

Premier Division	**Paul Hegarty** *(Dundee United)*
First Division	**Brian McLaughlin** *(Ayr United)*
Second Division	**Michael Leonard** *(Dunfermline Athletic)*
Young Player of the Year	**Raymond Stewart** *(Dundee United)*

1979/80

Premier Division	**Davie Provan** *(Celtic)*
First Division	**Sandy Clark** *(Airdrieonians)*
Second Division	**Paul Leetion** *(Falkirk)*
Young Player of the Year	**John MacDonald** *(Rangers)*

1980/81

Premier Division	**Mark McGhee** *(Aberdeen)*
First Division	**Eric Sinclair** *(Dundee)*
Second Division	**Jimmy Robertson** *(Queen of the South)*
Young Player of the Year	**Charlie Nicholas** *(Celtic)*

1981/82

Premier Division	**Sandy Clark** *(Airdrieonians)*
First Division	**Brian McLaughlin** *(Motherwell)*
Second Division	**Pat Nevin** *(Clyde)*
Young Player of the Year	**Frank McAvennie** *(St. Mirren)*

1982/83

Premier Division	**Charlie Nicholas** *(Celtic)*
First Division	**Gerry McCabe** *(Clydebank)*
Second Division	**John Colquhoun** *(Stirling Albion)*
Young Player of the Year	**Paul McStay** *(Celtic)*

1983/84

Premier Division	**Willie Miller** *(Aberdeen)*
First Division	**Gerry McCabe** *(Clydebank)*
Second Division	**Jim Liddle** *(Forfar Athletic)*
Young Player of the Year	**John Robertson** *(Heart of Midlothian)*

1984/85

Premier Division	**Jim Duffy** *(Morton)*
First Division	**Gerry McCabe** *(Clydebank)*
Second Division	**Bernie Slaven** *(Albion Rovers)*
Young Player of the Year	**Craig Levein** *(Heart of Midlothian)*

1985/86

Premier Division	**Richard Gough** *(Dundee United)*
First Division	**John Brogan** *(Hamilton Academical)*
Second Division	**Mark Smith** *(Queen's Park)*
Young Player of the Year	**Craig Levein** *(Heart of Midlothian)*

1986/87

Premier Division	**Brian McClair** *(Celtic)*
First Division	**Jim Holmes** *(Morton)*
Second Division	**John Sludden** *(Ayr United)*
Young Player of the Year	**Robert Fleck** *(Rangers)*

1987/88

Premier Division	**Paul McStay** *(Celtic)*
First Division	**Alex Taylor** *(Hamilton Academical)*
Second Division	**Henry Templeton** *(Ayr United)*
Young Player of the Year	**John Collins** *(Hibernian)*

1988/89

Premier Division	**Theo Snelders** *(Aberdeen)*
First Division	**Ross Jack** *(Dunfermline Athletic)*
Second Division	**Paul Hunter** *(East Fife)*
Young Player of the Year	**Billy McKinlay** *(Dundee United)*

1989/90

Premier Division	**Jim Bett** *(Aberdeen)*
First Division	**Ken Eadie** *(Clydebank)*
Second Division	**Willie Watters** *(Kilmarnock)*
Young Player of the Year	**Scott Crabbe** *(Heart of Midlothian)*

1990/91

Premier Division	**Paul Elliott** *(Celtic)*
First Division	**Simon Stainrod** *(Falkirk)*
Second Division	**Kevin Todd** *(Berwick Rangers)*
Young Player of the Year	**Eoin Jess** *(Aberdeen)*

1991/92

Premier Division	**Alistair McCoist** *(Rangers)*
First Division	**Gordon Dalziel** *(Raith Rovers)*
Second Division	**Andrew Thomson** *(Queen of the South)*
Young Player of the Year	**Philip O'Donnell** *(Motherwell)*

1992/93

Premier Division	**Andy Goram** *(Rangers)*
First Division	**Gordon Dalziel** *(Raith Rovers)*
Second Division	**Alexander Ross** *(Brechin City)*
Young Player of the Year	**Eoin Jess** *(Aberdeen)*

1993/94

Premier Division	**Mark Hateley** *(Rangers)*
First Division	**Richard Cadette** *(Falkirk)*
Second Division	**Andrew Thomson** *(Queen of the South)*
Young Player of the Year	**Philip O'Donnell** *(Motherwell)*

1994/95

Premier Division	**Brian Laudrup** *(Rangers)*
First Division	**Stephen Crawford** *(Raith Rovers)*
Second Division	**Derek McInnes** *(Greenock Morton)*
Third Division	**David Bingham** *(Forfar Athletic)*
Young Player of the Year	**Charlie Miller** *(Rangers)*

1995/96

Premier Division	**Paul Gascoigne** *(Rangers)*
First Division	**George O'Boyle** *(St. Johnstone)*
Second Division	**Stephen McCormick** *(Stirling Albion)*
Third Division	**Jason Young** *(Livingston)*
Young Player of the Year	**Jackie McNamara** *(Celtic)*

The Scottish Football Writers' Association

1965	**Billy McNeill** *(Celtic)*
1966	**John Greig** *(Rangers)*
1967	**Ronnie Simpson** *(Celtic)*
1968	**Gordon Wallace** *(Raith Rovers)*
1969	**Bobby Murdoch** *(Celtic)*
1970	**Pat Stanton** *(Hibernian)*
1971	**Martin Buchan** *(Aberdeen)*
1972	**Dave Smith** *(Rangers)*
1973	**George Connelly** *(Celtic)*
1974	**World Cup Squad**
1975	**Sandy Jardine** *(Rangers)*
1976	**John Greig** *(Rangers)*
1977	**Danny McGrain** *(Celtic)*
1978	**Derek Johnstone** *(Rangers)*
1979	**Andy Ritchie** *(Morton)*
1980	**Gordon Strachan** *(Aberdeen)*
1981	**Alan Rough** *(Partick Thistle)*
1982	**Paul Sturrock** *(Dundee United)*
1983	**Charlie Nicholas** *(Celtic)*
1984	**Willie Miller** *(Aberdeen)*
1985	**Hamish McAlpine** *(Dundee United)*
1986	**Sandy Jardine** *(Heart of Midlothian)*
1987	**Brian McClair** *(Celtic)*
1988	**Paul McStay** *(Celtic)*
1989	**Richard Gough** *(Rangers)*
1990	**Alex McLeish** *(Aberdeen)*
1991	**Maurice Malpas** *(Dundee United)*
1992	**Alistair McCoist** *(Rangers)*
1993	**Andy Goram** *(Rangers)*
1994	**Mark Hateley** *(Rangers)*
1995	**Brian Laudrup** *(Rangers)*
1996	**Paul Gascoigne** *(Rangers)*

Rangers – Tennents Scottish Cup Winners 1996. Photo: Courtesy of Evening Times.

Durie's Treble Delight

Rangers' spectacular Tennents Scottish Cup Final victory over Heart of Midlothian did much more than end the season in a perfect manner for Walter Smith and his players.

The stunning 5-1 outcome produced a stark reminder of just what the chasing clubs must achieve by way of standard to match the Bell's League Premier Division champions and also gave the Edinburgh club a fresh perspective on their progress. It was yet another game that underlined the good fortune that we have had in Scotland, to have world class players attracted to the domestic competitions and who deliver skills worth the admission money alone.

Almost 38,000 fans filed into Hampden Park, perhaps expecting Paul Gascoigne to run the show, and although the Player of the Year was impressive, it was the previous season's top award winner who grabbed centre stage. Brian Laudrup was simply magnificent, with pace, trickery and an accuracy with his distribution that would have defied opponents from any corner of the globe. Hearts could not afford him in that mood and while Gordon Durie's fine hat-trick captured the Sunday morning headlines, even he was quick to acknowledge the part that the Great Dane had played in providing the ammunition, which he used so professionally.

Hearts must reflect on their big day with the consolation that the same fate would probably have befallen most of the other teams in the Premier Division but it was, nevertheless, a shocked Tynecastle party that returned to the capital. Jim Jefferies' vastly improved side had, after all, not had it easy on their way to the National Stadium, with Partick Thistle, Kilmarnock, St. Johnstone and Aberdeen all having to be overcome. So it was hard to take as it quickly became clear that they were catching Rangers in their most dangerous mode particularly for their two fine young defenders, Paul Ritchie and Alan McManus.

Yet they had it easy compared to Gary Locke, who strode onto the pitch as the youngest ever Cup Final captain and just seven minutes into the game was stretchered off with knee ligament damage which will cost this fine prospect, much of this season. French goalkeeper, Gilles Rousset, was yet another victim of the day, when he allowed a cross-cum-shot from Brian Laudrup to slip through his legs and that after a first season at Tynecastle, when he had played a major part in Hearts' improvement. However, there have already been clear signs that all have recovered mentally from the ordeal and with Locke's recovery on course, Jefferies and his team can re-group to play a major part in the new season.

If the Final was one sided, the two Semi-Finals by comparison, contained all the nail biting excitement that has come to be an integral part of the Tennents Scottish Cup competition.

In the first Semi-Final tie, all the goals came late in the Aberdeen and Hearts match, with Duncan Shearer seemingly earning a replay when he cancelled out a John Robertson goal, but Allan Johnston struck virtually on the final whistle to end the Dons' hopes of a second prize for the season.

The Old Firm match the following day provided gripping entertainment, and if Celtic played well in the match, there somehow seemed an inevitability when goals from Ally McCoist and Brian Laudrup were too much for Celtic, although the Parkhead side set-up a late rally after Pierre Van Hooijdonk scored.

The Scottish Cup has never been short of romance and for two non League clubs, Keith and Whitehill Welfare, there was the thrill of meeting the Old Firm, with the appropriate substantial cheques.

Keith's reward for defeating Deveronvale 2-0 at the second attempt was a glittering home tie against Rangers (played at Pittodrie), where they were overrun by ten goals to one, but that didn't seem to matter as the whole town enjoyed a famous day out.

For Whitehill Welfare manager Dave Smith, the Scottish Cup run subsequently secured a job in League football at Montrose and he certainly had his players up for the job when they defeated Fraserburgh 2-1 away from home, after an earlier draw at Rosewall. Their reward was a Third Round tie at Easter Road, where they met Tommy Burns' Celtic, and put up a magnificent display of resistance until two Van Hooijdonk goals and one from Simon Donnelly, finally eroded their spirit.

Another club from the Highland region and one of The Scottish Football League's newest members, Caledonian Thistle, found even more resolve, for their exploits took them to the Quarter Final stage, where they would be pitted against the Premier Division champions, Rangers, this time at Tannadice Park.

They had to be tough to get there, for Jim Leishman's impressive Livingston were their first victims - 3-2 at home - before a penalty shoot-out victory at Bayview against East Fife, after two 1-1 draws had locked the teams together. That qualified them for a trip to Ochilview, where they defeated Cup specialists Stenhousemuir by a single goal and although they fell to Rangers 3-0 with Paul Gascoigne scoring twice, they had made their mark on the tournament.

Also at this stage, two goals in the last three minutes from Pierre Van Hooijdonk and Andreas Thom dramatically won Celtic the match against Dundee United after having trailed to an Owen Coyle goal for much of the match and set-up that Old Firm Semi-Final tie, whilst Dean Windass and Paul Bernard repaid Aberdeen some of their transfer fees with goals in the 2-1 win over Airdrieonians at Pittodrie. They had all been tight matches and the other Quarter Final tie at McDiarmid Park was no different as St. Johnstone stretched Hearts all the way, before strikes from Alan Lawrence and Dave McPherson were good enough to defeat a gallant Saints side that had levelled the tie with a George O'Boyle strike.

There were shocks in the early rounds as well, starting with Ross County's 2-0 victory over struggling Ayr United at Somerset Park, prior to their finding Forfar Athletic just too powerful in the Third Round, whilst on a difficult City Park in Edinburgh, Steve Archibald's East Fife made heavy work of coping with Spartans, drawing 0-0 in the capital before eventually succeeding back over the Forth through a slender 2-1 margin.

It was a miserable second half of the season for Hibernian and their Premier Division form was taken into the Cup by Alex Miller's players, when Paul Wright scored both Kilmarnock goals in a 2-0 Third Round victory at Easter Road.

Falkirk were Premier victims as well, when Terry Christie's Stenhousemuir side travelled to Brockville and created another cup upset triumphing 2-0. Motherwell also crashed out at the first time of asking, although there was no such shock tag losing 2-0 at home to Coca-Cola Cup winners, Aberdeen.

Mention should be made of Alex Smith's Clyde, who defeated Brechin City at Glebe Park in extra-time after a replay and then having Charlie Nicholas as a goalscorer in a 3-1 win over Coca-Cola Cup Finalists, Dundee. They then proceeded to give Rangers a competitive Fourth Round ninety minutes, leading the eventual Cup winners 1-0 with only 25 minutes remaining, until a combination of tired legs and some incisive play by Rangers saw the Ibrox club run out 4-1 winners.

It was a tournament that saw 164 goals being scored, almost an average of three per tie and there were hat-tricks for Rangers' trio Ian Ferguson, Alex Cleland and Gordon Durie as well as Queen's Park's Scott Edgar, in their 4-2 Second Round win at Queen of the South.

Outside the Hampden Semi-Finals and Final, Celtic twice had in excess of 30,000 for home ties against Raith Rovers and Dundee United, while Hearts vast travelling support ensured there were 14,173 for their Fourth Round victory at Rugby Park.

In the end, the Tennents Scottish Cup belonged to Rangers, and there are few who could deny them their May day glory after they had hit the net 24 times in five ties, and Celtic in the Semi-Final as well as for a spell against Clyde apart, had never been in trouble.

Indeed, they capped their whole campaign with a performance of breathtaking ruthlessness in that 5-1 victory, which established a new bench mark for the future. It will be fascinating to see if there is a team who can measure up to that standard during the course of the 1996/97 season.

RAY HEPBURN
(Freelance)

Brian Laudrup, Paul Gascoigne and Gordon Durie – Three nationalities, one cup.

FIRST ROUND

Saturday, 9th December, 1995

STRANRAER 0 — **LIVINGSTON 3**
Harvey (2), Duthie

Stranraer: Ross, Robertson, Reilly (McGuire), Howard, Gallagher, Duncan, Sloan, Grant (Ferguson), Kerrigan, Walker (McAulay), Henderson

Livingston: Douglas, S. Williamson, Alleyne, Davidson, Graham, McLeod, McMartin, Sorbie, Young, Harvey, Duthie (Thorburn)
Substitutes not used: Bailey, Callaghan
Attendance: 752

Tuesday, 12th December, 1995

STENHOUSEMUIR 2 — **ARBROATH 2**
McGeachie, Gardner (o.g.) — McCormick, Pew

Stenhousemuir: McKenzie, Sprott, Haddow, Armstrong, McGeachie, Christie, Bannon, Fisher (Roseburgh), Mathieson, Hutchison, I. Little
Substitutes not used: Hunter, G. Little

Arbroath: Dunn, McAulay, Peters, Ward (McCabe), Florence, Crawford, Pew (Elliot), Elder, McCormick, Watters, Gardner
Substitute not used: Porteous
Attendance: 424

Saturday, 16th December, 1995

GLASGOW UNIVERSITY 0 — **SPARTANS 1**
Burns

Glasgow University: Menzies, Mitchell (McLeod), B. Smith, Welsh (A. Smith), Duffy (McKinney), Gilchrist, Ventham, Guadagno, McIntosh, Sloan, Craig

Spartans: Oliver, Burns, Ettles (Mitchell), Findlay, Thomson, McKeating, Nixon (Johnstone), Galbraith (MacKinnon), Govan, McGovern, Durkin
Attendance: 273

ALBION ROVERS 0 — **DEVERONVALE 2**
Stewart, Heggie

Albion Rovers: Moffat, McDonald, Gallagher, Deeley, Speirs, Shanks, Bell, Crawford (Ryan), Young, McBride (McEwan), Willock
Substitute not used: Stewart

Deveronvale: I. Grant, Humphries, Cameron, Rattray, Cormack (Ironside), Simmers, Bell (Wolecki), A. Grant, Heggie, Stewart (Thornton), Dolan
Attendance: 484

FIRST ROUND REPLAY

Monday, 18th December, 1995

ARBROATH 0 — **STENHOUSEMUIR 1**
Mathieson

Arbroath: Hinchcliffe, Peters, Crawford, Middleton (Sexton), Ward, McAulay, Pew (Porteous), Elliot, McCormick, Watters, Gardner (McCabe)

Stenhousemuir: McKenzie, Sprott, Haddow, Armstrong, Bannon, Christie, Hunter (Aitken), Fisher, Mathieson, Hutchison, I. Little
Substitutes not used: G. Little, Brannigan
Attendance: 669

SECOND ROUND

Saturday, 6th January, 1996

AYR UNITED 0 — **ROSS COUNTY 2**
Robertson, Sharples (o.g.)

Ayr United: Duncan, Clarke (Byrne), Traynor, George, Jamieson, Sharples, Smith, Steel, Dalziel, Balfour, Kinnaird (S. Wilson)
Substitute not used: Barnstaple

Ross County: Hutchison, Herd, Mackay, Robertson, Bellshaw, Furphy (Andrew MacLeod), Ferries, Grant (Williamson), MacPherson (Milne), Connelly, Golabek
Attendance: 2,053

FORFAR ATHLETIC 3 — **LOSSIEMOUTH 1**
Bowes, Inglis, Mann — Clark

Forfar Athletic: Arthur, Hamilton, Henderson (Heddle), Mann, Craig, McPhee, Morgan, Inglis, Higgins, Bowes, Irvine
Substitutes not used: Hannigan, Donegan (Goalkeeper)

Lossiemouth: Pirie, Fiske, Cheyne, Masson, McKenzie, Gerrard (Kew), Still, Presslie (Shaw), Douglas (Kellas), Clark, Main
Attendance: 667

SPARTANS 0 — **EAST FIFE 0**

Spartans: Oliver, Burns, MacDonald, Findlay, Thomson, McKeating, Mitchell, Galbraith, Govan, McGovern (Nixon), Ettles (MacKinnon)
Substitute not used: Johnstone

East Fife: Hamilton, McStay, Gibb, Dixon, Beaton, Donaghy, Hutcheon (Andrew), Archibald, Scott, Allan, Hamill
Substitutes not used: Sneddon, Burns
Attendance: 997

DEVERONVALE 0 — **KEITH 0**

Deveronvale: I. Grant, Humphries, Cameron, Rattray, Cormack, Simmers, Bell (Schofield), Will, Heggie, Stewart (Morrison), Dolan
Substitute not used: Ironside

Keith: Thain, Thow, Wilson, Watt, Woolley, Gibson, Thomson, S. Taylor, Strachan (Cormie), Will (Nicol), Allan (Garden)
Attendance: 1,333

MONTROSE 2 — **COWDENBEATH 1**
Kennedy, P. Masson — Maratea

Montrose: Larter, Tosh, Tindal, P. Masson, Grant, Haro, MacDonald, Mailer, McGlashan, Kennedy (Smith), Ferrie (Taylor)
Substitute not used: Craib

Cowdenbeath: Russell, Maratea (Hamilton), Meldrum, Conn, Humphreys, Bowmaker, Steven, Millar (Brock), MacKenzie, Winter, Buckley (Soutar)
Attendance: 501

CALEDONIAN THISTLE 3 — **LIVINGSTON 2**
Ross, Teasdale, Hercher — Duthie, Harvey

Caledonian Thistle: Calder, MacArthur, Hastings, Bennett, Noble, Ross, Teasdale, Scott, Thomson, Christie, Hercher
Substitutes not used: Mitchell, McGinlay, McAllister

Livingston: Douglas, Sorbie (Callaghan), Alleyne (Coulston), Davidson, S. Williamson, McLeod, McMartin, Bailey (Thorburn), Young, Harvey, Duthie
Attendance: 1,923

WHITEHILL WELFARE 2 — **FRASERBURGH 2**
Gowrie (Pen), Tulloch — Killoh (2)

Whitehill Welfare: Cantley, Purves, Gowrie, Bennett (McCulloch) (Cameron), Steel, Millar, Smith, Bird, Sneddon, Brown, Tulloch
Substitute not used: O'Rourke

Fraserburgh: Gordon, Clark, Geddes, Young, Milne, Thomson, McCafferty (Norris), Killoh (McGruther), Keith, Hunter, Stephen
Substitute not used: Beaton
Attendance: 932

CLYDE 2 — **BRECHIN CITY 2**
Annand, Nicholas — Mitchell, Cairney (Pen)

Clyde: Hillcoat, Knox, Angus, Harrison (McCarron), McConnell, McCheyne, Dickson (Falconer), Nicholas, Annand, Watson, Ferguson
Substitute not used: Prunty

Brechin City: Allan, Mitchell, Brown, Cairney, Scott, Christie, McKellar, Farnan, Ross, Buick, McNeill (Smith)
Substitutes not used: Baillie, Garden (Goalkeeper)
Attendance: 903

QUEEN OF THE SOUTH 2 — **QUEEN'S PARK 4**
Mallan, Bryce (Pen) — Edgar (3), McGoldrick

Queen of the South: Butter, B. McKeown, Brown (Ramsay), C. Campbell (D. Campbell), D. McKeown, Bryce, Wilson, Cody, Graham (Harris), Kennedy, Mallan

Queen's Park: Chalmers, Callan, Arbuckle, Elder, Caven, Graham, Brodie (Orr), Fraser (Kennedy), Edgar, Ferry (McPhee), McGoldrick
Attendance: 1,034

STIRLING ALBION 3 — **ALLOA 1**
McCormick (2), Mitchell — Rixon

Stirling Albion: McGeown, A. Paterson, Deas, Mitchell, McQuilter, G. Paterson, Bone, McInnes (Tait), McCormick, Taggart, McLeod
Substitutes not used: Wood, Monaghan

Alloa: Balfour, McCormack, Bennett, Newbigging (Cully), McAneny, McAvoy, Mackay, Cadden (Whyte), Moffat, Gilmour (Hannah), Rixon
Attendance: 1,256

BERWICK RANGERS 3 — **ANNAN ATHLETIC 3**
Reid, Fraser, Irvine — Docherty (2), Muir
Berwick Rangers: Young, Valentine, Banks, Reid, Cowan, Fraser, Wilson, Neil, Kane, Irvine, Graham
Substitutes not used: McQueen (Goalkeeper), McGlynn, Walton
Annan Athletic: Burnett, Smith, Elliot, McGinlay, Hetherington, Sim, Patterson, Leslie, Docherty, (Learmont), Adams, Muir
Substitute not used: Hodgson, Middlemiss
Attendance: 421

Sunday, 7th January, 1996

EAST STIRLINGSHIRE 0 — **STENHOUSEMUIR 1**
I. Little
East Stirlingshire: McDougall, Russell, R. Lee, Watt (McBride), Sneddon (Stirling), Ross, I. Lee, Hunter (MacLean), Dwyer, Lamont, Neill
Stenhousemuir: McKenzie, Sprott, Haddow, Armstrong, McGeachie, Christie, Bannon, Fisher, Mathieson, Hutchison, I. Little
Substitutes not used: Aitken, Hunter, G. Little
Attendance: 901

SECOND ROUND REPLAYS

Tuesday, 9th January, 1996

BRECHIN CITY 0 — **CLYDE 0**
Match Abandoned after 94 Minutes
Brechin City: Allan, Mitchell, Brown, Cairney, Christie, Scott, McKellar, Farnan, Ross, Ferguson, McNeill
Substitutes not used: Buick, Baillie, Smith
Clyde: Hillcoat, Knox, Angus, McCarron (Thomson), McConnell, McCheyne, McCluskey (Dickson), Nicholas, Annand, Watson, Ferguson
Substitute not used: Falconer
Attendance: 596

Saturday, 13th January, 1996

EAST FIFE 2 — **SPARTANS 1**
Gibb, Allan — Nixon
East Fife: Hamilton, McStay, Gibb, Dixon, Beaton, Donaghy, Hamill, Hutcheon (Gartshore), Scott, Allan, Hope
Substitutes not used: Mair, McLeod
Spartans: Oliver, Burns, Ettles (Johnstone), Findlay, Thomson, McKeating, Mitchell (Harley), Galbraith, McGovern (Nixon), Govan, Durkin
Attendance: 1,135

KEITH 2 — **DEVERONVALE 0**
Nicol, Maver
Keith: Thain, Thow, Wilson, Watt, Woolley (Garden), Gibson, Thomson, S. Taylor, Strachan (Maver), Nicol (McPherson), Allan
Deveronvale: I. Grant, Humphries, Cameron (A. Grant), Rattray, Cormack, Simmers, Bell, Will (Morrison), Heggie, C. Stewart (M. Stewart), Dolan
Attendance: 1,899

FRASERBURGH 1 — **WHITEHILL WELFARE 2**
Stephen — Bird, Steel
Fraserburgh: Gordon, Clark, Michie, Young, Milne, Thomson (McCafferty), Geddes, Killoh (Beaton), Keith, Hunter, Stephen
Substitute not used: Norris
Whitehill Welfare: Cantley, Purves, Gowrie, Bennett (Cameron), Steel, Millar, Middlemist (O'Rourke), Bird, Sneddon, Brown, Tulloch
Substitute not used: Smith
Attendance: 2,027

ANNAN ATHLETIC 1 — **BERWICK RANGERS 2**
Sibbring — Kane (2)
Annan Athletic: Burnett, Smith, Stanley Leslie, McGinlay, Hetherington, Sim (Middlemiss), Paterson (Sibbring), Darrell (Learmont), Docherty, Steven Leslie, Muir
Berwick Rangers: Young, Wilson, Valentine, Reid, Cowan, Fraser, Kane (Forrester), Neil, McGlynn, Irvine, Graham
Substitutes not used: Walton, McQueen (Goalkeeper)
Attendance: 1,056

Monday, 15th January, 1996

BRECHIN CITY 1 — **CLYDE 3**
(A.E.T. - 0-0 After 90 Minutes)
Christie — McCheyne, McConnell, Annand
Brechin City: Allan, Mitchell, Brown, Cairney, Christie, Ferguson, McKellar, Farnan, Ross (Smith), Scott, McNeill
Substitutes not used: Baillie, Buick
Clyde: Hillcoat, Knox, Angus, Thomson, McConnell, McCheyne, Prunty, Nicholas, Annand, Watson (Brownlie) (McCluskey), Ferguson (Harrison)
Attendance: 1,033

THIRD ROUND

Saturday, 27th January, 1996

KEITH 1 — **RANGERS 10**
Garden — Ferguson (3), Cleland (3), Durie (Pen), Robertson, Miller, Mikhailitchenko
Keith: Thain, Thow, Wilson, Watt, Woolley, Gibson, Thomson, S. Taylor, Strachan (Garden), Nicol (G. Taylor), Allan (McPherson)
Rangers: Goram, Cleland (Durrant), Robertson, Gough (Brown), McLaren, Petric, Ferguson, McCall, Miller, Durie, Laudrup (Mikhailitchenko)
Attendance: 15,461

ROSS COUNTY 0 — **FORFAR ATHLETIC 3**
Bowes (2), Morgan
Ross County: Hutchison, Somerville (Williamson), Mackay, Herd, Bellshaw, Furphy, Ferries, Andrew MacLeod, Milne, Connelly, Golabek (Grant)
Substitute not used: MacPherson
Forfar Athletic: Arthur, Hamilton, McVicar, McPhee, Mann, Craig, Morgan, Allison (Glennie), Hannigan (Higgins), Bowes, Heddle
Substitute not used: Donegan (Goalkeeper)
Attendance: 2,283

HIBERNIAN 0 — **KILMARNOCK 2**
Wright (2)
Hibernian: Leighton, Millen, Tortolano, Farrell, Love, Mitchell (Harper), McAllister (Weir), C. Jackson, Wright, D. Jackson, O'Neill
Substitute not used: Renwick
Kilmarnock: Lekovic, MacPherson, Black (McKee), Reilly, Whitworth, Anderson, Mitchell, Henry, Wright (Montgomerie), Maskrey (Brown), Holt
Attendance: 8,366

RAITH ROVERS 3 — **QUEEN'S PARK 0**
Crawford (2), Lennon
Raith Rovers: Fridge, McMillan (McKilligan), Humphries, Kirkwood, Dennis, Sinclair (Coyle), Rougier, Cameron, Graham, Lennon, Crawford
Substitute not used: Buist
Queen's Park: Chalmers, Callan, Graham, Elder, Caven, Ferguson, Orr (Kennedy), Arbuckle, McPhee (Ferry), Brodie (Edgar), McGoldrick
Attendance: 2,665

CALEDONIAN THISTLE 1 — **EAST FIFE 1**
Stewart — Dwarika
Caledonian Thistle: Calder, MacArthur, Hastings, Bennett, Noble, Thomson, Teasdale, Scott (Mitchell), Stewart, Christie, Hercher (McGinlay)
Substitute not used: Ross
East Fife: Hamilton, McStay, Gibb, Dixon, Beaton, Donaghy, Cusick, Dwarika, Scott, Allan, Hamill
Substitutes not used: Hutcheon, Hope, Gartshore
Attendance: 2,320

Sunday, 28th January, 1996

WHITEHILL WELFARE 0 — **CELTIC 3**
Van Hooijdonk (2), Donnelly
Match played at Easter Road Stadium, Edinburgh
Whitehill Welfare: Cantley, Purves, Gowne, Bennett, Steel, Millar, Middlemist (Smith), Bird (Cameron), Sneddon, Brown, Tulloch (O'Rourke)
Celtic: Marshall, McNamara, McKinlay, Boyd (O'Neil), Hughes, Grant, Wieghorst, McStay, Van Hooijdonk, Walker (Donnelly), Collins (McLaughlin)
Attendance: 13,313

Tuesday, 30th January, 1996

FALKIRK 0 — **STENHOUSEMUIR 2**
I. Little, Hutchison

Falkirk: Parks, Weir, Munro (Kirk), Clark, James, Gray, McKenzie, Ferguson (Craig), Hagen, M. Johnston, Elliot
Substitute not used: McGowan

Stenhousemuir: McKenzie, Sprott, Scott (Roseburgh), Armstrong, Brannigan, Christie, Aitken, Fisher, Hunter, Hutchison, I. Little
Substitutes not used: G. Little, Logan
Attendance: 3,321

CLYDEBANK 0 — **STIRLING ALBION 1**
McCormick

Clydebank: Matthews, Lovering, Sutherland, Murdoch, Currie, Nicholls, Robertson (Flannigan), Connell, Teale, Lansdowne (Melvin), Bowman
Substitute not used: Jack

Stirling Albion: McGeown, A. Paterson (Gibson), Deas, Mitchell, McQuilter, G. Paterson, Bone, Tait, McCormick, Taggart, McLeod
Substitutes not used: Wood, Monaghan (Goalkeeper)
Attendance: 911

MOTHERWELL 0 — **ABERDEEN 2**
Windass, Shearer

Motherwell: Howie, May, McKinnon, Philliben, Martin, Denham, Lambert, Dolan, Arnott, Burns, McSkimming (Hendry)
Substitutes not used: McMillan, Krivokapic

Aberdeen: Watt, McKimmie, Glass, Grant, Irvine, Smith, Miller, Shearer (Dodds), Bernard, Windass, Jess
Substitutes not used: Snelders (Goalkeeper), Christie
Attendance: 6,035

DUMBARTON 1 — **AIRDRIEONIANS 3**
Mooney — Duffield (2), Smith

Dumbarton: MacFarlane, Burns, Fabiani (Granger), Melvin, Gow, Meechan, Mooney, McKinnon (McGarvey), Gibson, King, Ward (Dallas)

Airdrieonians: Rhodes, Boyle (Bonar), Stewart, Sandison, Sweeney, Black (J. McIntyre), Davies, Wilson, Cooper, Duffield, Smith
Substitute not used: Harvey
Attendance: 1,076

Wednesday, 31st January, 1996

HEART OF MIDLOTHIAN 1 — **PARTICK THISTLE 0**
Ritchie

Heart of Midlothian: Rousset, Locke, Ritchie, McPherson, McManus, Bruno, Johnston, Colquhoun, Robertson, Mackay, Pointon
Substitutes not used: Lawrence, P. Smith, Millar

Partick Thistle: Walker, Dinnie, Milne, Pittman (McWilliams), Welsh, Watson, W. Macdonald (Docherty), Foster, Henderson (Smith), Cameron, R. McDonald
Attendance: 13,770

HAMILTON ACADEMICAL 0 — **ST. JOHNSTONE 1**
Scott

Hamilton Academical: Cormack, Hillcoat, Renicks, Thomson (Sherry), Baptie, Craig, Quitongo (McKenzie), McEntegart, Geraghty, Hartley, McInulty
Substitute not used: Lorimer

St. Johnstone: Main, McQuillan, Preston, Sekerlioglu, Weir, McGowne, Scott, O'Neil, Grant, O'Boyle, Jenkinson
Substitutes not used: Cherry, Farquhar, Twaddle
Attendance: 1,394

CLYDE 3 — **DUNDEE 1**
Nicholas, Harrison, Annand — C. Duffy

Clyde: Hillcoat, Knox, Angus (Nisbet), Gillies, Thomson, Prunty, O'Neill (McCluskey), Nicholas (Patterson), Annand, Harrison, Ferguson

Dundee: Mathers, Smith, McQueen, C. Duffy, Magee (Tosh), McKeown, Shaw, Vrto, Britton, Hamilton, Cargill (Tully)
Substitute not used: Pageaud
Attendance: 2,039

Monday, 12th February, 1996

DUNFERMLINE ATHLETIC 3 — **ST. MIRREN 0**
Bingham, Petrie, A. Smith

Dunfermline Athletic: Van De Kamp, C. Miller, Fleming, Den Bieman, Tod, French, Moore, Robertson, A. Smith (Shaw), Petrie, Bingham (Farrell)
Substitute not used: Westwater (Goalkeeper)

St. Mirren: Money, Smith, McIntyre, McWhirter, Fenwick, Archdeacon (Taylor) (McLaughlin), Law, Gillies, Yardley, Lavety, Watson (Iwelumo)
Attendance: 4,899

Tuesday, 13th February, 1996

GREENOCK MORTON 1 — **MONTROSE 1**
Rajamaki — Kennedy

Greenock Morton: Wylie, Collins, McArthur, Anderson, McCahill, Lindberg, Lilley, Mahood, Hawke, Cormack, Rajamaki
Substitutes not used: Laing, McPherson, Blair

Montrose: Larter, Tosh, Tindal, Stephen, Grant, Haro, Kennedy (Cooper), Craib, McGlashan, Smith, Taylor (Ferrie)
Substitute not used: Kydd
Attendance: 2,707

Wednesday, 14th February, 1996

BERWICK RANGERS 1 — **DUNDEE UNITED 2**
Johnson (o.g.) — Coyle (2)

Berwick Rangers: McQueen, Valentine, Banks (Walton), Reid, Cowan, Fraser (Forrester), Wilson, Neil, Kane, Irvine, Graham
Substitute not used: McGlynn

Dundee United: Maxwell, Perry, Shannon, Pressley, Dailly, Johnson, Winters (McLaren), Robertson, McSwegan (Keith), Coyle, McQuilken
Substitute not used: McKinnon
Attendance: 2,077

THIRD ROUND REPLAYS

Wednesday, 7th February, 1996

EAST FIFE 1 — **CALEDONIAN THISTLE 1**
(A.E.T. - 1-1 after 90 minutes)
Scott — Hercher
Caledonian Thistle won 3-1 on Kicks from the Penalty Mark

East Fife: Hamilton, McStay, Gibb (Gartshore), Dixon, Demmin (Hutcheon), Hope, Donaghy, Archibald (Andrew), Scott, Allan, Hamill

Caledonian Thistle: Calder, MacArthur, Hastings, Bennett, Noble, Thomson (Mitchell), Teasdale (Ross), Scott (McGinlay), Stewart, Christie, Hercher
Attendance: 1,345

Wednesday, 14th February, 1996

MONTROSE 3 — **GREENOCK MORTON 2**
McGlashan (3) — Cormack, Lilley

Montrose: Larter, Tosh, Tindal, Stephen, Grant, Haro, Kennedy (Ferrie), Craib, McGlashan, Smith, MacDonald
Substitutes not used: Taylor, Kydd

Greenock Morton: Wylie, Collins, McArthur, Anderson, Johnstone, Lindberg, Lilley, Mahood (Blair), Hawke (Laing), Cormack, Rajamaki (McPherson)
Attendance: 682

FOURTH ROUND

Thursday, 15th February, 1996

CLYDE 1 — **RANGERS 4**
Angus — Miller (2), Van Vossen, Gascoigne

Clyde: Hillcoat, Knox, Angus, Gillies, Thomson, Harrison (Nisbet), O'Neill, Nicholas, Annand (Patterson), Watson, Ferguson (Prunty)

Rangers: Goram, Ferguson, Robertson, Moore, McLaren, Petric, Miller, Gascoigne, Van Vossen, McCall, Laudrup
Substitutes not used: Durrant, Brown, Scott (Goalkeeper)
Attendance: 5,722

Saturday, 17th February, 1996

STIRLING ALBION 0 — **ABERDEEN 2**
Windass, Shearer

Stirling Albion: McGeown, A. Paterson, Deas, Mitchell, McQuilter, G. Paterson, Bone, Tait (Wood), McCormick, Taggart, McLeod (Gibson)
Substitute not used: Monaghan (Goalkeeper)

Aberdeen: Watt, McKimmie, Glass, Grant, Irvine, Smith, Miller, Shearer, Windass, Dodds (Booth), Jess
Substitutes not used: Snelders (Goalkeeper), Inglis
Attendance: 3,808

CELTIC 2 — **RAITH ROVERS 0**
Thom, Donnelly

Celtic: Marshall, Boyd, McKinlay, McNamara, O'Neil, Grant, Donnelly (McLaughlin), McStay, Van Hooijdonk, Thom (Hay), Collins
Substitute not used: Wieghorst

Raith Rovers: Geddes, Kirkwood, Broddle, Coyle, Dennis, Sinclair, Rougier, Cameron, Crawford (Graham), Lennon (Dair), McInally Substitute not used: Fridge (Goalkeeper)
Attendance: 30,870

AIRDRIEONIANS 2 FORFAR ATHLETIC 2
Cooper, Duffield Inglis, Morgan
Airdrieonians: Martin, Stewart, Smith, Sandison, Sweeney, Black, Boyle, Davies, Cooper, Harvey (Wilson), Duffield (J. McIntyre)
Substitute not used: Bonar
Forfar Athletic: Arthur (Donegan), Irvine (Heddle), McVicar, Hamilton, McKillop, Glennie, Morgan, Allison, Hannigan, Bowes, Inglis
Substitute not used: Henderson
Attendance: 1,410

DUNDEE UNITED 1 DUNFERMLINE ATHLETIC 0
Brewster
Dundee United: Maxwell, Perry, Shannon, Pressley, Dailly, Malpas, Johnson, Robertson (McKinnon), McSwegan (Brewster), Coyle, Winters
Substitute not used: O'Hanlon (Goalkeeper)
Dunfermline Athletic: Van De Kamp, C. Miller, M. Millar, Den Bieman, Tod, French, Moore, Robertson, A. Smith, Petrie, Fleming (Shaw)
Substitutes not used: Farrell, Westwater (Goalkeeper)
Attendance: 7,342

KILMARNOCK 1 HEART OF MIDLOTHIAN 2
Anderson Ritchie, Berry
Kilmarnock: Lekovic, MacPherson, Black, Reilly, Montgomerie, Anderson, Mitchell, Henry, Wright, Brown, Holt (McKee)
Substitutes not used: Connor, Meldrum (Goalkeeper)
Heart of Midlothian: Rousset, Berry, Ritchie, McPherson, Mackay, Millar (McManus), Johnston (Robertson), Colquhoun, Lawrence, Fulton, Pointon
Substitute not used: Nelson (Goalkeeper)
Attendance: 14,173

STENHOUSEMUIR 0 CALEDONIAN THISTLE 1
Thomson
Stenhousemuir: McKenzie, Sprott, Bannon, Armstrong, Brannigan, Roseburgh (Hunter), Aitken, Fisher, Mathieson, Hutchison (Haddow), I. Little
Substitute not used: Scott
Caledonian Thistle: Calder, MacArthur, Hastings, Bennett, Noble, Thomson, Teasdale, Scott, Stewart, Christie, Hercher
Substitutes not used: Ross, McGinlay, Mitchell
Attendance: 1,634

ST. JOHNSTONE 3 MONTROSE 0
Scott (2),Grant
St. Johnstone: Main, McQuillan, Preston, Sekerlioglu (Irons), Weir, McGowne, Scott, O'Neil (Farquhar), Grant (Twaddle), O'Boyle, Jenkinson
Montrose: Larter, Tosh, Tindal, Stephen, Grant, Haro, Kennedy (Ferrie), Craib, McGlashan, Smith (Kydd), MacDonald (Taylor)
Attendance: 3,370

FOURTH ROUND REPLAY

Tuesday, 27th February, 1996

FORFAR ATHLETIC 0 AIRDRIEONIANS 0
(A.E.T.) Airdrieonians won 4-2 on Kicks from the Penalty Mark
Forfar Athletic: Arthur, McKillop, McVicar, McPhee, Mann (Hamilton), Glennie, Morgan, Allison (Donegan), Hannigan, Bowes (Higgins), Inglis
Airdrieonians: Martin, Stewart, (Bonar), Smith, Sandison, Sweeney, Davies, Boyle, Wilson, Cooper, Duffield, Harvey
Substitutes not used: T. McIntyre, Connelly
Attendance: 1,632

FIFTH ROUND

Thursday, 7th March, 1996

ST. JOHNSTONE 1 HEART OF MIDLOTHIAN 2
O'Boyle Lawrence, McPherson
St. Johnstone: Main, McQuillan, Preston, Sekerlioglu, Weir (Farquhar), McGowne, Griffin, O'Neil (Twaddle), Grant, O'Boyle, Jenkinson
Substitute not used: Robertson
Heart of Midlothian: Rousset, Locke, Ritchie, McPherson, Mackay (Johnston), Bruno, Lawrence, Colquhoun, Robertson (Millar), Fulton (McManus), Pointon
Attendance: 9,951

Saturday, 9th March, 1996

ABERDEEN 2 AIRDRIEONIANS 1
Windass, Bernard Bonar
Aberdeen: Watt, Grant, Woodthorpe, Bernard, Irvine, Smith, Miller (Shearer), Windass, Booth, Dodds, Glass
Substitutes not used: Snelders (Goalkeeper), Robertson
Airdrieonians: Martin, Stewart, Bonar, Sandison, Sweeney, Black (Wilson), Boyle, Davies, Cooper, Harvey, J. McIntyre
Substitutes not used: Jack, T. McIntyre
Attendance: 11,749

CALEDONIAN THISTLE 0 RANGERS 3
Gascoigne (2), Thomson (o.g.)
Match played at Tannadice Park, Dundee
Caledonian Thistle: Calder, MacArthur, Hastings, Bennett (Mitchell), Noble, Thomson (Ross), Teasdale, Scott, Stewart, Christie, Hercher (McGinlay)
Rangers: Goram, Moore, Robertson, Petric (Cleland), McLaren, Brown, Van Vossen (Durrant), Gascoigne, McCoist, Miller, Laudrup
Substitute not used: Mikhailitchenko
Attendance: 11,296

Sunday, 10th March, 1996

CELTIC 2 DUNDEE UNITED 1
Van Hooijdonk, Thom Coyle
Celtic: Marshall, O'Neil (O'Donnell), McKinlay, McNamara, Hughes, Grant, Donnelly, McStay, Van Hooijdonk, Thom, McLaughlin
Substitutes not used: Mackay, Bonner (Goalkeeper)
Dundee United: Maxwell, Perry, Malpas, Pressley, Welsh, Johnson, Coyle, Bowman, McSwegan (McLaren), Brewster (McKinnon), Winters
Substitute not used: Shannon
Attendance: 31,403

SEMI-FINALS

Saturday, 6th April, 1996

Hampden Park, Glasgow

ABERDEEN 1 HEART OF MIDLOTHIAN 2
Shearer Robertson, Johnston
Aberdeen: Watt, McKimmie, Woodthorpe, Glass, Inglis, Smith, Miller (Grant), Windass, Bernard, Dodds, Robertson (Shearer)
Substitute not used: Stillie (Goalkeeper)
Heart of Midlothian: Rousset, Locke, Ritchie, Mackay, McManus, Bruno, Johnston, Colquhoun, Lawrence (McPherson), Fulton (Robertson), Pointon
Substitute not used: Thomas
Attendance: 27,785

Sunday, 7th April, 1996

Hampden Park, Glasgow

CELTIC 1 RANGERS 2
Van Hooijdonk McCoist, Laudrup
Celtic: Marshall, Boyd, McKinlay, McNamara, Hughes, Grant, Donnelly, McStay, Van Hooijdonk, Thom, McLaughlin (Wieghorst)
Substitutes not used: O'Neil, Gray
Rangers: Goram, Cleland, Robertson, Petric, McLaren, Brown, Durie (Steven), Gascoigne, McCoist, McCall, Laudrup
Substitutes not used: Andersen, Scott (Goalkeeper)
Attendance: 36,333

FINAL

Saturday, 18th May, 1996

HAMPDEN PARK, GLASGOW

HEART OF MIDLOTHIAN 1 RANGERS 5

Heart of Midlothian: Rousset, Locke (Lawrence), Ritchie, McManus, McPherson, Bruno, (Robertson), Johnston, Mackay, Colquhoun, Fulton, Pointon
Substitute not used: Hogarth (Goalkeeper)
Rangers: Goram, Cleland, Robertson, Gough, McLaren, Brown, Durie, Gascoigne, Ferguson, (Durrant), McCall, Laudrup
Substitutes not used: Petric, Andersen
Scorers: Rangers: Laudrup (2), Durie (3)
Heart of Midlothian: Colquhoun
Referee: H. Dallas (Motherwell)
Attendance: 37,760

SEASON 1919/20

17th April, 1920 at Hampden Park; Attendance 95,000; Referee: Mr W. Bell (Hamilton)

KILMARNOCK 3 — Culley, Shortt, J. Smith
ALBION ROVERS 2 — Watson, Hillhouse

SEASON 1920/21

16th April, 1921 at Celtic Park; Attendance 28,294; Referee: Mr H. Humphreys (Greenock)

PARTICK THISTLE 1 — Blair
RANGERS 0

SEASON 1921/22

15th April, 1922 at Hampden Park; Attendance 75,000 Referee: Mr T. Dougray (Bellshill)

MORTON 1 — Gourlay
RANGERS 0

SEASON 1922/23

31th March, 1923 at Hampden Park; Attendance 80,100; Referee: Mr T. Dougray (Bellshill)

CELTIC 1 — Cassidy
HIBERNIAN 0

SEASON 1923/24

19th April, 1924 at Ibrox Stadium; Attendance 59,218; Referee: Mr T. Dougray (Bellshill)

AIRDRIEONIANS 2 — Russell (2)
HIBERNIAN 0

SEASON 1924/25

11th April, 1925 at Hampden Park; Attendance 75,137; Referee: Mr T. Dougray (Bellshill)

CELTIC 2 — Gallacher, McGrory
DUNDEE 1 — McLean

SEASON 1925/26

10th April, 1926 at Hampden Park; Attendance 98,620; Referee: Mr P. Craigmyle (Aberdeen)

ST. MIRREN 2 — McCrae, Howieson
CELTIC 0

SEASON 1926/27

16th April, 1927 at Hampden Park; Attendance 80,070; Referee: Mr T. Dougray (Bellshill)

CELTIC 3 — Robertson (o.g.), McLean, Connolly
EAST FIFE 1 — Wood

SEASON 1927/28

14th April, 1928 at Hampden Park; Attendance 118,115; Referee: Mr W. Bell (Motherwell)

RANGERS 4 — Meiklejohn (pen), McPhail, Archibald (2)
CELTIC 0

SEASON 1928/29

6th April, 1929 at Hampden Park; Attendance 114,708; Referee: Mr T. Dougray (Bellshill)

KILMARNOCK 2 — Aitken, Williamson
RANGERS 0

SEASON 1929/30

12th April, 1930 at Hampden Park; Attendance 107,475; Referee: Mr W. Bell (Motherwell)

RANGERS 0
PARTICK THISTLE 0

REPLAY

16th April, 1930 at Hampden Park; Attendance 103,686; Referee: Mr W. Bell (Motherwell)

RANGERS 2 — Marshall, Craig
PARTICK THISTLE 1 — Torbet

SEASON 1930/31

11th April, 1931 at Hampden Park; Attendance 104,803; Referee: Mr P. Craigmyle (Aberdeen)

CELTIC 2 — McGrory, Craig (o.g.)
MOTHERWELL 2 — Stevenson, McMenemy

REPLAY

15th April, 1931 at Hampden Park; Attendance 98,579; Referee: Mr P. Craigmyle (Aberdeen)

CELTIC 4 — R. Thomson (2), McGrory (2)
MOTHERWELL 2 — Murdoch, Stevenson

SEASON 1931/32

16th April, 1932 at Hampden Park; Attendance 111,982; Referee: Mr P. Craigmyle (Aberdeen)

RANGERS 1 — McPhail
KILMARNOCK 1 — Maxwell

REPLAY

20th April, 1932 at Hampden Park; Attendance 110,695; Referee: Mr P. Craigmyle (Aberdeen)

RANGERS 3 — Fleming, McPhail, English
KILMARNOCK 0

SEASON 1932/33

15th April, 1933 at Hampden Park; Attendance 102,339; Referee: Mr T. Dougray (Bellshill)

CELTIC 1 — McGrory
MOTHERWELL 0

SEASON 1933/34

21st April, 1934 at Hampden Park; Attendance 113,430; Referee: Mr M. C. Hutton (Glasgow)

RANGERS 5 — Nicholson (2), McPhail, Main, Smith
ST. MIRREN 0

SEASON 1934/35

20th April, 1935 at Hampden Park; Attendance 87,286; Referee: Mr H. Watson (Glasgow)

RANGERS 2 — Smith (2)
HAMILTON ACADEMICAL 1 — Harrison

SEASON 1935/36

18th April 1936 at Hampden Park; Attendance 88,859; Referee: Mr J. M. Martin (Ladybank)

RANGERS 1 — McPhail
THIRD LANARK 0

SEASON 1936/37

24th April, 1937 at Hampden Park; Attendance 147,365; Referee: Mr M. C. Hutton (Glasgow)

CELTIC 2 — Crum, Buchan
ABERDEEN 1 — Armstrong

SEASON 1937/38

23rd April, 1938 at Hampden Park; Attendance 80,091; Referee: Mr H. Watson (Glasgow)

EAST FIFE 1 — McLeod
KILMARNOCK 1 — McAvoy

REPLAY
27th April, 1938 at Hampden Park; Attendance 92,716; Referee: Mr H. Watson (Glasgow)

EAST FIFE 4	KILMARNOCK 2
McKerrell (2), McLeod, Miller	Thomson (pen), McGrogan
After extra-time	

SEASON 1938/39
22nd April, 1939 at Hampden Park; Attendance 94,799; Referee: Mr W. Webb (Glasgow)

CLYDE 4	MOTHERWELL 0
Wallace, Martin (2), Noble	

SEASON 1946/47
19th April, 1947 at Hampden Park; Attendance 82,140; Referee: Mr R. Calder (Glasgow)

ABERDEEN 2	HIBERNIAN 1
Hamilton, Williams	Cuthbertson

SEASON 1947/48
17th April, 1948 at Hampden Park; Attendance 129,176; Referee: Mr J. M. Martin (Blairgowrie)

RANGERS 1	MORTON 1
Gillick	Whyte
After extra-time	

REPLAY
21st April, 1948 at Hampden Park; Attendance 131,975; Referee: Mr J. M. Martin (Blairgowrie)

RANGERS 1	MORTON 0
Williamson	
After extra-time	

SEASON 1948/49
23rd April, 1949 at Hampden Park; Attendance 108,435; Referee: Mr R. G. Benzie (Irvine)

RANGERS 4	CLYDE 1
Young (2 (2 pens)), Williamson, Duncanson	Galletly

SEASON 1949/50
22nd April, 1950 at Hampden Park; Attendance 118,262 Referee: Mr J. A. Mowat (Burnside)

RANGERS 3	EAST FIFE 0
Findlay, Thornton (2)	

SEASON 1950/51
21st April, 1951 at Hampden Park; Attendance 131,943 Referee: Mr J. A. Mowat (Burnside)

CELTIC 1	MOTHERWELL 0
McPhail	

SEASON 1951/52
19th April, 1952 at Hampden Park; Attendance 136,304; Referee: Mr J. A. Mowat (Burnside)

MOTHERWELL 4	DUNDEE 0
Watson, Redpath, Humphries, Kelly	

SEASON 1952/53
25th April, 1953 at Hampden Park; Attendance 129,861; Referee: Mr J. A. Mowat (Burnside)

RANGERS 1	ABERDEEN 1
Prentice	Yorston

REPLAY
29th April, 1953 at Hampden Park; Attendance 112,619; Referee: Mr J. A. Mowat (Burnside)

RANGERS 1	ABERDEEN 0
Simpson	

SEASON 1953/54
24th April, 1954 at Hampden Park; Attendance 129,926; Referee: Mr C. E. Faultless (Giffnock)

CELTIC 2	ABERDEEN 1
Young (o.g.), Fallon	Buckley

SEASON 1954/55
23rd April, 1955 at Hampden Park; Attendance 106,111; Referee: Mr C. E. Faultless (Giffnock)

CLYDE 1	CELTIC 1
Robertson	Walsh

REPLAY
27th April, 1955 at Hampden Park; Attendance 68,735; Referee: Mr C. E. Faultless (Giffnock)

CLYDE 1	CELTIC 0
Ring	

SEASON 1955/56
21st April, 1956 at Hampden Park; Attendance 133,399; Referee: Mr R. H. Davidson (Airdrie)

HEART OF MIDLOTHIAN 3	CELTIC 1
Crawford (2), Conn	Haughney

SEASON 1956/57
20th April, 1957 at Hampden Park; Attendance 81,057; Referee: Mr J. A. Mowat (Burnside)

FALKIRK 1	KILMARNOCK 1
Prentice (pen)	Curlett

REPLAY
24th April, 1957 at Hampden Park; Attendance 79,785; Referee: Mr J. A. Mowat (Burnside)

FALKIRK 2	KILMARNOCK 1
Merchant, Moran	Curlett
After extra-time	

SEASON 1957/58
26th April, 1958 at Hampden Park; Attendance 95,123; Referee: Mr J. A. Mowat (Burnside)

CLYDE 1	HIBERNIAN 0
Coyle	

SEASON 1958/59
25th April 1959 at Hampden Park; Attendance 108,951; Referee: Mr J. A. Mowat (Burnside)

ST. MIRREN 3	ABERDEEN 1
Bryceland, Miller, Baker	Baird

SEASON 1959/60
23rd April, 1960 at Hampden Park; Attendance 108,017; Referee: Mr R. H. Davidson (Airdrie)

RANGERS 2	KILMARNOCK 0
Millar (2)	

SEASON 1960/61
22nd April, 1961 at Hampden Park; Attendance 113,618; Referee: Mr H. Phillips (Wishaw)

DUNFERMLINE ATHLETIC 0	CELTIC 0

REPLAY
26th April, 1961 at Hampden Park; Attendance 87,866; Referee: Mr H. Phillips (Wishaw)

DUNFERMLINE ATHLETIC 2	CELTIC 0
Thomson, Dickson	

SEASON 1961/62

21st April, 1962 at Hampden Park; Attendance 126,930;
Referee: Mr T. Wharton (Clarkston)

RANGERS 2 — **ST. MIRREN 0**
Brand, Wilson

SEASON 1962/63

4th May, 1963 at Hampden Park; Attendance 129,527;
Referee: Mr T. Wharton (Clarkston)

RANGERS 1 — **CELTIC 1**
Brand — Murdoch

REPLAY
15th May, 1963 at Hampden Park; Attendance 120,263;
Referee: Mr T. Wharton (Clarkston)

RANGERS 3 — **CELTIC 0**
Brand (2), Wilson

SEASON 1963/64

25th April, 1964 at Hampden Park; Attendance 120,982
Referee: Mr H. Phillips (Wishaw)

RANGERS 3 — **DUNDEE 1**
Millar (2), Brand — Cameron

SEASON 1964/65

24th April, 1965 at Hampden Park; Attendance 108,800;
Referee: Mr H. Phillips (Wishaw)

CELTIC 3 — **DUNFERMLINE ATHLETIC 2**
Auld (2), McNeill — Melrose, McLaughlin

SEASON 1965/66

23rd April, 1966 at Hampden Park; Attendance 126,559;
Referee: Mr T. Wharton (Clarkston)

RANGERS 0 — **CELTIC 0**

REPLAY
27th April, 1966 at Hampden Park; Attendance 96,862;
Referee: Mr T. Wharton (Clarkston)

RANGERS 1 — **CELTIC 0**
Johansen

SEASON 1966/67

29th April, 1967 at Hampden Park; Attendance 127,117;
Referee: Mr W. M. M. Syme (Glasgow)

CELTIC 2 — **ABERDEEN 0**
Wallace (2)

SEASON 1967/68

27th April, 1968 at Hampden Park; Attendance 56,365;
Referee: Mr W. Anderson (East Kilbride)

DUNFERMLINE ATHLETIC 3 — **HEART OF MIDLOTHIAN 1**
Gardner (2), Lister (pen) — Lunn (o.g.)

SEASON 1968/69

26th April, 1969 at Hampden Park; Attendance 132,870;
Referee: Mr J. Callaghan (Glasgow)

CELTIC 4 — **RANGERS 0**
McNeill, Lennox, Connelly, Chalmers

SEASON 1969/70

11th April, 1970 at Hampden Park; Attendance 108,434;
Referee: Mr R. H. Davidson (Airdrie)

ABERDEEN 3 — **CELTIC 1**
Harper (pen), McKay (2) — Lennox

SEASON 1970/71

8th May, 1971 at Hampden Park; Attendance 120,092;
Referee: Mr T. Wharton (Glasgow)

CELTIC 1 — **RANGERS 1**
Lennox — D. Johnstone

REPLAY
12th May, 1971 at Hampden Park; Attendance 103,332;
Referee: Mr T. Wharton (Glasgow)

CELTIC 2 — **RANGERS 1**
Macari, Hood (pen) — Callaghan (o.g.)

SEASON 1971/72

6th May, 1972 at Hampden Park; Attendance 106,102;
Referee: Mr A. MacKenzie (Larbert)

CELTIC 6 — **HIBERNIAN 1**
McNeill, Deans (3), Macari (2) — Gordon

SEASON 1972/73

5th May, 1973 at Hampden Park; Attendance 122,714;
Referee: Mr J. R. P. Gordon (Newport-on-Tay)

RANGERS 3 — **CELTIC 2**
Parlane, Conn, Forsyth — Dalglish, Connelly (pen)

SEASON 1973/74

4th May, 1974 at Hampden Park; Attendance 75,959;
Referee: Mr W. S. Black (Glasgow)

CELTIC 3 — **DUNDEE UNITED 0**
Hood, Murray, Deans

SEASON 1974/75

3rd May, 1975 at Hampden Park; Attendance 75,457;
Referee: Mr I. M. D. Foote (Glasgow)

CELTIC 3 — **AIRDRIEONIANS 1**
Wilson (2), McCluskey (pen) — McCann

SEASON 1975/76

1st May 1976 at Hampden Park; Attendance 85,354;
Referee: Mr R. H. Davidson (Airdrie)

RANGERS 3 — **HEART OF MIDLOTHIAN 1**
Johnstone (2), MacDonald — Shaw

SEASON 1976/77

7th May, 1977 at Hampden Park; Attendance 54,252;
Referee: Mr R. B. Valentine (Dundee)

CELTIC 1 — **RANGERS 0**
Lynch (pen)

SEASON 1977/78

6th May, 1978 at Hampden Park; Attendance 61,563;
Referee: Mr B. R. McGinlay (Glasgow)

RANGERS 2 — **ABERDEEN 1**
MacDonald, Johnstone — Ritchie

SEASON 1978/79

12th May, 1979 at Hampden Park; Attendance 50,610;
Referee: Mr B. R. McGinlay (Glasgow)

RANGERS 0 — **HIBERNIAN 0**

REPLAY

16th May, 1979 at Hampden Park; Attendance 33,504;
Referee: Mr B. R. McGinlay (Glasgow)

RANGERS 0 — **HIBERNIAN 0**
After extra–time

SECOND REPLAY

28th May, 1979 at Hampden Park; Attendance 30,602;
Referee: Mr I. M. D. Foote (Glasgow)

RANGERS 3 — **HIBERNIAN 2**
Johnstone (2), Duncan (o.g.) — Higgins, MacLeod (pen)
After extra–time – 2-2 After 90 Minutes

SEASON 1979/80

10th May, 1980 at Hampden Park; Attendance 70,303;
Referee: Mr G. B. Smith (Edinburgh)

CELTIC 1 — **RANGERS 0**
McCluskey
After extra–time

SEASON 1980/81

9th May, 1981 at Hampden Park; Attendance 53,000;
Referee: Mr I. M. D. Foote (Glasgow)

RANGERS 0 — **DUNDEE UNITED 0**
After extra–time

REPLAY

12th May, 1981 at Hampden Park; Attendance 43,099;
Referee: Mr I. M. D. Foote (Glasgow)

RANGERS 4 — **DUNDEE UNITED 1**
Cooper, Russell, MacDonald (2) — Dodds

SEASON 1981/82

22nd May, 1982 at Hampden Park; Attendance 53,788;
Referee: Mr B. R. McGinlay (Balfron)

ABERDEEN 4 — **RANGERS 1**
McLeish, McGhee, Strachan, Cooper — MacDonald
After extra–time – 1-1 after 90 minutes

SEASON 1982/83

21st May, 1983 at Hampden Park; Attendance 62,979;
Referee: Mr D. F. T. Syme (Rutherglen)

ABERDEEN 1 — **RANGERS 0**
Black
After extra–time

SEASON 1983/84

19th May 1984 at Hampden Park; Attendance 58,900;
Referee: Mr R. B. Valentine (Dundee)

ABERDEEN 2 — **CELTIC 1**
Black, McGhee — P. McStay
After extra–time – 1-1 after 90 minutes

SEASON 1984/85

18th May, 1985 at Hampden Park; Attendance 60,346;
Referee: Mr B. R. McGinlay (Balfron)

CELTIC 2 — **DUNDEE UNITED 1**
Provan, McGarvey — Beedie

SEASON 1985/86

10th May, 1986 at Hampden Park; Attendance 62,841;
Referee: Mr H. Alexander (Irvine)

ABERDEEN 3 — **HEART OF MIDLOTHIAN 0**
Hewitt (2), Stark

SEASON 1986/87

16th May, 1987 at Hampden Park; Attendance 51,782;
Referee: Mr K. J. Hope (Clarkston)

ST. MIRREN 1 — **DUNDEE UNITED 0**
Ferguson
After extra–time

SEASON 1987/88

14th May, 1988 at Hampden Park; Attendance 74,000;
Referee: Mr G. B. Smith (Edinburgh)

CELTIC 2 — **DUNDEE UNITED 1**
McAvennie (2) — Gallacher

SEASON 1988/89

20th May, 1989 at Hampden Park; Attendance 72,069;
Referee: Mr R. B. Valentine (Dundee)

CELTIC 1 — **RANGERS 0**
Miller

SEASON 1989/90

12th May, 1990 at Hampden Park; Attendance 60,493;
Referee: Mr G. B. Smith (Edinburgh)

ABERDEEN 0 — **CELTIC 0**
After extra–time. Aberdeen won 9–8 on Kicks from the Penalty Mark

SEASON 1990/91

18th May, 1991 at Hampden Park; Attendance 57,319;
Referee: Mr D. F. T. Syme (Rutherglen)

MOTHERWELL 4 — **DUNDEE UNITED 3**
Ferguson, O'Donnell, Angus, Kirk — Bowman, O'Neil, Jackson
After extra–time - 3-3 after 90 minutes

SEASON 1991/92

9th May 1992 at Hampden Park; Attendance 44,045;
Referee: Mr D. D. Hope (Erskine)

RANGERS 2 — **AIRDRIEONIANS 1**
Hateley, McCoist — Smith

SEASON 1992/93

29th May, 1993 at Celtic Park; Attendance 50,715;
Referee: Mr J. McCluskey (Stewarton)

RANGERS 2 — **ABERDEEN 1**
Murray, Hateley — Richardson

SEASON 1993/94

21st May, 1994 at Hampden Park; Attendance 37,709;
Referee: Mr D. D. Hope (Erskine)

DUNDEE UNITED 1 — **RANGERS 0**
Brewster

SEASON 1994/95

27th May, 1995 at Hampden Park; Attendance 38,672;
Referee: Mr L. W. Mottram (Forth)

CELTIC 1 — **AIRDRIEONIANS 0**
Van Hooijdonk

SEASON 1995/96

18th May, 1996 at Hampden Park; Attendance 37,760;
Referee: Mr H. Dallas (Motherwell)

RANGERS 5 — **HEART OF MIDLOTHIAN 1**
Laudrup (2), Durie (3) — Colquhoun

Stenhousemuir – The Challenge Cup Winners 1995

First for Stenhousemuir

When The Scottish Football League lost their title sponsor of The B & Q Cup, they decided it was time for a spot of DIY and set about funding the competition themselves.

Having bravely nailed their colours - and cash - to the mast, the League bosses must have been delighted to see last season's tournament continue to build on its own success story and, no team can have more reason to be grateful for the continued existence of this competition, which began life as The Centenary Cup back in 1990, than Second Division Stenhousemuir.

The Warriors from Larbert used The League Challenge Cup as their vehicle towards writing their own piece of history by lifting their first piece of silverware (or crystal in this case) since their formation in 1884.

In true Braveheart style, the Warriors had to overcome the might of First Division promotion challengers, Dundee United, to make McDiarmid Park on Sunday, 5th November, an occasion the little town will never forget.

Even veteran Warriors (and Stenhousemuir have made them their trademark) like Eamonn Bannon could not hide his delight, nor did he attempt to, as Terry Christie's side gallantly fought out a goalless draw before emerging victorious from a dramatic penalty shoot-out. It was the culmination of a giant-killing act which finally reaped rewards. Stenhousemuir had made their mark on cup competitions earlier in the year with a glory run in the Scottish Cup which saw them take the scalps of St. Johnstone and Aberdeen before finally falling to Hibernian.

So it was not without some justification that Christie and Co. entered last season's Challenge Cup brimful of confidence.

They had to accept the role of spectators for the First Round, courtesy of a bye, and the tie attracting the attention of the Warriors and the rest of the participating clubs was staged at Firhill where former winners, Hamilton Academical and holders Airdrieonians, locked horns. The score was tied at one apiece after 90 minutes and had doubled by the end of extra-time before Accies won the penalty shoot-out 4-3.

The other shock of the round saw Greenock Morton go down 1-0 to become the first ever Challenge Cup victims of the newest name in the competition, Livingston.

Favourites, Dundee United, emerged from their trip to Stranraer with a 2-0 win, while Dundee took the scoring honours defeating East Fife 4-2 with more than a little help from hat-trick hero Jim Hamilton.

The Dens Park men continued their scoring run with a 3-0 home win over Cowdenbeath in the first of the Second Round matches, with their Tannadice neighbours matching that scoreline against Hamilton.

Meanwhile, at sleepy Stenhousemuir, things were beginning to wake following a convincing 3-1 demolition job of Montrose. Gareth Hutchison was the rampant Warrior, pillaging all three goals.

By the time Bannon and his team-mates headed to Tayside to face Dundee in the Third Round, many believed their cup sojourn was about to hit the buffers. But, as Eamonn recalls, it was this trip which provided the catalyst for them to go all the way.

"Beating Dundee 3-1 at Dens saw our Cup run gain momentum because we knew this was a very good result and that we had deserved it," he said.

"It is a competition everyone in the lower divisions enjoys playing in as they believe that, without the presence of the Premier Division clubs, this is one trophy they really do have a chance of winning."

"And, the further you go in the competition, the more confident you become. Our win at Dundee meant we were into the Semi-Finals where we faced Stirling Albion, a team from our own division."

"Once again, we played well and

The Challenge Cup 1995 –
Jimmy Fisher, George McGeachie and Graeme Armstrong of Stenhousemuir – The Warriors Win

earned a 2-1 win to book our place in the Final."

Waiting for them there was Dundee United, a team considered to be of Premier status but making, what turned out, to be a fleeting visit to the lower divisions.

They had won through to the McDiarmid Park gala day thanks to a solitary goal from 18 year-old Ben Honeyman at Clydebank, followed by a comprehensive 4-0 dismissal of fellow promotion pushers Dunfermline Athletic in the other Semi-Final tie at East End Park.

Now, the experts would have had us believe, Billy Kirkwood's men only had to travel the short distance to Perth to collect the trophy and the £14,000 first prize.

But, in front of an enthusiastic crowd of almost 8,000, the Tangerine dream was quickly transformed into a Tangerine nightmare.

As a former United hero, Bannon knew all about his old team's cup tradition. He had helped them reach the UEFA Cup Final, the Semi-Final of the European Cup, win the Premier Division Championship, lift the League Cup on two occasions and, finish runners-up in too many Scottish Cup Finals for him to remember voluntarily.

Bannon knew relegation the previous season had hit United hard. But, under the guidance of his former team-mate Kirkwood, they were on the way back with a side which packed quality seldom seen at this level.

Admitted Bannon, "It seemed all of Stenhousemuir had travelled with us, and the party atmosphere was terrific. But, really, few people gave us much of a chance."

"I reckoned we would do well to hold United to half-time because, on paper, they had the better players."

"But, when we got in at the interval without any scoring, we realised we had not just been lucky. We had made good scoring chances ourselves and were right in the game. So, it was no surprise when we managed to hold our own to the end of the 90 minutes and then through extra-time."

"When you get to a penalty shoot-out, the team that started out as underdogs always fancies their chances."

It was at this point Lady Luck gave a final smile in the direction of the brave Warriors. Bannon offered some words of advice to Stenhousemuir 'keeper, Roddy McKenzie, and unwittingly handed the Warriors the trophy.

He told Roddy that Owen Coyle always hit his penalties to a goalkeeper's left. But, Eamonn hadn't noticed Owen was off the park by then and the United player about to take the penalty was, in fact, Craig Brewster.

S·F·L ©

Eamonn recalls: "Roddy saw that the man in front of him was about to hit the ball with his left foot, so reckoned it must be Owen and dived to his left."

"Fortunately for us, Craig did hit his penalty into that corner and Roddy was able to save it."

It was a case of mistaken identity which mattered little to the Stenhousemuir players who made their way back to Ochilview for a fireworks night party which was anything but a damp squib.

"We had a fabulous time celebrating," admitted Bannon, "and I enjoyed it all the more because I was at the stage of my career when winning trophies was not something I expected to be doing."

"I can honestly say winning the League Challenge Cup gave me as much pleasure as any other achievement in my career."

He was looking forward to leading Falkirk into this season's competition after making the short journey from the Stenhousemuir defence to the Brockville manager's chair during the summer.

However, an early exit from this season's tournaments put paid to that ambition, but nonetheless, he will always remember with great affection, the unexpected League Challenge Cup winners' medal that he won with Stenhousemuir in the autumn of his playing career.

RONNIE CULLY
(Evening Times)

Gareth Hutchison – "rampant Warrior"

FIRST ROUND

Saturday, 19th August, 1995

ALBION ROVERS 2 ROSS COUNTY 2
(A.E.T. - 1-1 After 90 Minutes)
M. Scott, J. McBride C. Milne, G. Connelly
Albion Rovers won 3-2 on Kicks from the Penalty Mark

Albion Rovers: D. Moonie, D. Riley, (D. McDonald), J. Gallagher, C. Shanks, M. Ryan, B. Strain, B. Deeley, L. Collins, M. Scott, J. McBride, (D. Seggie), G. Young
Substitute not used: J. Wight (Goalkeeper)

Ross County: S. Hutchison, C. Somerville, D. Mackay, R. Williamson, W. Herd, W. Furphy, (G. Campbell), K. Ferries, (R. McFee), B. Grant, (J. MacPherson), C. Milne, G. Connelly, D. Crainie
Attendance: 315

Tuesday, 22nd August, 1995

STIRLING ALBION 3 QUEEN'S PARK 0
T. Tait (2), S. McCormick
Stirling Albion: M. McGeown, M. McKechnie, P. Watson, C. Mitchell, R. McQuilter, T. Tait, I. McInnes, P. Deas, S. McCormick, (A. Farquhar), C. Taggart, J. McLeod
Substitutes not used: J. Gibson, M. Monaghan (Goalkeeper)

Queen's Park: J. Chalmers, D. Graham, K. McGoldrick, D. McGrath, G. Elder, K. Kennedy, D. Brodie, (C. Porter), R. Caven, S. Edgar, B. McPhee, (P. Ferguson), J. Matchett
Substitute not used: C. Bruce (Goalkeeper)
Attendance: 546

DUMBARTON 0 BRECHIN CITY 1
G. Mearns
Dumbarton: I. MacFarlane, H. Burns, R. Fabiani, S. Gow, (C. McKinnon), P. Martin, J. Marsland, M. Mooney, T. King, C. Gibson, J. Charnley, (M. McGarvey), A. Granger, (S. McGivern)

Brechin City: R. Allan, G. Mearns, R. Brown, H. Cairney, F. Conway, G. Christie, R. Brand, (R. Smith), C. Farnan, G. Price, W.D. Scott, S. Ferguson
Substitutes not used: S. Marr, R. Baillie
Attendance: 524

CLYDEBANK 2 ARBROATH 0
S. Kerrigan (2)
Clydebank: G. Matthews, C. Tomlinson, P. Lovering, S. Murdoch, T. Currie, D. Nicholls, S. Kerrigan, G. Connell, J. Grady, (P. Prior), J. Robertson, (G. Teale), G. Bowman
Substitute not used: D. Crawford

Arbroath: G. Dunn, T. McMillan, S. Florence, P. Clark, J. Fowler, J. Crawford, D. Pew, I. Porteous, (S. McCormick), C. McLean, A. Kennedy, J. McAulay, (S. Peters)
Substitute not used: C. Hinchcliffe (Goalkeeper)
Attendance: 345

QUEEN OF THE SOUTH 0 FORFAR ATHLETIC 1
R. Mann
Queen of the South: J. Butter, K. Hetherington, (S. Cody), J. Brown, B. McKeown, D. Kennedy, S. Ramsay, S. Wilson, A. McFarlane, C. Harris, D. Campbell (D. Jackson), T. Bryce, (S. Mallan)

Forfar Athletic: G. Arthur, S. Glennie, D. McVicar, (H. O'Neill), R. Mann, A. McKillop, D. Craig, A. Morgan, M. Bowes, P. Hannigan, D. Bingham, N. Irvine, (A. Paterson)
Substitute not used: J. Donegan (Goalkeeper)
Attendance: 1,087

CALEDONIAN THISTLE 1 ALLOA 2
N. MacMillan D. Diver, B. Moffat
Caledonian Thistle: M. McRitchie, D. Brennan, R. Hastings, M. Noble, R. Benson, N. MacMillan, D. Ross, M. Lisle, (G. Bennett), I. Stewart, C. Christie, D. Green
Substitutes not used: D. McGinlay, J. Scott

Alloa: P. Graham, G. Smith, D. Cully, J. McCormack, D. Lawrie, N. Bennett, S. Morrison, (R. Wylie), D. Diver, B. Moffat, S. Rixon, C. McKenzie, (M. Whyte)
Substitute not used: M. Nelson
Attendance: 878

EAST FIFE 2 DUNDEE 4
R. Scott (2) I. Anderson, J. Hamilton (3)
East Fife: L. Hamilton, J. McStay, A. Hamill, (S. Archibald), J. Cusick, D. Beaton, M. Donaghy, R. Hildersley, G. Allan, R. Scott, B. Andrew, D. Hope
Substitutes not used: D. Robertson (Goalkeeper), S. Hutcheon

Dundee: M. Pageaud, R. Farningham, T. McQueen, R. Manley, K. Bain, A. Cargill, I. Anderson, D. Vrto, (M. Wieghorst), G. Shaw, J. Hamilton, (G. Britton), N. McCann, (C. Tully)
Attendance: 1,157

HAMILTON ACADEMICAL 2 AIRDRIEONIANS 2
(A.E.T. - 1-1 After 90 Minutes)
G. Clark (2) J. Boyle, J. McIntyre
Hamilton Academical won 4-3 on Kicks from the Penalty Mark
Hamilton Academical: D. Cormack, P. McKenzie, S. McInulty, S. McEntegart, C. Paterson, M. McIntosh, P. Hartley, (C. Baptie), J. Sherry, S. McCormick, (D. McCarrison), J. McQuade, S. McCulloch, (G. Clark)

Airdrieonians: J. Martin, A. Stewart, P. Jack, (J. Boyle), J. Sandison, S. Sweeney, K. Black, (M. Wilson), G. Connelly, (J. McIntyre), J. Davies, S. Cooper, P. Duffield, A. Smith
Attendance: 883

CLYDE 0 ST. JOHNSTONE 2
P. Scott, J. O'Neil
Clyde: J. Hillcoat, G. Watson, I. Angus, (G. Ferguson), K. Gillies, K. Knox, J. Brown, M. O'Neill, C. Nicholas, E. Annand, T. Harrison, G. Parks, (I. McConnell)
Substitute not used: J. McQueen (Goalkeeper)

St. Johnstone: A. Main, J. McQuillan, A. Preston, M. Proctor, (G. Farquhar), D. Griffin, K. McGowne, P. Scott, R. Grant, (K. Twaddle), J. O'Neil, G. O'Boyle, S. Tosh, (D. Irons)
Attendance: 1,020

EAST STIRLINGSHIRE 0 ST. MIRREN 3
R. Dawson, B. Lavety (2)
East Stirlingshire: G. McDougall, L. Cuthbert, (D. Watt), R. Lee, M. McBride, S. Sneddon, A. Neill, S. MacLean, (D. Stirling), C. Scott, M. Geraghty, M. Abercromby, T. McKenna
Substitute not used: J. Orr

St. Mirren: A. Combe, R. Dawson, M. Baker, J. Fullarton, S. Watson, (J. Dick), B. Smith, R. Law, B. Hetherston, B. Lavety, A. Bone, (J. McMillan), J. Boyd, (G. McGrotty)
Attendance: 648

AYR UNITED 1 DUNFERMLINE ATHLETIC 2
(A.E.T. - 1-1 After 90 Minutes)
B. Bilsland M. Millar, J. McNamara
Ayr United: W. Lamont, R. Tannock, D. Boyce, C. MacFarlane, F. Rolling, J. Sharples, A. Shepherd, B. Bilsland, S. Wilson, S. Stainrod, (S. Connolly), V. Moore, (K. Biggart)
Substitute not used: K. McKay

Dunfermline Athletic: G. Van De Kamp, I. Den Bieman, M. Millar, N. McCathie, A. Tod, P. Smith, A. Moore, J. McNamara, (N. Cooper), G. Shaw, (D. Fleming), S. Petrie, P. Kinnaird, (M. McCulloch)
Attendance: 1,209

MONTROSE 2 BERWICK RANGERS 1
P. Masson, D. Grant A. Cole
Montrose: R. Massie, K. Tindal, L. Stephen, P. Masson, D. Grant, J. Tosh, I. MacDonald, N. McAvoy, (C. Cooper), C. McGlashan, S. Smith, C. MacRonald
Substitutes not used:I. Robertson, S. Taylor

Berwick Rangers: N. Young, C. Valentine, A. Banks, A. Cole, M. Cowan, G. Fraser, T. Graham, M. Neil, P. Rutherford, W. Irvine, K. Walton, (P. Forrester)
Substitutes not used: A. Reid, N. Clegg
Attendance: 420

Wednesday, 23rd August, 1995

STRANRAER 0 DUNDEE UNITED 2
C. Brewster, W. McKinlay
Stranraer: S. Ross, J. Hughes, G. Duncan, J. Robertson, J. McCaffrey, T. Callaghan, (D. McGuire), T. Sloan, W. Ferguson, (A. Grant), T. Walker, I. McAulay, D. Henderson
Substitute not used: P. McLean

Dundee United: A. Maxwell, M. Perry, R. Shannon, S. Pressley, B. Welsh, D. Bowman, A. McLaren, A. Robertson, (W. McKinlay), C. Brewster, S. Crabbe, (P. Connolly), N. Caldwell, (R. Winters)
Attendance: 576

LIVINGSTON 1 GREENOCK MORTON 0
W. Callaghan
Livingston: H. Stoute, T. Graham, M. Duthie, G. Davidson, S. Williamson, C. Smart, G. McMartin, G. Harvey, W. Callaghan, D. Alleyne, C. Sinclair, (S. Sorbie)
Substitutes not used: L. Bailey, J. Young

Greenock Morton: D. Wylie, D. Johnstone, (P. Blair), S. McArthur, J. Anderson, S. McCahill, J. Lindberg, D. Lilley, (W. Hawke), A. Mahood, D. Laing, D. McInnes, M. Rajamaki
Substitute not used: C. McPherson
Attendance: 303

SECOND ROUND

Monday, 11th September, 1995

DUNDEE 3 COWDENBEATH 0
A. Cargill, G. Shaw, I. Anderson
Dundee: M. Pageaud, R. Farningham, T. McQueen, C. Duffy, A. Cargill, R. McBain, (M. Teasdale), G. Shaw, (J. O'Driscoll), D. Vrto, P. Tosh, J. Hamilton, I. Anderson, (K. Bain)

Cowdenbeath: N. Russell, C. Winter, (C. Smith), G. Meldrum, M. Humphreys, B. McMahon, (E. Petrie), B. Malloy, G. Wood, S. Steven, D. Scott, M. Yardley, G. Buckley, (G. Soutar)
Attendance: 1,101

Tuesday, 12th September, 1995

ALBION ROVERS 1 BRECHIN CITY 3
P. Crawford R. Brown, R. Brand (2)
Albion Rovers: M. Osborne, D. McDonald, J. Gallagher, B. Strain, M. Ryan, (D. Miller), C. Shanks, L. Collins, (D. Seggie), B. Deeley, P. Crawford, J. McBride, R. Russell
Substitute not used: K. Quinn

Brechin City: R. Allan, B. Mitchell, R. Brown, H. Cairney, F. Conway, G. Christie, R. Smith, (G. Mearns), C. Farnan, A. Ross, W.D. Scott, R. Brand
Substitutes not used: S. Garden (Goalkeeper), S. Ferguson
Attendance: 214

ALLOA 2	STIRLING ALBION 4
B. Moffat (2)	J. Gibson, S. McCormick, C. Taggart, J. McLeod

Alloa: R. Balfour, K. Hannah, V. Conway, (M. Nelson), J. McCormack, R. Wylie, J. Gilmour, D. Kirkham, D. Diver, B. Moffat, M. Whyte, S. Cadden
Substitutes not used: S. Morrison, S. Rixon
Stirling Albion: M. McGeown, A. Paterson, P. Watson, C. Mitchell, R. McQuilter, T. Tait, J. Gibson, (M. McKechnie), P. Deas, S. McCormick, (W. Watters), C. Taggart, J. McLeod
Substitute not used: M. Monaghan (Goalkeeper)
Attendance: 722

DUNFERMLINE ATHLETIC 2	FORFAR ATHLETIC 1
G. Shaw, A. Tod	D. Bingham

Dunfermline Athletic: G. Van De Kamp, P. Fenwick, (A. Tod), D. Fleming, (P. Kinnaird), N. McCathie, C. Robertson, P. Smith, A. Moore, J. McNamara, G. Shaw, S. Petrie, M. Millar, (I. Den Bieman)
Forfar Athletic: G. Arthur, H. O'Neill, D. McVicar, R. Mann, A. McKillop, D. Craig, A. Morgan, M. Bowes, P. Hannigan, D. Bingham, I. McPhee
Substitutes not used: A. Paterson, J. Loney, J. Donegan (Goalkeeper)
Attendance: 2,083

DUNDEE UNITED 3	HAMILTON ACADEMICAL 0
I.G. Johnson, P. Connolly (2)	

Dundee United: K. O'Hanlon, M. Perry, R. Shannon, S. Pressley, C. Dailly, M. Malpas, P. Walker, W. McKinlay, S. Crabbe, (R. Winters), I.G. Johnson, P. Connolly
Substitutes not used: D. Craig, A. Maxwell (Goalkeeper)
Hamilton Academical: A. Ferguson, C. Hillcoat, S. Renicks, R. McStay, (D. Lorimer),C. Baptie, M. McIntosh, G. Clark, J. Sherry, D. McCarrison, I. McQuade, (P. Hartley), J.I. McParland, (P. McKenzie)
Attendance: 3,512

STENHOUSEMUIR 3	MONTROSE 1
G. Hutchison (3)	C. McGlashan

Stenhousemuir: R. McKenzie, E. Bannon, L. Haddow, G. Armstrong, G. McGeachie, J. Henderson, (A. Sprott), P. Logan, (D. Swanson), N. Aitken, (J. Clarke), M. Mathieson, G. Hutchison, I. Little
Montrose: D. Larter, C. MacRonald, (C. Cooper), L. Stephen, S. Smith, D. Grant, J. Tosh, I. MacDonald, N. McAvoy, C. McGlashan, S. Taylor, A. Ferrie
Substitute not used: R. Massie
Attendance: 280

CLYDEBANK 3	ST. JOHNSTONE 0
D. Nicholls, J. Grady (2)	

Clydebank: A. Monaghan, P. Agnew (I. McLaughlin), C. Sutherland, S. Murdoch, T. Currie, D. Nicholls, J. Robertson, G. Connell, C. Flannigan, (G. Teale), J. Grady, G. Bowman
Substitute not used: P. Lovering
St. Johnstone: A. Main, J. McQuillan, A. Preston, M. Proctor, P. Cherry, D. Irons, P. Scott, (R. Grant), J. O'Neil, K. Twaddle, (S. McLean), G. O'Boyle, G. Farquhar, (D. Griffin)
Attendance: 560

Wednesday, 13th September, 1995

LIVINGSTON 2	ST. MIRREN 0
C. Sinclair, J. Young	

Livingston: H. Stoute, C. McCartney, M. Duthie, G. Davidson, T. Graham, G. McLeod, G. McMartin, C. Smart, W. Callaghan, G. Harvey, (J. Young), C. Sinclair
Substitutes not used: L. Bailey, S. Sorbie
St. Mirren: A. Combe, R. Dawson, M. Baker, J. Dick, S. Watson, B. McLaughlin, R. Law, (S. Taylor), J. Fullarton, R. Gillies, A. Bone, (J. Boyd), G. McGrotty, (B. Hetherston)
Attendance: 469

THIRD ROUND

Monday, 25th September, 1995

DUNDEE 1	STENHOUSEMUIR 3
A. Cargill	M. Mathieson, I. Little, K. Bain (o.g.)

Dundee: P. Mathers, A. Matheson, M. Hutchison, (G. Shaw), J. Duffy, A. Cargill, R. McBain, I. Anderson, (G. Cadger), K. Bain, M. Dailly, J. Hamilton, N. McCann, (G. Britton)
Stenhousemuir: R. McKenzie, E. Bannon, L. Haddow, G. Armstrong, G. McGeachie, A. Sprott, P. Hunter, (P. Logan), J. Fisher, M. Mathieson, G. Hutchison, I. Little, (J. Henderson)
Substitute not used: N. Aitken
Attendance: 1,128

Tuesday, 26th September, 1995

DUNFERMLINE ATHLETIC 2	BRECHIN CITY 0
G. Shaw, S. Petrie	

Dunfermline Athletic: G. Van De Kamp, J. McNamara, D. Fleming, P. Fenwick, A. Tod, M. McCulloch, (P. Smith), A. Moore, (I. Den Bieman), C. Robertson, G. Shaw, S. Petrie, P. Kinnaird
Substitute not used: N. McCathie

Brechin City: R. Allan, B. Mitchell, R. Brown, H. Cairney, F. Conway, G. Christie, J. McKellar, C. Farnan, A. Ross, G. Mearns, S. Reid, (W. McNeill)
Substitutes not used: S. Marr, S. Garden (Goalkeeper)
Attendance: 2,006

CLYDEBANK 0	DUNDEE UNITED 1
	B. Honeyman

Clydebank: G. Matthews, C. Tomlinson, (P. Agnew), C. Sutherland, A. Lansdowne, T. Currie, D. Nicholls, G. Teale, G. Connell,S. Kerrigan, (C. Flannigan), J. Grady, G. Bowman
Substitute not used: P. Lovering
Dundee United: K. O'Hanlon, M. Perry, R. Shannon, D. Gray, C. Dailly, M. Malpas, N. Caldwell, I.G. Johnson, P. Walker, B. Honeyman, S. Gilmour
Substitutes not used: A. McLaren, R. Winters, A. Maxwell (Goalkeeper)
Attendance: 835

Wednesday, 27th September, 1995

LIVINGSTON 1	STIRLING ALBION 1
(A.E.T. - 1-1 After 90 Minutes)	
G. McLeod	J. McLeod

Stirling Albion Won 4-2 on Kicks from the Penalty Mark
Livingston: H. Stoute, S. Williamson, M. Duthie, G. Davidson, T. Graham, C. Smart, D. Alleyne, (S. Sorbie), G. Harvey, (J. Young), W. Callaghan, (L. Bailey), G. McLeod, G. McMartin
Stirling Albion: M. Monaghan, A. Paterson, J. Gibson, (P. Roberts), C. Mitchell, R. McQuilter, T. Tait, I. McInnes, P. Deas, S. McCormick, (W. Watters), C. Taggart, J. McLeod
Substitute not used: P. Watson
Attendance: 283

SEMI-FINALS

Wednesday, 4th October, 1995

STIRLING ALBION 1	STENHOUSEMUIR 2
S. McCormick	P. Logan, G. Hutchison

Stirling Albion: M. Monaghan, A. Paterson, J. Gibson, (W. Watters), C. Mitchell, R. McQuilter, T. Tait, I. McInnes, (P. Roberts), P. Deas, S. McCormick, C. Taggart, J. McLeod
Substitute not used: P. Watson
Stenhousemuir: R. McKenzie, E. Bannon, (N. Aitken), A. Sprott, (J. Henderson), G. Armstrong, K. Brannigan, P. Logan, (D. Swanson), P. Hunter, J. Fisher, M. Mathieson, G. Hutchison, I. Little
Attendance: 1,099

DUNFERMLINE ATHLETIC 0	DUNDEE UNITED 4
	C. Dailly, R. Winters (2), I.G. Johnson

Dunfermline Athletic: G. Van De Kamp, I. Den Bieman, D. Fleming, A. Tod, P. Fenwick, (N. McCathie), P. Smith, M. McCulloch, (G. Farrell), C. Robertson, G. Shaw, S. Petrie, P. Kinnaird
Substitute not used: I. Westwater (Goalkeeper)
Dundee United: K. O'Hanlon, M. Perry, R. Shannon, D. Gray, C. Dailly, M. Malpas, R. Winters, A. Robertson, B. Welsh, I.G. Johnson, A. McLaren, (P. Walker)
Substitutes not used: D. Mitchell, A. Maxwell (Goalkeeper)
Attendance: 4,900

FINAL

Sunday, 5th November, 1995

McDiarmid Park, Perth

STENHOUSEMUIR 0	DUNDEE UNITED 0

(A.E.T.) Stenhousemuir won 5-4 on Kicks from the Penalty Mark
Stenhousemuir: R. McKenzie, E. Bannon, L. Hadddow, G. Armstrong, G. McGeachie, A. Sprott, P. Hunter, J. Fisher, (T. Steel), M. Mathieson, G. Hutchison, I. Little
Substitutes not used: N. Aitken, P. Logan
Dundee United: A. Maxwell, R. Shannon, M. Malpas, S. Pressley, C. Dailly, R. McKinnon, A. McLaren, (J. McQuilken), I.G. Johnson, G. McSwegan, O. Coyle, (C. Brewster), R. Winters
Substitute not used: K. O'Hanlon (Goalkeeper)

Referee: J. Rowbotham (Kirkcaldy)

Attendance: 7,856

ROUND BY ROUND GOALS ANALYSIS

	No. of Goals Scored	Ties Played	Average Per Game
First Round	38	14	2.7
Second Round	28	8	3.5
Third Round	9	4	2.25
Semi-Finals	7	2	3.5
Final	0	1	0
Total No. of Goals Scored:		**82**	
Ties Played		**29**	
Average Goals per Game:		**2.8**	

League Challenge Cup Final Results Since 1990/91

(In Season 1990/91 known as The B&Q Centenary Cup; In Seasons 1991/92 to 1994/95 known as The B&Q Cup)

SEASON 1990/91
Sunday, 11th November, 1990 at Fir Park, Motherwell;
Attendance 11,506, Referee: K.J. Hope (Clarkston)

AYR UNITED 2 — **DUNDEE 3**
(AET - 2-2 After 90 Minutes)
D. Smyth, I. McAllister — W. Dodds (3)

SEASON 1991/92
Sunday, 8th December, 1991 at Fir Park, Motherwell;
Attendance 9,663, Referee: L.W. Mottram (Forth)

HAMILTON ACADEMICAL 1 — **AYR UNITED 0**
C. Harris

SEASON 1992/93
Sunday, 13th December, 1992 at St. Mirren Park, Paisley;
Attendance 7,391, Referee: J.J. Timmons (Kilwinning)

MORTON 2 — **HAMILTON ACADEMICAL 3**
R. Alexander (2) — C. Hillcoat, G. Clark (2)

SEASON 1993/94
Sunday, 12th December, 1993 at Fir Park, Motherwell;
Attendance 13,763, Referee: D.D. Hope (Erskine)

FALKIRK 3 — **ST. MIRREN 0**
C. Duffy, J. Hughes, R. Cadette

SEASON 1994/95
Sunday, 6th November, 1994 at McDiarmid Park, Perth;
Attendance 8,844, Referee: H.F. Williamson (Renfrew)

DUNDEE 2 — **AIRDRIEONIANS 3**
(AET - 2-2After 90 Minutes)
G. Britton, G. Hay (o.g.) — P. Harvey, J. Boyle, Andrew Smith

SEASON 1995/96
Sunday, 5th November, 1995 at McDiarmid Park, Perth;
Attendance 7,856, Referee: J. Rowbotham (Kirkcaldy)

STENHOUSEMUIR 0 — **DUNDEE UNITED 0 (A.E.T.)**
Stenhousemuir won 5-4 on Kicks from the Penalty Mark

Reserve League Cup – Season 1995/96

PRELIMINARY ROUND
15th August, 1995
DUNDEE UNITED 4 — MONTROSE 0
21st August, 1995
QUEEN OF THE SOUTH 1 — ST. JOHNSTONE 3

FIRST ROUND
7th August, 1995
STENHOUSEMUIR 2 — BERWICK RANGERS 0
15th August, 1995
ARBROATH 2 — AIRDRIEONIANS 1
19th September, 1995
DUMBARTON 9 — STRANRAER 2
20th September, 1995
HAMILTON ACADEMICAL 0 — EAST FIFE 1
(Match played at Bayview Park, Methil)
21st September, 1995
CLYDEBANK 4 — ALLOA 2
25th September, 1995
BRECHIN CITY 4 — QUEEN'S PARK 3
26th September, 1995
ST. MIRREN 2 — LIVINGSTON 1
27th September, 1995
CLYDE 1 — DUNDEE 1
(AET–1-1 After 90 minutes)
Clyde won 4-3 on Kicks from the Penalty Mark
DUNFERMLINE ATHLETIC 3COWDENBEATH 0
29th September, 1995
ST. JOHNSTONE 0 — DUNDEE UNITED 1
9th October, 1995
STIRLING ALBION 2 — GREENOCK MORTON 1
**FORFAR ATHLETIC -v- ALBION ROVERS

** PLEASE NOTE: Albion Rovers F.C. withdrew from all Reserve football after the draw for this competition was made and therefore, Forfar Athletic F.C. received a bye into the Second Round.

SECOND ROUND
16th October, 1995
CLYDE 2 — DUNDEE UNITED 3
17th October, 1995
CLYDEBANK 4 — ST. MIRREN 2
25th October, 1995
EAST FIFE 4 — DUMBARTON 1
30th October, 1995
BRECHIN CITY 0 — STENHOUSEMUIR 5
STIRLING ALBION 3 — FORFAR ATHLETIC 2
6th November, 1995
DUNFERMLINE ATHLETIC 4 — ARBROATH 0

THIRD ROUND
21st November, 1995
ABERDEEN 1 — HEART OF MIDLOTHIAN 1
(AET–1-1 After 90 minutes)
Heart of Midlothian won 4-2 on Kicks from the Penalty Mark
23rd November, 1995
KILMARNOCK 4 — STENHOUSEMUIR 2
27th November, 1995
PARTICK THISTLE 3 — RAITH ROVERS 2
29th November, 1995
DUNFERMLIINE ATHLETIC 3 — EAST FIFE 1
FALKIRK 2 — HIBERNIAN 1
30th November, 1995
CELTIC 5 — DUNDEE UNITED 0
STIRLING ALBION 2 — MOTHERWELL 2
(AET–1-1 After 90 minutes)
Stirling Albion won 4-3 on Kicks from the Penalty Mark
RANGERS 3 — CLYDEBANK 1

FOURTH ROUND
15th February, 1996
FALKIRK 1 — CELTIC 3
7th March, 1996
KILMARNOCK 1 — DUNFERMLINE ATHLETIC (
18th March, 1996
STIRLING ALBION 0 — PARTICK THISTLE 3
1st April, 1996
RANGERS 1 — HEART OF MIDLOTHIAN (

SEMI-FINALS
23rd April, 1996
KILMARNOCK 0 — RANGERS 1
30th April, 1996
PARTICK THISTLE 0 — CELTIC 2

FINAL
Thursday, 9th May, 1996 - St. Mirren Park, Paisley
RANGERS 0 — CELTIC 1 (AET)

Rangers: C. Scott, N. Murray, (L. Robertson), G. Shields, A. Mikhailitchenko, (B. McGinty), I. Nicolson, G. Petric, E.B. Andersen, I. Ferguson, (S. Boyack), C. Miller, I. Durrant, P. Van Vossen

Celtic: S. Kerr, D. Boyle, S. Gray, B. O'Neil, M. Mackay, G. Carberry, P. Kelly, (P. Dalglish), R. Vata, C. Hay, M. Anthony, B. McLaughlin
Substitutes not used: G. Morrison, P. Bonner (Goalkeeper)

Scorer: M. Anthony
Referee: I. M. Fyfe (Linlithgow)
Attendance: 5,304

EUROPEAN CHAMPIONSHIP QUALIFYING GROUP EIGHT

16th August, 1995 - Hampden Park, Glasgow

SCOTLAND 1 McCoist — **GREECE 0**

Scotland: J. Leighton, C. Calderwood, S. McKimmie, T. Boyd, C. Burley, S. McCall, G. McAllister, J. Collins, T. McKinlay, D. Jackson, (J. Robertson), D. Shearer, (A. McCoist)

Greece: Atmatzidis, Karataidis, Dabizas, Kalitzakis, Zagorakis, (Georgiadis), Apostolakis, Tsalouchidis, Tsartas, Kassapis, Vryzas, (Machlas), Batista, (Alexandris)

Attendance: 34,910

6th September, 1995 - Hampden Park, Glasgow

SCOTLAND 1 Booth — **FINLAND 0**

Scotland: J. Leighton, C. Calderwood, C. Hendry, T. Boyd, S. McKimmie, (W. McKinlay), A. McLaren, G. McAllister, J. Collins, T. McKinlay, S. Booth, (D. Jackson), J. Spencer, (A. McCoist)

Finland: Laukkanen, Kanerva, Suominen, Rissanen, Holmgren, Nieminen, (Gronlund), Myyry, Litmanen, Lindberg, Jarvinen, Hjelm

Attendance: 35,505

15th November, 1995
Hampden Park, Glasgow

SCOTLAND 5 Jess, Booth, McCoist, Nevin, Francini (o.g.) — **SAN MARINO 0**

Scotland: J. Leighton, A. McLaren, T. Boyd, C. Calderwood, C. Hendry, S. Gemmill, P. Nevin, S. Booth, (D. Jackson), E. Jess, G. McAllister, (A. McCoist), J. Collins, (W. McKinlay)

San Marino: Muccioli, Moroni, Gennari, Mazza, (Della Valle), Valentini, Guerra, (Montagna), Manzaroli, Matteoni, Bacciocchi, Mularoni, (Canti), Francini

Attendance: 30,306

FINAL GROUP TABLE

	P	W	D	L	F	A	Pts
Russia	10	8	2	0	34	5	26
Scotland	10	7	2	1	19	3	23
Greece	10	6	0	4	23	9	18
Finland	10	5	0	5	18	18	15
Faroe Islands	10	2	0	8	10	35	6
San Marino	10	0	0	10	2	36	0

Euro '96 England v Scotland – Gary McAllister outjumps Paul Ince

EURO '96 - GROUP A

8th June, 1996 - Wembley Stadium, London

ENGLAND 1 Shearer — **SWITZERLAND 1** Turkyilmaz (Pen)

Attendance: 76,567

10th June, 1996 - Villa Park, Birmingham

SCOTLAND 0 — **HOLLAND 0**

Scotland: A. Goram, S. McKimmie, (C. Burley), T. Boyd, C. Calderwood, C. Hendry, K. Gallacher, (W. McKinlay), S. McCall, G. McAllister, J. Collins, S. Booth, (J. Spencer), G. Durie

Holland: Van der Sar, Reiziger, de Kock, Bogarde, Davids, R de Boer, (Winter), Seedorf, Witschge, (Cocu), Taument, (Kluivert), Bergkamp, Cruyff

Attendance: 34,363

13th June, 1996 - Villa Park, Birmingham

HOLLAND 2 Cruyff, Bergkamp — **SWITZERLAND 0**

Attendance: 38,000

15th June, 1996 - Wembley Stadium, London

SCOTLAND 0 — **ENGLAND 2** Shearer, Gascoigne

Scotland: A. Goram, S. McKimmie, T. Boyd, C. Calderwood, C. Hendry, J. Spencer, (A. McCoist), S. McCall, G. McAllister, J. Collins T. McKinlay, (C. Burley), G. Durie, (E. Jess)

England: D. Seaman, G. Neville, S. Pearce, (J. Redknapp), (S. Campbell), P. Ince, (S. Stone), T. Adams, G. Southgate, P. Gascoigne, A. Shearer, E. Sheringham, D. Anderton, S. McManaman

Attendance: 76,864

18th June, 1996 - Wembley Stadium, London

HOLLAND 1 Kluivert — **ENGLAND 4** Shearer (2 (1 Pen)), Sheringham (2)

Attendance: 76,798

18th June, 1996 - Villa Park, Birmingham

SCOTLAND 1 McCoist — **SWITZERLAND 0**

Scotland: A. Goram, T. Boyd, C. Calderwood, C. Hendry, S. McCall, A. McCoist, (J. Spencer), G. McAllister, J. Collins, T. McKinlay, (S. Booth), G. Durie, C. Burley

Switzerland: Pascolo, Hottiger, Quentin, (Comisetti), Henchoz, Sforza, Chapuisat, (Fournier), Turkyilmaz, Vega, Koller, (Wicky), Vogel, Bonvin

Attendance: 39,000

GROUP A - TABLE

	P	W	D	L	F	A	Pts
England	3	2	1	0	7	2	7
Holland	3	1	1	1	3	4	4
Scotland	3	1	1	1	1	2	4
Switzerland	3	0	1	2	1	4	1

GROUP B

9th June, 1996 - Elland Road, Leeds

SPAIN 1 Alfonso — **BULGARIA 1** Stoichkov (Pen)

Attendance: 26,006

10th June, 1996 - St. James' Park, Newcastle

ROMANIA 0 — **FRANCE 1** Dugarry

Attendance: 26,323

13th June, 1996 - St. James' Park, Newcastle

BULGARIA 1 Stoichkov — **ROMANIA 0**

Attendance: 19,107

15th June, 1996 - Elland Road, Leeds

FRANCE 1 Djorkaeff — **SPAIN 1** Caminero

Attendance: 35,626

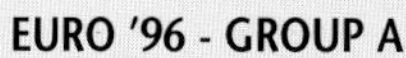

18th June, 1996 - St. James' Park, Newcastle

FRANCE 3 | **BULGARIA 1**
Blanc, Penev (o.g.), Loko | Stoichkov
Attendance: 26,976

18th June, 1996 - Elland Road, Leeds

ROMANIA 1 | **SPAIN 2**
Raducioiu | Manjarin, Amor
Attendance: 32,719

GROUP B - TABLE

	P	W	D	L	F	A	Pts
France	3	2	1	0	5	2	7
Spain	3	1	2	0	4	3	5
Bulgaria	3	1	1	1	3	4	4
Romania	3	0	0	3	1	4	0

GROUP C

9th June, 1996 - Old Trafford, Manchester

GERMANY 2 | **CZECH REPUBLIC 0**
Ziege, Moller
Attendance: 37,300

11th June, 1996 - Anfield, Liverpool

ITALY 2 | **RUSSIA 1**
Casiraghi (2) | Tsymbalar
Attendance: 35,120

14th June, 1996 - Anfield, Liverpool

CZECH REPUBLIC 2 | **ITALY 1**
Nedved, Bejbi | Chiesa
Attendance: 37,320

16th June, 1996 - Old Trafford, Manchester

RUSSIA 0 | **GERMANY 3**
Sammer, Klinsmann (2)
Attendance: 50,760

19th June, 1996 - Anfield, Liverpool

RUSSIA 3 | **CZECH REPUBLIC 3**
Mostovoi, Tetradze, Beschastnykh | Suchoparek, Kuka, Smicer
Attendance: 21,128

19th June, 1996 - Old Trafford, Manchester

ITALY 0 | **GERMANY 0**
Attendance: 53,740

GROUP C - TABLE

	P	W	D	L	F	A	Pts
Germany	3	2	1	0	5	0	7
Czech Republic	3	1	1	1	5	6	4
Italy	3	1	1	1	3	3	4
Russia	3	0	1	2	4	8	1

GROUP D

9th June, 1996 - Hillsborough, Sheffield

PORTUGAL 1 | **DENMARK 1**
Sa Pinto | B. Laudrup
Attendance: 34,993

11th June, 1996 - City Ground, Nottingham

TURKEY 0 | **CROATIA 1**
Vlaovic
Attendance: 22,460

14th June, 1996 - City Ground, Nottingham

PORTUGAL 1 | **TURKEY 0**
Couto
Attendance: 22,670

16th June, 1996 - Hillsborough, Sheffield

CROATIA 3 | **DENMARK 0**
Suker (2 (1 Pen)), Boban
Attendance: 33,671

19th June, 1996 - City Ground, Nottingham

CROATIA 0 | **PORTUGAL 3**
Figo, Pinto, Domingos
Attendance: 20,484

19th June, 1996 - Hillsborough, Sheffield

TURKEY 0 | **DENMARK 3**
B. Laudrup (2), Nielsen
Attendance: 28,951

GROUP D - TABLE

	P	W	D	L	F	A	Pts
Portugal	3	2	1	0	5	1	7
Croatia	3	2	0	1	4	3	6
Denmark	3	1	1	1	4	4	4
Turkey	3	0	0	3	0	5	0

QUARTER FINALS

22nd June, 1996 - Wembley Stadium, London

ENGLAND 0 | **SPAIN 0 (AET)**
England won 4-2 on Kicks from the Penalty Mark
Attendance: 75,440

22nd June, 1996 - Anfield, Liverpool

HOLLAND 0 | **FRANCE 0 (AET)**
France won 5-4 on Kicks from the Penalty Mark
Attendance: 37,465

23rd June, 1996 - Old Trafford, Manchester

GERMANY 2 | **CROATIA 1**
Klinsmann (Pen), Sammer | Suker
Attendance: 43,412

23rd June, 1996 - Villa Park, Birmingham

CZECH REPUBLIC 1 | **PORTUGAL 0**
Poborsky
Attendance: 26,832

SEMI-FINALS

26th June, 1996 - Old Trafford, Manchester

FRANCE 0 | **CZECH REPUBLIC 0 (AET)**
Czech Republic won 6-5 on Kicks from the Penalty Mark
Attendance: 43,877

26th June, 1996 - Wembley Stadium, London

ENGLAND 1 | **GERMANY 1**
(AET - 1-1 After 90 Minutes)
Shearer | Kuntz
Germany won 6-5 on Kicks from the Penalty Mark
Attendance: 75,862

FINAL

30th June, 1996 - Wembley Stadium, London

GERMANY 2 | **CZECH REPUBLIC 1**
(AET - 1-1 After 90 Minutes)
Bierhoff (2) | Berger (Pen)
Attendance: 73,611

FULL INTERNATIONAL FRIENDLY MATCHES

11th October, 1995 - Rasunda Stadium, Solna

SWEDEN 2 | **SCOTLAND 0**
Petterson, Schwarz

Sweden: B. Andersson, Lucic, P. Andersson, Bjorklund, Nilsson, Schwarz, Alexandersson, Gudmundsson, (Pringle), Petterson, K. Andersson, (Erlingmark), Brolin

Scotland: J. Leighton, (A. Goram), S. McKimmie, C, Calderwood, C. Hendry, C. Burley, (W. McKinlay), G. McAllister, (D. Jackson), A. McLaren, J. Collins, T. Boyd, J. Robertson, (P. Nevin), J. McGinlay, (E. Jess)

Attendance: 19,121

27th March, 1996 - Hampden Park, Glasgow

SCOTLAND 1 **AUSTRALIA 0**
McCoist

Scotland: J. Leighton, C. Burley, T. Boyd, B. O'Neil, (K. Gallacher), C. Hendry, W. McKinlay, (D. Jackson), J. Spencer, P. McStay, (S. Booth), A. McCoist, (P. Nevin), G. McAllister, J. Collins

Australia: Bosnich, T. Vidmar, Popovic, Van Blerk, Slater, Horvat, Arnold, A. Vidmar, Corica, Veart, (Tiatto), Tobin

Attendance: 20,608

24th April, 1996 - Parken Stadium, Copenhagen

DENMARK 2 **SCOTLAND 0**
M. Laudrup, B. Laudrup

Denmark: Schmeichel, (Krogh), Helveg, Rieper, Olsen, Risager, (Laursen), Schjonberg, Steen Nielsen, Thomsen, Beck, B. Laudrup, M. Laudrup, (A. Nielson)

Scotland: J. Leighton, (A. Goram), S. McKimmie, T. McKinlay, T. Boyd, C. Hendry, (W. McKinlay), S. McCall, (S. Gemmill), C. Burley, K. Gallacher, (A. McCoist), J. Spencer, (D. Jackson), G. McAllister, J. Collins

Attendance: 23,031

26th May, 1996 - Willowbrook Park, Connecticut

UNITED STATES OF AMERICA 2 **SCOTLAND 1**
Wynalda (Pen), Jones — Durie

United States of America: Sommer, Burns, Dooley, (Kirovski), Harkes, Ramos, Wynalda, Agoss, Jones, Balboa, Rayna, (McBride), Lalas

Scotland: J. Leighton, (J.N. Walker), T. Boyd, C. Burley, (S. McCall), C. Calderwood, C. Hendry, D. Whyte, E. Jess, D. Jackson, (J. Collins), S. Gemmill, (G. McAllister), S. Booth, G. Durie, (J. Spencer)

Attendance: 8,526

30th May, 1996 - The Orange Bowl, Miami

COLOMBIA 1 **SCOTLAND 0**
Asprilla

Colombia: Mondragon, Bermudez, Moreno, Ortiz, (Herrera), Cassiani, (Valderrama), Rincon, Estrada, (Mendoza), Serna, Mafla, (Asprilla), Valencia, (Aristizabal), Valencieno, (Alvarez)

Scotland: A. Goram, S. McKimmie, T. McKinlay, T. Boyd, C. Hendry, (C. Burley), C. Calderwood, J. Collins, G. McAllister, S. McCall, A. McCoist, (K. Gallacher), J. Spencer, (E. Jess)

Attendance: 12,000

UNDER 21 - EUROPEAN CHAMPIONSHIP

GROUP EIGHT

15th August, 1995 - Rugby Park, Kilmarnock

SCOTLAND 3 **GREECE 0**
McNamara, Liddell (Pen), Donnelly

Scotland: Stillie, McNamara, (McLaughlin), Gray, Fullarton, (Murray), Pressley, Hannah, Miller, Glass, Crawford, (Donnelly), Liddell, McCann

Greece: Karkanis, (Georgiou), Mavrogenidis, Kiassos, Theodoridis, (Lakis), Macheridis, (Grigoriou), Lygnos, Giannakopoulos, Passalis, Sapanis, Katsambis, Providas

Attendance: 2,517

6th September, 1995 - Broadwood Stadium, Cumbernauld

SCOTLAND 5 **FINLAND 0**
Harper (3), Hamilton, Locke

Scotland: Stillie, Murray, Fullarton, Locke, Handyside, Dailly, McNamara, Glass, Liddell, (Hamilton), Harper, (Crawford), McCann

Finland: Moilanen, Keula, Oinas, (Jalonen), Heinola, Nuorela, Hyypia, Javaja, (Huttunen), Karjalainen, Sumiala, Cottila, Vaisanen

Attendance: 2,571

14th November, 1995 - Firhill Stadium, Glasgow

SCOTLAND 1 **SAN MARINO 0**
Valentini (o.g.)

Scotland: Stillie, McNamara, (McNiven), Sheerin, Murray, Pressley, Handyside, Donnelly, Hamilton, (Freedman), Liddell, Dailly, McCann, (McLaughlin)

San Marino: Ceccoli, Giannini, Bacciocchi, Pelliccioni, Valentini, L. Gasperoni, B. Gasperoni, (Moretti), Muccioli, Ugolini, (Zucchi), Pancotti, (Zonzini), Gatti

Attendance: 3,000

FINAL GROUP TABLE

	P	W	D	L	F	A	Pts
Scotland	8	7	0	1	16	4	21
Finland	8	5	1	2	17	12	16
Russia	8	4	1	3	17	6	13
Greece	8	3	0	5	12	12	9
San Marino	8	0	0	8	1	29	0

QUARTER FINAL - First Leg

12th March, 1996 - Ulloi ut Stadium, Budapest

HUNGARY 2 **SCOTLAND 1**
Szanyo (pen), Zavadszky — Glass

Hungary: Szucs, Lendvai, Hrutkia, Sebok, Peto, Szatmari, (Zavadszky), Dombi, (Dardai), Lisztes, Sandor, (Preisinger), Szanyo, Egressy

Scotland: Stillie, McNamara, Glass, Ritchie, Pressley, Dailly, Donnelly, Murray, Crawford, (Fullarton), Liddell, Locke

Attendance: 15,000

Second Leg

26th March, 1996 - Easter Road Stadium, Edinburgh

SCOTLAND 3 **HUNGARY 1**
Dailly, Hamilton, Donnelly — Egressy

Scotland: Stillie, McNamara, (Hamilton), Gray, Marshall, Pressley, Dailly, (Crawford), Donnelly, Murray, (Baker), Liddell, Fullarton, McLaughlin

Hungary: Szucs, Molnar, Hrugka, Matyus, Peto, Sebok, Lendvai, Dardai, (Zavadszky), Lisztes, Szanyo, Egressy

Scotland Won 4-3 on Aggregate

Attendance: 9,173

SEMI-FINAL

28th May, 1996 - Barcelona

SPAIN 2 **SCOTLAND 1**
Oscar, De la Pena — Marshall

Spain: Mora, Mendieta, Aranzabal, Karanka, Santi, De la Pena, Roberto, Jose Ignacio, Oscar, (Morientes), Raul, Lardin

Scotland: Stillie, Dailly, Pressley, Marshall, McNamara, Miller, Gray, (Fullarton), Glass, Donnelly, Liddell, (Crawford), Johnston, (Hamilton)

Attendance: 15,500

THIRD AND FOURTH PLAY-OFF

31st May, 1996 - Barcelona

FRANCE 1 **SCOTLAND 0**
Moreau

France: Letizi, Candela, Bonnissel, La Ville, Moreau, Makelele, Dhorasso, Dacourt, Andre, (Corridon), Maurice, (Rott), Vairelles, (Wiltord)

Scotland: Stillie, (Meldrum), McNamara, Pressley, Marshall, Gray, Murray, Miller, Donnelly, Daily, (Crawford), Hamilton, (Liddell), Fullarton

Attendance: 10,000

"B" INTERNATIONAL MATCHES

10th October, 1995 - Stromvallen Stadium, Gavle

SWEDEN 1 **SCOTLAND 2**
Andreas Andersson — Shearer, Brown

Sweden: Hedman, (Green), Hansson, Y. Andersson, Jakobson, Sundgren, Wibran, Persson, Anders Andersson, (Pehrsson), Ljung, (Jonsson), Sahlin, Andreas Andersson

Scotland: J.N. Walker, (B. Gunn), B. Martin, D. Whyte, S. Tweed, R. McKinnon, P. Bernard, A. Rae, S. Gemmill, P. Telfer, D. Shearer, (T. Brown), G. Creaney, (K. Harper)

Attendance: 1,232

23rd April, 1996 - Idraetspark, Nykobing Falster

DENMARK 3 **SCOTLAND 0**
Larsen (2), Andersen

Denmark: Hogh, (Sorensen), Nielsen, Rytter, Tobiasen, (Sonksen), N. Jensen, J. Jensen, Larsen, Thomassen, Christensen, Christensen, Andersen, (Bjur)

Scotland: J.N. Walker, (M. Watt), J. McNamara, D. Whyte, P. Lambert, B. Martin, B. O'Neil, (J. Robertson), P. Nevin, E. Jess, J. McGinlay, (S. Booth), G. Durie, (D. Shearer), S. Glass, (C. Cameron)

Attendance: 3,796

1984/85

Premier Division
22 F. McDougall (Aberdeen)
19 B. McClair (Celtic)
17 E. Black (Aberdeen)
16 F. McAvennie (St. Mirren)
15 W. Stark (Aberdeen)
F. McGarvey (Celtic)
14 P. Sturrock (Dundee United)
M. Johnston (Celtic)
12 A. McCoist (Rangers)
10 E. Bannon (Dundee United)

First Division
22 G. McCoy (Falkirk)
21 D. MacCabe (Airdrieonians)
19 J. F. Frye (Clyde)
17 J. Flood (Airdrieonians)
K. Eadie (Brechin City)
14 K. Macdonald (Forfar Athletic)
A. Sprott (Meadowbank Thistle)
12 G. Murray (East Fife)
B. Millar (Kilmarnock)
A. Logan (Partick Thistle)

Second Division
27 B. Slaven (Albion Rovers)
22 K. Wright (Raith Rovers)
21 W. Irvine (Stirling Albion)
19 P. Smith (Raith Rovers)
18 J. Nicholson (Queen's Park)
16 D. Lloyd (Alloa)
K. Ward (Cowdenbeath)
15 J. Watson (Dunfermline Athletic)
12 I. Paterson (Cowdenbeath)
S. Maskrey (East Stirlingshire)
D. Somner (Montrose)

1985/86

Premier Division
24 A. McCoist (Rangers)
22 B. McClair (Celtic)
20 J. Robertson (Heart of Midlothian)
19 S. Cowan (Hibernian)
15 M. Johnston (Celtic)
14 F. McDougall (Aberdeen)
R. Stephen (Dundee)
12 D. Dodds (Dundee United)
A. Clark (Heart of Midlothian)
11 E. Bannon (Dundee United)
J. Brown (Dundee)

First Division
23 J. Brogan (Hamilton Academical)
22 K. Eadie (Brechin City)
15 J. Gilmour (Falkirk)
14 S. Kirk (East Fife)
I. Bryson (Kilmarnock)
J. McNeil (Morton)
13 G. McCoy (Dumbarton)
12 J. F. Frye (Clyde)
11 J. Flood (Airdrieonians)
M. Jamieson (Alloa)
S. Sorbie (Alloa)
J. McNaught (Hamilton Academical)
S. McGivern (Kilmarnock)
G. Smith (Partick Thistle)

Second Division
24 J. Watson (Dunfermline Athletic)
21 P. Smith (Raith Rovers)
K. Wright (Raith Rovers)
17 D. Jackson (Meadowbank Thistle)
A. Lawrence (Meadowbank Thistle)
W. Irvine (Stirling Albion)
15 C. McGlashan (Cowdenbeath)
I. M. Campbell (Dunfermline Athletic)
T. Bryce (Queen of the South)
S. Cochrane (Queen of the South)

1986/87

Premier Division
35 B. McClair (Celtic)
33 A. McCoist (Rangers)
23 M. Johnston (Celtic)
19 R. Fleck (Rangers)
16 J. Robertson (Heart of Midlothian)
I. Ferguson (Dundee United)
15 A. McInally (Celtic)
13 J. Colquhoun (Heart of Midlothian)
12 G. Harvey (Dundee)
W. Stark (Aberdeen)

First Division
23 R. Alexander (Morton)
21 G. McCoy (Dumbarton)
20 T. Bryce (Queen of the South)
18 D. Robertson (Morton)
17 O. Coyle (Dumbarton)
K. Macdonald (Forfar Athletic)
15 B. McNaughton (East Fife)
13 D. MacCabe (Airdrieonians)
J. Watson (Dunfermline Athletic)
12 C. Adam (Brechin City)
J. Murphy (Clyde)
S. Burgess (East Fife)

Second Division
26 J. Sludden (Ayr United)
25 W. Brown (St. Johnstone)
22 C. Harris (Raith Rovers)
21 J. McGachie (Meadowbank Thistle)
14 S. Sorbie (Alloa)
J. Fotheringham (Arbroath)
W. Blackie (Cowdenbeath)
R. Grant (Cowdenbeath)
13 R. Caven (Queen's Park)
K. Wright (Raith Rovers)
B. Cleland (Stranraer)

1987/88

Premier Division
33 T. Coyne (Dundee)
31 A. McCoist (Rangers)
26 J. Robertson (Heart of Midlothian)
A. Walker (Celtic)
15 J. Colquhoun (Heart of Midlothian)
F. McAvennie (Celtic)
K. Wright (Dundee)
13 C. Robertson (Dunfermline Athletic)
11 I. Ferguson (Dundee United)
10 J. Bett (Aberdeen)
P. Chalmers (St. Mirren)
I. Durrant (Rangers)
P. Kane (Hibernian)

First Division
25 G. Dalziel (Raith Rovers)
20 D. MacCabe (Airdrieonians)
K. Macdonald (Forfar Athletic)
17 J. Hughes (Queen of the South)
P. Hunter (East Fife)
16 C. Harkness (Kilmarnock)
C. McGlashan (Clyde)
D. Walker (Clyde)
15 C. Campbell (Airdrieonians)
14 O. Coyle (Dumbarton)
C. Harris (Raith Rovers)
J. McGachie (Meadowbank Thistle)

Second Division
31 J. Sludden (Ayr United)
23 J. Brogan (Stirling Albion)
H. Templeton (Ayr United)
19 T. Walker (Ayr United)
17 P. O'Brien (Queen's Park)
16 W. Watters (St. Johnstone)
15 G. Buckley (Brechin City)
14 P. Rutherford (Alloa)
13 T. Coyle (St. Johnstone)
C. Gibson (Stirling Albion)

1988/89

Premier Division
16 M. McGhee (Celtic)
C. Nicholas (Aberdeen)
14 S. Kirk (Motherwell)
13 S. Archibald (Hibernian)
12 K. Drinkell (Rangers)
F. McAvennie (Celtic)
11 P. Chalmers (St. Mirren)
10 M-M. Paatelainen (Dundee United)
9 T. Coyne (Dundee/Celtic)
K. Gallacher (Dundee United)
A. McCoist (Rangers)
W. Stark (Celtic)

First Division
22 K. Macdonald (Airdrieonians)
21 K. Eadie (Clydebank)
19 G. McCoy (Partick Thistle)
18 R. Jack (Dunfermline Athletic)
17 H. Templeton (Ayr United)
16 T. Bryce (Clydebank)
O. Coyle (Clydebank)
C. McGlashan (Clyde)
15 J. Sludden (Ayr United)
14 C. Campbell (Airdrieonians)
J. Watson (Dunfermline Athletic)

Second Division
23 C. Lytwyn (Alloa)
21 G. Murray (Montrose)
18 C. Gibson (Stirling Albion)
16 W. McNeill (East Stirlingshire)
15 C. Adam (Brechin City)
J. Brogan (Stirling Albion)
J. Chapman (Albion Rovers)
A. Graham (Albion Rovers)
13 S. MacIver (Dumbarton)
11 J. Fotheringham (Arbroath)
D. Lloyd (Stranraer)
P. Teevan (Albion Rovers)

1989/90

Premier Division
17 J. Robertson (Heart of Midlothian)
16 R. Jack (Dunfermline Athletic)
15 M. Johnston (Rangers)
14 A. McCoist (Rangers)
13 W. Dodds (Dundee)
12 S. Crabbe (Heart of Midlothian)
G. Torfason (St. Mirren)
11 N. Cusack (Motherwell)
C. Nicholas (Aberdeen)
K. Wright (Dundee)

First Division
27 O. Coyle (Airdrieonians/Clydebank)
21 K. Eadie (Clydebank)
20 G. Dalziel (Raith Rovers)
19 R. Grant (St. Johnstone)
18 C. Campbell (Partick Thistle)
17 D. McWilliams (Falkirk)
15 K. Macdonald (Raith Rovers/Airdrieonians)
13 A. Moore (St. Johnstone)
12 S. Maskrey (St. Johnstone)
11 R. Alexander (Morton)
J. Charnley (Partick Thistle)
C. McGlashan (Clyde)

Second Division
23 W. Watters (Kilmarnock)
20 C. Gibson (Dumbarton)
19 S. MacIver (Dumbarton)
16 J. Reid (Stirling Albion)
A. Ross (Cowdenbeath)
S. Sloan (Berwick Rangers)
15 D. Lloyd (Stirling Albion)
S. McCormick (Stenhousemuir)
14 P. Hunter (East Fife)
V. Moore (Stirling Albion)

1990/91

Premier Division
18 T. Coyne (Celtic)
14 D. Arnott (Motherwell)
H. Gillhaus (Aberdeen)
13 E. Jess (Aberdeen)
12 D. Jackson (Dundee United)
J. Robertson (Heart of Midlothian)
M. Walters (Rangers)
11 M. Johnston (Rangers)
A. McCoist (Rangers)
10 M. Hateley (Rangers)

First Division
29 K. Eadie (Clydebank)
25 G. Dalziel (Raith Rovers)
21 D. MacCabe (Morton)
20 O. Coyle (Airdrieonians)
18 K. Wright (Dundee)
16 S. Stainrod (Falkirk)
15 W. Dodds (Dundee)
S. McGivern (Falkirk)
D. Roseburgh (Meadowbank Thistle)
14 G. McCluskey (Hamilton Academical)
P. Ritchie (Brechin City)
R. Williamson (Kilmarnock)

Second Division
17 M. Hendry (Queen's Park)
A. Speirs (Stenhousemuir)
16 A.Ross (Cowdenbeath/Berwick Rangers)
15 A. MacKenzie (Cowdenbeath)
14 C. Harkness (Stranraer)
D. Lloyd (Stirling Albion)
J. McQuade (Dumbarton)
K. Todd (Berwick Rangers)
13 S. McCormick (Stenhousemuir)
V. Moore (Stirling Albion)

1991/92

Premier Division
34 A. McCoist (Rangers)
21 M. Hateley (Rangers)
C. Nicholas (Celtic)
18 P. Wright (St. Johnstone)
15 T. Coyne (Celtic)
S. Crabbe (Heart of Midlothian)
D. Ferguson (Dundee United)
14 G. Creaney (Celtic)
J. Robertson (Heart of Midlothian)
12 E. Jess (Aberdeen)

First Division
26 G. Dalziel (Raith Rovers)
22 K. Eadie (Clydebank)
19 W. Dodds (Dundee)
18 A. Mathie (Morton)
C. McGlashan (PartickThistle)
17 W. Watters (Stirling Albion)
14 G. Clark (Hamilton Academical)
A. Graham (Ayr United)
13 T. Smith (Hamilton Academical)
12 C. Brewster (Raith Rovers)
G. McCluskey (Hamilton Academical)

Second Division
26 A. Thomson (Queen of the South)
21 G. Buckley (Cowdenbeath)
J Sludden (East Fife)
19 J Gilmour (Dumbarton)
18 D. Diver (East Stirlingshire)
P. Lamont (Cowdenbeath)
17 S. McCormick (Queen's Park)
16 R. Scott (East Fife)
D. Thompson (Clyde)
14 T. Sloan (Stranraer)

1992/93

Premier Division
34 A. McCoist (Rangers)
22 D. Shearer (Aberdeen)
19 M. Hateley (Rangers)
16 P. Connolly (Dundee United)
W. Dodds (Dundee)
M-M. Paatelainen (Aberdeen)
14 P. Wright (St. Johnstone)
13 S. Booth (Aberdeen)
D. Jackson (Hibernian)
A. Payton (Celtic)

First Division
32 G. Dalziel (Raith Rovers)
22 C. Brewster (Raith Rovers)
21 C. Flannigan (Clydebank)
20 K. Eadie (Clydebank)
18 B. Lavety (St. Mirren)
15 J. McQuade (Dumbarton)
13 A. Mathie (Morton)
12 H. French (Dunfermline Athletic)
E. Gallagher (St. Mirren)
J. Henry (Clydebank)
M. Mooney (Dumbarton)

Second Division
26 M. Mathieson (Stenhousemuir)
23 A. Ross (Brechin City)
21 S. Petrie (Forfar Athletic)
A. Thomson (Queen of the South)
19 B. Moffat (Alloa)
T. Sloan (Stranraer)
S. Sorbie (Arbroath)
16 F. McGarvey (Clyde)
M. Scott (Albion Rovers)
R. Scott (East Fife)

1993/94

Premier Division
22 M. Hateley (Rangers)
17 D. Shearer (Aberdeen)
16 C. Brewster (Dundee United)
K. Wright (Hibernian)
14 A. Craig (Partick Thistle)
13 R. Grant (Partick Thistle)
12 T. Coyne (Motherwell)
G. Durie (Rangers)
10 P. McGinlay(Celtic)
J. Robertson (Heart of Midlothian)

First Division
19 P. Duffield (Hamilton Academical)
18 R. Cadette (Falkirk)
17 G. O'Boyle (Dunfermline Athletic)
15 H. French (Dunfermline Athletic)
13 C. Gibson (Dumbarton)
W. Watters (Stirling Albion)
12 S. McGivern (Ayr United)
11 R. Alexander (Greenock Morton)
K. Eadie (Clydebank)
C. Flannigan (Clydebank)
A. Tod (Dunfermline Athletic)

Second Division
29 A. Thomson (Queen of the South)
18 J. O'Neill (Queen's Park)
17 M. Scott (Albion Rovers)
16 D. Diver (2 for Alloa,10 for Arbroath, 4 for Stranraer)
T. Sloan (Stranraer)
15 W. Irvine (Berwick Rangers)
14 M. Mathieson (Stenhousemuir)
13 D. Bingham (Forfar Athletic)
J. Sludden (Stenhousemuir)
12 D. Grant (Montrose)
W. Hawke (Berwick Rangers)
I. Little (Meadowbank Thistle)
M. McCallum (East Stirlingshire)

1994/95

Premier Division
16 T. Coyne (Motherwell)
15 W. Dodds (Aberdeen)
13 M. Hateley (Rangers)
10 D. Arnott (Motherwell)
D. Jackson (Hibernian)
B. Laudrup (Rangers)
M. O'Neill (Hibernian)
J. Robertson (Heart of Midlothian)
K. Wright (Hibernian)
9 C. McDonald (Falkirk)

First Division
20 P. Duffield (Hamilton Academical)
19 G. O'Boyle (St. Johnstone)
16 G. Shaw (Dundee)
15 G. Dalziel (Raith Rovers)
14 S. Petrie (Dunfermline Athletic)
12 G. Britton (Dundee)
H. French (Dunfermline Athletic)
J. Hamilton (Dundee)
Andrew Smith (Airdrieonians)
11 S. Cooper (Airdrieonians)
S. Crawford (Raith Rovers)
A. Lawrence (Airdrieonians)

Second Division
17 M. Mooney (Dumbarton)
16 W. Hawke (Berwick Rangers)
D. Lilley (Greenock Morton)
15 W. Watters (Stirling Albion)
14 M. Rajamaki (Greenock Morton)
R. Scott (East Fife)
12 H. Ward (Dumbarton)
11 W. Irvine (Berwick Rangers)
10 J. Dickson (Clyde)
G. Hutchison (Stenhousemuir)

Third Division
23 M. Yardley (Cowdenbeath)
22 D. Bingham (Forfar Athletic)
19 C. McGlashan (Montrose)
17 A. Kennedy (Montrose)
16 M. Geraghty (East Stirlingshire)
13 B. Moffat (Alloa)
A. Ross (Forfar Athletic)
12 B. Grant (Ross County)
11 S. Tosh (Arbroath)
10 I. Lee (East Stirlingshire)
S. McCormick (Forfar Athletic)

1995/96

Premier Division
26 P. Van Hooijdonk (Celtic)
17 G. Durie (Rangers)
16 A. McCoist (Rangers)
14 P. Gascoigne (Rangers)
13 P. Wright (Kilmarnock)
11 C. Cameron (9 for Raith Rovers, 2 for Heart of Midlothian)
J. Collins (Celtic)
J. Robertson (Heart of Midlothian)
9 S. Booth (Aberdeen)
D. Jackson (Hibernian)
A. Johnston (Heart of Midlothian)
J. Miller (Aberdeen)
K. Wright (Hibernian)

First Division
21 G. O'Boyle (St. Johnstone)
17 C. Brewster (Dundee United)
G. McSwegan (Dundee United)
14 J. Hamilton (Dundee)
D. Lilley (Greenock Morton)
13 W. Hawke (Greenock Morton)
S. Petrie (Dunfermline Athletic)
12 G. Shaw (Dunfermline Athletic)
11 J. Grady (Clydebank)
P. Hartley (Hamilton Academical)
B. Lavety (St. Mirren)
M. Rajamaki (Greenock Morton)

Second Division
25 S. McCormick (Stirling Albion)
21 E. Annand (Clyde)
19 A. Bone (18 for Stirling Albion, 1 for St. Mirren)
16 C. McGlashan (Montrose)
13 W. Irvine (Berwick Rangers)
12 G. Higgins (Forfar Athletic)
S. Mallan (Queen of the South)
11 R. Scott (East Fife)
10 P. Forrester (Berwick Rangers)
M. Mathieson (Stenhousemuir)

Third Division
23 I. Stewart (Caledonian Thistle)
21 P. Dwyer (East Stirlingshire)
18 J. Young (Livingston)
15 C. Milne (Ross County)
12 C. Christie (Caledonian Thistle)
J. MacPherson (Ross County)
G. Young (Albion Rovers)
11 B. Grant (Ross County)
D. Scott (Cowdenbeath)
10 A. Hercher (Caledonian Thistle)

©

Leading Goalscorers – Club By Club Since 1981/82

ABERDEEN

Season	Div	No. of Goals	Player
1981-82	P	11	J. Hewitt
1982-83	P	16	M. McGhee
1983-84	P	13	M. McGhee
			G. Strachan
1984-85	P	22	F. McDougall
1985-86	P	14	F. McDougall
1986-87	P	12	W. Stark
1987-88	P	10	J. Bett
1988-89	P	16	C. Nicholas
1989-90	P	11	C. Nicholas
1990-91	P	14	H. Gillhaus
1991-92	P	12	E. Jess
1992-93	P	22	D. Shearer
1993-94	P	17	D. Shearer
1994-95	P	15	W. Dodds
1995-96	P	9	S. Booth
			J. Miller

AIRDRIEONIANS

Season	Div	No. of Goals	Player
1981-82	P	15	A. Clark
1982-83	F	12	B. Millar
1983-84	F	11	J. Flood
1984-85	F	21	D. MacCabe
1985-86	F	11	J. Flood
1986-87	F	13	D. MacCabe
1987-88	F	20	D. MacCabe
1988-89	F	22	K. Macdonald
1989-90	F	10	O. Coyle
1990-91	F	20	O. Coyle
1991-92	P	11	O. Coyle
1992-93	P	9	O. Coyle
1993-94	F	10	D. Kirkwood
1994-95	F	12	Andrew Smith
1995-96	F	9	J. McIntyre

ALBION ROVERS

Season	Div	No. of Goals	Player
1981-82	S	16	S. Evans
1982-83	S	13	S. Evans
1983-84	S	11	T. McGorm
1984-85	S	27	B. Slaven
1985-86	S	6	S. Conn
			V. Kasule
			A. Rodgers
1986-87	S	11	C. Wilson
1987-88	S	10	A. Graham
1988-89	S	15	J. Chapman
			A. Graham
1989-90	F	10	M. McAnenay
1990-91	S	12	M. McAnenay
1991-92	S	11	G. McCoy
1992-93	S	16	M. Scott
1993-94	S	17	M. Scott
1994-95	T	7	M. Scott
1995-96	T	12	G. Young

ALLOA

Season	Div	No. of Goals	Player
1981-82	S	14	S. Murray
1982-83	F	12	L. McComb
1983-84	F	10	D. Lloyd
1984-85	S	16	D. Lloyd
1985-86	F	11	M. Jamieson
			S. Sorbie
1986-87	S	14	S. Sorbie
1987-88	S	14	P. Rutherford
1988-89	S	23	C. Lytwyn
1989-90	F	9	P. Lamont
1990-91	S	11	J. Irvine
1991-92	S	12	M. Hendry
1992-93	S	19	B. Moffat
1993-94	S	7	W. Newbigging
1994-95	T	13	B. Moffat
1995-96	T	5	B. Moffat
			S. Rixon

ARBROATH

Season	Div	No. of Goals	Player
1981-82	S	21	D. Robb
1982-83	S	15	W. Gavine
			W. Steele
1983-84	S	18	J. Harley
1984-85	S	6	R. Brown
1985-86	S	14	M. McWalter
1986-87	S	14	J. Fotheringham
1987-88	S	13	A. McKenna
1988-89	S	11	J. Fotheringham
1989-90	S	12	J. Marshall
1990-91	S	10	M. Bennett
			S. Sorbie
1991-92	S	12	S. Sorbie
1992-93	S	19	S. Sorbie
1993-94	S	10	D. Diver
1994-95	T	11	S. Tosh
1995-96	T	8	S. McCormick
			D. Pew

AYR UNITED

Season	Div	No. of Goals	Player
1981-82	F	13	J. F. Frye
1982-83	F	7	J. F. Frye
			M. Larnach
			A. McInally
1983-84	F	15	A. McInally
1984-85	F	8	G. Collins
			J. McNiven
1985-86	F	6	D. Irons
1986-87	S	26	J. Sludden
1987-88	S	31	J. Sludden
1988-89	F	17	H. Templeton
1989-90	F	10	T. Bryce
1990-91	F	11	T. Bryce
1991-92	F	14	A. Graham
1992-93	F	9	A. Graham
1993-94	F	12	S. McGivern
1994-95	F	4	J. Jackson
1995-96	S	5	B. Bilsland
			I. English

BERWICK RANGERS

Season	Div	No. of Goals	Player
1981-82	S	16	M. Lawson
1982-83	S	8	I. Cashmore
			S. Romaines
1983-84	S	9	P. Davidson
			A. O'Hara
1984-85	S	9	P. Davidson
1985-86	S	12	J. Sokoluk
1986-87	S	8	E. Tait
1987-88	S	3	M. Cameron
			H. Douglas
			T. Graham
			G. Leitch
			C. Lytwyn
			M. Thompson
1988-89	S	10	J. Hughes
1989-90	S	16	S. Sloan
1990-91	S	14	K. Todd
1991-92	S	12	S. Bickmore
1992-93	S	11	D. Scott
1993-94	S	15	W. Irvine
1994-95	S	16	W. Hawke
1995-96	S	13	W. Irvine

BRECHIN CITY

Season	Div	No. of Goals	Player
1981-82	S	16	I. M. Campbell
1982-83	S	23	I. M. Campbell
1983-84	F	19	I. M. Campbell
1984-85	F	17	K. Eadie
1985-86	F	22	K. Eadie
1986-87	F	12	C. Adam
1987-88	S	15	G. Buckley
1988-89	S	15	C. Adam
1989-90	S	12	G. Lees
1990-91	F	14	P. Ritchie
1991-92	S	12	P. Ritchie
1992-93	S	23	A. Ross
1993-94	F	10	M. Miller
1994-95	S	6	G. Price
			R. Smith
1995-96	T	8	A. Ross

CALEDONIAN THISTLE

Season	Div	No. of Goals	Player
1994-95	T	6	C. Christie
			A. Hercher
1995-96	T	23	I. Stewart

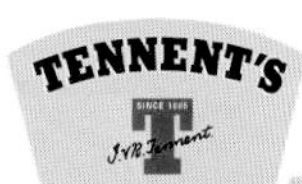

CELTIC

Season	Div	No. of Goals	Player
1981-82	P	21	G. McCluskey
1982-83	P	29	C. Nicholas
1983-84	P	23	B. McClair
1984-85	P	19	B. McClair
1985-86	P	22	B. McClair
1986-87	P	35	B. McClair
1987-88	P	26	A. Walker
1988-89	P	16	M. McGhee
1989-90	P	8	D. Dziekanowski
1990-91	P	18	T. Coyne
1991-92	P	21	C. Nicholas
1992-93	P	13	A. Payton
1993-94	P	10	P. McGinlay
1994-95	P	8	J. Collins
1995-96	P	26	P. Van Hooijdonk

CLYDE

Season	Div	No. of Goals	Player
1981-82	S	23	D. Masterton
1982-83	F	14	D. Masterton
1983-84	F	17	J. F. Frye
1984-85	F	19	J. F. Frye
1985-86	F	12	J. F. Frye
1986-87	F	12	J. Murphy
1987-88	F	16	C. McGlashan
			D. Walker
1988-89	F	16	C. McGlashan
1989-90	F	11	C. McGlashan
1990-91	F	8	S. Mallan
1991-92	S	16	D. Thompson
1992-93	S	16	F. McGarvey
1993-94	F	5	I. McConnell
			G. Parks
1994-95	S	10	J. Dickson
1995-96	S	21	E. Annand

CLYDEBANK

Season	Div	No. of Goals	Player
1981-82	F	20	B. Millar
1982-83	F	21	R. Williamson
1983-84	F	10	T. Coyne
1984-85	F	11	M. Conroy
1985-86	P	7	M. Conroy
			D. Lloyd
1986-87	P	9	M. Conroy
			S. Gordon
1987-88	F	11	M. Conroy
1988-89	F	21	K. Eadie
1989-90	F	21	K. Eadie
1990-91	F	29	K. Eadie
1991-92	F	22	K. Eadie
1992-93	F	21	C. Flannigan
1993-94	F	11	K. Eadie
			C. Flannigan
1994-95	F	9	K. Eadie
1995-96	F	11	J. Grady

COWDENBEATH

Season	Div	No. of Goals	Player
1981-82	S	16	G. Forrest
1982-83	S	13	W. Gibson
			C. McIntosh
1983-84	S	7	I. Paterson
1984-85	S	16	K. Ward
1985-86	S	15	C. McGlashan
1986-87	S	14	W. Blackie
			R. Grant
1987-88	S	11	R. Grant
1988-89	S	8	A. McGonigal
1989-90	S	16	A. Ross
1990-91	S	15	A. MacKenzie
1991-92	S	26	G. Buckley
1992-93	F	9	W. Callaghan
1993-94	S	11	W. Callaghan
1994-95	T	23	M. Yardley
1995-96	T	11	D. Scott

DUMBARTON

Season	Div	No. of Goals	Player
1981-82	F	9	R. Blair
1982-83	F	10	R. Blair
1983-84	F	15	J. Coyle
1984-85	P	7	J. Coyle
1985-86	F	13	G. McCoy
1986-87	F	21	G. McCoy
1987-88	F	14	O. Coyle
1988-89	S	13	S. MacIver
1989-90	S	20	C. Gibson
1990-91	S	14	J. McQuade
1991-92	S	19	J. Gilmour
1992-93	F	15	J. McQuade
1993-94	F	13	C. Gibson
1994-95	S	17	M. Mooney
1995-96	F	5	M. Mooney

DUNDEE

Season	Div	No. of Goals	Player
1981-82	P	12	I. Ferguson
1982-83	P	9	I. Ferguson
1983-84	P	13	W. McCall
1984-85	P	8	R. Stephen
1985-86	P	14	R. Stephen
1986-87	P	12	G. Harvey
1987-88	P	33	T. Coyne
1988-89	P	9	T. Coyne
1989-90	P	13	W. Dodds
1990-91	F	18	K. Wright
1991-92	F	19	W. Dodds
1992-93	P	16	W. Dodds
1993-94	P	6	D. Ristic
1994-95	F	16	G. Shaw
1995-96	F	14	J. Hamilton

DUNDEE UNITED

Season	Div	No. of Goals	Player
1981-82	P	15	P. Sturrock
1982-83	P	22	D. Dodds
1983-84	P	15	D. Dodds
1984-85	P	14	P. Sturrock
1985-86	P	12	D. Dodds
1986-87	P	16	I. Ferguson
1987-88	P	11	I. Ferguson
1988-89	P	10	M-M. Paatelainen
1989-90	P	7	D. Jackson
			M-M. Paatelainen
1990-91	P	12	D. Jackson
1991-92	P	17	D. Ferguson
1992-93	P	16	P. Connolly
1993-94	P	16	C. Brewster
1994-95	P	7	C. Brewster
1995-96	F	17	C. Brewster
			G. McSwegan

DUNFERMLINE ATHLETIC

Season	Div	No. of Goals	Player
1981-82	F	13	A. McNaughton
1982-83	F	8	R. Forrest
			S. Morrison
1983-84	S	9	S. Morrison
1984-85	S	15	J. Watson
1985-86	S	24	J. Watson
1986-87	F	13	J. Watson
1987-88	P	13	C. Robertson
1988-89	F	18	R. Jack
1989-90	P	16	R. Jack
1990-91	P	8	R. Jack
1991-92	P	6	D. Moyes
1992-93	F	12	H. French
1993-94	F	17	G. O'Boyle
1994-95	F	14	S. Petrie
1995-96	F	13	S. Petrie

EAST FIFE

Season	Div	No. of Goals	Player
1981-82	S	16	G. Scott
1982-83	S	14	R. Thomson
1983-84	S	16	G. Durie
1984-85	F	12	G. Murray
1985-86	F	14	S. Kirk
1986-87	F	15	B. McNaughton
1987-88	F	17	P. Hunter
1988-89	S	9	P. Hunter
1989-90	S	14	P. Hunter
1990-91	S	10	W. Brown
			R. Scott
1991-92	S	21	J. Sludden
1992-93	S	16	R. Scott
1993-94	S	10	R. Scott
1994-95	S	14	R. Scott
1995-96	S	11	R. Scott

EAST STIRLINGSHIRE

Season	Div	No. of Goals	Player
1981-82	F	4	J. Blair
			R. Edgar
			P. Lamont
1982-83	S	6	C. Gibson
1983-84	S	13	C. Gibson
1984-85	S	12	S. Maskrey
1985-86	S	12	S. Maskrey
1986-87	S	5	A. McGonigal
			J. Paisley
			D. Strange
1987-88	S	9	G. Murray
1988-89	S	16	W. McNeill
1989-90	S	4	W. McNeill
			D. Wilcox
			C. Wilson
1990-91	S	10	C. Lytwyn
			Dk. Walker
1991-92	S	18	D. Diver
1992-93	S	9	P. Roberts
1993-94	S	12	M. McCallum
1994-95	T	16	M. Geraghty
1995-96	T	21	P. Dwyer

FALKIRK

Season	Div	No. of Goals	Player
1981-82	F	10	W. Herd
1982-83	F	8	P. Houston
1983-84	F	11	K. McAllister
1984-85	F	22	G. McCoy
1985-86	F	15	J. Gilmour
1986-87	P	6	K. Eadie
1987-88	P	9	C. Baptie
1988-89	F	12	A. Rae
1989-90	F	17	D. McWilliams
1990-91	F	16	S. Stainrod
1991-92	P	9	K. McAllister
			E. May
1992-93	P	8	R. Cadette
1993-94	F	18	R. Cadette
1994-95	P	9	C. McDonald
1995-96	P	6	P. McGrillen

FORFAR ATHLETIC

Season	Div	No. of Goals	Player
1981-82	S	9	J. Clark
			S. Hancock
1982-83	S	16	K. Macdonald
1983-84	S	22	J. Liddle
1984-85	F	14	K. Macdonald
1985-86	F	10	J. Clark
1986-87	F	17	K. Macdonald
1987-88	F	20	K. Macdonald
1988-89	F	12	K. Ward
1989-90	F	8	C. Brewster
1990-91	F	12	G. Whyte
1991-92	F	8	G. Winter
1992-93	S	21	S. Petrie
1993-94	S	13	D. Bingham
1994-95	T	22	D. Bingham
1995-96	S	12	G. Higgins

GREENOCK MORTON

Season	Div	No. of Goals	Player
1981-82	P	6	A. Ritchie
1982-83	P	7	J. Rooney
1983-84	F	17	J. McNeil
1984-85	P	5	J. Gillespie
1985-86	F	14	J. McNeil
1986-87	F	23	R. Alexander
1987-88	P	8	Jim Boag
1988-89	F	11	R. Alexander
1989-90	F	11	R. Alexander
1990-91	F	21	D. MacCabe
1991-92	F	18	A. Mathie
1992-93	F	13	A. Mathie
1993-94	F	11	R. Alexander
1994-95	S	16	D. Lilley
1995-96	F	14	D. Lilley

HAMILTON ACADEMICAL

Season	Div	No. of Goals	Player
1981-82	F	10	J. Fairlie
1982-83	F	15	J. Fairlie
1983-84	F	9	D. Somner
1984-85	F	8	J. Brogan
			J. McGachie
1985-86	F	23	J. Brogan
1986-87	P	6	J. Brogan
1987-88	F	10	M. Caughey
1988-89	P	5	S. Gordon
			C. Harris
1989-90	F	9	C. Harris
1990-91	F	14	G. McCluskey
1991-92	F	14	G. Clark
1992-93	F	11	P. McDonald
1993-94	F	19	P. Duffield
1994-95	F	20	P. Duffield
1995-96	F	11	P. Hartley

HEART OF MIDLOTHIAN

Season	Div	No. of Goals	Player
1981-82	F	16	W. Pettigrew
1982-83	F	21	J. Robertson
1983-84	P	14	J. Robertson
1984-85	P	8	A. Clark
			J. Robertson
1985-86	P	20	J. Robertson
1986-87	P	16	J. Robertson
1987-88	P	26	J. Robertson
1988-89	P	5	J. Colquhoun
			I. Ferguson
1989-90	P	17	J Robertson
1990-91	P	12	J. Robertson
1991-92	P	15	S. Crabbe
1992-93	P	11	J. Robertson
1993-94	P	10	J. Robertson
1994-95	P	10	J. Robertson
1995-96	P	11	J. Robertson

HIBERNIAN

Season	Div	No. of Goals	Player
1981-82	P	11	G. Rae
1982-83	P	6	G. Murray
			G. Rae
			R. Thomson
1983-84	P	18	W. Irvine
1984-85	P	8	G. Durie
			P. Kane
1985-86	P	19	S. Cowan
1986-87	P	9	G. McCluskey
1987-88	P	10	P. Kane
1988-89	P	13	S. Archibald
1989-90	P	8	K. Houchen
1990-91	P	6	P. Wright
1991-92	P	11	M. Weir
1992-93	P	13	D. Jackson
1993-94	P	16	K. Wright
1994-95	P	10	D. Jackson
			M. O'Neill
			K. Wright
1995-96	P	9	D. Jackson
			K. Wright

KILMARNOCK

Season	Div	No. of Goals	Player
1981-82	F	14	J. Bourke
1982-83	P	9	B. Gallagher
1983-84	F	11	R. Clark
			B. Gallagher
1984-85	F	12	B. Millar
1985-86	F	14	I. Bryson
1986-87	F	10	I. Bryson
1987-88	F	16	C. Harkness
1988-89	F	12	W. Watters
1989-90	S	23	W. Watters
1990-91	F	14	R. Williamson
1991-92	F	10	C. Campbell
			A. Mitchell
1992-93	F	11	G. McCluskey
1993-94	P	7	R. Williamson
1994-95	P	6	C. McKee
1995-96	P	13	P. Wright

LIVINGSTON

FORMERLY MEADOWBANK THISTLE

Season	Div	No. of Goals	Player
1981-82	S	15	J. Jobson
1982-83	S	13	T. Hendrie
1983-84	F	10	C. Robertson
1984-85	F	14	A. Sprott
1985-86	S	17	D. Jackson
			A. Lawrence
1986-87	S	21	J. McGachie
1987-88	F	14	J. McGachie
1988-89	F	6	D. Roseburgh
1989-90	F	8	B. McNaughton
1990-91	F	15	D. Roseburgh
1991-92	F	8	D. Roseburgh
1992-93	F	9	P. Rutherford
1993-94	S	12	I. Little
1994-95	S	6	L. Bailey
1995-96	T	18	J. Young

MONTROSE

Season	Div	No. of Goals	Player
1981-82	S	9	I. Campbell
1982-83	S	12	E. Copland
1983-84	S	7	N. Burke
1984-85	S	12	D. Somner
1985-86	F	6	M. Allan
1986-87	F	10	I. Paterson
1987-88	S	11	H. Mackay
1988-89	S	21	G. S. Murray
1989-90	S	11	D. Powell
1990-91	S	11	G. Murray
1991-92	F	9	J. McGachie
1992-93	S	10	D. Grant
1993-94	S	12	D. Grant
1994-95	T	19	C. McGlashan
1995-96	S	16	C. McGlashan

MOTHERWELL

Season	Div	No. of Goals	Player
1981-82	F	20	W. Irvine
1982-83	P	11	B. McClair
1983-84	P	7	J. Gahagan
1984-85	F	9	A. Harrow
			R. Stewart
1985-86	P	9	J. Reilly
1986-87	P	10	S. Kirk
			A. Walker
1987-88	P	9	S. Cowan
1988-89	P	14	S. Kirk
1989-90	P	11	N. Cusack
1990-91	P	14	D. Arnott
1991-92	P	8	D. Arnott
1992-93	P	10	S. Kirk
1993-94	P	12	T. Coyne
1994-95	P	16	T. Coyne
1995-96	P	5	W. Falconer

PARTICK THISTLE

Season	Div	No. of Goals	Player
1981-82	P	9	M. Johnston
1982-83	F	22	M. Johnston
1983-84	F	13	K. McDowall
1984-85	F	12	A. Logan
1985-86	F	11	G. Smith
1986-87	F	10	C. West
1987-88	F	13	E. Gallagher
1988-89	F	19	G. McCoy
1989-90	F	18	C. Campbell
1990-91	F	13	D. Elliot
1991-92	F	18	C. McGlashan
1992-93	P	12	G. Britton
1993-94	P	14	A. Craig
1994-95	P	7	W. Foster
1995-96	P	5	A. Lyons
			R. McDonald

QUEEN OF THE SOUTH

Season	Div	No. of Goals	Player
1981-82	F	12	G. Phillips
1982-83	S	22	R. Alexander
1983-84	S	9	J. Robertson
1984-85	S	9	G. Cloy
1985-86	S	15	T. Bryce
			S. Cochrane
1986-87	F	20	T. Bryce
1987-88	F	17	J. Hughes
1988-89	F	7	G. Fraser
1989-90	S	8	S. Gordon
1990-91	S	11	A. Thomson
1991-92	S	26	A. Thomson
1992-93	S	21	A. Thomson
1993-94	S	29	A. Thomson
1994-95	S	9	D. Campbell
			S. Mallan
1995-96	S	12	S. Mallan

QUEEN'S PARK

Season	Div	No. of Goals	Player
1981-82	F	10	C. Crawley
1982-83	F	10	J. Gilmour
1983-84	S	17	A. Grant
1984-85	S	18	J. Nicholson
1985-86	S	11	G. Fraser
1986-87	S	13	R. Caven
1987-88	S	17	P. O'Brien
1988-89	S	9	M. Hendry
1989-90	S	10	M. Hendry
1990-91	S	17	M. Hendry
1991-92	S	17	S. McCormick
1992-93	S	11	R. Caven
1993-94	S	18	J. O'Neill
1994-95	T	8	S. McCormick
1995-96	T	6	S. Edgar
			K. McGoldrick

RAITH ROVERS

Season	Div	No. of Goals	Player
1981-82	F	12	I. Ballantyne
1982-83	F	18	C. Harris
1983-84	F	16	J. Kerr
1984-85	S	22	K. Wright
1985-86	S	21	P. Smith
			K. Wright
1986-87	S	22	C. Harris
1987-88	F	25	G. Dalziel
1988-89	F	11	G. Dalziel
1989-90	F	20	G. Dalziel
1990-91	F	25	G. Dalziel
1991-92	F	26	G. Dalziel
1992-93	F	32	G. Dalziel
1993-94	P	8	G. Dalziel
1994-95	F	15	G. Dalziel
1995-96	P	9	C. Cameron

RANGERS

Season	Div	No. of Goals	Player
1981-82	P	14	J. MacDonald
1982-83	P	10	J. MacDonald
1983-84	P	9	A.Clark
			A. McCoist
1984-85	P	12	A. McCoist
1985-86	P	24	A. McCoist
1986-87	P	33	A. McCoist
1987-88	P	31	A. McCoist
1988-89	P	12	K. Drinkell
1989-90	P	15	M. Johnston
1990-91	P	12	M. Walters
1991-92	P	34	A. McCoist
1992-93	P	34	A. McCoist
1993-94	P	22	M. Hateley
1994-95	P	13	M. Hateley
1995-96	P	17	G. Durie

ST. JOHNSTONE

Season	Div	No. of Goals	Player
1981-82	F	17	J. Morton
1982-83	F	26	J. Brogan
1983-84	P	9	J. Brogan
1984-85	F	9	J. Reid
1985-86	S	11	W. Brown
1986-87	S	25	W. Brown
1987-88	S	16	W. Watters
1988-89	F	12	S. Maskrey
1989-90	F	19	R. Grant
1990-91	P	9	H. Curran
1991-92	P	18	P. Wright
1992-93	P	14	P. Wright
1993-94	P	7	P. Wright
1994-95	F	19	G. O'Boyle
1995-96	F	21	G. O'Boyle

ST. MIRREN

Season	Div	No. of Goals	Player
1981-82	P	13	F. McAvennie
1982-83	P	9	F. McAvennie
1983-84	P	13	F. McDougall
1984-85	P	16	F. McAvennie
1985-86	P	7	G. Speirs
1986-87	P	10	F. McGarvey
1987-88	P	10	P. Chalmers
1988-89	P	11	P. Chalmers
1989-90	P	12	G. Torfason
1990-91	P	4	P. Kinnaird
			K. McDowall
			G. Torfason
1991-92	P	8	G. Torfason
1992-93	F	18	B. Lavety
1993-94	F	10	B. Lavety
1994-95	F	7	B. Lavety
1995-96	F	11	B. Lavety

STENHOUSEMUIR

Season	Div	No. of Goals	Player
1981-82	S	8	B. Jenkins
1982-83	S	15	G. Murray
1983-84	S	14	G. Forrest
1984-85	S	6	H. Erwin
			A. McNaughton
1985-86	S	11	J. Sinnet
1986-87	S	5	A. Bateman
			P. Russell
1987-88	S	10	T. Condie
1988-89	S	9	C. Walker
1989-90	S	15	S. McCormick
1990-91	S	17	A. Speirs
1991-92	S	6	M. Mathieson
1992-93	S	26	M. Mathieson
1993-94	S	14	M. Mathieson
1994-95	S	10	G. Hutchison
1995-96	S	10	M. Mathieson

ROSS COUNTY

Season	Div	No. of Goals	Player
1994-95	T	12	B. Grant
1995-96	T	15	C. Milne

Scotland's top scorer last season Pierre Van Hooijdonk (Celtic).

STIRLING ALBION

Season	Div	No. of Goals	Player
1981-82	S	13	J. Colquhoun
1982-83	S	21	J. Colquhoun
1983-84	S	12	W. Irvine
1984-85	S	21	W. Irvine
1985-86	S	17	W. Irvine
1986-87	S	7	S. Gavin
			C. Gibson
1987-88	S	23	J. Brogan
1988-89	S	18	C. Gibson
1989-90	S	16	J. Reid
1990-91	S	14	D. Lloyd
1991-92	F	17	W. Watters
1992-93	F	11	W. Watters
1993-94	F	13	W. Watters
1994-95	S	15	W. Watters
1995-96	S	25	S. McCormick

STRANRAER

Season	Div	No. of Goals	Player
1981-82	S	11	S. Sweeney
1982-83	S	12	S. Sweeney
1983-84	S	11	J. McGuire
1984-85	S	10	J. Sweeney
1985-86	S	8	J. McGuire
			S. Mauchlen
1986-87	S	13	B. Cleland
1987-88	S	8	B. Cleland
1988-89	S	11	D. Lloyd
1989-90	S	13	C. Harkness
1990-91	S	14	C. Harkness
1991-92	S	14	T. Sloan
1992-93	S	19	T. Sloan
1993-94	S	16	T. Sloan
1994-95	F	4	D. Henderson
			T. Sloan
1995-96	S	6	A. Grant

The following section details the League Championship careers, appearances and goals of all players currently registered with each Premier Division club for season 1996/97 as at 16th September, 1996 that have played at senior first team level. It should be noted that all appearances include both full League appearances and substitute League appearances made by players. All club names shown in italics are for League appearances made when a player moved to a club on a Temporary Transfer basis with the player's registration subsequently reverting back to his original club.

AITKEN, Robert Sime
Born : Irvine 24/11/58

SEASON	CLUB	LEAGUE APPEARANCES	GOALS
1975-76	Celtic	12	-
1976-77	Celtic	33	5
1977-78	Celtic	33	2
1978-79	Celtic	36	5
1979-80	Celtic	35	3
1980-81	Celtic	33	4
1981-82	Celtic	33	3
1982-83	Celtic	33	6
1983-84	Celtic	31	5
1984-85	Celtic	33	3
1985-86	Celtic	36	-
1986-87	Celtic	42	1
1987-88	Celtic	43	1
1988-89	Celtic	32	-
1989-90	Celtic	18	2
1989-90	Newcastle United	22	1
1990-91	Newcastle United	32	-
1991-92	St. Mirren	34	1
1992-93	Aberdeen	26	2
1993-94	Aberdeen	1	-
1994-95	Aberdeen	2	-
1995-96	Aberdeen	-	-

ALBERTZ, Jorg
Born : Monchengladbach, Germany 29/01/71
from Hamburger SV

ANDERSEN, Erik Bo
Born : Randers, Denmark 14/11/70
from Aalborg Boldspilklub A/S

SEASON	CLUB	LEAGUE APPEARANCES	GOALS
1995-96	Rangers	6	6

ANDERSON, Derek Christopher
Born : Paisley 15/05/72

SEASON	CLUB	LEAGUE APPEARANCES	GOALS
1991-92	Greenock Morton	-	-
1993-94	Kilmarnock	-	-
1994-95	Kilmarnock	20	-
1995-96	Kilmarnock	28	-

ARNOTT, Douglas
Born : Lanark 05/08/61

SEASON	CLUB	LEAGUE APPEARANCES	GOALS
1986-87	Motherwell	1	-
1987-88	Motherwell	2	-
1988-89	Motherwell	14	1
1989-90	Motherwell	30	5
1990-91	Motherwell	29	14
1991-92	Motherwell	26	8
1992-93	Motherwell	33	6
1993-94	Motherwell	29	8
1994-95	Motherwell	27	10
1995-96	Motherwell	27	3

BECKFORD, Darren
Born : Manchester 12/05/67

SEASON	CLUB	LEAGUE APPEARANCES	GOALS
1984-85	Manchester City	4	-
1985-86	Manchester City	3	-
1985-86	*Bury*	12	5
1986-87	Manchester City	4	-
1986-87	*Port Vale*	11	4
1987-88	Port Vale	40	9
1988-89	Port Vale	42	20
1989-90	Port Vale	42	17
1990-91	Port Vale	43	22
1991-92	Norwich City	30	7
1992-93	Norwich City	8	1
1992-93	Oldham Athletic	7	3
1993-94	Oldham Athletic	22	6
1994-95	Oldham Athletic	3	-
1995-96	Oldham Athletic	20	2

BENNEKER, Armand
Born : Tongeren, Belgium 25/06/69
from MVV Maastricht

BERNARD, Paul
Born : Edinburgh 30/12/72

SEASON	CLUB	LEAGUE APPEARANCES	GOALS
1990-91	Oldham Athletic	2	1
1991-92	Oldham Athletic	21	5
1992-93	Oldham Athletic	33	4
1993-94	Oldham Athletic	32	5
1994-95	Oldham Athletic	17	2
1995-96	Oldham Athletic	7	1
1995-96	Aberdeen	31	1

BINGHAM, David Thomas
Born : Dunfermline 03/09/70

SEASON	CLUB	LEAGUE APPEARANCES	GOALS
1989-90	St. Johnstone	1	-
1990-91	St. Johnstone	7	2
1991-92	St. Johnstone	9	1
1992-93	St. Johnstone	-	-
1992-93	Forfar Athletic	20	6
1993-94	Forfar Athletic	38	13
1994-95	Forfar Athletic	36	22
1995-96	Forfar Athletic	5	3
1995-96	Dunfermline Athletic	15	3

BJORKLUND, Joachim
Born : Vaxjo, Sweden 15/03/71
from Vicenza Calcio

BOLLAN, Gary
Born : Dundee 24/03/73

SEASON	CLUB	LEAGUE APPEARANCES	GOALS
1987-88	Celtic	-	-
1988-89	Celtic	-	-
1989-90	Celtic	-	-
1990-91	Dundee United	2	-
1991-92	Dundee United	10	1
1992-93	Dundee United	15	3
1993-94	Dundee United	12	-
1994-95	Dundee United	7	-
1994-95	Rangers	6	-
1995-96	Rangers	4	-

BONAR, Paul
Born : Glasgow 28/12/76

SEASON	CLUB	LEAGUE APPEARANCES	GOALS
1995-96	Airdrieonians	12	-
1995-96	Raith Rovers	5	-

BONNER, Patrick Joseph
Born : Donegal 24/05/60

SEASON	CLUB	LEAGUE APPEARANCES	GOALS
1978-79	Celtic	2	-
1979-80	Celtic	-	-
1980-81	Celtic	36	-
1981-82	Celtic	36	-
1982-83	Celtic	36	-
1983-84	Celtic	33	-
1984-85	Celtic	34	-
1985-86	Celtic	30	-
1986-87	Celtic	43	-
1987-88	Celtic	32	-
1988-89	Celtic	26	-
1989-90	Celtic	36	-
1990-91	Celtic	36	-
1991-92	Celtic	19	-
1992-93	Celtic	33	-
1993-94	Celtic	31	-
1994-95	Celtic	20	-
1995-96	Celtic	-	-

BOOTH, Scott
Born : Aberdeen 16/12/71

SEASON	CLUB	LEAGUE APPEARANCES	GOALS
1988-89	Aberdeen	-	-
1989-90	Aberdeen	2	-
1990-91	Aberdeen	19	6
1991-92	Aberdeen	33	5
1992-93	Aberdeen	29	13
1993-94	Aberdeen	25	4
1994-95	Aberdeen	12	6
1995-96	Aberdeen	24	9

BOWMAN, David
Born : Tunbridge Wells 10/03/64

SEASON	CLUB	LEAGUE APPEARANCES	GOALS
1980-81	Heart of Midlothian	17	1
1981-82	Heart of Midlothian	16	1
1982-83	Heart of Midlothian	39	5
1983-84	Heart of Midlothian	33	-
1984-85	Heart of Midlothian	11	1
1984-85	Coventry City	10	-
1985-86	Coventry City	30	2
1986-87	Dundee United	29	-
1987-88	Dundee United	39	1
1988-89	Dundee United	29	1
1989-90	Dundee United	24	1
1990-91	Dundee United	20	1
1991-92	Dundee United	41	3
1992-93	Dundee United	24	-
1993-94	Dundee United	35	2
1994-95	Dundee United	31	-
1995-96	Dundee United	17	-

BOYD, Thomas
Born : Glasgow 24/11/65

SEASON	CLUB	LEAGUE APPEARANCES	GOALS
1983-84	Motherwell	13	-
1984-85	Motherwell	36	-
1985-86	Motherwell	31	-
1986-87	Motherwell	31	-
1987-88	Motherwell	42	2
1988-89	Motherwell	36	1
1989-90	Motherwell	33	1
1990-91	Motherwell	30	2
1991-92	Chelsea	23	-
1991-92	Celtic	13	1
1992-93	Celtic	42	-
1993-94	Celtic	38	-
1994-95	Celtic	35	1
1995-96	Celtic	34	-

BRITTON, Gerard Joseph
Born : Glasgow 20/10/70

SEASON	CLUB	LEAGUE APPEARANCES	GOALS
1987-88	Celtic	-	-
1988-89	Celtic	-	-
1989-90	Celtic	-	-
1990-91	Celtic	2	-
1991-92	Celtic	-	-
1991-92	*Reading*	2	-
1992-93	Celtic	-	-
1992-93	Partick Thistle	40	12
1993-94	Partick Thistle	22	3
1993-94	Dundee	17	1
1994-95	Dundee	26	12
1995-96	Dundee	25	2

BROWN, John
Born : Stirling 26/01/62

SEASON	CLUB	LEAGUE APPEARANCES	GOALS
1979-80	Hamilton Academical	19	-
1980-81	Hamilton Academical	38	6
1981-82	Hamilton Academical	28	5
1982-83	Hamilton Academical	9	-
1983-84	Hamilton Academical	39	-
1984-85	Dundee	34	7
1985-86	Dundee	29	11
1986-87	Dundee	31	10
1987-88	Dundee	20	3
1987-88	Rangers	9	2
1988-89	Rangers	29	1
1989-90	Rangers	27	1
1990-91	Rangers	27	1
1991-92	Rangers	25	4
1992-93	Rangers	39	4
1993-94	Rangers	24	-
1994-95	Rangers	13	1
1995-96	Rangers	14	-

BROWN, Thomas
Born : Glasgow 01/04/68

SEASON	CLUB	LEAGUE APPEARANCES	GOALS
1991-92	Queen of the South	-	-
1993-94	Kilmarnock	31	5
1994-95	Kilmarnock	27	4
1995-96	Kilmarnock	25	6

BROWNE, Paul
Born : Glasgow 17/02/75

SEASON	CLUB	LEAGUE APPEARANCES	GOALS
1993-94	Aston Villa	-	-
1994-95	Aston Villa	-	-
1995-96	Aston Villa	2	-

BRUNO, Pasquale
Born : Lecce, Italy 19/06/62
from Fiorentina

SEASON	CLUB	LEAGUE APPEARANCES	GOALS
1995-96	Heart of Midlothian	22	1

BUCHAN, Martin James
Born : Manchester 03/04/77

SEASON	CLUB	LEAGUE APPEARANCES	GOALS
1994-95	Aberdeen	-	-
1995-96	Aberdeen	4	1

BURNS, Alexander
Born : Bellshill 04/08/73

SEASON	CLUB	LEAGUE APPEARANCES	GOALS
1991-92	Motherwell	-	-
1992-93	Motherwell	-	-
1993-94	Motherwell	4	1
1994-95	Motherwell	14	3
1995-96	Motherwell	28	3

CADETE (Reis), Jorge Paulo Santos
Born : Mozambique 27/08/68
from Sporting Lisbon

SEASON	CLUB	LEAGUE APPEARANCES	GOALS
1995-96	Celtic	6	5

CALLAGHAN, Stuart
Born : Calderbank 20/07/76

SEASON	CLUB	LEAGUE APPEARANCES	GOALS
1992-93	Heart of Midlothian	-	-
1993-94	Heart of Midlothian	-	-
1994-95	Heart of Midlothian	-	-
1995-96	Heart of Midlothian	1	-

CAMERON, Colin
Born : Kirkcaldy 23/10/72

SEASON	CLUB	LEAGUE APPEARANCES	GOALS
1990-91	Raith Rovers	-	-
1991-92	Sligo Rovers	-	-
1992-93	Raith Rovers	16	1
1993-94	Raith Rovers	42	6
1994-95	Raith Rovers	34	7
1995-96	Raith Rovers	30	9
1995-96	Heart of Midlothian	4	2

CAMERON, Ian
Born : Glasgow 24/08/66

SEASON	CLUB	LEAGUE APPEARANCES	GOALS
1983-84	St. Mirren	8	-
1984-85	St. Mirren	9	1
1985-86	St. Mirren	12	-
1986-87	St. Mirren	31	6
1987-88	St. Mirren	41	8
1988-89	St. Mirren	26	2
1989-90	Aberdeen	11	-
1990-91	Aberdeen	10	1
1991-92	Aberdeen	6	-
1992-93	Partick Thistle	41	5
1993-94	Partick Thistle	41	1
1994-95	Partick Thistle	34	3
1995-96	Partick Thistle	35	1

CHRISTIE, Kevin
Born : Aberdeen 01/04/76

SEASON	CLUB	LEAGUE APPEARANCES	GOALS
1994-95	Aberdeen	-	-
1995-96	Aberdeen	2	-

CLARK, John
Born : Edinburgh 22/09/64

SEASON	CLUB	LEAGUE APPEARANCES	GOALS
1981-82	Dundee United	-	-
1982-83	Dundee United	1	-
1983-84	Dundee United	9	1
1984-85	Dundee United	10	3
1985-86	Dundee United	11	1
1986-87	Dundee United	30	3
1987-88	Dundee United	28	3
1988-89	Dundee United	20	2
1989-90	Dundee United	29	1
1990-91	Dundee United	18	2
1991-92	Dundee United	35	1
1992-93	Dundee United	37	2
1993-94	Dundee United	14	-
1993-94	Stoke City	12	-
1994-95	Stoke City	5	-
1994-95	Falkirk	31	8
1995-96	Falkirk	17	2
1995-96	Dunfermline Athletic	11	1

CLELAND, Alexander
Born : Glasgow 10/12/70

SEASON	CLUB	LEAGUE APPEARANCES	GOALS
1987-88	Dundee United	1	-
1988-89	Dundee United	9	-
1989-90	Dundee United	15	-
1990-91	Dundee United	20	2
1991-92	Dundee United	31	4
1992-93	Dundee United	24	-
1993-94	Dundee United	33	1
1994-95	Dundee United	18	1
1994-95	Rangers	10	-
1995-96	Rangers	25	1

COLQUHOUN, John Mark
Born : Stirling 14/07/63

SEASON	CLUB	LEAGUE APPEARANCES	GOALS
1980-81	Stirling Albion	13	-
1981-82	Stirling Albion	37	13
1982-83	Stirling Albion	39	21
1983-84	Stirling Albion	15	11
1983-84	Celtic	12	2
1984-85	Celtic	20	2
1985-86	Heart of Midlothian	36	8
1986-87	Heart of Midlothian	43	13
1987-88	Heart of Midlothian	44	15
1988-89	Heart of Midlothian	36	5
1989-90	Heart of Midlothian	36	6
1990-91	Heart of Midlothian	36	7
1991-92	Millwall	27	3
1992-93	Sunderland	20	-
1993-94	Heart of Midlothian	41	6
1994-95	Heart of Midlothian	31	2
1995-96	Heart of Midlothian	31	4

COYLE, Owen Columba
Born : Paisley 14/07/66

SEASON	CLUB	LEAGUE APPEARANCES	GOALS
1985-86	Dumbarton	16	5
1986-87	Dumbarton	43	17
1987-88	Dumbarton	41	14
1988-89	Dumbarton	3	-
1988-89	Clydebank	36	16
1989-90	Clydebank	27	17
1989-90	Airdrieonians	10	10
1990-91	Airdrieonians	28	20
1991-92	Airdrieonians	43	11
1992-93	Airdrieonians	42	9
1993-94	Bolton Wanderers	30	7
1994-95	Bolton Wanderers	19	5
1995-96	Bolton Wanderers	5	-
1995-96	Dundee United	28	5

COYNE, Thomas
Born : Glasgow 14/11/62

SEASON	CLUB	LEAGUE APPEARANCES	GOALS
1981-82	Clydebank	31	9
1982-83	Clydebank	38	18
1983-84	Clydebank	11	10
1983-84	Dundee United	18	3
1984-85	Dundee United	21	3
1985-86	Dundee United	13	2
1986-87	Dundee	20	9
1987-88	Dundee	43	33
1988-89	Dundee	26	9
1988-89	Celtic	7	-
1989-90	Celtic	23	7
1990-91	Celtic	26	18
1991-92	Celtic	39	15
1992-93	Celtic	10	3
1992-93	Tranmere Rovers	12	1
1993-94	Tranmere Rovers	-	-
1993-94	Motherwell	26	12
1994-95	Motherwell	31	16
1995-96	Motherwell	14	4

CRABBE, Scott
Born : Edinburgh 12/08/68

SEASON	CLUB	LEAGUE APPEARANCES	GOALS
1986-87	Heart of Midlothian	5	-
1987-88	Heart of Midlothian	5	-
1988-89	Heart of Midlothian	1	-
1989-90	Heart of Midlothian	35	12
1990-91	Heart of Midlothian	21	3
1991-92	Heart of Midlothian	41	15
1992-93	Heart of Midlothian	8	1
1992-93	Dundee United	27	4
1993-94	Dundee United	21	2
1994-95	Dundee United	9	-
1995-96	Dundee United	2	-a

CRAIG, David William
Born : Glasgow 11/06/69

SEASON	CLUB	LEAGUE APPEARANCES	GOALS
1989-90	Partick Thistle	9	1
1990-91	Partick Thistle	3	-
1991-92	Partick Thistle	-	-
1991-92	East Stirlingshire	34	-
1992-93	East Stirlingshire	16	2
1993-94	East Stirlingshire	38	4
1994-95	Dundee United	6	-
1995-96	Dundee United	-	-
1995-96	Hamilton Academical	17	1

CRAIG, Michael
Born : Glasgow 20/09/77

SEASON	CLUB	LEAGUE APPEARANCES	GOALS
1995-96	Aberdeen	1	-

CURRAN, Henry
Born : Glasgow 09/10/66

SEASON	CLUB	LEAGUE APPEARANCES	GOALS
1984-85	Dumbarton	2	-
1985-86	Dumbarton	6	-
1986-87	Dumbarton	8	-
1986-87	Dundee United	3	-
1987-88	Dundee United	6	-
1988-89	Dundee United	6	-
1989-90	St. Johnstone	31	3
1990-91	St. Johnstone	35	9
1991-92	St. Johnstone	39	8
1992-93	St. Johnstone	34	8
1993-94	St. Johnstone	39	3
1994-95	St. Johnstone	26	4
1995-96	Partick Thistle	8	-

DARGO, Craig Peter
Born : Edinburgh 03/01/78

SEASON	CLUB	LEAGUE APPEARANCES	GOALS
1995-96	Raith Rovers	1	-

DAVIES, William McIntosh
Born : Glasgow 31/05/64

SEASON	CLUB	LEAGUE APPEARANCES	GOALS
1980-81	Rangers	-	-
1981-82	Rangers	4	-
1982-83	Rangers	4	-
1983-84	Rangers	3	1
1984-85	Rangers	-	-
1985-86	Rangers	-	-
1987-88	St. Mirren	18	-
1988-89	St. Mirren	27	4
1989-90	St. Mirren	29	1
1990-91	St. Mirren	-	-
1990-91	Leicester City	6	-
1990-91	Dunfermline Athletic	26	-
1991-92	Dunfermline Athletic	33	-
1992-93	Dunfermline Athletic	41	10
1993-94	Dunfermline Athletic	4	-
1993-94	Motherwell	10	-
1994-95	Motherwell	31	4
1995-96	Motherwell	33	2

DEN BIEMAN, Ivo Johannes
Born : Wamel, Holland 04/02/67
from SV Leones

SEASON	CLUB	LEAGUE APPEARANCES	GOALS
1990-91	Montrose	36	5
1991-92	Montrose	42	6
1992-93	Dundee	24	3
1993-94	Dunfermline Athletic	41	3
1994-95	Dunfermline Athletic	31	5
1995-96	Dunfermline Athletic	26	1

DENHAM, Greig Paterson
Born : Glasgow 05/10/76

SEASON	CLUB	LEAGUE APPEARANCES	GOALS
1993-94	Motherwell	-	-
1994-95	Motherwell	-	-
1995-96	Motherwell	13	-

DENNIS, Shaun
Born : Kirkcaldy 20/12/69

SEASON	CLUB	LEAGUE APPEARANCES	GOALS
1988-89	Raith Rovers	10	-
1989-90	Raith Rovers	18	-
1990-91	Raith Rovers	35	1
1991-92	Raith Rovers	42	-

SEASON	CLUB	LEAGUE APPEARANCES	GOALS
1992-93	Raith Rovers	31	1
1993-94	Raith Rovers	43	3
1994-95	Raith Rovers	26	1
1995-96	Raith Rovers	25	-

DI CANIO, Paolo
Born : Rome, Italy 08/07/68
from AC Milan

DODDS, William
Born: New Cumnock 05/02/69

SEASON	CLUB	LEAGUE APPEARANCES	GOALS
1986-87	Chelsea	1	-
1987-88	Chelsea	-	-
1987-88	*Partick Thistle*	30	9
1988-89	Chelsea	2	-
1989-90	Dundee	30	13
1990-91	Dundee	37	15
1991-92	Dundee	42	19
1992-93	Dundee	41	16
1993-94	Dundee	24	6
1993-94	St. Johnstone	20	6
1994-95	Aberdeen	35	15
1995-96	Aberdeen	31	7

DODS, Darren
Born : Edinburgh 07/06/75

SEASON	CLUB	LEAGUE APPEARANCES	GOALS
1992-93	Hibernian	-	-
1993-94	Hibernian	-	-
1994-95	Hibernian	1	-
1995-96	Hibernian	15	-

DOLAN, James
Born : Salsburgh 22/02/69

SEASON	CLUB	LEAGUE APPEARANCES	GOALS
1987-88	Motherwell	-	-
1988-89	Motherwell	5	-
1989-90	Motherwell	12	-
1990-91	Motherwell	8	1
1991-92	Motherwell	32	2
1992-93	Motherwell	25	2
1993-94	Motherwell	36	-
1994-95	Motherwell	31	-
1995-96	Motherwell	27	-

DONALD, Graeme Still
Born : Stirling 14/04/74

SEASON	CLUB	LEAGUE APPEARANCES	GOALS
1991-92	Hibernian	5	3
1992-93	Hibernian	4	-
1993-94	Hibernian	6	-
1994-95	Hibernian	-	-
1995-96	Hibernian	13	1

DONNELLY, Simon
Born : Glasgow 01/12/74

SEASON	CLUB	LEAGUE APPEARANCES	GOALS
1993-94	Celtic	12	5
1994-95	Celtic	17	-
1995-96	Celtic	35	6

DOW, Andrew James
Born : Dundee 07/02/73

SEASON	CLUB	LEAGUE APPEARANCES	GOALS
1990-91	Dundee	-	-
1991-92	Dundee	4	-
1992-93	Dundee	14	1
1993-94	Chelsea	14	-
1994-95	Chelsea	-	-
1994-95	*Bradford City*	5	-
1995-96	Chelsea	1	-
1995-96	Hibernian	8	1

DUFFIELD, Peter
Born : Middlesbrough 04/02/69

SEASON	CLUB	LEAGUE APPEARANCES	GOALS
1986-87	Middlesbrough	-	-
1987-88	Sheffield United	11	1
1987-88	*Halifax Town*	12	6
1988-89	Sheffield United	38	11
1989-90	Sheffield United	5	2
1990-91	Sheffield United	2	-
1990-91	*Rotherham United*	17	4
1991-92	Sheffield United	2	-
1992-93	Sheffield United	-	-
1992-93	*Blackpool*	5	1
1992-93	*Bournemouth*	-	-
1992-93	*Stockport County*	7	4
1992-93	*Crewe Alexandria*	2	-
1993-94	Sheffield United	-	-
1993-94	Hamilton Academical	36	19
1994-95	Hamilton Academical	36	20
1995-96	Airdrieonians	24	6
1995-96	Raith Rovers	9	5

DUFFY, Cornelius
Born : Glasgow 05/06/67

SEASON	CLUB	LEAGUE APPEARANCES	GOALS
1984-85	Dundee United	-	-
1985-86	Dundee United	-	-
1989-90	Dundee United	-	-
1990-91	Dundee United	-	-
1990-91	Falkirk	25	2
1991-92	Falkirk	39	2
1992-93	Falkirk	34	5
1993-94	Falkirk	23	10
1993-94	Dundee	12	2
1994-95	Dundee	24	3
1995-96	Dundee	19	3

DURIE, Gordon Scott
Born : Paisley 06/12/65

SEASON	CLUB	LEAGUE APPEARANCES	GOALS
1981-82	East Fife	13	1
1982-83	East Fife	25	2
1983-84	East Fife	34	16
1984-85	East Fife	9	7
1984-85	Hibernian	22	8
1985-86	Hibernian	25	6
1985-86	Chelsea	1	-
1986-87	Chelsea	25	5
1987-88	Chelsea	26	12
1988-89	Chelsea	32	17
1989-90	Chelsea	15	5
1990-91	Chelsea	24	12
1991-92	Tottenham Hotspur	31	7
1992-93	Tottenham Hotspur	17	3
1993-94	Tottenham Hotspur	10	1
1993-94	Rangers	24	12
1994-95	Rangers	20	6
1995-96	Rangers	27	17

DURRANT, Ian
Born : Glasgow 29/10/66

SEASON	CLUB	LEAGUE APPEARANCES	GOALS
1984-85	Rangers	5	-
1985-86	Rangers	30	2
1986-87	Rangers	39	4
1987-88	Rangers	40	10
1988-89	Rangers	8	2
1989-90	Rangers	-	-
1990-91	Rangers	4	1
1991-92	Rangers	13	-
1992-93	Rangers	30	3
1993-94	Rangers	23	-
1994-95	Rangers	26	4
1995-96	Rangers	15	-

ESSANDOH, Roy
Born : Belfast 17/02/76
from Glentoran

SEASON	CLUB	LEAGUE APPEARANCES	GOALS
1994-95	Motherwell	-	-
1995-96	Motherwell	4	-

FALCONER, William Henry
Born : Aberdeen 05/04/66

SEASON	CLUB	LEAGUE APPEARANCES	GOALS
1982-83	Aberdeen	1	-
1983-84	Aberdeen	8	1
1984-85	Aberdeen	16	4
1985-86	Aberdeen	8	-
1986-87	Aberdeen	8	-
1987-88	Aberdeen	36	8
1988-89	Watford	33	5
1989-90	Watford	30	3
1990-91	Watford	35	4
1991-92	Middlesbrough	25	5
1992-93	Middlesbrough	28	5
1993-94	Middlesbrough	-	-
1993-94	Sheffield United	23	3
1993-94	Celtic	14	1
1994-95	Celtic	26	4
1995-96	Celtic	2	-
1995-96	Motherwell	15	5

FARRELL, Gerard James
Born : Glasgow 14/06/75

SEASON	CLUB	LEAGUE APPEARANCES	GOALS
1993-94	Dumbarton	1	-
1994-95	Dumbarton	1	-
1995-96	Dunfermline Athletic	6	-

FERGUSON, Ian
Born : Glasgow 15/03/67

SEASON	CLUB	LEAGUE APPEARANCES	GOALS
1984-85	Clyde	2	-
1985-86	Clyde	19	4
1986-87	Clyde	5	-
1986-87	St. Mirren	35	4
1987-88	St. Mirren	22	6
1987-88	Rangers	8	1
1988-89	Rangers	30	6
1989-90	Rangers	24	-
1990-91	Rangers	11	1
1991-92	Rangers	16	1
1992-93	Rangers	30	4
1993-94	Rangers	35	5
1994-95	Rangers	16	1
1995-96	Rangers	18	2

FERGUSON, Steven
Born : Edinburgh 18/05/77

SEASON	CLUB	LEAGUE APPEARANCES	GOALS
1995-96	Dunfermline Athletic	1	-

FERRERI, Juan Francisco
Born : Florida, Uruguay 13/07/70
from Denfensor Sporting Club

SEASON	CLUB	LEAGUE APPEARANCES	GOALS
1994-95	Dundee United	1	-
1995-96	Dundee United	-	-

FINDLAY, William McCall
Born : Kilmarnock 29/08/70

SEASON	CLUB	LEAGUE APPEARANCES	GOALS
1987-88	Hibernian	-	-
1988-89	Hibernian	3	1
1989-90	Hibernian	10	-
1990-91	Hibernian	26	2
1991-92	Hibernian	9	-
1992-93	Hibernian	7	-
1993-94	Hibernian	20	3
1994-95	Hibernian	18	1
1994-95	Kilmarnock	9	-
1995-96	Kilmarnock	3	-

FLEMING, Derek
Born : Falkirk 05/12/73

SEASON	CLUB	LEAGUE APPEARANCES	GOALS
1992-93	Meadowbank Thistle	4	-
1993-94	Meadowbank Thistle	38	2
1994-95	Meadowbank Thistle	7	1
1994-95	Dunfermline Athletic	29	1
1995-96	Dunfermline Athletic	33	3

FRAIL, Stephen Charles
Born : Glasgow 10/08/69

SEASON	CLUB	LEAGUE APPEARANCES	GOALS
1985-86	Dundee	-	-
1986-87	Dundee	-	-
1987-88	Dundee	4	-
1988-89	Dundee	23	1
1989-90	Dundee	6	-
1990-91	Dundee	26	-
1991-92	Dundee	3	-
1992-93	Dundee	7	-
1993-94	Dundee	32	-
1993-94	Heart of Midlothian	9	2
1994-95	Heart of Midlothian	25	2
1995-96	Heart of Midlothian	-	-

FRENCH, Hamish Mackie
Born : Aberdeen 07/02/64

SEASON	CLUB	LEAGUE APPEARANCES	GOALS
1987-88	Dundee United	20	2
1988-89	Dundee United	18	3
1989-90	Dundee United	12	2
1990-91	Dundee United	19	3
1991-92	Dundee United	6	1
1991-92	Dunfermline Athletic	31	2
1992-93	Dunfermline Athletic	38	12
1993-94	Dunfermline Athletic	36	15
1994-95	Dunfermline Athletic	25	12
1995-96	Dunfermline Athletic	23	4

FULTON, Stephen
Born: Greenock 10/08/70

SEASON	CLUB	LEAGUE APPEARANCES	GOALS
1986-87	Celtic	-	-
1987-88	Celtic	-	-
1988-89	Celtic	3	-
1989-90	Celtic	16	-
1990-91	Celtic	21	-
1991-92	Celtic	30	2
1992-93	Celtic	6	-
1993-94	Bolton Wanderers	4	-
1994-95	Falkirk	28	3
1995-96	Falkirk	5	-
1995-96	Heart of Midlothian	26	2

GASCOIGNE, Paul
Born : Gateshead 27/05/67

SEASON	CLUB	LEAGUE APPEARANCES	GOALS
1984-85	Newcastle United	2	-
1985-86	Newcastle United	31	9
1986-87	Newcastle United	24	5
1987-88	Newcastle United	35	7
1988-89	Tottenham Hotspur	32	6
1989-90	Tottenham Hotspur	34	6
1990-91	Tottenham Hotspur	26	7
1991-92	Tottenham Hotspur	-	-
1992-93	Lazio Societa Sportiva	22	4
1993-94	Lazio Societa Sportiva	17	2
1994-95	Lazio Societa Sportiva	2	-
1995-96	Rangers	28	14

GEDDES, Alexander Robert
Born : Inverness 12/08/60

SEASON	CLUB	LEAGUE APPEARANCES	GOALS
1977-78	Dundee	-	-
1978-79	Dundee	-	-
1979-80	Dundee	-	-
1980-81	Dundee	20	-
1981-82	Dundee	28	-
1982-83	Dundee	1	-
1983-84	Dundee	24	-
1984-85	Dundee	16	-
1985-86	Dundee	36	-
1986-87	Dundee	44	-
1987-88	Dundee	38	-
1988-89	Dundee	34	-
1989-90	Dundee	12	-
1990-91	Kilmarnock	38	-
1991-92	Kilmarnock	33	-
1992-93	Kilmarnock	44	-
1993-94	Kilmarnock	44	-
1994-95	Kilmarnock	12	-
1995-96	Kilmarnock	2	-
1995-96	Raith Rovers	9	-

GLASS, Stephen
Born : Dundee 23/05/76

SEASON	CLUB	LEAGUE APPEARANCES	GOALS
1994-95	Aberdeen	19	1
1995-96	Aberdeen	32	3

GORAM, Andrew Lewis
Born : Bury 13/04/64

SEASON	CLUB	LEAGUE APPEARANCES	GOALS
1981-82	Oldham Athletic	3	-
1982-83	Oldham Athletic	38	-
1983-84	Oldham Athletic	22	-
1984-85	Oldham Athletic	41	-
1985-86	Oldham Athletic	41	-
1986-87	Oldham Athletic	41	-
1987-88	Oldham Athletic	9	-
1987-88	Hibernian	33	1
1988-89	Hibernian	36	-
1989-90	Hibernian	34	-
1990-91	Hibernian	35	-
1991-92	Rangers	44	-
1992-93	Rangers	34	-
1993-94	Rangers	8	-
1994-95	Rangers	19	-
1995-96	Rangers	30	-

GOSS, Jeremy
Born : Oekolia, Cyprus 11/05/65

SEASON	CLUB	LEAGUE APPEARANCES	GOALS
1982-83	Norwich City	-	-
1983-84	Norwich City	1	-
1984-85	Norwich City	5	-
1985-86	Norwich City	-	-
1986-87	Norwich City	1	-
1987-88	Norwich City	22	2
1988-89	Norwich City	-	-
1989-90	Norwich City	7	-
1990-91	Norwich City	19	1
1991-92	Norwich City	33	1
1992-93	Norwich City	25	1
1993-94	Norwich City	34	6
1994-95	Norwich City	25	2
1995-96	Norwich City	16	1

GOUGH, Charles Richard
Born : Stockholm, Sweden 05/04/62

SEASON	CLUB	LEAGUE APPEARANCES	GOALS
1980-81	Dundee United	4	-
1981-82	Dundee United	30	1
1982-83	Dundee United	34	8
1983-84	Dundee United	33	3
1984-85	Dundee United	33	6
1985-86	Dundee United	31	5
1986-87	Tottenham Hotspur	40	2
1987-88	Tottenham Hotspur	9	-
1987-88	Rangers	31	5
1988-89	Rangers	35	4
1989-90	Rangers	26	-
1990-91	Rangers	26	-
1991-92	Rangers	33	2
1992-93	Rangers	25	2
1993-94	Rangers	37	3
1994-95	Rangers	25	1
1995-96	Rangers	29	3

GRANT, Brian
Born : Bannockburn 19/06/64

SEASON	CLUB	LEAGUE APPEARANCES	GOALS
1981-82	Stirling Albion	1	-
1982-83	Stirling Albion	1	-
1983-84	Stirling Albion	24	3
1984-85	Aberdeen	-	-
1985-86	Aberdeen	-	-
1986-87	Aberdeen	15	4
1987-88	Aberdeen	7	1
1988-89	Aberdeen	26	1
1989-90	Aberdeen	31	6
1990-91	Aberdeen	32	2
1991-92	Aberdeen	33	6
1992-93	Aberdeen	29	3
1993-94	Aberdeen	30	2
1994-95	Aberdeen	32	2
1995-96	Aberdeen	25	-

GRANT, Peter
Born : Bellshill 30/08/65

SEASON	CLUB	LEAGUE APPEARANCES	GOALS
1982-83	Celtic	-	-
1983-84	Celtic	3	-
1984-85	Celtic	20	4
1985-86	Celtic	30	1
1986-87	Celtic	37	1
1987-88	Celtic	37	2
1988-89	Celtic	21	-
1989-90	Celtic	26	-
1990-91	Celtic	27	-
1991-92	Celtic	22	-
1992-93	Celtic	31	2
1993-94	Celtic	28	-
1994-95	Celtic	28	2
1995-96	Celtic	31	3

Peter Grant

GRAY, Stuart Edward
Born : Harrogate 18/12/73

SEASON	CLUB	LEAGUE APPEARANCES	GOALS
1992-93	Celtic	1	-
1993-94	Celtic	-	-
1994-95	Celtic	11	-
1995-96	Celtic	5	1

HANNAH, David
Born : Airdrie 04/08/73

SEASON	CLUB	LEAGUE APPEARANCES	GOALS
1991-92	Dundee United	-	-
1992-93	Dundee United	5	-
1993-94	Dundee United	10	2
1994-95	Dundee United	32	2
1995-96	Dundee United	7	1

HARPER, Kevin Patrick
Born : Oldham 15/01/76

SEASON	CLUB	LEAGUE APPEARANCES	GOALS
1992-93	Hibernian	-	-
1993-94	Hibernian	2	-
1994-95	Hibernian	23	5
1995-96	Hibernian	16	3

HARVEY, Paul Edward
Born : Glasgow 28/08/68

SEASON	CLUB	LEAGUE APPEARANCES	GOALS
1986-87	Manchester United	-	-
1987-88	Manchester United	-	-
1987-88	Clydebank	29	1
1988-89	Clydebank	29	1
1989-90	Clydebank	34	3
1990-91	Clydebank	36	2
1991-92	Clydebank	41	4
1992-93	Clydebank	39	5
1993-94	Clydebank	26	3
1993-94	Airdrieonians	13	1
1994-95	Airdrieonians	33	2
1995-96	Airdrieonians	34	2

HAY, Christopher Drummond
Born : Glasgow 28/08/74

SEASON	CLUB	LEAGUE APPEARANCES	GOALS
1993-94	Celtic	2	-
1994-95	Celtic	5	-
1995-96	Celtic	4	-

HEGARTY, Ryan Michael
Born : Edinburgh 08/03/76

SEASON	CLUB	LEAGUE APPEARANCES	GOALS
1994-95	Dundee United	-	-
1995-96	Dunfermline Athletic	9	1

HENDRY, John
Born: Glasgow 06/01/70

SEASON	CLUB	LEAGUE APPEARANCES	GOALS
1988-89	Dundee	2	-
1989-90	Dundee	-	-
1989-90	*Forfar Athletic*	10	6
1990-91	Tottenham Hotspur	4	2
1991-92	Tottenham Hotspur	5	1
1991-92	*Charlton Athletic*	5	1
1992-93	Tottenham Hotspur	5	2
1993-94	Tottenham Hotspur	3	-
1994-95	Tottenham Hotspur	-	-
1995-96	Motherwell	16	2

HENRY, John
Born: Vale of Leven 31/12/71

SEASON	CLUB	LEAGUE APPEARANCES	GOALS
1990-91	Clydebank	3	1
1991-92	Clydebank	35	8
1992-93	Clydebank	32	12
1993-94	Clydebank	44	6
1994-95	Kilmarnock	30	4
1995-96	Kilmarnock	29	3

HOGARTH, Myles
Born : Falkirk 30/03/75

SEASON	CLUB	LEAGUE APPEARANCES	GOALS
1995-96	Heart of Midlothian	1	-

HOLT, Gary
Born : Irvine 09/03/73

SEASON	CLUB	LEAGUE APPEARANCES	GOALS
1994-95	Stoke City	-	-
1995-96	Kilmarnock	26	-

HOWIE, Scott
Born : Glasgow 04/01/72

SEASON	CLUB	LEAGUE APPEARANCES	GOALS
1991-92	Clyde	15	-
1992-93	Clyde	39	-
1993-94	Clyde	1	-
1993-94	Norwich City	2	-
1994-95	Norwich City	-	-
1994-95	Motherwell	3	-
1995-96	Motherwell	36	-

HUGHES, John
Born : Edinburgh 09/09/64

SEASON	CLUB	LEAGUE APPEARANCES	GOALS
1988-89	Berwick Rangers	27	10
1989-90	Berwick Rangers	14	4
1989-90	Swansea City	24	4
1990-91	Swansea City	-	-
1990-91	Falkirk	32	2
1991-92	Falkirk	38	2
1992-93	Falkirk	15	-
1993-94	Falkirk	29	3
1994-95	Falkirk	20	-
1995-96	Celtic	26	2

HUMPHRIES, Mark
Born : Glasgow 23/12/71

SEASON	CLUB	LEAGUE APPEARANCES	GOALS
1990-91	Aberdeen	-	-
1991-92	Aberdeen	2	-
1992-93	Aberdeen	-	-
1993-94	Leeds United	-	-
1994-95	Bristol City	4	-
1995-96	Bristol City	-	-
1995-96	Raith Rovers	9	-

HUNTER, Gordon
Born : Wallyford 03/05/67

SEASON	CLUB	LEAGUE APPEARANCES	GOALS
1983-84	Hibernian	1	-
1984-85	Hibernian	6	-
1985-86	Hibernian	25	-
1986-87	Hibernian	29	-
1987-88	Hibernian	35	-
1988-89	Hibernian	33	1
1989-90	Hibernian	34	-
1990-91	Hibernian	20	1
1991-92	Hibernian	37	2
1992-93	Hibernian	23	-
1993-94	Hibernian	29	1
1994-95	Hibernian	29	2
1995-96	Hibernian	22	-

INGLIS, John
Born : Edinburgh 16/10/66

SEASON	CLUB	LEAGUE APPEARANCES	GOALS
1983-84	East Fife	4	1
1984-85	East Fife	9	-
1985-86	East Fife	30	-
1986-87	East Fife	13	-
1986-87	Brechin City	15	-
1987-88	Brechin City	26	3
1988-89	Brechin City	12	1
1988-89	Meadowbank Thistle	12	1
1989-90	Meadowbank Thistle	38	3
1990-91	St. Johnstone	31	1
1991-92	St. Johnstone	40	-
1992-93	St. Johnstone	39	-
1993-94	St. Johnstone	25	1
1994-95	St. Johnstone	5	-
1994-95	Aberdeen	17	1
1995-96	Aberdeen	24	1

IRELAND, Craig
Born : Dundee 29/11/75

SEASON	CLUB	LEAGUE APPEARANCES	GOALS
1994-95	Aberdeen	-	-
1995-96	Aberdeen	-	-
1995-96	Dunfermline Athletic	10	-

IRVINE, Brian Alexander
Born : Bellshill 24/05/65

SEASON	CLUB	LEAGUE APPEARANCES	GOALS
1983-84	Falkirk	3	-
1984-85	Falkirk	35	-
1985-86	Aberdeen	1	-
1986-87	Aberdeen	20	1
1987-88	Aberdeen	16	1
1988-89	Aberdeen	27	2
1989-90	Aberdeen	31	1
1990-91	Aberdeen	29	2
1991-92	Aberdeen	41	4
1992-93	Aberdeen	39	5
1993-94	Aberdeen	42	7
1994-95	Aberdeen	17	1
1995-96	Aberdeen	18	3

JACKSON, Christopher
Born : Edinburgh 29/10/73

SEASON	CLUB	LEAGUE APPEARANCES	GOALS
1992-93	Hibernian	1	-
1993-94	Hibernian	12	-
1994-95	Hibernian	-	-
1995-96	Hibernian	23	2

JACKSON, Darren
Born : Edinburgh 25/07/66

SEASON	CLUB	LEAGUE APPEARANCES	GOALS
1985-86	Meadowbank Thistle	39	17
1986-87	Meadowbank Thistle	9	5
1986-87	Newcastle United	23	3
1987-88	Newcastle United	31	2
1988-89	Newcastle United	15	2
1988-89	Dundee United	1	-
1989-90	Dundee United	25	7
1990-91	Dundee United	33	12
1991-92	Dundee United	28	11
1992-93	Hibernian	36	13
1993-94	Hibernian	39	7
1994-95	Hibernian	31	10
1995-96	Hibernian	36	9

JOHNSON, Ian Grant
Born : Dundee 24/03/72

SEASON	CLUB	LEAGUE APPEARANCES	GOALS
1990-91	Dundee United	-	-
1991-92	Dundee United	10	1
1992-93	Dundee United	17	1
1993-94	Dundee United	10	-
1994-95	Dundee United	13	1
1995-96	Dundee United	28	4

KEITH, Marino
Born : Peterhead 16/12/74

SEASON	CLUB	LEAGUE APPEARANCES	GOALS
1995-96	Dundee United	4	-

KEY, Lance
Born : Kettering 13/05/68

SEASON	CLUB	LEAGUE APPEARANCES	GOALS
1991-92	Sheffield Wednesday	-	-
1991-92	*York City*	-	-
1992-93	Sheffield Wednesday	-	-
1993-94	Sheffield Wednesday	-	-
1993-94	*Oldham Athletic*	2	-
1993-94	*Portsmouth*	-	-
1994-95	Sheffield Wednesday	-	-
1994-95	*Oxford United*	6	-
1995-96	Sheffield Wednesday	-	-
1995-96	*Lincoln City*	5	-
1995-96	*Hartlepool United*	1	-
1995-96	*Rochdale*	14	-

KIRIAKOV, Ilian
Born : Pavlikeni, Bulgaria 04/08/67
from Anorthosis

KIRK, Stephen David
Born : Kirkcaldy 03/01/63

SEASON	CLUB	LEAGUE APPEARANCES	GOALS
1979-80	East Fife	25	2
1980-81	Stoke City	-	-
1981-82	Stoke City	12	-
1982-83	Partick Thistle	-	-
1982-83	East Fife	25	8
1983-84	East Fife	33	5
1984-85	East Fife	38	8
1985-86	East Fife	39	14
1986-87	Motherwell	35	10
1987-88	Motherwell	38	4
1988-89	Motherwell	33	14
1989-90	Motherwell	34	8
1990-91	Motherwell	29	2
1991-92	Motherwell	38	6
1992-93	Motherwell	40	10
1993-94	Motherwell	36	7
1994-95	Motherwell	18	2
1994-95	Falkirk	11	5
1995-96	Falkirk	20	4
1995-96	Raith Rovers	7	1

KIRKWOOD, David Stewart
Born : St. Andrews 27/08/67

SEASON	CLUB	LEAGUE APPEARANCES	GOALS
1983-84	East Fife	14	2
1984-85	East Fife	17	4
1985-86	East Fife	34	2
1986-87	East Fife	35	2
1987-88	Rangers	4	-
1988-89	Rangers	2	-
1989-90	Heart of Midlothian	19	-
1990-91	Heart of Midlothian	9	1
1991-92	Airdrieonians	36	9
1992-93	Airdrieonians	27	2
1993-94	Airdrieonians	29	10
1994-95	Raith Rovers	19	1
1995-96	Raith Rovers	28	2

KOMBOUARE, Antoine
Born : Noumea 16/11/63
from F.C. Sion

KPEDEKPO, Malcolm
Born : Aberdeen 27/08/76

SEASON	CLUB	LEAGUE APPEARANCES	GOALS
1994-95	Aberdeen	1	-
1995-96	Aberdeen	5	-

KRIVOKAPIC, Miodrag
Born : Niksic Crna Gora 06/09/59
From Red Star Belgrade

SEASON	CLUB	LEAGUE APPEARANCES	GOALS
1988-89	Dundee United	24	1
1989-90	Dundee United	26	-
1990-91	Dundee United	24	-
1991-92	Dundee United	-	-
1992-93	Dundee United	8	-
1993-94	Motherwell	42	1
1994-95	Motherwell	16	-
1995-96	Motherwell	13	-
1995-96	Raith Rovers	5	-

LANDELS, Graeme John
Born : Broxburn 27/03/78

SEASON	CLUB	LEAGUE APPEARANCES	GOALS
1995-96	Raith Rovers	1	-

LAUCHLAN, James Harley
Born : Glasgow 02/02/77

SEASON	CLUB	LEAGUE APPEARANCES	GOALS
1994-95	Kilmarnock	2	-
1995-96	Kilmarnock	5	-

LAUDRUP, Brian
Born : Vienna, Austria 22/02/69

SEASON	CLUB	LEAGUE APPEARANCES	GOALS
1986-89	Brondby IF	49	13
1989-90	Bayern Uerdingen	34	6
1990-92	FC Bayern Munich	53	11
1992-93	AC Fiorentina	31	5
1993-94	*AC Milan*	9	1
From AC Fiorentina			
1994-95	Rangers	33	10
1995-96	Rangers	22	2

LAVETY, Barry
Born : Johnstone 21/08/74

SEASON	CLUB	LEAGUE APPEARANCES	GOALS
1991-92	St. Mirren	5	2
1992-93	St. Mirren	42	18
1993-94	St. Mirren	42	10
1994-95	St. Mirren	31	7
1995-96	St. Mirren	29	11

LEIGHTON, James
Born : Johnstone 24/07/58

SEASON	CLUB	LEAGUE APPEARANCES	GOALS
1978-79	Aberdeen	11	-
1979-80	Aberdeen	1	-
1980-81	Aberdeen	35	-
1981-82	Aberdeen	36	-
1982-83	Aberdeen	35	-
1983-84	Aberdeen	36	-
1984-85	Aberdeen	34	-
1985-86	Aberdeen	26	-
1986-87	Aberdeen	42	-
1987-88	Aberdeen	44	-
1988-89	Manchester United	38	-
1989-90	Manchester United	35	-
1990-91	Manchester United	-	-
1990-91	*Arsenal*	-	-

SEASON	CLUB	LEAGUE APPEARANCES	GOALS
1991-92	Manchester United	-	-
1991-92	*Reading*	8	-
1991-92	Dundee	13	-
1992-93	Dundee	8	-
1993-94	Hibernian	44	-
1994-95	Hibernian	36	-
1995-96	Hibernian	36	-

LEKOVIC, Dragoje
Born : Sivac, Montenegro 21/11/67

From Buducnost Podgorica

SEASON	CLUB	LEAGUE APPEARANCES	GOALS
1994-95	Kilmarnock	20	-
1995-96	Kilmarnock	33	-

LEMAJIC, Zoran
Born : Niksic 08/11/60

from C.S. Maritimo

LENNON, Daniel Joseph
Born : Whitburn 06/04/69

SEASON	CLUB	LEAGUE APPEARANCES	GOALS
1987-88	Hibernian	1	-
1988-89	Hibernian	1	-
1989-90	Hibernian	-	-
1990-91	Hibernian	6	-
1991-92	Hibernian	11	1
1992-93	Hibernian	13	-
1993-94	Hibernian	5	1
1993-94	Raith Rovers	7	-
1994-95	Raith Rovers	20	-
1995-96	Raith Rovers	33	5

LEVEIN, Craig William
Born : Dunfermline 22/10/64

SEASON	CLUB	LEAGUE APPEARANCES	GOALS
1981-82	Cowdenbeath	15	-
1982-83	Cowdenbeath	30	-
1983-84	Cowdenbeath	15	-
1983-84	Heart of Midlothian	22	-
1984-85	Heart of Midlothian	36	1
1985-86	Heart of Midlothian	33	2
1986-87	Heart of Midlothian	12	-
1987-88	Heart of Midlothian	21	-
1988-89	Heart of Midlothian	9	-
1989-90	Heart of Midlothian	35	-
1990-91	Heart of Midlothian	33	4
1991-92	Heart of Midlothian	36	2
1992-93	Heart of Midlothian	37	3
1993-94	Heart of Midlothian	30	3
1994-95	Heart of Midlothian	24	-
1995-96	Heart of Midlothian	1	-

LOCKE, Gary
Born : Edinburgh 16/06/75

SEASON	CLUB	LEAGUE APPEARANCES	GOALS
1992-93	Heart of Midlothian	1	-
1993-94	Heart of Midlothian	33	-
1994-95	Heart of Midlothian	9	-
1995-96	Heart of Midlothian	29	4

LOVE, Graeme
Born : Bathgate 07/12/73

SEASON	CLUB	LEAGUE APPEARANCES	GOALS
1991-92	Hibernian	1	-
1992-93	Hibernian	1	-
1993-94	Hibernian	4	-
1994-95	Hibernian	12	-
1995-96	Hibernian	14	-

MACKAY, Gary
Born : Edinburgh 23/01/64

SEASON	CLUB	LEAGUE APPEARANCES	GOALS
1980-81	Heart of Midlothian	12	-
1981-82	Heart of Midlothian	17	2
1982-83	Heart of Midlothian	34	6
1983-84	Heart of Midlothian	31	4
1984-85	Heart of Midlothian	17	2
1985-86	Heart of Midlothian	32	4
1986-87	Heart of Midlothian	37	7
1987-88	Heart of Midlothian	41	5
1988-89	Heart of Midlothian	29	2
1989-90	Heart of Midlothian	33	1
1990-91	Heart of Midlothian	30	3
1991-92	Heart of Midlothian	43	1
1992-93	Heart of Midlothian	37	2
1993-94	Heart of Midlothian	36	1
1994-95	Heart of Midlothian	34	2
1995-96	Heart of Midlothian	26	2

MACKAY, Malcolm George
Born: Bellshill 19/02/72

SEASON	CLUB	LEAGUE APPEARANCES	GOALS
1989-90	Queen's Park	-	-
1990-91	Queen's Park	10	-
1991-92	Queen's Park	27	3
1992-93	Queen's Park	33	3
1993-94	Celtic	-	-
1994-95	Celtic	1	-
1995-96	Celtic	11	1

MacPHERSON, Angus Ian
Born : Glasgow 11/10/68

SEASON	CLUB	LEAGUE APPEARANCES	GOALS
1988-89	Rangers	-	-
1989-90	Rangers	-	-
1989-90	*Exeter City*	11	1
1990-91	Kilmarnock	11	-
1991-92	Kilmarnock	43	3
1992-93	Kilmarnock	40	5
1993-94	Kilmarnock	43	2
1994-95	Kilmarnock	33	1
1995-96	Kilmarnock	35	1

MALPAS, Maurice Daniel Robert
Born : Dunfermline 03/08/62

SEASON	CLUB	LEAGUE APPEARANCES	GOALS
1979-80	Dundee United	-	-
1980-81	Dundee United	-	-
1981-82	Dundee United	19	-
1982-83	Dundee United	34	1
1983-84	Dundee United	34	2
1984-85	Dundee United	35	2
1985-86	Dundee United	36	2
1986-87	Dundee United	36	-
1987-88	Dundee United	44	-
1988-89	Dundee United	36	1
1989-90	Dundee United	30	2
1990-91	Dundee United	36	1
1991-92	Dundee United	44	3
1992-93	Dundee United	37	-
1993-94	Dundee United	35	-
1994-95	Dundee United	31	-
1995-96	Dundee United	30	2

MARSHALL, Gordon George Banks
Born : Edinburgh 19/04/64

SEASON	CLUB	LEAGUE APPEARANCES	GOALS
1980-81	Rangers	-	-
1981-82	Rangers	-	-
1982-83	Rangers	-	-
1982-83	*East Stirlingshire*	15	-
1982-83	East Fife	10	-
1983-84	East Fife	34	-
1984-85	East Fife	39	-
1985-86	East Fife	39	-
1986-87	East Fife	36	-
1986-87	Falkirk	10	-
1987-88	Falkirk	44	-
1988-89	Falkirk	39	-
1989-90	Falkirk	39	-
1990-91	Falkirk	39	-
1991-92	Celtic	25	-
1992-93	Celtic	11	-
1993-94	Celtic	1	-
1993-94	*Stoke City*	10	-
1994-95	Celtic	16	-
1995-96	Celtic	36	-

MARTIN, Brian
Born : Bellshill 24/02/63

SEASON	CLUB	LEAGUE APPEARANCES	GOALS
1980-81	Albion Rovers	10	-
1980-81	Stenhousemuir	2	-
1985-86	Falkirk	25	1
1986-87	Falkirk	34	1
1986-87	Hamilton Academical	7	-
1987-88	Hamilton Academical	23	-
1987-88	St. Mirren	12	1
1988-89	St. Mirren	34	2
1989-90	St. Mirren	35	2
1990-91	St. Mirren	31	2
1991-92	St. Mirren	17	2
1991-92	Motherwell	25	-
1992-93	Motherwell	44	3
1993-94	Motherwell	43	2
1994-95	Motherwell	32	2
1995-96	Motherwell	33	2

MAXWELL, Alastair Espie
Born : Hamilton 16/02/65

SEASON	CLUB	LEAGUE APPEARANCES	GOALS
1981-82	Motherwell	-	-
1982-83	Motherwell	-	-
1983-84	Motherwell	4	-
1984-85	Motherwell	15	-
1985-86	Motherwell	4	-
1986-87	Motherwell	21	-
1987-88	Motherwell	1	-
1987-88	*Clydebank*	1	-
1988-89	Motherwell	17	-
1989-90	Motherwell	36	-
1990-91	Motherwell	36	1
1991-92	Motherwell	-	-
1991-92	*Liverpool*	-	-
1991-92	*Bolton Wanderers*	3	-
1992-93	Rangers	10	-
1993-94	Rangers	32	-
1994-95	Rangers	11	-
1995-96	Dundee United	34	-

MAY, Edward
Born : Edinburgh 30/08/67

SEASON	CLUB	LEAGUE APPEARANCES	GOALS
1983-84	Dundee United	-	-
1984-85	Dundee United	-	-
1984-85	Hibernian	-	-
1985-86	Hibernian	19	1
1986-87	Hibernian	30	5
1987-88	Hibernian	35	2
1988-89	Hibernian	25	2
1989-90	Brentford	30	8
1990-91	Brentford	17	2
1990-91	Falkirk	13	6
1991-92	Falkirk	36	9
1992-93	Falkirk	42	6
1993-94	Falkirk	38	9
1994-95	Falkirk	24	2
1994-95	Motherwell	10	2
1995-96	Motherwell	28	1

McALLISTER, Kevin
Born : Falkirk 08/11/62

SEASON	CLUB	LEAGUE APPEARANCES	GOALS
1983-84	Falkirk	35	11
1984-85	Falkirk	29	7
1985-86	Chelsea	20	-
1986-87	Chelsea	8	-
1987-88	Chelsea	5	-
1987-88	*Falkirk*	6	3
1988-89	Chelsea	36	6
1989-90	Chelsea	24	1
1990-91	Chelsea	13	1
1991-92	Falkirk	42	9
1992-93	Falkirk	41	3
1993-94	Hibernian	36	6
1994-95	Hibernian	23	1
1995-96	Hibernian	31	4

McCALL, Stuart
Born : Leeds 10/06/64

SEASON	CLUB	LEAGUE APPEARANCES	GOALS
1982-83	Bradford City	28	4
1983-84	Bradford City	46	5

Stuart McCall

SEASON	CLUB	LEAGUE APPEARANCES	GOALS
1984-85	Bradford City	46	8
1985-86	Bradford City	38	4
1986-87	Bradford City	36	7
1987-88	Bradford City	44	9
1988-89	Everton	33	-
1989-90	Everton	37	3
1990-91	Everton	33	3
1991-92	Rangers	36	1
1992-93	Rangers	36	5
1993-94	Rangers	34	3
1994-95	Rangers	30	2
1995-96	Rangers	21	3

McCANN, Neil Docherty
Born : Greenock 11/08/74

SEASON	CLUB	LEAGUE APPEARANCES	GOALS
1991-92	Dundee	-	-
1992-93	Dundee	3	-
1993-94	Dundee	22	1
1994-95	Dundee	32	2
1995-96	Dundee	22	2

McCART, Christopher
Born : Motherwell 17/04/67

SEASON	CLUB	LEAGUE APPEARANCES	GOALS
1984-85	Motherwell	-	-
1985-86	Motherwell	13	-
1986-87	Motherwell	-	-
1987-88	Motherwell	1	-
1988-89	Motherwell	26	-
1989-90	Motherwell	34	1
1990-91	Motherwell	36	-
1991-92	Motherwell	22	2
1992-93	Motherwell	29	3
1993-94	Motherwell	36	-
1994-95	Motherwell	24	-
1995-96	Motherwell	20	-

McCOIST, Alistair
Born : Bellshill 24/09/62

SEASON	CLUB	LEAGUE APPEARANCES	GOALS
1978-79	St. Johnstone	4	-
1979-80	St. Johnstone	15	-
1980-81	St. Johnstone	38	22
1981-82	Sunderland	28	2
1982-83	Sunderland	28	6
1983-84	Rangers	30	9
1984-85	Rangers	25	12
1985-86	Rangers	33	24
1986-87	Rangers	44	33
1987-88	Rangers	40	31
1988-89	Rangers	19	9
1989-90	Rangers	34	14
1990-91	Rangers	26	11
1991-92	Rangers	38	34
1992-93	Rangers	34	34
1993-94	Rangers	21	7
1994-95	Rangers	9	1
1995-96	Rangers	25	16

McCULLOCH, Greig
Born : Girvan 18/04/76

SEASON	CLUB	LEAGUE APPEARANCES	GOALS
1994-95	Aberdeen	-	-
1995-96	Raith Rovers	7	1

McCULLOCH, Lee
Born : Bellshill 14/05/78

SEASON	CLUB	LEAGUE APPEARANCES	GOALS
1994-95	Motherwell	-	-
1995-96	Motherwell	1	-

McCULLOCH, Mark Ross
Born : Inverness 19/05/75

SEASON	CLUB	LEAGUE APPEARANCES	GOALS
1994-95	Dunfermline Athletic	9	-
1995-96	Dunfermline Athletic	10	-

McGINLAY, Patrick David
Born : Glasgow 30/05/67

SEASON	CLUB	LEAGUE APPEARANCES	GOALS
1985-86	Blackpool	-	-
1986-87	Blackpool	12	1
1987-88	Hibernian	-	-
1988-89	Hibernian	2	-
1989-90	Hibernian	28	3
1990-91	Hibernian	32	1
1991-92	Hibernian	43	9
1992-93	Hibernian	40	10
1993-94	Celtic	41	10

SEASON	CLUB	LEAGUE APPEARANCES	GOALS
1994-95	Celtic	8	1
1994-95	Hibernian	24	7
1995-96	Hibernian	31	5

McGINTY, Brian
Born : East Kilbride 10/12/76

SEASON	CLUB	LEAGUE APPEARANCES	GOALS
1993-94	Rangers	-	-
1994-95	Rangers	1	-
1995-96	Rangers	2	-

McGOWNE, Kevin
Born : Kilmarnock 16/12/69

SEASON	CLUB	LEAGUE APPEARANCES	GOALS
1988-89	St. Mirren	-	-
1989-90	St. Mirren	2	-
1990-91	St. Mirren	10	-
1991-92	St. Mirren	36	1
1992-93	St. Johnstone	26	1
1993-94	St. Johnstone	41	-
1994-95	St. Johnstone	30	1
1995-96	St. Johnstone	23	2

McINALLY, James Edward
Born : Glasgow 19/02/64

SEASON	CLUB	LEAGUE APPEARANCES	GOALS
1982-83	Celtic	1	-
1983-84	Celtic	-	-
1983-84	*Dundee*	11	2
1984-85	Nottingham Forest	24	-
1985-86	Nottingham Forest	12	-
1985-86	Coventry City	5	-
1986-87	Dundee United	32	1
1987-88	Dundee United	36	2
1988-89	Dundee United	29	1
1989-90	Dundee United	35	3
1990-91	Dundee United	33	1
1991-92	Dundee United	32	4
1992-93	Dundee United	32	-
1993-94	Dundee United	31	-
1994-95	Dundee United	25	-
1995-96	Raith Rovers	25	-

McINNES, Derek John
Born : Paisley 05/07/71

SEASON	CLUB	LEAGUE APPEARANCES	GOALS
1987-88	Greenock Morton	2	-
1988-89	Greenock Morton	29	1
1989-90	Greenock Morton	23	1
1990-91	Greenock Morton	31	3
1991-92	Greenock Morton	42	7
1992-93	Greenock Morton	40	2
1993-94	Greenock Morton	16	1
1994-95	Greenock Morton	26	3
1995-96	Greenock Morton	12	1
1995-96	Rangers	6	-

McINTYRE, James
Born : Alexandria 24/05/72

SEASON	CLUB	LEAGUE APPEARANCES	GOALS
1991-92	Bristol City	1	-
1992-93	Bristol City	-	-
1992-93	*Exeter City*	15	3
1993-94	Airdrieonians	13	-
1994-95	Airdrieonians	12	1
1995-96	Airdrieonians	29	9
1995-96	Kilmarnock	7	2

McKEE, Colin
Born : Glasgow 22/08/73

SEASON	CLUB	LEAGUE APPEARANCES	GOALS
1991-92	Manchester United	-	-
1992-93	Manchester United	-	-
1992-93	*Bury*	2	-
1993-94	Manchester United	1	-
1994-95	Manchester United	-	-
1994-95	Kilmarnock	25	6
1995-96	Kilmarnock	28	4

McKENZIE, Roderick
Born : Bellshill 08/08/75

SEASON	CLUB	LEAGUE APPEARANCES	GOALS
1993-94	Heart of Midlothian	-	-
1994-95	Heart of Midlothian	-	-
1995-96	Stenhousemuir	36	-

McKIMMIE, Stewart
Born : Aberdeen 27/10/62

SEASON	CLUB	LEAGUE APPEARANCES	GOALS
1980-81	Dundee	17	-
1981-82	Dundee	16	-

SEASON	CLUB	LEAGUE APPEARANCES	GOALS
1982-83	Dundee	31	-
1983-84	Dundee	16	-
1983-84	Aberdeen	18	1
1984-85	Aberdeen	34	3
1985-86	Aberdeen	34	3
1986-87	Aberdeen	37	-
1987-88	Aberdeen	42	-
1988-89	Aberdeen	35	-
1989-90	Aberdeen	33	-
1990-91	Aberdeen	26	1
1991-92	Aberdeen	39	-
1992-93	Aberdeen	14	-
1993-94	Aberdeen	40	-
1994-95	Aberdeen	34	1
1995-96	Aberdeen	29	-

McKINLAY, Thomas Valley
Born : Glasgow 03/12/64

SEASON	CLUB	LEAGUE APPEARANCES	GOALS
1981-82	Dundee	-	-
1982-83	Dundee	1	-
1983-84	Dundee	36	3
1984-85	Dundee	34	3
1985-86	Dundee	22	-
1986-87	Dundee	32	2
1987-88	Dundee	19	-
1988-89	Dundee	18	-
1988-89	Heart of Midlothian	17	1
1989-90	Heart of Midlothian	29	1
1990-91	Heart of Midlothian	33	2
1991-92	Heart of Midlothian	39	2
1992-93	Heart of Midlothian	34	-
1993-94	Heart of Midlothian	43	-
1994-95	Heart of Midlothian	11	-
1994-95	Celtic	17	-
1995-96	Celtic	32	-

McKINNON, Raymond
Born : Dundee 05/08/70

SEASON	CLUB	LEAGUE APPEARANCES	GOALS
1987-88	Dundee United	-	-
1988-89	Dundee United	1	-
1989-90	Dundee United	10	-
1990-91	Dundee United	17	2
1991-92	Dundee United	25	4
1992-93	Nottingham Forest	6	1
1993-94	Nottingham Forest	-	-
1993-94	Aberdeen	5	-
1994-95	Aberdeen	20	-
1995-96	Aberdeen	1	-
1995-96	Dundee United	9	-

McKNIGHT, Paul
Born : Belfast 08/02/77

SEASON	CLUB	LEAGUE APPEARANCES	GOALS
1993-94	Rangers	-	-
1994-95	Rangers	1	-
1995-96	Rangers	-	-

McLAREN, Alan James
Born : Edinburgh 04/01/71

SEASON	CLUB	LEAGUE APPEARANCES	GOALS
1987-88	Heart of Midlothian	1	-
1988-89	Heart of Midlothian	12	1
1989-90	Heart of Midlothian	27	1
1990-91	Heart of Midlothian	23	1
1991-92	Heart of Midlothian	38	1
1992-93	Heart of Midlothian	34	-
1993-94	Heart of Midlothian	37	1
1994-95	Heart of Midlothian	10	1
1994-95	Rangers	24	2
1995-96	Rangers	36	3

McLAREN, Andrew
Born : Glasgow 05/06/73

SEASON	CLUB	LEAGUE APPEARANCES	GOALS
1989-90	Dundee United	-	-
1990-91	Dundee United	-	-
1991-92	Dundee United	13	-
1992-93	Dundee United	5	-
1993-94	Dundee United	27	2
1994-95	Dundee United	20	-
1995-96	Dundee United	31	3

McLAUGHLIN, Brian
Born : Bellshill 14/05/74

SEASON	CLUB	LEAGUE APPEARANCES	GOALS
1992-93	Celtic	-	-
1993-94	Celtic	8	-

SEASON	CLUB	LEAGUE APPEARANCES	GOALS
1994-95	Celtic	21	-
1995-96	Celtic	26	4

McLAUGHLIN, Joseph
Born : Greenock 02/06/60

SEASON	CLUB	LEAGUE APPEARANCES	GOALS
1977-78	Morton	-	-
1978-79	Morton	-	-
1979-80	Morton	30	2
1980-81	Morton	34	1
1981-82	Morton	36	-
1982-83	Morton	34	-
1983-84	Chelsea	41	-
1984-85	Chelsea	36	1
1985-86	Chelsea	40	1
1986-87	Chelsea	36	2
1987-88	Chelsea	36	1
1988-89	Chelsea	31	-
1989-90	Charlton Athletic	31	-
1990-91	Watford	24	1
1991-92	Watford	22	1
1992-93	Watford	-	-
1992-93	Falkirk	8	1
1993-94	Falkirk	37	2
1994-95	Falkirk	28	2
1995-96	Falkirk	16	1
1995-96	Hibernian	9	-

McLEISH, Alexander
Born : Glasgow 21/01/59

SEASON	CLUB	LEAGUE APPEARANCES	GOALS
1977-78	Aberdeen	1	-
1978-79	Aberdeen	19	1
1979-80	Aberdeen	35	2
1980-81	Aberdeen	32	3
1981-82	Aberdeen	32	5
1982-83	Aberdeen	34	2
1983-84	Aberdeen	32	2
1984-85	Aberdeen	30	1
1985-86	Aberdeen	34	3
1986-87	Aberdeen	40	3
1987-88	Aberdeen	36	1
1988-89	Aberdeen	34	-
1989-90	Aberdeen	32	2
1990-91	Aberdeen	33	-
1991-92	Aberdeen	7	-
1992-93	Aberdeen	27	-
1993-94	Aberdeen	35	-
1994-95	Motherwell	2	-
1995-96	Motherwell	1	-

McMANUS, Allan William
Born : Paisley 17/11/74

SEASON	CLUB	LEAGUE APPEARANCES	GOALS
1992-93	Heart of Midlothian	-	-
1993-94	Heart of Midlothian	-	-
1994-95	Heart of Midlothian	-	-
1995-96	Heart of Midlothian	18	2

McMillan, Stephen
Born : Edinburgh 19/01/76

SEASON	CLUB	LEAGUE APPEARANCES	GOALS
1993-94	Motherwell	1	-
1994-95	Motherwell	3	-
1995-96	Motherwell	12	-

McNAMARA, Jackie
Born : Glasgow 24/10/73

SEASON	CLUB	LEAGUE APPEARANCES	GOALS
1991-92	Dunfermline Athletic	-	-
1992-93	Dunfermline Athletic	3	-
1993-94	Dunfermline Athletic	39	-
1994-95	Dunfermline Athletic	30	2
1995-96	Dunfermline Athletic	7	1
1995-96	Celtic	26	1

McPHERSON, David
Born : Paisley 28/01/64

SEASON	CLUB	LEAGUE APPEARANCES	GOALS
1980-81	Rangers	-	-
1981-82	Rangers	-	-
1982-83	Rangers	18	1
1983-84	Rangers	36	2
1984-85	Rangers	31	-
1985-86	Rangers	34	5
1986-87	Rangers	42	7
1987-88	Rangers	44	4
1988-89	Heart of Midlothian	32	4
1989-90	Heart of Midlothian	35	4
1990-91	Heart of Midlothian	34	2
1991-92	Heart of Midlothian	44	2
1992-93	Rangers	34	2
1993-94	Rangers	28	1
1994-95	Rangers	9	-
1994-95	Heart of Midlothian	23	2
1995-96	Heart of Midlothian	26	1

McQUILKEN, James Charles
Born : Glasgow 03/10/74

SEASON	CLUB	LEAGUE APPEARANCES	GOALS
1992-93	Celtic	1	-
1993-94	Celtic	-	-
1994-95	Celtic	-	-
1995-96	Celtic	4	-
1995-96	Dundee United	9	-

McSKIMMING, Shaun Peter
Born : Stranraer 29/05/70

SEASON	CLUB	LEAGUE APPEARANCES	GOALS
1986-87	Stranraer	-	-
1987-88	Dundee	-	-
1988-89	Dundee	-	-
1989-90	Dundee	7	-
1990-91	Dundee	16	3
1991-92	Kilmarnock	30	1
1992-93	Kilmarnock	35	5
1993-94	Kilmarnock	40	3
1994-95	Kilmarnock	8	-
1994-95	Motherwell	14	2
1995-96	Motherwell	15	1

McSTAY, Paul Michael Lyons
Born : Hamilton 22/10/64

SEASON	CLUB	LEAGUE APPEARANCES	GOALS
1981-82	Celtic	10	1
1982-83	Celtic	36	6
1983-84	Celtic	34	3
1984-85	Celtic	32	4
1985-86	Celtic	34	8
1986-87	Celtic	43	3
1987-88	Celtic	44	5
1988-89	Celtic	33	5
1989-90	Celtic	35	3
1990-91	Celtic	30	2
1991-92	Celtic	31	7
1992-93	Celtic	43	4
1993-94	Celtic	35	2
1994-95	Celtic	29	1
1995-96	Celtic	30	2

McSWEGAN, Gary
Born : Glasgow 24/09/70

SEASON	CLUB	LEAGUE APPEARANCES	GOALS
1986-87	Rangers	-	-
1987-88	Rangers	1	-
1988-89	Rangers	1	-
1989-90	Rangers	-	-
1990-91	Rangers	3	-
1991-92	Rangers	4	-
1992-93	Rangers	9	4
1993-94	Notts County	37	15
1994-95	Notts County	22	6
1995-96	Notts County	3	-
1995-96	Dundee United	25	17

MELDRUM, Colin George
Born : Kilmarnock 26/11/75

SEASON	CLUB	LEAGUE APPEARANCES	GOALS
1993-94	Kilmarnock	-	-
1994-95	Kilmarnock	4	-
1995-96	Kilmarnock	1	-

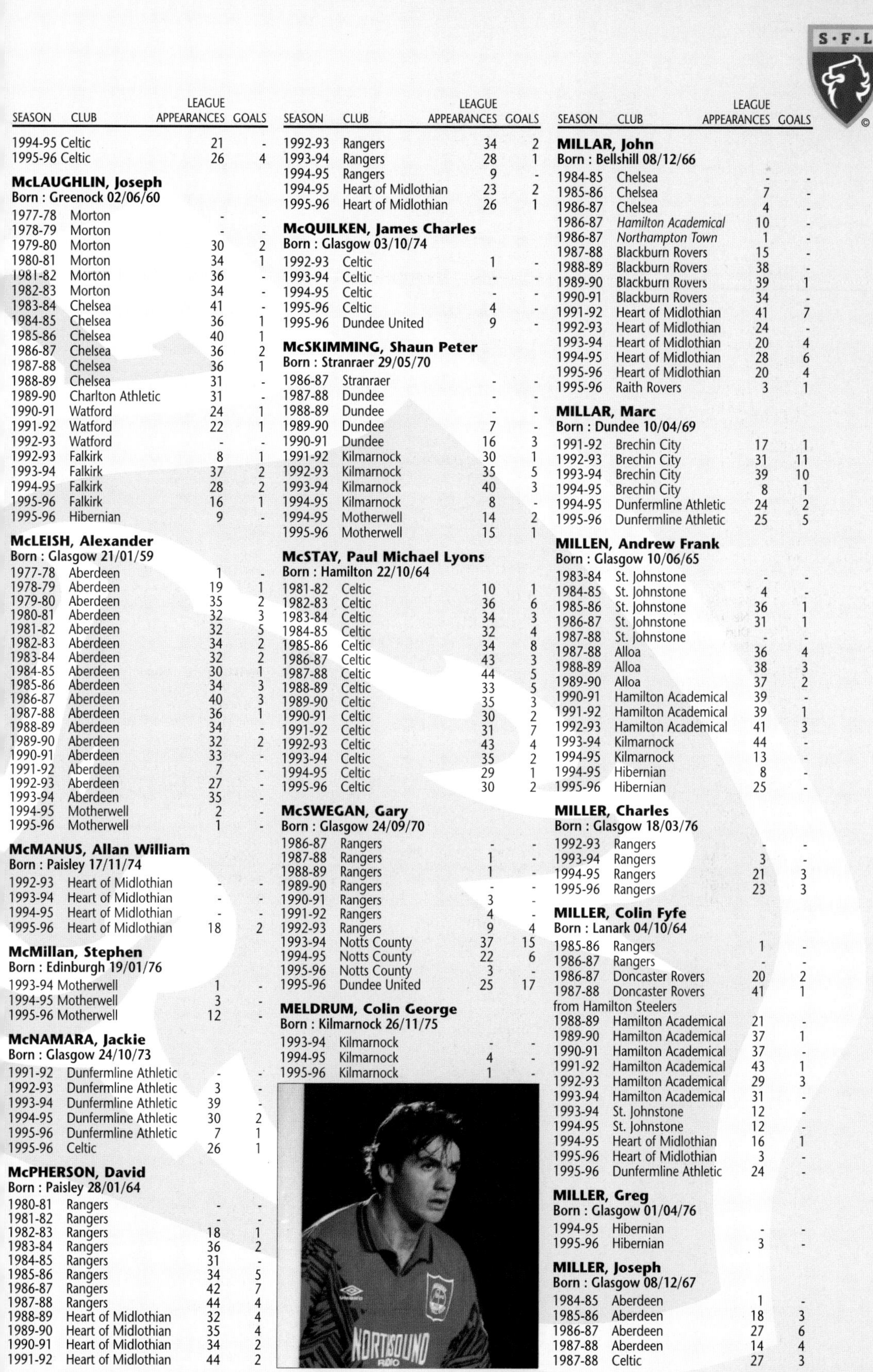

Joe Miller

MILLAR, John
Born : Bellshill 08/12/66

SEASON	CLUB	LEAGUE APPEARANCES	GOALS
1984-85	Chelsea	-	-
1985-86	Chelsea	7	-
1986-87	Chelsea	4	-
1986-87	*Hamilton Academical*	10	-
1986-87	*Northampton Town*	1	-
1987-88	Blackburn Rovers	15	-
1988-89	Blackburn Rovers	38	-
1989-90	Blackburn Rovers	39	1
1990-91	Blackburn Rovers	34	-
1991-92	Heart of Midlothian	41	7
1992-93	Heart of Midlothian	24	-
1993-94	Heart of Midlothian	20	4
1994-95	Heart of Midlothian	28	6
1995-96	Heart of Midlothian	20	4
1995-96	Raith Rovers	3	1

MILLAR, Marc
Born : Dundee 10/04/69

SEASON	CLUB	LEAGUE APPEARANCES	GOALS
1991-92	Brechin City	17	1
1992-93	Brechin City	31	11
1993-94	Brechin City	39	10
1994-95	Brechin City	8	1
1994-95	Dunfermline Athletic	24	2
1995-96	Dunfermline Athletic	25	5

MILLEN, Andrew Frank
Born : Glasgow 10/06/65

SEASON	CLUB	LEAGUE APPEARANCES	GOALS
1983-84	St. Johnstone	-	-
1984-85	St. Johnstone	4	-
1985-86	St. Johnstone	36	1
1986-87	St. Johnstone	31	1
1987-88	St. Johnstone	-	-
1987-88	Alloa	36	4
1988-89	Alloa	38	3
1989-90	Alloa	37	2
1990-91	Hamilton Academical	39	-
1991-92	Hamilton Academical	39	1
1992-93	Hamilton Academical	41	3
1993-94	Kilmarnock	44	-
1994-95	Kilmarnock	13	-
1994-95	Hibernian	8	-
1995-96	Hibernian	25	-

MILLER, Charles
Born : Glasgow 18/03/76

SEASON	CLUB	LEAGUE APPEARANCES	GOALS
1992-93	Rangers	-	-
1993-94	Rangers	3	-
1994-95	Rangers	21	3
1995-96	Rangers	23	3

MILLER, Colin Fyfe
Born : Lanark 04/10/64

SEASON	CLUB	LEAGUE APPEARANCES	GOALS
1985-86	Rangers	1	-
1986-87	Rangers	-	-
1986-87	Doncaster Rovers	20	2
1987-88	Doncaster Rovers	41	1
from Hamilton Steelers			
1988-89	Hamilton Academical	21	-
1989-90	Hamilton Academical	37	1
1990-91	Hamilton Academical	37	-
1991-92	Hamilton Academical	43	1
1992-93	Hamilton Academical	29	3
1993-94	Hamilton Academical	31	-
1993-94	St. Johnstone	12	-
1994-95	St. Johnstone	12	-
1994-95	Heart of Midlothian	16	1
1995-96	Heart of Midlothian	3	-
1995-96	Dunfermline Athletic	24	-

MILLER, Greg
Born : Glasgow 01/04/76

SEASON	CLUB	LEAGUE APPEARANCES	GOALS
1994-95	Hibernian	-	-
1995-96	Hibernian	3	-

MILLER, Joseph
Born : Glasgow 08/12/67

SEASON	CLUB	LEAGUE APPEARANCES	GOALS
1984-85	Aberdeen	1	-
1985-86	Aberdeen	18	3
1986-87	Aberdeen	27	6
1987-88	Aberdeen	14	4
1987-88	Celtic	27	3

SEASON	CLUB	LEAGUE APPEARANCES	GOALS
1988-89	Celtic	22	8
1989-90	Celtic	24	5
1990-91	Celtic	30	8
1991-92	Celtic	26	2
1992-93	Celtic	23	2
1993-94	Aberdeen	27	4
1994-95	Aberdeen	27	-
1995-96	Aberdeen	31	9

MILLER, William Nesbit
Born : Edinburgh 01/11/69

SEASON	CLUB	LEAGUE APPEARANCES	GOALS
1989-90	Hibernian	11	-
1990-91	Hibernian	25	1
1991-92	Hibernian	30	-
1992-93	Hibernian	34	-
1993-94	Hibernian	37	-
1994-95	Hibernian	34	-
1995-96	Hibernian	13	-

MITCHELL, Alistair Robert
Born : Kirkcaldy 03/12/68

SEASON	CLUB	LEAGUE APPEARANCES	GOALS
1988-89	East Fife	18	4
1989-90	East Fife	35	12
1990-91	East Fife	34	7
1991-92	Kilmarnock	42	10
1992-93	Kilmarnock	32	6
1993-94	Kilmarnock	34	5
1994-95	Kilmarnock	35	4
1995-96	Kilmarnock	30	3

MONTGOMERIE, Samuel Raymond
Born : Irvine 17/04/61

SEASON	CLUB	LEAGUE APPEARANCES	GOALS
1980-81	Newcastle United	-	-
1981-82	Dumbarton	20	5
1982-83	Dumbarton	25	2
1983-84	Dumbarton	39	1
1984-85	Dumbarton	6	-
1985-86	Dumbarton	24	-
1986-87	Dumbarton	35	-
1987-88	Dumbarton	31	-
1988-89	Kilmarnock	31	2
1989-90	Kilmarnock	35	3
1990-91	Kilmarnock	37	-
1991-92	Kilmarnock	30	1
1992-93	Kilmarnock	42	-
1993-94	Kilmarnock	42	-
1994-95	Kilmarnock	12	-
1995-96	Kilmarnock	14	-

MOORE, Allan
Born : Glasgow 25/12/64

SEASON	CLUB	LEAGUE APPEARANCES	GOALS
1983-84	Dumbarton	4	-
1984-85	Dumbarton	4	-
1985-86	Dumbarton	33	4
1986-87	Dumbarton	18	3
1986-87	Heart of Midlothian	10	-
1987-88	Heart of Midlothian	7	1
1988-89	Heart of Midlothian	12	2
1989-90	St. Johnstone	33	13
1990-91	St. Johnstone	31	5
1991-92	St. Johnstone	21	1
1992-93	St. Johnstone	26	3
1993-94	St. Johnstone	13	1
1993-94	Dunfermline Athletic	8	-
1994-95	Dunfermline Athletic	12	1
1995-96	Dunfermline Athletic	28	5

MOORE, Craig Andrew
Born : Canterbury, Australia 12/12/75

SEASON	CLUB	LEAGUE APPEARANCES	GOALS
1993-94	Rangers	1	-
1994-95	Rangers	21	2
1995-96	Rangers	11	1

MURRAY, Neil
Born : Bellshill 21/02/73

SEASON	CLUB	LEAGUE APPEARANCES	GOALS
1989-90	Rangers	-	-
1990-91	Rangers	-	-
1991-92	Rangers	-	-
1992-93	Rangers	16	-
1993-94	Rangers	22	-
1994-95	Rangers	20	1
1995-96	Rangers	5	-

NAYSMITH, Gary Andrew
Born : Edinburgh 16/11/78

SEASON	CLUB	LEAGUE APPEARANCES	GOALS
1995-96	Heart of Midlothian	1	-

O'DONNELL, Philip
Born : Bellshill 25/03/72

SEASON	CLUB	LEAGUE APPEARANCES	GOALS
1990-91	Motherwell	12	-
1991-92	Motherwell	42	4
1992-93	Motherwell	32	4
1993-94	Motherwell	35	7
1994-95	Motherwell	3	-
1994-95	Celtic	27	6
1995-96	Celtic	15	3

O'NEIL, Brian
Born : Paisley 06/09/72

SEASON	CLUB	LEAGUE APPEARANCES	GOALS
1991-92	Celtic	28	1
1992-93	Celtic	17	3
1993-94	Celtic	27	2
1994-95	Celtic	26	-
1995-96	Celtic	5	-

PERRY, Mark George
Born : Aberdeen 07/02/71

SEASON	CLUB	LEAGUE APPEARANCES	GOALS
1988-89	Dundee United	-	-
1989-90	Dundee United	-	-
1990-91	Dundee United	-	-
1991-92	Dundee United	-	-
1992-93	Dundee United	18	1
1993-94	Dundee United	9	-
1994-95	Dundee United	9	-
1995-96	Dundee United	20	2

PETRIC, Gordan
Born : Belgrade, Yugoslavia 30/07/69
From Belgrade, FC Partizan Belgrade

SEASON	CLUB	LEAGUE APPEARANCES	GOALS
1993-94	Dundee United	27	1
1994-95	Dundee United	33	2
1995-96	Rangers	33	1

PETRIE, Stewart James John
Born : Dundee 27/02/70

SEASON	CLUB	LEAGUE APPEARANCES	GOALS
1988-89	Forfar Athletic	-	-
1989-90	Forfar Athletic	-	-
1990-91	Forfar Athletic	36	6
1991-92	Forfar Athletic	41	7
1992-93	Forfar Athletic	37	21
1993-94	Forfar Athletic	3	-
1993-94	Dunfermline Athletic	37	6
1994-95	Dunfermline Athletic	33	14
1995-96	Dunfermline Athletic	34	13

PHILLIBEN, John
Born : Stirling 14/03/64

SEASON	CLUB	LEAGUE APPEARANCES	GOALS
1980-81	Stirling Albion	15	-
1981-82	Stirling Albion	37	1
1982-83	Stirling Albion	34	-
1983-84	Stirling Albion	23	-
1983-84	Doncaster Rovers	12	-
1984-85	Doncaster Rovers	36	1
1985-86	Doncaster Rovers	22	-
1985-86	*Cambridge United*	6	-
1986-87	Doncaster Rovers	1	-
1986-87	Motherwell	37	-
1987-88	Motherwell	35	2
1988-89	Motherwell	19	-
1989-90	Motherwell	24	-
1990-91	Motherwell	11	1
1991-92	Motherwell	32	1
1992-93	Motherwell	31	-
1993-94	Motherwell	28	2
1994-95	Motherwell	31	-
1995-96	Motherwell	24	-

POINTON, Neil Geoffrey
Born : Church Warsop 28/11/67

SEASON	CLUB	LEAGUE APPEARANCES	GOALS
1981-82	Scunthorpe United	5	-
1982-83	Scunthorpe United	46	1
1983-84	Scunthorpe United	45	1
1984-85	Scunthorpe United	46	-
1985-86	Scunthorpe United	17	-
1985-86	Everton	15	-
1986-87	Everton	12	1
1987-88	Everton	33	3
1988-89	Everton	23	-
1989-90	Everton	19	1
1990-91	Manchester City	35	1
1991-92	Manchester City	39	1
1992-93	Oldham Athletic	34	3
1993-94	Oldham Athletic	24	-
1994-95	Oldham Athletic	32	-
1995-96	Oldham Athletic	4	-
1995-96	Heart of Midlothian	22	3

PRESSLEY, Steven John
Born : Elgin 11/10/73

SEASON	CLUB	LEAGUE APPEARANCES	GOALS
1990-91	Rangers	-	-
1991-92	Rangers	1	-
1992-93	Rangers	8	-
1993-94	Rangers	23	1
1994-95	Rangers	2	1
1994-95	Coventry City	19	1
1995-96	Dundee United	35	2

REID, Christopher Thomas
Born : Edinburgh 04/11/71

SEASON	CLUB	LEAGUE APPEARANCES	GOALS
1989-90	Hibernian	2	-
1990-91	Hibernian	1	-
1991-92	Hibernian	9	-
1992-93	Hibernian	14	-
1993-94	Hibernian	-	-
1994-95	Hibernian	-	-
1995-96	Hibernian	-	-

REILLY, Mark
Born : Bellshill 30/03/69

SEASON	CLUB	LEAGUE APPEARANCES	GOALS
1988-89	Motherwell	-	-
1989-90	Motherwell	4	-
1990-91	Motherwell	-	-
1991-92	Kilmarnock	19	-
1992-93	Kilmarnock	19	3
1993-94	Kilmarnock	38	-
1994-95	Kilmarnock	32	-
1995-96	Kilmarnock	28	-

RENWICK, Michael
Born : Edinburgh 29/02/76

SEASON	CLUB	LEAGUE APPEARANCES	GOALS
1992-93	Hibernian	-	-
1993-94	Hibernian	-	-
1994-95	Hibernian	1	-
1995-96	Hibernian	2	-

RICE, Brian
Born : Bellshill 11/10/63

SEASON	CLUB	LEAGUE APPEARANCES	GOALS
1980-81	Hibernian	1	-
1981-82	Hibernian	1	-
1982-83	Hibernian	22	2
1983-84	Hibernian	25	5
1984-85	Hibernian	35	4
1985-86	Nottingham Forest	19	3
1986-87	Nottingham Forest	3	1
1986-87	*Grimsby Town*	4	-
1987-88	Nottingham Forest	30	2
1988-89	Nottingham Forest	20	1
1988-89	*West Bromwich Albion*	3	-
1989-90	Nottingham Forest	18	2
1990-91	Nottingham Forest	1	-
1990-91	*Stoke City*	18	1
1991-92	Falkirk	16	1
1992-93	Falkirk	17	2
1993-94	Falkirk	37	3
1994-95	Falkirk	26	2
1995-96	Falkirk	5	-
1995-96	Dunfermline Athletic	6	-

RITCHIE, Innes
Born : Edinburgh 24/08/73

SEASON	CLUB	LEAGUE APPEARANCES	GOALS
1992-93	Motherwell	-	-
1993-94	Motherwell	-	-
1994-95	Motherwell	1	-
1995-96	Motherwell	10	-

RITCHIE, Paul Simon
Born : Kirkcaldy 21/08/75

SEASON	CLUB	LEAGUE APPEARANCES	GOALS
1992-93	Heart of Midlothian	-	-
1993-94	Heart of Midlothian	-	-

SEASON	CLUB	LEAGUE APPEARANCES	GOALS
1994-95	Heart of Midlothian	-	-
1995-96	Heart of Midlothian	28	1

ROBERTS, Mark Kingsley
Born : Irvine 29/10/75

SEASON	CLUB	LEAGUE APPEARANCES	GOALS
1991-92	Kilmarnock	1	-
1992-93	Kilmarnock	5	-
1993-94	Kilmarnock	13	2
1994-95	Kilmarnock	4	1
1995-96	Kilmarnock	11	-

ROBERTSON, Alexander
Born : Edinburgh 26/04/71

SEASON	CLUB	LEAGUE APPEARANCES	GOALS
1987-88	Rangers	-	-
1988-89	Rangers	2	-
1989-90	Rangers	1	-
1990-91	Rangers	15	1
1991-92	Rangers	6	-
1992-93	Rangers	2	-
1993-94	Rangers	-	-
1993-94	Coventry City	-	-
1994-95	Coventry City	1	-
1995-96	Coventry City	-	-
1995-96	Dundee United	4	-

ROBERTSON, Craig Peter
Born : Dunfermline 22/04/63

SEASON	CLUB	LEAGUE APPEARANCES	GOALS
1979-80	Heart of Midlothian	-	-
1980-81	Raith Rovers	-	-
1981-82	Raith Rovers	11	-
1982-83	Raith Rovers	22	-
1983-84	Raith Rovers	38	3
1984-85	Raith Rovers	39	11
1985-86	Raith Rovers	25	2
1986-87	Raith Rovers	35	3
1987-88	Dunfermline Athletic	42	13
1988-89	Dunfermline Athletic	13	5
1988-89	Aberdeen	4	1
1989-90	Aberdeen	22	2
1990-91	Aberdeen	8	1
1991-92	Dunfermline Athletic	33	1
1992-93	Dunfermline Athletic	34	3
1993-94	Dunfermline Athletic	40	3
1994-95	Dunfermline Athletic	35	6
1995-96	Dunfermline Athletic	28	5

ROBERTSON, David
Born : Aberdeen 17/10/68

SEASON	CLUB	LEAGUE APPEARANCES	GOALS
1986-87	Aberdeen	34	-
1987-88	Aberdeen	23	-
1988-89	Aberdeen	23	-
1989-90	Aberdeen	20	1
1990-91	Aberdeen	35	1
1991-92	Rangers	42	1
1992-93	Rangers	39	3
1993-94	Rangers	32	1
1994-95	Rangers	23	3
1995-96	Rangers	25	3

ROBERTSON, Hugh Scott
Born : Aberdeen 19/03/75

SEASON	CLUB	LEAGUE APPEARANCES	GOALS
1993-94	Aberdeen	8	-
1994-95	Aberdeen	3	2
1995-96	Aberdeen	11	-

ROBERTSON, John Grant
Born : Edinburgh 02/10/64

SEASON	CLUB	LEAGUE APPEARANCES	GOALS
1980-81	Heart of Midlothian	-	-
1981-82	Heart of Midlothian	1	-
1982-83	Heart of Midlothian	23	19
1983-84	Heart of Midlothian	35	15
1984-85	Heart of Midlothian	33	8
1985-86	Heart of Midlothian	35	20
1986-87	Heart of Midlothian	37	16
1987-88	Heart of Midlothian	39	26
1987-88	Newcastle United	-	-
1988-89	Newcastle United	12	-
1988-89	Heart of Midlothian	15	4
1989-90	Heart of Midlothian	32	17
1990-91	Heart of Midlothian	31	12
1991-92	Heart of Midlothian	42	14
1992-93	Heart of Midlothian	42	11
1993-94	Heart of Midlothian	36	8
1994-95	Heart of Midlothian	31	10
1995-96	Heart of Midlothian	33	11

RODDIE, Andrew Robert
Born : Glasgow 04/11/71

SEASON	CLUB	LEAGUE APPEARANCES	GOALS
1988-89	Aberdeen	-	-
1989-90	Aberdeen	-	-
1990-91	Aberdeen	-	-
1991-92	Aberdeen	10	2
1992-93	Aberdeen	11	2
1993-94	Aberdeen	6	1
1994-95	Aberdeen	-	-
1994-95	Motherwell	19	-
1995-96	Motherwell	24	-

ROSS, Ian
Born : Broxburn 27/08/74

SEASON	CLUB	LEAGUE APPEARANCES	GOALS
1993-94	Motherwell	-	-
1994-95	Motherwell	-	-
1995-96	Motherwell	1	-

ROUGIER, Anthony Leo
Born : Trinidad and Tobago 17/07/71

From Trinity Pros

SEASON	CLUB	LEAGUE APPEARANCES	GOALS
1994-95	Raith Rovers	4	-
1995-96	Raith Rovers	23	1

ROUSSET, Gilles
Born : Hyeres, France 22/08/63

from Rennes

SEASON	CLUB	LEAGUE APPEARANCES	GOALS
1995-96	Heart of Midlothian	25	-

ROWSON, David A.
Born : Aberdeen 14/09/76

SEASON	CLUB	LEAGUE APPEARANCES	GOALS
1994-95	Aberdeen	-	-
1995-96	Aberdeen	9	-

SALVATORE, Stefano
Born : Rome 29/12/67

from Atalanta

SELLARS, Neil Andrew
Born : Kirkcaldy 09/05/77

SEASON	CLUB	LEAGUE APPEARANCES	GOALS
1994-95	Raith Rovers	-	-
1995-96	Raith Rovers	1	-

SHANNON, Robert
Born : Bellshill 20/04/66

SEASON	CLUB	LEAGUE APPEARANCES	GOALS
1982-83	Dundee	-	-
1983-84	Dundee	6	-
1984-85	Dundee	3	-
1985-86	Dundee	33	-
1986-87	Dundee	39	5
1987-88	Dundee	41	-
1988-89	Dundee	29	1
1989-90	Dundee	36	1
1990-91	Dundee	37	2
1991-92	Dundee	3	-
1991-92	*Middlesbrough*	1	-
1991-92	Dunfermline Athletic	27	-
1992-93	Dunfermline Athletic	42	-
1993-94	Motherwell	43	-
1994-95	Motherwell	25	3
1995-96	Dundee United	26	1

SHAW, Gregory
Born : Dumfries 15/02/70

SEASON	CLUB	LEAGUE APPEARANCES	GOALS
1988-89	Ayr United	2	-
1989-90	Ayr United	3	-
1990-91	Ayr United	9	-
1991-92	Ayr United	39	10
1992-93	Ayr United	5	-
1992-93	*Liverpool*	-	-
1992-93	Falkirk	6	2
1993-94	Falkirk	28	10
1994-95	Falkirk	3	-
1994-95	Dunfermline Athletic	6	-
1995-96	Dunfermline Athletic	28	12

SHEARER, Duncan
Born : Fort William 28/08/62

SEASON	CLUB	LEAGUE APPEARANCES	GOALS
1983-84	Chelsea	-	-
1984-85	Chelsea	-	-
1985-86	Chelsea	2	1
1985-86	Huddersfield Town	8	7
1986-87	Huddersfield Town	42	21
1987-88	Huddersfield Town	33	10
1988-89	Swindon Town	36	14
1989-90	Swindon Town	42	20
1990-91	Swindon Town	44	22
1991-92	Swindon Town	37	22
1991-92	Blackburn Rovers	6	1
1992-93	Aberdeen	34	22
1993-94	Aberdeen	43	17
1994-95	Aberdeen	23	7
1995-96	Aberdeen	30	3

SHIELDS, Greg
Born : Falkirk 21/08/76

SEASON	CLUB	LEAGUE APPEARANCES	GOALS
1994-95	Rangers	-	-
1995-96	Rangers	1	-

SKILLING, Mark James
Born : Irvine 06/10/72

SEASON	CLUB	LEAGUE APPEARANCES	GOALS
1992-93	Kilmarnock	40	4
1993-94	Kilmarnock	23	3
1994-95	Kilmarnock	17	3
1995-96	Kilmarnock	15	1

SMITH, Andrew Mark
Born : Aberdeen 22/11/68

SEASON	CLUB	LEAGUE APPEARANCES	GOALS
1990-91	Airdrieonians	28	3
1991-92	Airdrieonians	29	4
1992-93	Airdrieonians	34	4
1993-94	Airdrieonians	38	7
1994-95	Airdrieonians	36	12
1995-96	Dunfermline Athletic	19	9

SNELDERS, Theodorus G.A.
Born : Westervoort, Holland 07/12/63

From FC Twente

SEASON	CLUB	LEAGUE APPEARANCES	GOALS
1988-89	Aberdeen	36	-
1989-90	Aberdeen	23	-
1990-91	Aberdeen	21	-
1991-92	Aberdeen	42	-
1992-93	Aberdeen	41	-
1993-94	Aberdeen	33	-
1994-95	Aberdeen	24	-
1995-96	Aberdeen	7	-
1995-96	Rangers	2	-

STEVEN, Trevor
Born : Berwick Upon Tweed 21/09/63

SEASON	CLUB	LEAGUE APPEARANCES	GOALS
1980-81	Burnley	1	-
1981-82	Burnley	36	3
1982-83	Burnley	39	8
1983-84	Everton	27	1
1984-85	Everton	40	12
1985-86	Everton	41	9
1986-87	Everton	41	14
1987-88	Everton	36	6
1988-89	Everton	29	6
1989-90	Rangers	34	3
1990-91	Rangers	19	2
1991-92	Rangers	2	1
1991-92	Marseille	27	3
1992-93	Rangers	24	5
1993-94	Rangers	32	4
1994-95	Rangers	11	-
1995-96	Rangers	6	-

STILLIE, Derek
Born : Irvine 03/12/73

SEASON	CLUB	LEAGUE APPEARANCES	GOALS
1990-91	Aberdeen	-	-
1991-92	Aberdeen	-	-
1992-93	Aberdeen	-	-
1993-94	Aberdeen	5	1
1994-95	Aberdeen	-	-
1995-96	Aberdeen	-	-

STUBBS, Alan
Born : Kirkby 06/10/71

SEASON	CLUB	LEAGUE APPEARANCES	GOALS
1990-91	Bolton Wanderers	23	-
1991-92	Bolton Wanderers	32	1
1992-93	Bolton Wanderers	42	2
1993-94	Bolton Wanderers	41	1
1994-95	Bolton Wanderers	39	1

SEASON	CLUB	LEAGUE APPEARANCES	GOALS
1995-96	Bolton Wanderers	25	4

TAYLOR, Alexander
Born : Baillieston 13/06/62

SEASON	CLUB	LEAGUE APPEARANCES	GOALS
1980-81	Dundee United	-	-
1981-82	Dundee United	-	-
1982-83	Dundee United	3	-
1983-84	Dundee United	9	1
1984-85	Dundee United	21	5
1986-87	Hamilton Academical	25	1
1987-88	Hamilton Academical	41	4
1988-89	Walsall	13	3
1989-90	Walsall	32	3
1990-91	Walsall	-	-
1990-91	Falkirk	29	2
1991-92	Falkirk	22	1
1992-93	Falkirk	8	1
1992-93	Partick Thistle	8	1
1993-94	Partick Thistle	32	4
1994-95	Partick Thistle	23	2
1995-96	Raith Rovers	9	-

THOM, Andreas
Born : Rudersdorf, Germany 07/09/65
from TSV Bayer 04 Leverkusen

SEASON	CLUB	LEAGUE APPEARANCES	GOALS
1995-96	Celtic	32	5

THOMAS, Kevin Roderick
Born : Edinburgh 25/04/75

SEASON	CLUB	LEAGUE APPEARANCES	GOALS
1992-93	Heart of Midlothian	4	2
1993-94	Heart of Midlothian	12	-
1994-95	Heart of Midlothian	18	5
1995-96	Heart of Midlothian	3	-

THOMSON, Scott Munro
Born : Aberdeen 29/01/72

SEASON	CLUB	LEAGUE APPEARANCES	GOALS
1990-91	Brechin City	30	3
1991-92	Brechin City	11	3
1991-92	Aberdeen	-	-
1992-93	Aberdeen	2	-
1993-94	Aberdeen	3	-
1994-95	Aberdeen	10	1
1995-96	Aberdeen	4	-
1995-96	Raith Rovers	9	1

THOMSON, Scott Yuill
Born : Edinburgh 08/11/66

SEASON	CLUB	LEAGUE APPEARANCES	GOALS
1984-85	Dundee United	-	-
1985-86	Dundee United	-	-
1985-86	*Raith Rovers*	1	-
1986-87	Dundee United	3	-
1987-88	Dundee United	-	-
1988-89	Dundee United	1	-
1989-90	Dundee United	2	-
1990-91	Dundee United	-	-
1990-91	*Barnsley*	-	-
1991-92	Forfar Athletic	44	-
1992-93	Forfar Athletic	39	-
1993-94	Forfar Athletic	5	-
1993-94	Raith Rovers	34	-
1994-95	Raith Rovers	35	-
1995-96	Raith Rovers	26	-

TOD, Andrew
Born : Dunfermline 04/11/71

SEASON	CLUB	LEAGUE APPEARANCES	GOALS
1993-94	Dunfermline Athletic	22	11
1994-95	Dunfermline Athletic	35	6
1995-96	Dunfermline Athletic	36	5

TORTOLANO, Joseph
Born : Stirling 06/04/66

SEASON	CLUB	LEAGUE APPEARANCES	GOALS
1983-84	West Bromich Albion	-	-
1984-85	West Bromich Albion	-	-
1985-86	Hibernian	20	3
1986-87	Hibernian	33	-
1987-88	Hibernian	21	4
1988-89	Hibernian	25	-
1989-90	Hibernian	7	-
1990-91	Hibernian	18	1
1991-92	Hibernian	25	1
1992-93	Hibernian	21	3
1993-94	Hibernian	18	1
1994-95	Hibernian	18	-
1995-96	Hibernian	15	-

TWADDLE, Kevin
Born : Edinburgh 31/10/71

SEASON	CLUB	LEAGUE APPEARANCES	GOALS
1994-95	St. Johnstone	25	6
1995-96	St. Johnstone	26	4

TZVETANOV, Tzanko
Born : Svichtov, Bulgaria 06/01/70
from SV Waldof Mannheim

VAN DE KAMP, Guido
Born : 's Hertogenbosch, Holland 08/02/64
From BVV Den Bosch

SEASON	CLUB	LEAGUE APPEARANCES	GOALS
1991-92	Dundee United	27	-
1992-93	Dundee United	1	-
1993-94	Dundee United	25	-
1994-95	Dunfermline Athletic	13	-
1995-96	Dunfermline Athletic	26	-

VAN DER GAAG, Mitchell
Born : Zutphen, Holland 27/10/71
from PSV Eindhoven

SEASON	CLUB	LEAGUE APPEARANCES	GOALS
1994-95	Motherwell	2	-
1995-96	Motherwell	12	1

VAN HOOIJDONK, Pierre
Born : Steenbergen, Holland 29/11/69
From NAC Breda

SEASON	CLUB	LEAGUE APPEARANCES	GOALS
1994-95	Celtic	14	4
1995-96	Celtic	34	26

VAN VOSSEN, Peter Jacobus
Born : Zierikzee, Holland 21/04/68
from Istanbulspor Kulubu

SEASON	CLUB	LEAGUE APPEARANCES	GOALS
1995-96	Rangers	7	-

WALKER, Joseph Nicol
Born : Aberdeen 29/09/62

SEASON	CLUB	LEAGUE APPEARANCES	GOALS
1980-81	Leicester City	-	-
1981-82	Leicester City	6	-
1982-83	Motherwell	16	-
1983-84	Motherwell	15	-
1983-84	Rangers	8	-
1984-85	Rangers	14	-
1985-86	Rangers	34	-
1986-87	Rangers	2	-
1986-87	*Falkirk*	8	-
1987-88	Rangers	5	-
1987-88	*Dunfermline Athletic*	1	-
1988-89	Rangers	12	-
1989-90	Heart of Midlothian	-	-
1990-91	Heart of Midlothian	13	-
1991-92	Heart of Midlothian	-	-
1991-92	*Burnley*	6	-
1992-93	Heart of Midlothian	18	-
1993-94	Heart of Midlothian	17	-
1994-95	Heart of Midlothian	2	-
1994-95	Partick Thistle	20	-
1995-96	Partick Thistle	33	-

WALKER, Paul
Born : Kilwinning 20/08/77

SEASON	CLUB	LEAGUE APPEARANCES	GOALS
1994-95	Dundee United	-	-
1995-96	Dundee United	2	-

WARD, Kenneth
Born : Blairhall 16/03/63

SEASON	CLUB	LEAGUE APPEARANCES	GOALS
1983-84	Cowdenbeath	31	5
1984-85	Cowdenbeath	36	16
1985-86	Cowdenbeath	16	8
1985-86	Forfar Athletic	14	1
1986-87	Forfar Athletic	33	4
1987-88	Forfar Athletic	37	7
1988-89	Forfar Athletic	35	12
1989-90	Forfar Athletic	2	-
1989-90	St. Johnstone	18	4
1990-91	St. Johnstone	10	1
1991-92	St. Johnstone	12	1
1991-92	Hamilton Academical	12	5
1992-93	Hamilton Academical	34	10
1993-94	Hamilton Academical	30	8
1994-95	Dunfermline Athletic	23	4
1995-96	Dunfermline Athletic	-	-

WATT, Michael
Born : Aberdeen 27/11/70

SEASON	CLUB	LEAGUE APPEARANCES	GOALS
1989-90	Aberdeen	7	-
1990-91	Aberdeen	10	-
1991-92	Aberdeen	2	-
1992-93	Aberdeen	3	-
1993-94	Aberdeen	4	-
1994-95	Aberdeen	14	-
1995-96	Aberdeen	30	-

WEIR, David Gillespie
Born : Falkirk 10/05/70

SEASON	CLUB	LEAGUE APPEARANCES	GOALS
1992-93	Falkirk	30	1
1993-94	Falkirk	37	3
1994-95	Falkirk	32	1
1995-96	Falkirk	34	3

WEIR, Michael Graham
Born : Edinburgh 16/01/66

SEASON	CLUB	LEAGUE APPEARANCES	GOALS
1982-83	Hibernian	-	-
1983-84	Hibernian	-	-
1984-85	Hibernian	12	-
1985-86	Hibernian	7	-
1986-87	Hibernian	24	4
1987-88	Hibernian	5	1
1987-88	Luton Town	8	-
1987-88	Hibernian	13	2
1988-89	Hibernian	7	-
1989-90	Hibernian	18	3
1990-91	Hibernian	20	1
1991-92	Hibernian	31	11
1992-93	Hibernian	33	5
1993-94	Hibernian	-	-
1994-95	Hibernian	19	1
1995-96	Hibernian	9	1

WELSH, Brian
Born : Edinburgh 23/02/69

SEASON	CLUB	LEAGUE APPEARANCES	GOALS
1986-87	Dundee United	1	-
1987-88	Dundee United	1	1
1988-89	Dundee United	1	-
1989-90	Dundee United	5	-
1990-91	Dundee United	17	-
1991-92	Dundee United	11	1
1992-93	Dundee United	15	1
1993-94	Dundee United	37	1
1994-95	Dundee United	27	4
1995-96	Dundee United	23	1

WESTWATER, Ian
Born : Loughborough 08/11/63

SEASON	CLUB	LEAGUE APPEARANCES	GOALS
1980-81	Heart of Midlothian	2	-
1981-82	Heart of Midlothian	-	-
1982-83	Heart of Midlothian	-	-
1983-84	Heart of Midlothian	-	-
1984-85	Dunfermline Athletic	8	-
1985-86	Dunfermline Athletic	38	-
1986-87	Dunfermline Athletic	42	-
1987-88	Dunfermline Athletic	28	-
1988-89	Dunfermline Athletic	39	-
1989-90	Dunfermline Athletic	36	-
1990-91	Dunfermline Athletic	1	-
1991-92	Falkirk	40	-
1992-93	Falkirk	24	-
1993-94	Falkirk	3	-
1993-94	Dunfermline Athletic	9	-
1994-95	Dunfermline Athletic	17	-
1995-96	Dunfermline Athletic	11	-

WHITWORTH, Neil
Born : Wigan 12/04/72

SEASON	CLUB	LEAGUE APPEARANCES	GOALS
1989-90	Wigan Athletic	2	-
1990-91	Wigan Athletic	-	-
1990-91	Manchester United	2	-
1991-92	Manchester United	-	-
1991-92	*Preston North End*	6	-
1991-92	*Barnsley*	11	-
1992-93	Manchester United	-	-
1993-94	*Rotherham United*	8	1

SEASON	CLUB	LEAGUE APPEARANCES	GOALS
1993-94	*Blackpool*	-	-
1994-95	Manchester United	-	-
1994-95	Kilmarnock	30	3
1995-96	Kilmarnock	28	-

WIEGHORST, Morten
Born : Glostrup, Denmark 25/02/71

SEASON	CLUB	LEAGUE APPEARANCES	GOALS
From Lyngby			
1992-93	Dundee	23	2
1993-94	Dundee	24	2
1994-95	Dundee	29	3
1995-96	Dundee	14	4
1995-96	Celtic	11	1

WILKINS, Raymond Colin
Born : Hillingdon 14/09/56

SEASON	CLUB	LEAGUE APPEARANCES	GOALS
1973-74	Chelsea	6	-
1974-75	Chelsea	21	2
1975-76	Chelsea	42	11
1976-77	Chelsea	42	7
1977-78	Chelsea	33	7
1978-79	Chelsea	35	3
1979-80	Manchester United	37	2
1980-81	Manchester United	13	-
1981-82	Manchester United	42	1
1982-83	Manchester United	26	1
1983-84	Manchester United	42	3
1984-85	AC Milan	28	-
1985-86	AC Milan	29	2
1986-87	AC Milan	16	-
from Paris St. Germain			
1987-88	Rangers	24	1
1988-89	Rangers	31	1
1989-90	Rangers	15	-
1989-90	Queens Park Rangers	23	1
1990-91	Queens Park Rangers	38	2
1991-92	Queens Park Rangers	27	1
1992-93	Queens Park Rangers	27	2
1993-94	Queens Park Rangers	39	1
1994-95	Crystal Palace	1	-
1994-95	Queens Park Rangers	2	-
1995-96	Queens Park Rangers	15	-

WINDASS, Dean
Born : Hull 01/04/69

SEASON	CLUB	LEAGUE APPEARANCES	GOALS
1991-92	Hull City	32	6
1992-93	Hull City	41	7
1993-94	Hull City	43	23
1994-95	Hull City	44	17
1995-96	Hull City	16	4
1995-96	Aberdeen	20	6

WINTERS, Robert
Born : East Kilbride 04/11/74

SEASON	CLUB	LEAGUE APPEARANCES	GOALS
1991-92	Dundee United	-	-
1992-93	Dundee United	-	-
1993-94	Dundee United	-	-
1994-95	Dundee United	13	2
1995-96	Dundee United	35	7

WISHART, Fraser
Born : Johnstone 01/03/65

SEASON	CLUB	LEAGUE APPEARANCES	GOALS
1983-84	Motherwell	6	-
1984-85	Motherwell	-	-
1985-86	Motherwell	26	-
1986-87	Motherwell	44	3
1987-88	Motherwell	43	1
1988-89	Motherwell	35	1
1989-90	St. Mirren	20	-
1990-91	St. Mirren	22	-
1991-92	St. Mirren	9	-
1992-93	Falkirk	24	2
1993-94	Rangers	5	-
1994-95	Rangers	4	-
1994-95	Heart of Midlothian	8	-
1995-96	Heart of Midlothian	1	-

WOODS, Stephen Gerard
Born : Glasgow 23/02/70

SEASON	CLUB	LEAGUE APPEARANCES	GOALS
1989-90	Hibernian	-	-
1990-91	Hibernian	-	-
1991-92	Hibernian	-	-
1991-92	Clydebank	5	-
1992-93	Clydebank	42	-
1993-94	Clydebank	10	-
1993-94	Preston North End	20	-
1994-95	Motherwell	33	-
1995-96	Motherwell	-	-

WOODTHORPE, Colin
Born : Liverpool 13/01/69

SEASON	CLUB	LEAGUE APPEARANCES	GOALS
1986-87	Chester City	30	2
1987-88	Chester City	35	-
1988-89	Chester City	44	3
1989-90	Chester City	46	1
1990-91	Norwich City	1	-
1991-92	Norwich City	15	1
1992-93	Norwich City	7	-
1993-94	Norwich City	20	-
1994-95	Aberdeen	14	-
1995-96	Aberdeen	15	1

WRIGHT, Keith
Born : Edinburgh 17/05/65

SEASON	CLUB	LEAGUE APPEARANCES	GOALS
1983-84	Raith Rovers	37	5
1984-85	Raith Rovers	38	22
1985-86	Raith Rovers	39	21
1986-87	Raith Rovers	17	13
1986-87	Dundee	20	10
1987-88	Dundee	42	15
1988-89	Dundee	35	8
1989-90	Dundee	34	11
1990-91	Dundee	36	18
1991-92	Hibernian	40	9
1992-93	Hibernian	42	11
1993-94	Hibernian	42	16
1994-95	Hibernian	19	10
1995-96	Hibernian	28	9

WRIGHT, Paul Hamilton
Born : East Kilbride 17/08/67

SEASON	CLUB	LEAGUE APPEARANCES	GOALS
1983-84	Aberdeen	1	-
1984-85	Aberdeen	-	-
1985-86	Aberdeen	10	2
1986-87	Aberdeen	25	4
1987-88	Aberdeen	9	4
1988-89	Aberdeen	23	6
1989-90	Queens Park Rangers	15	5
1989-90	Hibernian	3	1
1990-91	Hibernian	33	6
1991-92	St. Johnstone	41	18
1992-93	St. Johnstone	42	14
1993-94	St. Johnstone	17	7
1994-95	St. Johnstone	12	1
1994-95	Kilmarnock	7	1
1995-96	Kilmarnock	36	13

WRIGHT, Stephen
Born : Bellshill 27/08/71

SEASON	CLUB	LEAGUE APPEARANCES	GOALS
1987-88	Aberdeen	-	-
1988-89	Aberdeen	-	-
1989-90	Aberdeen	1	-
1990-91	Aberdeen	17	1
1991-92	Aberdeen	23	-
1992-93	Aberdeen	36	-
1993-94	Aberdeen	36	-
1994-95	Aberdeen	34	1
1995-96	Rangers	6	-

OFFICIAL LIST OF CLASS 1 REFEREES 1996/97

Graeme R. Alison (Dumfries)
Kevin R. Bisset (Inverness)
Thomas Brown (Edinburgh)
Kenneth W. Clark (Paisley)
Martin A. Clark (Edinburgh)
George T. Clyde (Bearsden)
William N. M. Crombie (Edinburgh)
Hugh Dallas (Motherwell)
Stuart Dougal (Burnside)
Ian S. Elmslie (Aberdeen)
Gerard A. Evans (Bishopbriggs)
John Fleming (Glasgow)
Alan Freeland (Aberdeen)
Ian M. Fyfe (Linlithgow)
Alan C. Gemmill (Linlithgow)
James A. Herald (Newton Mearns)
James McCluskey (Stewarton)
T. Michael McCurry (Glasgow)
Eric Martindale (Newlands)
Garry P. Mitchell (Arbroath)
Leslie W. Mottram (Forth)
Robert Orr (Kilbarchan)
Michael F. Pocock (Aberdeen)
John Rowbotham (Kirkcaldy)
Alexander M. Roy (Aberdeen)
George H. Simpson (Peterhead)
J. Douglas K. Smith (Troon)
Robert T. Tait (East Kilbride)
Ian Taylor (Edinburgh)
Kevin E. Toner (Glasgow)
John R. Underhill (Edinburgh)
Andrew W. Waddell (Edinburgh)
John A. Young (Thornliebank)
William S. G. Young (Clarkston)

Bell's League Fixtures 1996/97

Saturday, August 10th, 1996
Aberdeen v Celtic
Dundee United v Motherwell
Hibernian v Kilmarnock
Rangers v Raith Rovers

Saturday, August 17th, 1996
Celtic v Raith Rovers
Dundee United v Hibernian
Dunfermline Athletic v Rangers
Heart of Midlothian v Kilmarnock
Motherwell v Aberdeen

East Fife v St. Mirren
Greenock Morton v Clydebank
Partick Thistle v Dundee
St. Johnstone v Falkirk
Stirling Albion v Airdrieonians

Ayr United v Hamilton Academical
Clyde v Berwick Rangers
Dumbarton v Stranraer
Livingston v Queen of the South
Stenhousemuir v Brechin City

Albion Rovers v Forfar Athletic
Arbroath v Ross County
Inverness Cal. Th. v Cowdenbeath
Montrose v Alloa
Queen's Park v East Stirlingshire

Friday, August 23rd, 1996
East Stirlingshire v Albion Rovers

Saturday, August 24th, 1996
Hibernian v Dunfermline Athletic
Kilmarnock v Celtic
Raith Rovers v Motherwell
Rangers v Dundee United

Airdrieonians v East Fife
Clydebank v Stirling Albion
Dundee v Greenock Morton
Falkirk v Partick Thistle
St. Mirren v St. Johnstone

Berwick Rangers v Stenhousemuir
Brechin City v Ayr United
Hamilton Academical v Clyde
Queen of the South v Dumbarton
Stranraer v Livingston

Alloa v Arbroath
Cowdenbeath v Montrose
Forfar Athletic v Inverness Cal. Th.
Ross County v Queen's Park

Sunday, August 25th, 1996
Aberdeen v Heart of Midlothian

Saturday, August 31st, 1996
Greenock Morton v Falkirk
Partick Thistle v St. Mirren
Stirling Albion v Dundee

Ayr United v Berwick Rangers
Clyde v Queen of the South
Dumbarton v Brechin City
Livingston v Hamilton Academical
Stenhousemuir v Stranraer

Albion Rovers v Cowdenbeath
Arbroath v East Stirlingshire
Inverness Cal. Th. v Alloa
Montrose v Ross County
Queen's Park v Forfar Athletic

Tuesday, September 3rd, 1996
East Fife v Clydebank

Saturday, September 7th, 1996
Celtic v Hibernian
Heart of Midlothian v Dundee United
Kilmarnock v Dunfermline Athletic
Motherwell v Rangers
Raith Rovers v Aberdeen

Clydebank v St. Mirren
Dundee v Airdrieonians
Greenock Morton v East Fife
St. Johnstone v Partick Thistle
Stirling Albion v Falkirk

Berwick Rangers v Queen of the South
Clyde v Dumbarton
Livingston v Brechin City
Stenhousemuir v Ayr United
Stranraer v Hamilton Academical

Albion Rovers v Inverness Cal. Th.
Cowdenbeath v Queen's Park
East Stirlingshire v Forfar Athletic
Montrose v Arbroath
Ross County v Alloa

Tuesday, September 10th, 1996
Dunfermline Athletic v Heart of Midlothian

Saturday, September 14th, 1996
Aberdeen v Kilmarnock
Dundee United v Celtic
Dunfermline Athletic v Motherwell
Hibernian v Raith Rovers
Rangers v Heart of Midlothian

Airdrieonians v Greenock Morton
East Fife v St. Johnstone
Falkirk v Clydebank
Partick Thistle v Stirling Albion
St. Mirren v Dundee

Ayr United v Clyde
Brechin City v Stranraer
Dumbarton v Livingston
Hamilton Academical v Berwick Rangers
Queen of the South v Stenhousemuir

Alloa v Cowdenbeath
Arbroath v Albion Rovers
Forfar Athletic v Ross County
Inverness Cal. Th. v East Stirlingshire
Queen's Park v Montrose

Saturday, September 21st, 1996
Aberdeen v Hibernian
Celtic v Dunfermline Athletic
Heart of Midlothian v Motherwell
Kilmarnock v Rangers
Raith Rovers v Dundee United

Airdrieonians v Partick Thistle
Clydebank v St. Johnstone
Dundee v East Fife
St. Mirren v Falkirk
Stirling Albion v Greenock Morton

Berwick Rangers v Dumbarton
Brechin City v Hamilton Academical
Queen of the South v Ayr United
Stenhousemuir v Livingston
Stranraer v Clyde

Albion Rovers v Alloa
Cowdenbeath v Ross County
East Stirlingshire v Montrose
Forfar Athletic v Arbroath
Inverness Cal. Th. v Queen's Park

Tuesday, September 24th, 1996
St. Johnstone v Airdrieonians

Saturday, September 28th, 1996
Dundee United v Aberdeen
Dunfermline Athletic v Raith Rovers
Hibernian v Heart of Midlothian
Motherwell v Kilmarnock
Rangers v Celtic

East Fife v Stirling Albion
Falkirk v Airdrieonians
Greenock Morton v St. Mirren
Partick Thistle v Clydebank
St. Johnstone v Dundee

Ayr United v Stranraer
Clyde v Brechin City
Dumbarton v Stenhousemuir
Hamilton Academical v Queen of the South
Livingston v Berwick Rangers

Alloa v East Stirlingshire
Arbroath v Cowdenbeath
Montrose v Forfar Athletic
Queen's Park v Albion Rovers
Ross County v Inverness Cal. Th.

Saturday, October 5th, 1996
Airdrieonians v St. Mirren
Dundee v Clydebank
East Fife v Falkirk
Greenock Morton v Partick Thistle
Stirling Albion v St. Johnstone

Brechin City v Berwick Rangers
Dumbarton v Ayr United
Livingston v Clyde
Stenhousemuir v Hamilton Academical
Stranraer v Queen of the South

Albion Rovers v Montrose
East Stirlingshire v Ross County
Forfar Athletic v Cowdenbeath
Inverness Cal. Th. v Arbroath
Queen's Park v Alloa

Saturday, October 12th, 1996
Aberdeen v Dunfermline Athletic
Celtic v Motherwell
Dundee United v Kilmarnock
Hibernian v Rangers
Raith Rovers v Heart of Midlothian

Clydebank v Airdrieonians
Falkirk v Dundee
Partick Thistle v East Fife
St. Johnstone v Greenock Morton
St. Mirren v Stirling Albion

Ayr United v Livingston
Berwick Rangers v Stranraer
Clyde v Stenhousemuir
Hamilton Academical v Dumbarton
Queen of the South v Brechin City

Alloa v Forfar Athletic
Arbroath v Queen's Park
Cowdenbeath v East Stirlingshire
Montrose v Inverness Cal. Th.
Ross County v Albion Rovers

Saturday, October 19th, 1996
Dunfermline Athletic v Dundee United
Kilmarnock v Raith Rovers
Motherwell v Hibernian
Rangers v Aberdeen

Airdrieonians v Stirling Albion
Clydebank v Greenock Morton
Dundee v Partick Thistle
Falkirk v St. Johnstone
St. Mirren v East Fife

Berwick Rangers v Clyde
Brechin City v Stenhousemuir
Hamilton Academical v Ayr United
Queen of the South v Livingston
Stranraer v Dumbarton

Alloa v Montrose
Cowdenbeath v Inverness Cal. Th.
East Stirlingshire v Queen's Park
Forfar Athletic v Albion Rovers
Ross County v Arbroath

Sunday, October 20th, 1996

Heart of Midlothian v Celtic

Saturday, October 26th, 1996

Aberdeen v Raith Rovers
Dundee United v Heart of Midlothian
Dunfermline Athletic v Kilmarnock
Hibernian v Celtic
Rangers v Motherwell

East Fife v Airdrieonians
Greenock Morton v Dundee
Partick Thistle v Falkirk
St. Johnstone v St. Mirren
Stirling Albion v Clydebank

Ayr United v Brechin City
Clyde v Hamilton Academical
Dumbarton v Queen of the South
Livingston v Stranraer
Stenhousemuir v Berwick Rangers

Arbroath v Alloa
Forfar Athletic v Inverness Cal. Th.
Montrose v Cowdenbeath
Queen's Park v Ross County

Sunday, October 27th, 1996

Albion Rovers v East Stirlingshire

Saturday, November 2nd, 1996

Celtic v Aberdeen
Heart of Midlothian v Dunfermline Athletic
Kilmarnock v Hibernian
Motherwell v Dundee United
Raith Rovers v Rangers

Clydebank v Falkirk
Dundee v St. Mirren
Greenock Morton v Airdrieonians
St. Johnstone v East Fife
Stirling Albion v Partick Thistle

Berwick Rangers v Hamilton Academical
Clyde v Ayr United
Livingston v Dumbarton
Stenhousemuir v Queen of the South
Stranraer v Brechin City

Albion Rovers v Arbroath
Cowdenbeath v Alloa
East Stirlingshire v Inverness Cal. Th.
Montrose v Queen's Park
Ross County v Forfar Athletic

Saturday, November 9th, 1996

Airdrieonians v Dundee
East Fife v Greenock Morton
Falkirk v Stirling Albion
Partick Thistle v St. Johnstone
St. Mirren v Clydebank

Ayr United v Stenhousemuir
Brechin City v Livingston
Dumbarton v Clyde
Hamilton Academical v Stranraer
Queen of the South v Berwick Rangers

Alloa v Ross County
Arbroath v Montrose
Forfar Athletic v East Stirlingshire
Inverness Cal. Th. v Albion Rovers
Queen's Park v Cowdenbeath

Thursday, November 14th, 1996

Celtic v Rangers

Saturday, November 16th, 1996

Aberdeen v Dundee United
Heart of Midlothian v Hibernian
Kilmarnock v Motherwell
Raith Rovers v Dunfermline Athletic

Airdrieonians v Falkirk
Clydebank v Partick Thistle
Dundee v St. Johnstone
St. Mirren v Greenock Morton
Stirling Albion v East Fife

Berwick Rangers v Livingston
Brechin City v Clyde
Queen of the South v Hamilton Academical
Stenhousemuir v Dumbarton
Stranraer v Ayr United

Albion Rovers v Queen's Park
Cowdenbeath v Arbroath
East Stirlingshire v Alloa
Forfar Athletic v Montrose
Inverness Cal. Th. v Ross County

Saturday, November 23rd, 1996

Dundee United v Raith Rovers
Dunfermline Athletic v Celtic
Hibernian v Aberdeen
Motherwell v Heart of Midlothian
Rangers v Kilmarnock

East Fife v Dundee
Falkirk v St. Mirren
Greenock Morton v Stirling Albion
Partick Thistle v Airdrieonians
St. Johnstone v Clydebank

Ayr United v Queen of the South
Clyde v Stranraer
Dumbarton v Berwick Rangers
Hamilton Academical v Brechin City
Livingston v Stenhousemuir

Alloa v Albion Rovers
Arbroath v Forfar Athletic
Montrose v East Stirlingshire
Queen's Park v Inverness Cal. Th.
Ross County v Cowdenbeath

Saturday, November 30th, 1996

Celtic v Heart of Midlothian
Dundee United v Dunfermline Athletic
Hibernian v Motherwell
Raith Rovers v Kilmarnock

Clydebank v Dundee
Falkirk v East Fife
Partick Thistle v Greenock Morton
St. Johnstone v Stirling Albion
St. Mirren v Airdrieonians

Ayr United v Dumbarton
Berwick Rangers v Brechin City
Clyde v Livingston
Hamilton Academical v Stenhousemuir
Queen of the South v Stranraer

Alloa v Queen's Park
Arbroath v Inverness Cal. Th.
Cowdenbeath v Forfar Athletic
Montrose v Albion Rovers
Ross County v East Stirlingshire

Sunday, December 1st, 1996

Aberdeen v Rangers

Saturday, December 7th, 1996

Dunfermline Athletic v Aberdeen
Heart of Midlothian v Raith Rovers
Kilmarnock v Dundee United
Motherwell v Celtic
Rangers v Hibernian

Airdrieonians v Clydebank
Dundee v Falkirk
East Fife v Partick Thistle
Greenock Morton v St. Johnstone
Stirling Albion v St. Mirren

Tuesday, December 10th, 1996

Dundee United v Rangers

Wednesday, December 11th, 1996

Celtic v Kilmarnock
Dunfermline Athletic v Hibernian
Heart of Midlothian v Aberdeen
Motherwell v Raith Rovers

Saturday, December 14th, 1996

Aberdeen v Motherwell
Hibernian v Dundee United
Kilmarnock v Heart of Midlothian
Raith Rovers v Celtic
Rangers v Dunfermline Athletic

Airdrieonians v St. Johnstone
Dundee v Stirling Albion
Falkirk v Greenock Morton
St. Mirren v Partick Thistle

Brechin City v Queen of the South
Dumbarton v Hamilton Academical
Livingston v Ayr United
Stenhousemuir v Clyde
Stranraer v Berwick Rangers

Albion Rovers v Ross County
East Stirlingshire v Cowdenbeath
Forfar Athletic v Alloa
Inverness Cal. Th. v Montrose
Queen's Park v Arbroath

Saturday, December 21st, 1996

Celtic v Dundee United
Heart of Midlothian v Rangers
Kilmarnock v Aberdeen
Motherwell v Dunfermline Athletic
Raith Rovers v Hibernian

Clydebank v East Fife
Stirling Albion v Airdrieonians

Clyde v Berwick Rangers
Stenhousemuir v Brechin City

Inverness Cal. Th. v Cowdenbeath
Montrose v Alloa
Queen's Park v East Stirlingshire

Thursday, December 26th, 1996

Aberdeen v Celtic
Dundee United v Motherwell
Dunfermline Athletic v Heart of Midlothian
Hibernian v Kilmarnock
Rangers v Raith Rovers

East Fife v St. Mirren
Greenock Morton v Clydebank
Partick Thistle v Dundee
St. Johnstone v Falkirk

Ayr United v Hamilton Academical
Dumbarton v Stranraer
Livingston v Queen of the South

Albion Rovers v Forfar Athletic
Arbroath v Ross County

Saturday, December 28th, 1996

Aberdeen v Hibernian
Celtic v Dunfermline Athletic
Heart of Midlothian v Motherwell
Kilmarnock v Rangers
Raith Rovers v Dundee United

Airdrieonians v Partick Thistle
Clydebank v St. Johnstone
Dundee v East Fife
St. Mirren v Falkirk
Stirling Albion v Greenock Morton

Berwick Rangers v Ayr United
Brechin City v Dumbarton
Hamilton Academical v Livingston
Queen of the South v Clyde
Stranraer v Stenhousemuir

Alloa v Inverness Cal. Th.
Cowdenbeath v Albion Rovers
East Stirlingshire v Arbroath
Forfar Athletic v Queen's Park
Ross County v Montrose

Wednesday, January 1st, 1997

Dundee United v Aberdeen
Dunfermline Athletic v Raith Rovers
Hibernian v Heart of Midlothian
Motherwell v Kilmarnock

East Fife v Stirling Albion
Falkirk v Airdrieonians
Greenock Morton v St. Mirren
Partick Thistle v Clydebank
St. Johnstone v Dundee

Ayr United v Stranraer
Clyde v Brechin City
Dumbarton v Stenhousemuir
Hamilton Academical v Queen of the South
Livingston v Berwick Rangers

Alloa v East Stirlingshire
Arbroath v Cowdenbeath
Montrose v Forfar Athletic
Queen's Park v Albion Rovers
Ross County v Inverness Cal. Th.

Thursday, January 2nd, 1997

Rangers v Celtic

Saturday, January 4th, 1997

Aberdeen v Dunfermline Athletic
Celtic v Motherwell
Dundee United v Kilmarnock
Hibernian v Rangers
Raith Rovers v Heart of Midlothian

Airdrieonians v Greenock Morton
East Fife v St. Johnstone
Falkirk v Clydebank
Partick Thistle v Stirling Albion
St. Mirren v Dundee

Saturday, January 11th, 1997

Dunfermline Athletic v Dundee United
Heart of Midlothian v Celtic
Kilmarnock v Raith Rovers
Motherwell v Hibernian

Clydebank v St. Mirren
Dundee v Airdrieonians
Greenock Morton v East Fife
St. Johnstone v Partick Thistle
Stirling Albion v Falkirk

Berwick Rangers v Dumbarton
Brechin City v Hamilton Academical
Queen of the South v Ayr United
Stenhousemuir v Livingston
Stranraer v Clyde

Albion Rovers v Alloa
Cowdenbeath v Ross County
East Stirlingshire v Montrose
Forfar Athletic v Arbroath
Inverness Cal. Th. v Queen's Park

Sunday, January 12th, 1997

Rangers v Aberdeen

Saturday, January 18th, 1997

Celtic v Hibernian
Heart of Midlothian v Dundee United
Kilmarnock v Dunfermline Athletic
Motherwell v Rangers
Raith Rovers v Aberdeen

Airdrieonians v St. Mirren
Dundee v Clydebank
East Fife v Falkirk
Greenock Morton v Partick Thistle
Stirling Albion v St. Johnstone

Brechin City v Berwick Rangers
Dumbarton v Ayr United
Livingston v Clyde
Stenhousemuir v Hamilton Academical
Stranraer v Queen of the South

Albion Rovers v Montrose
East Stirlingshire v Ross County
Forfar Athletic v Cowdenbeath
Inverness Cal. Th. v Arbroath
Queen's Park v Alloa

Saturday, February 1st, 1997

Aberdeen v Kilmarnock
Dundee United v Celtic
Dunfermline Athletic v Motherwell
Hibernian v Raith Rovers
Rangers v Heart of Midlothian

Clydebank v Airdrieonians
Falkirk v Dundee
Partick Thistle v East Fife
St. Johnstone v Greenock Morton
St. Mirren v Stirling Albion

Ayr United v Livingston
Berwick Rangers v Stranraer
Clyde v Stenhousemuir
Hamilton Academical v Dumbarton
Queen of the South v Brechin City

Alloa v Forfar Athletic
Arbroath v Queen's Park
Cowdenbeath v East Stirlingshire
Montrose v Inverness Cal. Th.
Ross County v Albion Rovers

Saturday, February 8th, 1997

Celtic v Raith Rovers
Dundee United v Hibernian
Dunfermline Athletic v Rangers
Heart of Midlothian v Kilmarnock
Motherwell v Aberdeen

East Fife v Clydebank
Greenock Morton v Falkirk
Partick Thistle v St. Mirren
St. Johnstone v Airdrieonians
Stirling Albion v Dundee

Ayr United v Clyde
Brechin City v Stranraer
Dumbarton v Livingston
Hamilton Academical v Berwick Rangers
Queen of the South v Stenhousemuir

Alloa v Coiwdenbeath
Arbroath v Albion Rovers
Forfar Athletic v Ross County
Inverness Cal. Th. v East Stirlingshire
Queen's Park v Montrose

Tuesday, February 11th, 1997

Hibernian v Dunfermline Athletic
Kilmarnock v Celtic
Raith Rovers v Motherwell

Wednesday, February 12th, 1997

Aberdeen v Heart of Midlothian
Rangers v Dundee United

Saturday, February 15th, 1997

Berwick Rangers v Queen of the South
Clyde v Dumbarton
Livingston v Brechin City
Stenhousemuir v Ayr United
Stranraer v Hamilton Academical

Albion Rovers v Inverness Cal. Th.
Cowdenbeath v Queen's Park
East Stirlingshire v Forfar Athletic
Montrose v Arbroath
Ross County v Alloa

Saturday, February 22nd, 1997

Dunfermline Athletic v Aberdeen
Heart of Midlothian v Raith Rovers
Kilmarnock v Dundee United
Motherwell v Celtic
Rangers v Hibernian

Airdrieonians v East Fife
Clydebank v Stirling Albion
Dundee v Greenock Morton
Falkirk v Partick Thistle
St. Mirren v St. Johnstone

Berwick Rangers v Stenhousemuir
Brechin City v Ayr United
Hamilton Academical v Clyde
Queen of the South v Dumbarton
Stranraer v Livingston

Alloa v Arbroath
Cowdenbeath v Montrose
Inverness Cal. Th. v Forfar Athletic
Ross County v Queen's Park

Sunday, February 23rd, 1997

East Stirlingshire v Albion Rovers

Saturday, March 1st, 1997

Aberdeen v Rangers
Celtic v Heart of Midlothian
Dundee United v Dunfermline Athletic
Hibernian v Motherwell
Raith Rovers v Kilmarnock

East Fife v Dundee
Falkirk v St. Mirren
Greenock Morton v Stirling Albion
Partick Thistle v Airdrieonians
St. Johnstone v Clydebank

Ayr United v Berwick Rangers
Clyde v Queen of the South
Dumbarton v Brechin City
Livingston v Hamilton Academical
Stenhousemuir v Stranraer

Albion Rovers v Cowdenbeath
Arbroath v East Stirlingshire
Inverness Cal. Th. v Alloa
Montrose v Ross County
Queen's Park v Forfar Athletic

Saturday, March 8th, 1997

Ayr United v Queen of the South
Clyde v Stranraer
Dumbarton v Berwick Rangers
Hamilton Academical v Brechin City
Livingston v Stenhousemuir

Alloa v Albion Rovers
Arbroath v Forfar Athletic
Montrose v East Stirlingshire
Queen's Park v Inverness Cal. Th.
Ross County v Cowdenbeath

Saturday, March 15th, 1997

Aberdeen v Dundee United
Heart of Midlothian v Hibernian
Kilmarnock v Motherwell
Raith Rovers v Dunfermline Athletic

Airdrieonians v Falkirk
Clydebank v Partick Thistle
Dundee v St. Johnstone
St. Mirren v Greenock Morton
Stirling Albion v East Fife

Berwick Rangers v Livingston
Brechin City v Clyde
Queen of the South v Hamilton Academical
Stenhousemuir v Dumbarton
Stranraer v Ayr United

Albion Rovers v Queen's Park
Cowdenbeath v Arbroath
East Stirlingshire v Alloa
Forfar Athletic v Montrose
Inverness Cal. Th. v Ross County

Sunday, March 16th, 1997

Celtic v Rangers

Saturday, March 22nd, 1997

Dundee United v Raith Rovers
Dunfermline Athletic v Celtic
Hibernian v Aberdeen
Motherwell v Heart of Midlothian
Rangers v Kilmarnock

Clydebank v Dundee
Falkirk v East Fife
Partick Thistle v Greenock Morton
St. Johnstone v Stirling Albion
St. Mirren v Airdrieonians

Ayr United v Dumbarton
Berwick Rangers v Brechin City
Clyde v Livingston
Hamilton Academical v Stenhousemuir
Queen of the South v Stranraer

Alloa v Queen's Park
Arbroath v Inverness Cal. Th.
Cowdenbeath v Forfar Athletic
Montrose v Albion Rovers
Ross County v East Stirlingshire

Saturday, April 5th, 1997

Aberdeen v Motherwell
Hibernian v Dundee United
Kilmarnock v Heart of Midlothian
Raith Rovers v Celtic
Rangers v Dunfermline Athletic

Airdrieonians v Clydebank
Dundee v Falkirk
East Fife v Partick Thistle
Greenock Morton v St. Johnstone
Stirling Albion v St. Mirren

Brechin City v Queen of the South
Dumbarton v Hamilton Academical
Livingston v Ayr United
Stenhousemuir v Clyde
Stranraer v Berwick Rangers

Albion Rovers v Ross County
East Stirlingshire v Cowdenbeath
Forfar Athletic v Alloa
Inverness Cal. Th. v Montrose
Queen's Park v Arbroath

Saturday, April 12th, 1997

Celtic v Kilmarnock
Dundee United v Rangers
Dunfermline Athletic v Hibernian
Heart of Midlothian v Aberdeen
Motherwell v Raith Rovers

Airdrieonians v Dundee
East Fife v Greenock Morton
Falkirk v Stirling Albion
Partick Thistle v St. Johnstone
St. Mirren v Clydebank

Ayr United v Stenhousemuir
Brechin City v Livingston
Dumbarton v Clyde
Hamilton Academical v Stranraer
Queen of the South v Berwick Rangers

Alloa v Ross County
Arbroath v Montrose
Forfar Athletic v East Stirlingshire
Inverness Cal. Th. v Albion Rovers
Queen's Park v Cowdenbeath

Saturday, April 19th, 1997

Celtic v Aberdeen
Heart of Midlothian v Dunfermline Athletic
Kilmarnock v Hibernian
Motherwell v Dundee United
Raith Rovers v Rangers

Clydebank v Falkirk
Dundee v St. Mirren
Greenock Morton v Airdrieonians
St. Johnstone v East Fife
Stirling Albion v Partick Thistle

Berwick Rangers v Hamilton Academical
Clyde v Ayr United
Livingston v Dumbarton
Stenhousemuir v Queen of the South
Stranraer v Brechin City

Albion Rovers v Arbroath
Cowdenbeath v Alloa
East Stirlingshire v Inverness Cal. Th.
Montrose v Queen's Park
Ross County v Forfar Athletic

Saturday, April 26th, 1997

Airdrieonians v Stirling Albion
Clydebank v Greenock Morton
Dundee v Partick Thistle
Falkirk v St. Johnstone
St. Mirren v East Fife

Berwick Rangers v Clyde
Brechin City v Stenhousemuir
Hamilton Academical v Ayr United
Queen of the South v Livingston
Stranraer v Dumbarton

Alloa v Montrose
Cowdenbeath v Inverness Cal. Th.
East Stirlingshire v Queen's Park
Forfar Athletic v Albion Rovers
Ross County v Arbroath

Friday, May 2nd, 1997

Albion Rovers v East Stirlingshire

Saturday, May 3rd, 1997

Aberdeen v Raith Rovers
Dundee United v Heart of Midlothian
Dunfermline Athletic v Kilmarnock
Hibernian v Celtic
Rangers v Motherwell

East Fife v Airdrieonians
Greenock Morton v Dundee
Partick Thistle v Falkirk
St. Johnstone v St. Mirren
Stirling Albion v Clydebank

Ayr United v Brechin City
Clyde v Hamilton Academical
Dumbarton v Queen of the South
Livingston v Stranraer
Stenhousemuir v Berwick Rangers

Arbroath v Alloa
Inverness Cal. Th. v Forfar Athletic
Montrose v Cowdenbeath
Queen's Park v Ross County

Saturday, May 10th, 1997

Celtic v Dundee United
Heart of Midlothian v Rangers
Kilmarnock v Aberdeen
Motherwell v Dunfermline Athletic
Raith Rovers v Hibernian

Airdrieonians v St. Johnstone
Clydebank v East Fife
Dundee v Stirling Albion
Falkirk v Greenock Morton
St. Mirren v Partick Thistle

Berwick Rangers v Ayr United
Brechin City v Dumbarton
Hamilton Academical v Livingston
Queen of the South v Clyde
Stranraer v Stenhousemuir

Alloa v Inverness Cal. Th.
Cowdenbeath v Albion Rovers
East Stirlingshire v Arbroath
Forfar Athletic v Queen's Park
Ross County v Montrose

Coca-Cola Cup Draw Season 1996/97

TENNENT'S LAGER

S·F·L

The Coca-Cola Cup

1st Round

Clyde	-v-	Inverness Caledonian Thistle
Ayr United	-v-	Livingston
Cowdenbeath	-v-	Forfar Athletic
Stranraer	-v-	Queen of the South
Brechin City	-v-	Montrose
Queen's Park	-v-	Ross County
East Stirlingshire	-v-	Alloa
Albion Rovers	-v-	Arbroath

Above ties to be played on Saturday, 3rd August, 1996

2nd Round

Partick Thistle	-v-	Cowdenbeath or Forfar Athletic
Queen's Park or Ross County	-v-	Aberdeen
Greenock Morton	-v-	Hamilton Academical
Airdrieonains	-v-	Raith Rovers
St. Mirren	-v-	Berwick Rangers
East Fife	-v-	St. Johnstone
Dundee	-v-	Dumbarton
Kilmarnock	-v-	Ayr United or Livingston
Stirling Albion	-v-	Dundee United
Motherwell	-v-	East Stirlingshire or Alloa
Falkirk	-v-	Albion Rovers or Arbroath

Above ties to be played on Tuesday, 13th August, 1996

Heart of Midlothian	-v-	Stenhousemuir
Clydebank	-v-	Rangers
Clyde or Inverness Cal. Th.	-v-	Celtic
*Stranraer or Queen of the South	-v-	Dunfermline Athletic
†Brechin City or Montrose	-v-	Hibernian

Above ties to be played on Wednesday, 14th August, 1996

**(If Queen of the South win their 1st Round Tie, the above match will be played on Tuesday, 13th August, 1996)*

†(If Brechin City win their 1st Round Tie, the above match will be played on Tuesday, 13th August, 1996)

3rd Round

.... -v- ....
.... -v- ....
.... -v- ....
.... -v- ....
.... -v- ....
.... -v- ....
.... -v- ....
.... -v- ....

Ties to be played on Tuesday, 3rd or Wednesday, 4th September, 1996

4th Round

.... -v- ....
.... -v- ....
.... -v- ....
.... -v- ....

Ties to be played on Tuesday, 17th or Wednesday, 18th September, 1996

Semi–Finals

.... -v- ....
.... -v- ....

Ties to be played on Tuesday, 22nd or Wednesday, 23rd October, 1996

COCA–COLA CUP FINAL

.... -v- ....

To be played on Sunday, 24th November, 1996

In the event of a draw after normal time in all rounds, extra-time of 30 minutes (i.e. 15 minutes each way) will take place and thereafter, if necessary, Kicks from the Penalty Mark in accordance with the Rules laid down by the International Football Association Board will be taken.

THE COCA-COLA CUP INCENTIVES

The Coca-Cola Man of the Match Award

A player will be chosen at every game in The Coca-Cola Cup, by selected members of the media attending each game, to be presented with The Coca-Cola Cup Man of the Match award.
Each player selected to receive The Coca-Cola Cup Man of the Match award will be presented with a 'Coca-Cola' Mountain Bike.

The Fastest Goal per Round

The scorer of the fastest goal in every round of The Coca-Cola Cup in 1996/97* will be awarded £250.00. The player will also nominate a youth or school team, which is a current member of a League or Association, affiliated to The Scottish Football Association, and in The Under 14's age category. The team shall be presented with a 'Coca-Cola' Big Red Bag.
The 'Coca-Cola' Big Red Bag contains portable goals, footballs, cones, training tops, everything necessary to organise training and coaching exercises for the team. The 'Coca-Cola' Big Red Bag provides a self contained coaching package, purpose designed for youth and school teams.
** The fastest goal per round in The Coca-Cola Cup 1996/97 will be the goal scored in the shortest elapsed period of time after Kick-Off, in any fixture in The Coca-Cola Cup 1996/97, during each round, 1st, 2nd, 3rd, 4th, Semi & Final in this competition, in accordance with the officially recorded Statistics of The Scottish Football League.*

Fastest Goal in The Coca-Cola Cup 1996/97

The player scoring the fastest goal overall* in The Coca-Cola Cup 1996/97 will be awarded £500.00. The player will also nominate a youth or school team, which is a current member of a League or Association, affiliated to The Scottish Football Association, and in The Under 14's age category. The team shall be presented with a full set of team kit.
** The fastest goal overall in The Coca-Cola Cup 1996/97 will be the goal scored in the shortest period of time after Kick-Off, in any fixture in The Coca-Cola Cup 1996/97, in accordance with the officially recorded Statistics of The Scottish Football League.*

Top Scorer Award

The player scoring the most number of goals in The Coca-Cola Cup Competition 1996/97 will be awarded £1,000.00 cash.*
The player will also select a local secondary school, which is a a member of The Scottish Football Association, who shall be presented with a full set of team kit, for use for their football team.

*** FOOTNOTE:**

For the purpose of the aforementioned Incentives, all goals must be scored during regulation time or extra-time, but will exclude own goals and Kicks from the Penalty Mark in accordance with the Rules laid down by The International Football Association Board.

Challenge Cup Draw

SEASON 1996/97

1st Round

Dundee	-v-	Stenhousemuir
Albion Rovers	-v-	St. Johnstone
Cowdenbeath	-v-	Falkirk
Livingston	-v-	Inverness Cal. Thistle
Alloa	-v-	Clyde
Hamilton Academical	-v-	St. Mirren
Brechin City	-v-	Stirling Albion
Montrose	-v-	Dumbarton
Partick Thistle	-v-	Queen's Park
Arbroath	-v-	Queen of the South
Berwick Rangers	-v-	Stranraer
Clydebank	-v-	East Stirlingshire
Forfar Athletic	-v-	Greenock Morton
Ross County	-v-	Ayr United

BYES: Airdrieonians and East Fife

Above ties to be played on Saturday, 10th August, 1996

2nd Round

.... -v- ....
.... -v- ....
.... -v- ....
.... -v- ....
.... -v- ....
.... -v- ....
.... -v- ....
.... -v- ....

Above ties to be played on Tuesday, 27th or Wednesday, 28th August, 1996

3rd Round

.... -v- ....
.... -v- ....
.... -v- ....
.... -v- ....

Above ties to be played on Tuesday, 10th or Wednesday, 11th September, 1996

Semi–Finals

.... -v- ....
.... -v- ....

Above ties to be played on Tuesday, 1st or Wednesday, 2nd October, 1996

FINAL TIE

.... -v- ....

To be played on Sunday, 3rd November, 1996

In the event of a draw after normal time in all rounds, extra-time of 30 minutes (i.e. 15 minutes each way) will take place and thereafter, if necessary, Kicks from the Penalty Mark in accordance with the Rules laid down by the International Football Association Board will be taken.

BREAKDOWN OF HOW ALL THE SPONSORSHIP MONIES WILL BE ALLOCATED DURING SEASON 1996/97

BELL'S LEAGUE CHAMPIONSHIP

DISTRIBUTION OF BELL'S LEAGUE CHAMPIONSHIP MONIES

Each Premier Division Club will receive	£40,000
Each First Division Club will receive	£17,000
Each Second Division Club will receive	£10,000
Each Third Division Club will receive	£ 8,500

The Coca-Cola Cup

DISTRIBUTION OF COCA–COLA CUP MONIES

8	First Round Losers will each receive	£ 5,000
16	Second Round Losers will each receive	£ 7,000
8	Third Round Losers will each receive	£11,000
4	Fourth Round Losers will each receive	£16,000
2	Semi-Final Losers will each receive	£22,000
	The Runner-Up will receive	£40,000
	The Winner will receive	£60,000

DISTRIBUTION OF CHALLENGE CUP MONIES

14	First Round Losers will each receive	£ 2,125
8	Second Round Losers will each receive	£ 3,200
4	Third Round Losers will each receive	£ 4,400
2	Semi-Final Losers will each receive	£ 5,750
	The Runner-Up will receive	£10,000
	The Winner will receive	£14,000

Dates for your Diary Season 1996/97

TENNENTS SCOTTISH CUP 1996/97

First Round	7th December, 1996
Second Round	4th January, 1997
Third Round	25th January, 1997
Fourth Round	15th February, 1997
Fifth Round	8th March, 1997
Semi-Finals	12th April, 1997
Final	24th May, 1997

F.I.F.A. WORLD CUP 1998 QUALIFYING MATCHES

Austria	-v-	Scotland	Saturday, 31st August, 1996
Latvia	-v-	Scotland	Saturday, 5th October, 1996
Estonia	-v-	Scotland	Wednesday, 9th October, 1996
Scotland	-v-	Sweden	Sunday, 10th November, 1996
Scotland	-v-	Estonia	Saturday, 29th March, 1997
Scotland	-v-	Austria	Wednesday, 2nd April, 1997
Sweden	-v-	Scotland	Wednesday, 30th April, 1997
Belarus	-v-	Scotland	Sunday, 8th June, 1997

EUROPEAN "UNDER 21" CHAMPIONSHIP 1996/98 (QUALIFYING MATCHES)

Austria	-v-	Scotland	Friday, 30th August, 1996
Latvia	-v-	Scotland	Sunday, 6th October, 1996
Estonia	-v-	Scotland	Tuesday, 8th October, 1996
Scotland	-v-	Sweden	Saturday, 9th November, 1996
Scotland	-v-	Estonia	Friday, 28th March, 1997
Scotland	-v-	Austria	Tuesday, 1st April, 1997
Sweden	-v-	Scotland	Tuesday, 29th April, 1997
Belarus	-v-	Scotland	Saturday, 7th June, 1997

EUROPEAN "UNDER 18" CHAMPIONSHIP 1996/97 QUALIFYING MATCHES – MINI TOURNAMENT

The Netherlands, Lithuania, Wales and Scotland — 14th-20th October, 1996 (The Netherlands)

FOUR NATIONS YOUTH TOURNAMENT FOR "UNDER 17" PLAYERS

Denmark, Belgium, The Netherlands and Scotland — 2nd–8th September, 1996 (Denmark)

EUROPEAN "UNDER 16" CHAMPIONSHIP 1996/97 QUALIFYING MATCHES – MINI TOURNAMENT

Poland, Wales, Norway and Scotland — 30th September - 6th October, 1996 (Poland)

"UNDER 16" INTERNATIONAL CHALLENGE MATCHES

Denmark -v- Scotland 17th and 19th September, 1996

CHAMPIONS LEAGUE

EUROPEAN CHAMPION CLUBS' CUP

Qualifying Round: Knock-out system in August 1996

First-leg matches	Wednesday, 7th August, 1996
Second-leg matches	Wednesday, 21st August,1996

Group Matches: Championship system between Sept 1996 and Dec 1996

1st match day:	Wednesday, 11th September, 1996
2nd match day:	Wednesday, 25th September, 1996
3rd match day:	Wednesday, 16th October, 1996
4th match day:	Wednesday, 30th October, 1996
5th match day:	Wednesday, 20th November, 1996
6th match day:	Wednesday, 4th December, 1996

Quarter-Finals: Knock-out system in March 1997

First-leg matches:	Wednesday, 5th March, 1997
Second-leg matches:	Wednesday, 19th March, 1997

Semi-Finals: Knock-out system in April 1997

First-leg matches:	Wednesday, 9th April, 1997
Second-leg matches:	Wednesday, 23rd April, 1997

Final: Wednesday, 28th May 1997

U.E.F.A. CUP

Qualifying Round:	
First-leg matches:	Tuesday, 6th August, 1996
Second-leg matches:	Tuesday, 20th August, 1996
First Round:	
First-leg matches:	Tuesday, 10th September, 1996
Second-leg matches:	Tuesday, 24th September, 1996
Second Round:	
First-leg matches:	Tuesday, 15th October, 1996
Second-leg matches:	Tuesday, 29th October, 1996
Third Round:	
First-leg matches:	Tuesday, 19th November, 1996
Second-leg matches:	Tuesday, 3rd December, 1996
Quarter-Finals :	
First-leg matches:	Tuesday, 4th March, 1997
Second-leg matches:	Tuesday, 18th March, 1997
Semi-Finals:	
First-leg matches:	Tuesday, 8th April, 1997
Second-leg matches:	Tuesday, 22nd April, 1997
Final:	
First-leg match:	Wednesday 7th May, 1997
Second-leg match:	Wednesday 21st May, 1997

EUROPEAN CUP WINNERS' CUP

Qualifying Round:	
First-leg matches:	Thursday, 8th August, 1996
Second-leg matches:	Thursday, 22nd August, 1996
First Round:	
First-leg matches:	Thursday, 12th September, 1996
Second-leg matches:	Thursday, 26th September, 1996
Second Round:	
First-leg matches:	Thursday, 17th October, 1996
Second-leg matches:	Thursday, 31st October, 1996
Quarter-Finals :	
First-leg matches:	Thursday, 6th March, 1997
Second-leg matches:	Thursday, 20th March, 1997
Semi-Finals:	
First-leg matches:	Thursday, 10th April, 1997
Second-leg matches:	Thursday, 24th April, 1997
Final:	Wednesday, 14th May, 1997

Careers of Scottish League Managers

S·F·L ©

Premier Division

■ **ABERDEEN**
ROY AITKEN
Player: Celtic, Newcastle United, St. Mirren, Aberdeen, Scotland
Manager: Aberdeen

■ **CELTIC**
TOMMY BURNS
Player: Celtic, Kilmarnock, Scotland
Manager: Kilmarnock, Celtic

■ **DUNDEE UNITED**
TOMMY McLEAN
Player: Kilmarnock, Rangers, Scotland
Manager: Greenock Morton, Motherwell, Heart of Midlothian, Raith Rovers, Dundee United

■ **DUNFERMLINE ATHLETIC**
BERT PATON
Player: Leeds United, Dunfermline Athletic
Manager: Cowdenbeath, Raith Rovers, Dunfermline Athletic

■ **HEART OF MIDLOTHIAN**
JIM JEFFERIES
Player: Heart of Midlothian, Berwick Rangers
Manager: Berwick Rangers, Falkirk, Heart of Midlothian

■ **HIBERNIAN**

Player:
Manager:

■ **KILMARNOCK**
ALEX TOTTEN
Player: Liverpool, Dundee, Dunfermline Athletic, Falkirk, Queen of the South, Alloa
Manager: Alloa, Falkirk, Dumbarton, St. Johnstone, East Fife, Kilmarnock

■ **MOTHERWELL**
ALEX McLEISH
Player: Aberdeen, Motherwell, Scotland
Manager: Motherwell

■ **RAITH ROVERS**
IAIN MUNRO
Player: St. Mirren, Hibernian, Rangers, St. Mirren, Stoke City, Sunderland, Dundee United, Hibernian, Scotland
Manager: Dunfermline Athletic, Dundee, Hamilton Academical, Raith Rovers

■ **RANGERS**
WALTER SMITH
Player: Dundee United, Dumbarton, Dundee United
Manager: Rangers

First Division

■ **AIRDRIEONIANS**
ALEX MacDONALD
Player: St. Johnstone, Rangers, Heart of Midlothian, Scotland
Manager: Heart of Midlothian, Airdrieonians

■ **CLYDEBANK**
BRIAN WRIGHT
Player: Hamilton Academical, Motherwell, Clydebank, Partick Thistle, Clydebank, Queen of the South, Clydebank
Coach: Clydebank

■ **DUNDEE**
JAMES DUFFY
Player: Celtic, Greenock Morton, Dundee, Partick Thistle, Dundee
Manager: Falkirk, Dundee

■ **EAST FIFE**

Player:
Manager:

■ **FALKIRK**
EAMONN BANNON
Player: Heart of Midlothian, Chelsea, Dundee United, Heart of Midlothian, Hibernian, Heart of Midlothian, Stenhousemuir, Scotland
Manager: Falkirk

■ **GREENOCK MORTON**
ALLAN McGRAW
Player: Greenock Morton, Hibernian, Linfield (Northern Ireland)
Manager: Greenock Morton

■ **PARTICK THISTLE**
MURDO MacLEOD
Player: Dumbarton, Celtic, Borussia Dortmund (Germany), Hibernian, Dumbarton, Partick Thistle, Scotland
Manager: Dumbarton, Partick Thistle

■ **ST. JOHNSTONE**
PAUL STURROCK
Player: Dundee United, Scotland
Manager: St. Johnstone

■ **ST. MIRREN**
TONY FITZPATRICK
Player: St. Mirren, Bristol City, St. Mirren
Manager: St. Mirren (Twice)

■ **STIRLING ALBION**
KEVIN DRINKELL
Player: Grimsby Town, Norwich City, Rangers, Coventry City, Falkirk, Stirling Albion
Manager: Stirling Albion

Second Division

■ **AYR UNITED**
GORDON DALZIEL
Player: Rangers, Manchester City, Partick Thistle, East Stirlingshire, Raith Rovers, Ayr United
Manager: Ayr United

■ **BERWICK RANGERS**
IAN ROSS
Player: Liverpool, Aston Villa, Notts County, Northampton Town, Peterborough United, Wolverhampton Wanderers, Hereford United
Manager: Valur, KR (both Iceland), Huddersfield Town, Berwick Rangers

■ **BRECHIN CITY**
JOHN YOUNG
Player: St. Mirren, Brechin City, Arbroath
Manager: Brechin City

■ **CLYDE**

Player:
Manager:

■ **DUMBARTON**
JIM FALLON
Player: Clydebank
Manager: Clydebank (Coach), Dumbarton

■ **HAMILTON ACADEMICAL**
SANDY CLARK
Player: Airdrieonians, West Ham United, Rangers, Heart of Midlothian, Partick Thistle, Dunfermline Athletic, Heart of Midlothian
Manager: Partick Thistle, Heart of Midlothian, Hamilton Academical

■ **LIVINGSTON**
JIM LEISHMAN
Player: Dunfermline Athletic, Cowdenbeath
Manager: Dunfermline Athletic, Inverness Thistle, Montrose, Livingston (Formerly Meadowbank Thistle)

■ **QUEEN OF THE SOUTH**
CO-MANAGERS:
ROWAN ALEXANDER & MARK SHANKS
Rowan Alexander
Player: Queen of the South, St. Mirren, Brentford, Greenock Morton, Queen of the South
Manager: Queen of the South
Mark Shanks
Player: Ayr United, Dumbarton, Queen of the South
Manager: Queen of the South

■ **STENHOUSEMUIR**
TERRY CHRISTIE
Player: Dundee, Raith Rovers, Stirling Albion
Manager: Meadowbank Thistle, Stenhousemuir

■ **STRANRAER**
CAMPBELL MONEY
Player: St. Mirren, Stranraer
Manager: Stranraer

Third Division

■ **ALBION ROVERS**
VINNIE MOORE
Player: Clydebank, Airdrieonians, Stirling Albion, Ayr United, Albion Rovers
Manager: Albion Rovers

■ **ALLOA**
THOMAS HENDRIE
Player: Meadowbank Thistle, Berwick Rangers
Manager: Berwick Rangers, Alloa

■ **ARBROATH**
JOHN BROGAN
Player: Albion Rovers, St. Johnstone, Hibernian, Ayr United, Hamilton Academical, Stirling Albion
Manager: Stirling Albion, Arbroath

■ **COWDENBEATH**
TOM STEVEN
Player: Hibernian, Hamilton Academical, Berwick Rangers
Manager: Cowdenbeath

■ **EAST STIRLINGSHIRE**
BILLY LITTLE
Player: Aberdeen, Falkirk, Stirling Albion, East Stirlingshire
Manager: Falkirk, Queen of the South, East Stirlingshire (twice)

■ **FORFAR ATHLETIC**
TOM CAMPBELL
Player: Did Not Play at Senior Level
Manager: Forfar Athletic

■ **INVERNESS CALEDONIAN THISTLE**
STEVE PATERSON
Player: Manchester United, Sheffield United, Hong Kong Rangers, Sydney Olympic, Yorniuri Tokyo
Manager: Inverness Caledonian Thistle

■ **MONTROSE**
DAVE SMITH
Player: Dunfermline Athletic
Manager: Montrose

■ **QUEEN'S PARK**
HUGH McCANN
Player: Celtic, Alloa, Berwick Rangers, East Stirlingshire
Coach: Alloa (Manager), Queen's Park

■ **ROSS COUNTY**
NEALE COOPER
Player: Aberdeen, Aston Villa, Rangers, Reading, Dunfermline Athletic, Ross County
Manager: Ross County

INFORMATION COMPILED BY JIM JEFFREY

The Season in Camera

S·F·L

1. Hearts v Aberdeen. Tennents Scottish Cup Semi-Final. The Hearts bench celebrate
2. Scotland manager, Craig Brown. Bell's Manager of the Month, November 1995
3. Aberdeen celebrations. Tennents Scottish Cup. Quarter-Final v Airdrieonians
4. Euro '96. Scotland v Holland
5. The Old Firm – another epic tussle.